Teach Yourself VISUALLY™ FrontPage® 2002

From
maranGraphics®

&

HUNGRY MINDS, INC.
New York, NY • Cleveland, OH • Indianapolis, IN
Chicago, IL • Foster City, CA • San Francisco, CA

Teach Yourself VISUALLY™ FrontPage® 2002

Published by
Hungry Minds, Inc.
909 Third Avenue
New York, NY 10022
www.hungryminds.com

Library of Congress Control Number: 2001089087
ISBN: 0-7645-3590-0
Printed in the United States of America
10 9 8 7 6 5 4 3 2 1

1K/RW/QU/QR/MG

Distributed in the United States by Hungry Minds, Inc.
Distributed by CDG Books Canada Inc. for Canada; by Transworld Publishers Limited in the United Kingdom; by IDG Norge Books for Norway; by IDG Sweden Books for Sweden; by IDG Books Australia Publishing Corporation Pty. Ltd. for Australia and New Zealand; by TransQuest Publishers Pte Ltd. for Singapore, Malaysia, Thailand, Indonesia, and Hong Kong; by Gotop Information Inc. for Taiwan; by ICG Muse, Inc. for Japan; by Intersoft for South Africa; by Eyrolles for France; by International Thomson Publishing for Germany, Austria and Switzerland; by Distribuidora Cuspide for Argentina; by LR International for Brazil; by Galileo Libros for Chile; by Ediciones ZETA S.C.R. Ltda. for Peru; by WS Computer Publishing Corporation, Inc. for the Philippines; by Contemporanea de Ediciones for Venezuela; by Express Computer Distributors for the Caribbean and West Indies; by Micronesia Media Distributor, Inc. for Micronesia; by Chips Computadoras S.A. de C.V. for Mexico; by Editorial Norma de Panama S.A. for Panama; by American Bookshops for Finland.
For U.S. corporate orders, please call maranGraphics at 800-469-6616 or fax 905-890-9434.
For general information on Hungry Minds' products and services, please contact our Customer Care Department within the U.S. at 800-762-2974, outside the U.S. at 317-572-3993 or fax 317-572-4002.
For sales inquiries and reseller information, including discounts, premium and bulk quantity sales, and foreign-language translations, please contact our Customer Care Department at 800-434-3422, fax 317-572-4002, or write to Hungry Minds, Inc., Attn: Customer Care Department, 10475 Crosspoint Boulevard, Indianapolis, IN 46256.
For information on licensing foreign or domestic rights, please contact our Sub-Rights Customer Care Department at 650-653-7098.
For information on using Hungry Minds' products and services in the classroom or for ordering examination copies, please contact our Educational Sales Department at 800-434-2086 or fax 317-572-4005.
Please contact our Public Relations Department at 212-884-5163 for press review copies or 212-884-5000 for author interviews and other publicity information or fax 212-884-5400.
For authorization to photocopy items for corporate, personal, or educational use, please contact Copyright Clearance Center, 222 Rosewood Drive, Danvers, MA 01923, or fax 978-750-4470.

Trademark Acknowledgments

Permissions

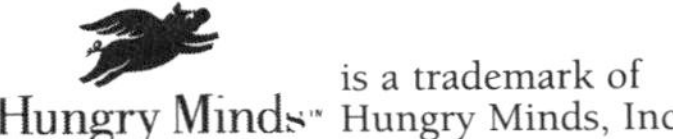

is a trademark of Hungry Minds, Inc.

U.S. Corporate Sales
Contact maranGraphics at (800) 469-6616 or fax (905) 890-9434.

U.S. Trade Sales
Contact Hungry Minds at (800) 434-3422 or fax (317) 572-4002.

Some comments from our readers...

"I have to praise you and your company on the fine products you turn out. I have twelve of the *Teach Yourself VISUALLY* and *Simplified* books in my house. They were instrumental in helping me pass a difficult computer course. Thank you for creating books that are easy to follow."

–Gordon Justin (Brielle, NJ)

"I commend your efforts and your success. I teach in an outreach program for the Dr. Eugene Clark Library in Lockhart, TX. Your *Teach Yourself VISUALLY* books are incredible and I use them in my computer classes. All my students love them!"

–Michele Schalin (Lockhart, TX)

"Thank you so much for helping people like me learn about computers. The Maran family is just what the doctor ordered. Thank you, thank you, thank you."

–Carol Moten (New Kensington, PA)

"I would like to take this time to compliment maranGraphics on creating such great books. Thank you for making it clear. Keep up the good work."

–Kirk Santoro (Burbank, CA)

"I write to extend my thanks and appreciation for your books. They are clear, easy to follow, and straight to the point. Keep up the good work!"

–Seward Kollie (Dakar, Senegal)

"What fantastic teaching books you have produced! Congratulations to you and your staff. You deserve the Nobel prize in Education in the Software category. Thanks for helping me to understand computers."

–Bruno Tonon (Melbourne, Australia)

"Over time, I have bought a number of your 'Read Less, Learn More' books. For me, they are THE way to learn anything easily."

–José A. Mazón (Cuba, NY)

"I was introduced to maranGraphics about four years ago and YOU ARE THE GREATEST THING THAT EVER HAPPENED TO INTRODUCTORY COMPUTER BOOKS!"

–Glenn Nettleton (Huntsville, AL)

"Compliments To The Chef!! Your books are extraordinary! Or, simply put, Extra-Ordinary, meaning way above the rest! THANK YOU THANK YOU THANK YOU! for creating these."

–Christine J. Manfrin (Castle Rock, CO)

"I'm a grandma who was pushed by an 11-year-old grandson to join the computer age. I found myself hopelessly confused and frustrated until I discovered the Visual series. I'm no expert by any means now, but I'm a lot further along than I would have been otherwise. Thank you!"

–Carol Louthain (Logansport, IN)

"Thank you, thank you, thank you...for making it so easy for me to break into this high-tech world. I now own four of your books. I recommend them to anyone who is a beginner like myself. Now... if you could just do one for programming VCRs, it would make my day!"

–Gay O'Donnell (Calgary, Alberta, Canada)

"You're marvelous! I am greatly in your debt."

–Patrick Baird (Lacey, WA)

maranGraphics is a family-run business
located near Toronto, Canada.

At **maranGraphics**, we believe in producing great computer books–one book at a time.

Each maranGraphics book uses the award-winning communication process that we have been developing over the last 25 years. Using this process, we organize screen shots, text and illustrations in a way that makes it easy for you to learn new concepts and tasks.

We spend hours deciding the best way to perform each task, so you don't have to! Our clear, easy-to-follow screen shots and instructions walk you through each task from beginning to end.

Our detailed illustrations go hand-in-hand with the text to help reinforce the information. Each illustration is a labor of love–some take up to a week to draw!

We want to thank you for purchasing what we feel are the best computer books money can buy. We hope you enjoy using this book as much as we enjoyed creating it!

Sincerely,

The Maran Family

Please visit us on the Web at:
www.maran.com

CREDITS

Author:
Ruth Maran

Copy Editor:
Roxanne Van Damme

Copy Editor & Screen Captures:
Stacey Morrison

Project Manager:
Judy Maran

Editing & Screen Captures:
Teri Lynn Pinsent
Luis Lee
Norm Schumacher
Faiza Jagot

Layout Designer:
Treena Lees

Illustrations & Screens:
Russ Marini
Sean Johannesen
Steven Schaerer
Natalie Tweedie
Paul Baker
Dave Thornhill

Indexer:
Teri Lynn Pinsent

Permissions Coordinator:
Jennifer Amaral

Senior Vice President and Publisher, Hungry Minds Technology Publishing Group:
Richard Swadley

Publishing Director, Hungry Minds Technology Publishing Group:
Barry Pruett

Editorial Support, Hungry Minds Technology Publishing Group:
Martine Edwards
Lindsay Sandman
Sandy Rodrigues

Post Production
Robert Maran

ACKNOWLEDGMENTS

Thanks to the dedicated staff of maranGraphics, including Jennifer Amaral, Roderick Anatalio, Paul Baker, Cathy Benn, Joel Desamero, Faiza Jagot, Sean Johannesen, Kelleigh Johnson, Wanda Lawrie, Luis Lee, Treena Lees, Jill Maran, Judy Maran, Robert Maran, Ruth Maran, Russ Marini, Suzana G. Miokovic, Stacey Morrison, Teri Lynn Pinsent, Steven Schaerer, Norm Schumacher, Raquel Scott, Natalie Tweedie, Roxanne Van Damme and Paul Whitehead.

Finally, to Richard Maran who originated the easy-to-use graphic format of this guide. Thank you for your inspiration and guidance.

TABLE OF CONTENTS

Chapter 1 — GETTING STARTED

Chapter 2 — FRONTPAGE BASICS

Chapter 3 — WORK WITH WEB PAGES

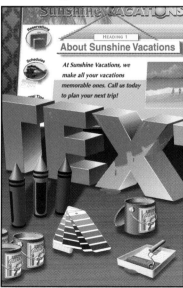

TABLE OF CONTENTS

Chapter 6 — ADD IMAGES

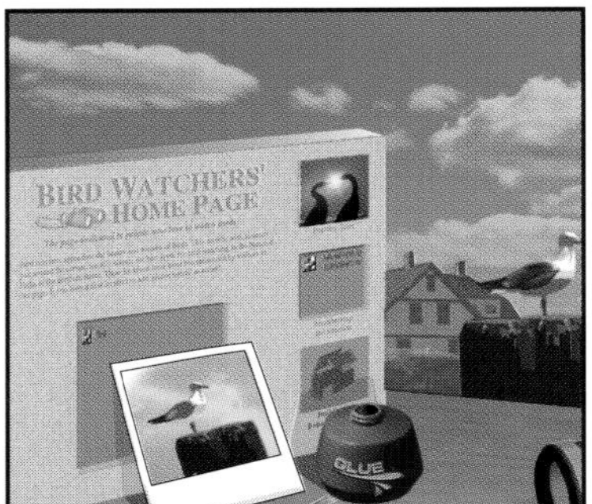

Chapter 7 — CUSTOMIZE IMAGES

Chapter 8 — CREATE LINKS

Chapter 9

CREATE TABLES

Chapter 10

WORK WITH NAVIGATIONAL STRUCTURE

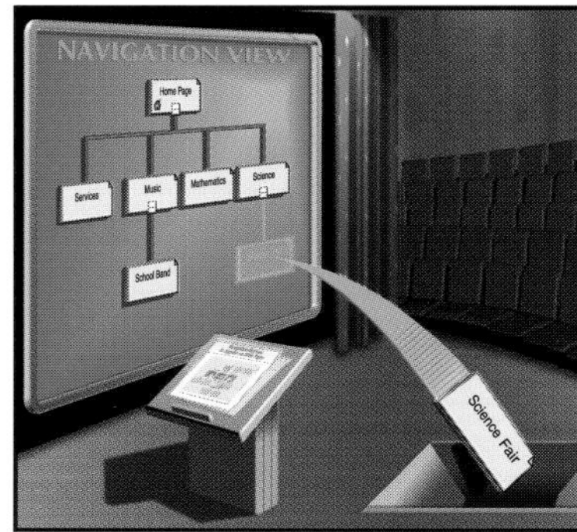

Chapter 11 — CREATE FRAMES

Chapter 12 — CREATE FORMS

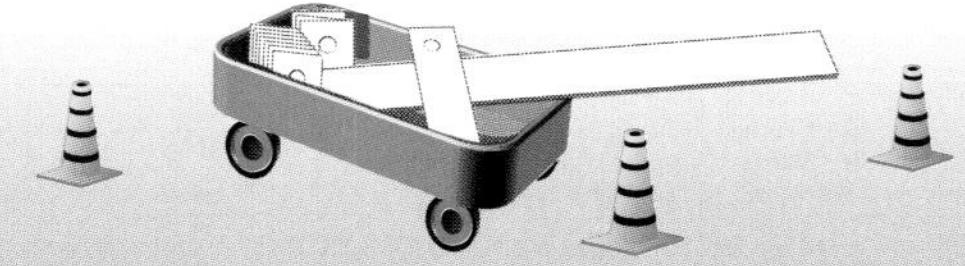

Chapter 13 ADD WEB PAGE EFFECTS

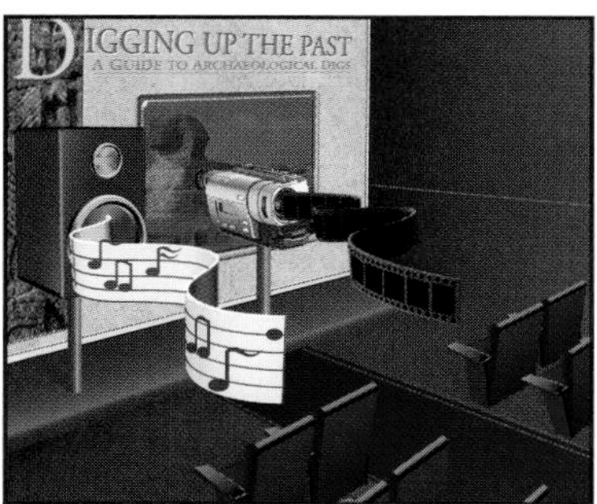

Chapter 14 MANAGE WEB PAGES

Chapter 15 PUBLISH WEB PAGES

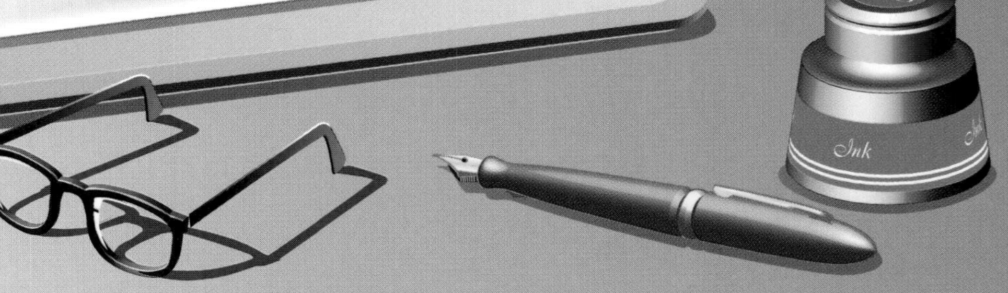
FRONTPAGE
Ink

CHAPTER 1

Getting Started

Are you thinking about creating Web pages? This chapter will help you get started.

FrontPage allows you to create, edit, manage and publish Web pages.

EDIT AND FORMAT TEXT

FrontPage offers many features to help you edit and format text on your Web pages. You can add, delete and re-arrange text as well as check your Web pages for spelling errors. You can enhance information by using various fonts, sizes, styles and colors and apply a theme to instantly give your Web pages a professional look.

ADD IMAGES

You can add images to your Web pages to illustrate concepts or enhance the appearance of your pages. FrontPage includes a large selection of ready-made clip art images, simple shapes and text effects that you can add to your Web pages. FrontPage also offers many ways to customize images, such as adding text and cropping images.

CREATE LINKS

You can create links to connect a word, phrase or image on a Web page to another Web page. You can also create links that visitors can select to send you an e-mail message. FrontPage can check all the links in your Web site to determine if the links are working properly.

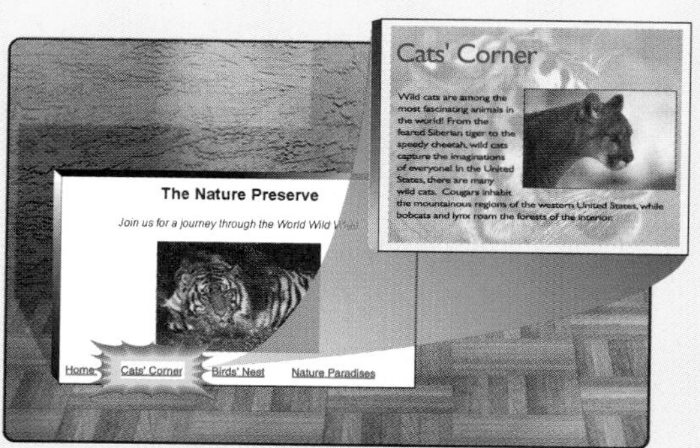

CREATE TABLES

You can create a table to neatly display information on a Web page. Tables are also useful for controlling the placement of text and images on a Web page. FrontPage offers many ready-to-use designs that can instantly enhance the appearance of a table you create.

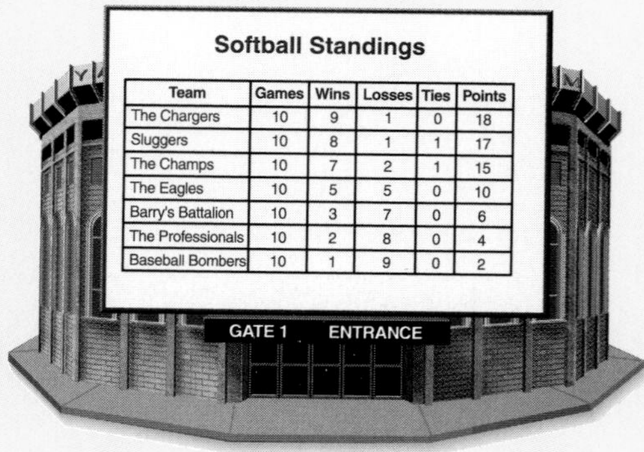

Softball Standings

Team	Games	Wins	Losses	Ties	Points
The Chargers	10	9	1	0	18
Sluggers	10	8	1	1	17
The Champs	10	7	2	1	15
The Eagles	10	5	5	0	10
Barry's Battalion	10	3	7	0	6
The Professionals	10	2	8	0	4
Baseball Bombers	10	1	9	0	2

WORK WITH NAVIGATIONAL STRUCTURE

You can work with the navigational structure of your Web site to define how the pages in your site are related. Once you set up the navigational structure of your Web site, you can add navigation buttons to your Web pages. Navigation buttons are links visitors can select to easily move through the pages in your Web site.

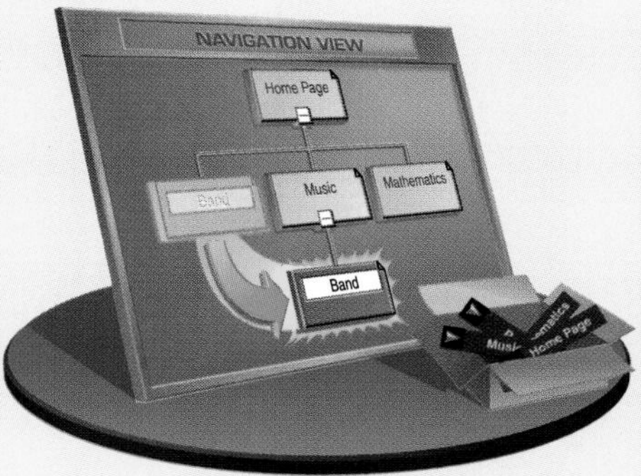

CREATE FRAMES

You can create frames to divide a Web browser window into sections. Each section will display a different Web page. Frames allow you to keep information such as an advertisement or navigational tools on the screen while visitors browse through your Web pages.

CREATE FORMS

Forms allow you to gather information from visitors who view your Web pages. You can create forms that allow visitors to send you questions or comments about your Web pages. You can also create forms that allow visitors to purchase your products and services on the Web.

PUBLISH WEB PAGES

When you finish creating your Web pages, FrontPage helps you transfer the pages to a Web server to make the pages available on the Web. Once your Web pages are stored on a Web server, you can notify friends, family, colleagues and people on the Web about your Web pages.

The World Wide Web is part of the Internet and consists of a huge collection of documents stored on computers around the world.

The World Wide Web is also called the Web.

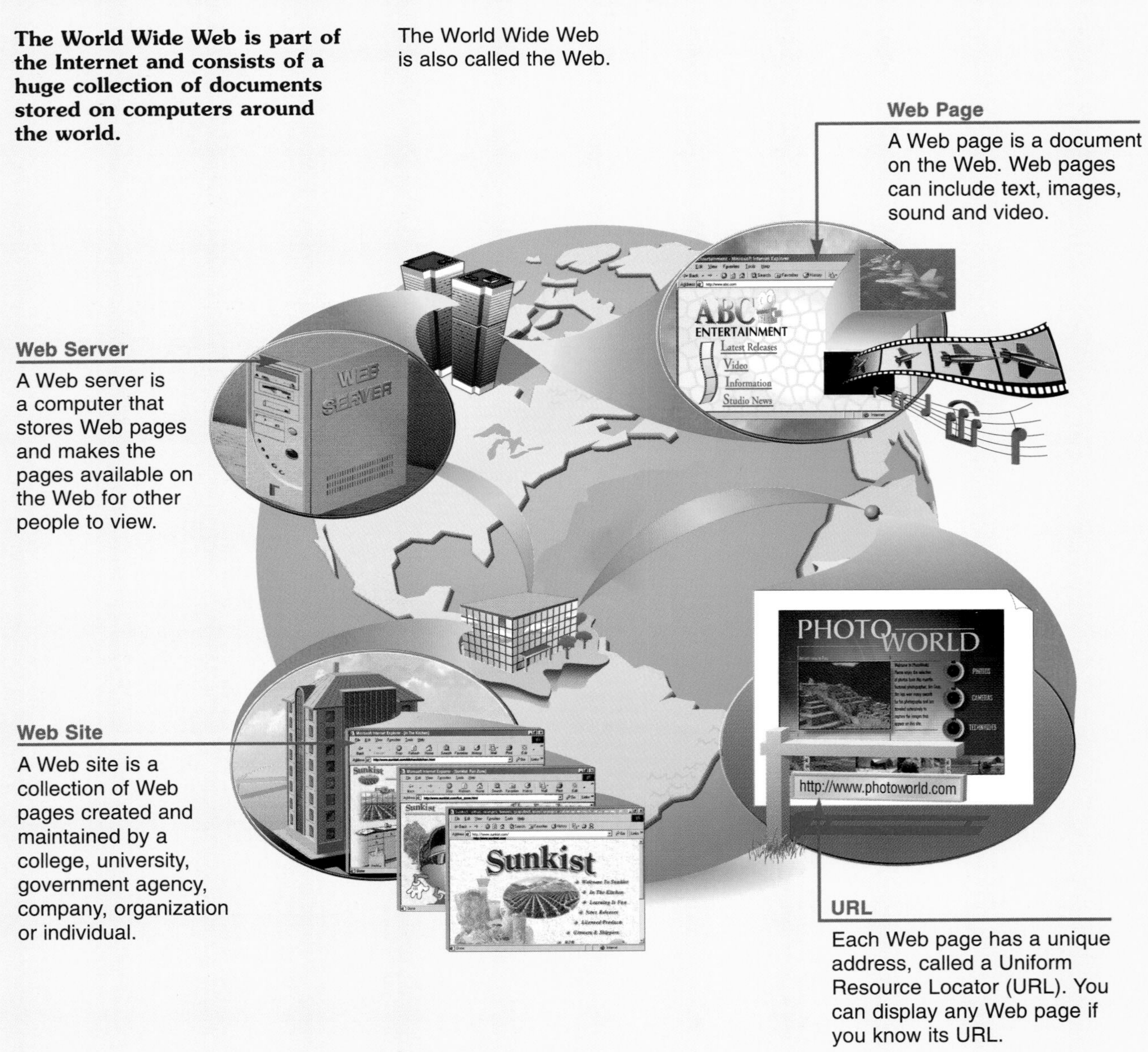

Web Page

A Web page is a document on the Web. Web pages can include text, images, sound and video.

Web Server

A Web server is a computer that stores Web pages and makes the pages available on the Web for other people to view.

Web Site

A Web site is a collection of Web pages created and maintained by a college, university, government agency, company, organization or individual.

URL

Each Web page has a unique address, called a Uniform Resource Locator (URL). You can display any Web page if you know its URL.

LINKS

Web pages contain links, which are highlighted text or images on a Web page that connect to other pages on the Web. You can select a link to display a Web page located on the same computer or on a computer across the city, country or world.

Links allow you to easily navigate through a vast amount of information by jumping from one Web page to another. Links are also known as hyperlinks.

WEB BROWSERS

A Web browser is a program that allows you to view and explore information on the Web.

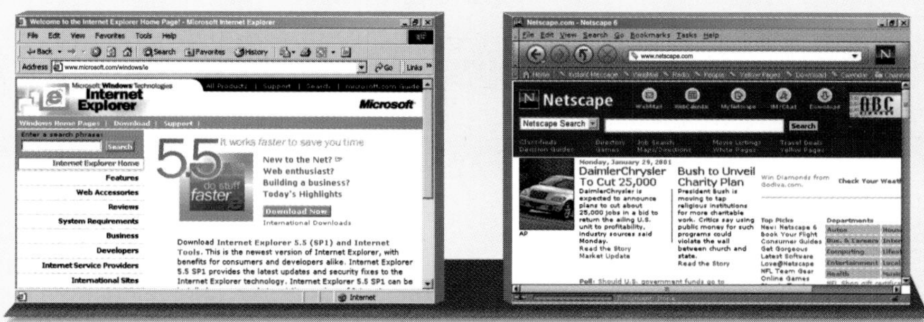

Microsoft Internet Explorer

Microsoft Internet Explorer is a popular Web browser that comes with the latest versions of Windows. You can also obtain Internet Explorer at the www.microsoft.com/windows/ie Web page.

Netscape Navigator

Netscape Navigator is a popular Web browser that you can obtain at the www.netscape.com Web site or at computer stores.

HTML

HyperText Markup Language (HTML) is a computer language used to create Web pages. Web pages are HTML documents that consist of text and special instructions called tags. A Web browser interprets the tags in an HTML document to determine how to display the Web page. When you create a Web page in FrontPage, the HTML tags are hidden from view.

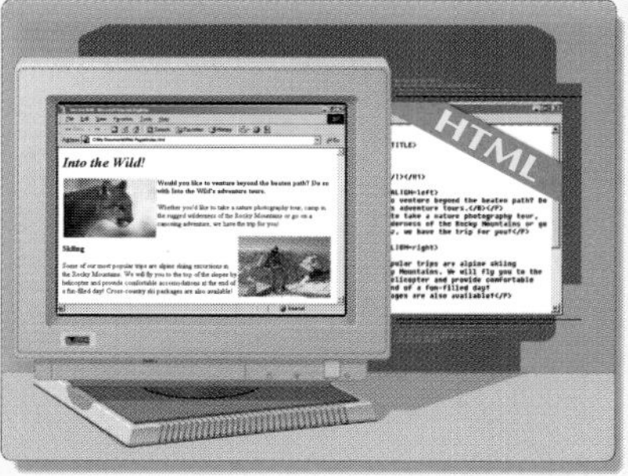

PROOFREAD INFORMATION

Carefully check your Web pages for spelling and grammar errors. If your Web pages contain spelling mistakes, visitors may assume that the information on your pages is inaccurate. You may want to print your Web pages to help you proofread the pages.

PUT IMPORTANT INFORMATION FIRST

Always display the most important information at the top of each Web page. Some visitors may not scroll through a Web page to read all the information. These visitors will miss important information if you do not display the information at the top of a Web page.

PAGE LENGTH

Web pages should not be too short or too long. If the information on a Web page is shorter than half a screen, try to combine the information with another Web page. If a Web page is longer than five screens, try to break up the page into several shorter pages.

INCLUDE CONTACT INFORMATION

Always include your name and e-mail address on Web pages you create. This allows visitors to contact you if they have questions or comments about your Web pages.

PROVIDE A FAQ

A FAQ is a list of Frequently Asked Questions about a topic. Providing a FAQ in your Web site allows you to provide answers to common questions that people have about your Web pages. A FAQ can also help prevent people from sending you e-mail messages that repeatedly ask the same questions.

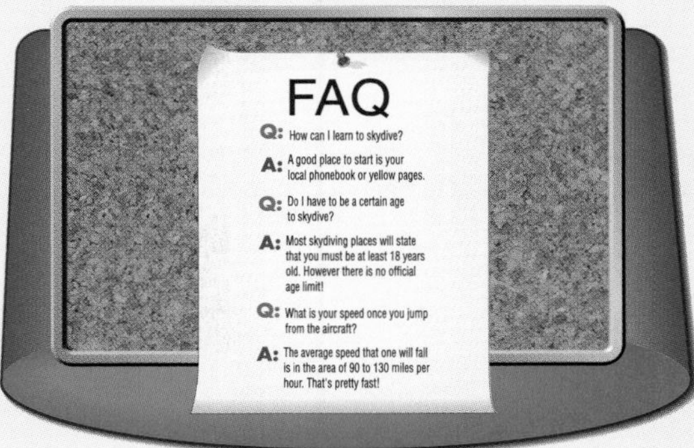

COPYRIGHT CONSIDERATIONS

If you plan to use information or images you did not create yourself, make sure the information or images are not copyrighted. Many pages on the Web offer information and images you can use that do not have copyright restrictions.

UPDATE INFORMATION

You should update your Web pages on a regular basis. If the information on your Web pages never changes, people may only read the pages once and never visit the pages again. You should include the date on your Web pages to let visitors know when you last updated the pages.

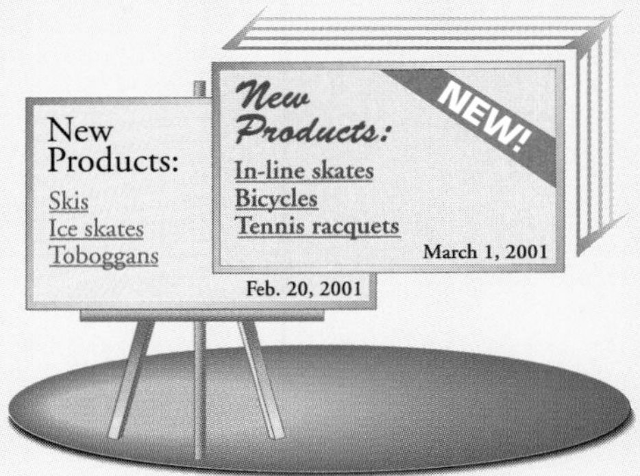

TRANSFER SPEED

When creating your Web pages, try to keep the file size of the pages and images as small as possible. This will reduce the time your Web pages take to transfer and appear on a visitor's screen. If your Web pages take too long to appear, visitors may leave your Web site.

PLAN A HOME PAGE

The home page is the main Web page in a Web site. The home page is usually the first page people will see when they visit a Web site.

When you create a Web site, FrontPage automatically names your home page index.htm.

SUMMARY

Always include a brief summary of your Web site on your home page. You should state the purpose of your Web site, such as whether you want to entertain or inform visitors.

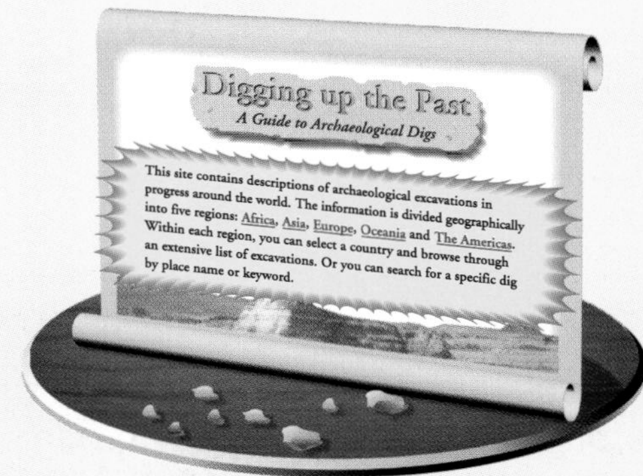

TABLE OF CONTENTS

Your home page should include a table of contents that lists the information contained in your Web site. You can include links that visitors can select to quickly access information of interest.

BOOKMARK REMINDER

Web browsers have a feature called bookmarks or favorites that allow people to store the addresses of Web pages they often visit. You can include an image or phrase on your home page to remind visitors to bookmark your home page. This allows visitors to quickly return to your Web site.

QUICK TRANSFER SPEED

You should try to keep the file size of your home page and the images on the page as small as possible. This will reduce the time your home page takes to appear on a visitor's screen. If your home page takes too long to appear, visitors may leave your Web site.

START FRONTPAGE

You can start FrontPage to begin creating Web pages that you can publish on the Web.

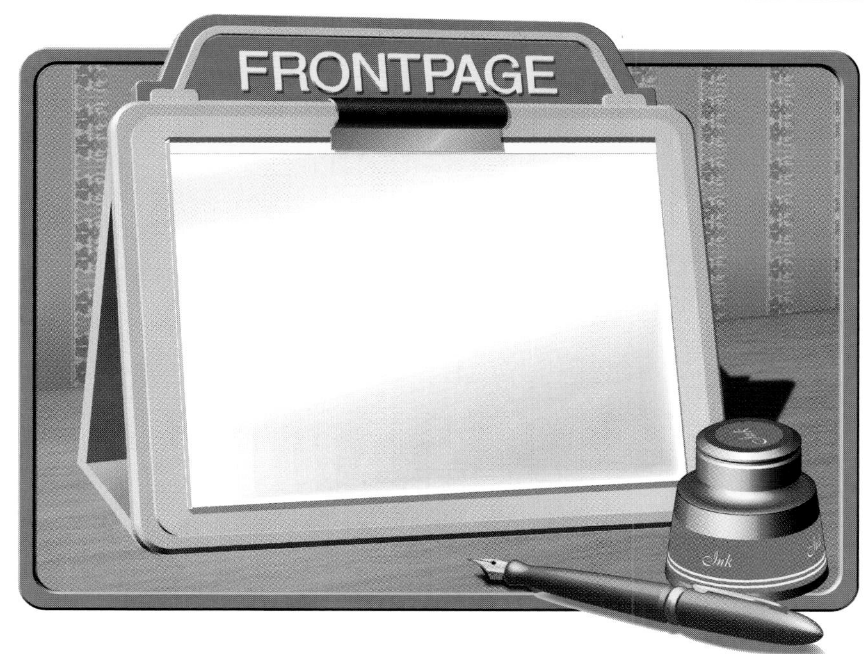

START FRONTPAGE

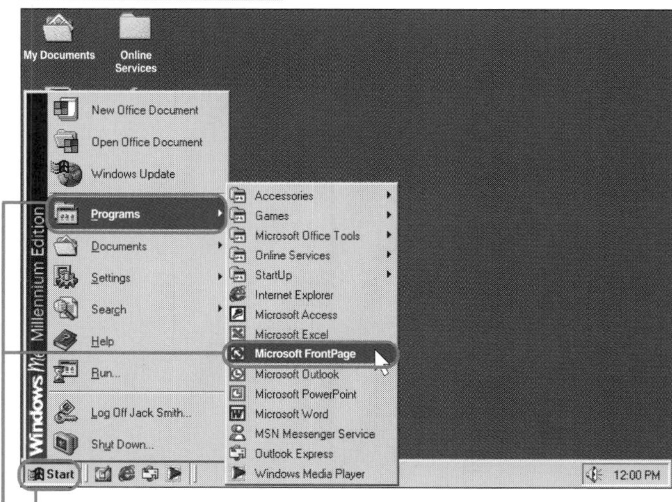

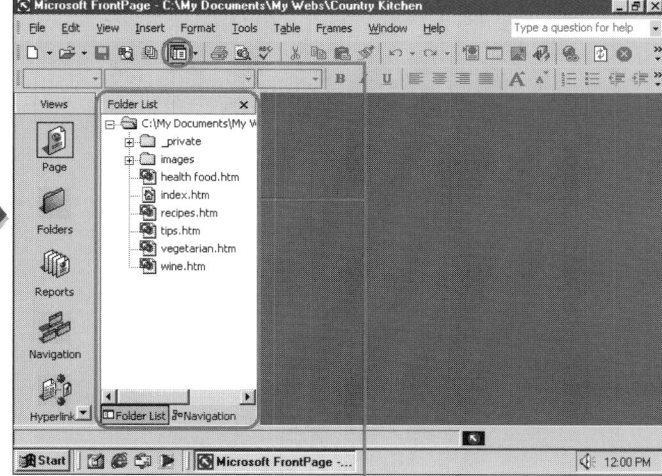

1 Click **Start**.

2 Click **Programs**.

3 Click **Microsoft FrontPage**.

Note: If Microsoft FrontPage does not appear on the menu, position the mouse over the bottom of the menu to display all the menu options.

■ The Microsoft FrontPage window appears.

■ If you have previously used FrontPage, the last Web site you worked with opens.

■ This area lists the Web pages, folders and other items in the Web site.

■ If the list does not appear, click to display the list.

The FrontPage window displays many items you can use to create and work with your Web site.

Web Page Tabs

Each tab displays the file name of an open Web page. The displayed Web page has a white tab.

Scroll Bars

Allow you to browse through a Web page.

Title Bar

Shows the location and name of the displayed Web site.

Menu Bar

Provides access to lists of commands available in FrontPage and displays an area where you can type a question to get help information.

Standard Toolbar

Contains buttons you can use to select common commands, such as Save and Print.

Formatting Toolbar

Contains buttons you can use to select common formatting commands, such as Bold and Italic.

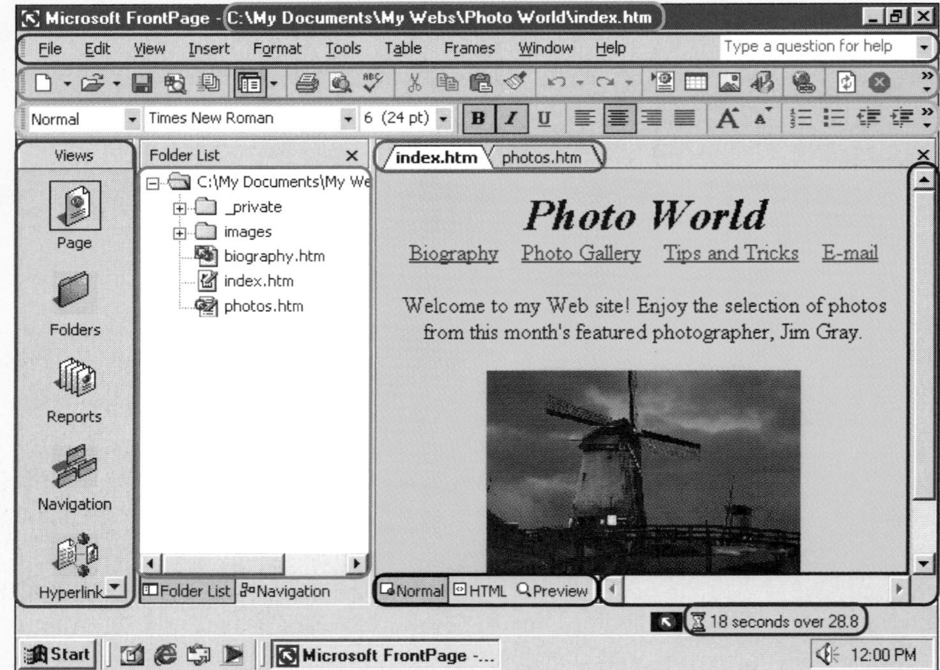

Views Bar

Provides access to six different views of your Web site.

Folder List

Lists the folders, Web pages and other items in your Web site.

Web Page Views

Provides access to three different views of your Web pages.

Estimated Download Time

Indicates how many seconds the displayed Web page will take to transfer to a visitor's computer when using a 28.8 Kbps modem.

EXIT FRONTPAGE

When you finish using FrontPage, you can exit the program.

You should always exit FrontPage and all other programs before turning off your computer.

EXIT FRONTPAGE

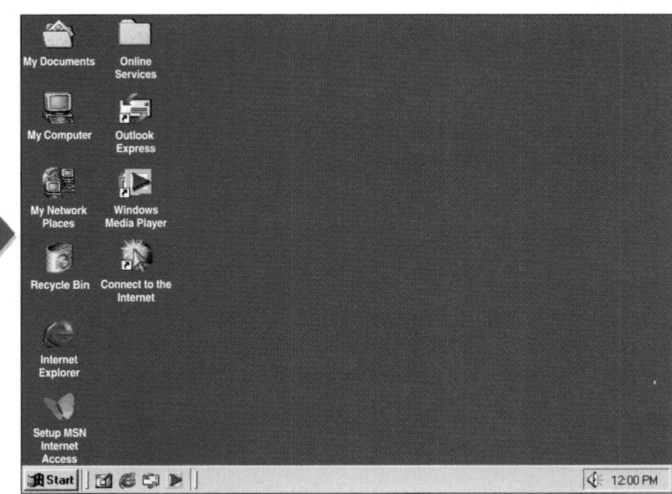

■ Before exiting FrontPage, you should save all the Web pages in your Web site. To save a Web page, see page 28.

1 Click ☒ to exit FrontPage.

■ The Microsoft FrontPage window disappears from your screen.

■ If you have more than one Web site open, you will need to repeat step 1 for each Web site.

GETTING HELP

If you do not know how to perform a task in FrontPage, you can search for help information on the task.

GETTING HELP

1 Click this area and type the task you want to get help information on. Then press the Enter key.

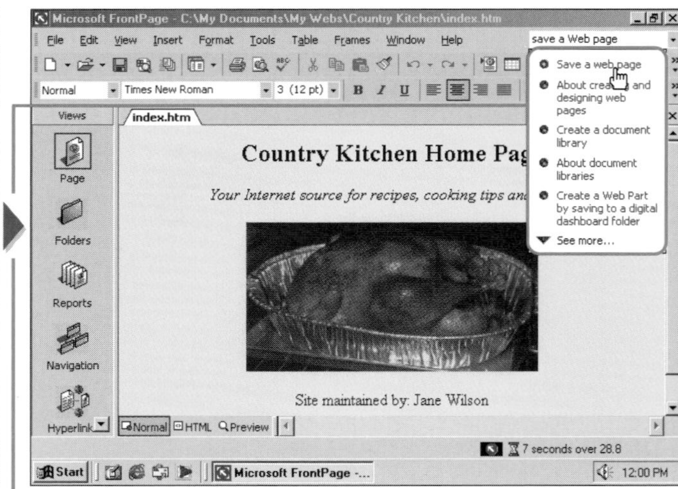

■ A list of related help topics appears.

2 Click a help topic of interest.

*Note: If the help topic you want does not appear in the list, you can click **See more** to view additional help topics.*

What other ways can I obtain help?

In the Microsoft FrontPage Help window, you can use the following tabs to obtain help information.

Contents
You can double-click a book icon ( ) or click a page icon ( ) to browse through the contents of FrontPage Help.

Answer Wizard
You can type a question about a topic of interest. A list of help topics related to your question will appear.

Index
You can type a word of interest or double-click a word in an alphabetical list of help topics. A list of related help topics will appear.

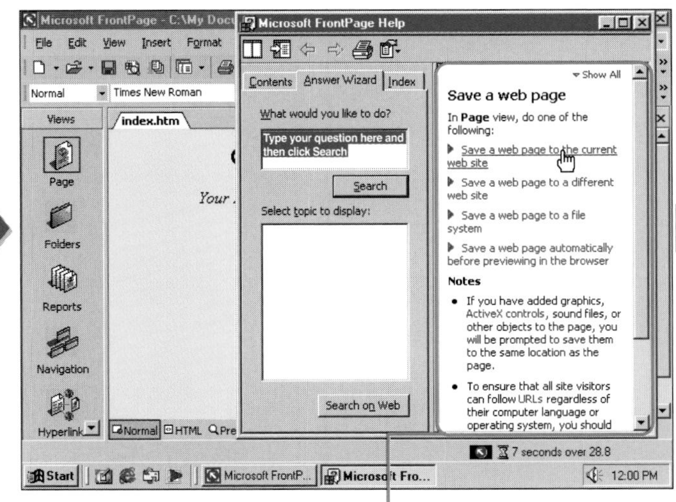

■ The Microsoft FrontPage Help window appears.

Note: To maximize the Microsoft FrontPage Help window to fill your screen, click ▢ in the top right corner of the window.

■ This area displays information about the help topic you selected.

■ To display additional information for a word or phrase that appears in color, click the text.

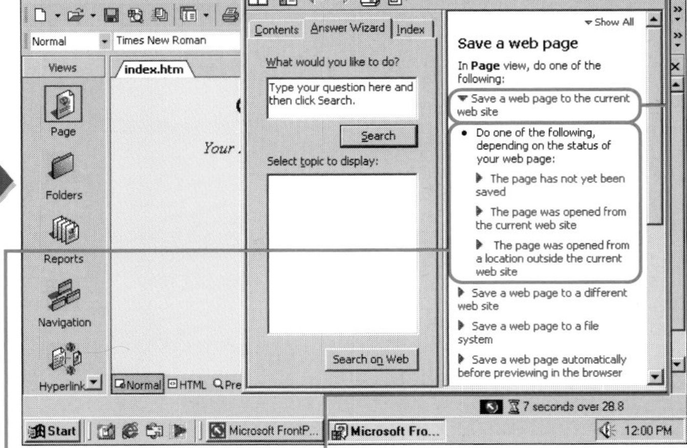

■ The additional information appears.

Note: Selecting a colored word or phrase will display information such as a definition, tips or a list of steps.

■ To once again hide the information, click the colored word or phrase.

3 When you finish reviewing the help information, click ☒ to close the Microsoft FrontPage Help window.

Navigation Pane
Home Page
Sedans
SUVs
Vans
Sports Cars
National Parks
The United States is home to a wide variety of wildlife from coast to coast.
One of the best ways to discover this country's wildlife is to visit one of the many National or State Parks.
Whether your're interested in bird watching, hiking or just getting some fresh air, these parks will provide the perfect
Links
Information
Contact
nature preserve
Rare & Endangered Species
Exotic Birds & Insects
National Parks

CHAPTER 2

FrontPage Basics

Are you ready to begin creating your Web pages? This chapter will provide you with the basics you need to work with FrontPage.

CREATE A NEW WEB SITE

You can use a template or wizard to create a new Web site. Templates and wizards provide the layout and design for the Web pages in a Web site.

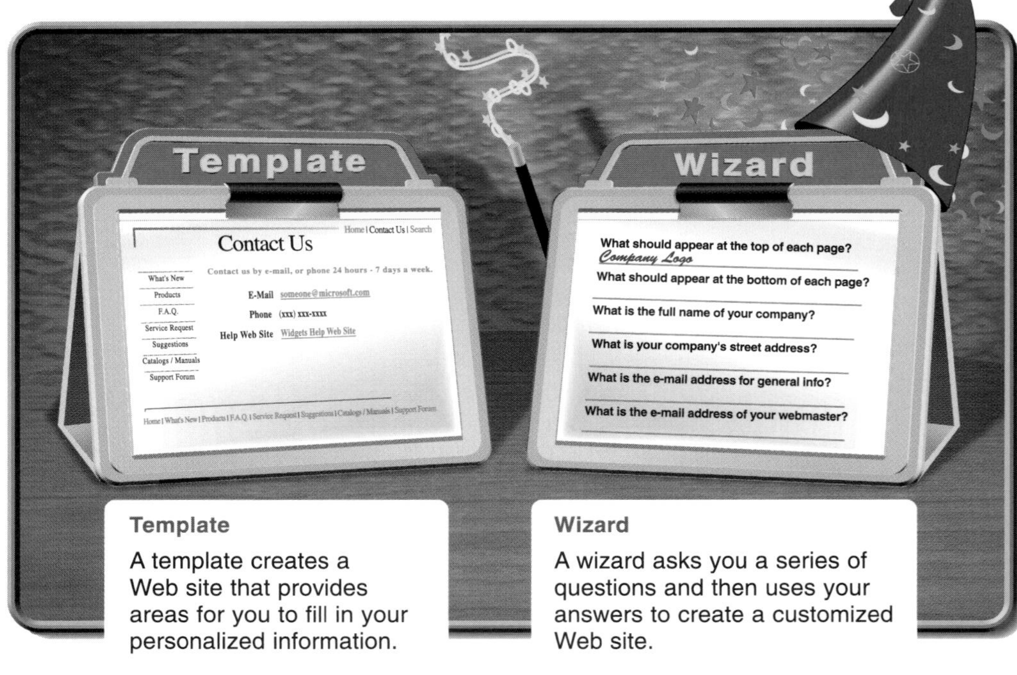

Template

A template creates a Web site that provides areas for you to fill in your personalized information.

Wizard

A wizard asks you a series of questions and then uses your answers to create a customized Web site.

CREATE A NEW WEB SITE

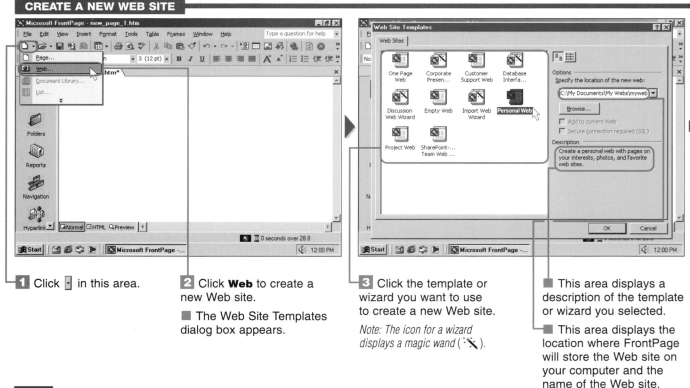

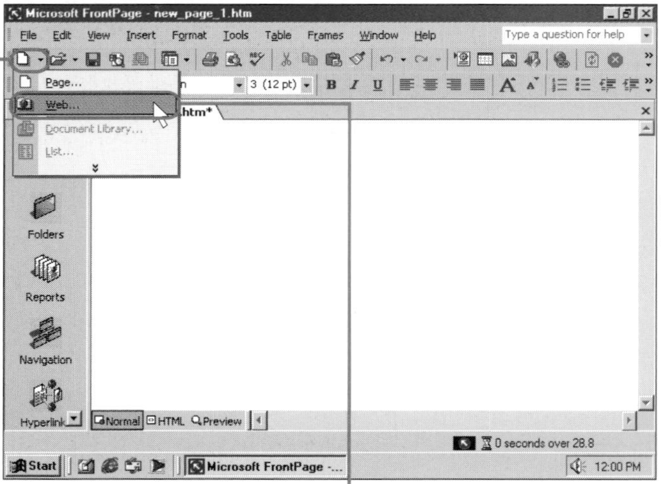

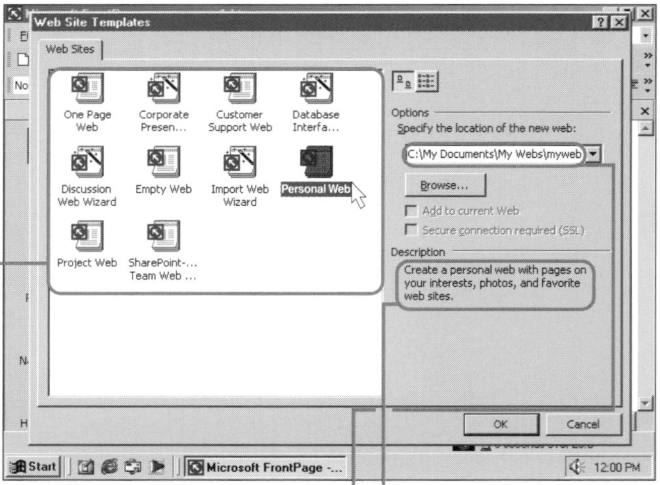

1 Click ▾ in this area.

2 Click **Web** to create a new Web site.

■ The Web Site Templates dialog box appears.

3 Click the template or wizard you want to use to create a new Web site.

Note: The icon for a wizard displays a magic wand (✨ *).*

■ This area displays a description of the template or wizard you selected.

■ This area displays the location where FrontPage will store the Web site on your computer and the name of the Web site.

How can I create a blank Web site?

You can use one of the following templates to create a Web site that does not contain any sample text or images. A blank Web site gives you the most flexibility and control.

The **One Page Web** template creates a Web site containing one blank Web page.

The **Empty Web** template creates an empty Web site that does not contain any Web pages. You can add the Web pages you need.

Where will FrontPage store my Web sites?

When you first opened FrontPage on your computer, a folder called My Webs was automatically created in the My Documents folder. FrontPage stores your Web sites in this folder.

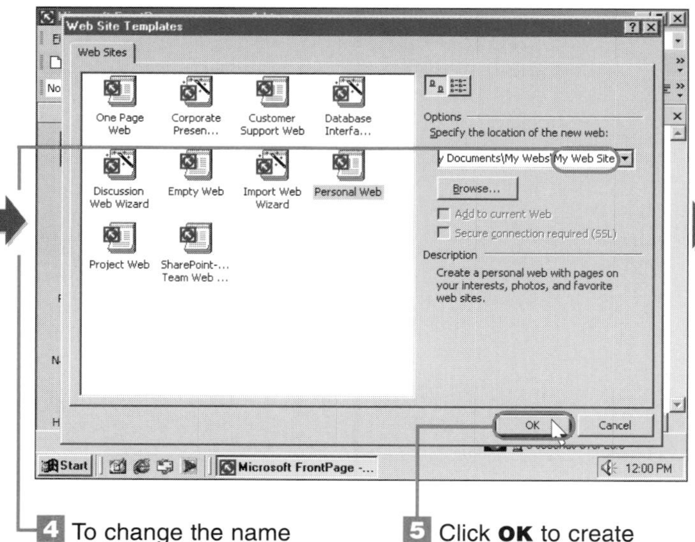

4 To change the name of the Web site, drag the mouse I over the existing name and then type a new name.

5 Click **OK** to create the Web site.

*Note: If you selected a wizard in step **3**, FrontPage will ask you a series of questions before creating the Web site.*

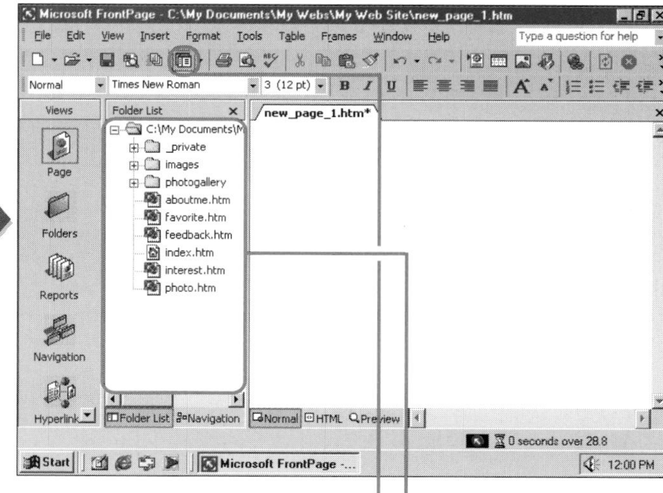

■ FrontPage creates the Web site.

■ If you already had a Web site open, the new Web site appears in a new Microsoft FrontPage window. You can click the buttons on the taskbar to switch between the Web sites.

■ This area lists the Web pages in the Web site.

■ If the list does not appear, click ▤ to display the list.

DISPLAY OR HIDE THE FOLDER LIST

You can display or hide a list of all the Web pages, folders and other items in your Web site.

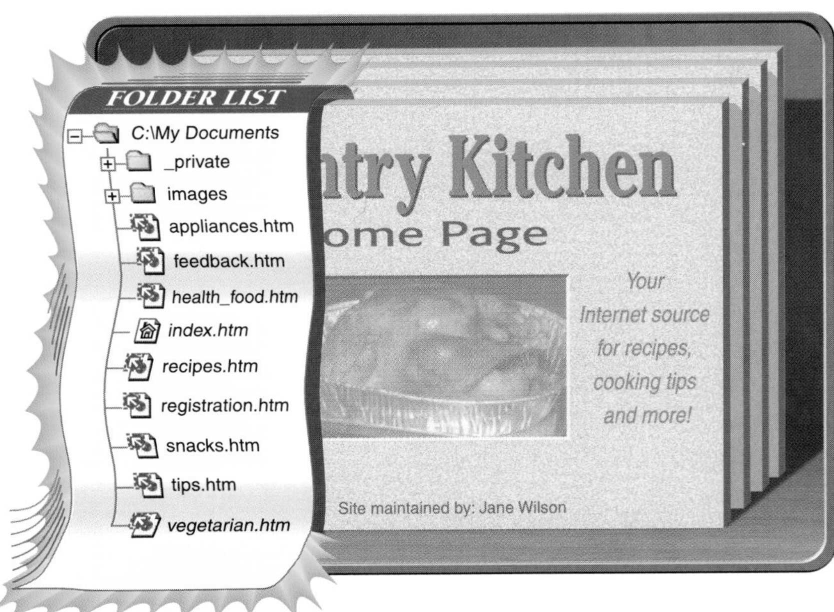

DISPLAY OR HIDE THE FOLDER LIST

1 Click .

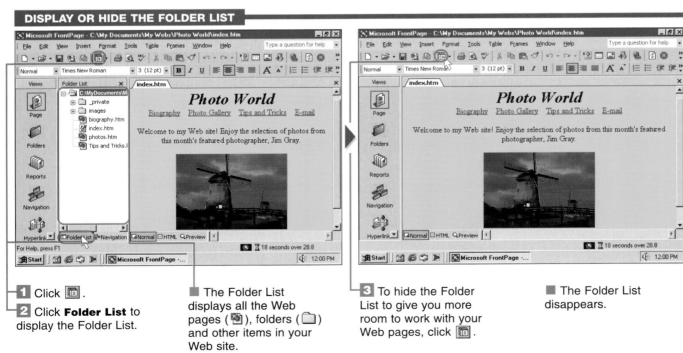

2 Click **Folder List** to display the Folder List.

■ The Folder List displays all the Web pages ( ), folders ( ) and other items in your Web site.

3 To hide the Folder List to give you more room to work with your Web pages, click .

■ The Folder List disappears.

DISPLAY OR HIDE THE NAVIGATION PANE

You can display or hide the Navigation Pane, which shows the navigational structure of your Web site.

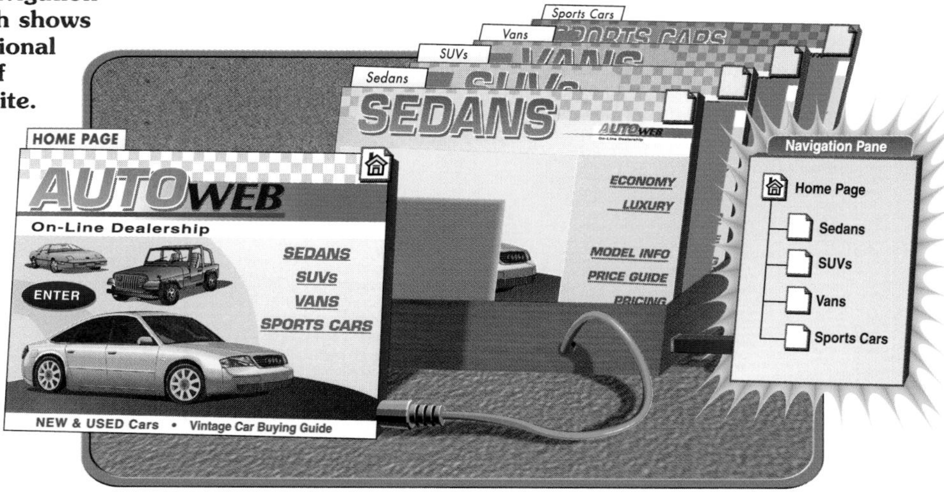

The navigational structure of your Web site defines how the Web pages in your Web site are related. For information on working with the navigational structure of your Web site, see pages 178 to 187.

DISPLAY OR HIDE THE NAVIGATION PANE

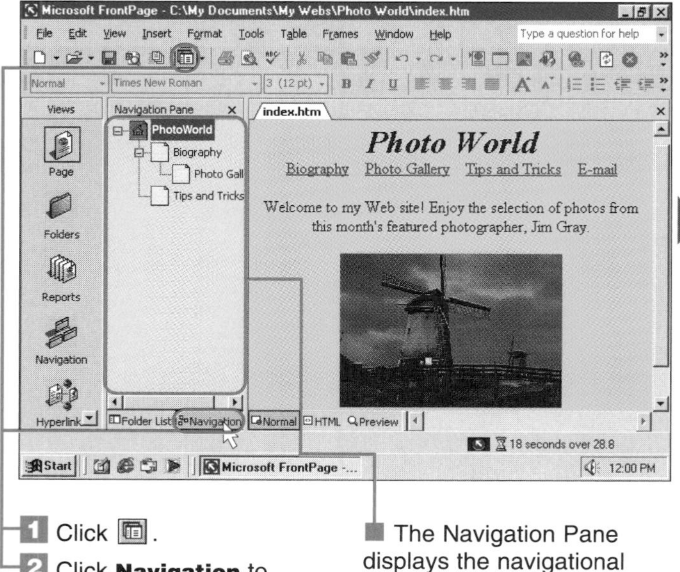

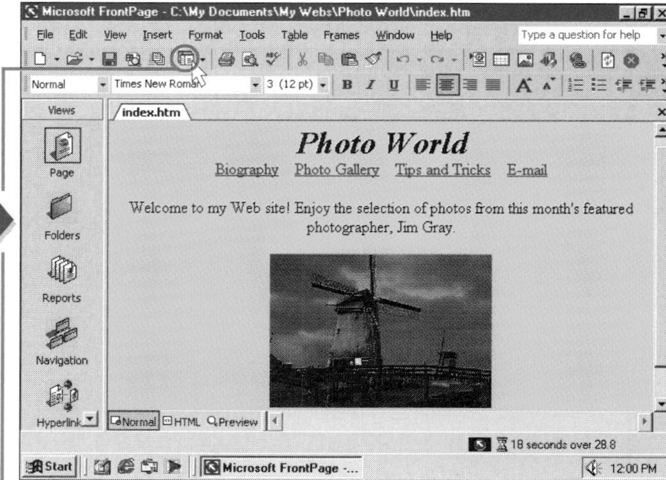

1 Click [icon].

2 Click **Navigation** to display the Navigation Pane.

■ The Navigation Pane displays the navigational structure of the Web pages in your Web site.

3 To hide the Navigation Pane to give you more room to work with your Web pages, click [icon].

■ The Navigation Pane disappears.

OPEN A WEB PAGE

You can open a Web page to view the page on your screen. This allows you to review and make changes to the Web page.

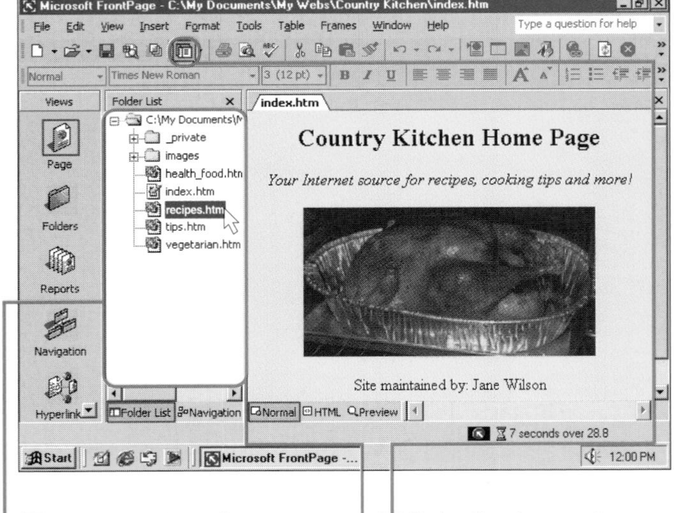

■ This area lists all the Web pages ( ), folders ( ) and other items in your Web site.

Note: Each Web page that is currently open displays a pencil ( ) on its icon.

■ If the list does not appear, click to display the list.

1 Double-click the Web page you want to open.

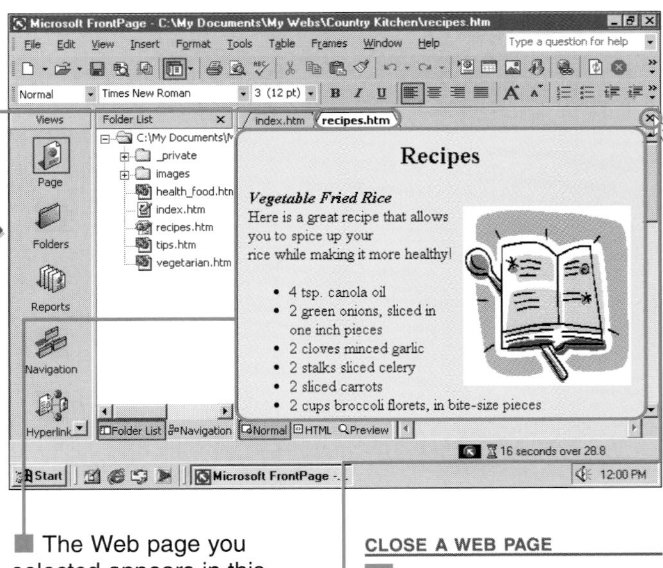

■ The Web page you selected appears in this area. You can now review and edit the Web page.

■ A tab displays the file name of the Web page.

CLOSE A WEB PAGE

1 When you finish working with a Web page, click to close the Web page.

■ The Web page disappears from your screen.

SWITCH BETWEEN WEB PAGES

You can have several Web pages in your Web site open at once. FrontPage allows you to easily switch from one open Web page to another.

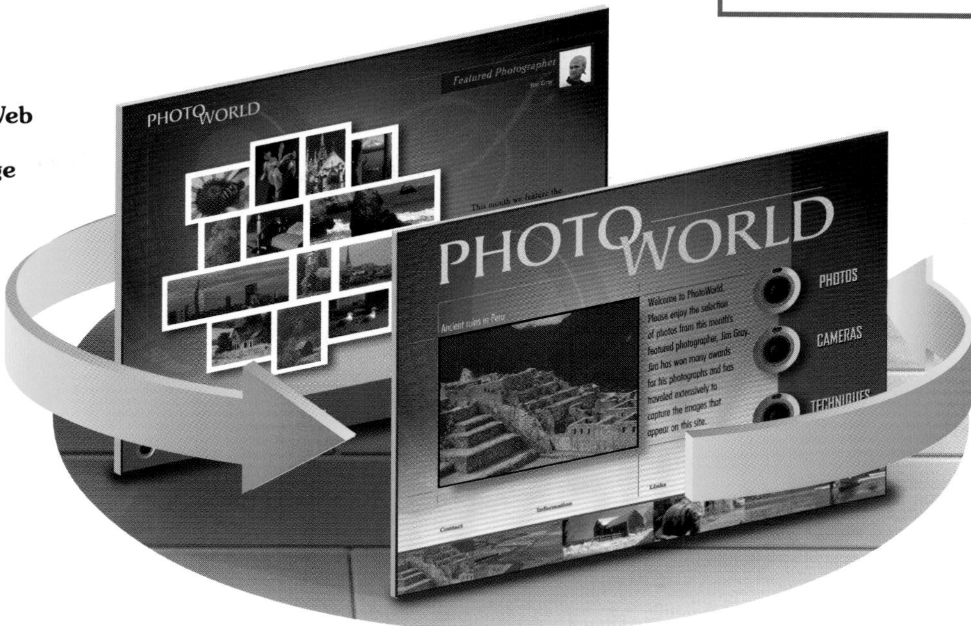

SWITCH BETWEEN WEB PAGES

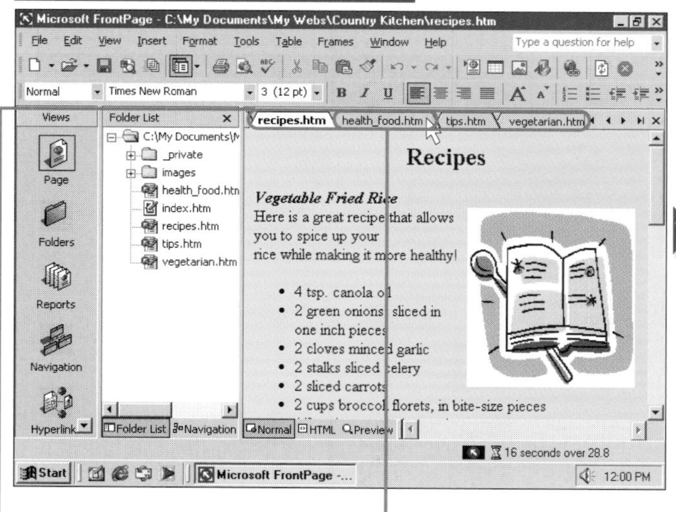

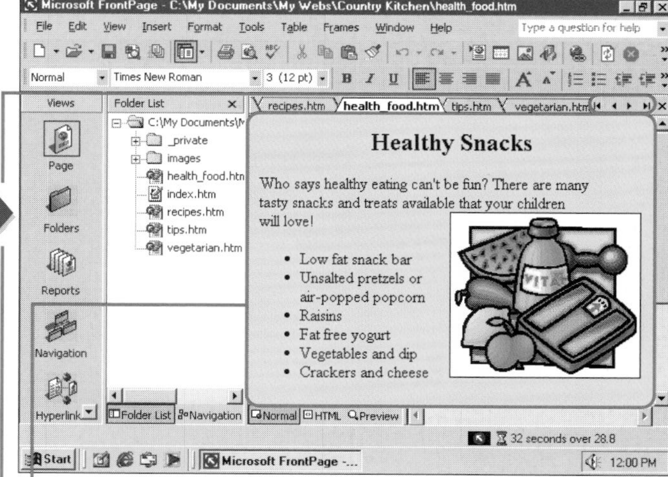

■ This area displays a tab for each open Web page. The displayed Web page has a white tab.

1 Click the tab for the Web page you want to display.

■ The Web page you selected appears. You can now review and edit the Web page.

■ These buttons appear if you have several Web pages open and FrontPage cannot display the tabs for all the open pages. To browse through the tabs, click one of the following buttons.

- Display first tab
- Display previous tab
- Display next tab
- Display last tab

DISPLAY OR HIDE A TOOLBAR

FrontPage offers several toolbars that you can display or hide at any time. Toolbars contain buttons that you can select to quickly perform common tasks.

When you first start FrontPage, the **Standard** and **Formatting** toolbars appear on your screen.

DISPLAY OR HIDE A TOOLBAR

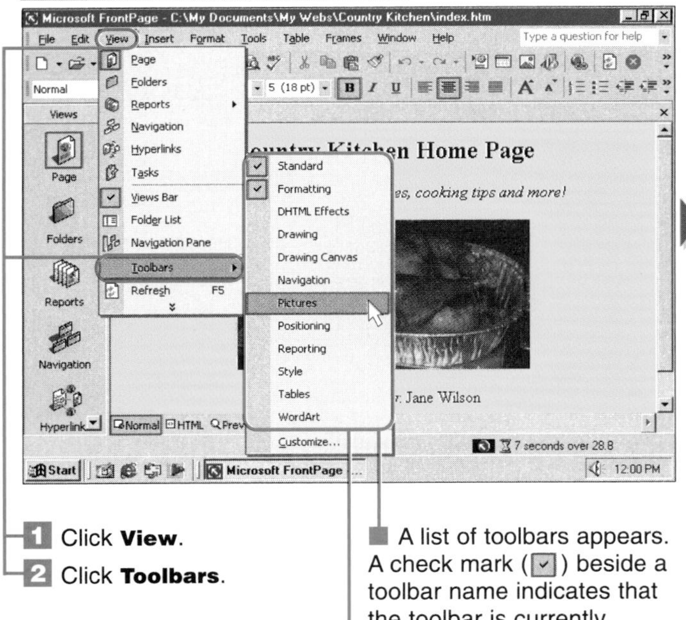

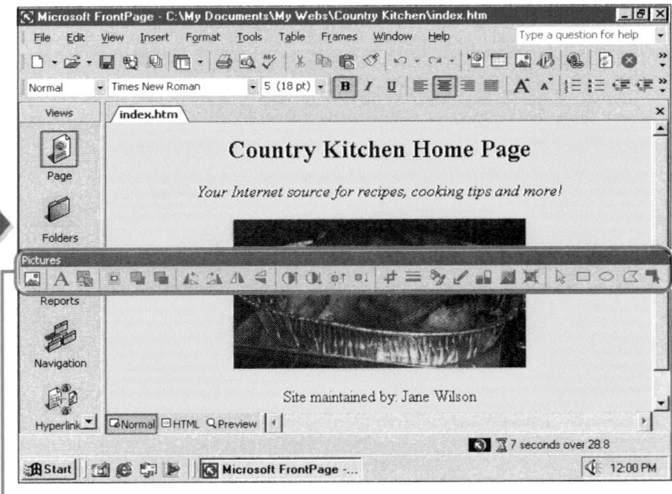

1 Click **View**.

2 Click **Toolbars**.

■ A list of toolbars appears. A check mark (☑) beside a toolbar name indicates that the toolbar is currently displayed.

3 Click the name of the toolbar you want to display or hide.

■ FrontPage displays or hides the toolbar you selected.

Note: A screen displaying fewer toolbars provides a larger and less cluttered working area.

CREATE A BLANK WEB PAGE

You can add a blank Web page to your Web site to provide information about a new topic.

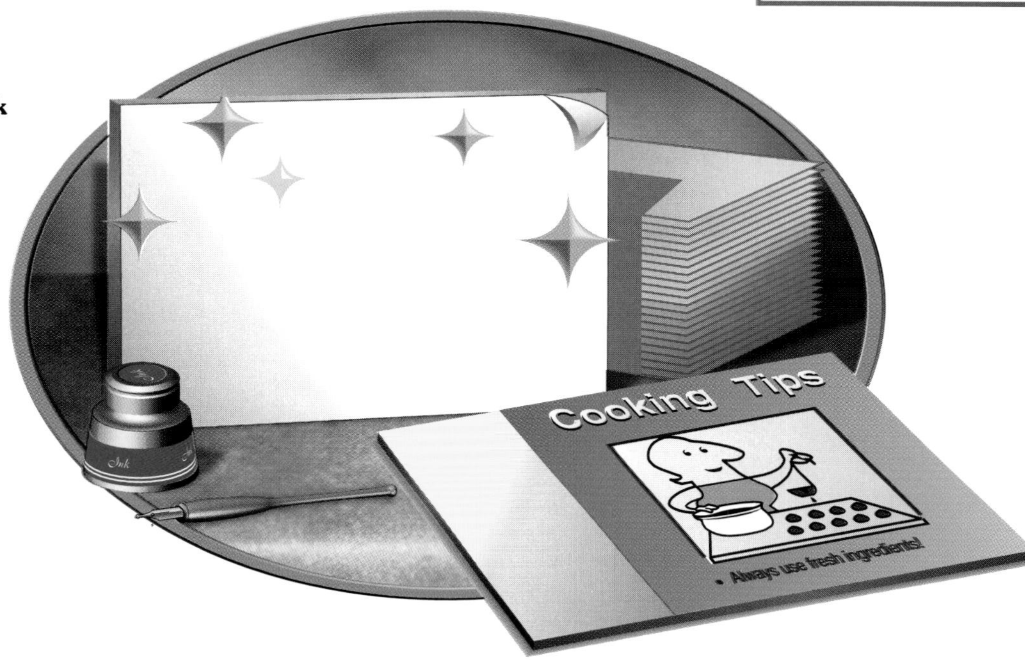

CREATE A BLANK WEB PAGE

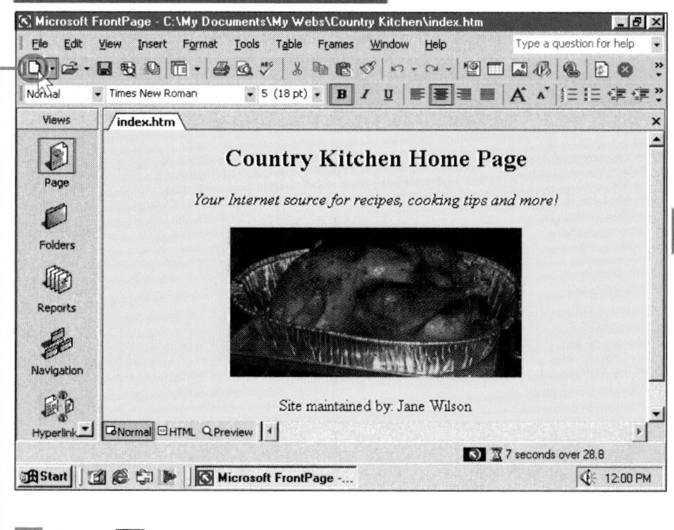

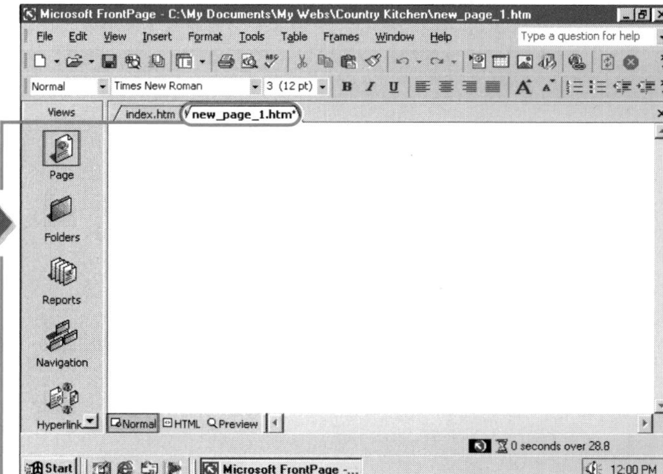

1 Click [new page icon] to create a blank Web page.

■ A blank Web page appears.

■ A tab displays a temporary file name for the Web page. To save and name the Web page, see page 28.

■ You can immediately add information to the Web page.

CREATE A WEB PAGE USING A TEMPLATE

FrontPage provides several ready-to-use templates that you can use to quickly create a new Web page.

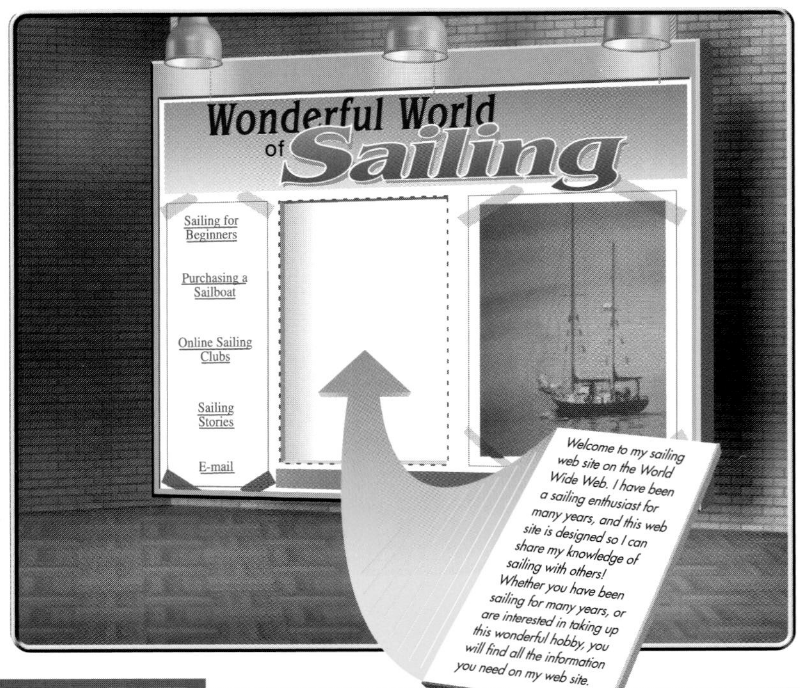

CREATE A WEB PAGE USING A TEMPLATE

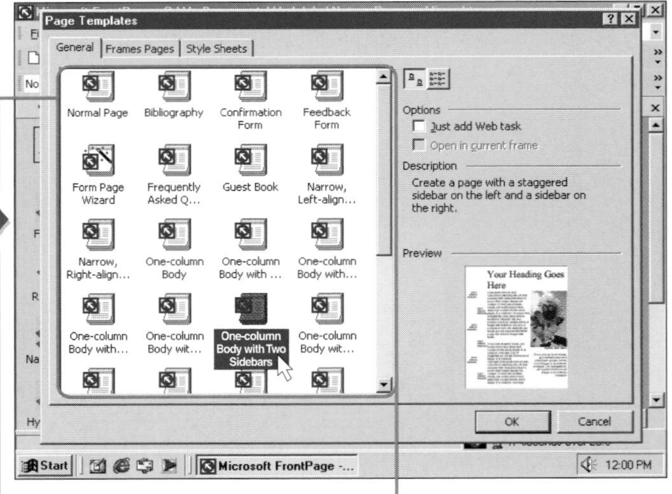

1 Click ▾ in this area.

2 Click **Page**.

■ The Page Templates dialog box appears.

■ This area displays the templates you can use to create your Web page.

3 Click the template you want to use.

Why would I use a template to create a new Web page?

If you are new to creating Web pages, templates can provide a good starting point for the layout and design of your Web pages. Templates provide sample text that can help you determine what text you should include on a Web page. You can replace the sample text with your own personalized information. FrontPage offers a variety of templates, such as a bibliography, feedback form, guest book and table of contents.

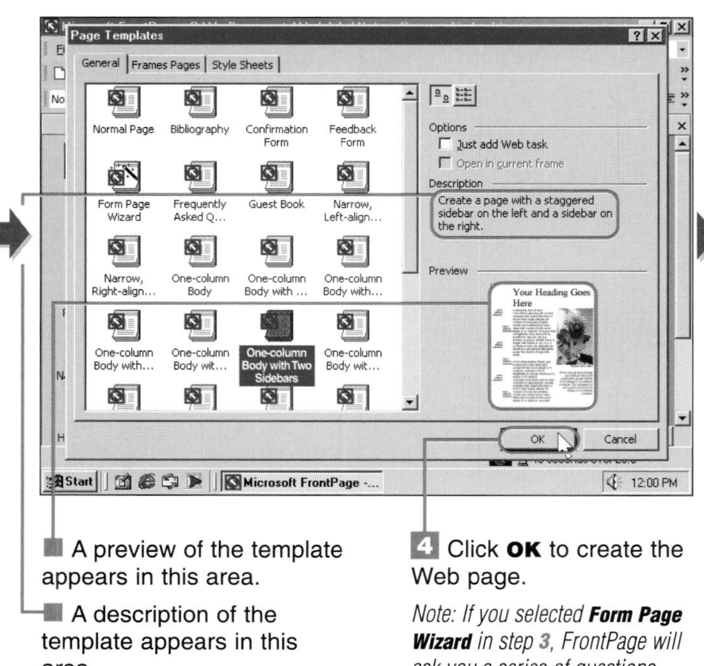

■ A preview of the template appears in this area.

■ A description of the template appears in this area.

4 Click **OK** to create the Web page.

*Note: If you selected **Form Page Wizard** in step 3, FrontPage will ask you a series of questions before creating the Web page.*

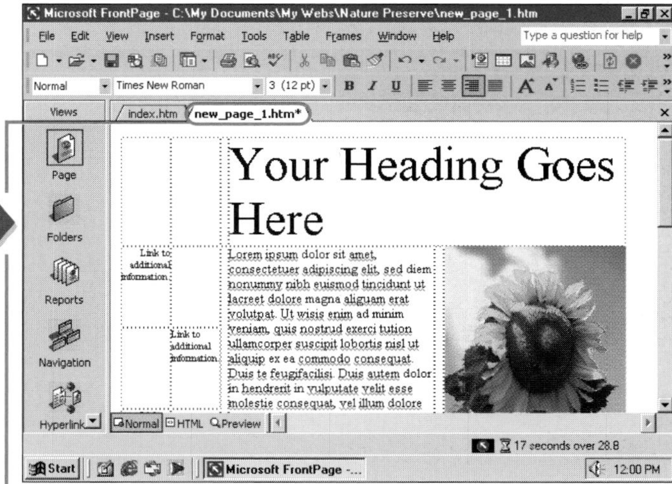

■ The Web page appears.

■ A tab displays a temporary file name for the Web page. To save and name the Web page, see page 28.

■ You can replace the existing text and images on the Web page with your own information.

SAVE A WEB PAGE

You should save a Web page to store the page for future use. Saving a Web page allows you to later review and edit the page.

If your Web page contains images, FrontPage will ask you to save the images when you save the Web page.

You should regularly save changes you make to your Web pages to avoid losing your work.

SAVE A WEB PAGE

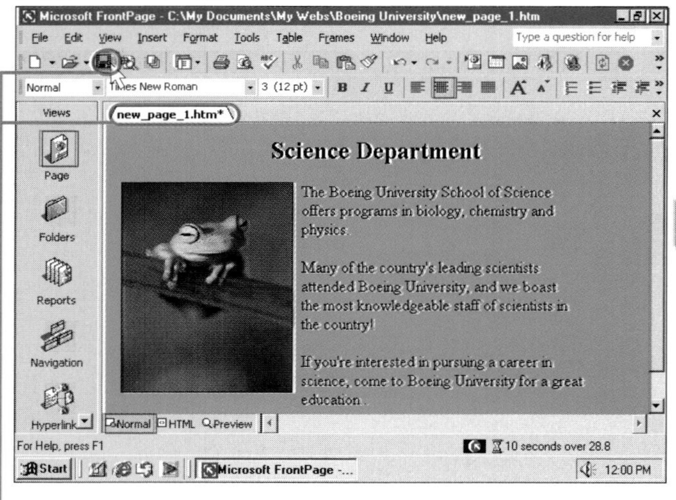

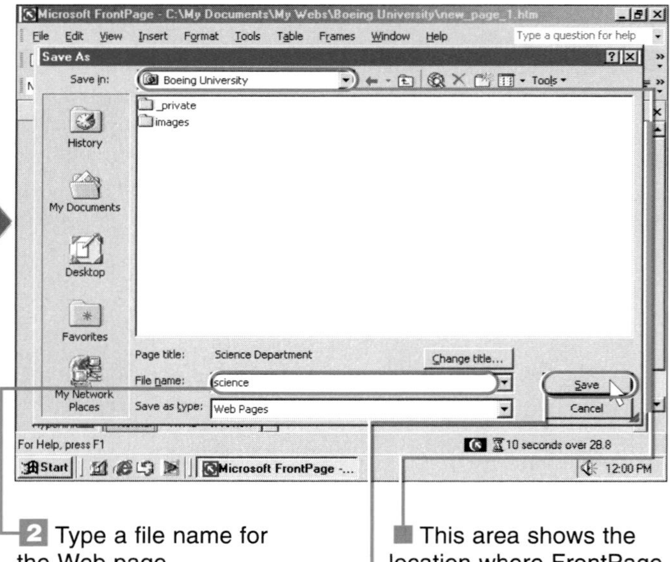

■ If you have not saved changes you have made to a Web page, an asterisk (*) appears on the tab for the page.

1 Click ▣ to save the displayed Web page.

■ The Save As dialog box appears.

Note: If you previously saved the Web page, the Save As dialog box will not appear since you have already named the page.

2 Type a file name for the Web page.

*Note: A Web page file name should not include spaces or the characters * : ? # > < | or ".*

■ This area shows the location where FrontPage will store your Web page.

3 Click **Save** to save the Web page.

Where will FrontPage store a Web page on my computer?

When you first opened FrontPage on your computer, a folder called My Webs was automatically created in the My Documents folder. The My Webs folder contains a separate folder for each Web site you create. When you save a Web page, FrontPage will store the Web page in the folder for the current Web site.

When I save a Web page, why do I need to save the images displayed on the page?

When you add an image to a Web page, you must save the image as part of your Web site. FrontPage will store a copy of the image in the same folder that stores all the Web pages for your Web site. This ensures the image will transfer with your Web site when you publish your Web pages.

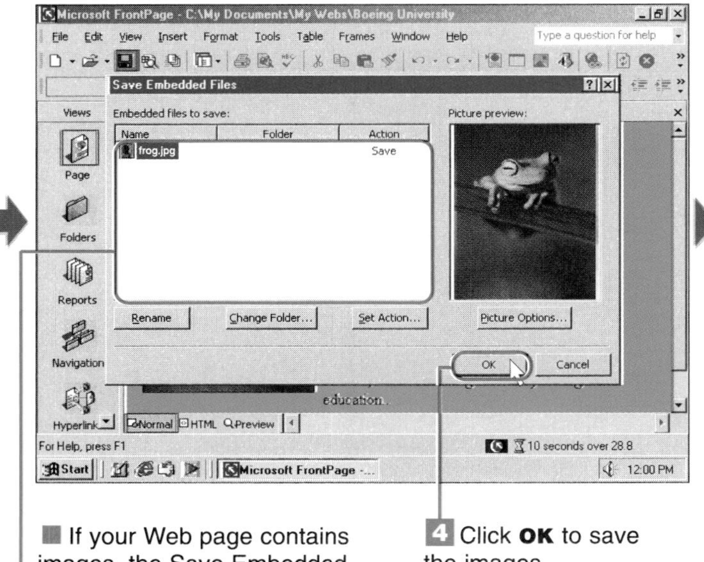

■ If your Web page contains images, the Save Embedded Files dialog box appears.

■ This area lists the images you added to the Web page.

4 Click **OK** to save the images.

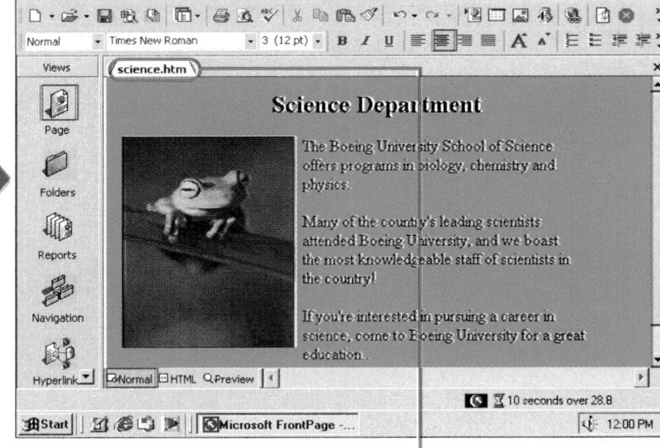

■ FrontPage saves your Web page and the images displayed on the page.

■ The tab for the Web page displays the file name you specified.

USING THE TASK PANE

You can use the task panes that come with FrontPage to perform common tasks. A task pane appears when you first start FrontPage.

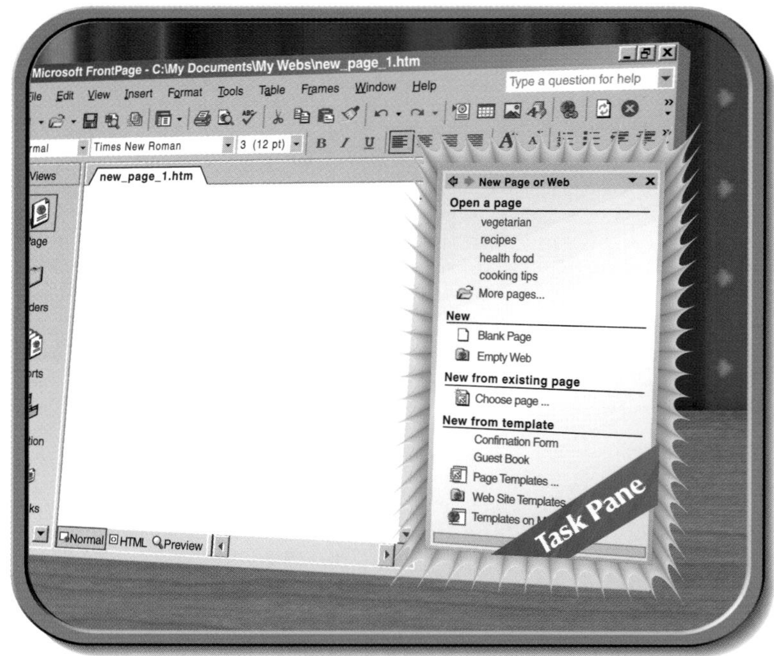

USING THE TASK PANE

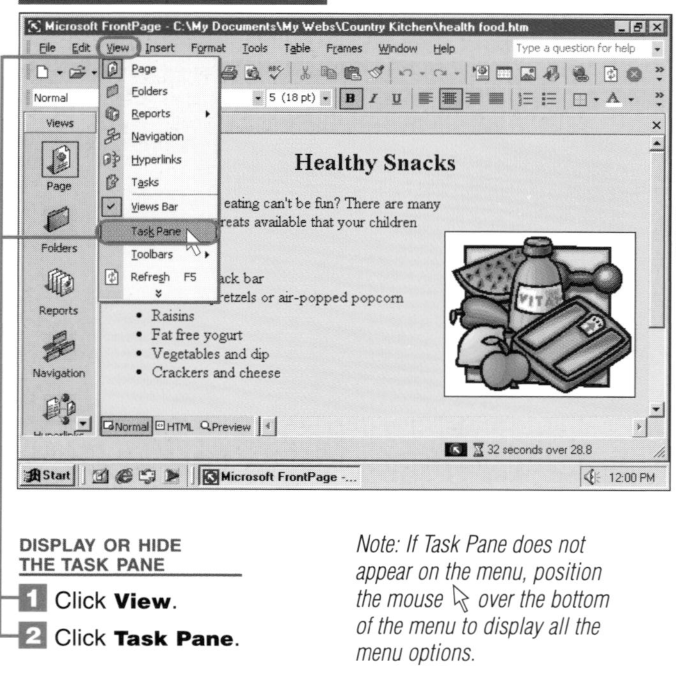

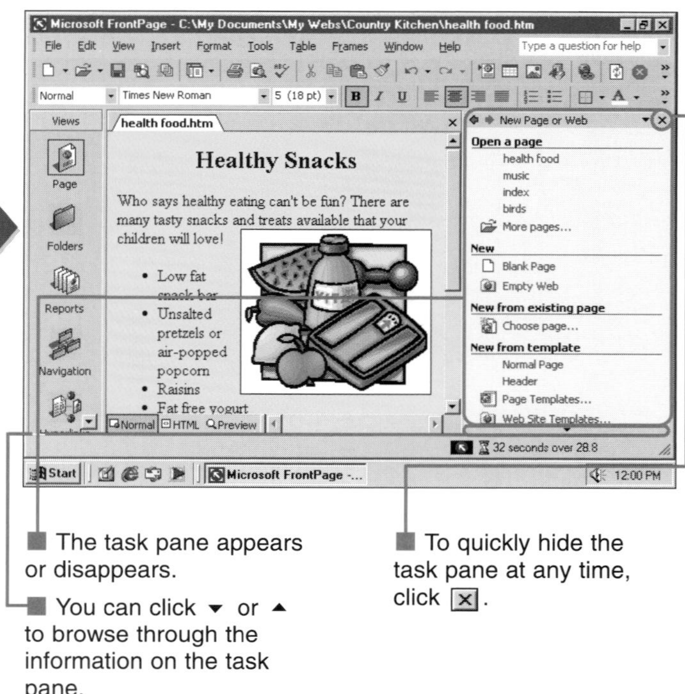

DISPLAY OR HIDE THE TASK PANE

1 Click **View**.

2 Click **Task Pane**.

Note: If Task Pane does not appear on the menu, position the mouse over the bottom of the menu to display all the menu options.

■ The task pane appears or disappears.

■ You can click ▾ or ▴ to browse through the information on the task pane.

■ To quickly hide the task pane at any time, click ☒.

What task panes are available in FrontPage?

New Page or Web

Allows you to perform common tasks in FrontPage, such as opening a Web page and creating a new Web page. To perform a task, click the task you want to perform.

Clipboard

Displays each item you have selected to move or copy. For information on moving and copying text, see page 56. To place a clipboard item on a Web page, click the item.

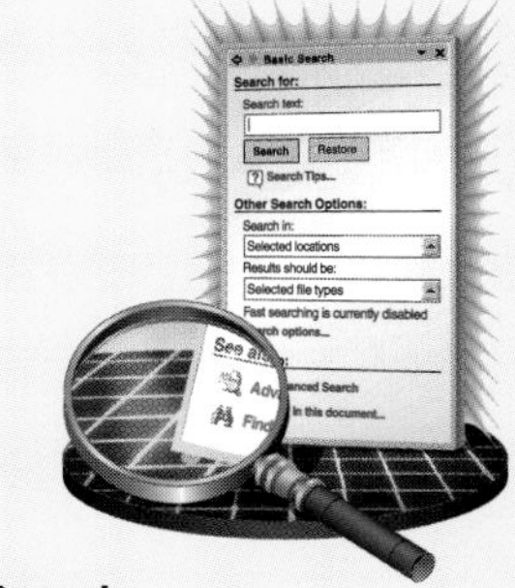

Search

Allows you to search for Web pages and other types of files on your computer. For information on searching for Web pages and other types of files, see page 50.

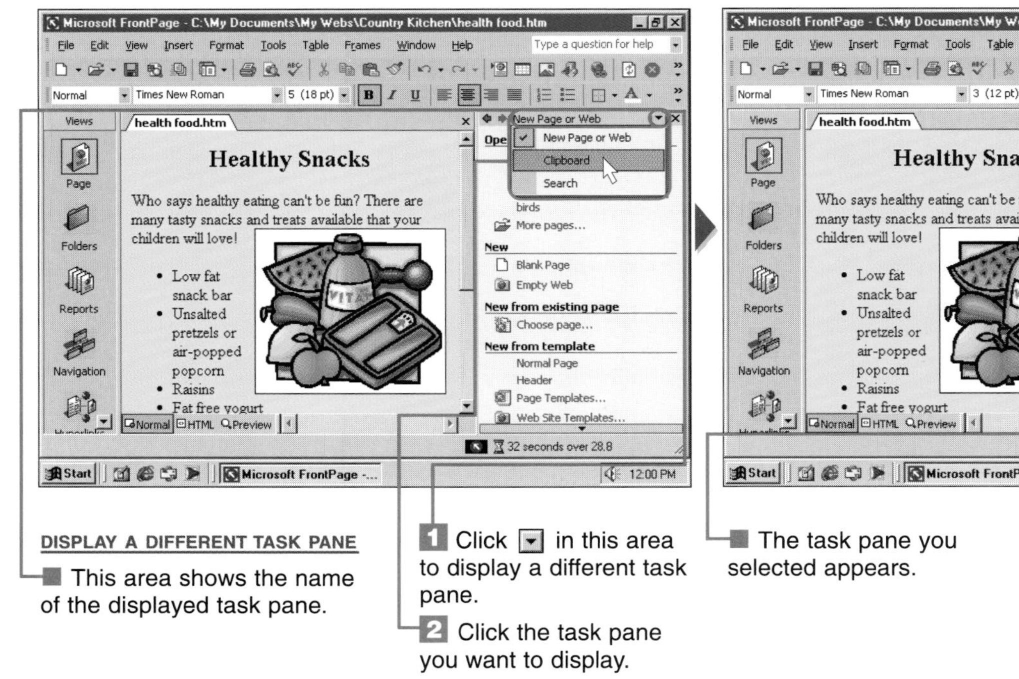

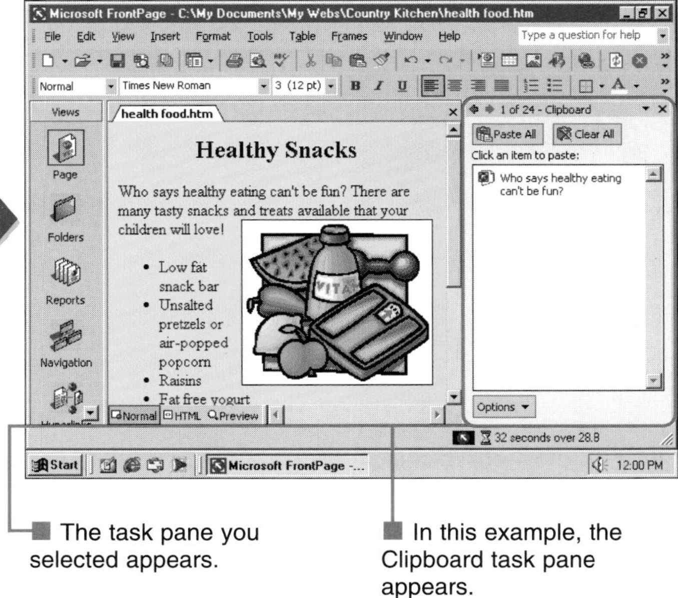

DISPLAY A DIFFERENT TASK PANE

■ This area shows the name of the displayed task pane.

1 Click ▾ in this area to display a different task pane.

2 Click the task pane you want to display.

■ The task pane you selected appears.

■ In this example, the Clipboard task pane appears.

CHANGE THE VIEW OF A WEB SITE

FrontPage offers six different views of your Web site that you can use to create and organize your Web pages.

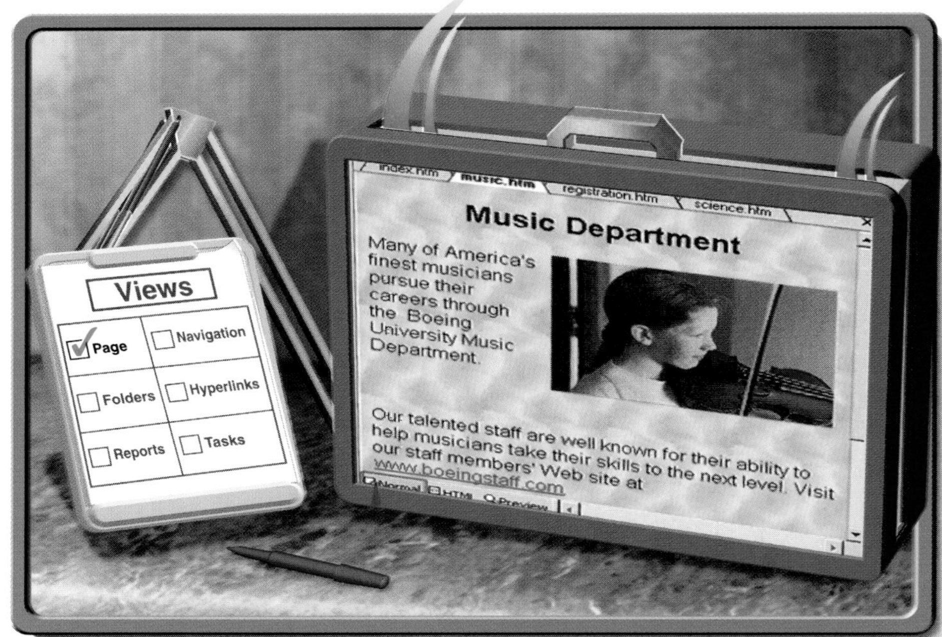

CHANGE THE VIEW OF A WEB SITE

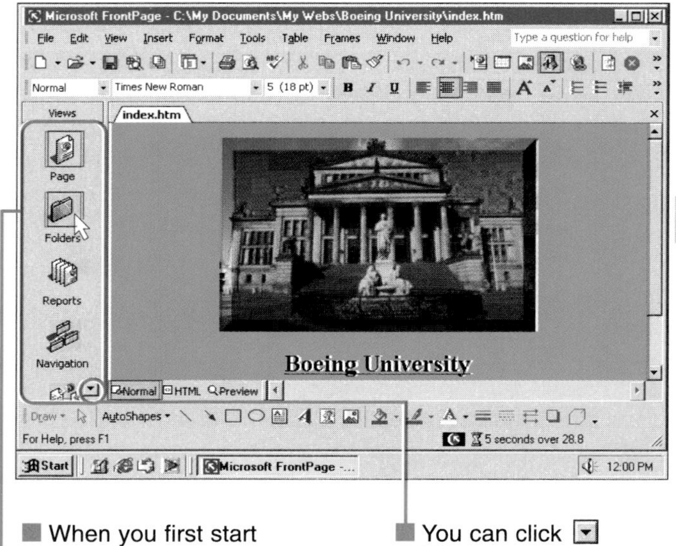

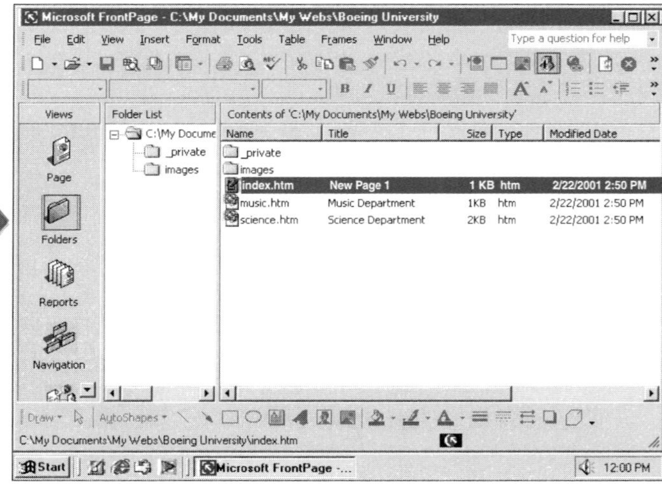

■ When you first start FrontPage, your Web site appears in the Page view.

1 To change the view of your Web site, click the icon for the view you want to use.

■ You can click ▼ or ▲ to browse through the views.

■ Your Web site appears in the view you selected.

THE WEB SITE VIEWS

Page

The Page view allows you to enter, edit and format the information on your Web pages.

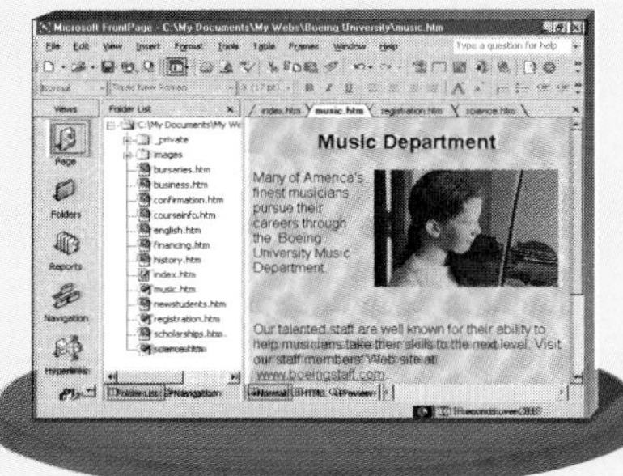

Folders

The Folders view displays the organization of the folders in your Web site and lists information about the Web pages, images and other items in your Web site.

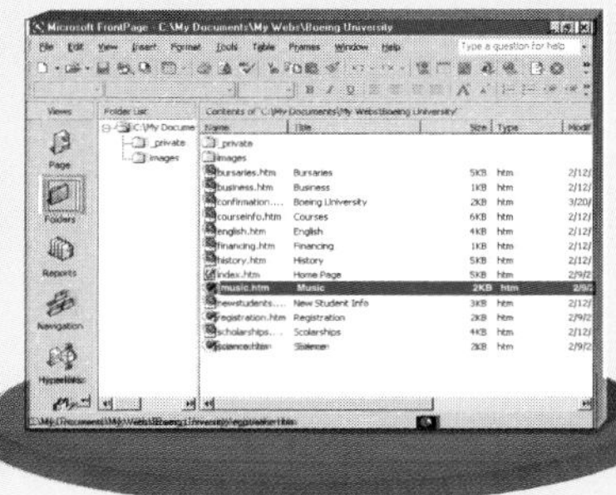

Reports

The Reports view allows you to display various reports that analyze and summarize information about your Web site.

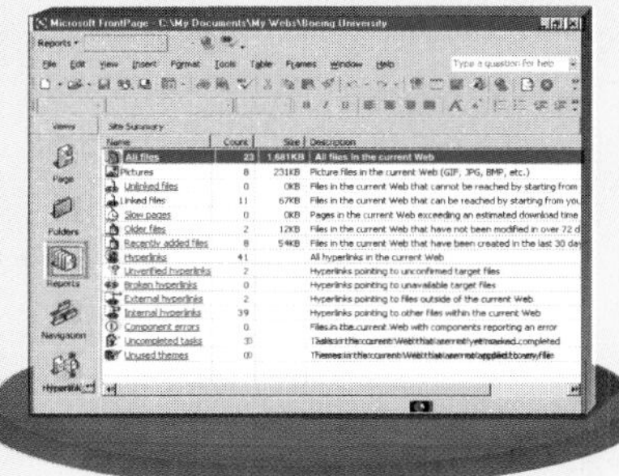

Navigation

The Navigation view allows you to view and work with the navigational structure of the Web pages in your Web site.

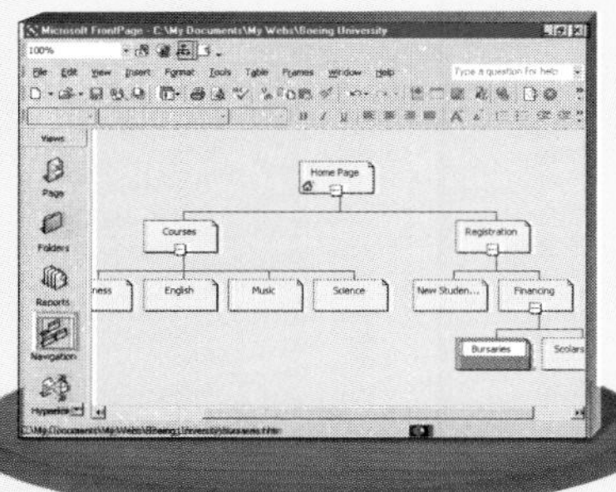

Hyperlinks

The Hyperlinks view allows you to view the links that connect the Web pages in your Web site.

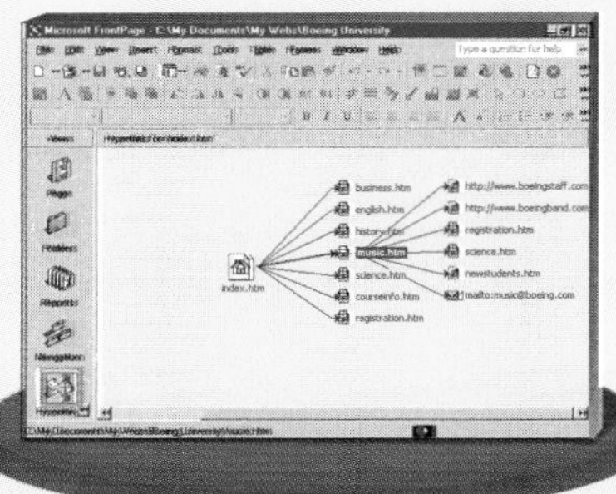

Tasks

The Tasks view allows you to create a to-do list to keep track of tasks you need to accomplish to complete your Web site.

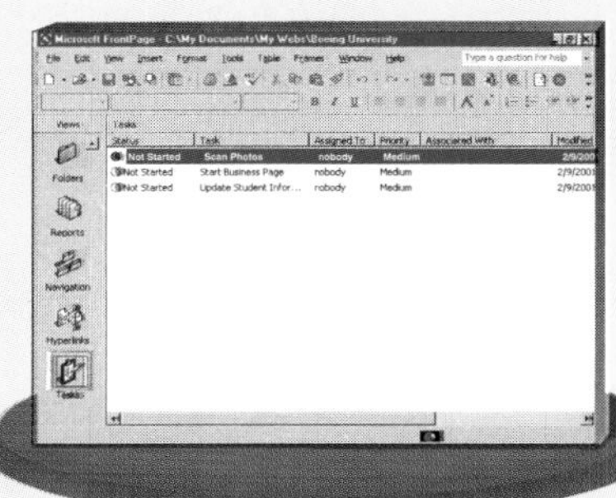

OPEN A WEB SITE

You can open a Web site so you can review and make changes to the site.

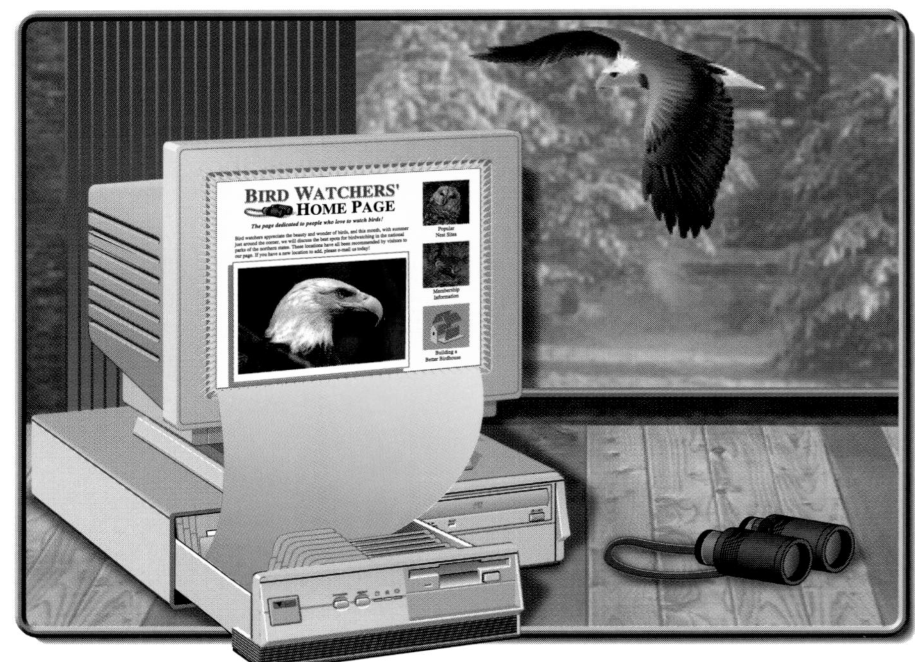

OPEN A WEB SITE

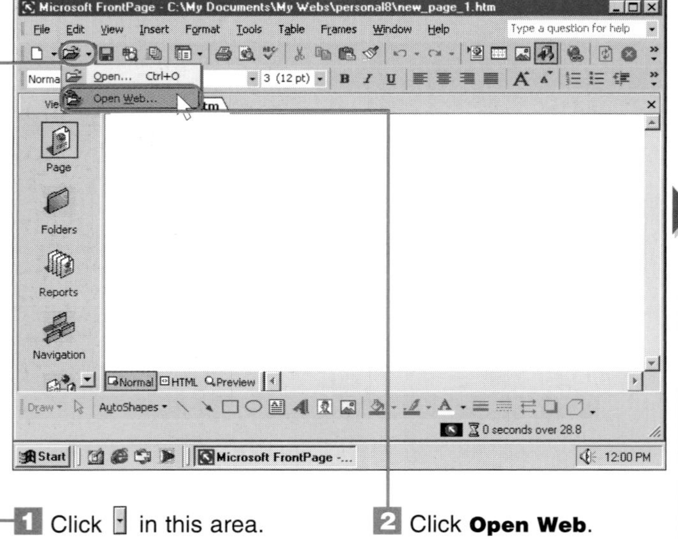

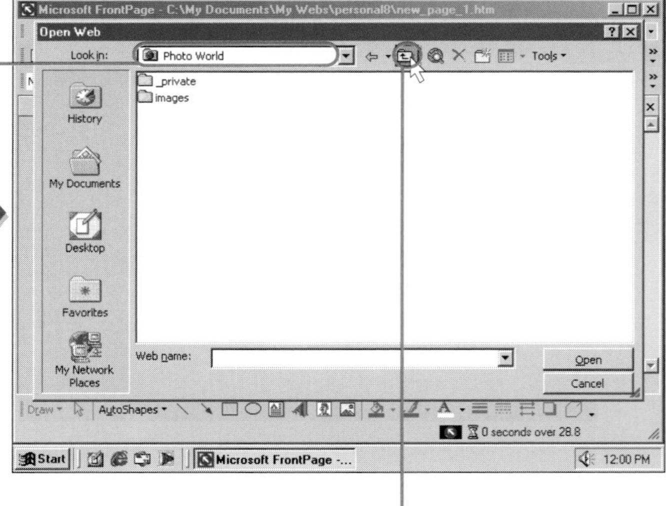

1 Click ▾ in this area.

2 Click **Open Web**.

■ The Open Web dialog box appears.

■ This area shows the location of the displayed folders.

3 Click the up-folder button to display the contents of the My Webs folder.

Note: FrontPage automatically stores your Web sites in the My Webs folder.

How can I quickly open a Web site I recently worked with?

FrontPage remembers the names of the last four Web sites you worked with. You can quickly open any of these Web sites.

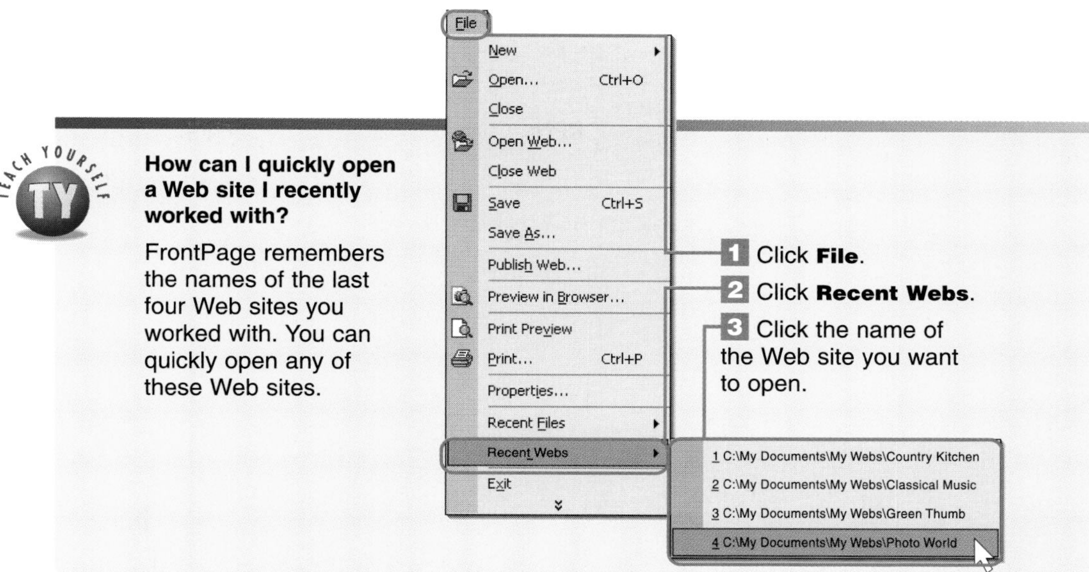

1 Click **File**.

2 Click **Recent Webs**.

3 Click the name of the Web site you want to open.

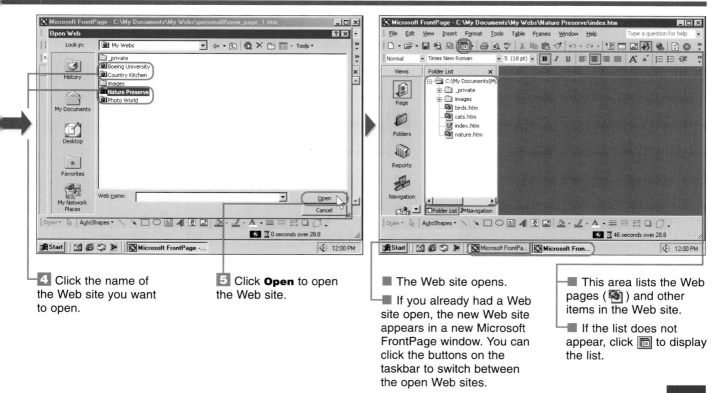

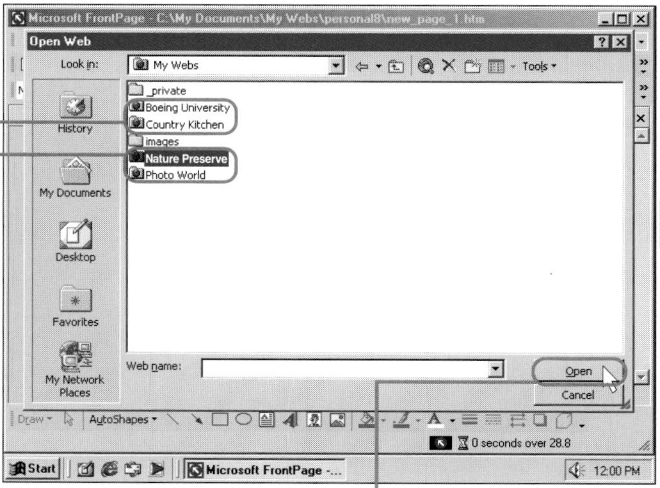

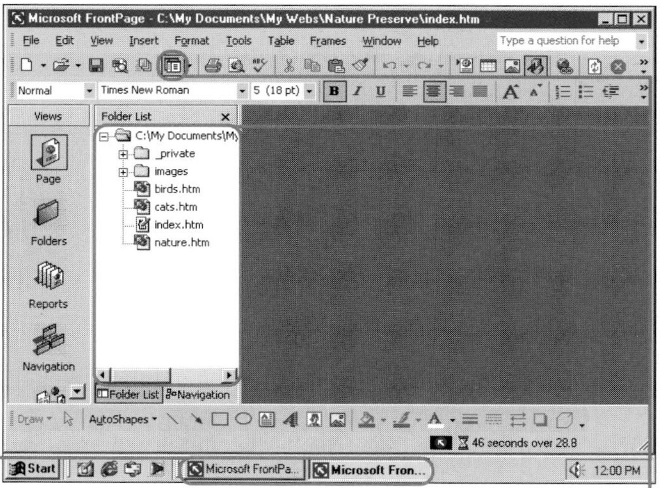

4 Click the name of the Web site you want to open.

5 Click **Open** to open the Web site.

■ The Web site opens.

■ If you already had a Web site open, the new Web site appears in a new Microsoft FrontPage window. You can click the buttons on the taskbar to switch between the open Web sites.

■ This area lists the Web pages ( ) and other items in the Web site.

■ If the list does not appear, click to display the list.

PHOTO WORLD
PHOTOS
CAMERAS
TECHNIQUES
Welcome to PhotoWorld. Please enjoy the selection of photos from this month's featured photographer, Jim Gray. Jim has won many awards for his photographs and has traveled extensively to capture the images that appear on this site.
Home
Music
Science
Mathematics
Law
Student Services
Registration Forms

CHAPTER 3

Work With Web Pages

Would you like to print, rename and delete your Web pages? This chapter shows you how to perform these tasks and more.

FrontPage allows you to add text to a Web page quickly and easily.

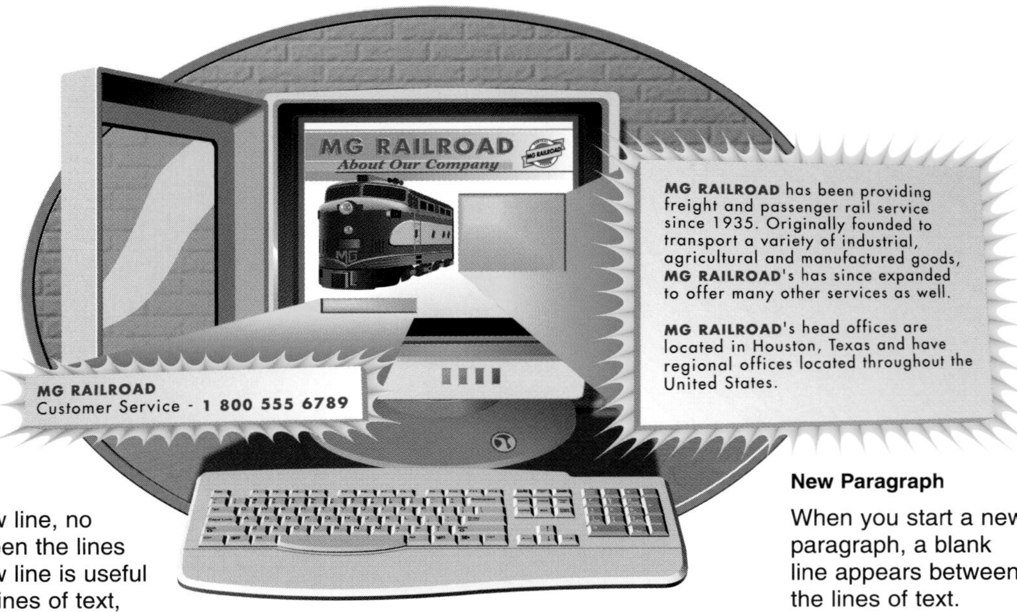

New Line

When you start a new line, no space appears between the lines of text. Starting a new line is useful when entering short lines of text, such a mailing address or poem.

New Paragraph

When you start a new paragraph, a blank line appears between the lines of text.

ENTER TEXT

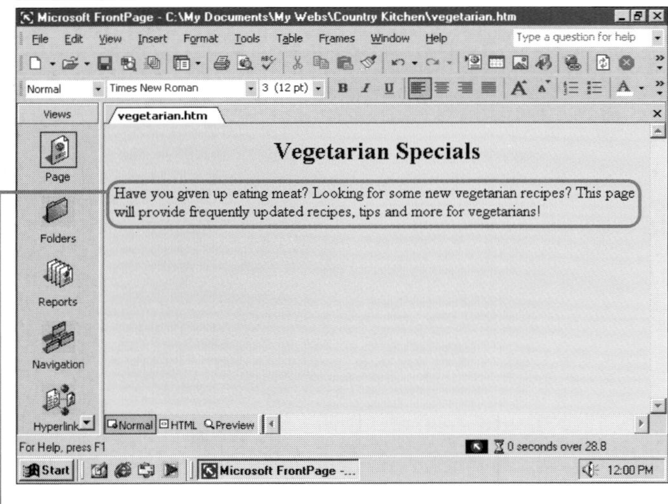

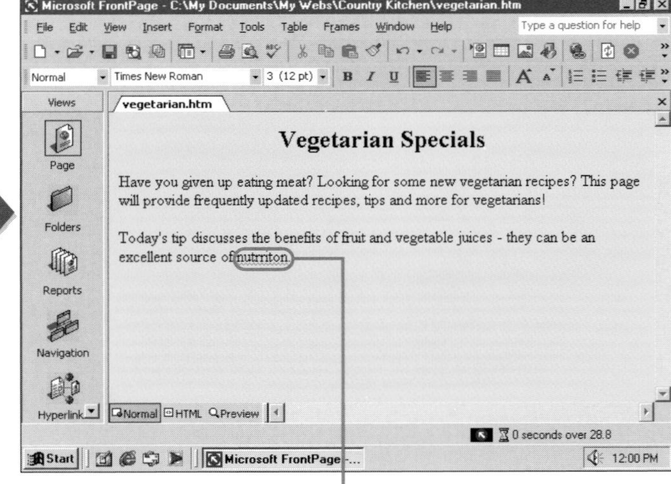

1 Type the text you want to display on your Web page.

■ The text you type will appear where the insertion point flashes on your screen.

2 To start a new paragraph, press the Enter key.

■ To start a new line, press and hold down the Shift key as you press the Enter key.

■ FrontPage automatically underlines misspelled words in red. The underlines will not appear when you publish your Web pages. To correct misspelled words, see page 60.

You can remove text you no longer need from a Web page.

When you remove text from a Web page, the remaining text in the line or paragraph will move to fill the empty space.

DELETE TEXT

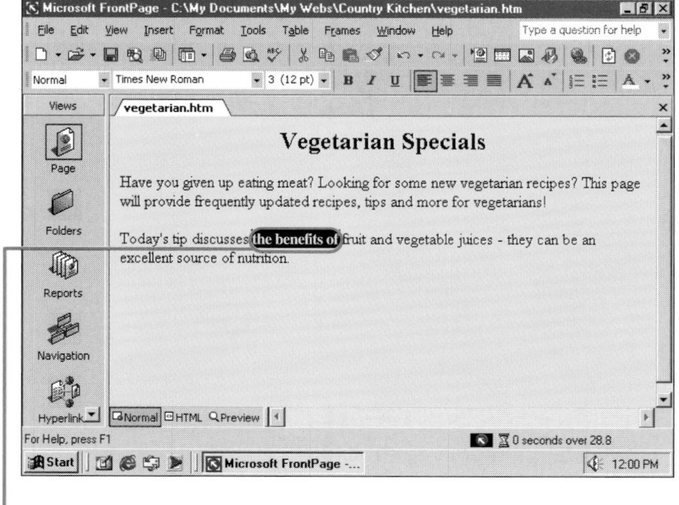

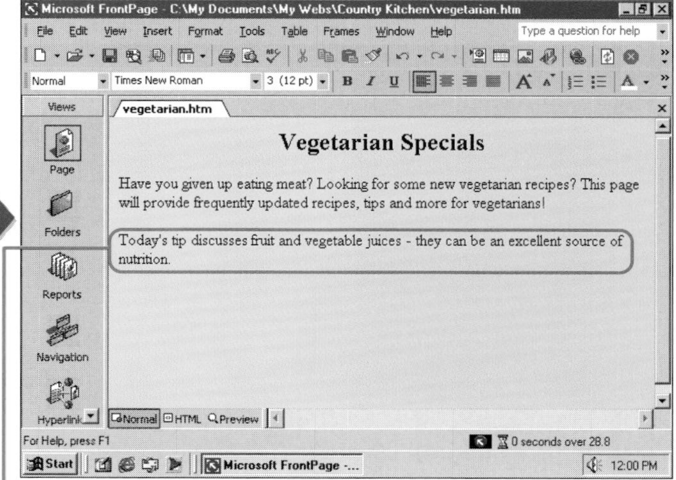

1 Select the text you want to delete. To select text, see page 54.

2 Press the Delete key to remove the text.

■ The text disappears. The remaining text in the line or paragraph moves to fill the empty space.

■ To delete a single character, click to the right of the character you want to delete and then press the ←Backspace key. FrontPage deletes the character to the left of the flashing insertion point.

PRINT A WEB PAGE

You can produce a paper copy of the Web page displayed on your screen. This is useful if you want to review and edit the Web page.

Before printing a Web page, make sure your printer is turned on and contains paper.

PRINT A WEB PAGE

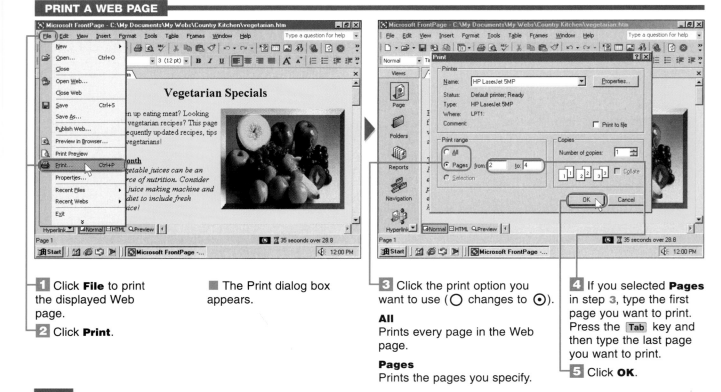

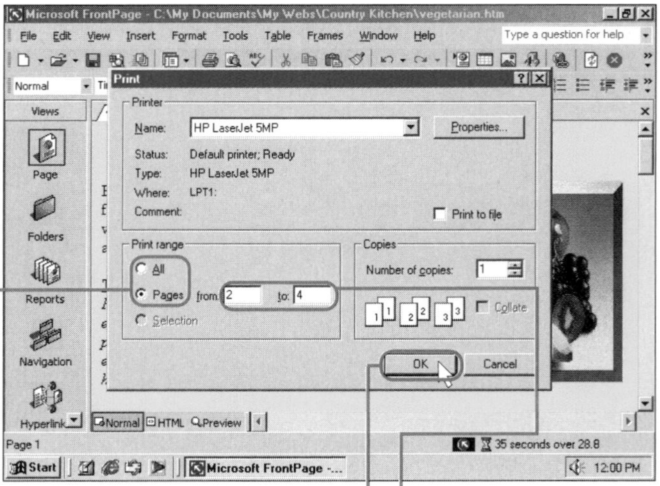

1 Click **File** to print the displayed Web page.

2 Click **Print**.

■ The Print dialog box appears.

3 Click the print option you want to use (○ changes to ⦿).

All
Prints every page in the Web page.

Pages
Prints the pages you specify.

4 If you selected **Pages** in step 3, type the first page you want to print. Press the Tab key and then type the last page you want to print.

5 Click **OK**.

DISPLAY WEB PAGE DOWNLOAD TIME

FrontPage displays the estimated amount of time a Web page will take to transfer to a visitor's computer.

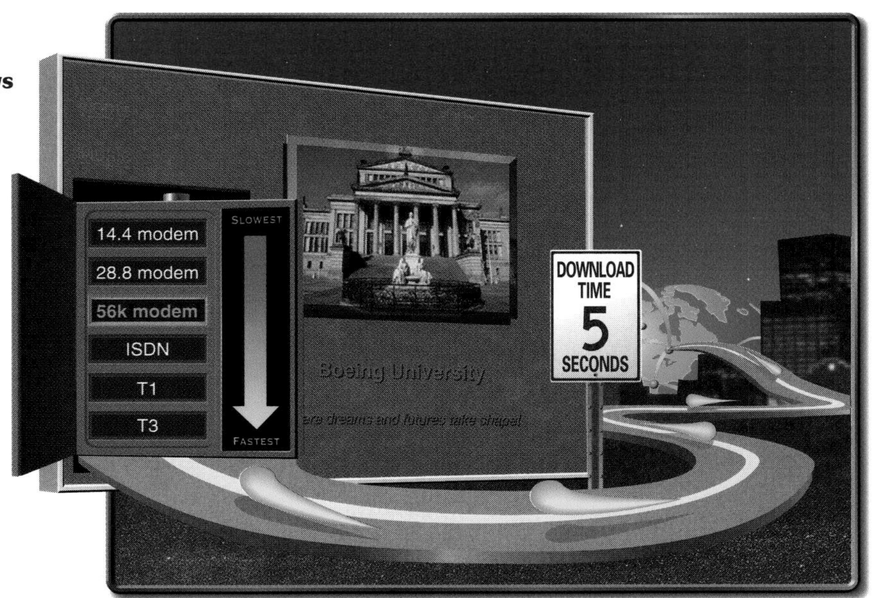

You can display the estimated download time for various types of connections. Faster types of connections will download a Web page more quickly.

DISPLAY WEB PAGE DOWNLOAD TIME

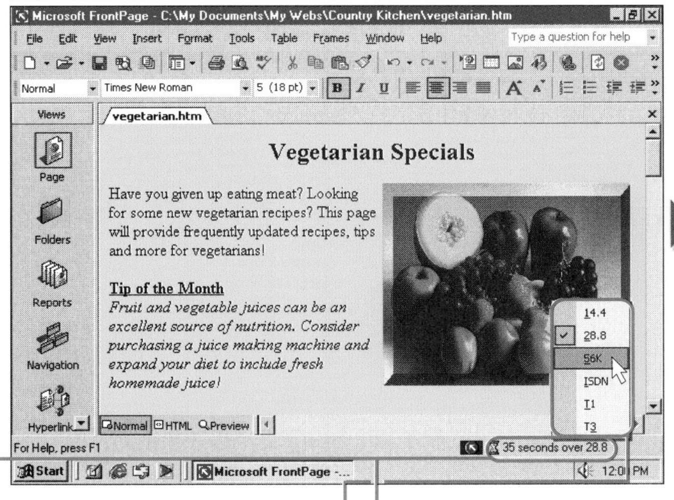

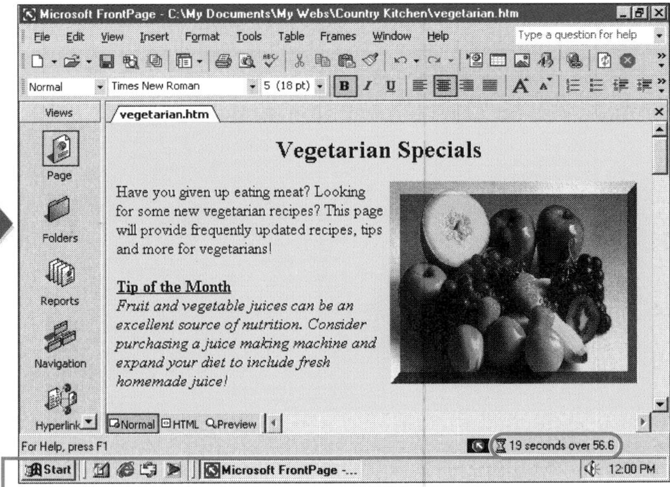

■ This area displays the estimated amount of time the displayed Web page will take to transfer to a visitor's computer using a 28.8 Kbps modem.

1 To view the estimated amount of time for another type of connection, click this area. A list of connection types appears.

2 Click the connection type of interest.

■ This area displays the estimated amount of time the displayed Web page will take to transfer to a visitor's computer using the connection type you selected.

Note: Web pages with more text, images and other items will take longer to transfer to a visitor's computer.

CHANGE THE VIEW OF A WEB PAGE

FrontPage offers three different ways that you can view your Web pages.

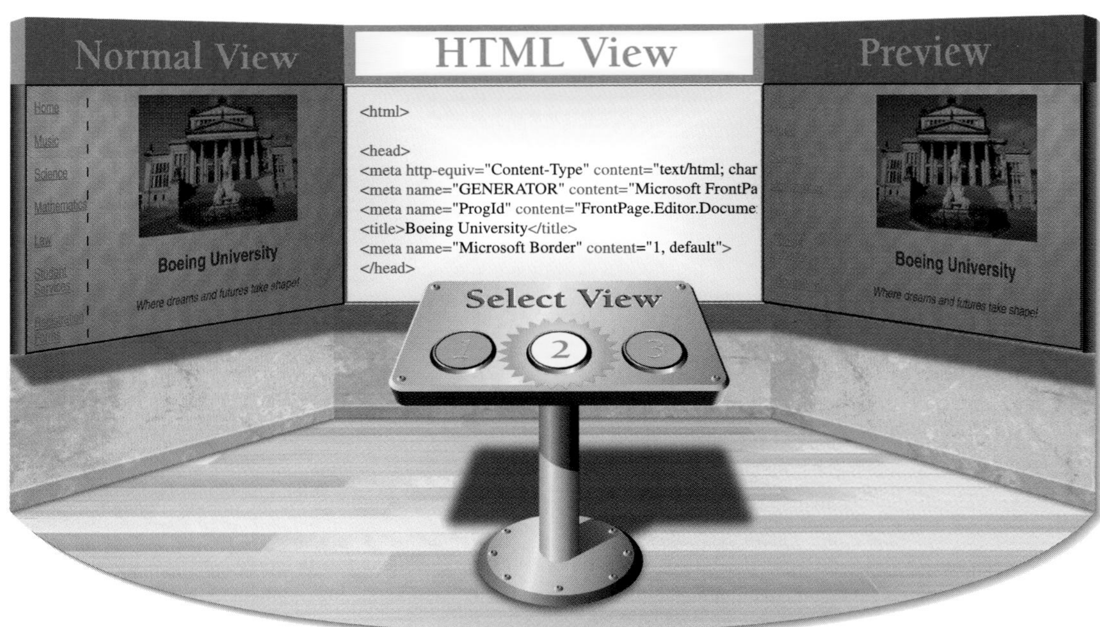

CHANGE THE VIEW OF A WEB PAGE

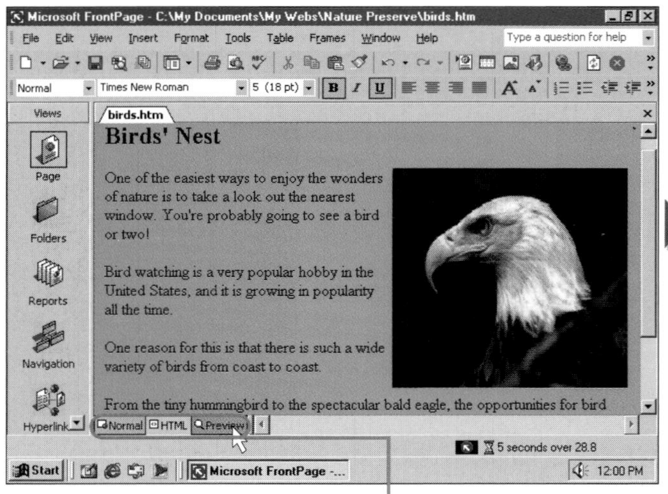

■ By default, Web pages appear in the Normal view.

1 Click a button to display a Web page in a different view.

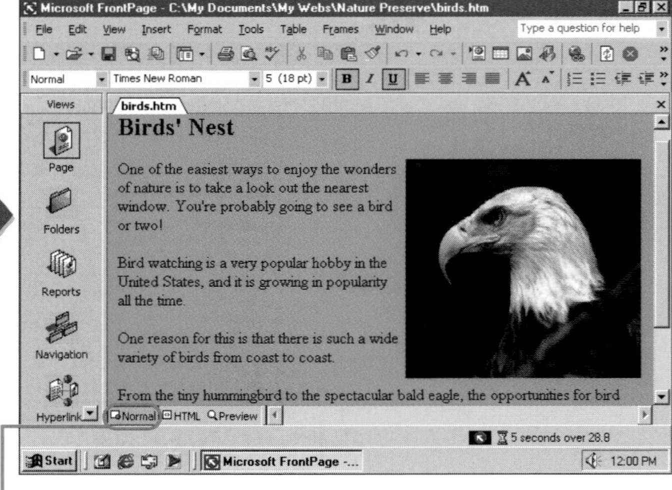

NORMAL

■ The Normal view allows you to enter, edit and format the information on a Web page.

How are HTML tags used to create a Web page?

Each tag gives a specific instruction and is surrounded by angle brackets < >. Most tags have an opening tag and a closing tag that affect the text between the tags. The closing tag has a forward slash (/). Some tags have only an opening tag. Here are some common tags.

Tag	Description
<b>	Bolds text
<blockquote>	Separates a section of text from the main text
<body>	Identifies the main content of a Web page
<i>	Italicizes text
<p>	Starts a new paragraph
<title>	Creates a title for a Web page

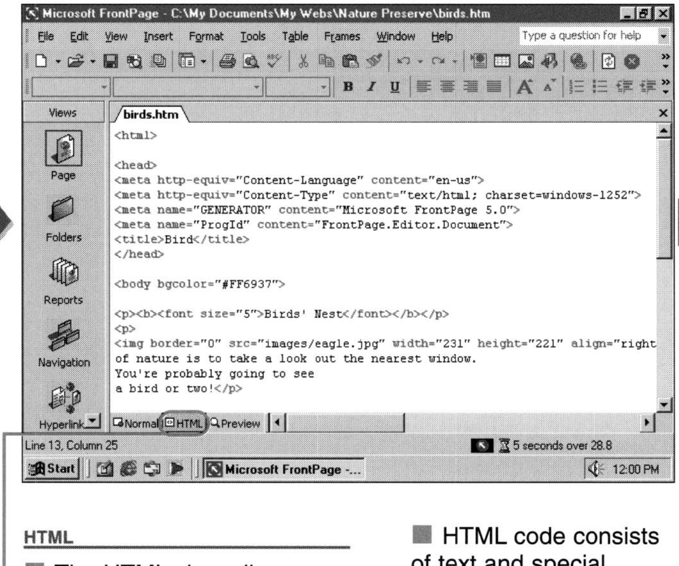

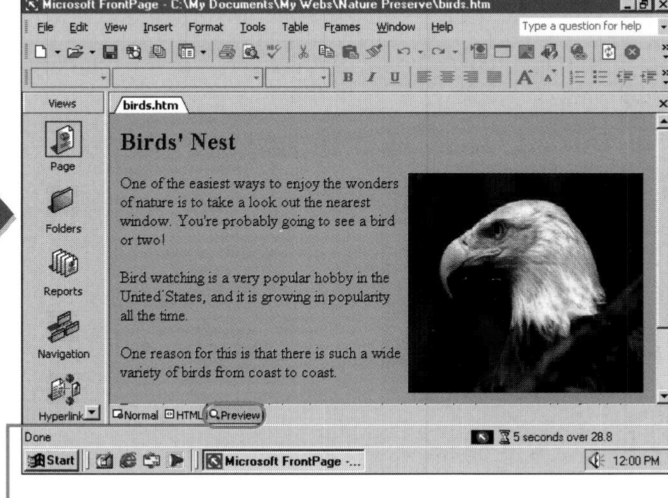

HTML

■ The HTML view allows you to see the HTML code used to create a Web page.

■ As you enter information in the Normal view, FrontPage automatically creates the HTML code for the Web page.

■ HTML code consists of text and special instructions called tags. Tags are shown in blue.

PREVIEW

■ The Preview view allows you to see how a Web page will appear on the Web.

Note: The Preview view may not properly display some items on a Web page, such as a hit counter.

DISPLAY A WEB PAGE IN A WEB BROWSER

You can display a Web page in a Web browser to see how the page will appear on the Web.

A Web browser is a program that allows people to view and explore information on the Web.

DISPLAY A WEB PAGE IN A WEB BROWSER

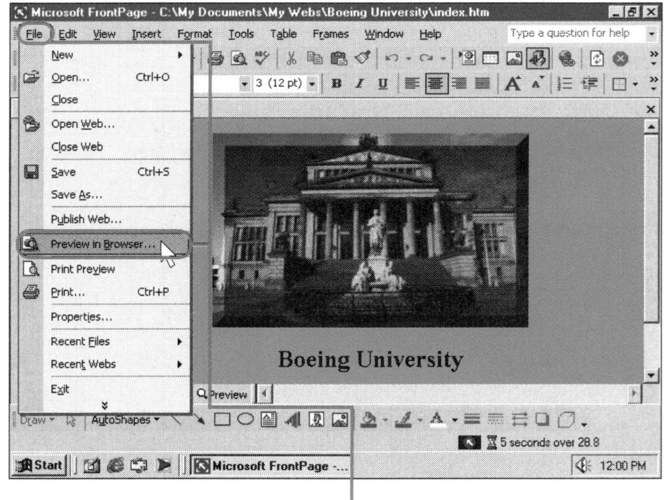

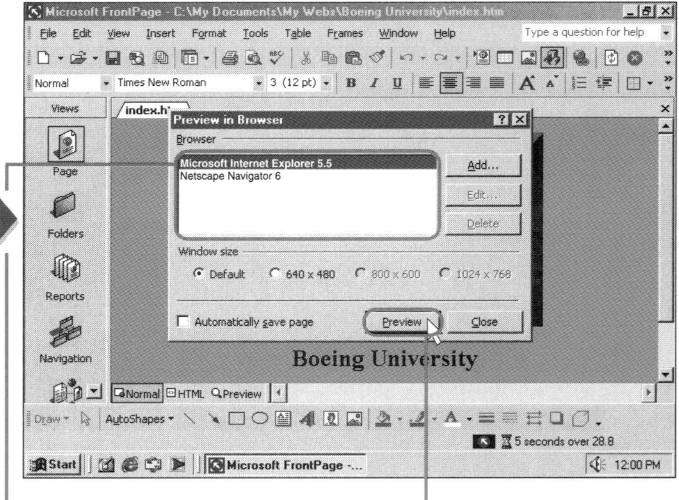

1 Click 💾 to save any changes you made to your Web page.

Note: For information on saving a Web page, see page 28.

2 Click **File** to display the Web page in a Web browser.

3 Click **Preview in Browser**.

■ The Preview in Browser dialog box appears.

■ This area lists the Web browsers FrontPage detects on your computer.

4 Click the Web browser you want to use to display the Web page.

5 Click **Preview**.

*Note: A dialog box appears if the Web page contains items that will only preview correctly when you publish your Web pages. Click **OK** to continue.*

Should I display my Web pages in more than one Web browser?

You should display and test your Web pages in several Web browsers. This allows you to make sure the pages will look and work the way you planned in different Web browsers. The most popular Web browsers are Microsoft Internet Explorer and Netscape Navigator.

Microsoft Internet Explorer

Microsoft Internet Explorer comes with the latest versions of Windows. You can also obtain Internet Explorer at the www.microsoft.com/windows/ie Web page.

Netscape Navigator

You can obtain Netscape Navigator at the www.netscape.com Web site and at computer stores.

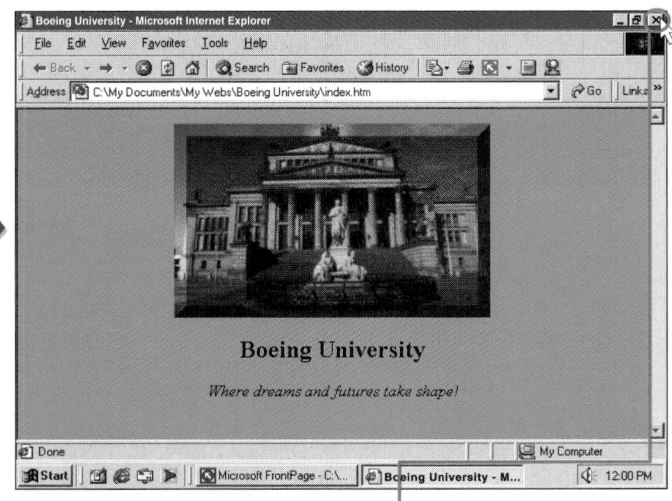

■ The Web browser opens and displays the Web page. You can now review the Web page.

6 When you finish reviewing the Web page, click ☒ to close the Web browser window.

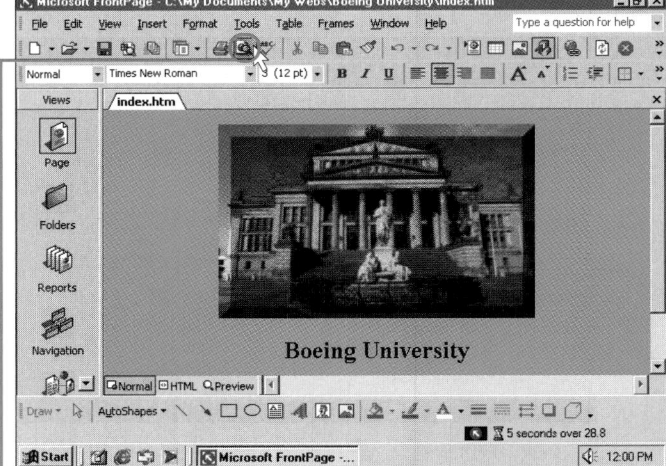

QUICKLY DISPLAY A WEB PAGE IN A WEB BROWSER

1 Click 🔍 to quickly view the displayed Web page in a Web browser.

■ The Web page will appear in the Web browser you last used to display a Web page.

USING THE FOLDERS VIEW

You can use the Folders view to display information about the Web pages, images and other items in your Web site.

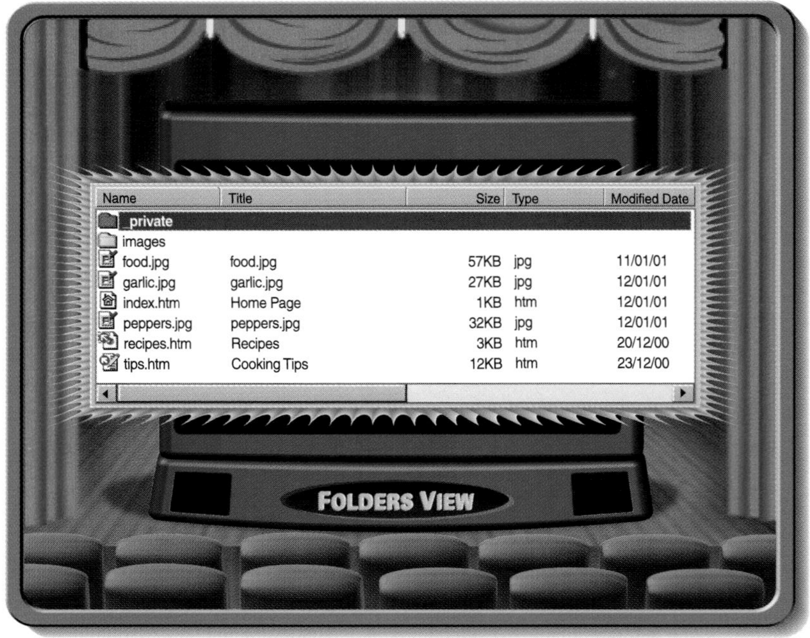

Name | Title | Size | Type | Modified Date
_private
images
food.jpg | food.jpg | 57KB | jpg | 11/01/01
garlic.jpg | garlic.jpg | 27KB | jpg | 12/01/01
index.htm | Home Page | 1KB | htm | 12/01/01
peppers.jpg | peppers.jpg | 32KB | jpg | 12/01/01
recipes.htm | Recipes | 3KB | htm | 20/12/00
tips.htm | Cooking Tips | 12KB | htm | 23/12/00
FOLDERS VIEW

USING THE FOLDERS VIEW

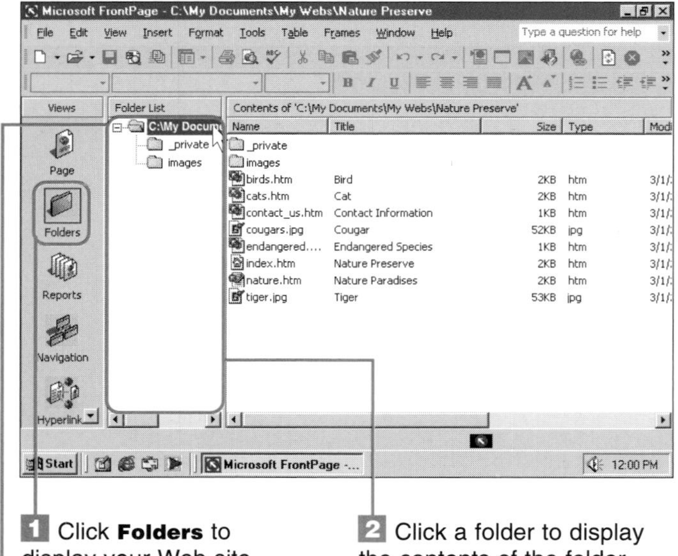

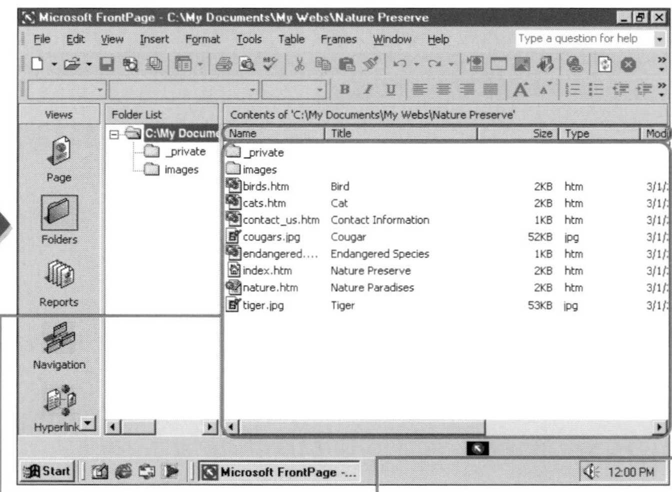

1 Click **Folders** to display your Web site in the Folders view.

■ This area displays the organization of the folders in your Web site.

2 Click a folder to display the contents of the folder.

Note: To display the contents of your entire Web site, click the top folder.

■ This area displays the contents of the folder you selected. FrontPage displays information about the Web pages ( ), images ( ) and other items in the folder.

■ To view the items in a different order, click the heading of the column you want to use to sort the items.

Note: You can click the heading of the column again to sort the items in the opposite order.

CHANGE A WEB PAGE TITLE

You can give a Web page a title that describes the contents of the page. The title appears at the top of a Web browser window when a visitor views the page.

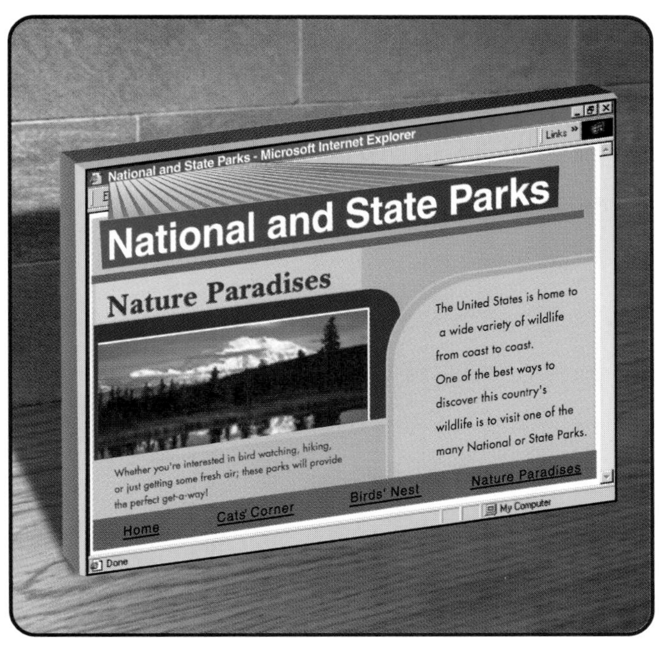

If you do not specify a title for a Web page, FrontPage will use the phrase "New Page" or the first line of text on the page as the title.

You should use a brief, descriptive title that will interest people in reading your Web page. Use a title such as "Favorite Golf Getaways" rather than a less descriptive title such as "My Home Page."

CHANGE A WEB PAGE TITLE

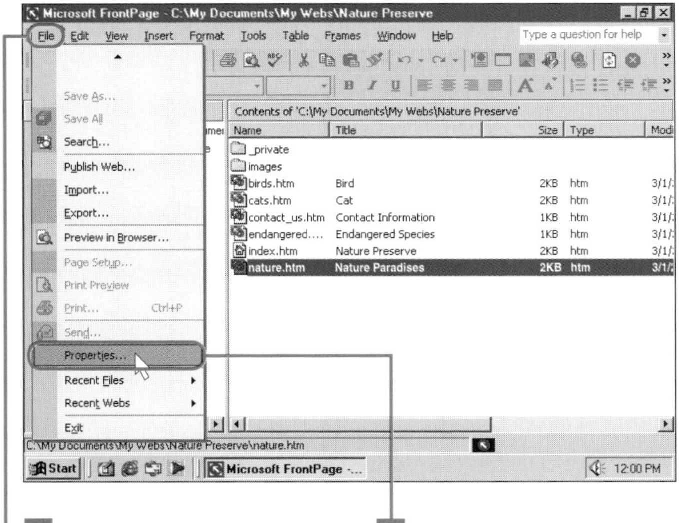

1 Click **File** to change the title of the displayed Web page.

2 Click **Properties**.

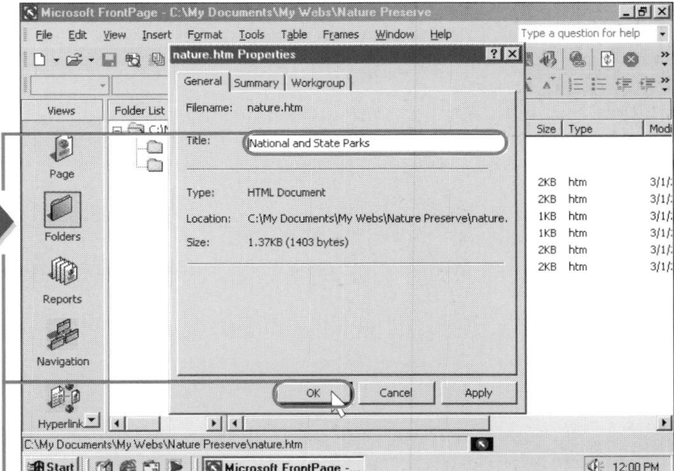

■ The Page Properties dialog box appears.

3 Type a title for the Web page.

4 Click **OK** to confirm the title you entered.

■ When a visitor displays the Web page, the title will appear at the top of the Web browser window. To preview a Web page in a Web browser, see page 44.

RENAME A WEB PAGE

You can rename a Web page to better describe the contents of the page.

You should not rename the Web page named index.htm since this is your home page. If you rename this Web page, visitors may get an error message when they visit your Web site.

RENAME A WEB PAGE

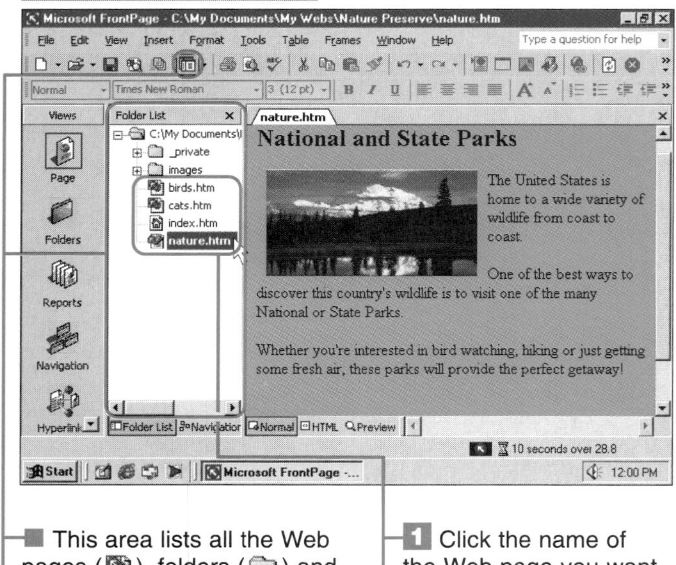

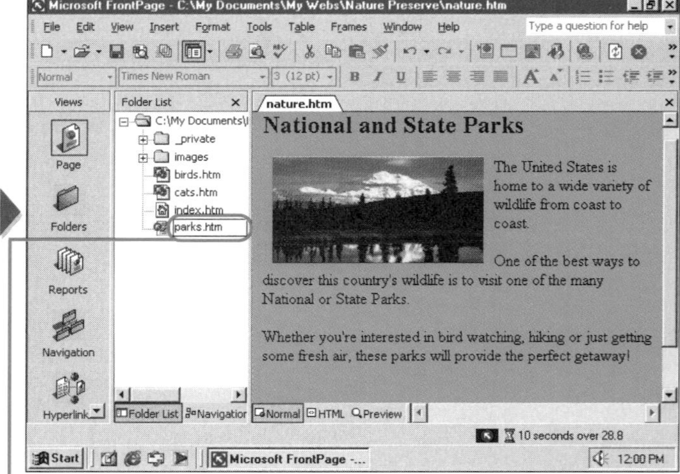

- This area lists all the Web pages ( ), folders ( ) and other items in your Web site.
- If the list does not appear, click to display the list.

1. Click the name of the Web page you want to rename.
2. Wait a moment and then click the name of the Web page again.

- The name of the Web page appears in a box.

3. Type a new name for the Web page. Make sure you add the **.htm** extension to the end of the Web page name. Then press the Enter key.

*Note: A dialog box will appear if the Web page is linked to other pages in your Web site. Click **Yes** to have FrontPage automatically update the linked Web pages.*

DELETE A WEB PAGE

You can delete a Web page you no longer want to include in your Web site.

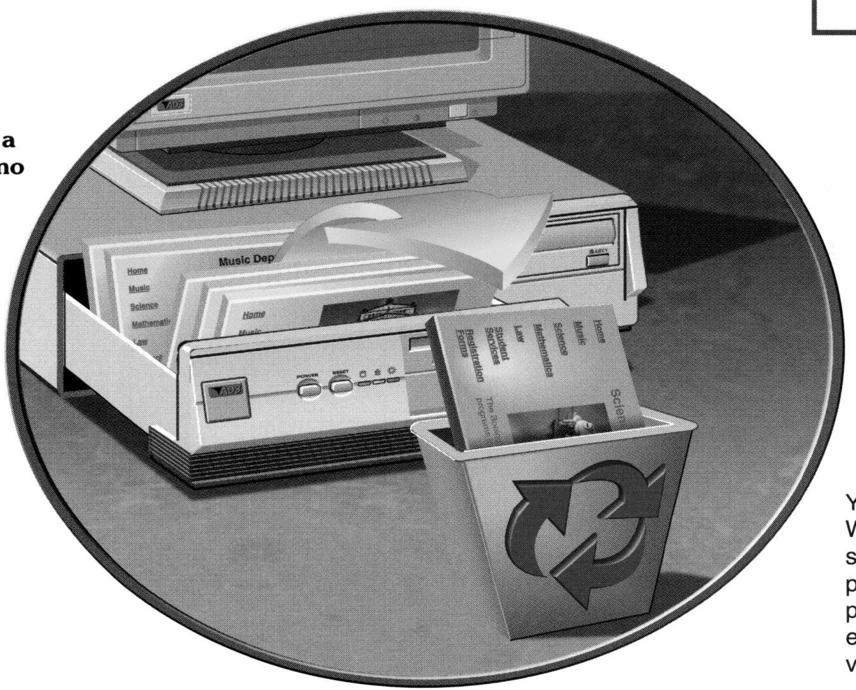

You should not delete the Web page named index.htm since this is your home page. If you delete this Web page, visitors may get an error message when they visit your Web site.

DELETE A WEB PAGE

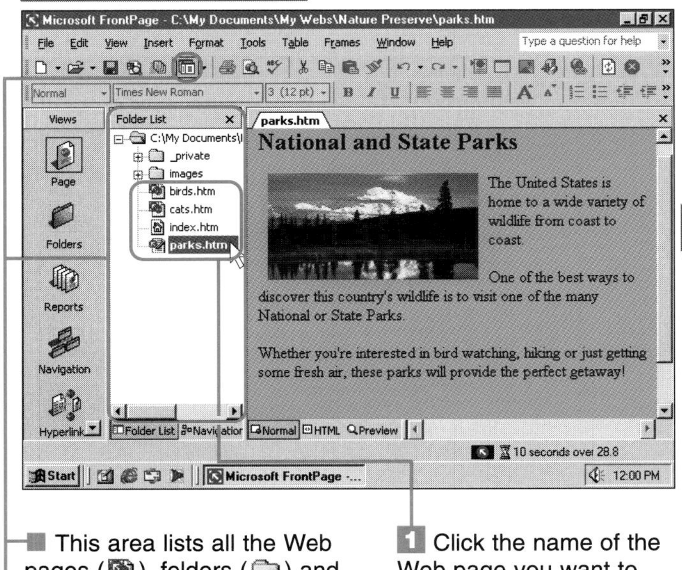

■ This area lists all the Web pages (icon), folders (icon) and other items in your Web site.

■ If the list does not appear, click (icon) to display the list.

1 Click the name of the Web page you want to delete.

2 Press the Delete key.

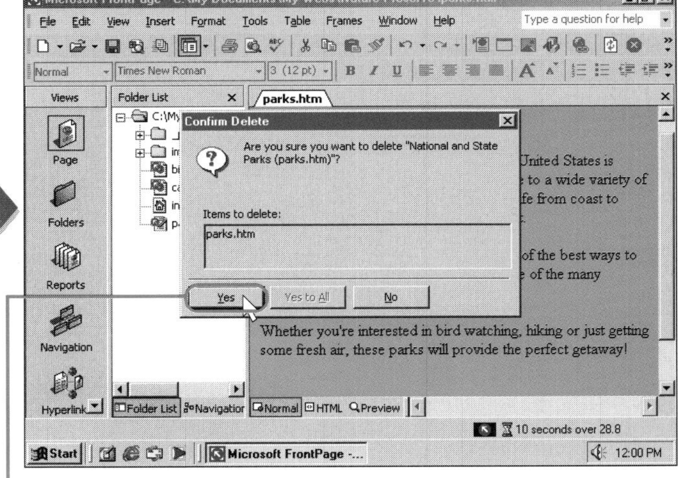

■ A confirmation dialog box appears.

3 Click **Yes** to delete the Web page.

■ FrontPage deletes the Web page.

SEARCH FOR A WEB PAGE

If you cannot remember the name or location of a Web page you want to work with, you can search for the Web page on your computer.

SEARCH FOR A WEB PAGE

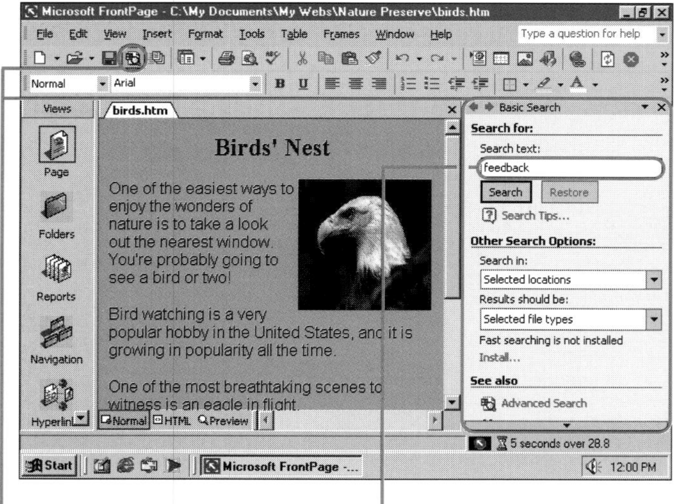

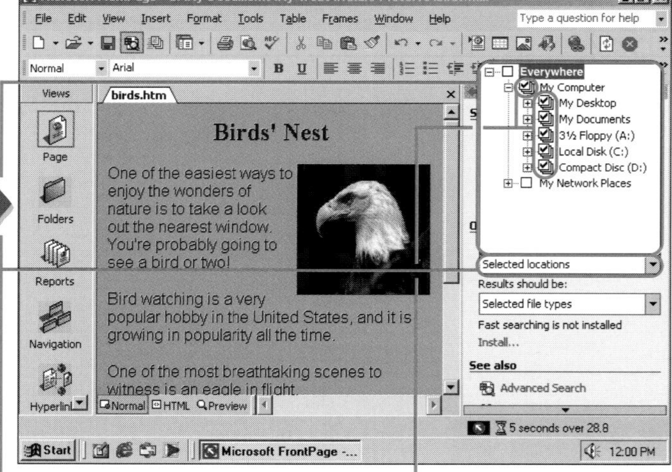

1 Click [icon] to search for a Web page on your computer.

■ The Search task pane appears.

2 Click this area and type one or more words you want to search for.

3 Click [▾] in this area to select the locations you want to search.

■ A check mark (✔) appears beside each location that FrontPage will search.

Note: By default, FrontPage will search all the drives and folders on your computer.

4 If you do not want to search a specific location, click the box (☑) beside the location (☑ changes to ☐).

5 Click outside the menu to close the menu.

How will FrontPage use the words I specify to search for Web pages?

FrontPage will search the contents of Web pages and the file names of Web pages for the words you specify. When searching the contents of Web pages, FrontPage will search for various forms of the words. For example, searching for "run" will find "run," "running" and "ran."

When selecting the locations and types of files I want to search for, how can I display more items?

Each item that displays a plus sign (⊞) contains hidden items. To display the hidden items, click the plus sign (⊞) beside the item (⊞ changes to ⊟). To once again hide the items, click the minus sign (⊟) beside the item.

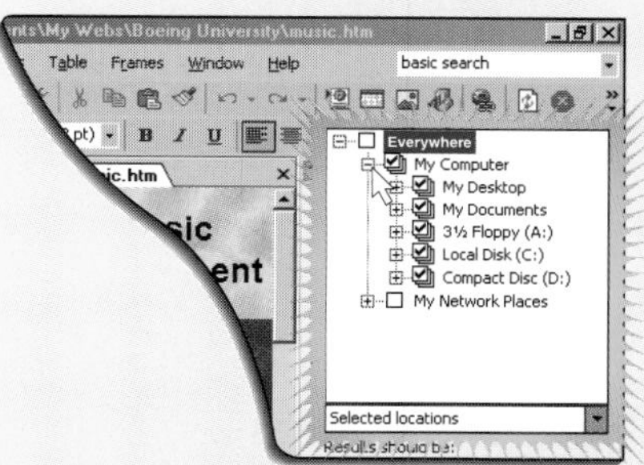

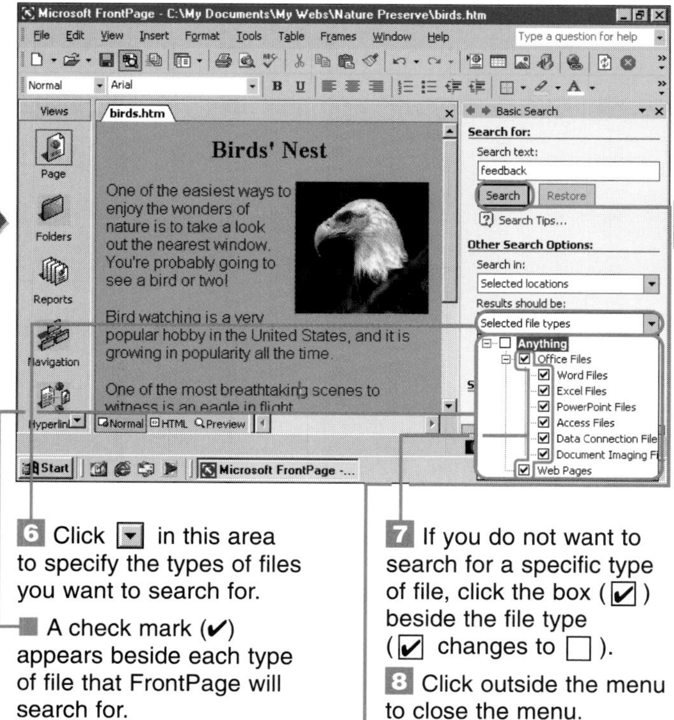

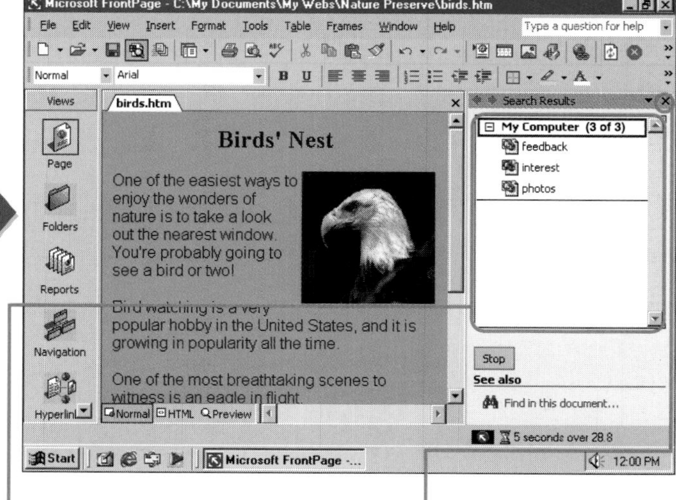

6 Click ▼ in this area to specify the types of files you want to search for.

■ A check mark (✔) appears beside each type of file that FrontPage will search for.

7 If you do not want to search for a specific type of file, click the box (✔) beside the file type (✔ changes to ☐).

8 Click outside the menu to close the menu.

9 Click **Search** to start the search.

■ This area lists the Web pages and other files that contain the words you specified.

■ To open a Web page or other type of file in the list, click the file.

■ To close the Search task pane at any time, click ☒.

Stephenson
Stephenson
Racing Page
Stevensen
Stevensen
Stephenson
Stevensen

CHAPTER 4

Edit Text

Would you like to edit the text in your Web pages or check your Web pages for spelling errors? This chapter teaches you how.

SELECT TEXT

Before performing many tasks in FrontPage, you must select the text you want to work with. Selected text appears highlighted on your screen.

SELECT TEXT

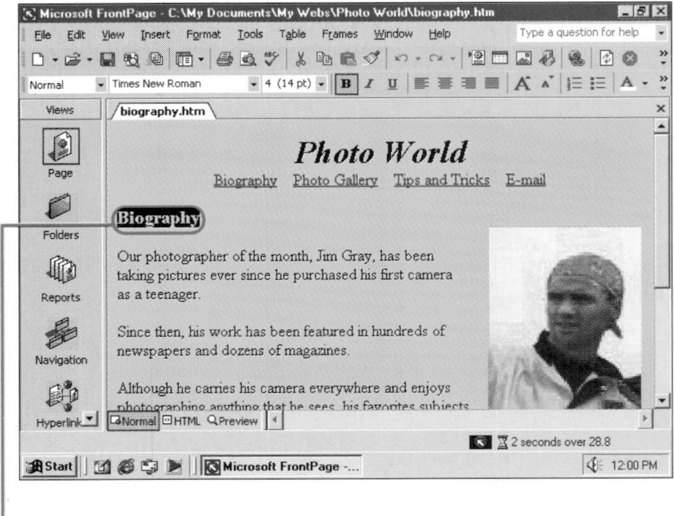

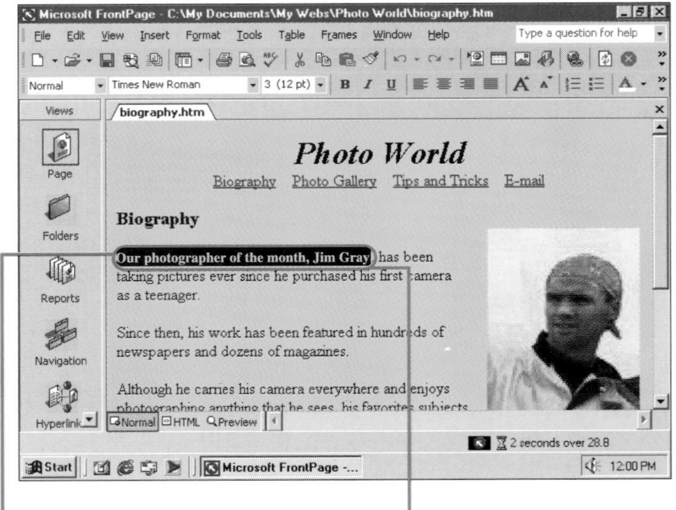

SELECT A WORD

1 Double-click the word you want to select.

■ To deselect text, click outside the selected area.

SELECT ANY AMOUNT OF TEXT

1 Position the mouse I to the left of the first word you want to select.

2 Drag the mouse I over the text until you highlight all the text you want to select.

UNDO CHANGES

FrontPage remembers the last changes you made to your Web pages. If you regret these changes, you can cancel them by using the Undo feature.

The Undo feature can cancel up to 30 of your last editing and formatting changes.

UNDO CHANGES

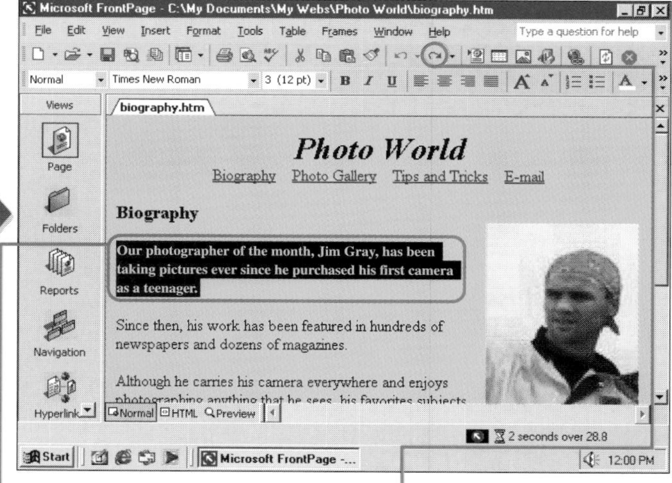

1 Click ↶ to undo the last change you made to your Web page.

■ FrontPage cancels the last change you made to your Web page.

■ You can repeat step **1** to cancel previous changes you made.

■ To reverse the results of using the Undo feature, click ↷.

MOVE OR COPY TEXT

You can move or copy text to a new location on a Web page.

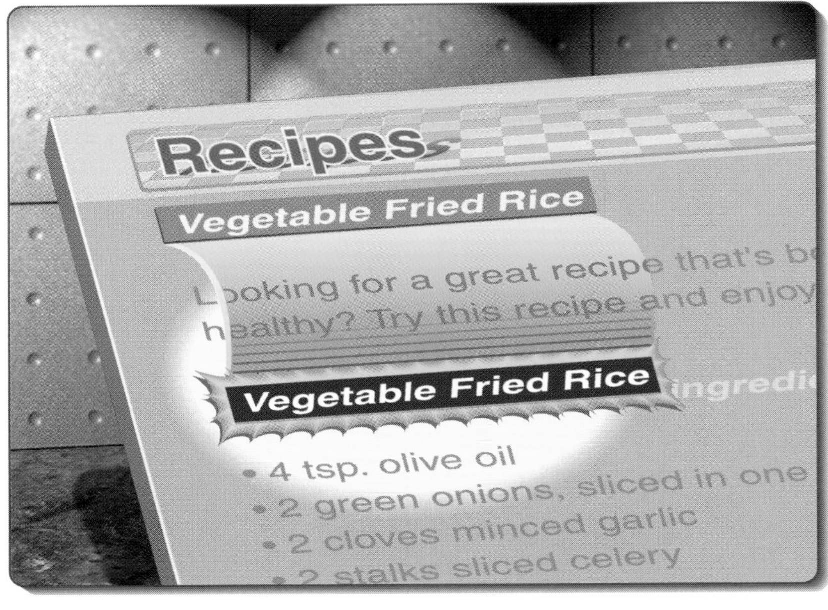

Moving text allows you to re-arrange text on a Web page. When you move text, the text disappears from its original location.

Copying text allows you to repeat information on a Web page without having to retype the text. When you copy text, the text appears in both the original and new locations.

MOVE OR COPY TEXT

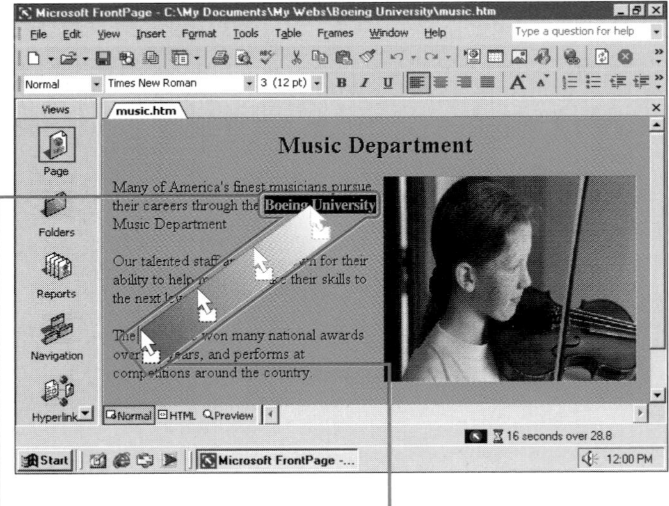

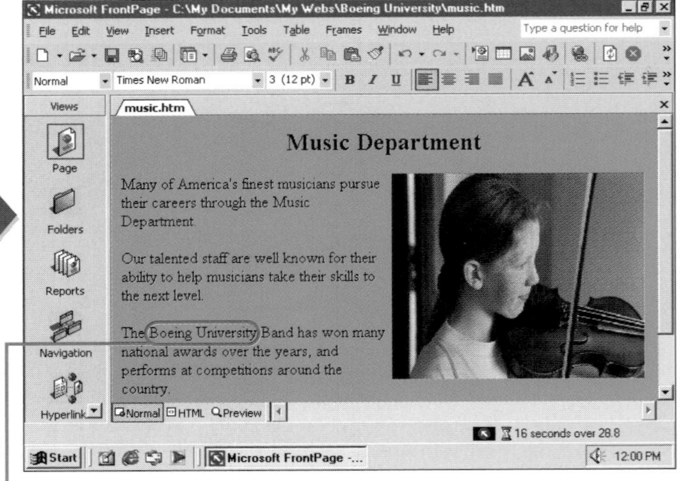

USING DRAG AND DROP

1 Select the text you want to move. To select text, see page 54.

2 Position the mouse I over the selected text (I changes to ↖).

3 To move the text, drag the mouse to where you want to place the text.

Note: The text will appear where you position the dotted insertion point on your screen.

■ The text moves to the new location.

■ To copy text, perform steps 1 to 3, except press and hold down the Ctrl key as you perform step 3.

How can copying text help me edit my Web pages?

If you plan to make major changes to a paragraph, you may want to copy the paragraph before you begin. This gives you two copies of the paragraph—the original paragraph and a copy of the paragraph that you can edit. If you are pleased with the changes you make, you can delete the original paragraph. To delete text, see page 39.

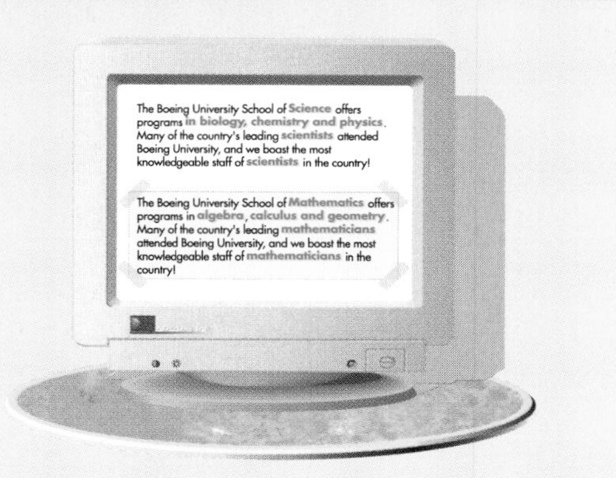

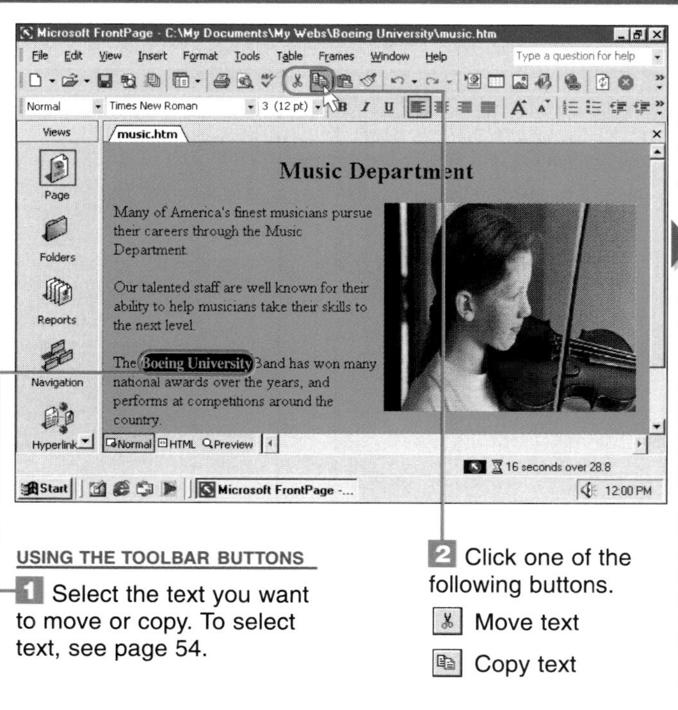

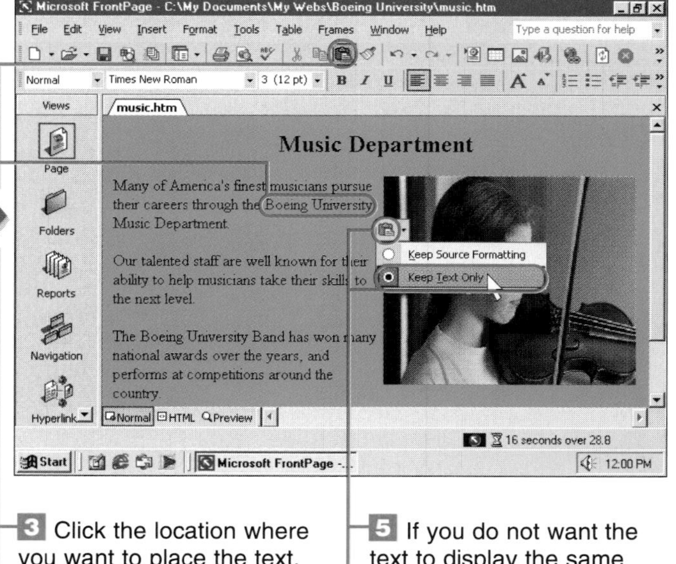

USING THE TOOLBAR BUTTONS

1 Select the text you want to move or copy. To select text, see page 54.

2 Click one of the following buttons.

- Move text
- Copy text

3 Click the location where you want to place the text.

4 Click the paste button to place the text in the new location.

- The text appears in the new location.

5 If you do not want the text to display the same formatting as the original text, click the paste options button.

6 Click **Keep Text Only**.

Note: The paste options button is available only until you perform another task.

ADD SYMBOLS

You can add symbols or special characters that do not appear on your keyboard to your Web pages.

ADD SYMBOLS

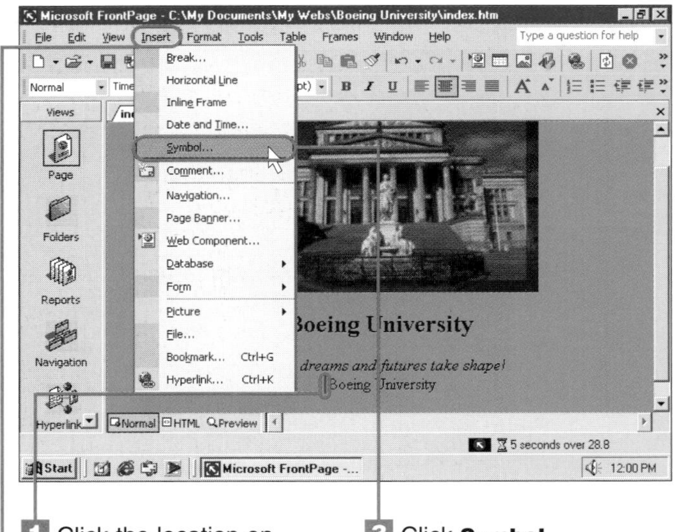

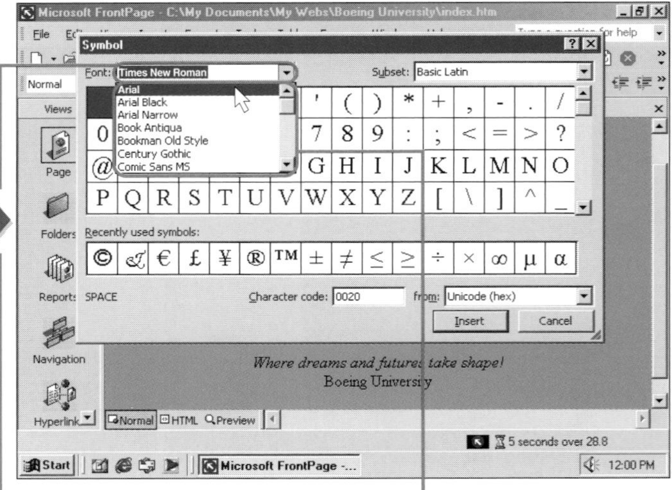

1 Click the location on your Web page where you want a symbol to appear.

2 Click **Insert**.

3 Click **Symbol**.

Note: If Symbol does not appear on the menu, position the mouse over the bottom of the menu to display all the menu options.

■ The Symbol dialog box appears, displaying the symbols for the current font.

4 To display the symbols for another font, click ▾ in this area.

5 Click the font that provides the symbols you want to display.

After I add a symbol to a Web page, why does the text I type appear unusual?

When you add a symbol to a Web page, the text you type after the symbol may appear in the same font you selected for the symbol. If you want the text to appear as the text on the rest of the Web page, you need to change the font of the text. To change the font of text, see page 70.

What should I consider when adding a symbol to a Web page?

If the font for a symbol is not available on a visitor's computer, the symbol may not appear properly on their computer. To avoid this problem, select a symbol from a commonly used font, such as Arial or Times New Roman.

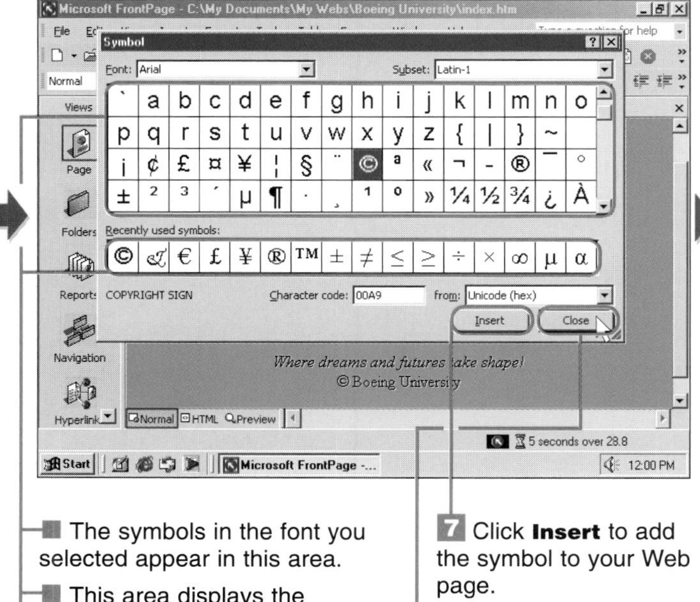

- The symbols in the font you selected appear in this area.
- This area displays the most recently used symbols.

6 Click the symbol you want to place on your Web page.

7 Click **Insert** to add the symbol to your Web page.

8 Click **Close** to close the Symbol dialog box.

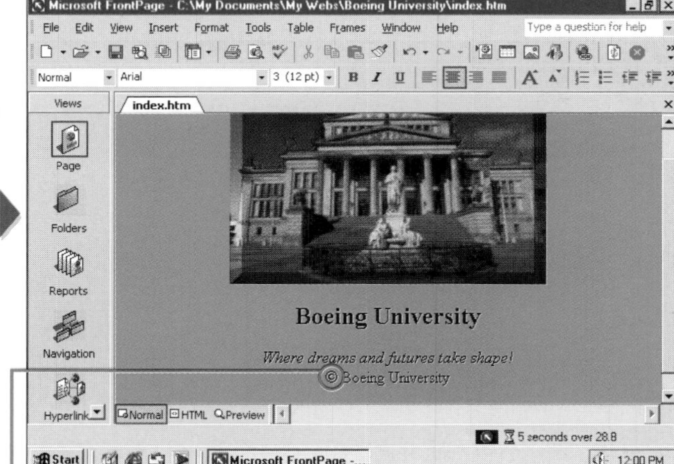

- The symbol appears on your Web page.

- To remove a symbol from a Web page, drag the mouse I over the symbol until you highlight the symbol and then press the Delete key.

CHECK SPELLING

You can quickly find and correct all the spelling errors on a Web page.

FrontPage automatically checks your Web pages for spelling errors as you type. Misspelled words display a wavy red underline. The underlines will not appear when you publish your Web pages.

CHECK SPELLING

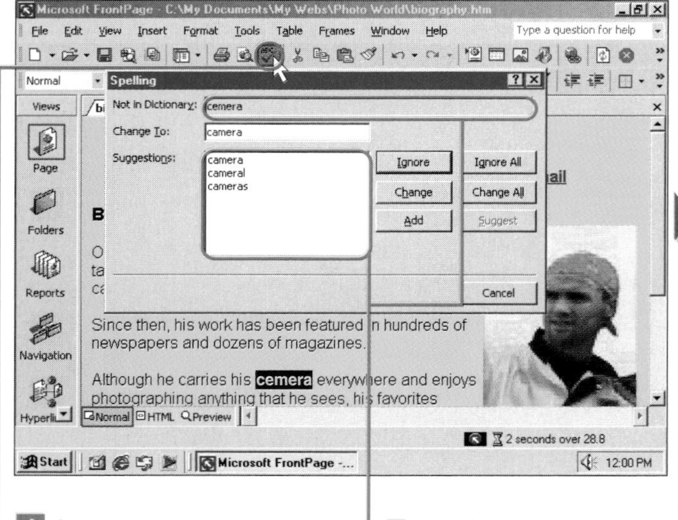

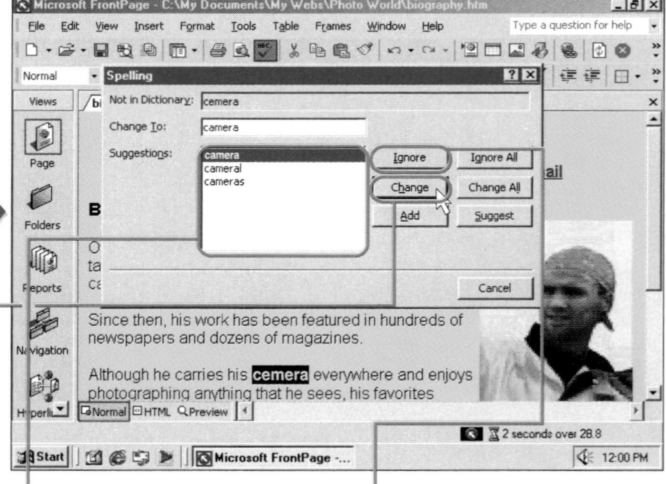

1 Click anywhere on the Web page you want to spell check.

2 Click the spelling button to start the spell check.

■ The Spelling dialog box appears if FrontPage finds a misspelled word on your Web page.

■ This area displays the misspelled word.

■ This area displays suggestions for correcting the word.

3 Click the word you want to use to correct the misspelled word.

4 Click **Change** to replace the word on your Web page with the word you selected.

■ To skip the word and continue checking your Web page, click **Ignore**.

*Note: To skip the word and all other occurrences of the word on your Web page, click **Ignore All**.*

How does FrontPage find spelling errors on a Web page?

FrontPage compares every word on a Web page to words in its own dictionary. If a word does not exist in the dictionary, the word is considered misspelled.

FrontPage will not find a correctly spelled word used in the wrong context, such as "My niece is **sit** years old." You should carefully review your Web pages to find this type of error.

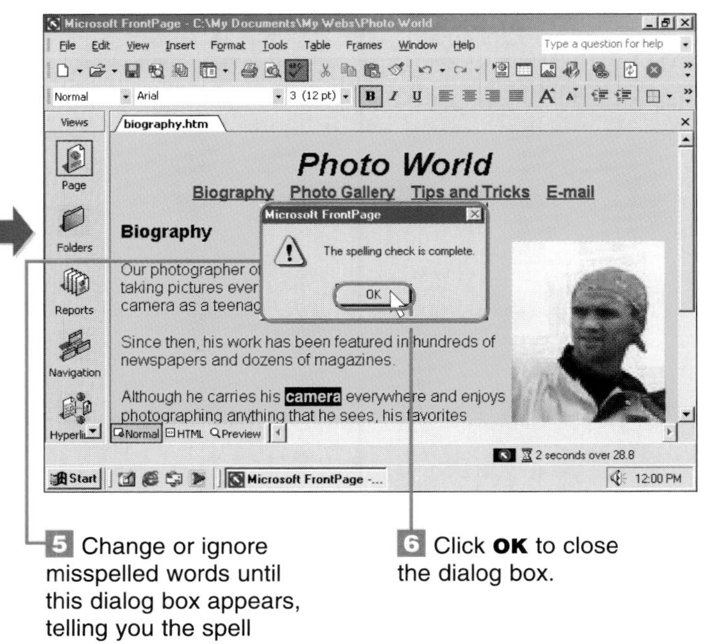

5 Change or ignore misspelled words until this dialog box appears, telling you the spell check is complete.

6 Click **OK** to close the dialog box.

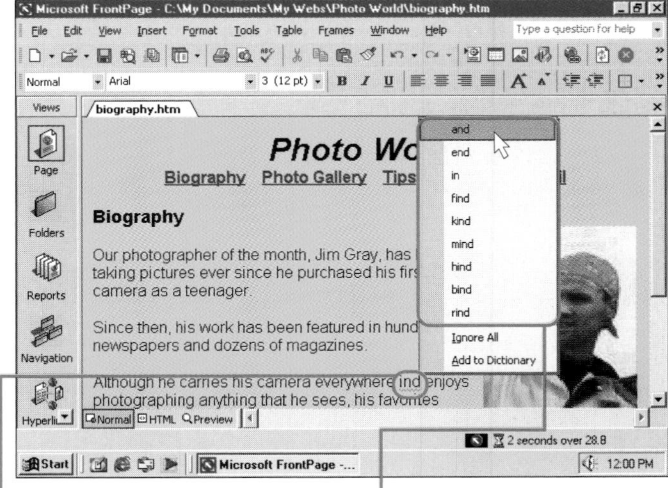

CORRECT ONE MISSPELLED WORD

1 Right-click the misspelled word you want to correct.

■ A menu appears with suggestions to correct the word.

2 To replace the word on your Web page with one of the suggestions, click the suggestion.

Note: If you do not want to replace the word, click outside the menu to close the menu.

USING THE THESAURUS

You can use the thesaurus to replace a word on your Web page with a more suitable word.

USING THE THESAURUS

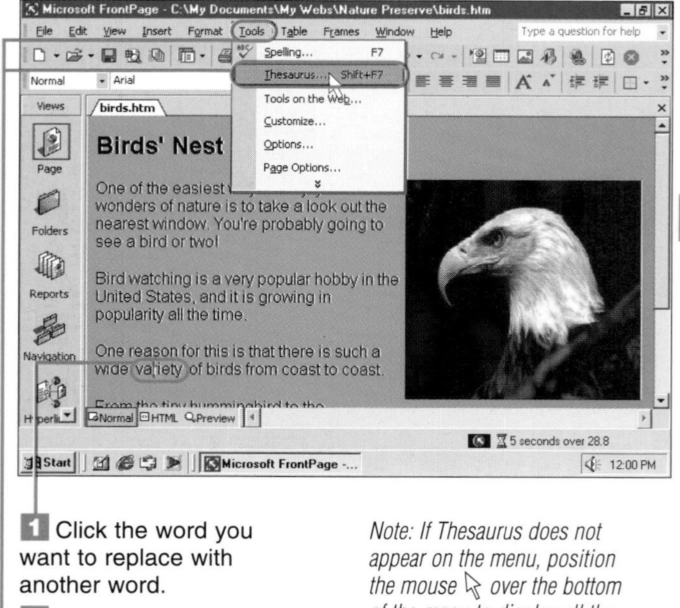

1 Click the word you want to replace with another word.

2 Click **Tools**.

3 Click **Thesaurus**.

Note: If Thesaurus does not appear on the menu, position the mouse over the bottom of the menu to display all the menu options.

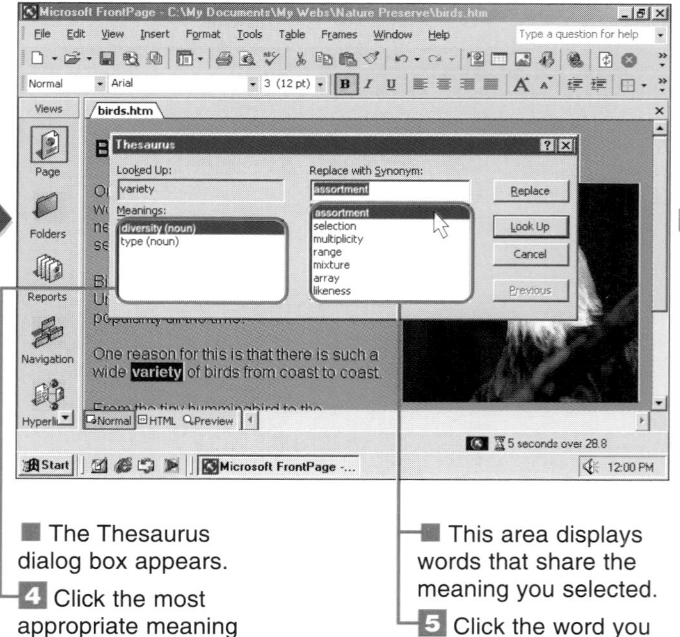

■ The Thesaurus dialog box appears.

4 Click the most appropriate meaning of the word.

■ This area displays words that share the meaning you selected.

5 Click the word you want to use on your Web page.

How can the thesaurus help me?

Many people use the thesaurus to replace a word that appears repeatedly on a Web page. Replacing repeated words can help add variety to your writing. You may also want to use the thesaurus to find a word that more clearly explains a concept. Using the thesaurus included with FrontPage is faster and more convenient than searching through a printed thesaurus.

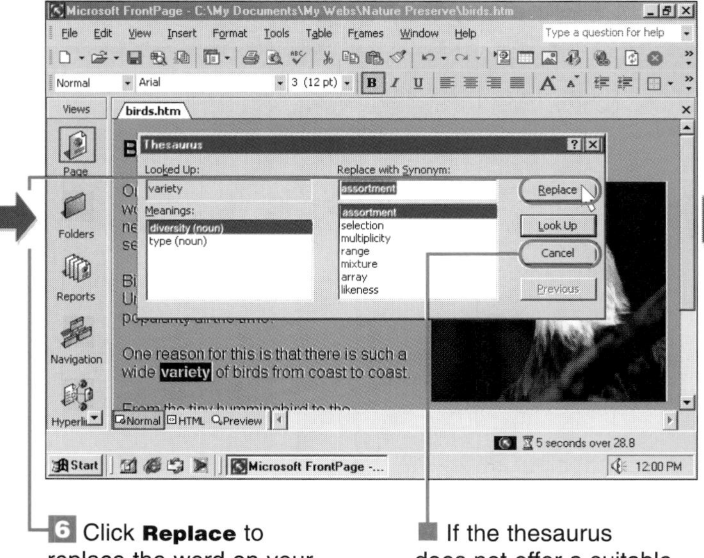

6 Click **Replace** to replace the word on your Web page with the word you selected.

■ If the thesaurus does not offer a suitable replacement for the word, click **Cancel** to close the Thesaurus dialog box.

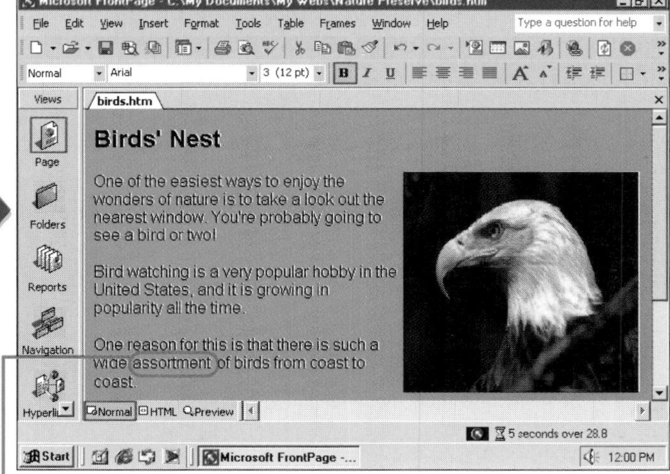

■ The word you selected replaces the word on your Web page.

■ To deselect text, click outside the selected area.

FIND AND REPLACE TEXT

You can find and replace every occurrence of a word or phrase on a Web page. This is useful if you have frequently misspelled a name.

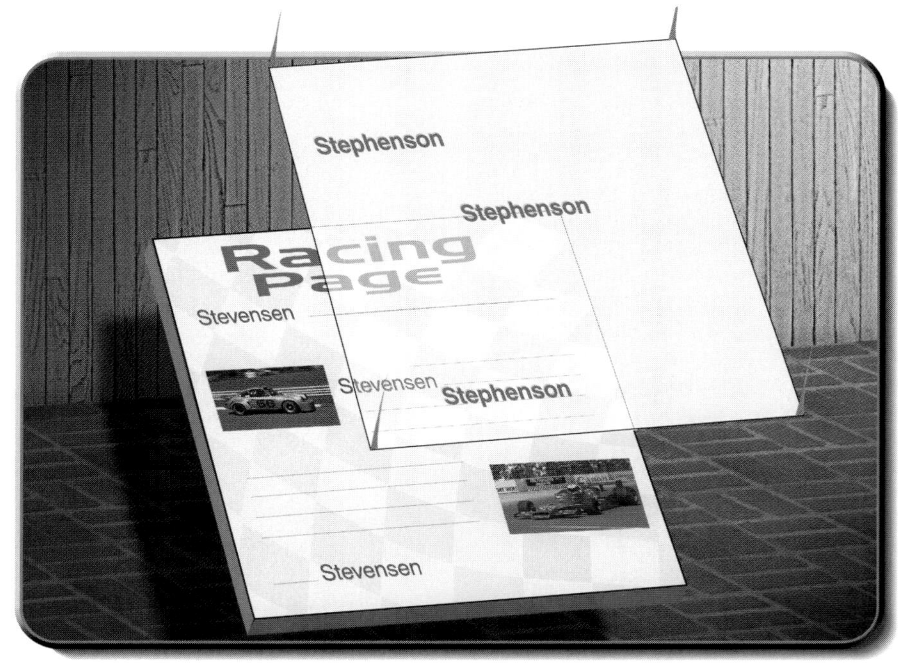

FIND AND REPLACE TEXT

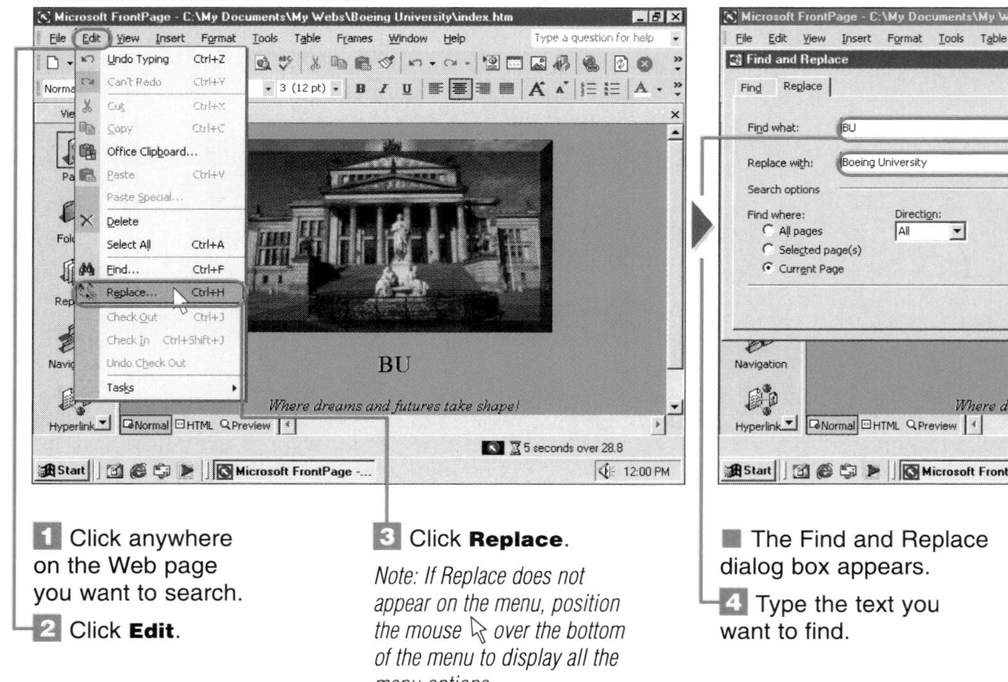

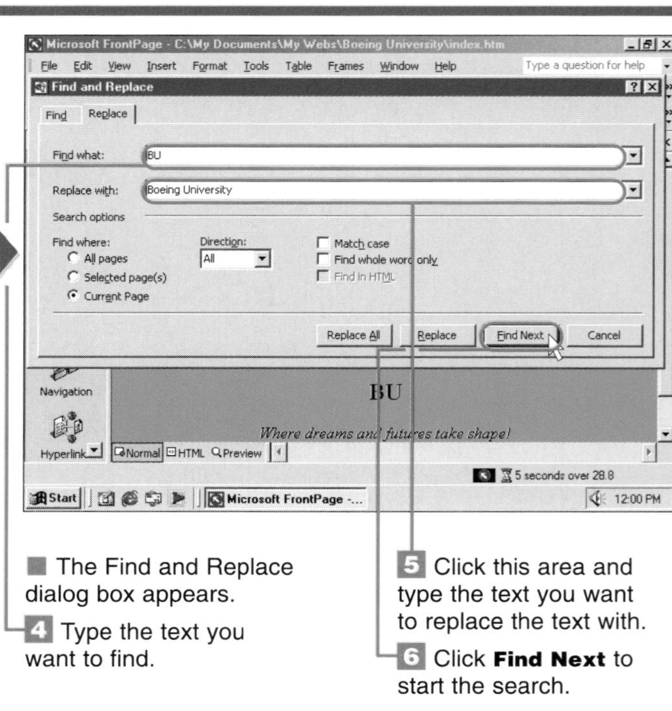

1 Click anywhere on the Web page you want to search.

2 Click **Edit**.

3 Click **Replace**.

Note: If Replace does not appear on the menu, position the mouse over the bottom of the menu to display all the menu options.

■ The Find and Replace dialog box appears.

4 Type the text you want to find.

5 Click this area and type the text you want to replace the text with.

6 Click **Find Next** to start the search.

Can I use the Find and Replace feature to quickly enter text?

Yes. You can type a short form of a word or phrase, such as UM, throughout a Web page. You can then use the Find and Replace feature to replace the short form with the full word or phrase, such as University of Massachusetts.

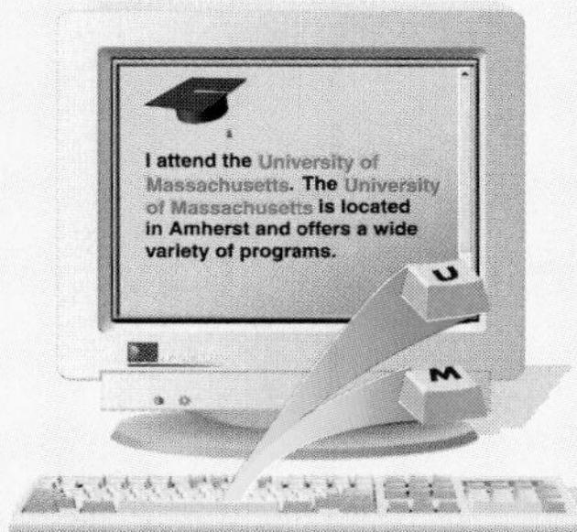

How can I speed up my search?

In the Find and Replace dialog box, you can select one of the following options to speed up your search.

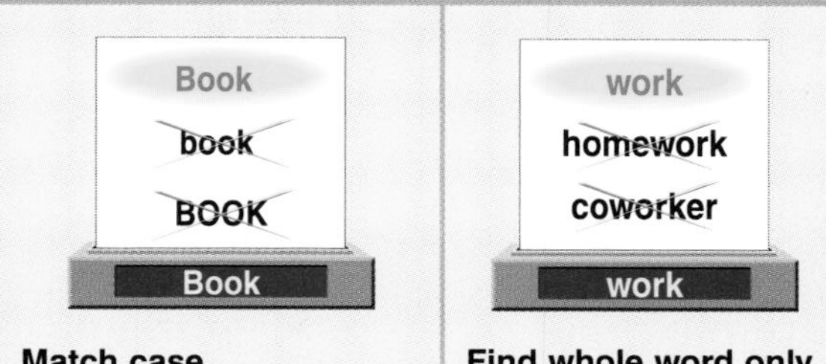

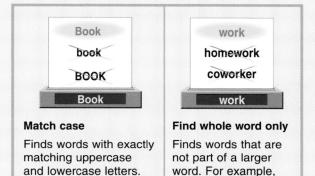

Match case

Finds words with exactly matching uppercase and lowercase letters. For example, "Book" will not find "book" or "BOOK."

Find whole word only

Finds words that are not part of a larger word. For example, "work" will not find "homework" or "coworker."

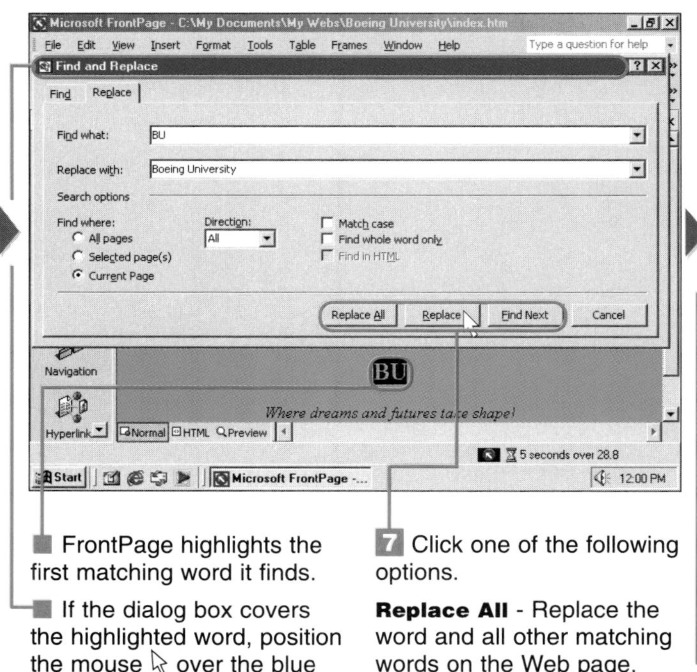

■ FrontPage highlights the first matching word it finds.

■ If the dialog box covers the highlighted word, position the mouse over the blue title bar and then drag the dialog box to a new location.

7 Click one of the following options.

Replace All - Replace the word and all other matching words on the Web page.

Replace - Replace the word.

Find Next - Ignore the word.

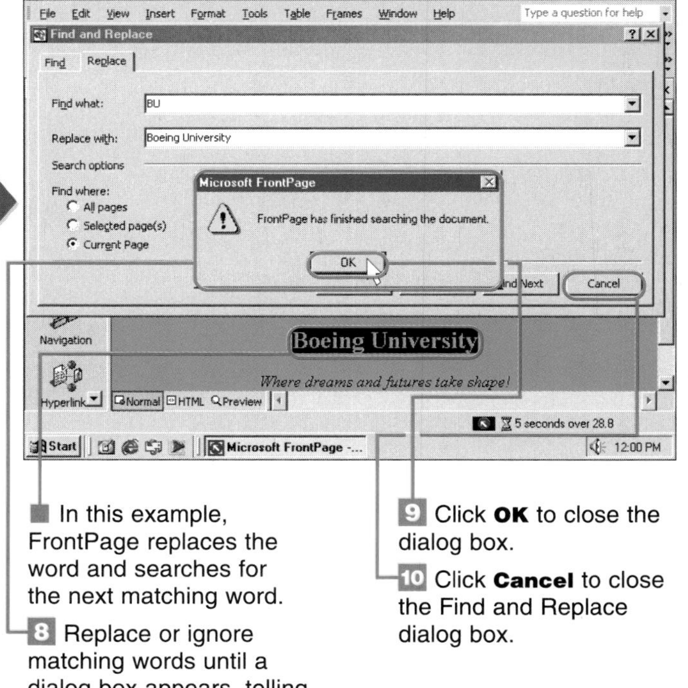

■ In this example, FrontPage replaces the word and searches for the next matching word.

8 Replace or ignore matching words until a dialog box appears, telling you the search is complete.

9 Click **OK** to close the dialog box.

10 Click **Cancel** to close the Find and Replace dialog box.

HEADING 1
About Sunshine Vacations
Schedules
At Sunshine Vacations, we make all your vacations memorable ones. Call us today to plan your next trip!
TEXT
Ultra Gloss

CHAPTER 5

Format Web Pages

Do you want to change the appearance of text on your Web pages? This chapter shows you how to change the size and color of text, create lists, apply a theme and much more.

BOLD, ITALICIZE OR UNDERLINE TEXT

You can bold, italicize or underline text to emphasize information on a Web page.

Be careful when underlining text, since visitors may mistake the text for a link. For information on links, see pages 134 to 153.

BOLD, ITALICIZE OR UNDERLINE TEXT

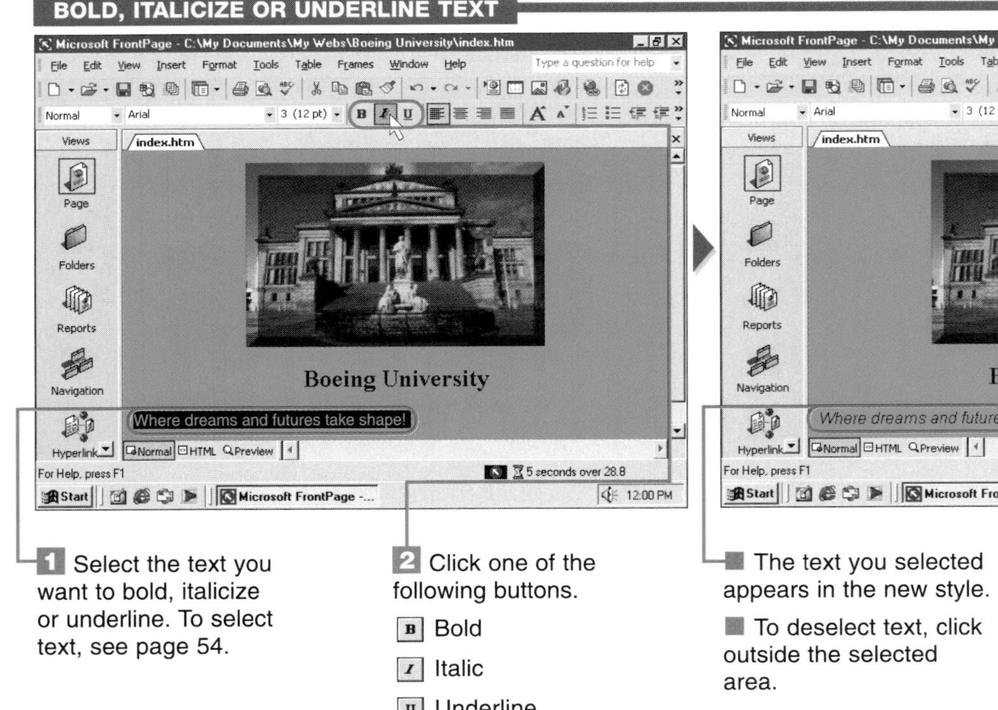

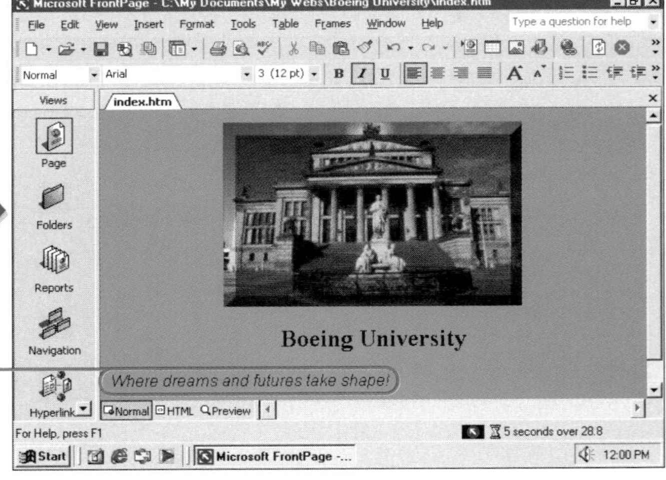

1 Select the text you want to bold, italicize or underline. To select text, see page 54.

2 Click one of the following buttons.

- **B** Bold
- *I* Italic
- U Underline

■ The text you selected appears in the new style.

■ To deselect text, click outside the selected area.

■ To remove a bold, italic or underline style, repeat steps **1** and **2**.

CHANGE ALIGNMENT OF TEXT

You can enhance the appearance of a Web page by aligning text in different ways.

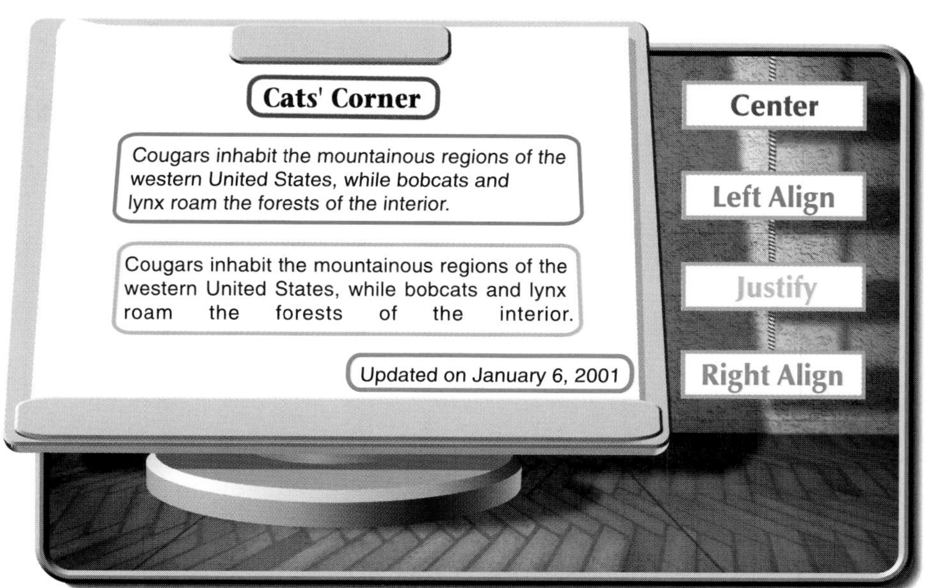
Cats' Corner
Cougars inhabit the mountainous regions of the western United States, while bobcats and lynx roam the forests of the interior.
Cougars inhabit the mountainous regions of the western United States, while bobcats and lynx roam the forests of the interior.
Updated on January 6, 2001
Center
Left Align
Justify
Right Align

CHANGE ALIGNMENT OF TEXT

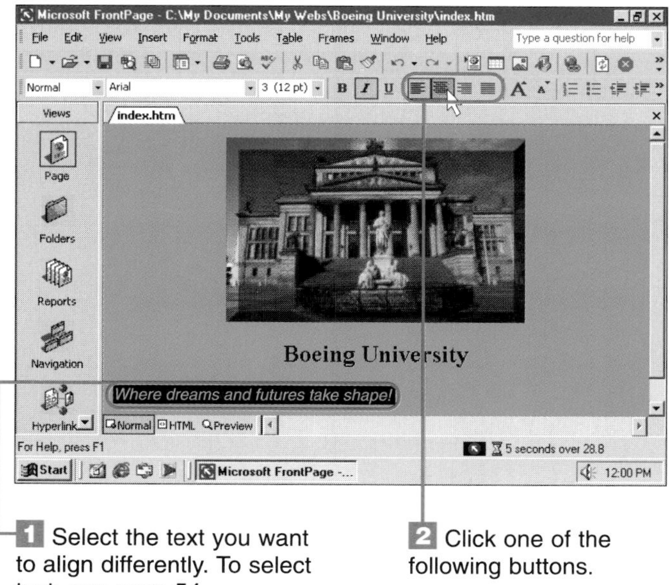
Boeing University
Where dreams and futures take shape!

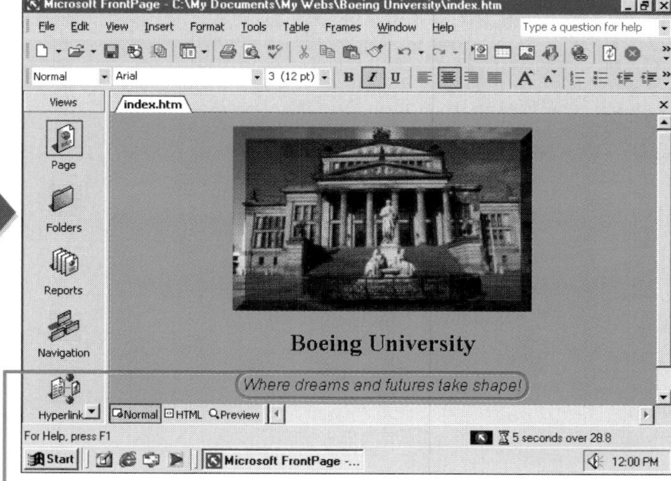
Boeing University
Where dreams and futures take shape!

1 Select the text you want to align differently. To select text, see page 54.

2 Click one of the following buttons.

- Left align
- Center
- Right align
- Justify

■ The text appears in the new alignment.

■ To deselect text, click outside the selected area.

CHANGE FONT OF TEXT

You can change the font of text to enhance the appearance of your Web page.

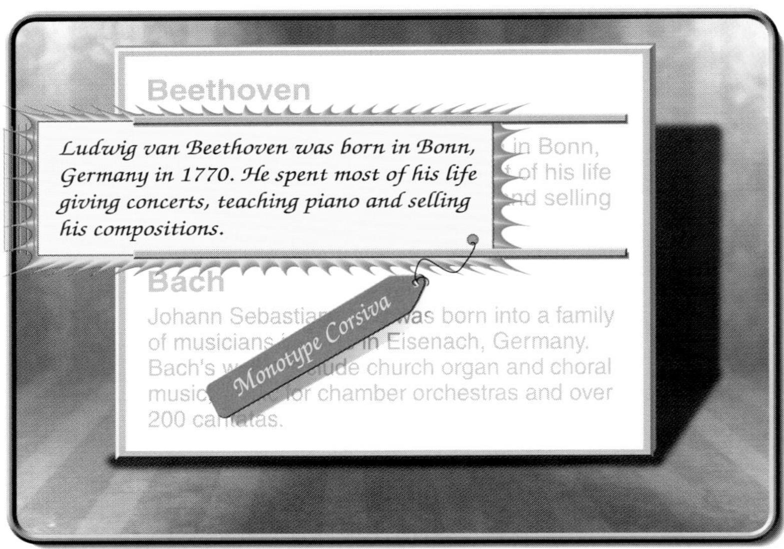

You should choose common fonts for your Web pages, such as Arial or Times New Roman. If a font you choose is not available on a visitor's computer, their Web browser will use a different font and your text may not appear the way you expected.

CHANGE FONT OF TEXT

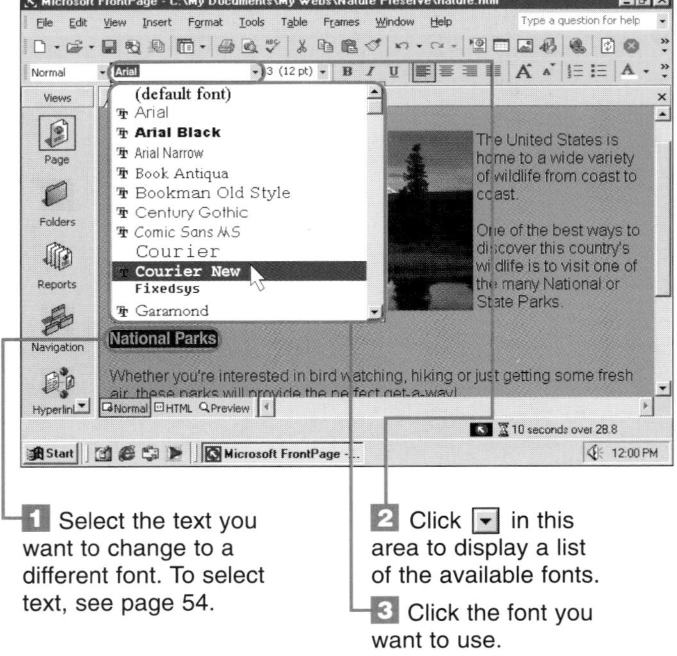

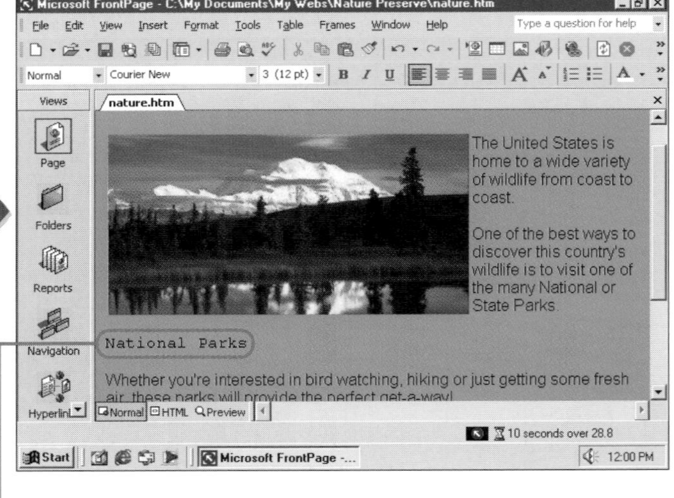

1 Select the text you want to change to a different font. To select text, see page 54.

2 Click ▾ in this area to display a list of the available fonts.

3 Click the font you want to use.

■ The text you selected changes to the new font.

■ To deselect text, click outside the selected area.

■ To return the text to the original font, repeat steps 1 to 3, selecting **(default font)** in step 3.

CHANGE SIZE OF TEXT

You can increase or decrease the size of text on a Web page.

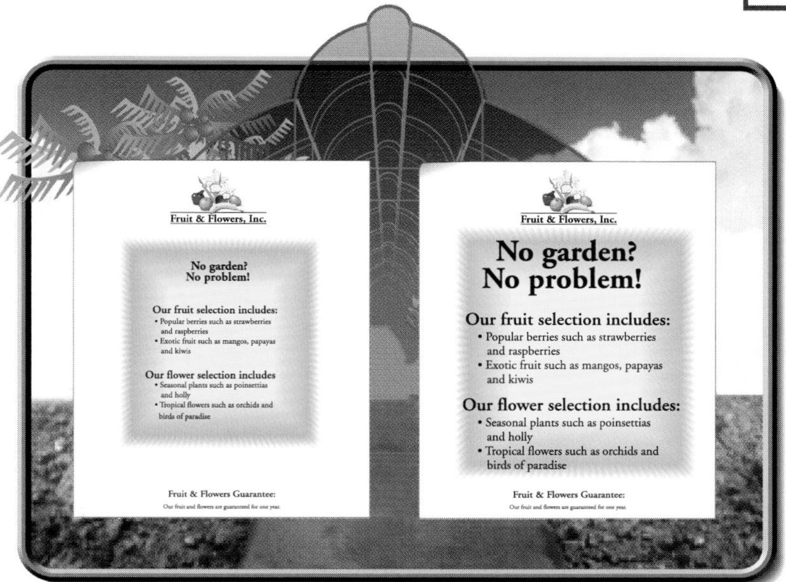

Larger text is easier to read, but smaller text allows you to fit more information on a screen.

CHANGE SIZE OF TEXT

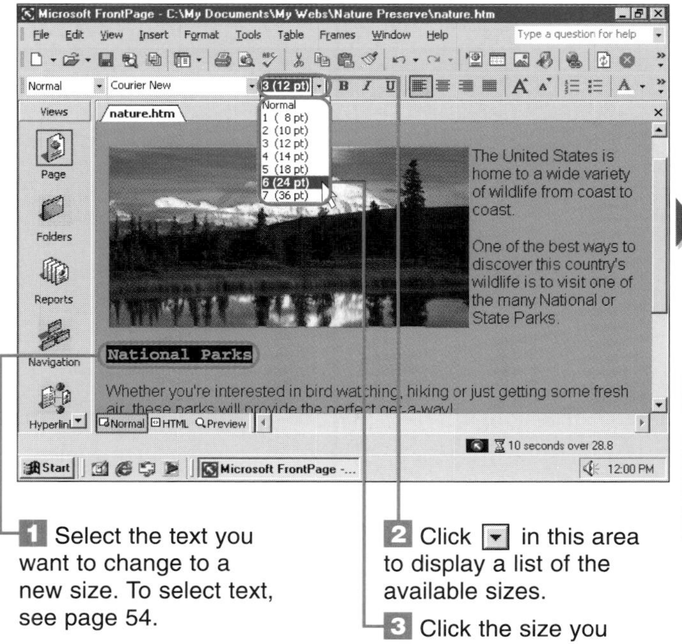

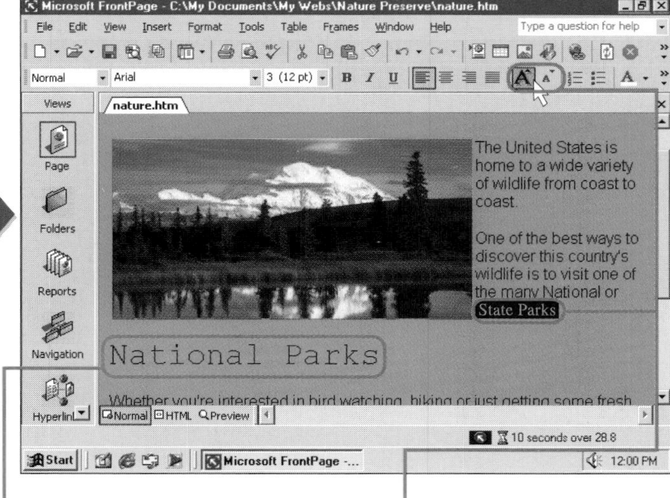

1 Select the text you want to change to a new size. To select text, see page 54.

2 Click ▾ in this area to display a list of the available sizes.

3 Click the size you want to use.

■ The text you selected changes to the new size.

■ To deselect text, click outside the selected area.

■ To return the text to the original size, repeat steps 1 to 3, selecting **Normal** in step 3.

QUICKLY CHANGE SIZE OF TEXT

1 Select the text you want to change to a new size.

2 Click A or A to increase or decrease the size of the text.

CHANGE COLOR OF TEXT

You can change the color of text to draw attention to headings or important information on a Web page.

CHANGE COLOR OF TEXT

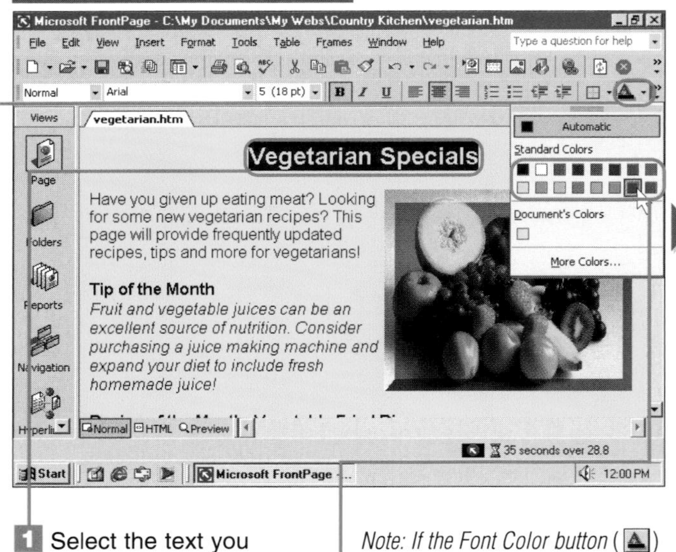

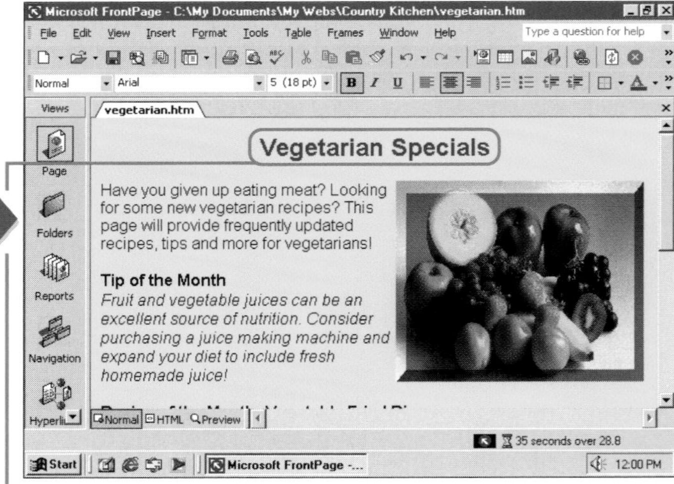

1 Select the text you want to change to a different color. To select text, see page 54.

2 Click ▾ in this area to display the available colors.

Note: If the Font Color button (A) is not displayed, click » on the Formatting toolbar to display all the buttons.

3 Click the color you want to use.

■ The text appears in the color you selected.

■ To deselect text, click outside the selected area.

■ To return text to its original color, repeat steps 1 to 3, selecting **Automatic** in step 3.

HIGHLIGHT TEXT

You can highlight text that you want to stand out on a Web page.

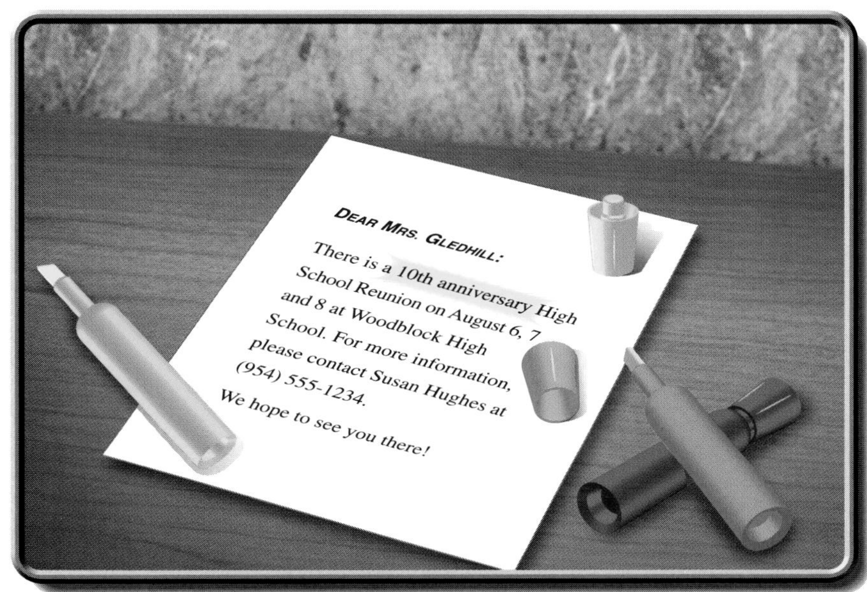

Highlighting text is also useful for marking information you want to review or verify later.

HIGHLIGHT TEXT

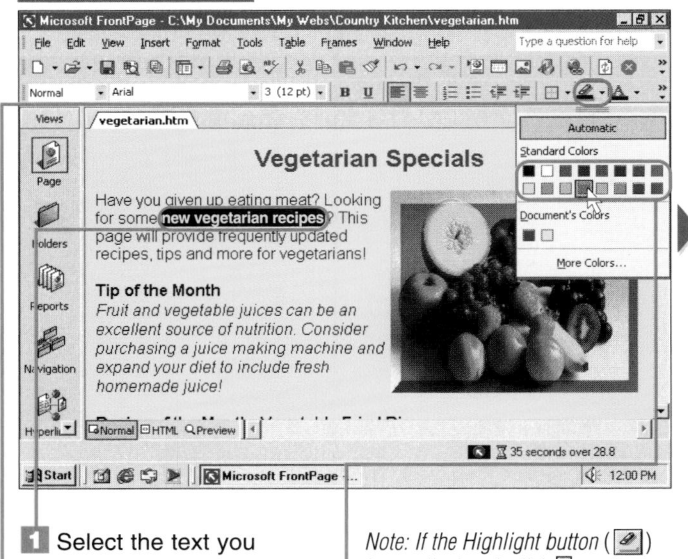

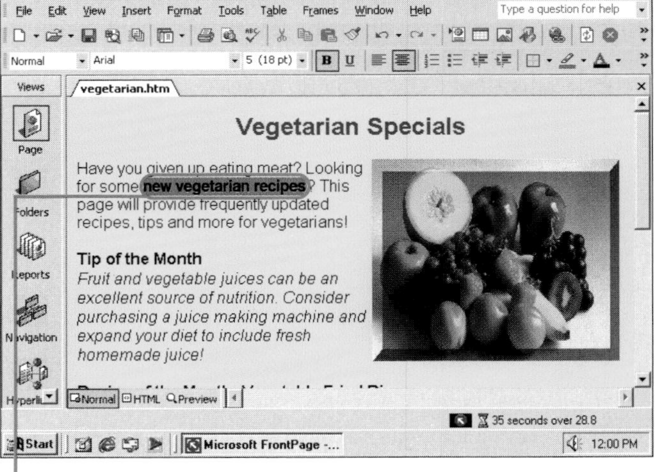

1 Select the text you want to highlight. To select text, see page 54.

2 Click ▾ in this area to display the available highlight colors.

Note: If the Highlight button (✎) is not displayed, click » on the Formatting toolbar to display all the buttons.

3 Click the highlight color you want to use.

■ The text appears highlighted in the color you selected.

■ To deselect text, click outside the selected area.

■ To remove a highlight from text, repeat steps 1 to 3, selecting **Automatic** in step 3.

CHANGE APPEARANCE OF TEXT

You can make text on a Web page look more attractive by using various fonts, styles, sizes, effects and colors.

CHANGE APPEARANCE OF TEXT

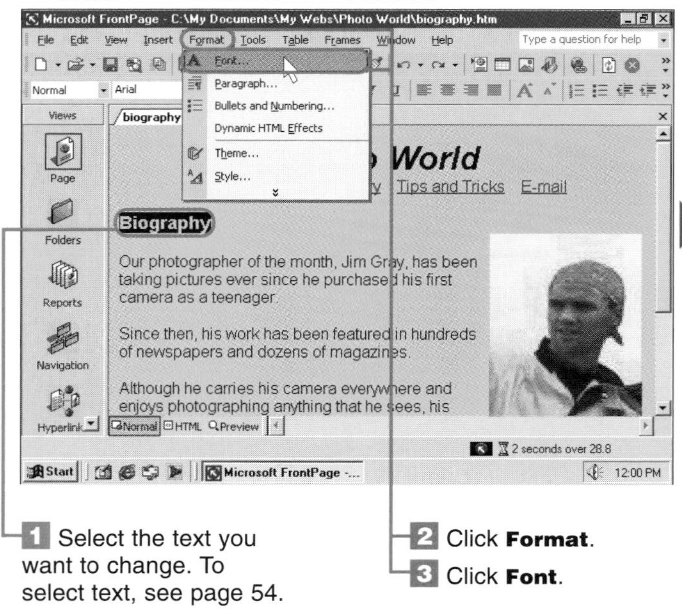

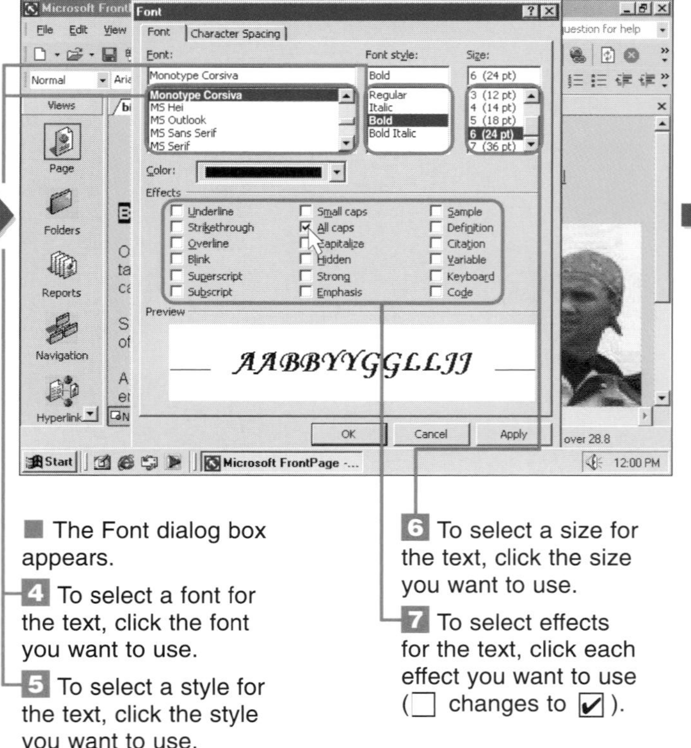

1 Select the text you want to change. To select text, see page 54.

2 Click **Format**.

3 Click **Font**.

■ The Font dialog box appears.

4 To select a font for the text, click the font you want to use.

5 To select a style for the text, click the style you want to use.

6 To select a size for the text, click the size you want to use.

7 To select effects for the text, click each effect you want to use (☐ changes to ☑).

What are some effects that I can add to text on a Web page?

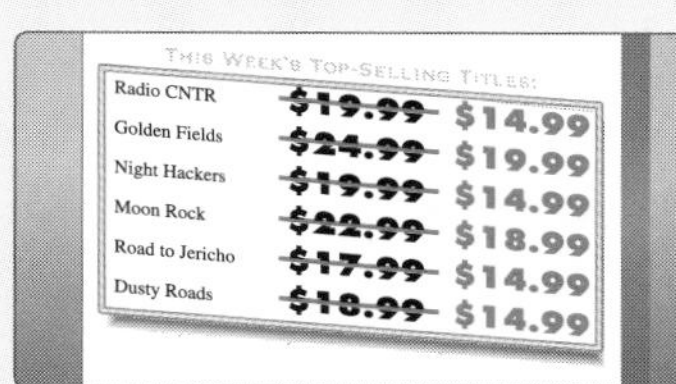

Strikethrough

This effect places a line through text. Companies often use this effect to strike out old prices to show that new prices are lower.

Blink

This effect blinks text on and off. Blinking text is useful for drawing attention to information on a Web page. The Internet Explorer Web browser cannot display blinking text.

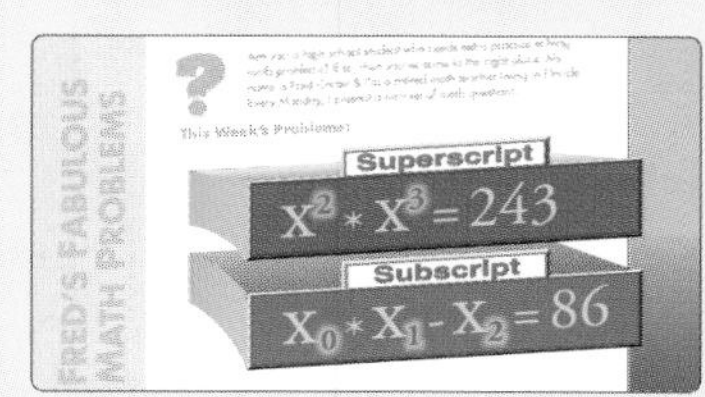

Superscript and Subscript

These effects place text or numbers slightly above or below text on a Web page. These effects are useful for displaying mathematical equations.

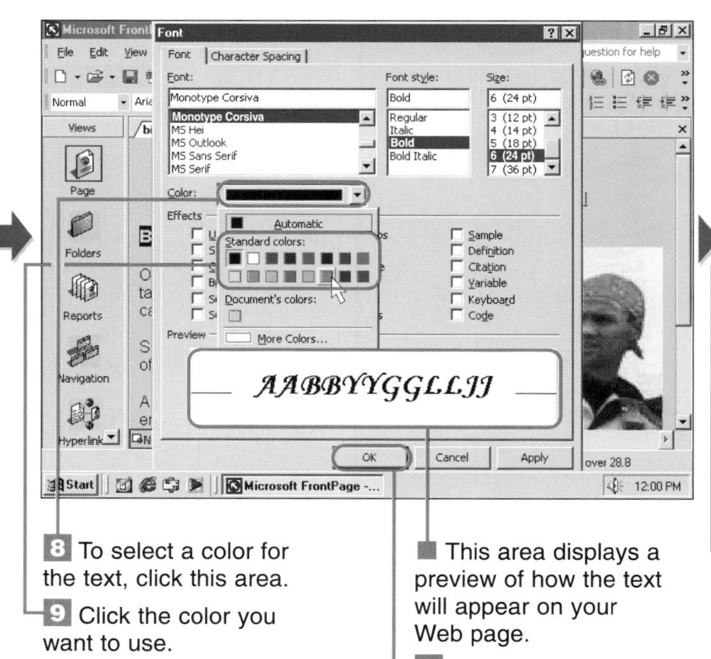

8 To select a color for the text, click this area.

9 Click the color you want to use.

■ This area displays a preview of how the text will appear on your Web page.

10 Click **OK** to confirm your changes.

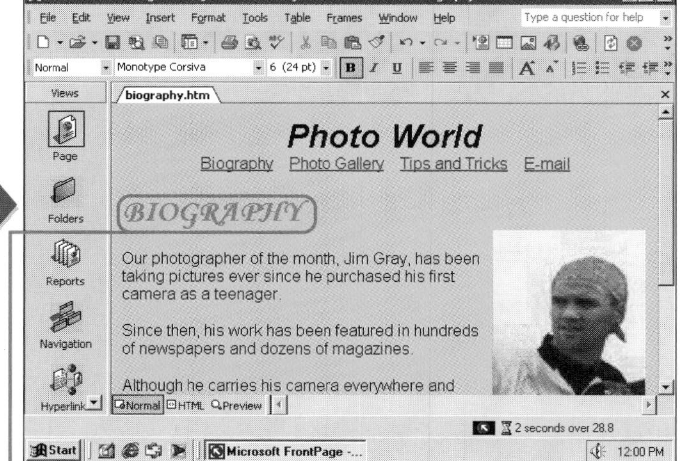

■ The text you selected displays the changes.

■ To deselect text, click outside the selected area.

■ To return the text to its original appearance, repeat steps 1 to 3, except select **Remove Formatting** in step 3.

INDENT TEXT

You can indent text to make paragraphs on a Web page stand out.

INDENT TEXT

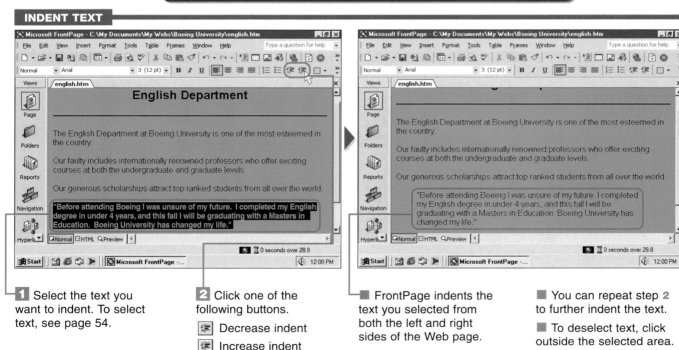

1 Select the text you want to indent. To select text, see page 54.

2 Click one of the following buttons.

- Decrease indent
- Increase indent

■ FrontPage indents the text you selected from both the left and right sides of the Web page.

■ You can repeat step **2** to further indent the text.

■ To deselect text, click outside the selected area.

ADD BORDERS TO TEXT

You can add borders to text to draw attention to information on a Web page.

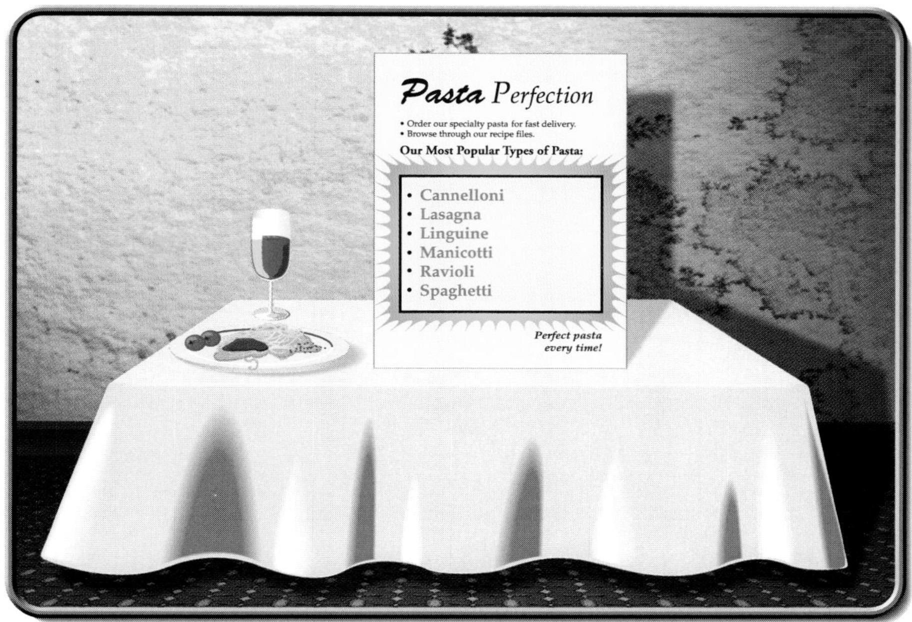

ADD BORDERS TO TEXT

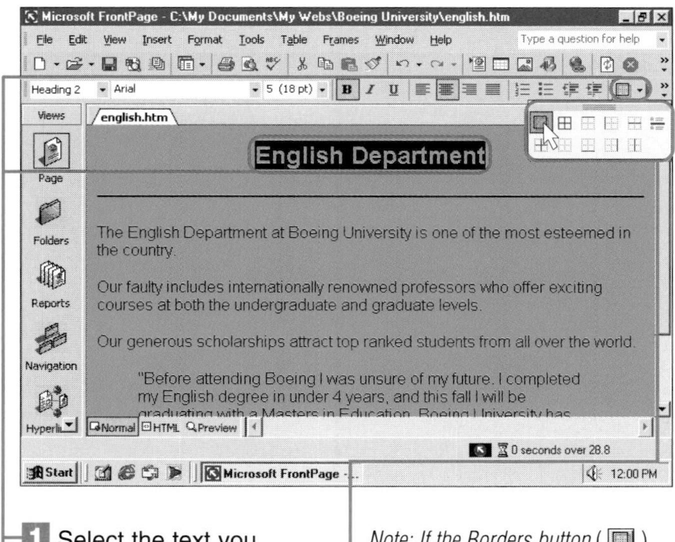

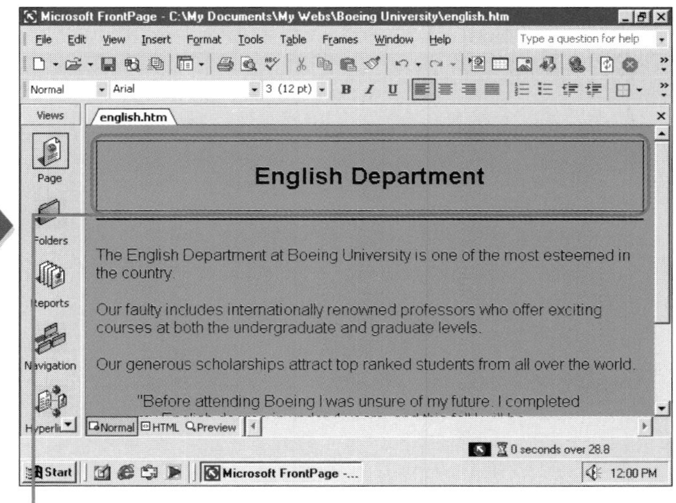

1 Select the text you want to add a border to. To select text, see page 54.

2 Click ▾ in this area to display the available types of borders.

Note: If the Borders button ( ) is not displayed, click » on the Formatting toolbar to display all the buttons.

3 Click the type of border you want to add.

Note: You cannot add some types of borders to text.

■ The text displays the border you selected.

■ To deselect text, click outside the selected area.

■ To remove borders from text, repeat steps 1 to 3, selecting ▢ in step 3.

COPY FORMATTING

You can copy the formatting of text to make one area of text on a Web page look exactly like another.

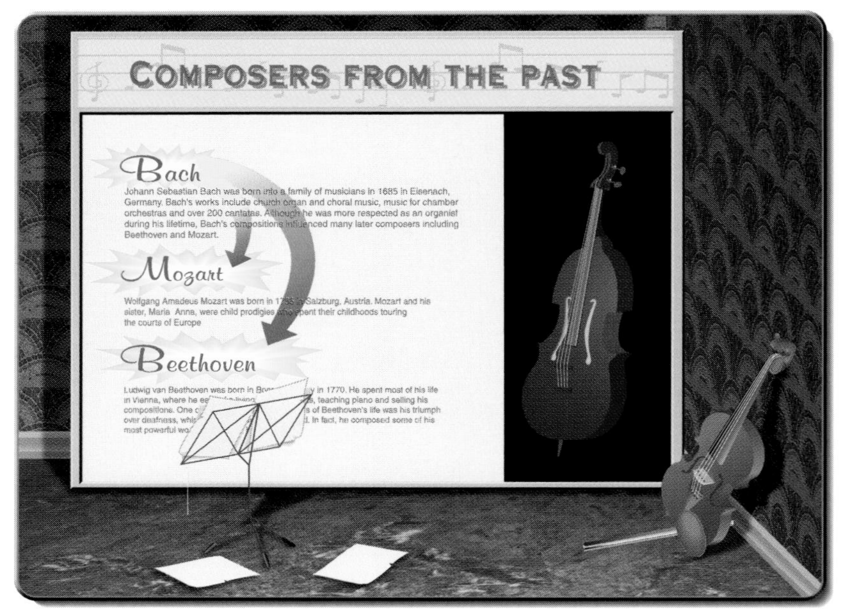

You may want to copy the formatting of text to make all the headings or important words on a Web page look the same. This will give the text on a Web page a consistent appearance.

COPY FORMATTING

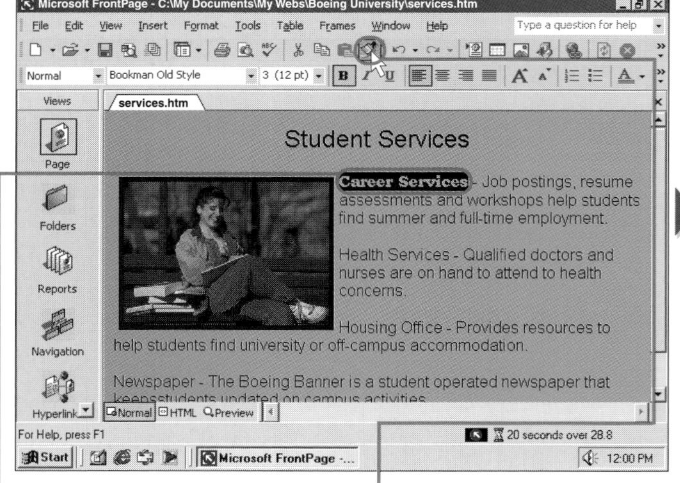

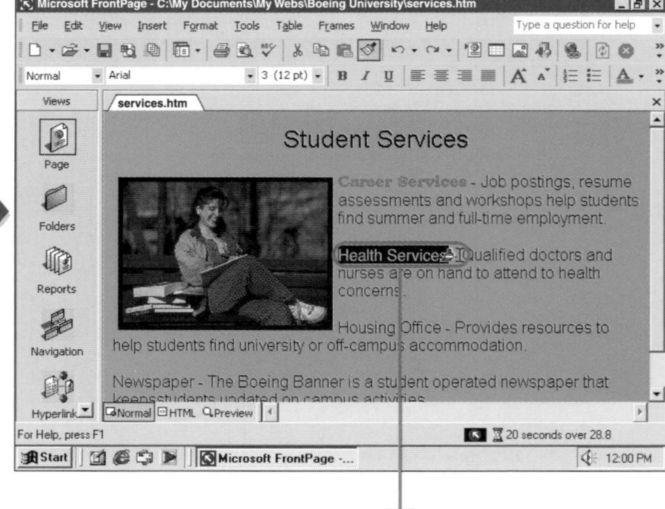

1 Select the text that displays the formatting you want to copy. To select text, see page 54.

2 Click the Format Painter button to copy the formatting of the text.

■ The mouse I changes to the Format Painter pointer when over your Web page.

3 Select the text you want to display the same formatting.

Can I copy the formatting of a link?

You can copy the formatting of a link to another word or phrase on your Web page. The text you copy the formatting to will link to the same destination as the original text.

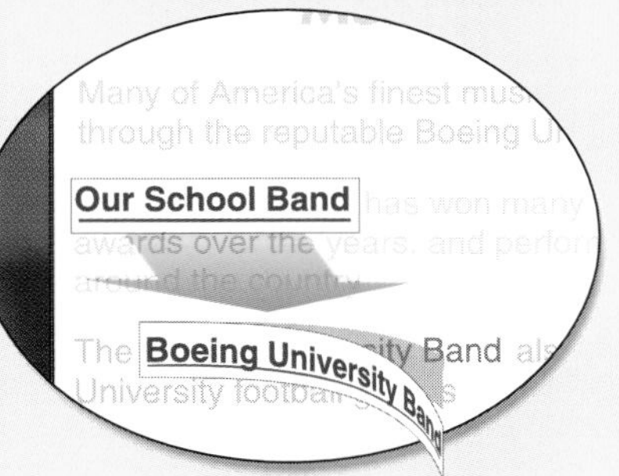

How can I remove the formatting from text?

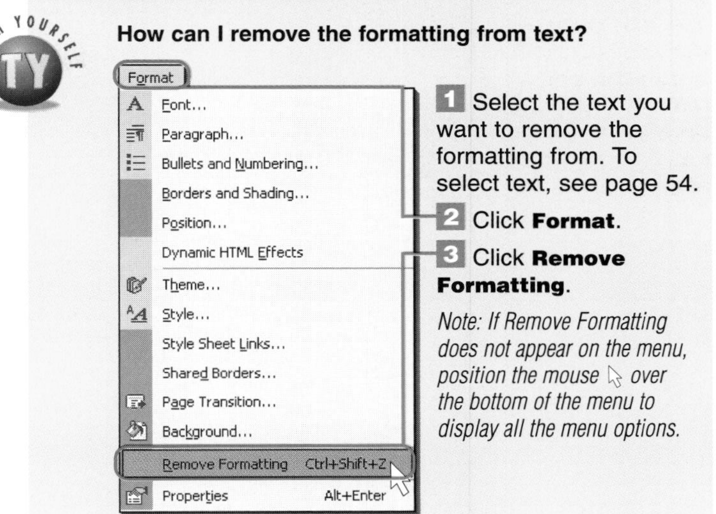

1 Select the text you want to remove the formatting from. To select text, see page 54.

2 Click **Format**.

3 Click **Remove Formatting**.

Note: If Remove Formatting does not appear on the menu, position the mouse over the bottom of the menu to display all the menu options.

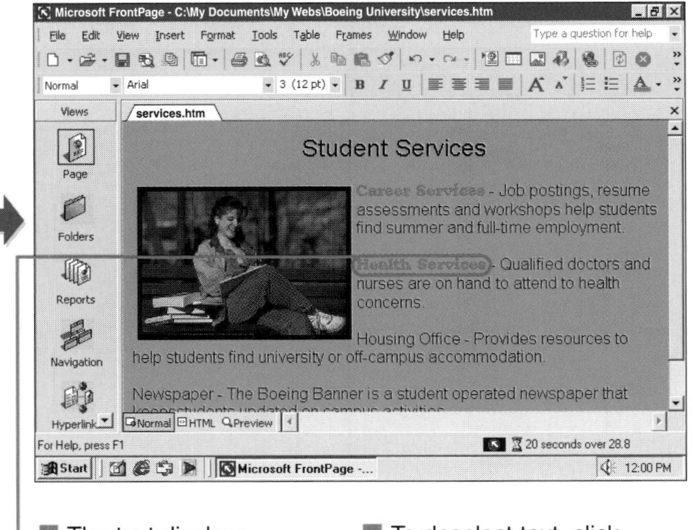

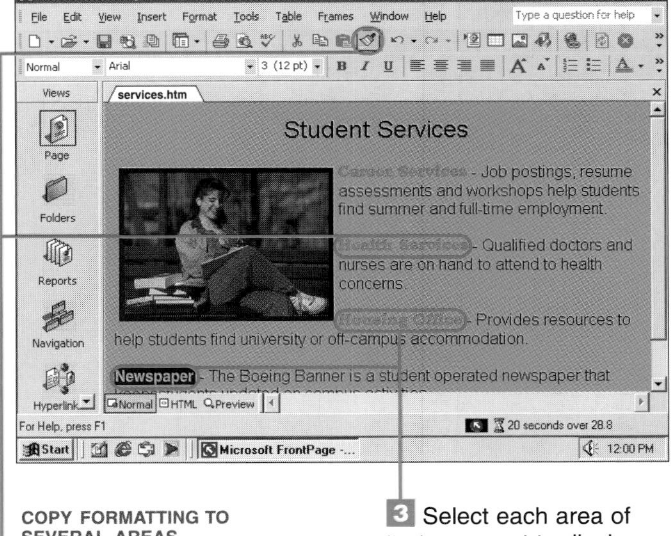

■ The text displays the same formatting.

■ To deselect text, click outside the selected area.

COPY FORMATTING TO SEVERAL AREAS

1 Select the text that displays the formatting you want to copy.

2 Double-click to copy the formatting of the text.

3 Select each area of text you want to display the same formatting.

4 When you finish selecting all the text you want to display the same formatting, press the Esc key.

ADD A HEADING

You can use headings to help organize the information on a Web page. There are six heading sizes you can use.

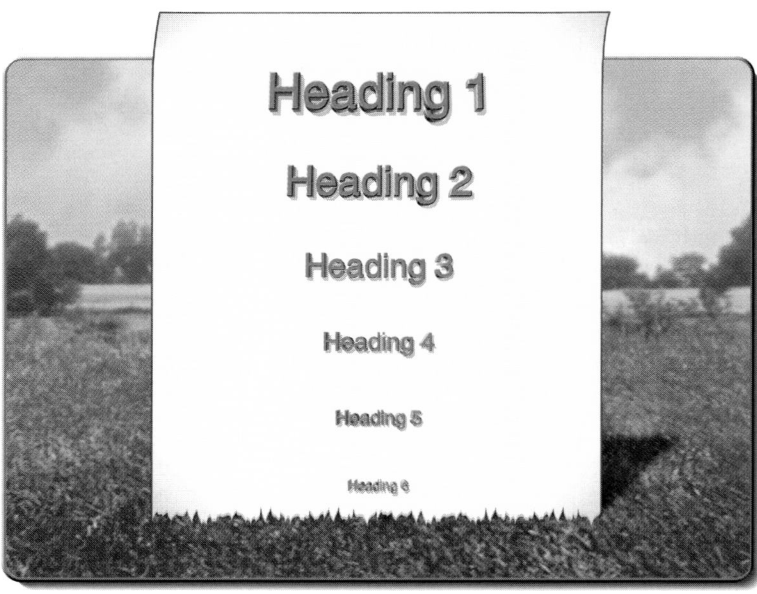

Headings can help visitors quickly locate topics of interest.

Since different Web browsers display headings in slightly different ways, you should only use headings to signify the importance of information on a Web page and not to change the appearance of text.

ADD A HEADING

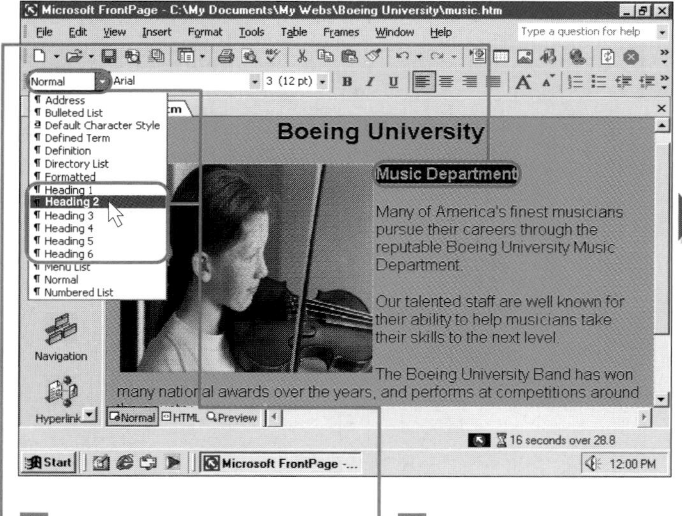

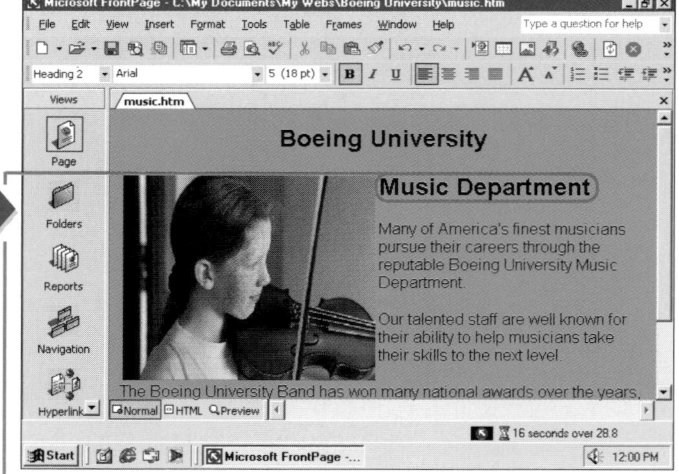

1 Select the text you want to make a heading. To select text, see page 54.

2 Click this area to display a list of the available heading sizes.

3 Click the heading size you want to use.

■ The text appears as a heading on your Web page.

■ To deselect text, click outside the selected area.

■ To remove the heading style from text, repeat steps 1 to 3, selecting **Normal** in step 3.

CREATE A DEFINITION LIST

You can create a definition list to display terms and their definitions. This type of list is ideal for displaying a glossary.

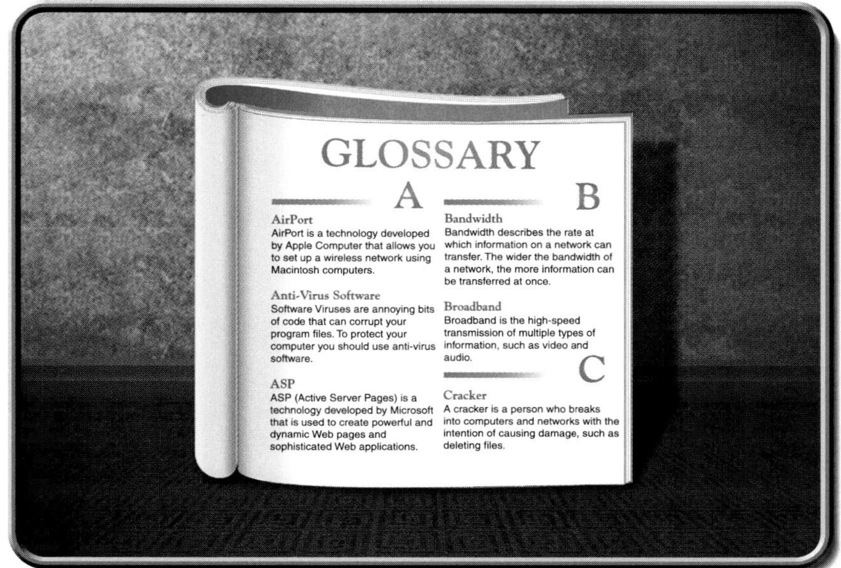

CREATE A DEFINITION LIST

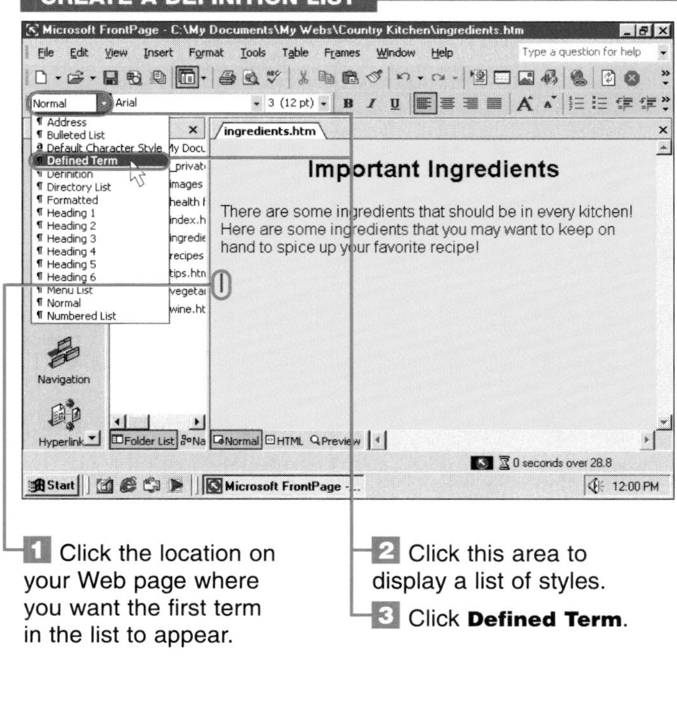

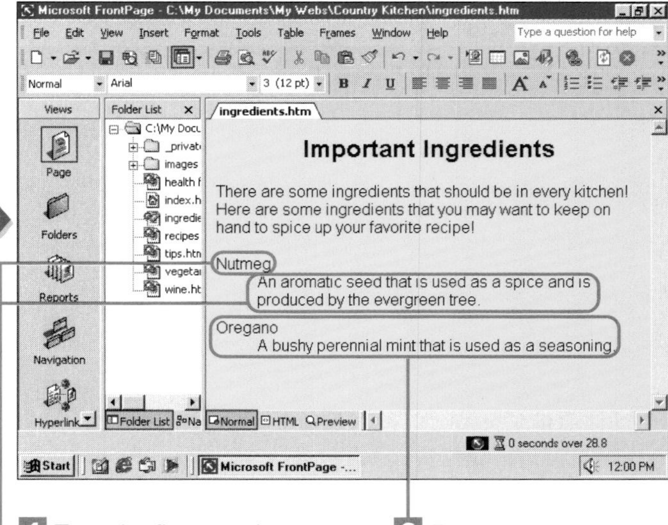

1 Click the location on your Web page where you want the first term in the list to appear.

2 Click this area to display a list of styles.

3 Click **Defined Term**.

4 Type the first term in the list and then press the Enter key.

■ FrontPage automatically adds an indent for the definition of the term.

5 Type the definition of the term and then press the Enter key.

6 Repeat steps 4 and 5 for each term you want to include in the list.

■ When you complete the list, press the Enter key twice.

CREATE A BULLETED OR NUMBERED LIST

You can separate items in a list by beginning each item with a bullet or number.

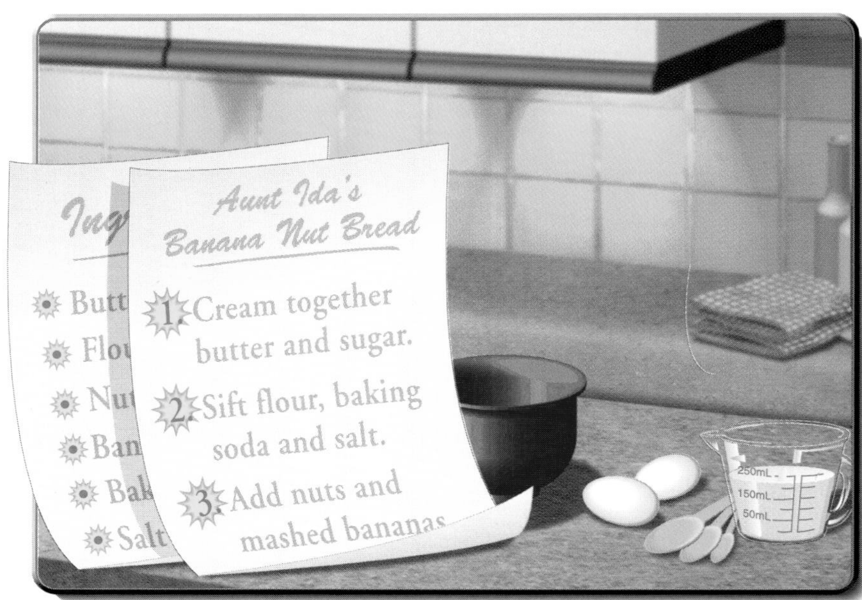

Bulleted List

Bulleted lists are useful for items in no particular order, such as a list of products or Web pages. Bulleted lists are also known as unordered lists.

Numbered List

Numbered lists are useful for items in a specific order, such as a set of instructions or a table of contents. Numbered lists are also known as ordered lists.

CREATE A BULLETED OR NUMBERED LIST

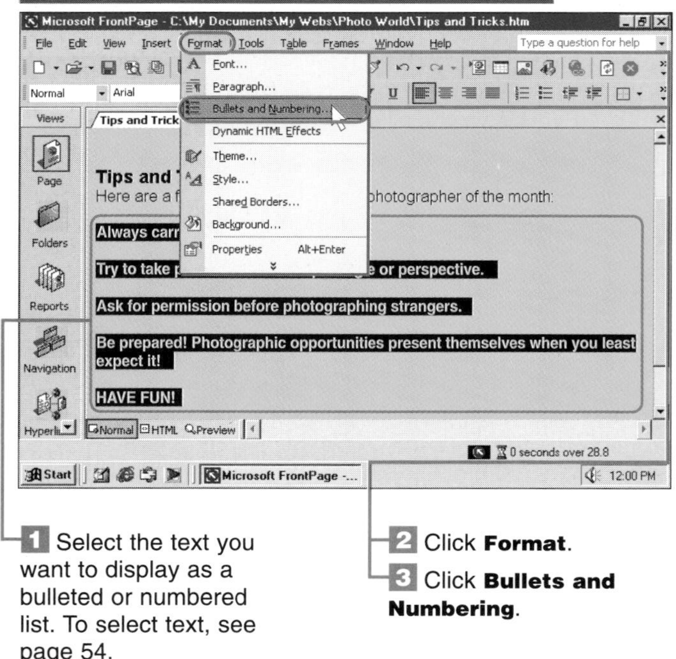

1 Select the text you want to display as a bulleted or numbered list. To select text, see page 54.

2 Click **Format**.

3 Click **Bullets and Numbering**.

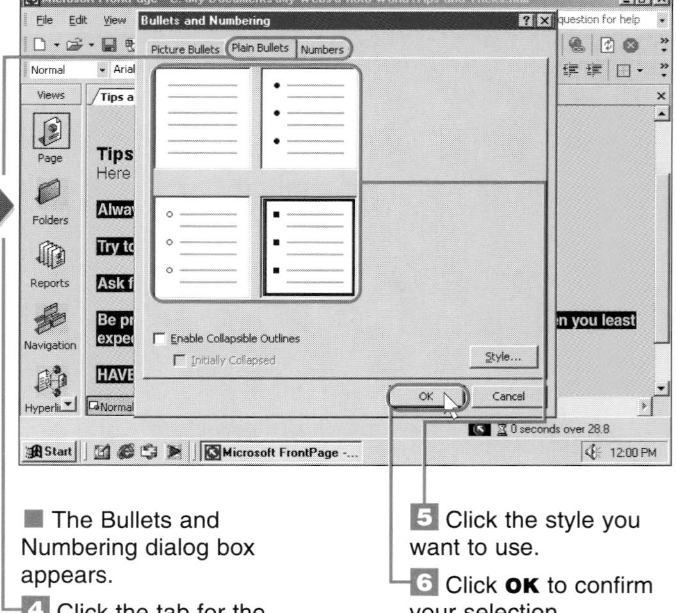

■ The Bullets and Numbering dialog box appears.

4 Click the tab for the type of list you want to create.

5 Click the style you want to use.

6 Click **OK** to confirm your selection.

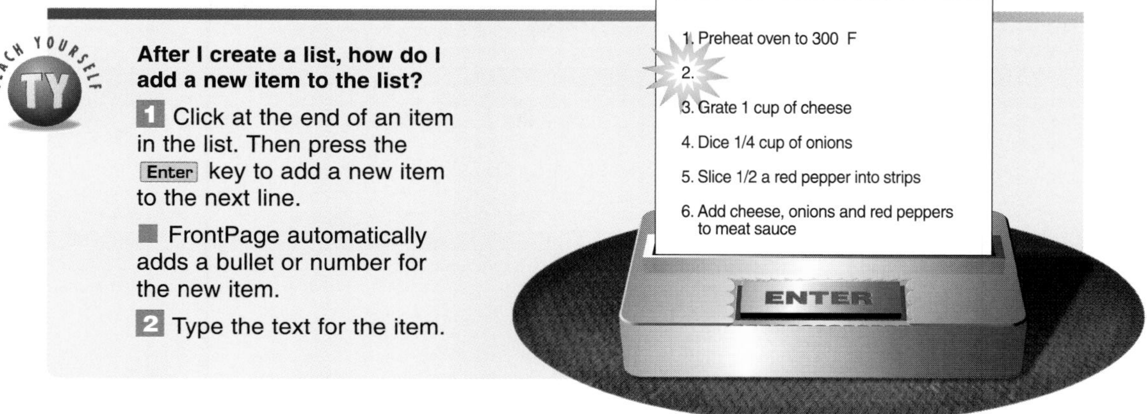

After I create a list, how do I add a new item to the list?

1 Click at the end of an item in the list. Then press the Enter key to add a new item to the next line.

■ FrontPage automatically adds a bullet or number for the new item.

2 Type the text for the item.

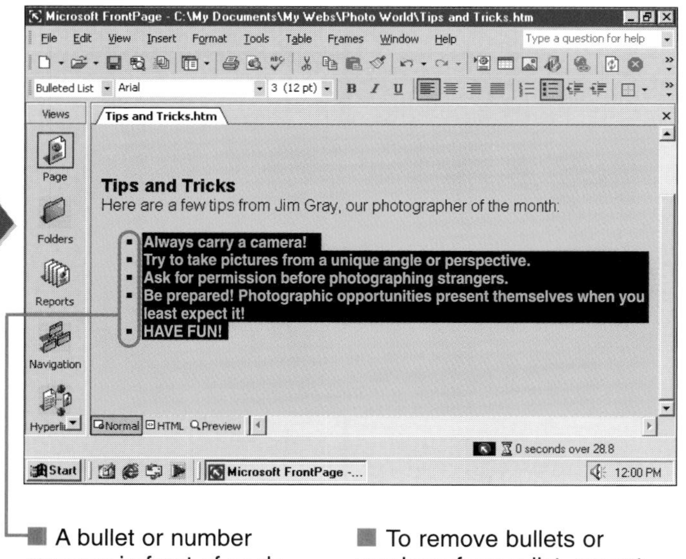

■ A bullet or number appears in front of each item in the list.

■ To deselect the text in the list, click outside the selected area.

■ To remove bullets or numbers from a list, repeat steps 1 to 6, selecting the top left style in step 5.

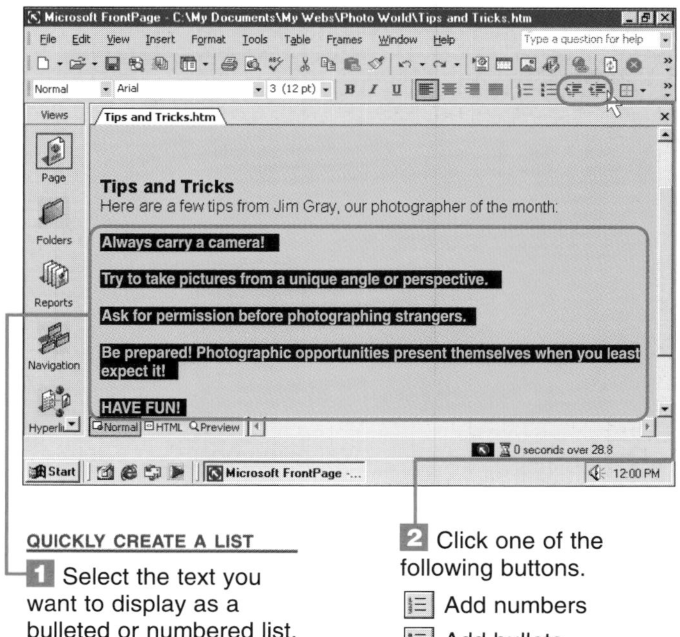

QUICKLY CREATE A LIST

1 Select the text you want to display as a bulleted or numbered list.

2 Click one of the following buttons.

Add numbers

Add bullets

CREATE A LIST WITH PICTURE BULLETS

You can create an eye-catching list on a Web page that uses images as bullets.

You should use a small image for picture bullets that will fit neatly beside each item in a list.

CREATE A LIST WITH PICTURE BULLETS

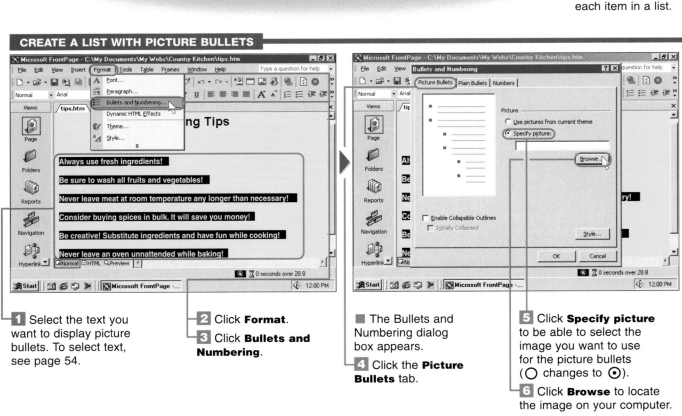

1 Select the text you want to display picture bullets. To select text, see page 54.

2 Click **Format**.

3 Click **Bullets and Numbering**.

■ The Bullets and Numbering dialog box appears.

4 Click the **Picture Bullets** tab.

5 Click **Specify picture** to be able to select the image you want to use for the picture bullets (○ changes to ⊙).

6 Click **Browse** to locate the image on your computer.

Where can I obtain images that I can use as bullets in a list?

You can use a graphics program to create your own picture bullets. Many Web sites also offer images that you can use as picture bullets. You can find picture bullets at the following Web sites.

www.abcgiant.com

www.grapholina.com/Graphics

www.theshockzone.com

Is there a faster way to add picture bullets to a list?

When you apply a theme to your Web pages, FrontPage will automatically add picture bullets to bulleted lists you have created. To create a bulleted list, see page 82. To apply a theme to Web pages, see page 88.

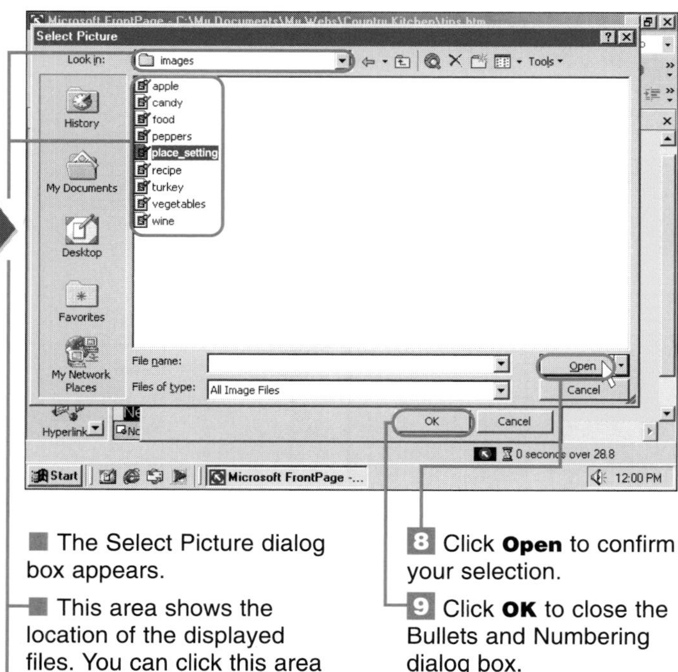

- The Select Picture dialog box appears.
- This area shows the location of the displayed files. You can click this area to change the location.

7 Click the image you want to use for the picture bullets.

8 Click **Open** to confirm your selection.

9 Click **OK** to close the Bullets and Numbering dialog box.

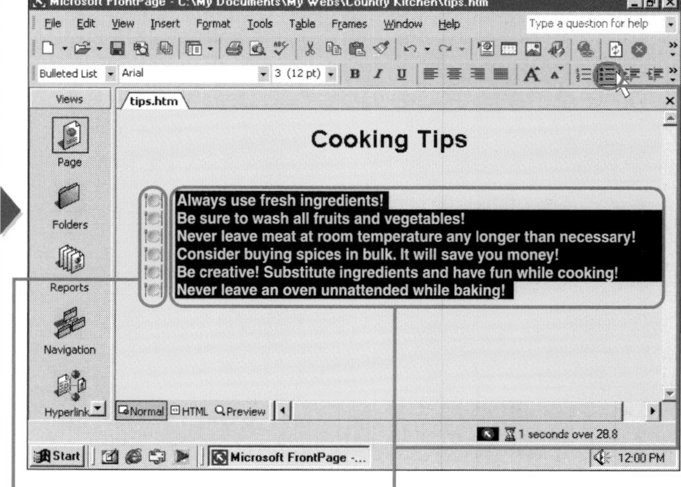

- A picture bullet appears in front of each item in the list.
- To deselect the text, click outside the selected area.

Note: When you save the Web page, FrontPage will ask you to save the image as part of your Web site. To save a Web page, see page 28.

REMOVE PICTURE BULLETS

1 Select the text that displays the picture bullets.

2 Click the bullets button to remove the images from the list.

You can change the background color of a Web page to customize the appearance of the page.

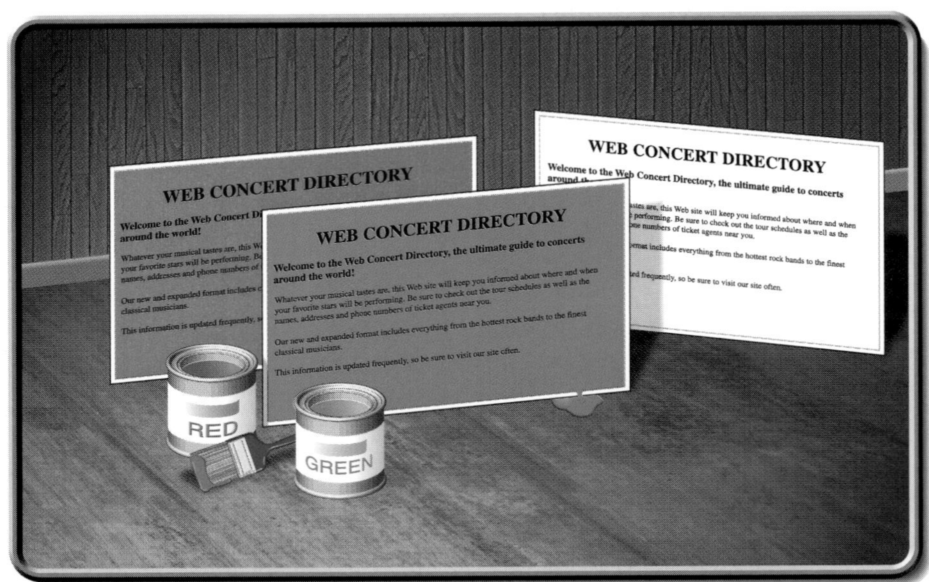

CHANGE BACKGROUND COLOR

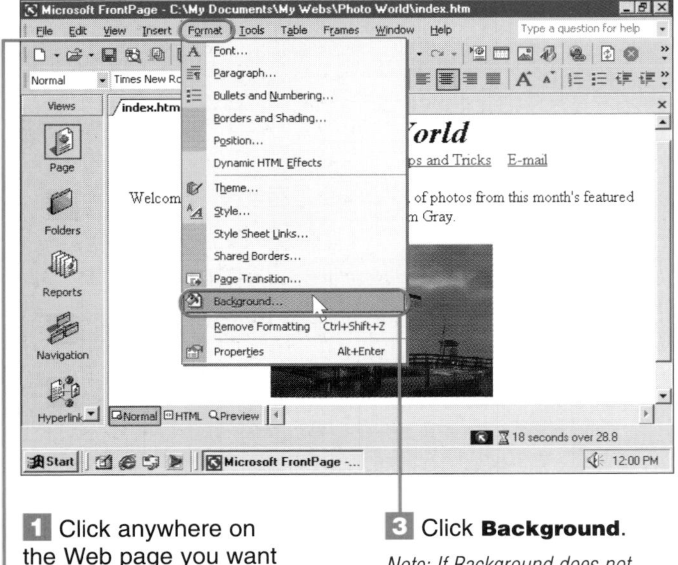

1 Click anywhere on the Web page you want to add a background color to.

2 Click **Format**.

3 Click **Background**.

Note: If Background does not appear on the menu, position the mouse over the bottom of the menu to display all the menu options.

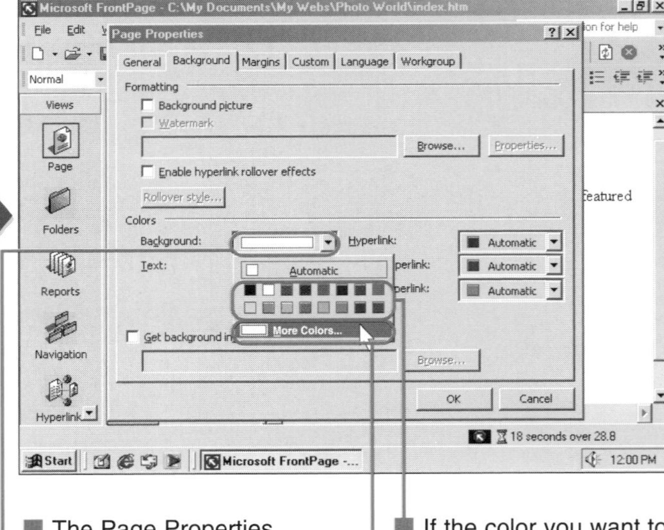

■ The Page Properties dialog box appears.

4 Click this area to select a background color for your Web page.

■ If the color you want to use appears in this area, click the background color and then skip to step 8.

5 To display additional colors that you can use, click **More Colors**.

What should I consider when changing the background color of my Web pages?

Make sure you select a background color that works well with the color of your text. For example, red text on a blue background can be difficult to read. To make the text on your Web pages easy to read, try to use dark text on a light background or light text on a dark background. To change the color of text, see page 72.

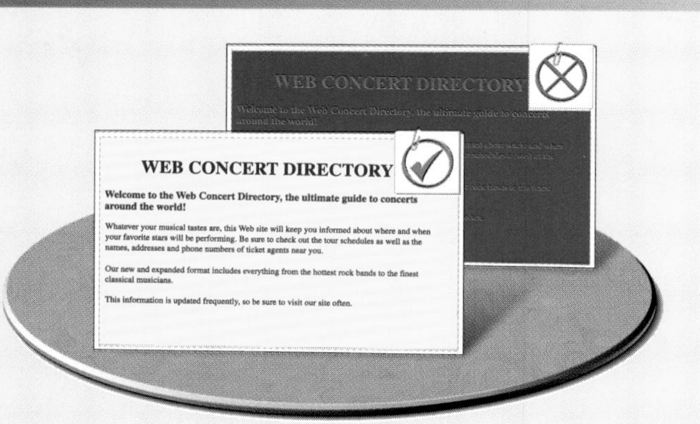

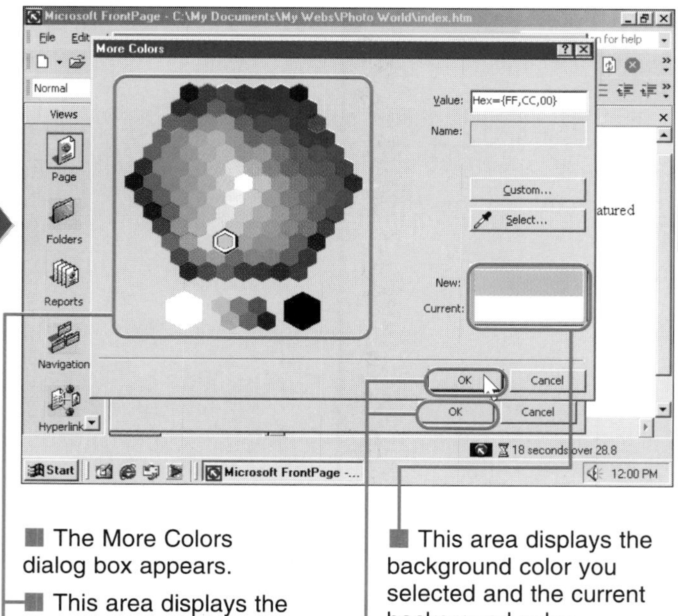

■ The More Colors dialog box appears.

■ This area displays the available background colors.

6 Click the background color you want to use.

■ This area displays the background color you selected and the current background color.

7 Click **OK** to confirm your selection.

8 Click **OK** in the Page Properties dialog box to change the background color of your Web page.

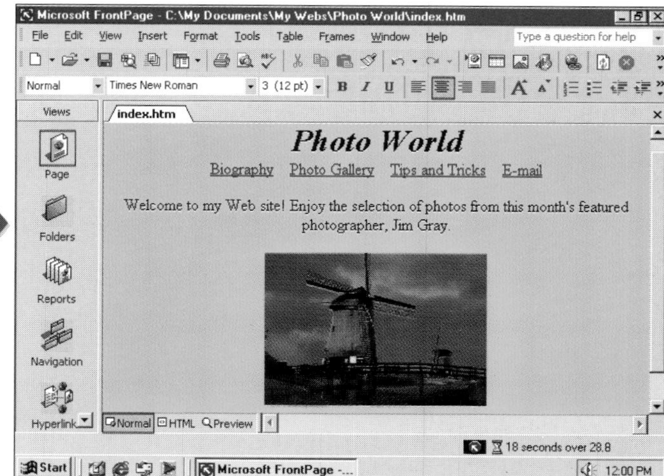

■ The Web page background displays the color you selected.

■ To return to the original background color, repeat steps 1 to 5, except select **Automatic** in step 5. Then perform step 8.

APPLY A THEME

FrontPage offers many themes that you can choose from to give your Web pages a professional appearance.

A theme will change the way fonts, colors, bullets and lines appear on your Web pages.

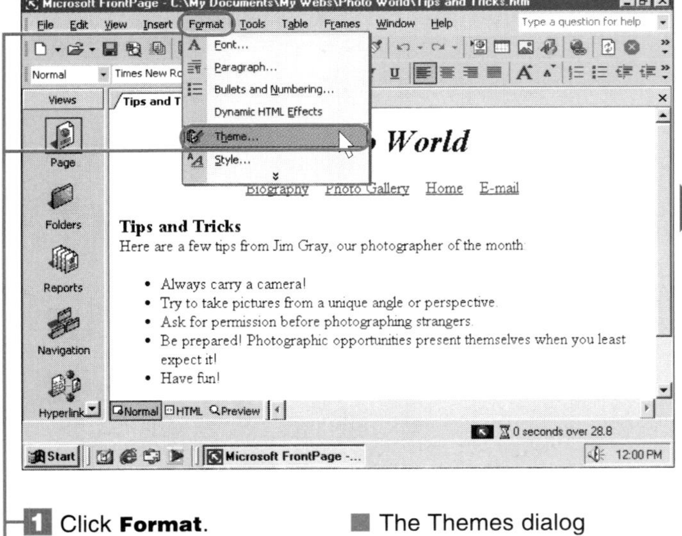

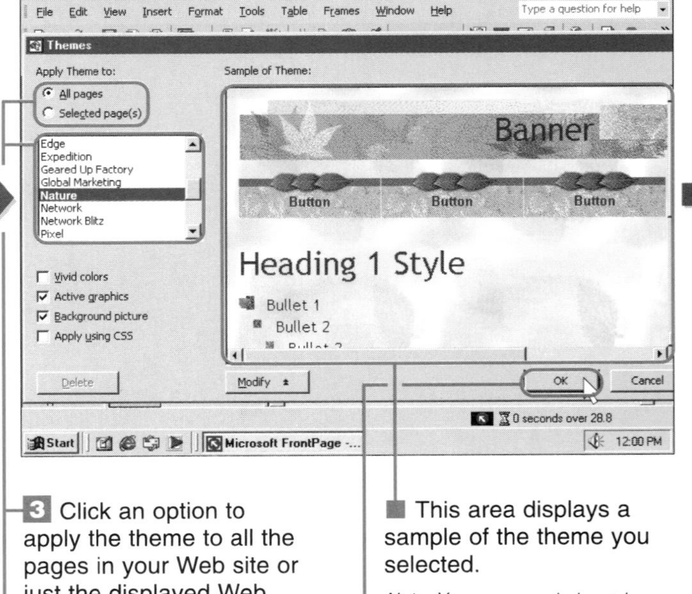

1 Click **Format**.

2 Click **Theme**.

■ The Themes dialog box appears.

3 Click an option to apply the theme to all the pages in your Web site or just the displayed Web page (○ changes to ⦿).

4 Click the theme you want to use.

■ This area displays a sample of the theme you selected.

Note: You can repeat step 4 to view a sample of a different theme.

5 Click **OK** to apply the selected theme.

How can I change the appearance of a theme?

In the Themes dialog box, FrontPage provides additional options you can select to customize themes. You can click an option to turn the option on (☑) or off (☐).

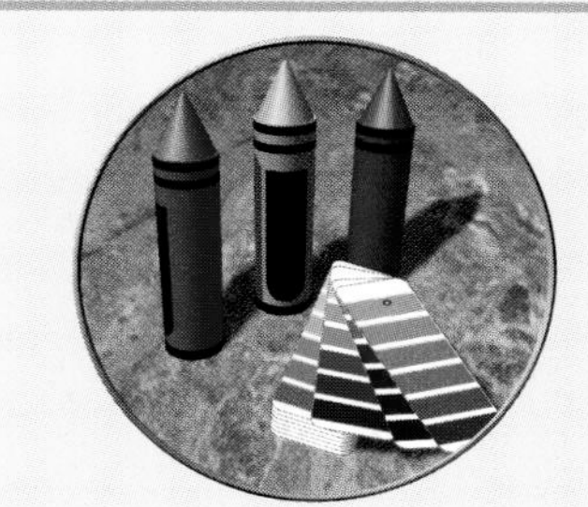

Vivid colors

Use brighter colors.

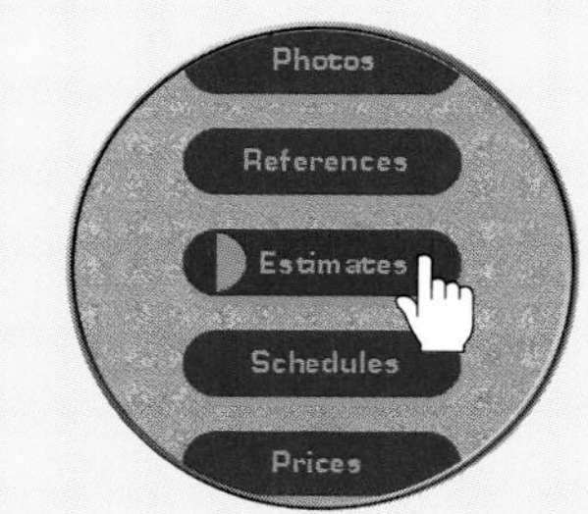

Active graphics

Use animated graphics.

Background picture

Use a background image.

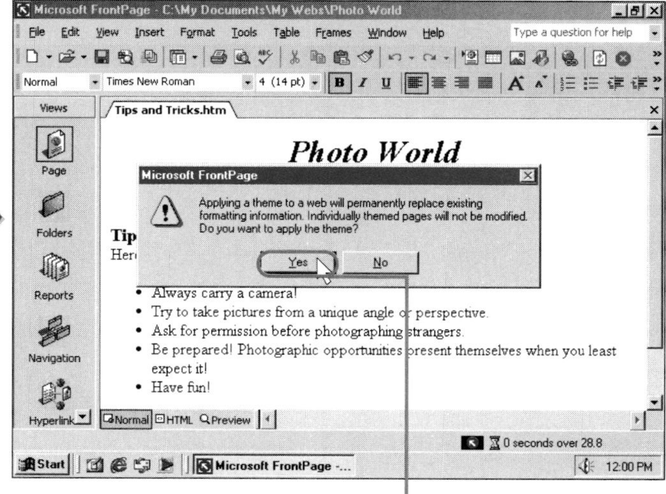

■ A dialog box may appear, stating that applying a theme will change the appearance of all your Web pages and permanently replace some of the formatting changes you previously made.

6 Click **Yes** to continue.

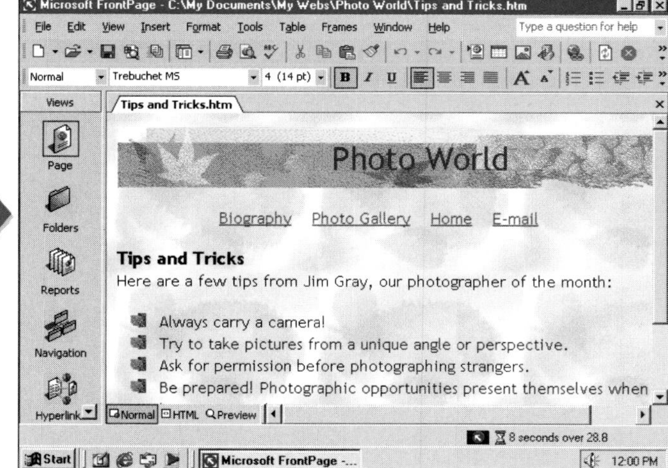

■ The Web page(s) you specified display the theme.

■ To remove a theme from Web pages, repeat steps **1** to **6**, selecting **(No Theme)** in step **4**.

BIRD WATCHERS' HOME PAGE
The page dedicated to people who love to watch birds!
Bird watchers appreciate the beauty and wonder of birds. This month, with summer just around the corner, we will discuss the best spots for bird-watching in the National Parks of the northern States. These locations have been recommended by visitors to our page. If you have a new location to add, please e-mail us today!
Bird

Popular Sites

Membership Information

Membership Information

GLUE

CHAPTER 6

Add Images

Would you like to add images to your Web pages? Read this chapter to learn how.

REASONS FOR USING IMAGES

ILLUSTRATIONS

You can add images to your Web pages to display drawings, paintings and computer-generated art. Adding images can help illustrate a concept that is difficult to explain with words. For example, you can include a map to give directions, a chart to show financial trends or a diagram to point out parts of a product.

PHOTOGRAPHS

You can display photographs of your family, pets or favorite celebrities on your Web pages. Many companies include photographs of their products so people around the world can view their products without having to visit a store or wait for a catalog to arrive in the mail.

TYPES OF IMAGES

When you save a Web page, FrontPage automatically converts any images you added to the page to the GIF or JPEG format. The GIF and JPEG formats are the most popular image formats on the Web.

GIF

Graphics Interchange Format (GIF) images are limited to 256 colors and are often used for logos, banners and computer-generated art. GIF images have the .gif extension, such as logo.gif.

JPEG

Joint Photographic Experts Group (JPEG) images can have millions of colors and are often used for photographs and very large images. JPEG images have the .jpg extension, such as stonehenge.jpg.

OBTAIN IMAGES

INTERNET

Many Web sites offer images you can use free of charge on your Web pages. Make sure you have permission to use any images you obtain on the Web. You can find images at the following Web sites.

www.allfree-clipart.com

www.free-graphics.com

www.noeticart.com

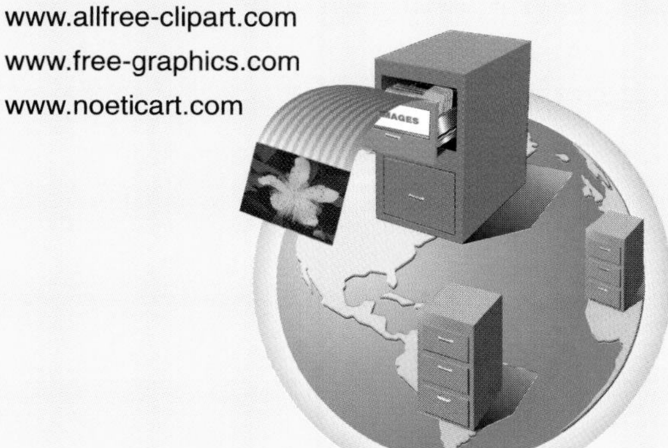

SCAN IMAGES

If you have existing images that you want to add to your Web pages, you can use a scanner to scan the images into your computer. You can scan photographs, logos and drawings and then place the scanned images on your Web pages. If you do not have a scanner, many service bureaus will scan images for a fee.

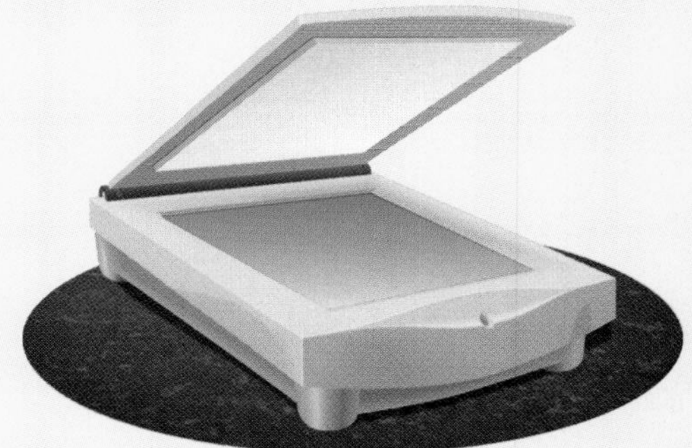

CREATE IMAGES

You can use an image editing program to create your own images. Creating your own images allows you to design images that best suit your Web pages. Popular image editing programs include Adobe Photoshop (www.adobe.com) and Jasc Paint Shop Pro (www.jasc.com). If you are creating a Web site for your company, you may want to hire a graphic artist to create images for you.

IMAGE COLLECTIONS

You can purchase collections of ready-made images at computer stores. Image collections can include cartoons, drawings, photographs and computer-generated art.

You can add an image to illustrate a concept or enhance the appearance of a Web page.

ADD AN IMAGE

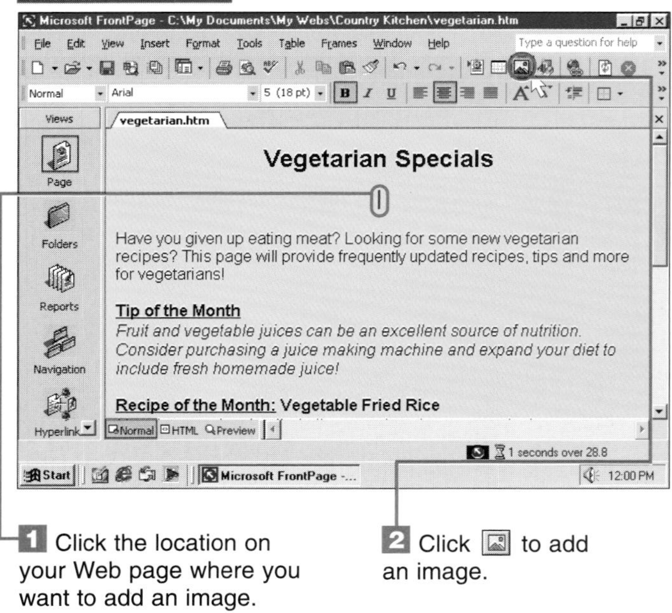

1 Click the location on your Web page where you want to add an image.

2 Click 🖼 to add an image.

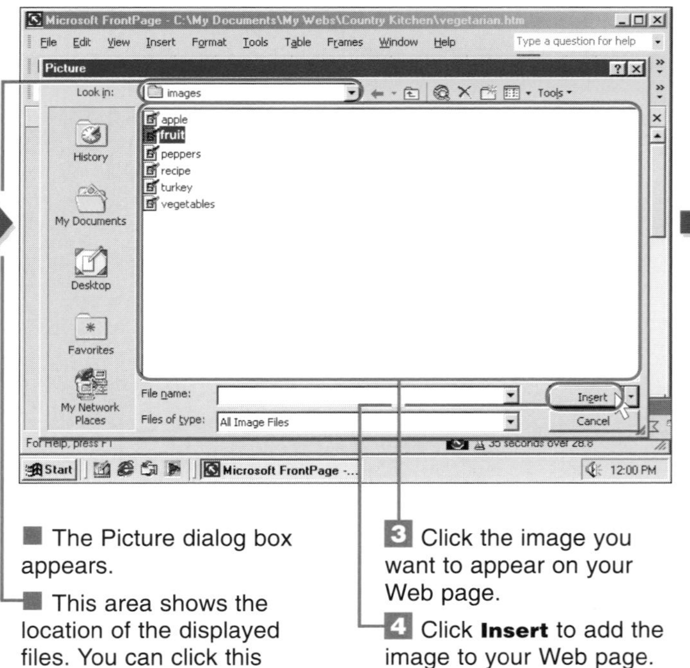

■ The Picture dialog box appears.

■ This area shows the location of the displayed files. You can click this area to change the location.

3 Click the image you want to appear on your Web page.

4 Click **Insert** to add the image to your Web page.

What should I consider when adding an image to a Web page?

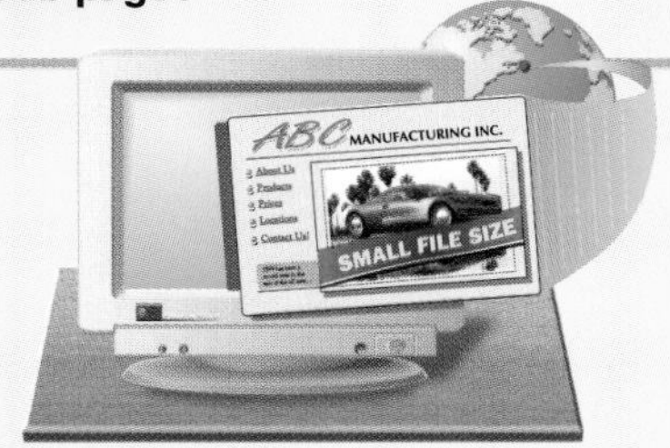

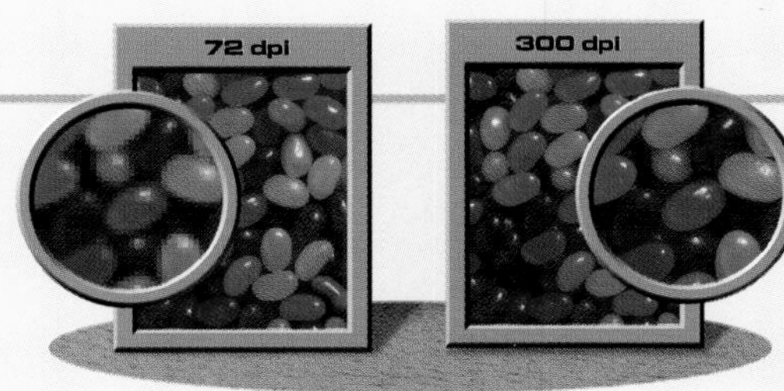

Image Size

Images increase the time Web pages take to appear on a visitor's screen. If a Web page takes too long to appear, visitors may lose interest and move to another page. Whenever possible, you should use images with small file sizes since these images will transfer faster.

Image Resolution

The resolution of an image refers to the clarity of the image. Higher resolution images are sharper and more detailed, but take longer to transfer to a visitor's computer. Since most computer monitors display images at a resolution of 72 dots per inch (dpi), images you add to your Web pages do not need to have a resolution higher than 72 dpi.

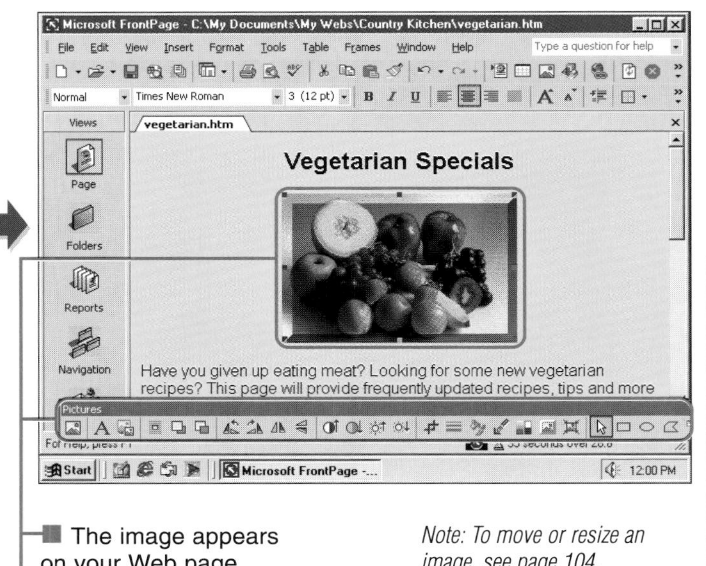

■ The image appears on your Web page.

■ The Pictures toolbar appears, displaying buttons that allow you to change the appearance of the image.

Note: To move or resize an image, see page 104.

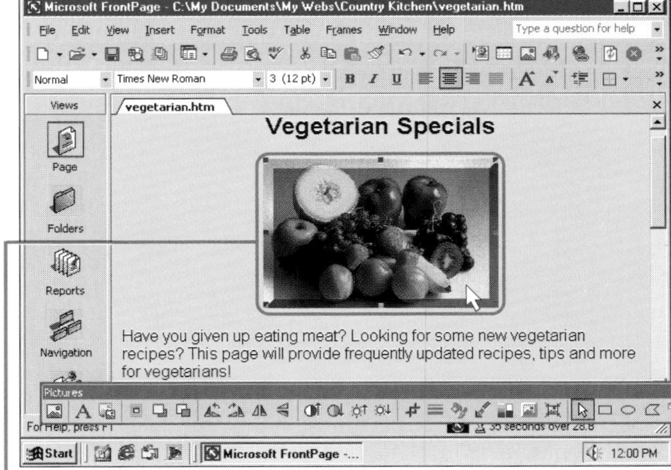

DELETE AN IMAGE

1 Click the image you want to delete. Handles (■) appear around the image.

2 Press the Delete key to delete the image.

ADD AN AUTOSHAPE

FrontPage provides many ready-made shapes, called AutoShapes, that you can add to a Web page.

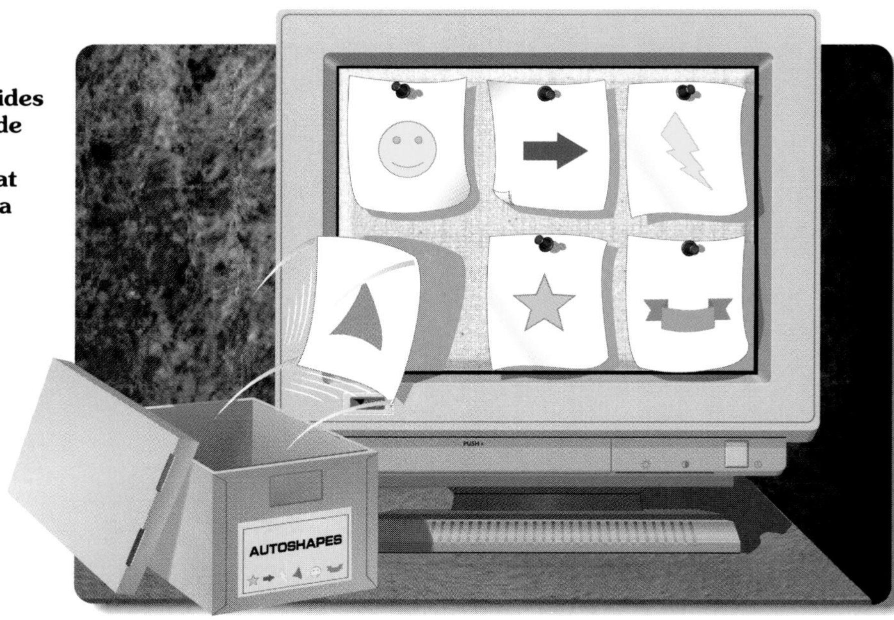

FrontPage offers several types of AutoShapes such as Lines, Block Arrows, Stars and Banners.

ADD AN AUTOSHAPE

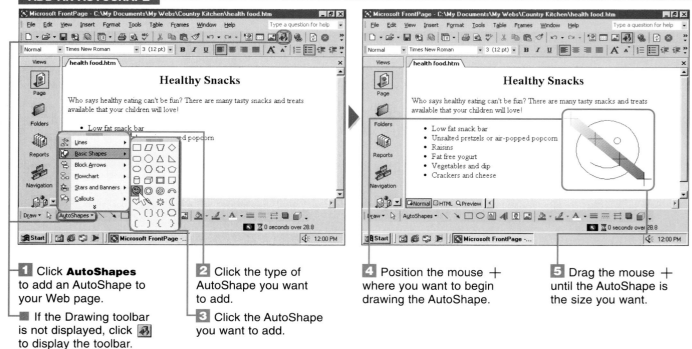

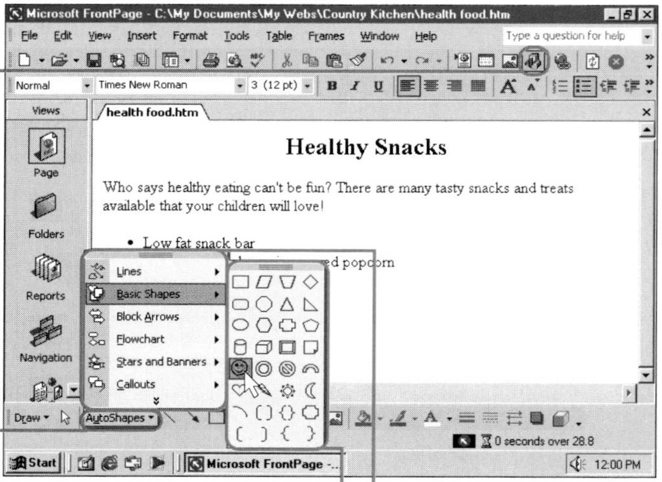

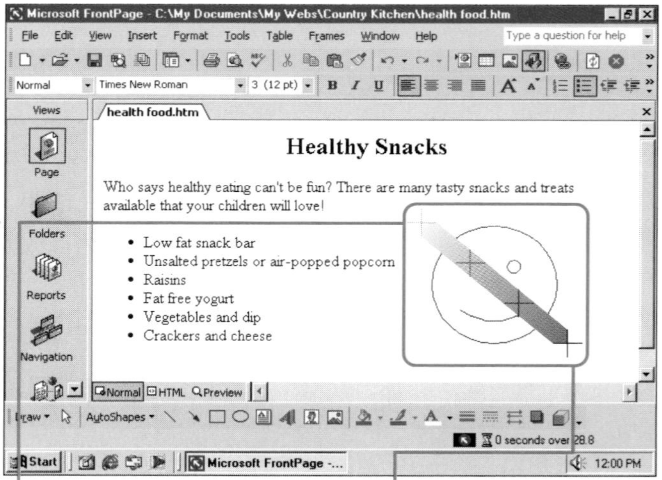

1. Click **AutoShapes** to add an AutoShape to your Web page.

■ If the Drawing toolbar is not displayed, click [icon] to display the toolbar.

2. Click the type of AutoShape you want to add.

3. Click the AutoShape you want to add.

4. Position the mouse + where you want to begin drawing the AutoShape.

5. Drag the mouse + until the AutoShape is the size you want.

Why do green and yellow dots appear on some AutoShapes?

You can use the green and yellow dots to change the appearance of an AutoShape.

To rotate an AutoShape, position the mouse over the green dot (●) and then drag the mouse ↻ to a new position.

To change the design of an AutoShape, position the mouse over the yellow dot (◇) and then drag the mouse ▷ until the shape displays the design you want.

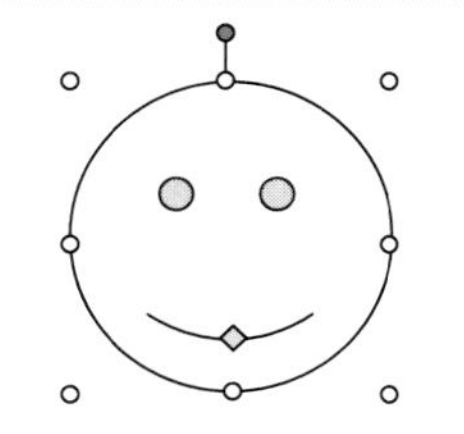

How do I delete an AutoShape?

To delete an AutoShape, click the edge of the AutoShape and then press the Delete key.

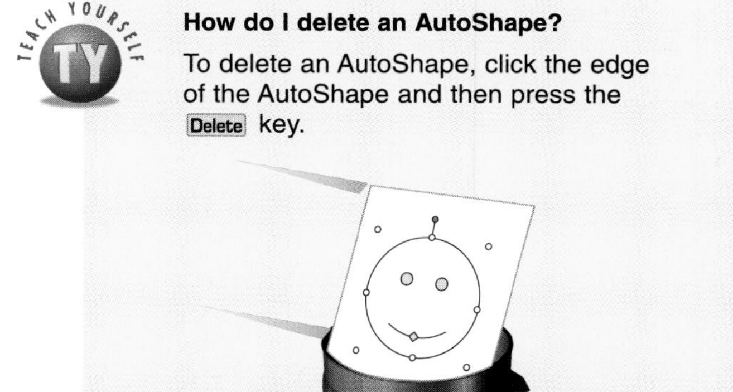

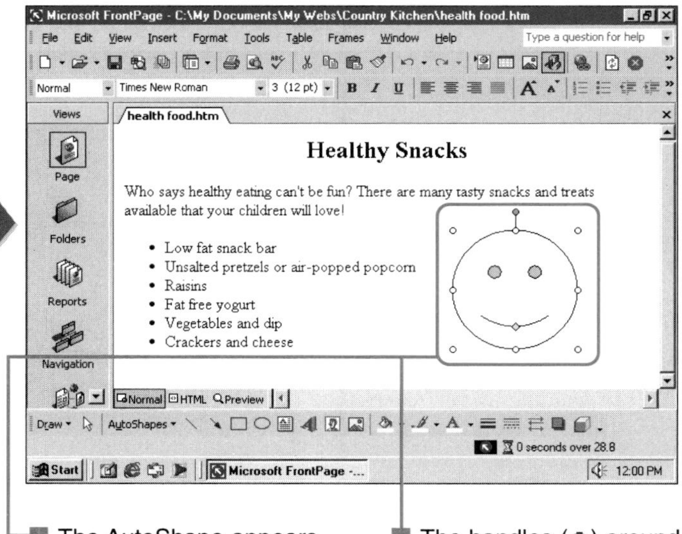

■ The AutoShape appears on your Web page.

Note: If you selected an AutoShape from the Callouts category, you can type the text you want to display in the AutoShape.

■ The handles (○) around the AutoShape allow you to change the size of the AutoShape. To move or resize an AutoShape, see page 104.

■ To deselect an AutoShape, click outside the AutoShape.

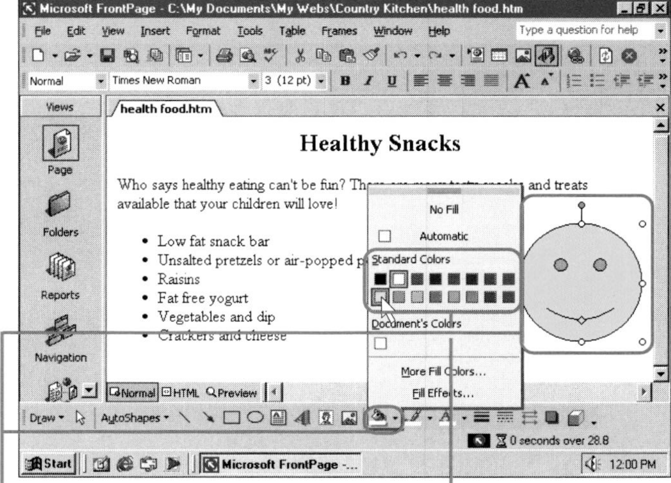

ADD COLOR TO AN AUTOSHAPE

1 Click the AutoShape you want to add color to.

2 Click ▾ in this area to display the available colors.

3 Click the color you want to use.

■ The AutoShape displays the color you selected.

ADD WORDART

You can add WordArt to a Web page to display a decorative title or draw attention to important information.

ADD WORDART

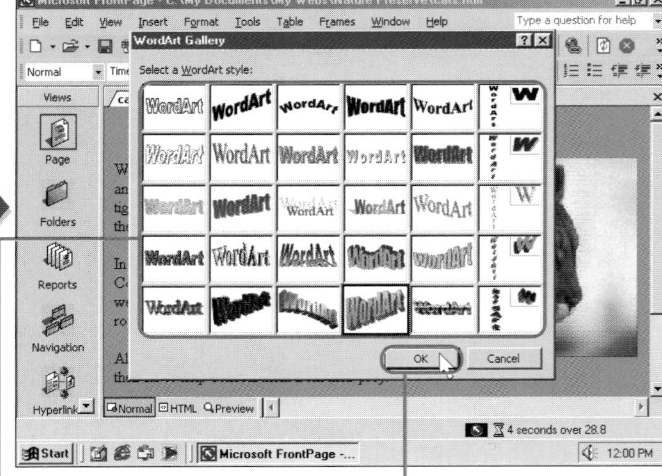

1 Click the location on your Web page where you want to add WordArt.

2 Click **Insert**.

3 Click **Picture**.

4 Click **WordArt**.

Note: If WordArt does not appear on the menu, position the mouse over the bottom of the menu to display all the menu options.

■ The WordArt Gallery dialog box appears.

5 Click the WordArt style you want to use.

6 Click **OK** to confirm your selection.

How do I edit WordArt text?

To edit WordArt text, double-click the WordArt to redisplay the Edit WordArt Text dialog box. Then perform steps 7 and 8 below to specify the text you want the WordArt to display.

When I add WordArt to a Web page, why does the WordArt toolbar appear?

The WordArt toolbar contains buttons that allow you to change the appearance of WordArt. For example, you can click one of the following buttons to alter the appearance of WordArt.

	Display all the letters in the WordArt at the same height.
	Display the WordArt text vertically rather than horizontally.

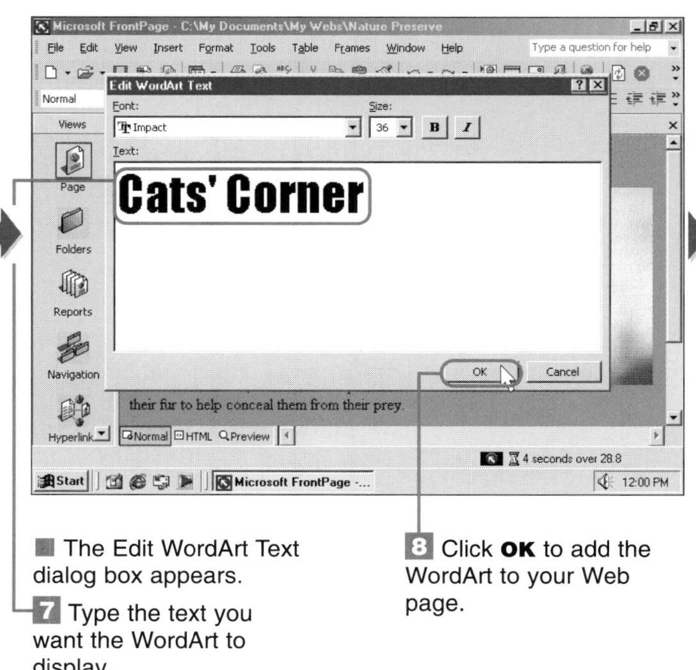

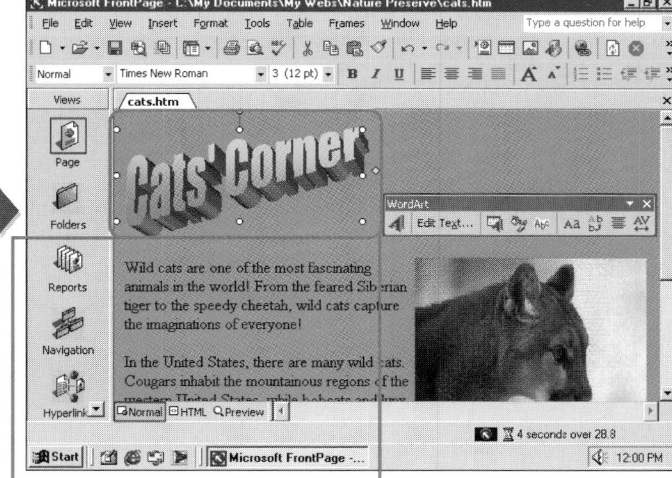

■ The Edit WordArt Text dialog box appears.

7 Type the text you want the WordArt to display.

8 Click **OK** to add the WordArt to your Web page.

■ The WordArt appears on your Web page.

■ The handles (○) around the WordArt allow you to change the size of the WordArt. To move or resize WordArt, see page 104.

■ To deselect WordArt, click outside the WordArt.

DELETE WORDART

1 Click the WordArt you want to delete and then press the Delete key.

ADD A CLIP ART IMAGE

You can add a professionally designed clip art image to a Web page to make the page more interesting.

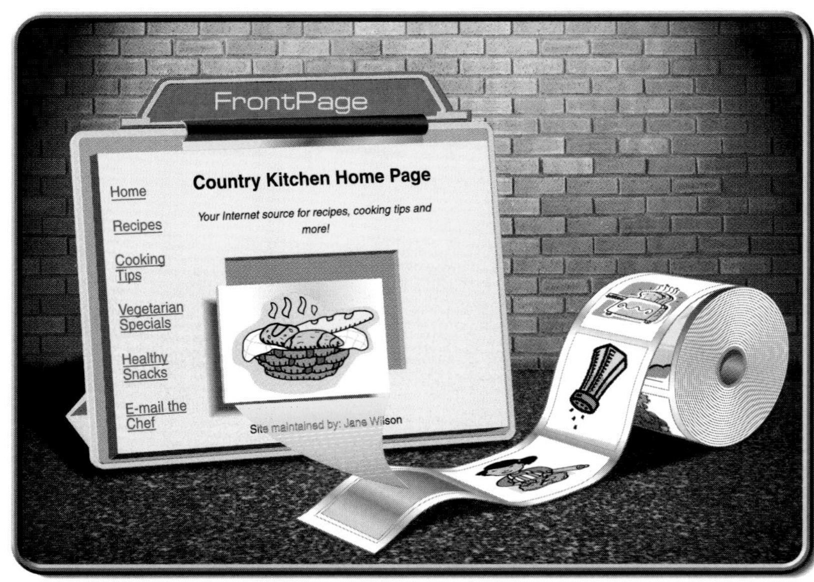

FrontPage includes the Clip Organizer, which organizes the image, sound and video files on your computer. You can use the Clip Organizer to add a clip art image to a Web page.

ADD A CLIP ART IMAGE

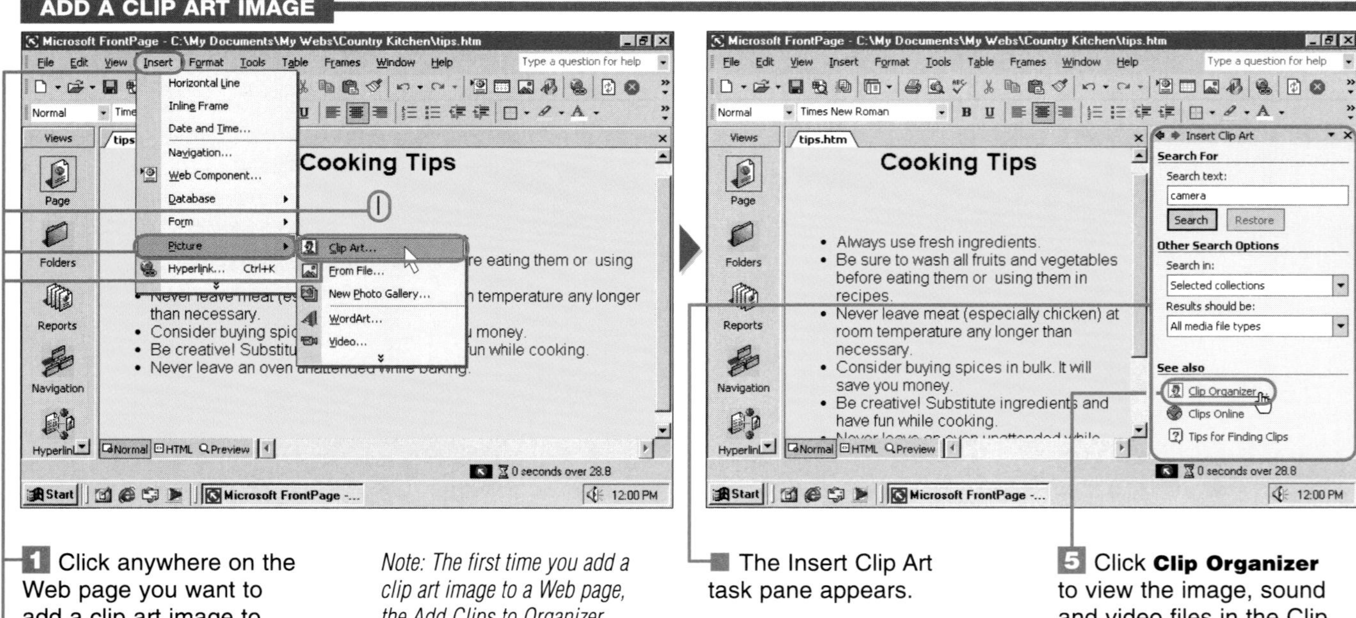

1 Click anywhere on the Web page you want to add a clip art image to.

2 Click **Insert**.

3 Click **Picture**.

4 Click **Clip Art**.

*Note: The first time you add a clip art image to a Web page, the Add Clips to Organizer dialog box appears. Click **Now** in the dialog box to catalog the image, sound and video files on your computer.*

■ The Insert Clip Art task pane appears.

5 Click **Clip Organizer** to view the image, sound and video files in the Clip Organizer.

■ The Microsoft Clip Organizer window appears.

How does the Clip Organizer arrange my image, sound and video files?

The Clip Organizer arranges your media files into three main folders.

My Collections

Displays the media files you have specified as your favorites and media files that came with Microsoft Windows.

Office Collections

Displays the media files that came with Microsoft Office.

Web Collections

Displays the media files that are available at Microsoft's Web site and Web sites in partnership with Microsoft.

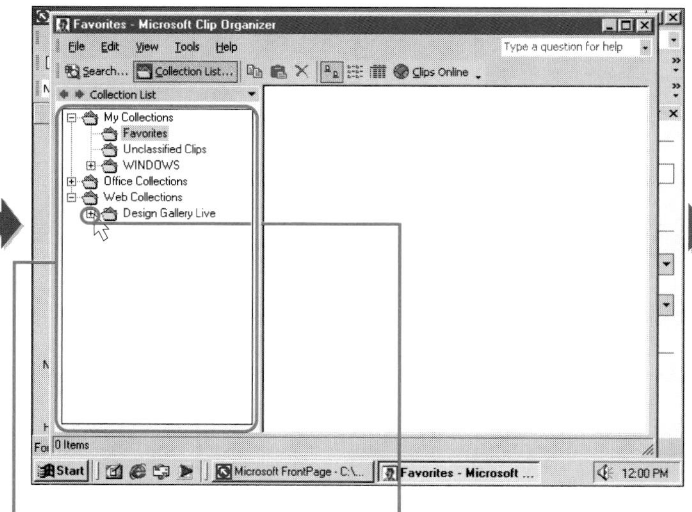

- This area lists the folders that contain image, sound and video files that you can add to your Web page.
- A folder displaying a plus sign (⊞) contains hidden folders.

6 To display the hidden folders within a folder, click a plus sign (⊞) beside a folder (⊞ changes to ⊟).

Note: You must be connected to the Internet to view the contents of the Web Collections folder.

- The hidden folders appear.

Note: To once again hide the folders within a folder, click a minus sign (⊟) beside a folder.

7 Click a folder of interest.

- This area displays the contents of the folder you selected.

8 Click the image you want to add to your Web page.

CONTINUED

ADD A CLIP ART IMAGE

After you locate an image in the Clip Organizer that you want to add to your Web page, you can copy the image and then place the image on your page.

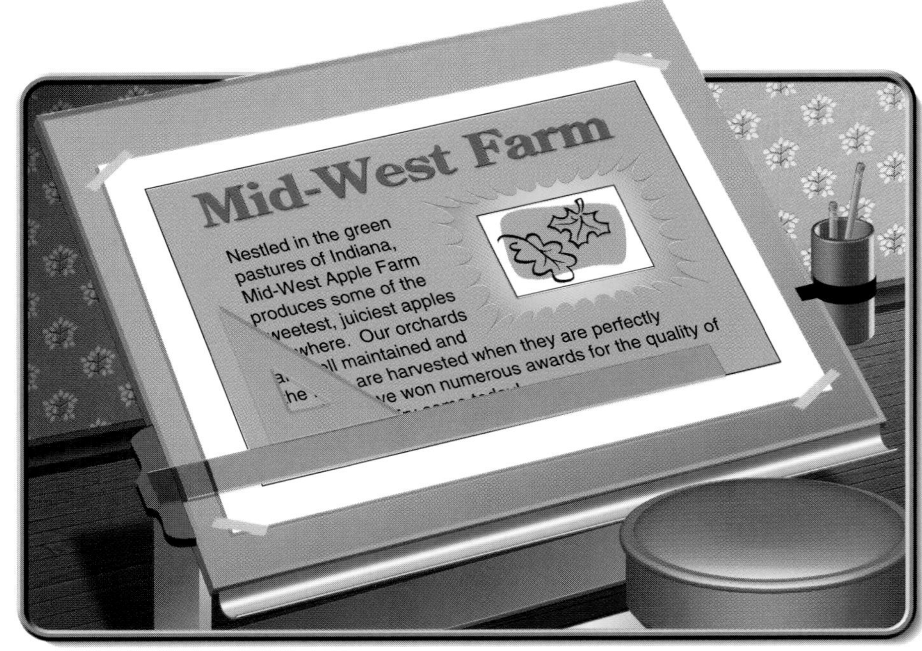

ADD A CLIP ART IMAGE (CONTINUED)

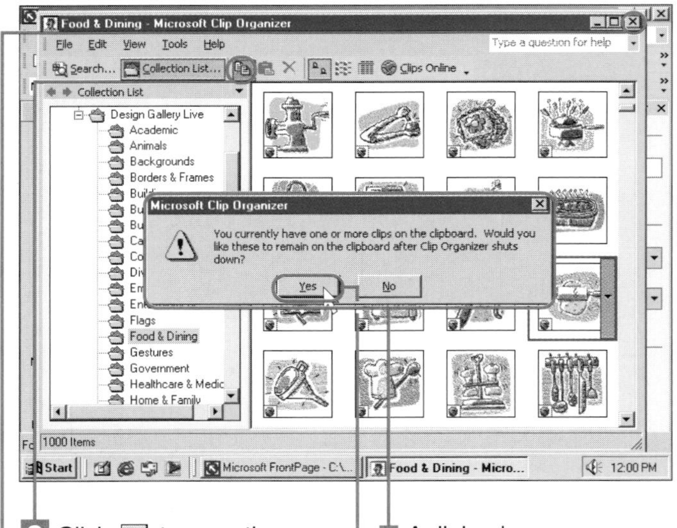

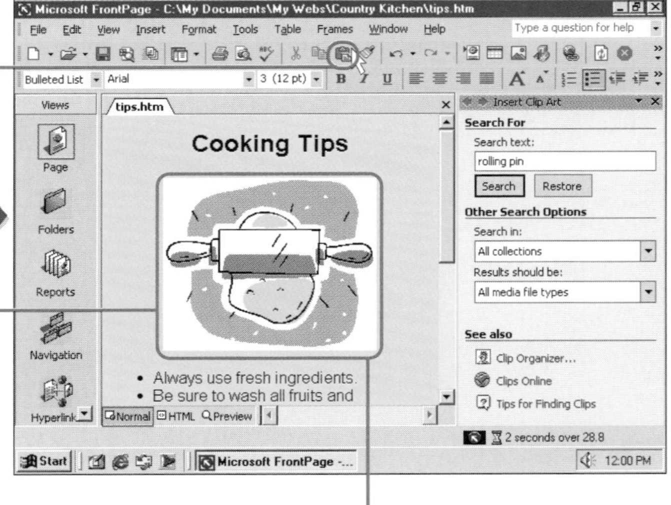

9 Click [copy icon] to copy the image you selected.

10 Click [close icon] to close the Microsoft Clip Organizer window.

■ A dialog box appears, stating that you have one or more clip art images on the clipboard.

Note: The clipboard temporarily stores information you have selected to move or copy.

11 Click **Yes** to keep the image on the clipboard.

12 Click the location on your Web page where you want to add the image.

13 Click [paste icon] to place the image on your Web page.

■ The image appears on your Web page.

Note: To move or resize the image, see page 104.

■ To delete the image, click the image and then press the Delete key.

How does FrontPage search for clip art images?

When you search for clip art images, FrontPage compares the words you specified to the keywords assigned to the clip art images and the file names of the clip art images. When a match is found, the clip art image appears in the results of the search.

Where can I obtain more clip art images?

You can buy collections of clip art images at computer stores. Many Web sites, such as www.allfree-clipart.com and www.free-graphics.com, also offer clip art images you can use for free on your Web pages.

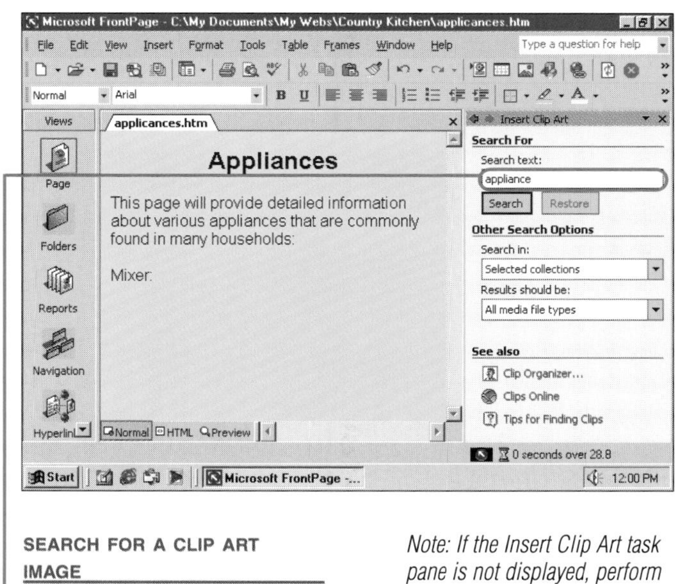

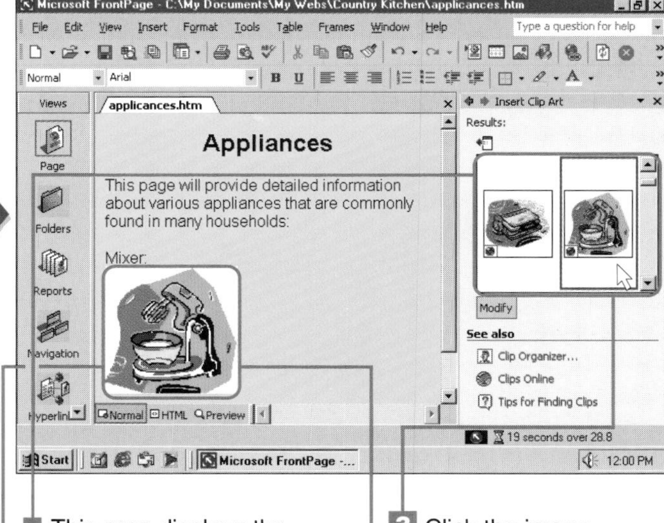

SEARCH FOR A CLIP ART IMAGE

You can search for clip art images by specifying one or more words of interest.

1 Click this area and then type one or more words that describe the clip art image you want to find. Then

Note: If the Insert Clip Art task pane is not displayed, perform steps 1 to 4 on page 100 to display the task pane.

■ This area displays the images that match the words you specified.

2 Click the location on your Web page where you want to add an image.

3 Click the image you want to add to your Web page.

■ The image appears on your Web page.

Note: To move or resize the image, see page 104.

MOVE OR RESIZE AN IMAGE

You can change the location and size of an image on a Web page.

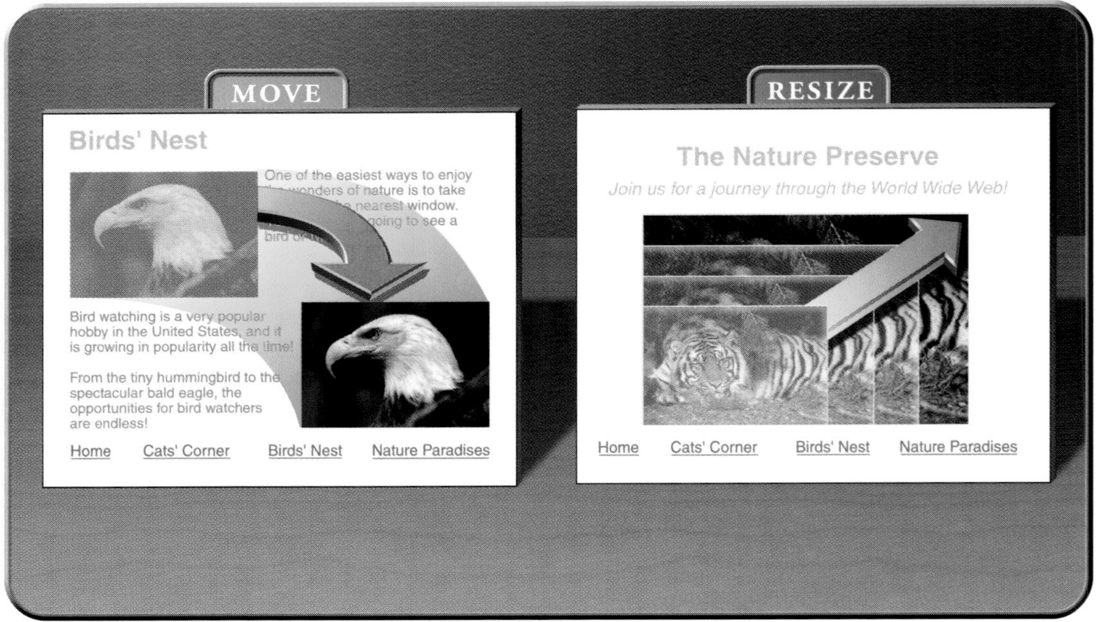

MOVE AN IMAGE

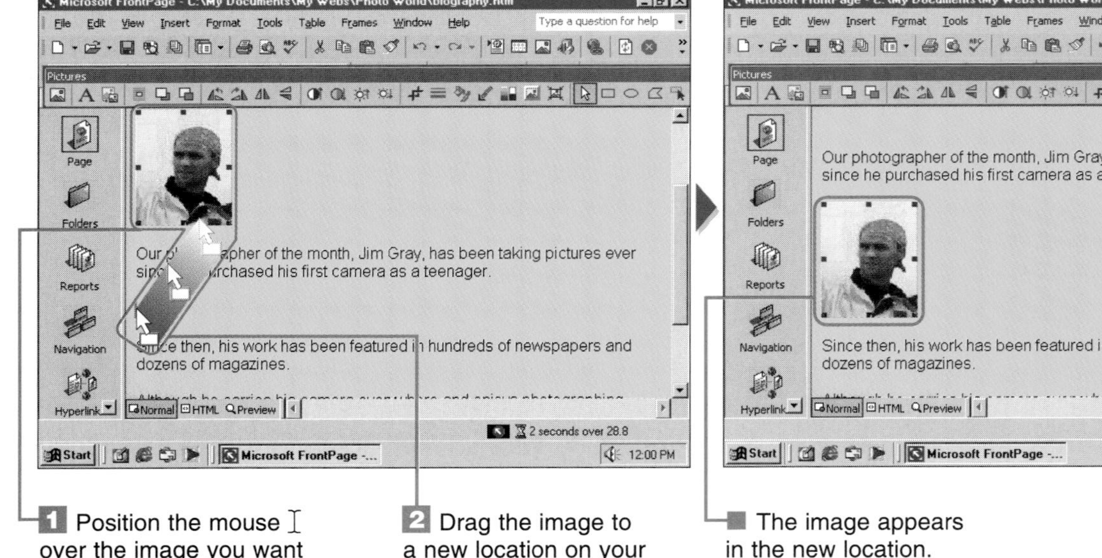

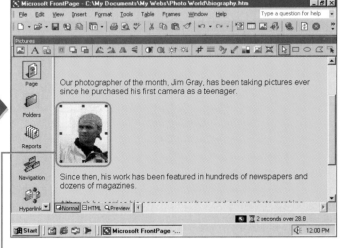

1 Position the mouse I over the image you want to move (I changes to ↖).

2 Drag the image to a new location on your Web page.

Note: The dotted insertion point indicates where the image will appear.

■ The image appears in the new location.

How can I make an image I resized appear less distorted?

After you resize an image, you can resample the image to make the image appear less distorted. To resample an image, click the image and then click the Resample button ( ) on the Pictures toolbar.

When you resample an image you increased in size, the file size of the image increases. When you resample an image you reduced in size, the file size of the image decreases. Keep in mind that the file size of an image determines how fast an image transfers and appears on a visitor's computer.

RESIZE AN IMAGE

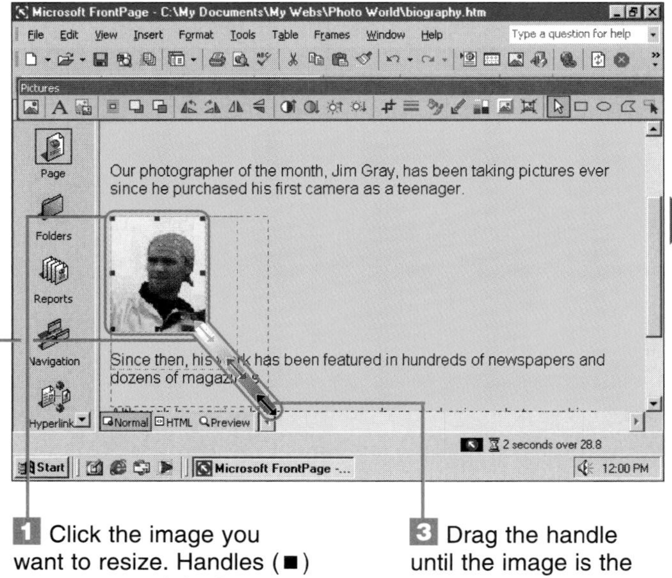

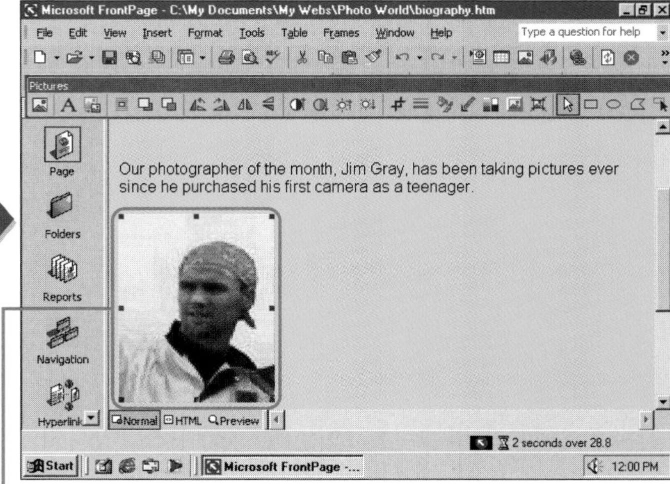

1 Click the image you want to resize. Handles (■) appear around the image.

2 Position the mouse ↖ over one of the handles (↖ changes to ↘, ↔ or ↕).

3 Drag the handle until the image is the size you want.

Note: To keep the image in proportion, drag a corner handle.

■ The image appears in the new size.

Note: If you make an image too large, the image may appear distorted.

PROVIDE ALTERNATIVE TEXT

You can provide text that you want to display if an image does not appear on a Web page. This will give visitors who do not see the image information about the missing image.

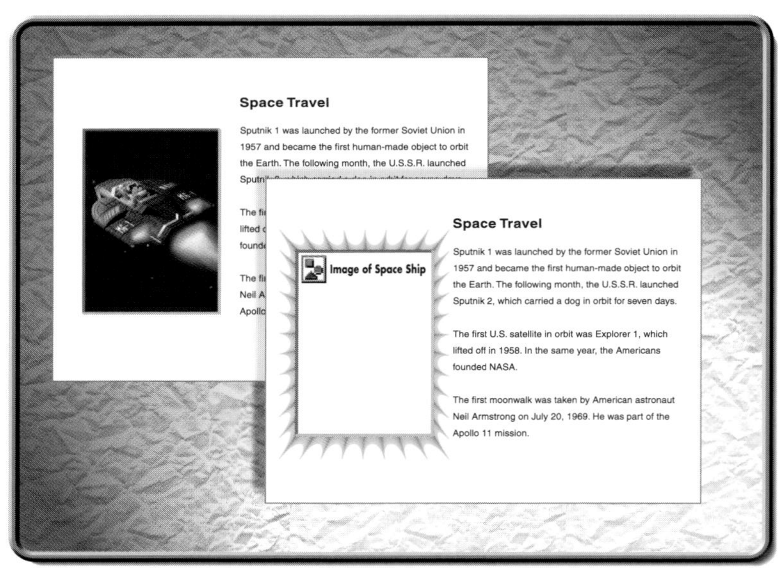

Some visitors use Web browsers that cannot display images, while others turn off the display of images to browse through information on the Web more quickly.

PROVIDE ALTERNATIVE TEXT

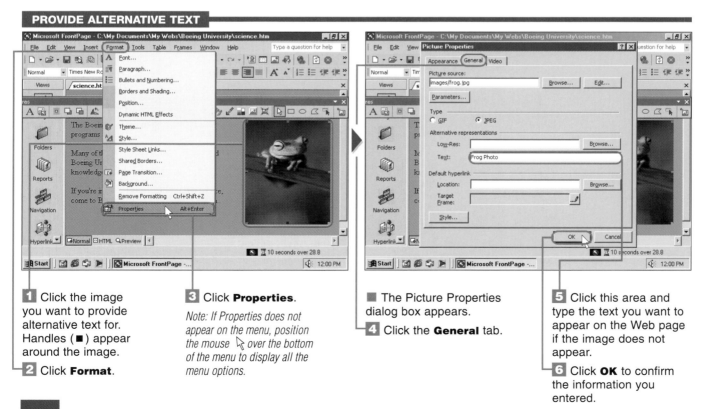

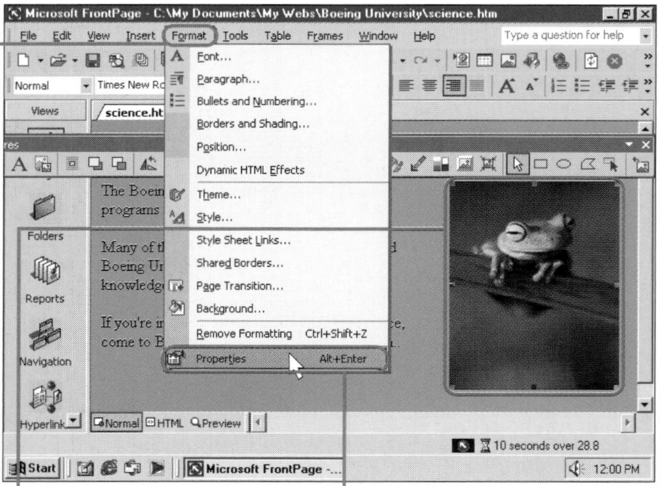

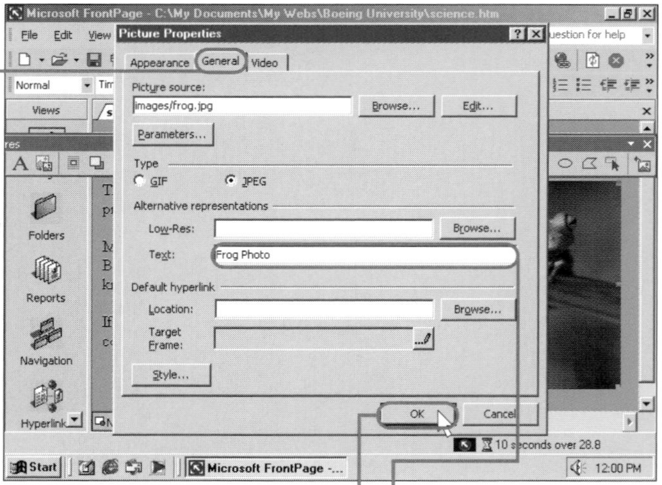

1 Click the image you want to provide alternative text for. Handles (■) appear around the image.

2 Click **Format**.

3 Click **Properties**.

Note: If Properties does not appear on the menu, position the mouse over the bottom of the menu to display all the menu options.

■ The Picture Properties dialog box appears.

4 Click the **General** tab.

5 Click this area and type the text you want to appear on the Web page if the image does not appear.

6 Click **OK** to confirm the information you entered.

ADD A HORIZONTAL LINE

You can add a horizontal line to visually separate sections of a Web page.

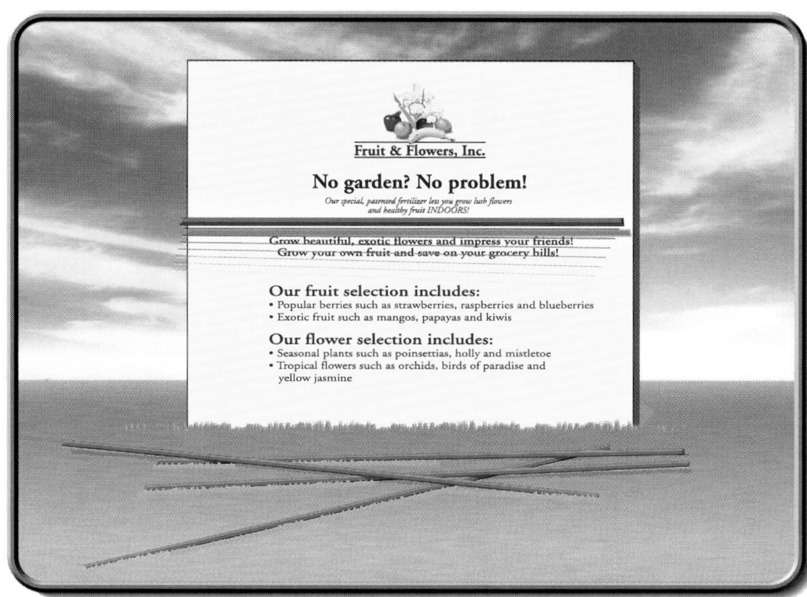

You should not overuse horizontal lines on your Web pages since this can distract your visitors and make your Web pages difficult to read. Try not to place more than one horizontal line on each screen.

ADD A HORIZONTAL LINE

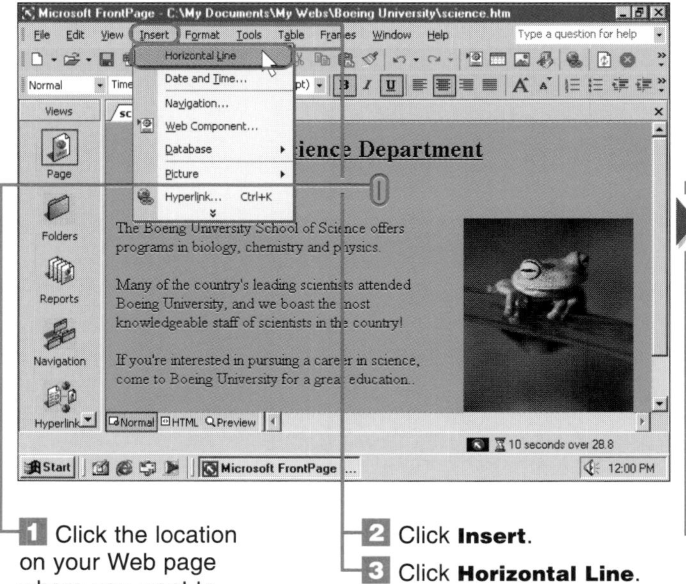

1 Click the location on your Web page where you want to add a horizontal line.

2 Click **Insert**.

3 Click **Horizontal Line**.

■ The horizontal line appears on your Web page.

■ To remove a horizontal line, click the line and then press the Delete key.

Note: To customize a horizontal line, see page 108.

CUSTOMIZE A HORIZONTAL LINE

You can customize the appearance of a horizontal line on a Web page.

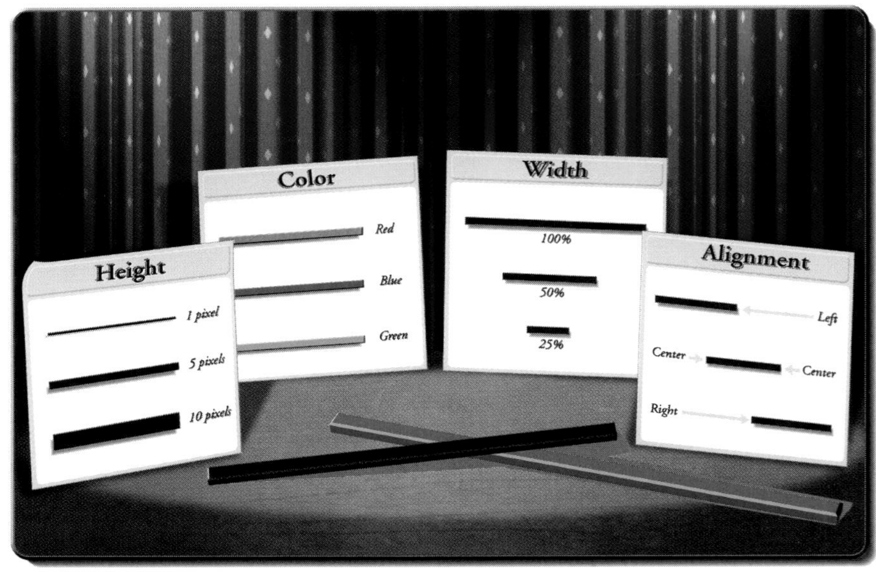

You can change the height, color, width and alignment of a horizontal line.

If you have applied a theme to your Web pages, you cannot customize a horizontal line. For information on themes, see page 88.

CUSTOMIZE A HORIZONTAL LINE

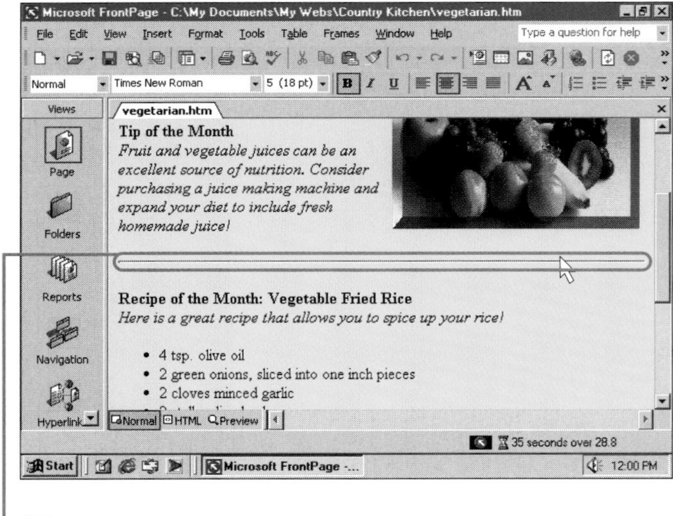

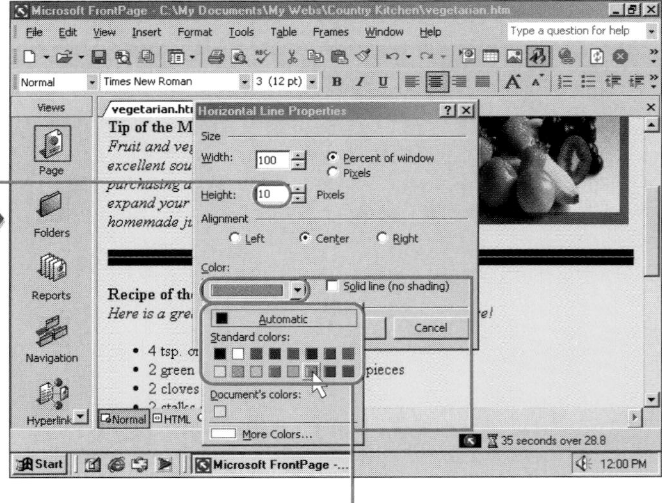

1 Double-click the horizontal line you want to customize.

■ The Horizontal Line Properties dialog box appears.

2 To change the height of the horizontal line, double-click the text in this area and type a number for the height in pixels.

Note: A pixel is a dot on a computer screen.

3 To change the color of the horizontal line, click this area to display the available colors.

4 Click the color you want to use.

How can I add a more decorative horizontal line to a Web page?

You can use an image instead of a horizontal line to visually separate sections of a Web page. You can create your own horizontal line images in an image editing program or obtain images on the Web. The following Web sites offer images that you can use as horizontal lines.

members.nbci.com/SSWebGraphics/lines/lines.htm

www.coolgraphics.com/gallery/lines.shtml

www.theskull.com/hor_rule.html

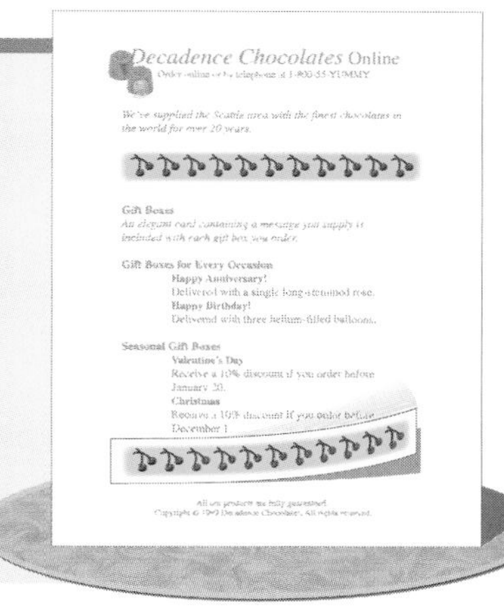

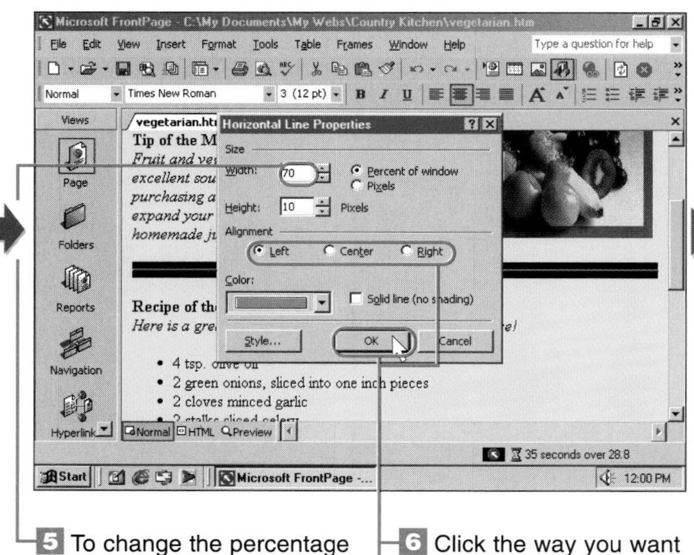

5 To change the percentage of the Web page that the horizontal line extends across, double-click the text in this area and type a percentage.

*Note: To extend the horizontal line across half your Web page, type **50**.*

6 Click the way you want to align the horizontal line (○ changes to ⦿).

Note: Selecting an alignment will have no effect if the horizontal line extends across 100 percent of the Web page.

7 Click **OK**.

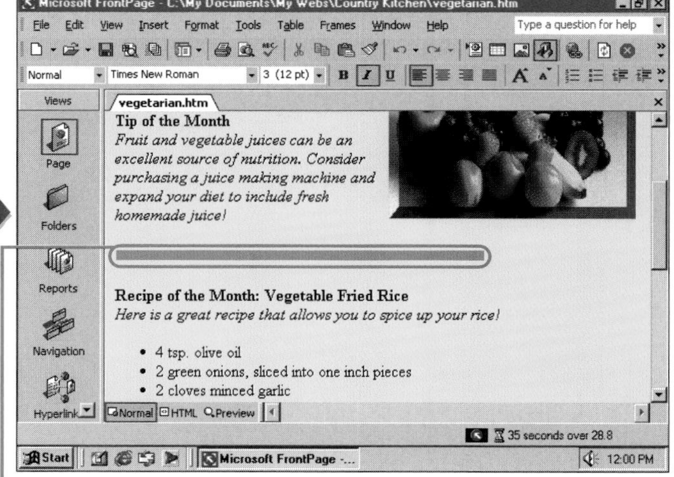

■ The horizontal line displays the changes you specified.

Note: The Netscape Navigator Web browser cannot display a horizontal line in color.

■ To deselect a horizontal line, click outside the horizontal line.

You can have a small image repeat to fill an entire Web page. This can add an interesting background design to a Web page.

Many Web sites offer background images you can use for free on your Web pages. You can find background images at the following Web sites:

imagine.metanet.com

www.ip.pt/webground/index_02.html

www.nepthys.com/textures

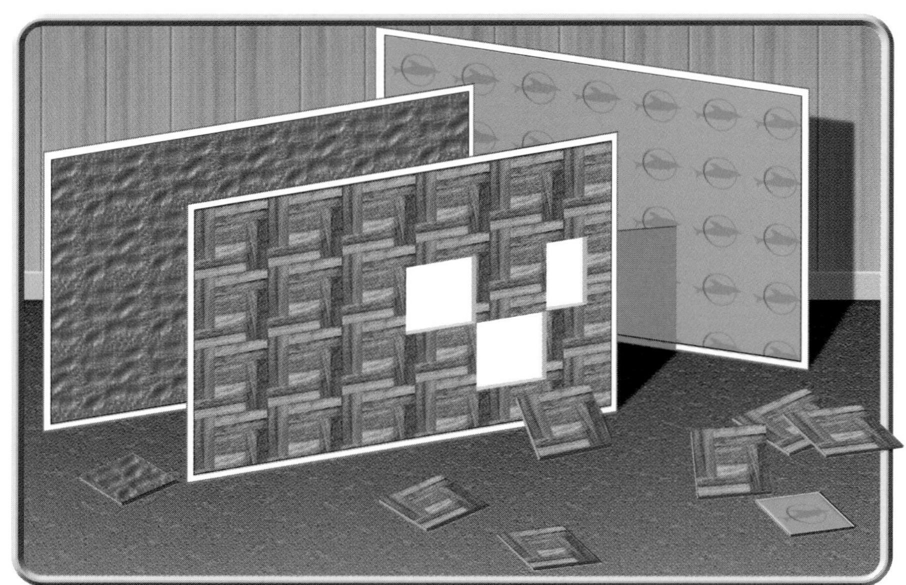

ADD A BACKGROUND IMAGE

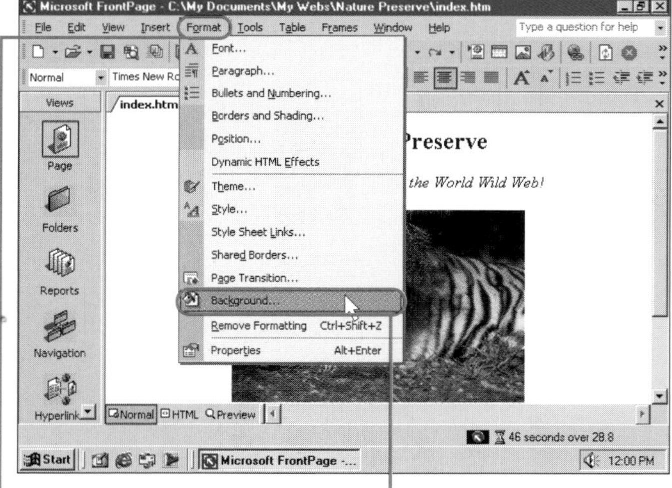

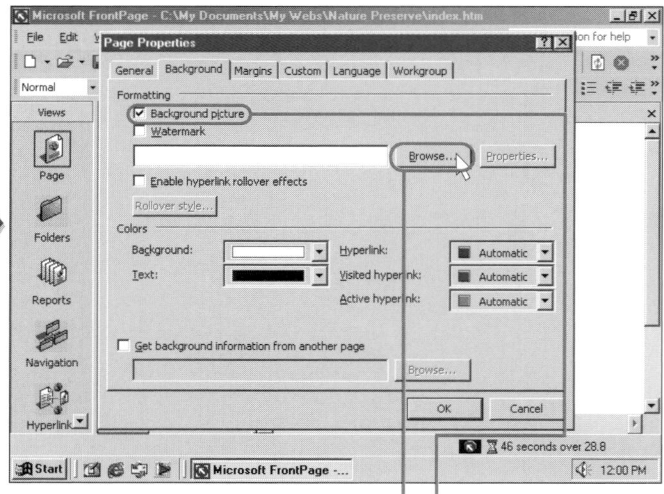

1 Click anywhere on the Web page you want to add a background image to.

2 Click **Format**.

3 Click **Background**.

Note: If Background does not appear on the menu, position the mouse ⇖ over the bottom of the menu to display all the menu options.

■ The Page Properties dialog box appears.

*Note: A different dialog box appears if the Web page uses a theme. You must remove the theme before you can add a background image. Click **OK** to close the dialog box. For information on themes, see page 88.*

4 Click **Background picture** to add a background image to your Web page (☐ changes to ☑).

5 Click **Browse** to locate the image you want to use.

What type of image should I use as a background image?

Small File Size

Since background images increase the time Web pages take to appear on a visitor's screen, you should choose an image with a small file size that will transfer faster.

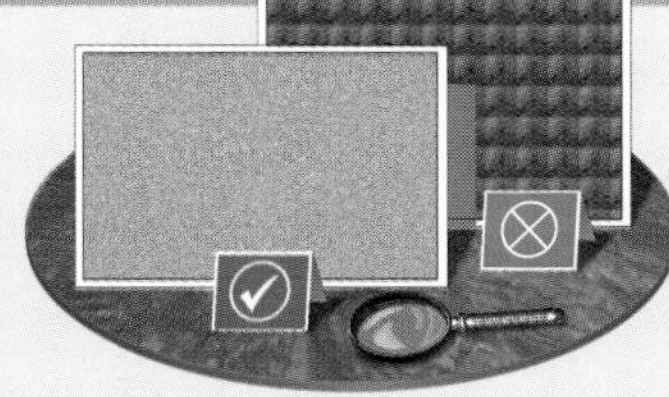

Seamless Background

A good background image should have invisible edges. When the image repeats to fill the Web page, you should not be able to tell where the edges of the images meet.

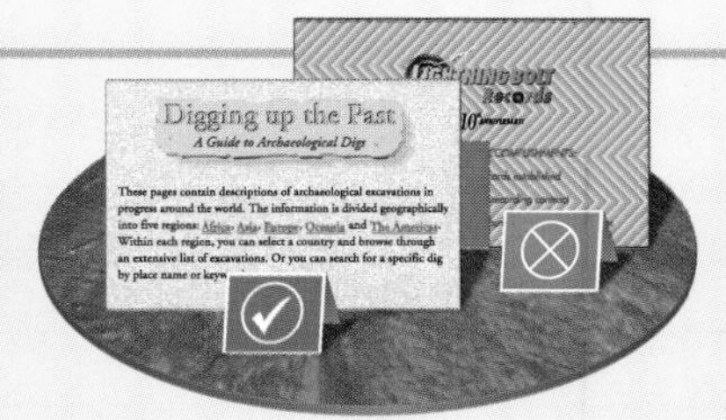

Web Page Readability

Make sure the background image you choose does not affect the readability of your Web page. You may need to change the color of text to make the Web page easier to read. To change the color of text, see page 72.

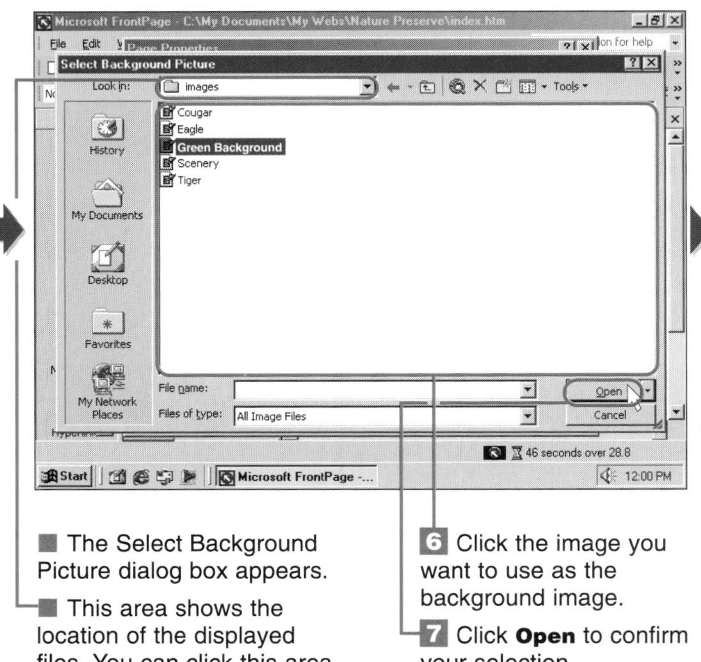

■ The Select Background Picture dialog box appears.

■ This area shows the location of the displayed files. You can click this area to change the location.

6 Click the image you want to use as the background image.

7 Click **Open** to confirm your selection.

■ This area displays the location and name of the background image you selected.

8 Click **OK** to add the background image to your Web page.

■ The image will repeat to fill your entire Web page.

■ To remove a background image from a Web page, repeat steps 1 to 4 (☑ changes to ☐ in step 4). Then perform step 8.

CREATE A PHOTO GALLERY

You can create a photo gallery to neatly display several images on a Web page.

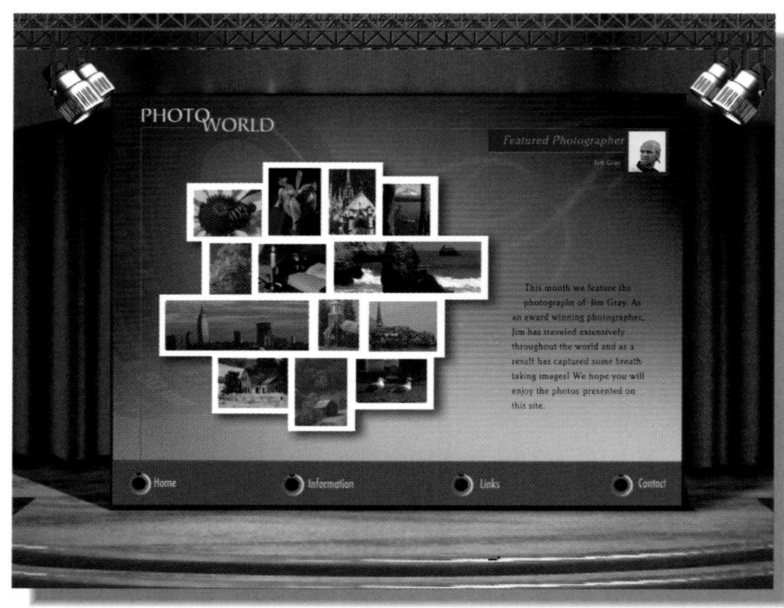

When you create a photo gallery, FrontPage automatically creates thumbnails of your images. A thumbnail image is a small version of an image that visitors can select to display a larger version of the image.

CREATE A PHOTO GALLERY

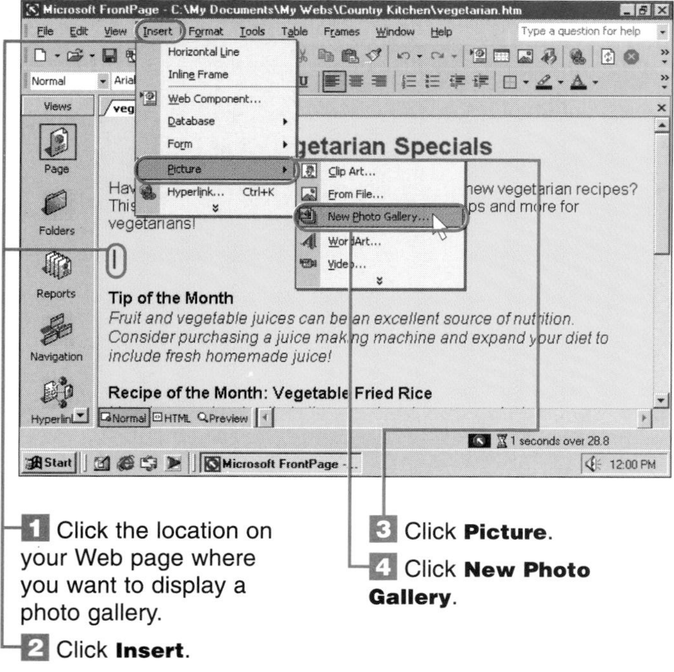

1 Click the location on your Web page where you want to display a photo gallery.

2 Click **Insert**.

3 Click **Picture**.

4 Click **New Photo Gallery**.

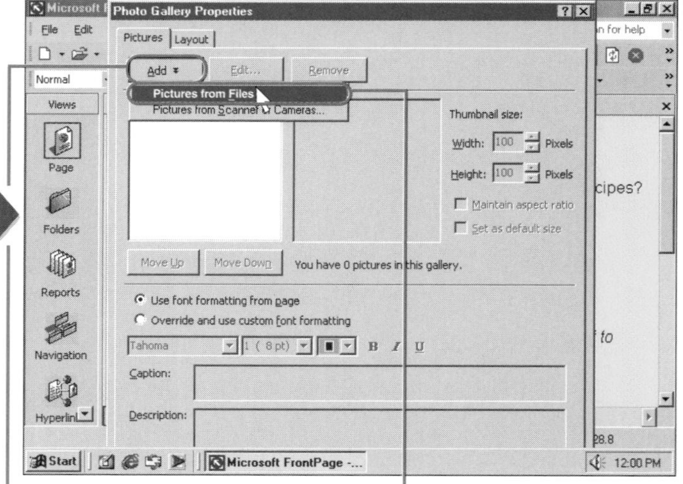

■ The Photo Gallery Properties dialog box appears.

5 Click **Add** to select an image that you want to add to the photo gallery.

6 Click **Pictures from Files** to locate an image on your computer that you want to add to the photo gallery.

How many images can I add to a photo gallery?

You can add as many images as you like to a photo gallery. Keep in mind that adding more images to a photo gallery will increase the time the Web page takes to transfer and appear on a visitor's computer screen.

How can I remove an image from a photo gallery?

You may want to remove an image from a photo gallery if you accidentally added the wrong image or if you no longer want to display a particular image.

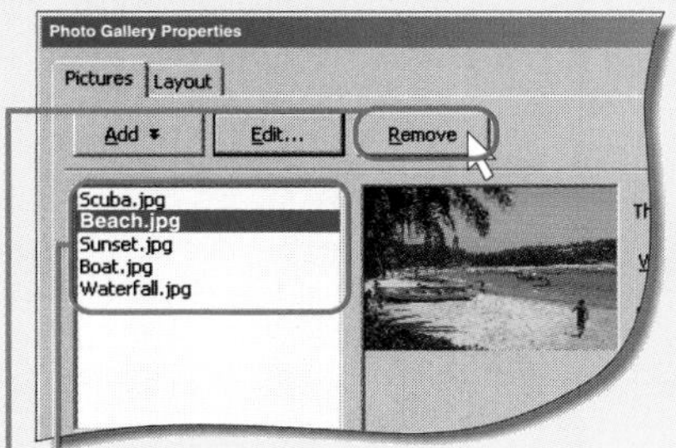

1 In the Photo Gallery Properties dialog box, click the name of the image you want to remove from the photo gallery.

2 Click **Remove** to remove the image.

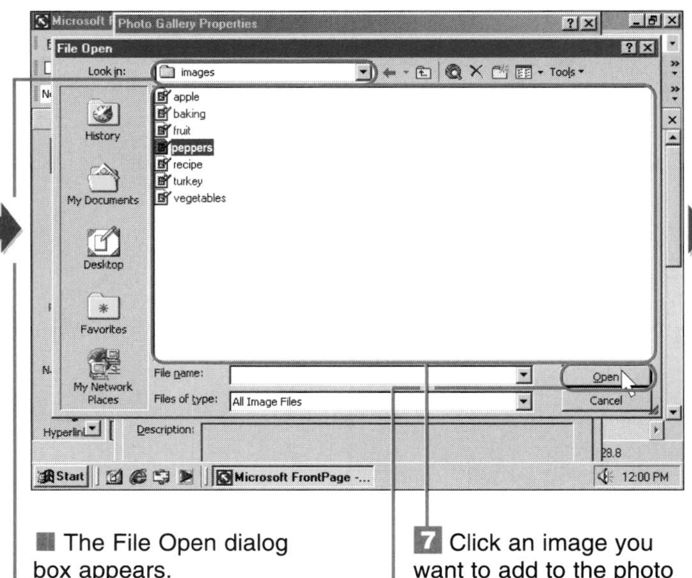

■ The File Open dialog box appears.

■ This area shows the location of the displayed files. You can click this area to change the location.

7 Click an image you want to add to the photo gallery.

8 Click **Open** to select the image.

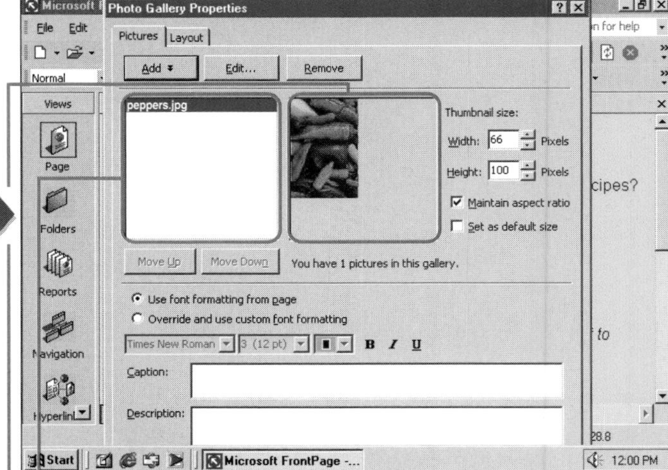

■ The name of the image appears in this area.

■ This area displays a preview of the image.

9 To select the other images that you want to add to the photo gallery, repeat steps 5 to 8 for each image.

CONTINUED

When creating a photo gallery, you can provide a title and description that you want to display beside each image.

Providing a title and description is useful if your photo gallery displays images you want to describe to your visitors, such as photographs of your products or family vacation.

CREATE A PHOTO GALLERY (CONTINUED)

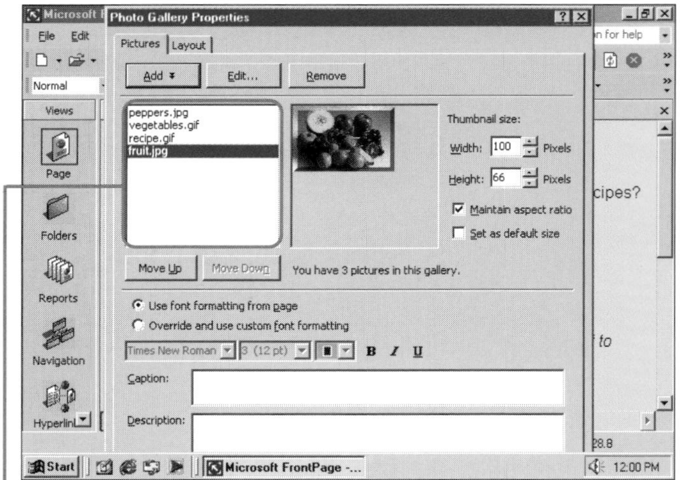

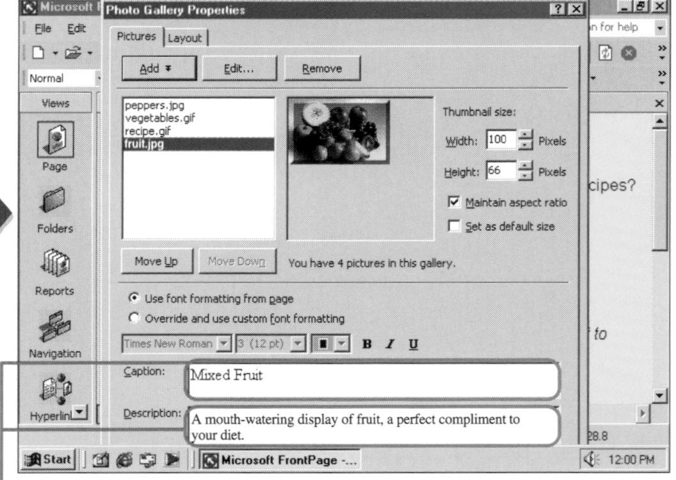

10 If you want to display a title and description beside each image in the photo gallery, click the name of an image in this area.

*Note: If you do not want to display a title and description beside any images in the photo gallery, skip to step **14**.*

11 Click this area and type a title for the image.

12 Click this area and type a description for the image.

Note: If you wish, you can specify just a title or just a description for the image.

13 To specify a title and description for the other images in the photo gallery, repeat steps **10** to **12** for each image.

What layouts are available for the photo gallery?

Horizontal Layout

The images appear in rows. The titles and descriptions of the images appear below each image.

Montage Layout

The images appear in a collage pattern. When a visitor positions the mouse over an image, the title of the image appears in a small, yellow box. This layout does not display the descriptions of images.

Slide Show

The images appear in a row that visitors can scroll through. When a visitor clicks an image, a larger version of the image appears. The title and description of the selected image appears below the full-size image.

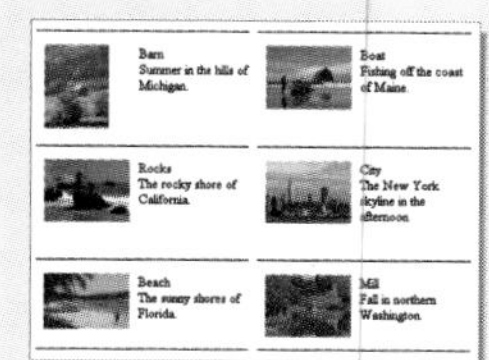

Vertical Layout

The images appear in columns. The titles and descriptions of the images appear to the right of each image.

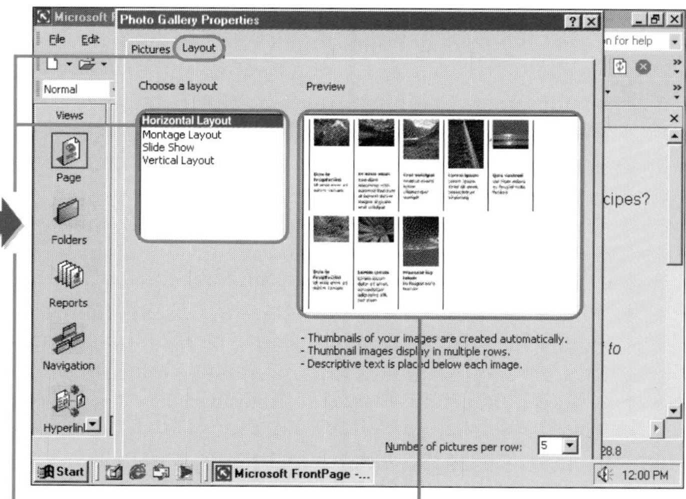

14 Click the **Layout** tab.

15 Click the layout you want to use for the photo gallery.

■ This area shows a preview of the layout you selected.

16 Click **OK** or press the Enter key to create the photo gallery.

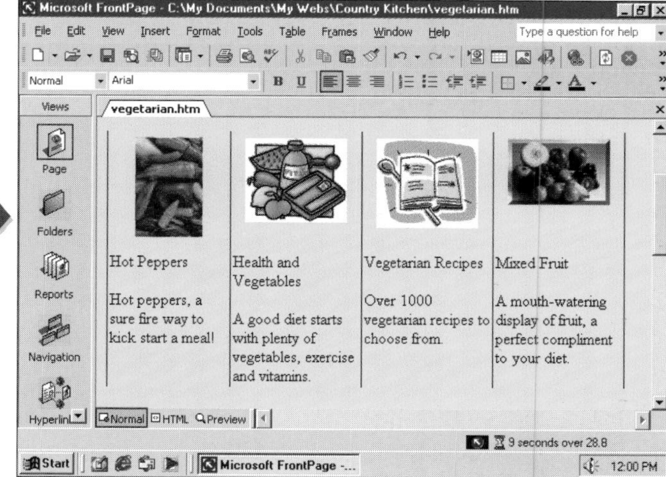

■ The photo gallery appears on your Web page.

Note: To test the photo gallery, you can use the Preview view. For information on the Preview view, see page 42.

■ To make changes to the photo gallery, double-click the photo gallery and then repeat steps **5** to **16**.

■ To delete a photo gallery, click the photo gallery and then press the Delete key.

BIRD WATCHERS'
Eagle
Popular
Nest Sites
Membership
Information
Building a
Better Birdhouse

CHAPTER 7

Customize Images

Do you want to customize your images? This chapter shows you how to add a border to an image, create an image map and more.

ROTATE OR FLIP AN IMAGE

You can rotate or flip an image to change the way the image appears on a Web page.

ROTATE OR FLIP AN IMAGE

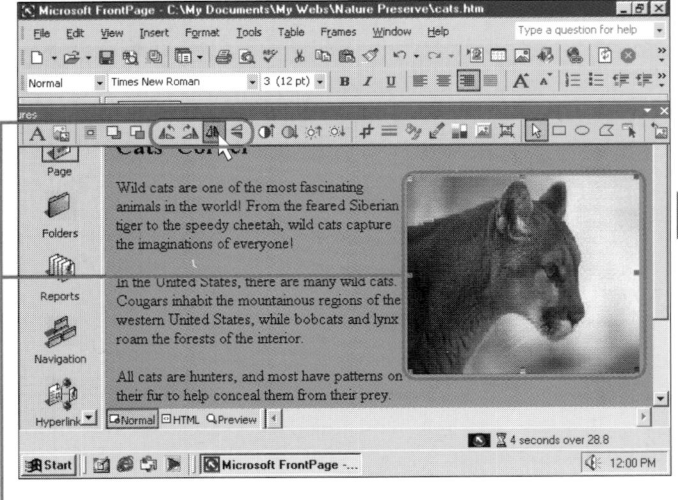

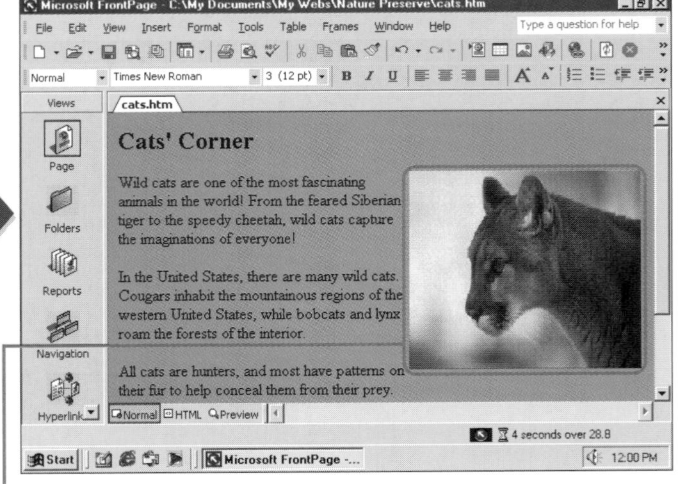

1 Click the image you want to rotate or flip.

2 Click one of the following buttons.

- Rotate left
- Rotate right
- Flip horizontal
- Flip vertical

Note: If the Pictures toolbar is not displayed, see page 24 to display the toolbar.

■ FrontPage rotates or flips the image.

■ To deselect the image, click outside the image.

ADD TEXT TO AN IMAGE

You can add text to an image to provide a title or description for the image.

You can only add text to a GIF image. For information on GIF images, see page 92.

ADD TEXT TO AN IMAGE

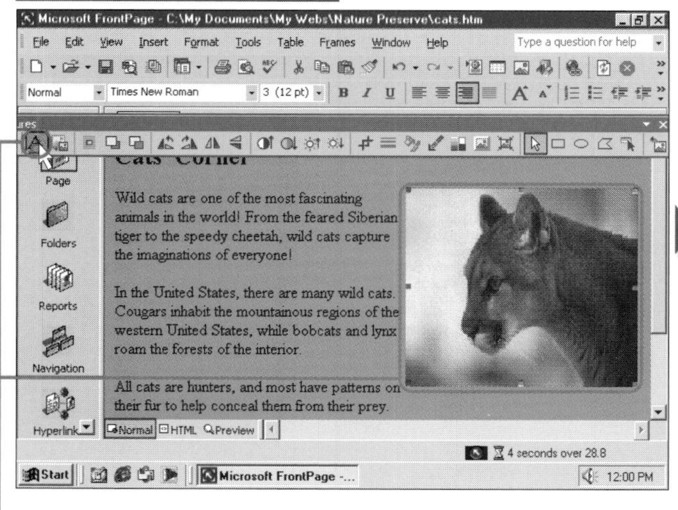

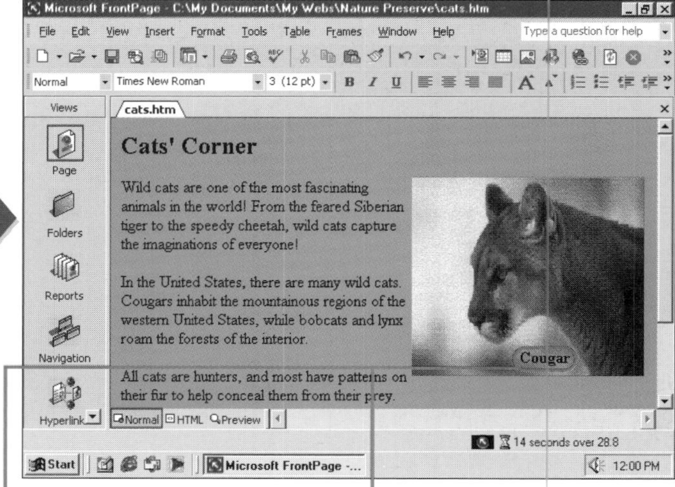

1 Click the image you want to add text to.

2 Click A to add text to the image.

Note: A dialog box appears if the image you selected is not a GIF image. To add text to the image, FrontPage will need to convert the image to a GIF image. Click ***OK*** *to convert the image or click* ***Cancel*** *to choose not to convert the image.*

■ A text box appears on the image.

3 Type the text you want to add to the image.

4 When you finish typing the text, click outside the image.

Note: You can move or resize a text box as you would move or resize any image. To move or resize an image, see page 104.

■ To delete the text, click the text and then press the Delete key.

ADD A BORDER TO AN IMAGE

You can add a border to an image on a Web page. Adding a border allows you to place a frame around the image.

ADD A BORDER TO AN IMAGE

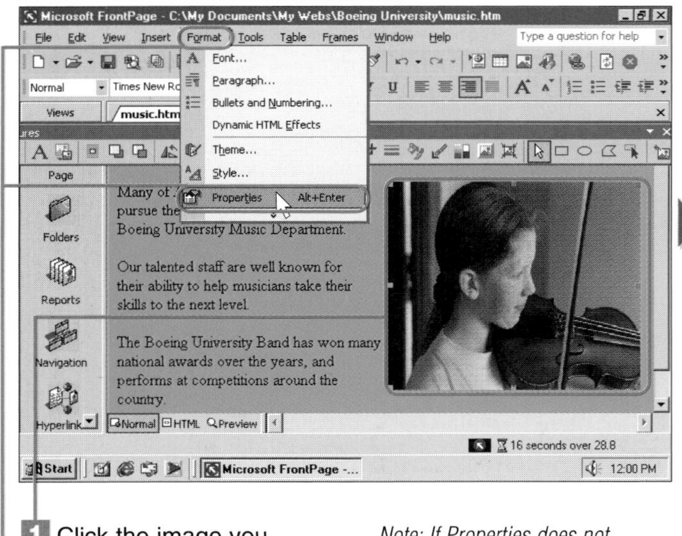

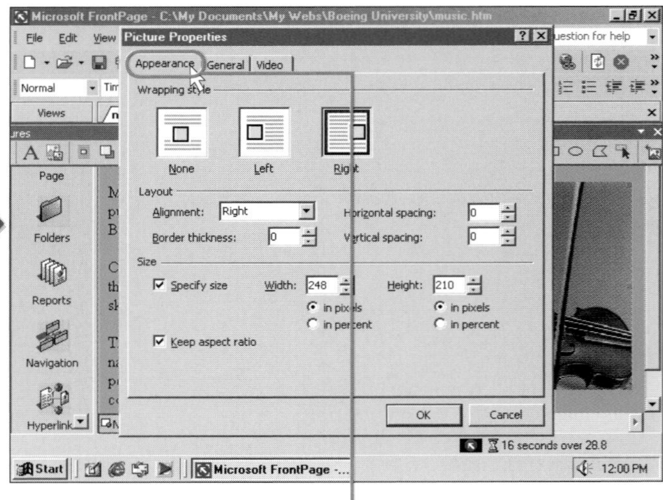

1 Click the image you want to add a border to.

2 Click **Format**.

3 Click **Properties**.

Note: If Properties does not appear on the menu, position the mouse over the bottom of the menu to display all the menu options.

■ The Picture Properties dialog box appears.

4 Click the **Appearance** tab.

What color border will appear around an image?

A black border will appear around an image, unless the image is a link. By default, a linked image displays a blue border to help people quickly recognize that the image is a link. If you change the color of links on a Web page, the borders around linked images will display the color you specify for links. To create an image link that visitors can click to display another Web page, see page 134. To change link colors, see page 144.

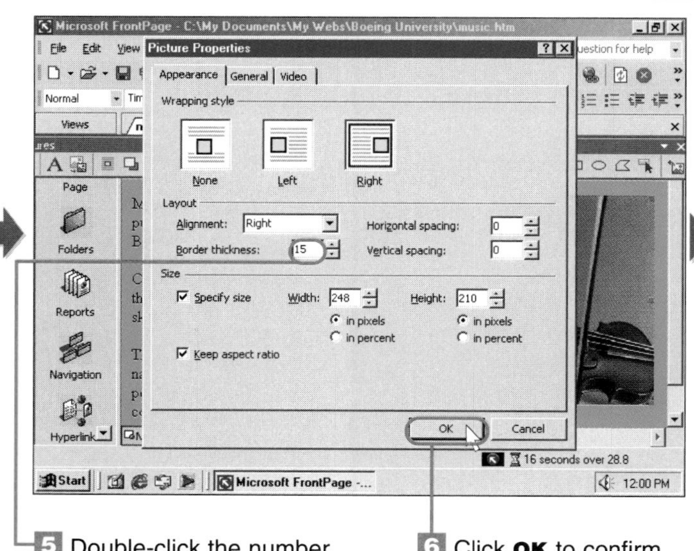

5 Double-click the number in this area and then type a thickness for the border in pixels.

Note: A pixel is a dot on a computer screen.

6 Click **OK** to confirm your change.

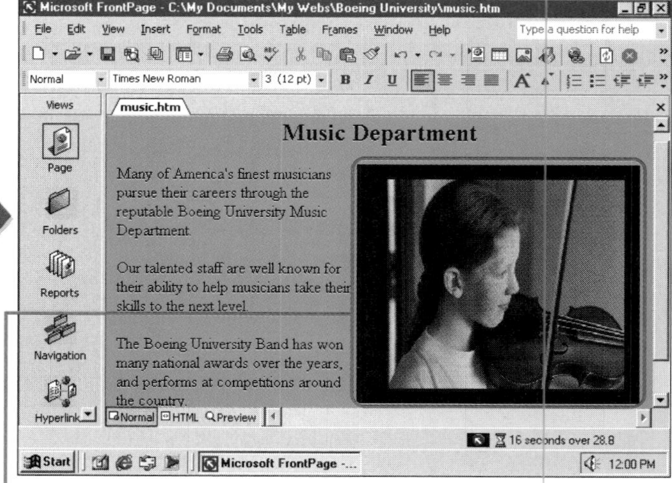

■ A border appears around the image.

■ To deselect an image, click outside the image.

■ To remove a border from an image, repeat steps **1** to **6**, typing **0** in step **5**.

ALIGN AN IMAGE WITH TEXT

You can change the way an image appears in relation to surrounding text on a Web page.

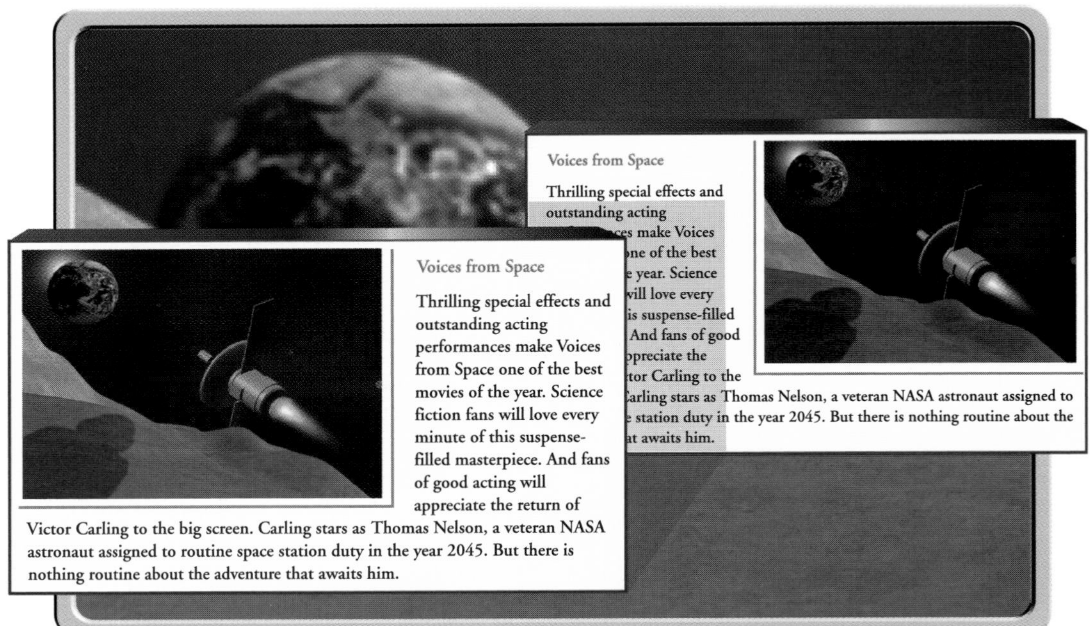

ALIGN AN IMAGE WITH TEXT

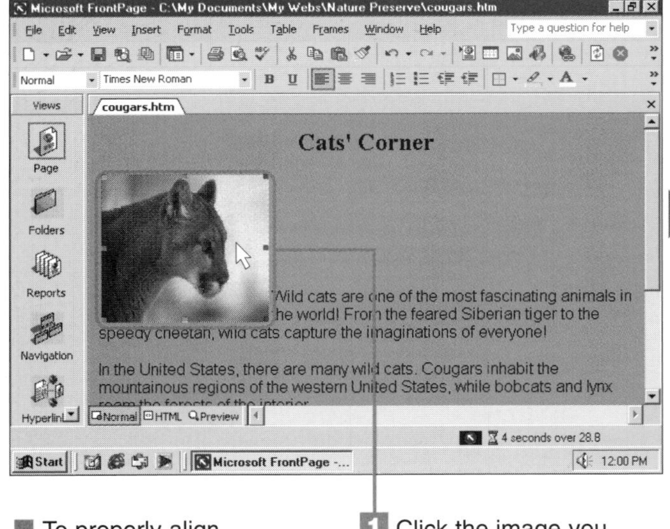

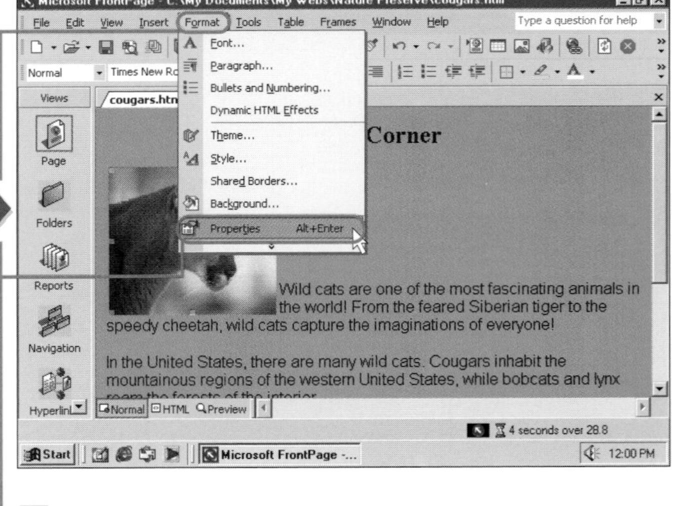

■ To properly align an image with text, the image must appear at the beginning of the text. To move an image on your Web page, see page 104.

1 Click the image you want to align with text.

2 Click **Format**.

3 Click **Properties**.

Note: If Properties does not appear on the menu, position the mouse over the bottom of the menu to display all the menu options.

■ The Picture Properties dialog box appears.

What are some of the alignment options that FrontPage offers?

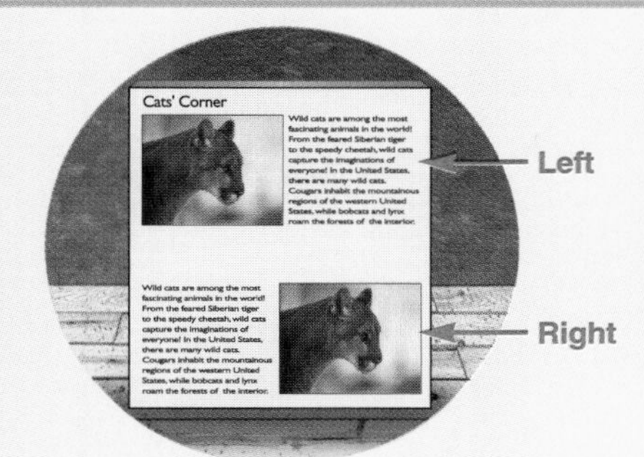

You can use the Left and Right options to wrap text around an image. The Left option places the image on the left side of the text. The Right option places the image on the right side of the text.

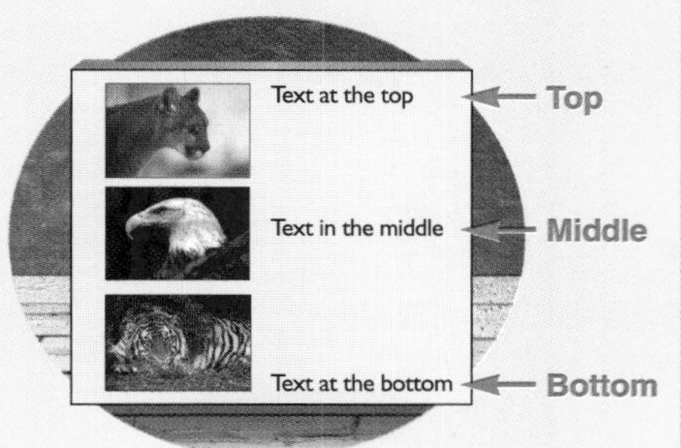

You can use the Top, Middle and Bottom options to vertically align an image with a single line of text.

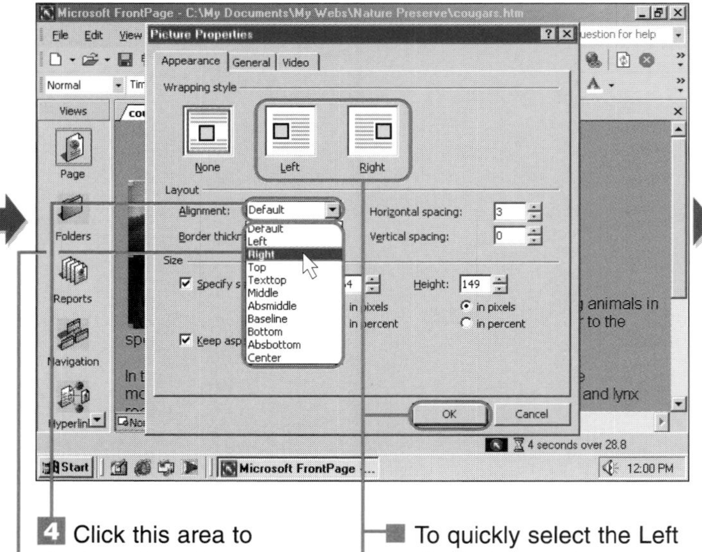

4 Click this area to display a list of the alignment options.

5 Click the alignment option you want to use.

■ To quickly select the Left or Right alignment option, click the appropriate option in this area.

6 Click **OK** to confirm your selection.

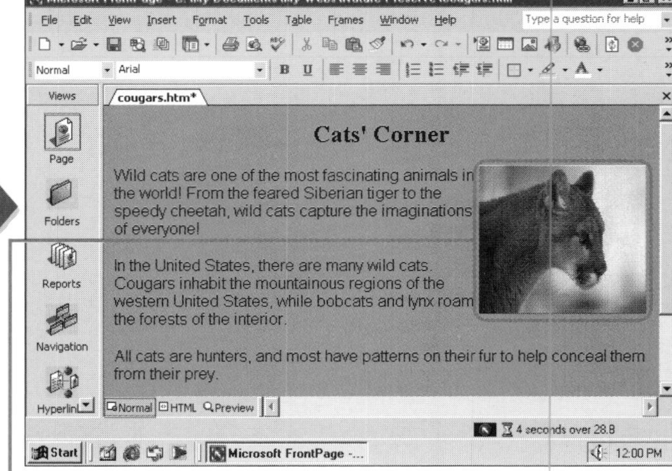

■ The image appears aligned with the text.

■ To increase the amount of space between an image and the surrounding text, see page 124.

■ If you no longer want to align an image with text, repeat steps 1 to 6, selecting **Default** in step 5.

ADD SPACE AROUND AN IMAGE

You can increase the amount of space between an image and other elements on a Web page.

ADD SPACE AROUND AN IMAGE

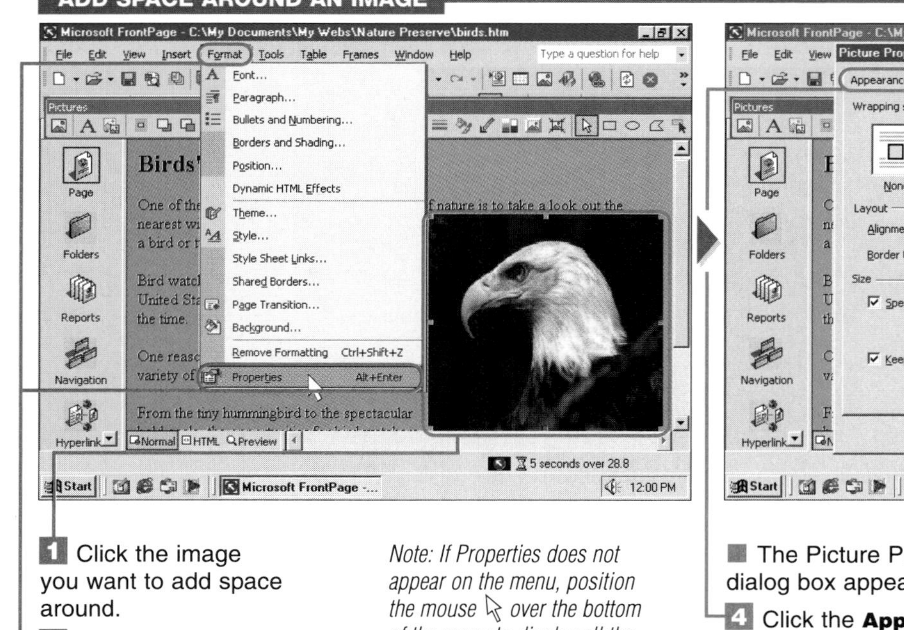

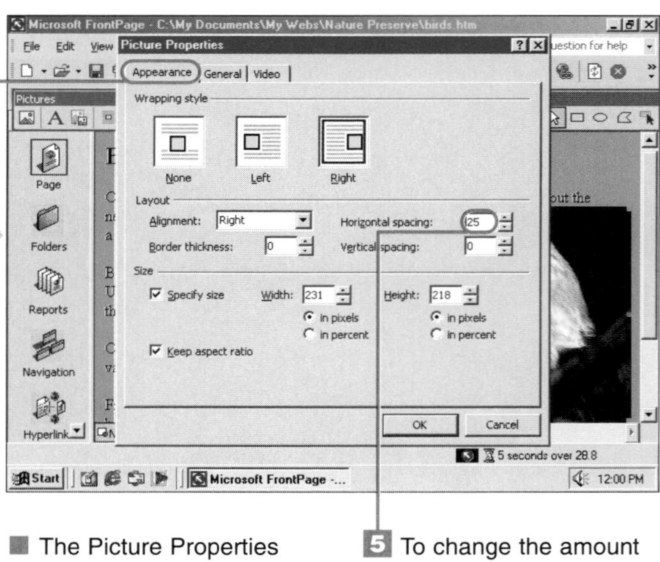

1 Click the image you want to add space around.

2 Click **Format**.

3 Click **Properties**.

Note: If Properties does not appear on the menu, position the mouse over the bottom of the menu to display all the menu options.

■ The Picture Properties dialog box appears.

4 Click the **Appearance** tab.

5 To change the amount of space on both the left and right sides of the image, double-click this area and type a number for the amount of space in pixels.

Can I increase the amount of space on just one side of an image?

No. You cannot increase the amount of space on just one side of an image. The horizontal spacing option defines the amount of space for both the left and right sides of an image. The vertical spacing option defines the amount of space for both the top and bottom of an image.

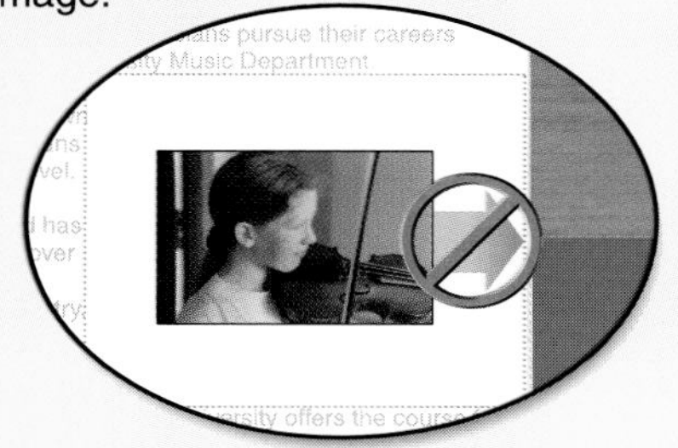

How do I specify the amount of space around an image?

You specify the amount of space around an image in pixels. A pixel is a dot on a computer screen. The word "pixel" comes from **pic**ture **el**ement.

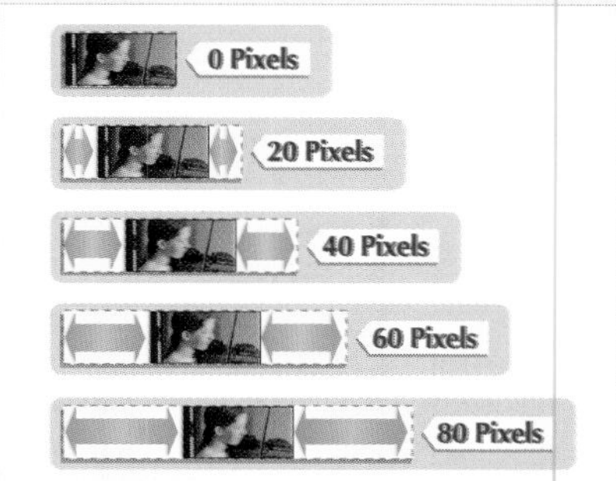

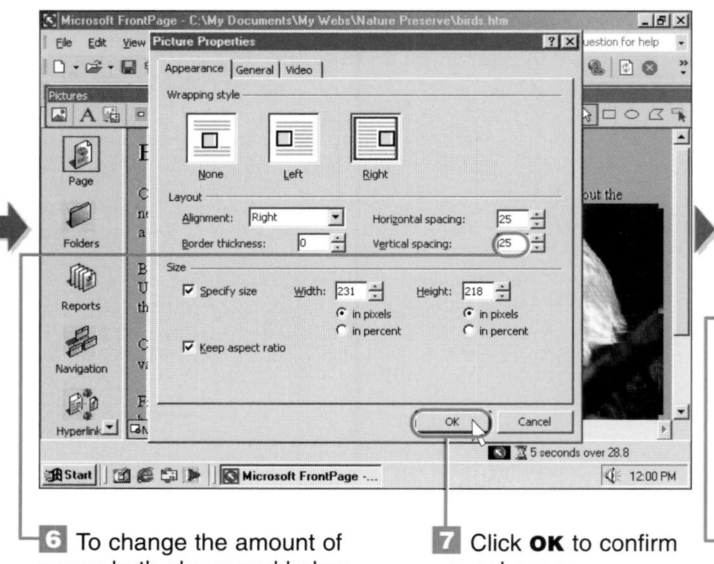

6 To change the amount of space both above and below the image, double-click this area and type a number for the amount of space in pixels.

7 Click **OK** to confirm your changes.

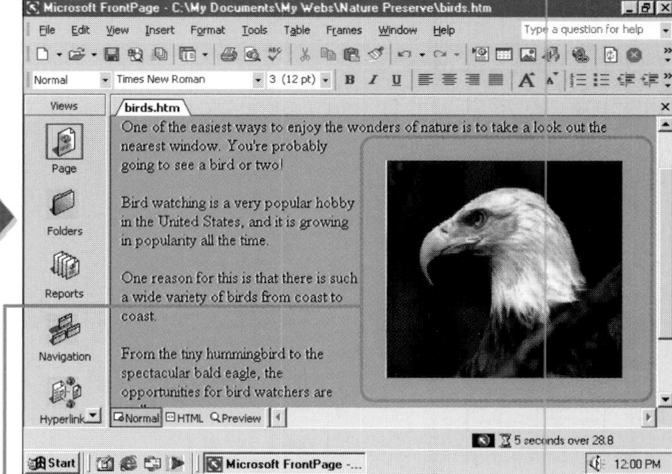

■ The image appears with the spacing you specified.

CROP AN IMAGE

You can crop an image to remove parts of the image that you do not want to show on a Web page.

CROP AN IMAGE

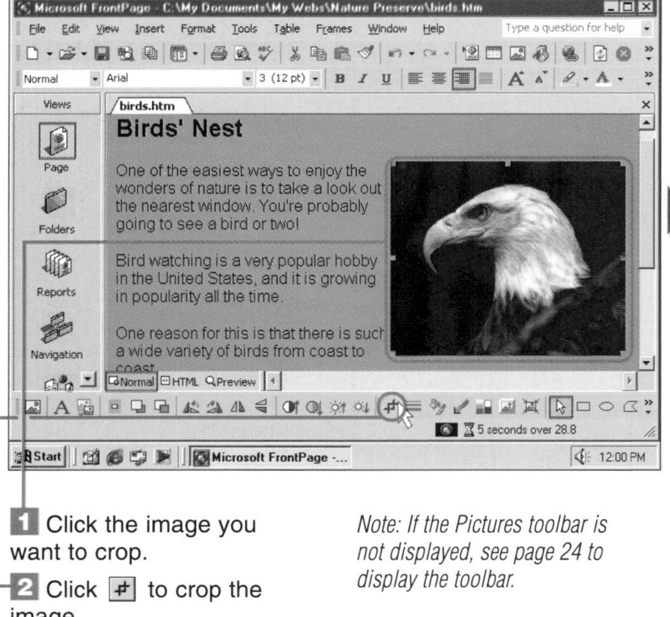

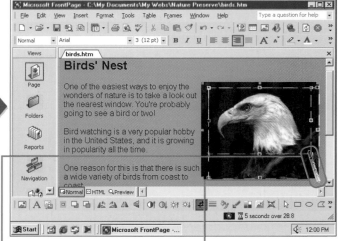

1 Click the image you want to crop.

2 Click ⌗ to crop the image.

Note: If the Pictures toolbar is not displayed, see page 24 to display the toolbar.

■ A dashed line appears around the image. Handles (■) appear on the dashed line.

3 Position the mouse + over a handle (+ changes to ↘, ↔ or ↕).

4 Drag the handle until the dashed line surrounds the part of the image you want to keep.

*Note: If you make a mistake when selecting the area, click outside of the image and then repeat steps **1** to **4**.*

When would I want to crop an image?

Cropping an image is useful when you want to focus a visitor's attention on an important part of the image. You may also want to crop an image to make the image fit better on your Web page.

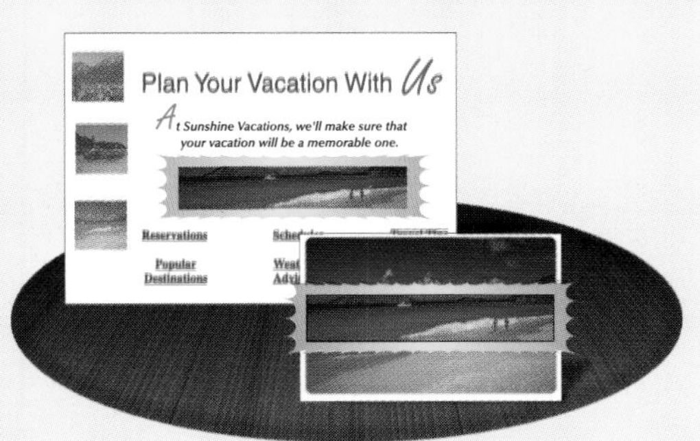

Will cropping an image change the file size of the image?

When you crop an image, you reduce the file size of the image. This allows the image to transfer more quickly to a visitor's computer.

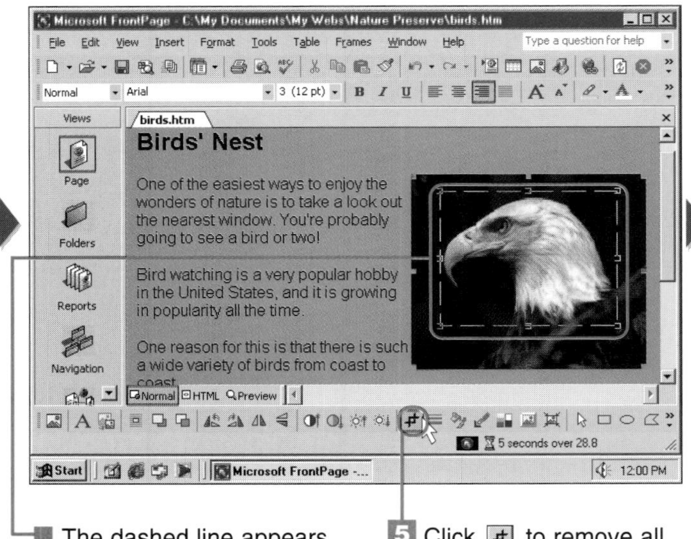

■ The dashed line appears around the area that will remain on the Web page.

5 Click ⌗ to remove all parts of the image outside of the selected area.

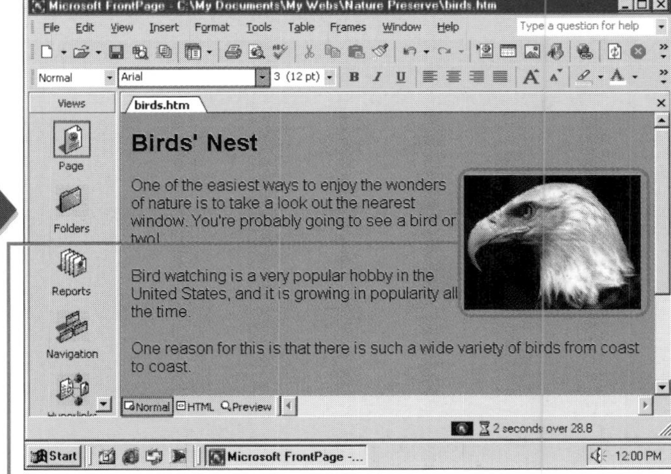

■ All parts of the image outside of the selected area disappear.

Note: If the image appears on several Web pages, the image will appear cropped on each Web page.

CREATE A THUMBNAIL IMAGE

You can create a thumbnail image on a Web page. A thumbnail image is a small version of an image that visitors can select to display a larger version of the image.

Thumbnail images allow visitors to quickly view a smaller image and decide if they want to wait to view a larger version of the image. Thumbnail images transfer faster and appear on a visitor's screen more quickly.

CREATE A THUMBNAIL IMAGE

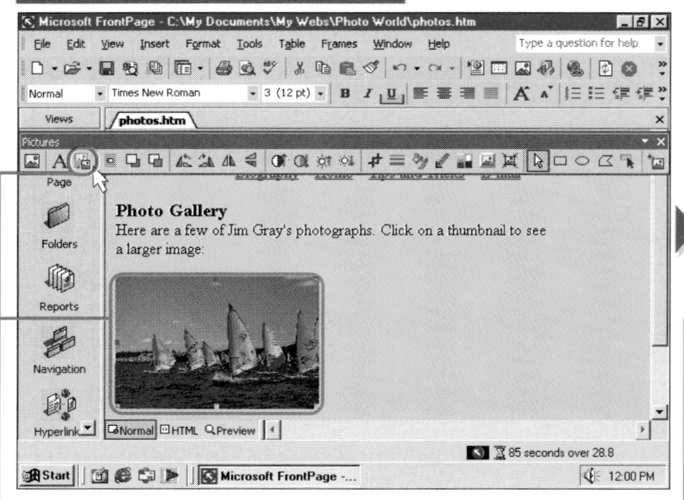

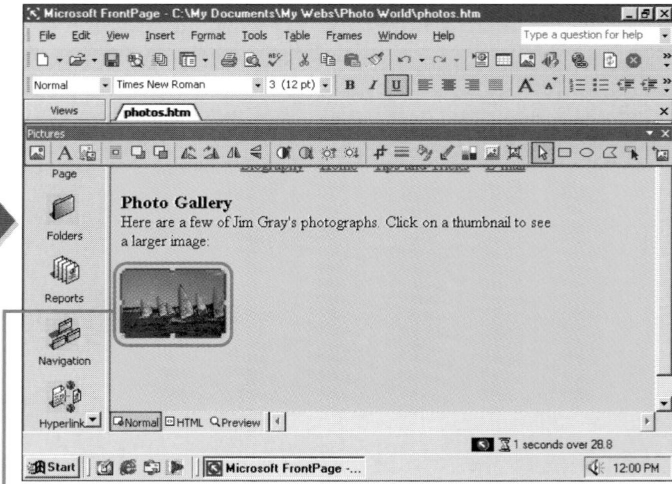

1 Click the image you want to display as a thumbnail image.

2 Click [icon] to create a thumbnail image.

Note: If the Pictures toolbar is not displayed, see page 24 to display the toolbar.

■ A dialog box appears if the image is too small or if the image is already a link. Click **OK** to close the dialog box.

■ A smaller version of the image appears on your Web page.

■ A visitor can click the image to view the larger version of the image.

Note: To test the thumbnail image, you can use the Preview view. For information on the Preview view, see page 42.

■ When you save the Web page, FrontPage will save the new thumbnail image as part of your Web site.

MAKE AN IMAGE BACKGROUND TRANSPARENT

You can make the background of an image transparent so the background will blend into a Web page.

Making an image background transparent works best when the entire background of the image is one color.

You can only make the background of a GIF image transparent. For information on GIF images, see page 92.

MAKE AN IMAGE BACKGROUND TRANSPARENT

1 Click the image with the background you want to make transparent.

2 Click the set transparent color button to select the background color you want to make transparent.

Note: If the Pictures toolbar is not displayed, see page 24 to display the toolbar.

3 Position the mouse over the background of the image and then click to select the background color.

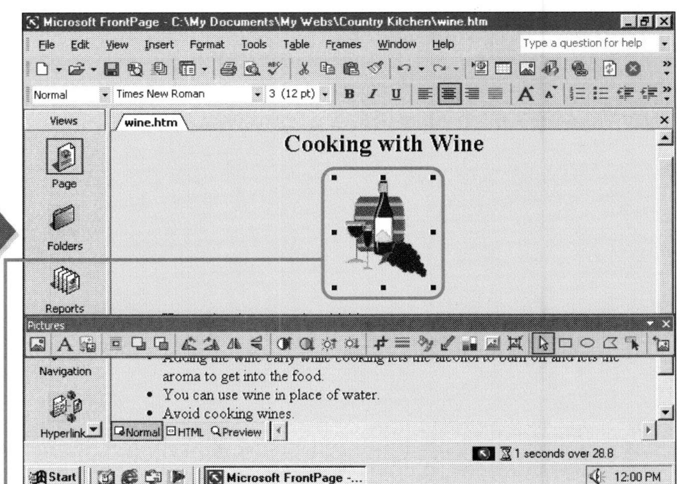

■ The image displays a transparent background.

Note: When you make the background of an image transparent, every part of the image that displays the background color will also be transparent.

CREATE AN IMAGE MAP

You can create an image map that divides an image into different areas, called hotspots, that each link to a different Web page.

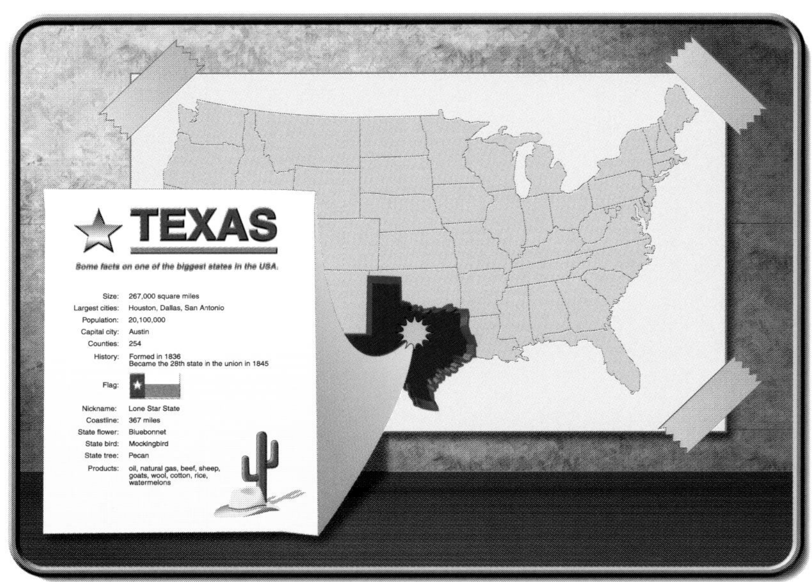

Creating an image map is useful for an image such as a floor plan or map that you want to contain links to different Web pages.

CREATE AN IMAGE MAP

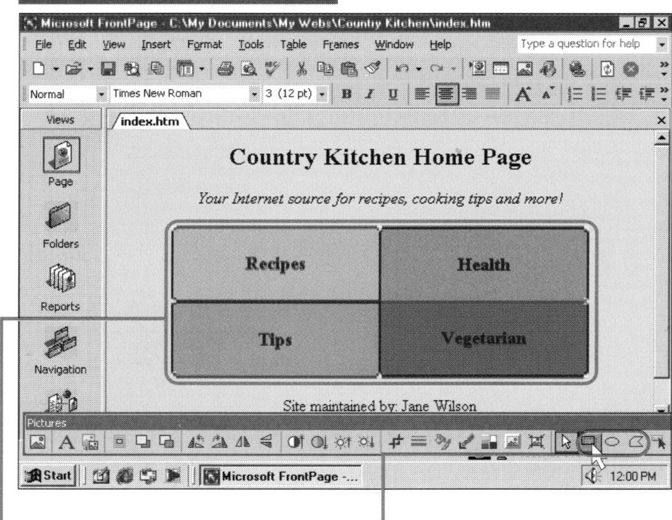

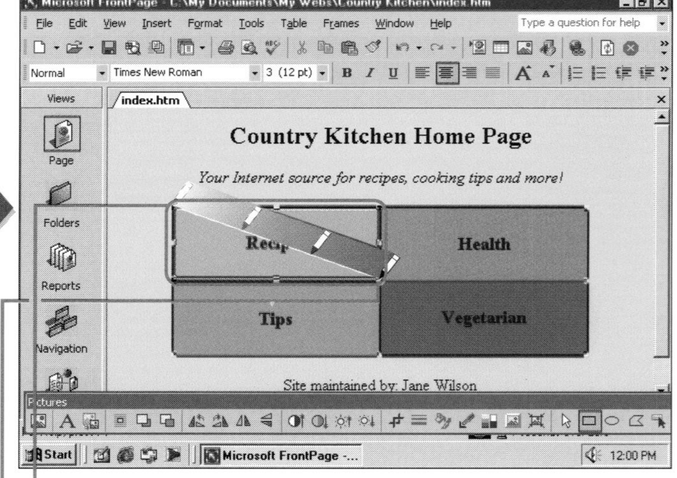

1 Click the image you want to use as an image map. Handles (■) appear around the image.

2 Click the shape you want to use to create a hotspot on the image.

- Rectangle
- Circle
- Irregular shape

Note: If the Pictures toolbar is not displayed, see page 24 to display the toolbar.

3 Position the mouse I over the area of the image you want to make a hotspot (I changes to ✎).

4 Drag the mouse ✎ until the hotspot is the size you want.

■ If you selected the Irregular shape in step 2, repeat steps 3 and 4 until you finish drawing all the lines for the hotspot. Then double-click the mouse to complete the hotspot.

Note: A hotspot cannot extend beyond the edge of an image.

What should I consider when choosing an image for an image map?

When creating an image map, you should use an image that has several distinct areas that visitors can select. Photographs do not usually make good image maps.

How do I move, resize or delete a hotspot on an image map?

You can move or resize a hotspot as you would move or resize any image on a Web page. To move or resize an image, see page 104.

To delete a hotspot, click the hotspot and then press the Delete key.

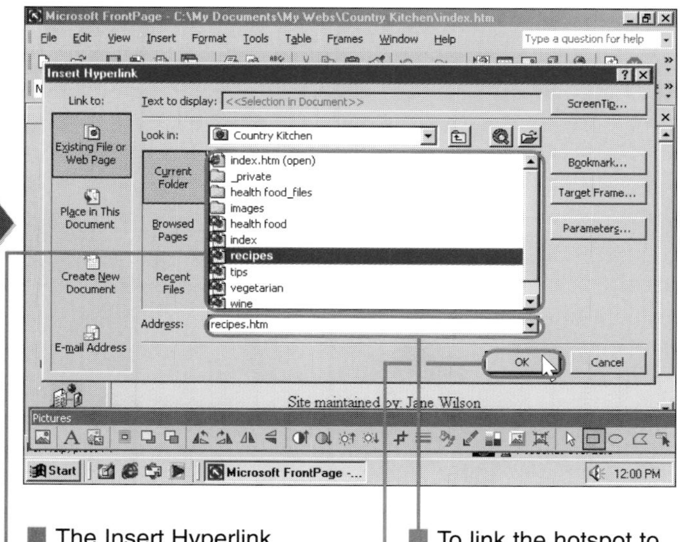

■ The Insert Hyperlink dialog box appears.

5 To link the hotspot to a page in your Web site, click the Web page ( ) in this area. The area lists all the Web pages in the current Web site.

■ To link the hotspot to a page on the Web, type the address of the Web page in this area.

6 Click **OK** to create the link.

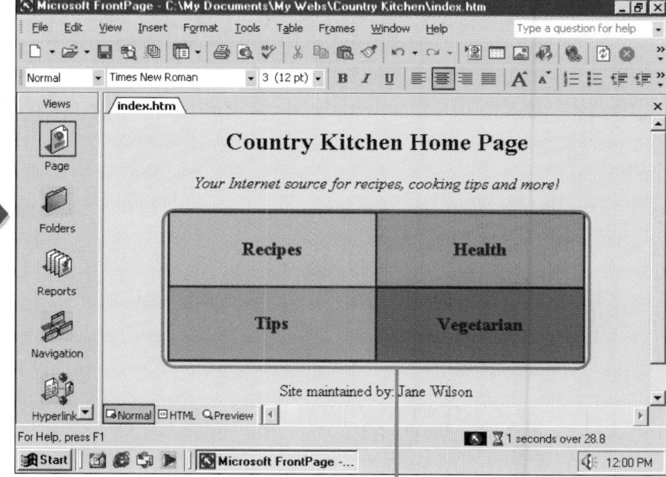

■ You can repeat steps 1 to 6 for each hotspot you want to create on the image.

■ To deselect the image and hide the hotspots, click outside the image.

Note: To once again display the hotspots, click the image.

■ A visitor can click a hotspot to display the Web page you specified.

Note: To test hotspots, you can use the Preview view. For information on the Preview view, see page 42.

Science Today
Chapter 1 - Introduction to Our World
Chapter 2 - Nature Now and Then
Chapter 3 - Chemistry of the Environment
Chapter 4 - The Water Around Us
Chapter 5 - How Healthy Are We?
Chapter 6 - Solar Energy

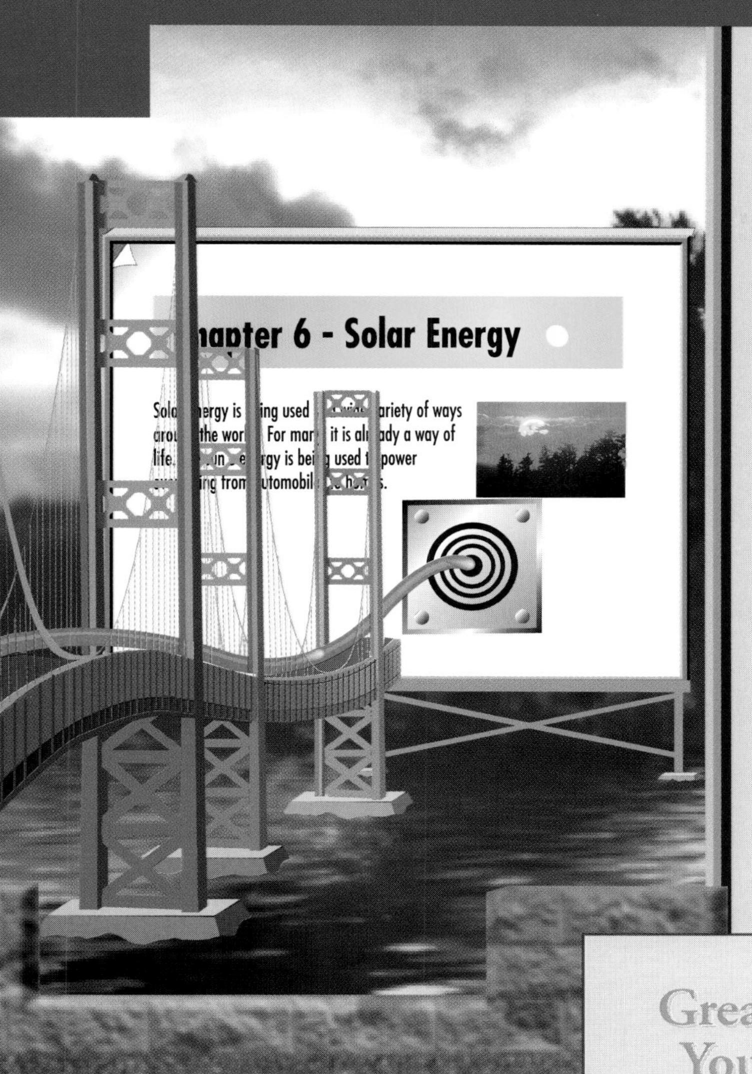

CHAPTER 8

Create Links

Do you want to create links that will connect your Web pages to other information on the Internet? Learn how in this chapter.

Great Web Sites You Can Visit!

1 Bank of America
2 Wal-Mart
3 McDonald's
4 NBC News
5 NFL Football
6 Sunkist
7 Pepsi
8 BMW

CREATE A LINK TO ANOTHER WEB PAGE

You can create a link to connect a word, phrase or image on a Web page to another page on the Web.

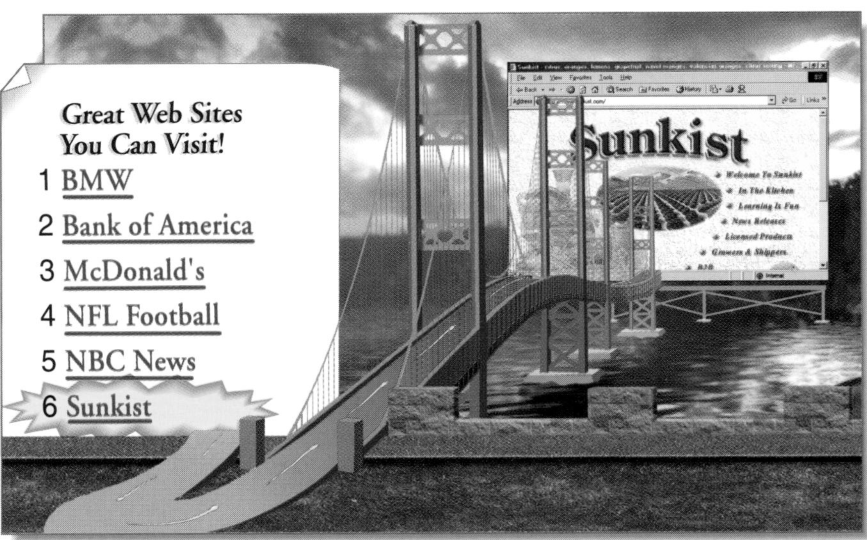

You can create a link to a Web page in your own Web site or to a Web page created by another person or company.

CREATE A LINK TO ANOTHER WEB PAGE

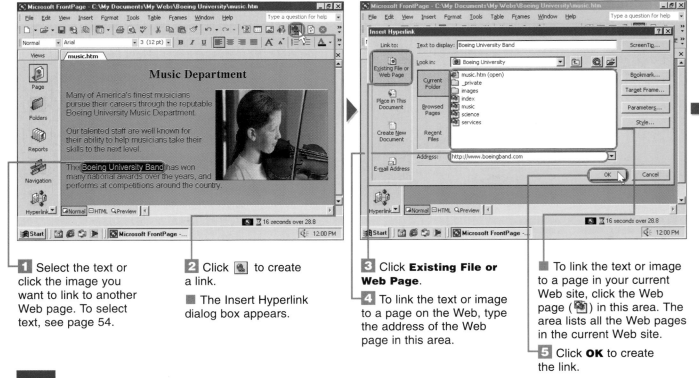

1 Select the text or click the image you want to link to another Web page. To select text, see page 54.

2 Click [icon] to create a link.

■ The Insert Hyperlink dialog box appears.

3 Click **Existing File or Web Page**.

4 To link the text or image to a page on the Web, type the address of the Web page in this area.

■ To link the text or image to a page in your current Web site, click the Web page ([icon]) in this area. The area lists all the Web pages in the current Web site.

5 Click **OK** to create the link.

What should I consider when creating a link to another Web page?

Be Descriptive

Make sure the text or image you use for a link clearly indicates where the link will take your visitors. Do not use the phrase "Click Here" for a link, since this phrase is not very informative.

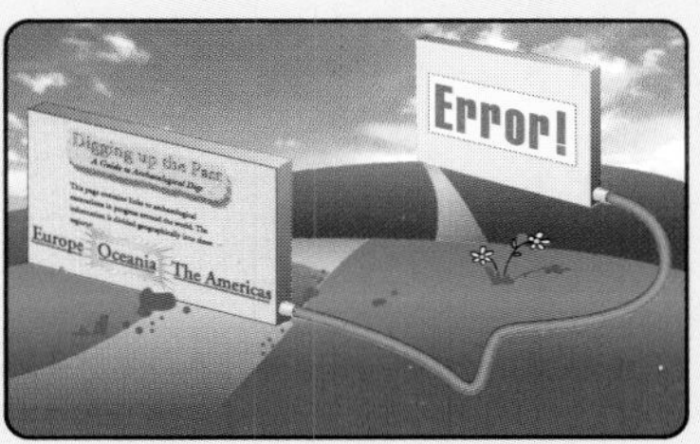

Check Your Links

When you create links, you should check the links on a regular basis. You will frustrate visitors who select a link that no longer connects to relevant information or displays an error message. To have FrontPage check the links in your Web site, see page 148.

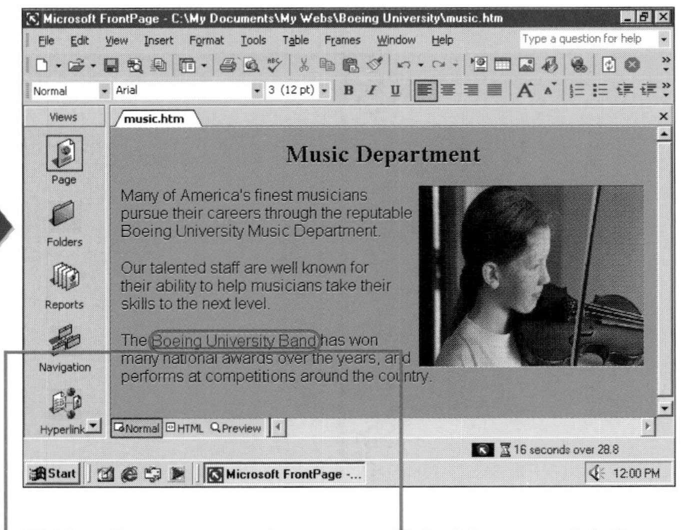

■ FrontPage creates the link. Text links appear underlined and in color.

■ To deselect the link, click outside the link.

■ A visitor can click the link to display the Web page you specified.

Note: To test the link, you can use the Preview view. For information on the Preview view, see page 42.

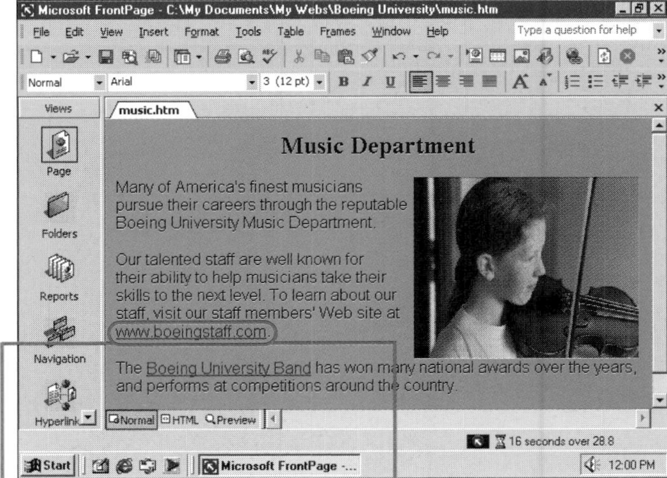

CREATE A LINK AUTOMATICALLY

1 Type the address of a Web page.

2 Press the **Spacebar** or the Enter key.

■ FrontPage automatically changes the Web page address to a link.

CREATE A LINK TO A WEB PAGE AREA

You can create a link that visitors can select to display a specific area on a Web page. This allows visitors to quickly display information of interest.

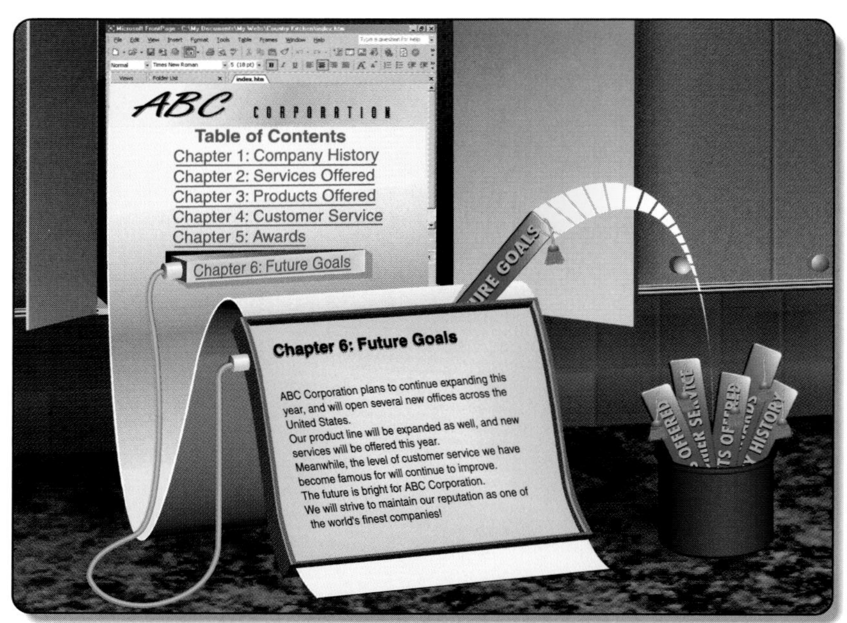

Before you can create a link to a specific area on a Web page, you must create a bookmark. A bookmark identifies the area of the Web page that you want visitors to be able to quickly display.

CREATE A LINK TO A WEB PAGE AREA

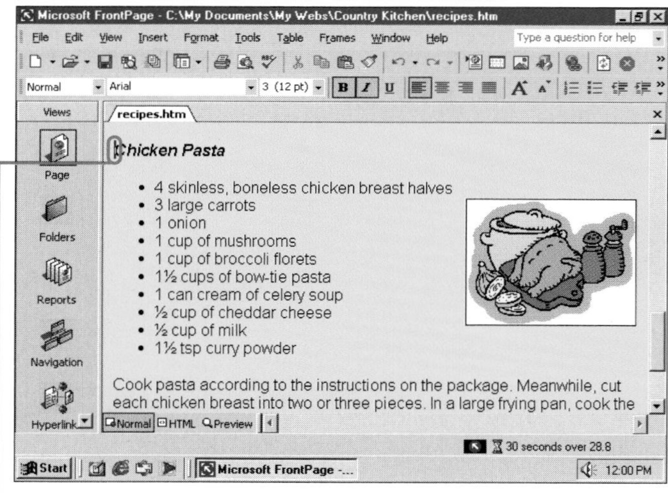

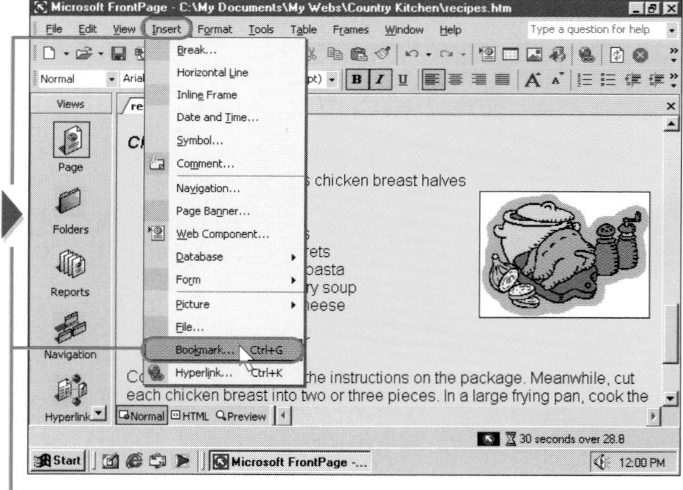

CREATE A BOOKMARK

1. Click the location on the Web page you want visitors to be able to quickly display.
2. Click **Insert**.
3. Click **Bookmark**.

Note: If Bookmark does not appear on the menu, position the mouse over the bottom of the menu to display all the menu options.

When would I create a link to a Web page area?

You may want to create a link that takes visitors to a specific area within the same Web page. For example, you can create a table of contents at the top of a Web page that contains links to various sections of the same page.

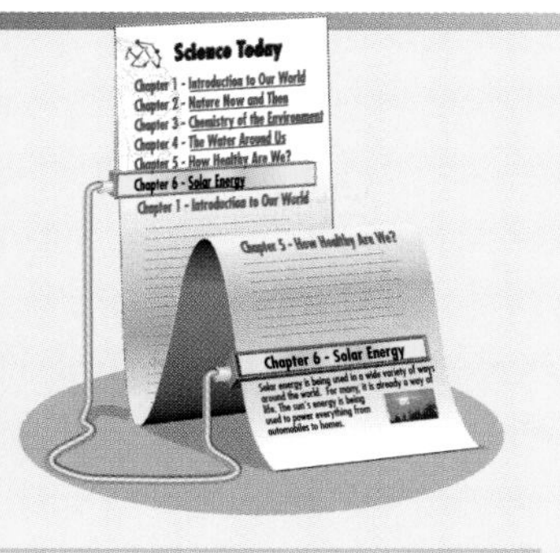

You can also create a link that will take visitors to a specific area on a different Web page in your Web site. For example, you can create a glossary of terms on one Web page that contains links to specific definitions on another page.

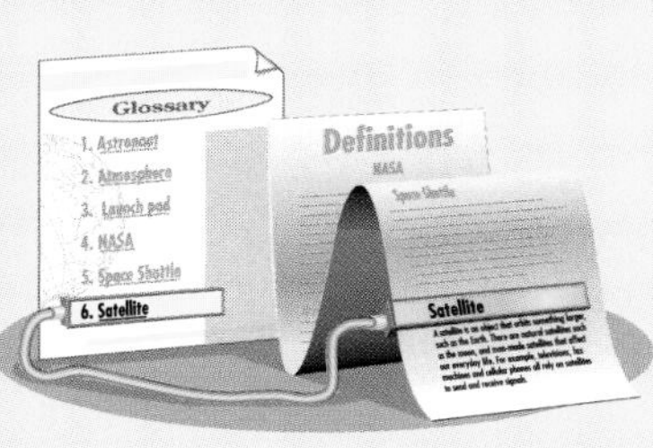

How do I delete a bookmark?

To delete a bookmark from a Web page, drag the mouse I over the flag ( ) for the bookmark until you highlight the flag and then press the Delete key. Deleting a bookmark will not remove the link connected to the bookmark.

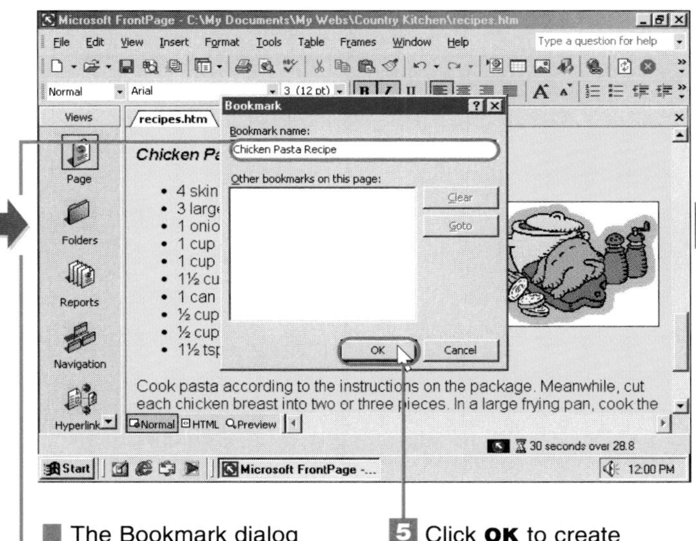

■ The Bookmark dialog box appears.

4 Type a name for the bookmark. Make sure the name clearly describes the Web page area.

5 Click **OK** to create the bookmark.

■ A flag ( ) appears on your Web page to indicate the location of the bookmark. The flag will not appear when you publish your Web pages.

6 Save the Web page to save your changes. For information on saving a Web page, see page 28.

■ You now need to create a link that visitors can select to display the Web page area you have bookmarked.

CONTINUED

CREATE A LINK TO A WEB PAGE AREA

After you create a bookmark to identify an area of a Web page, you will need to create a link that visitors can select to display the area.

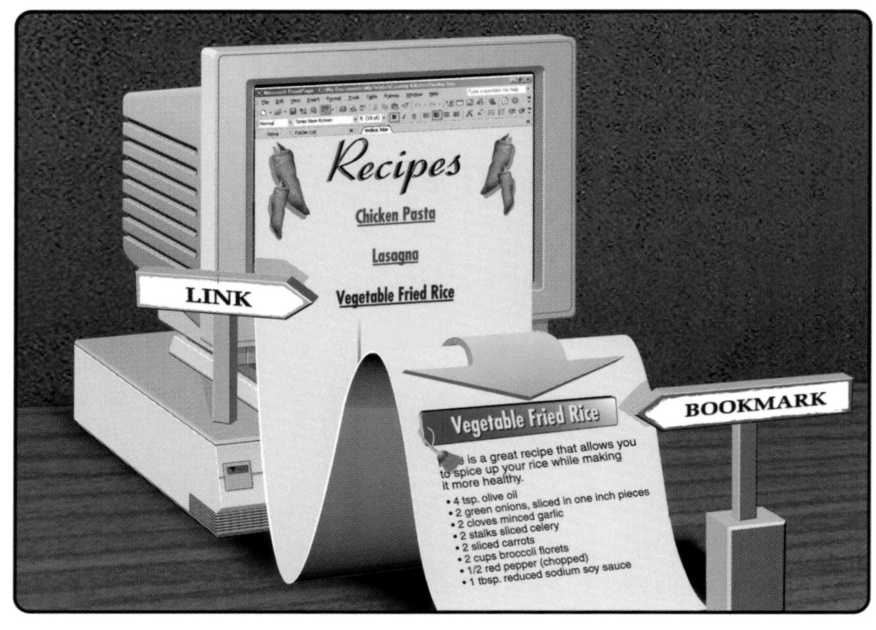

Make sure the text or image you use for the link clearly indicates where the link will take your visitors.

CREATE A LINK TO A WEB PAGE AREA (CONTINUED)

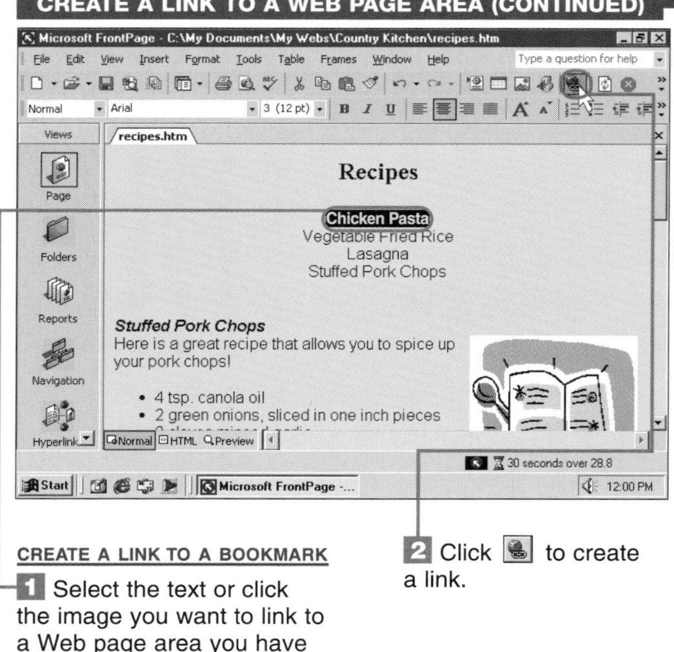

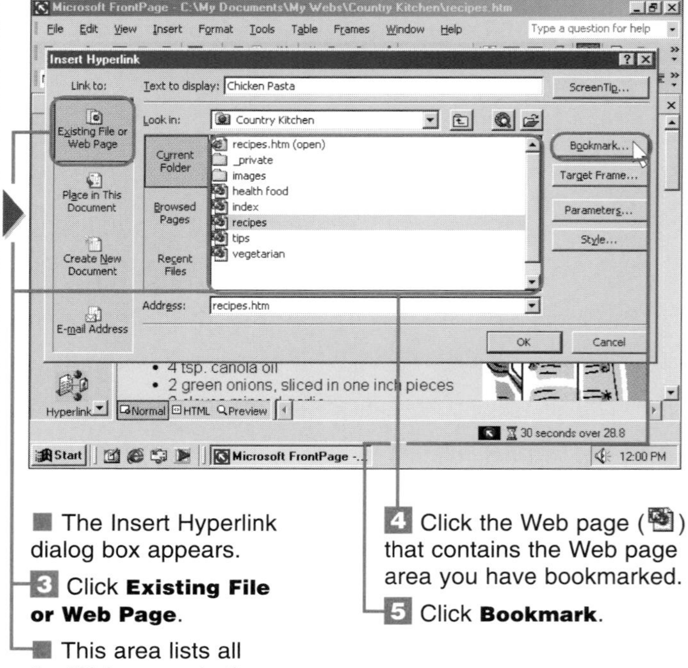

CREATE A LINK TO A BOOKMARK

1 Select the text or click the image you want to link to a Web page area you have bookmarked. To select text, see page 54.

2 Click to create a link.

■ The Insert Hyperlink dialog box appears.

3 Click **Existing File or Web Page**.

■ This area lists all the Web pages in the current Web site.

4 Click the Web page () that contains the Web page area you have bookmarked.

5 Click **Bookmark**.

What should I consider when adding links to a Web page?

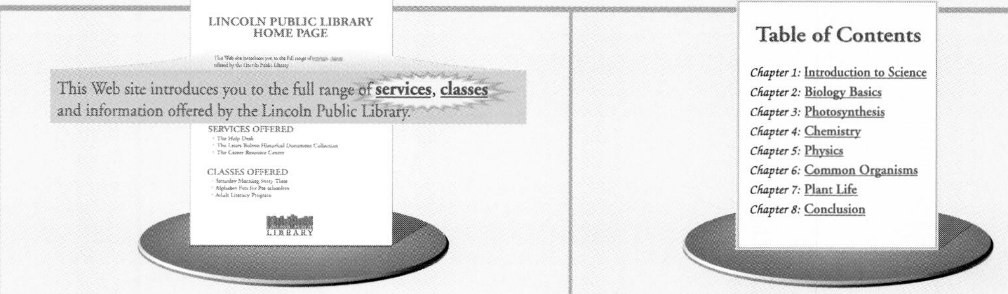

Separate Links

Do not place two text links beside each other on a Web page. When two text links appear side by side, visitors may see one long link rather than two separate links.

Use Link Menus

If you plan to include many links on a Web page, you should consider displaying the links in a menu format, like a table of contents in a book.

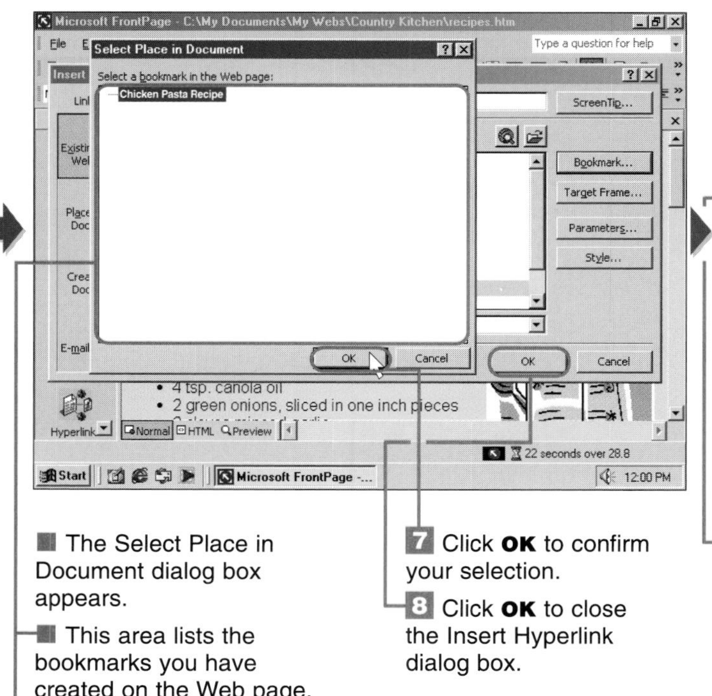

■ The Select Place in Document dialog box appears.

■ This area lists the bookmarks you have created on the Web page.

6 Click the bookmark you want to link the text or image to.

7 Click **OK** to confirm your selection.

8 Click **OK** to close the Insert Hyperlink dialog box.

■ FrontPage creates the link. Text links appear underlined and in color.

■ To deselect the link, click outside the link.

■ A visitor can click the link to display the Web page area you specified.

Note: To test the link, you can use the Preview view. For information on the Preview view, see page 42.

CREATE AN E-MAIL LINK

You can create a link on a Web page that allows visitors to quickly send you an e-mail message.

When a visitor selects an e-mail link, a blank message addressed to you will appear.

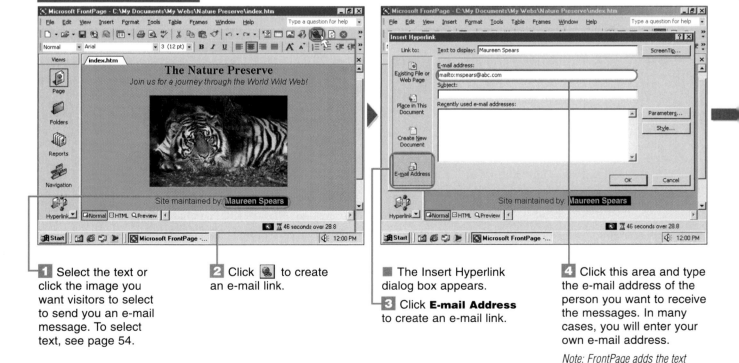

CREATE AN E-MAIL LINK

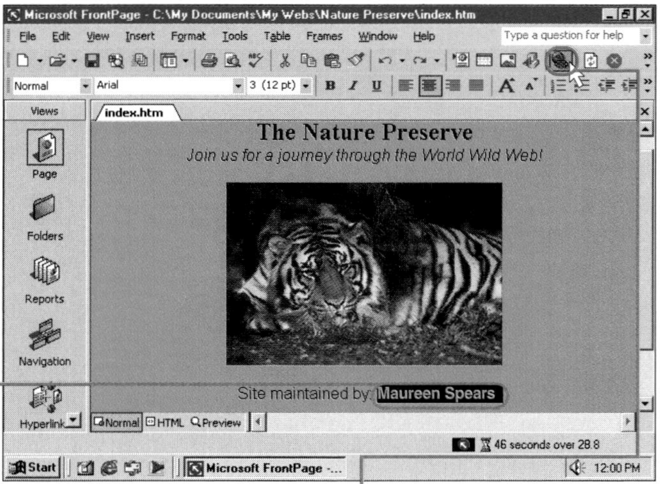

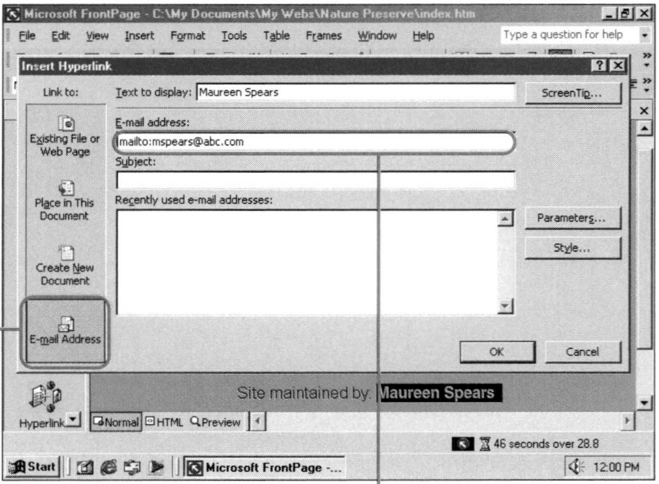

1 Select the text or click the image you want visitors to select to send you an e-mail message. To select text, see page 54.

2 Click to create an e-mail link.

■ The Insert Hyperlink dialog box appears.

3 Click **E-mail Address** to create an e-mail link.

4 Click this area and type the e-mail address of the person you want to receive the messages. In many cases, you will enter your own e-mail address.

Note: FrontPage adds the text "mailto:" in front of the e-mail address you type.

Why should I include an e-mail link on a Web page?

An e-mail link allows visitors to send you questions and comments that can help you improve your Web pages. Many companies include a list of e-mail links that allows visitors to contact employees in different departments.

Can FrontPage automatically create an e-mail link?

When you type an e-mail address on your Web page and then press the Enter key or the **Spacebar**, FrontPage will automatically change the address to a link for you.

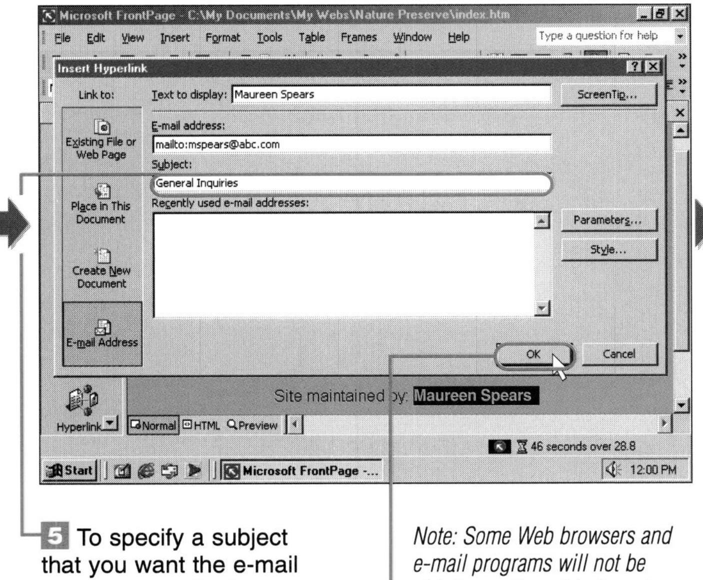

5 To specify a subject that you want the e-mail messages to display, click this area and type a subject.

Note: Some Web browsers and e-mail programs will not be able to use the subject you type.

6 Click **OK** to create the e-mail link.

■ FrontPage creates the e-mail link. Text e-mail links appear underlined and in color.

■ To deselect the e-mail link, click outside the link.

■ A visitor can click the e-mail link to send a message to the e-mail address you specified.

Note: To test the link, you can use the Preview view. For information on the Preview view, see page 42.

REMOVE A LINK

You can remove a link from text or an image on a Web page. Removing a link will not remove the text or image from your Web page.

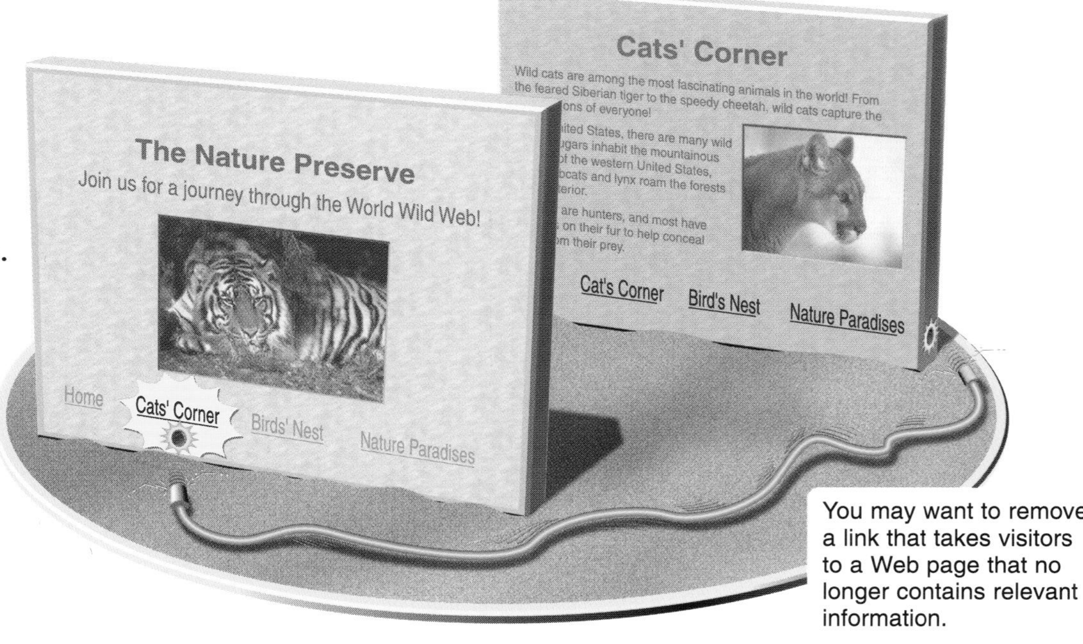

You may want to remove a link that takes visitors to a Web page that no longer contains relevant information.

REMOVE A LINK

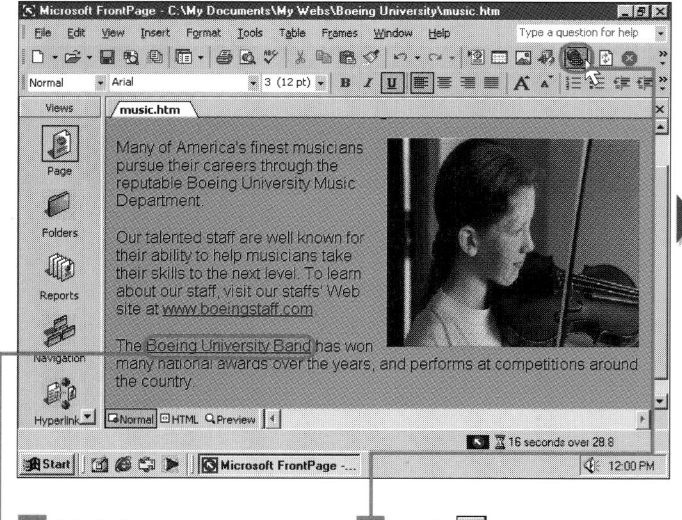

1 Click the text or image you no longer want to be a link.

2 Click [icon] to remove the link.

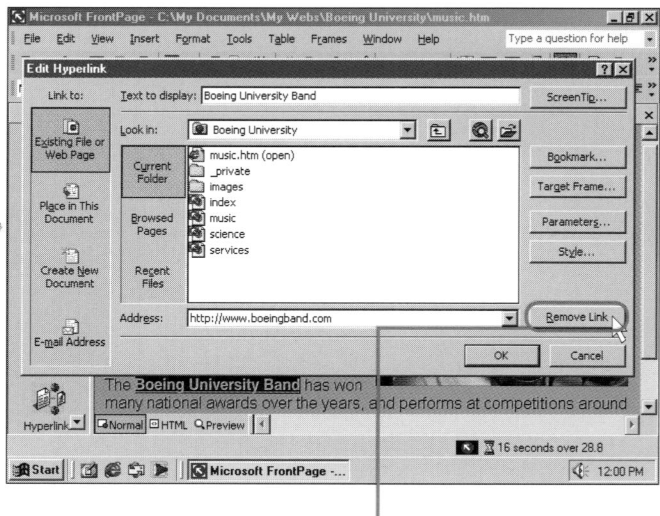

■ The Edit Hyperlink dialog box appears.

3 Click **Remove Link** to remove the link from the text or image.

Can I make changes to a link without removing the link?

Change Text for a Link

To edit the text for a link, drag the mouse over the text you want to change until you highlight the text and then type the new text. For example, you could change "www.maran.com" to "maranGraphics."

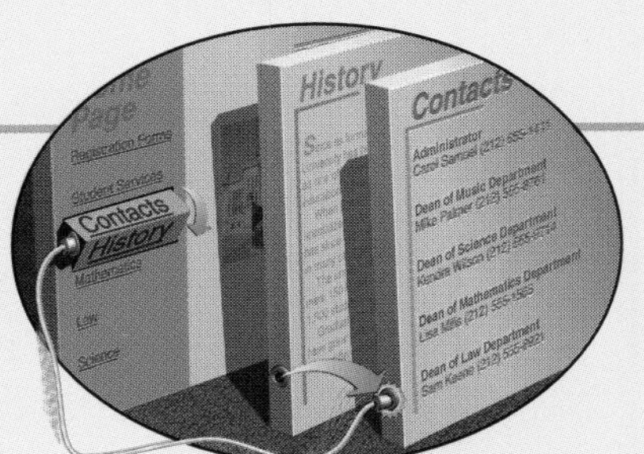

Change Linked Web Page

You can change the address of the Web page that a link connects to. This is useful if you typed the Web page address incorrectly when you created the link or if you want the link to connect to a different Web page. To edit a link, repeat steps 1 to 5 on page 134.

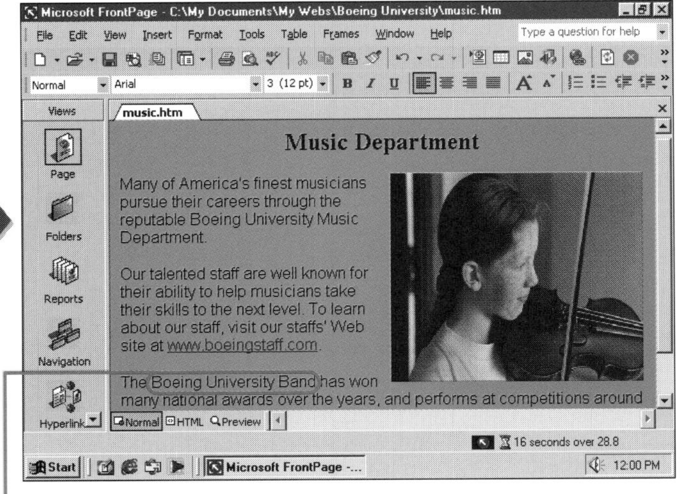

■ FrontPage removes the link from the text or image.

■ Text links no longer appear underlined and in color. The appearance of image links does not change.

■ To deselect the link, click outside the link.

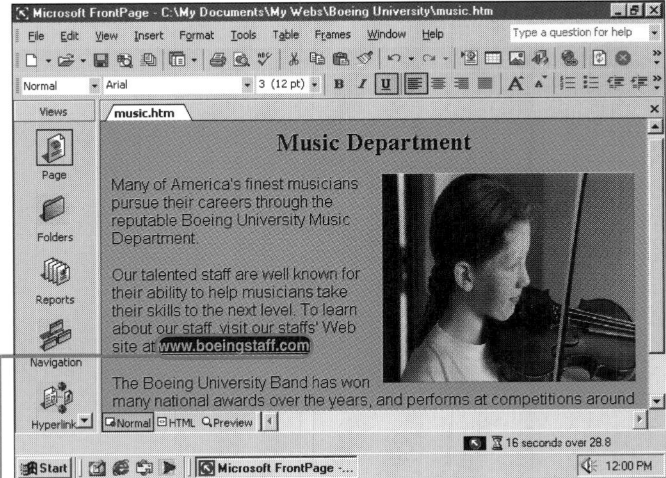

REMOVE ENTIRE LINK

1 To remove a link as well as the text or image for the link, select the text or click the image and then press the Delete key. To select text, see page 54.

CHANGE LINK COLORS

You can change the color of links on a Web page.

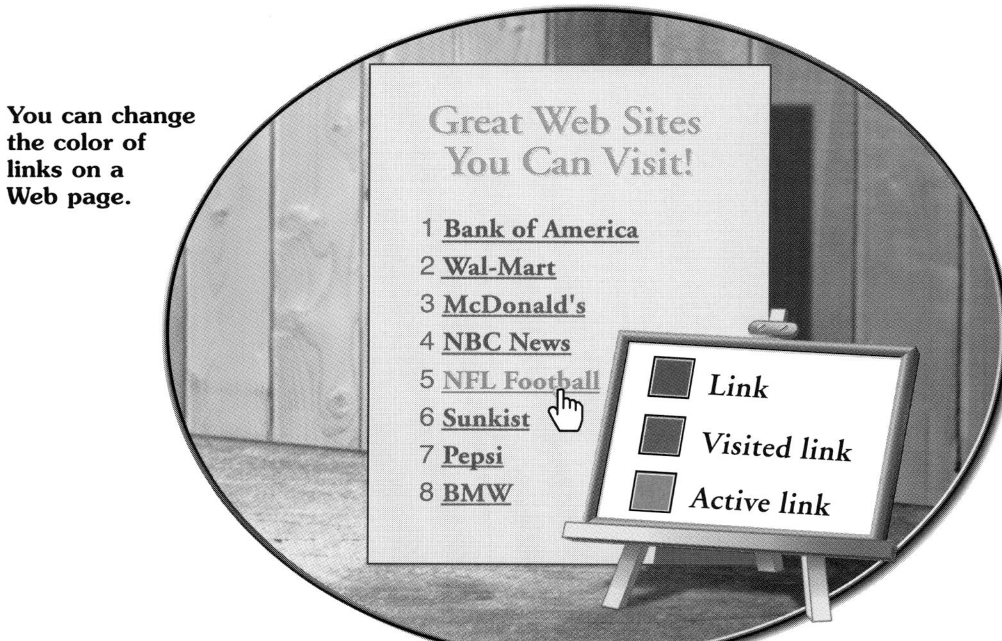

A Web page can contain three types of links.

Link
A link a visitor has not yet selected.

Visited link
A link a visitor has previously selected.

Active link
A link a visitor is currently selecting.

CHANGE LINK COLORS

1 Click anywhere on the Web page you want to use different link colors.

2 Click **Format**.

3 Click **Background**.

Note: If Background does not appear on the menu, position the mouse over the bottom of the menu to display all the menu options.

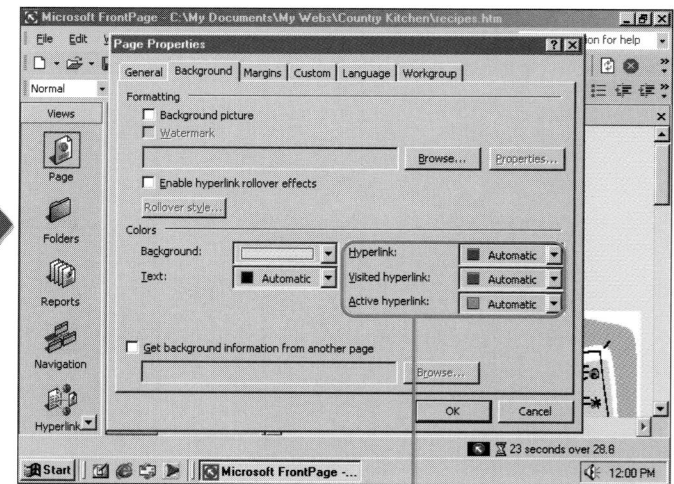

■ The Page Properties dialog box appears.

*Note: A different dialog box appears if the Web page uses a theme. You must remove the theme before you can change the link colors. Click **OK** to close the dialog box. For information on themes, see page 88.*

■ This area displays the colors currently used for links, visited links and active links.

What should I consider when changing the color of links?

Change Only When Necessary

You should change the link colors only when necessary, such as when the background color of the Web page makes the links difficult to read. You may confuse some visitors if you do not use the standard link colors.

Choose Different Colors

Make sure you choose different colors for links, visited links and active links. This allows visitors to clearly distinguish between the different types of links. FrontPage initially displays links in blue, visited links in purple and active links in red.

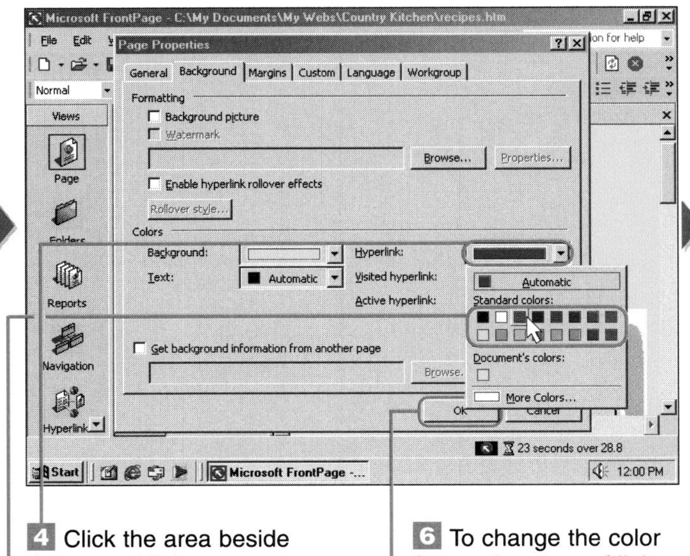

4 Click the area beside the type of link you want to display in a different color.

5 Click the color you want to use.

6 To change the color for another type of link, repeat steps 4 and 5.

7 Click **OK** to confirm your changes.

■ The links on your Web page appear in the colors you selected.

■ To return a link to its original color, repeat steps 1 to 7, selecting **Automatic** in step 5.

Note: To test a link, you can use the Preview view. For information on the Preview view, see page 42.

USING THE HYPERLINKS VIEW

You can use the Hyperlinks view to display the links that connect the Web pages in your Web site.

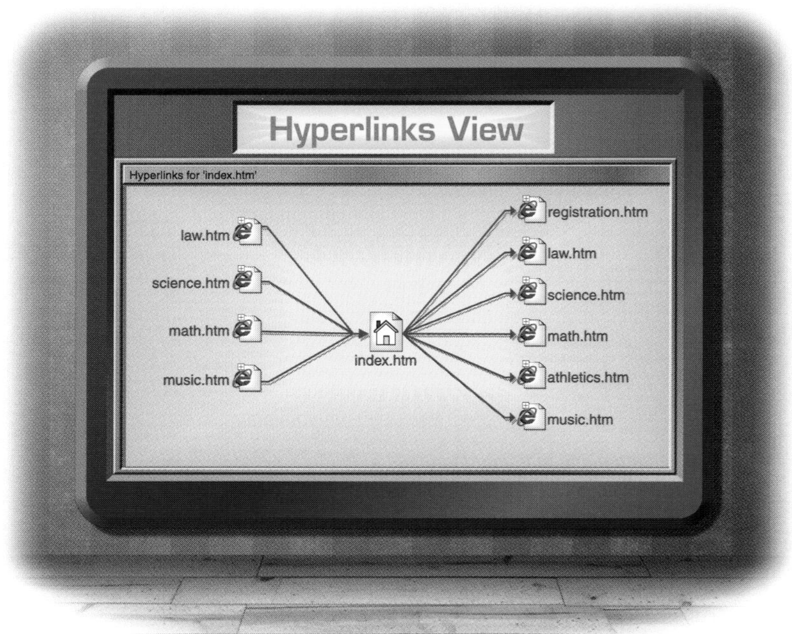

The Hyperlinks view helps you determine if your Web pages contain the necessary links that will allow visitors to easily navigate through your Web site.

Before using the Hyperlinks view, make sure you save all your Web pages to ensure that you will view the most recent links you added to the pages. To save Web pages, see page 28.

USING THE HYPERLINKS VIEW

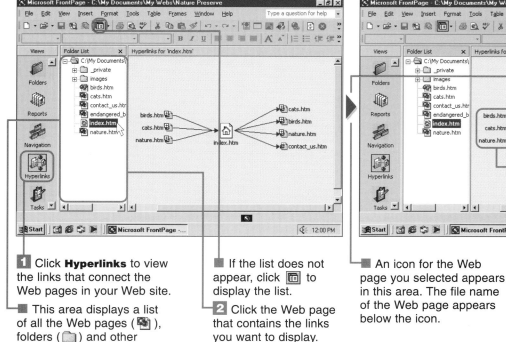

1 Click **Hyperlinks** to view the links that connect the Web pages in your Web site.

■ This area displays a list of all the Web pages ( ), folders ( ) and other items in your Web site.

■ If the list does not appear, click to display the list.

2 Click the Web page that contains the links you want to display.

■ An icon for the Web page you selected appears in this area. The file name of the Web page appears below the icon.

■ FrontPage displays the links to and from the Web page.

What does each icon represent in the Hyperlinks view?

Here are the most common icons you will see in the Hyperlinks view.

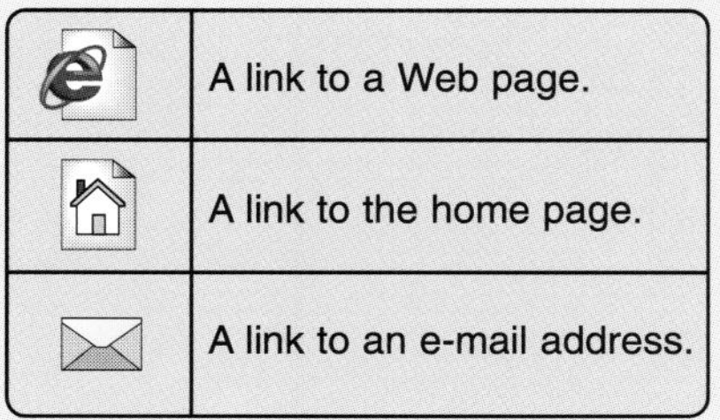

	A link to a Web page.
	A link to the home page.
	A link to an e-mail address.

Why does my Web site contain links that I didn't create?

When you use a template or wizard to create a Web site, FrontPage may automatically add links to the Web pages for you. To create a Web site using a template or wizard, see page 26.

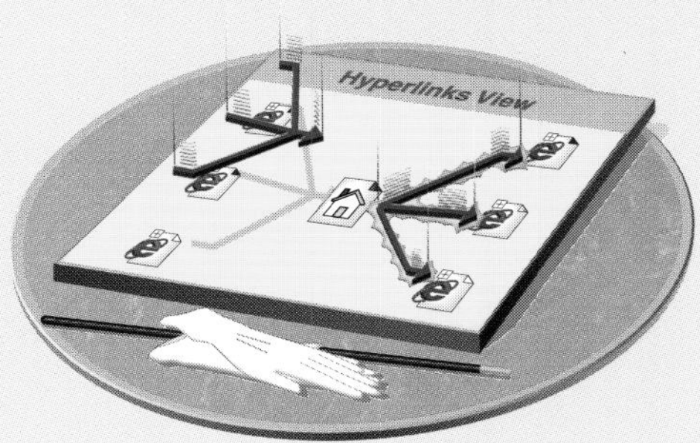

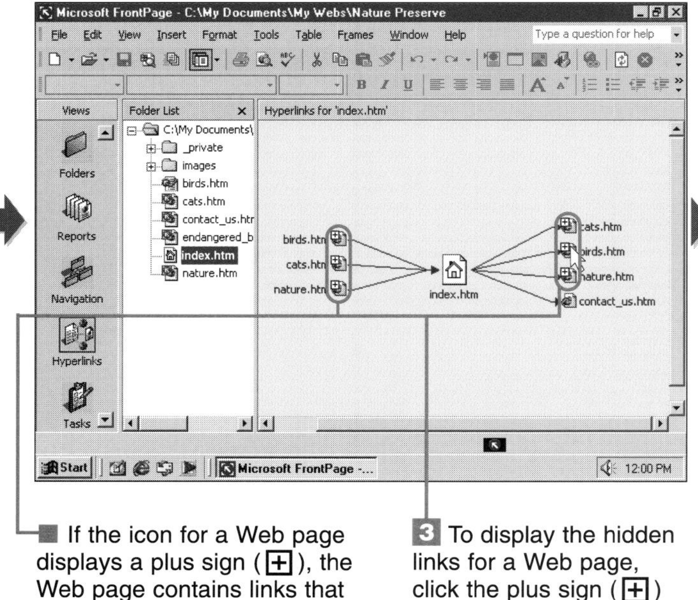

■ If the icon for a Web page displays a plus sign (⊞), the Web page contains links that are not shown.

3 To display the hidden links for a Web page, click the plus sign (⊞) on the Web page icon (⊞ changes to ⊟).

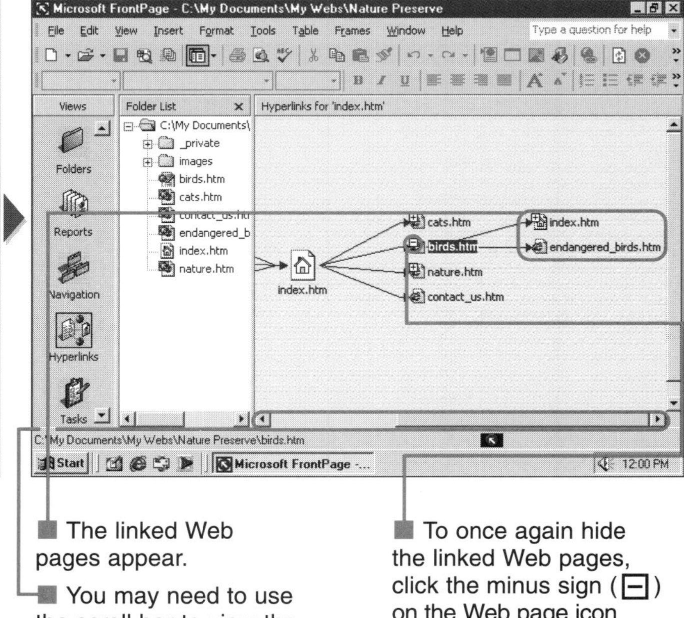

■ The linked Web pages appear.

■ You may need to use the scroll bar to view the linked Web pages.

■ To once again hide the linked Web pages, click the minus sign (⊟) on the Web page icon (⊟ changes to ⊞).

CHECK LINKS

You can check all the links in your Web site to determine if the links are working properly.

Before checking the links in your Web site, make sure you save all your Web pages. This ensures that FrontPage will check the links on the most recent versions of the pages.

CHECK LINKS

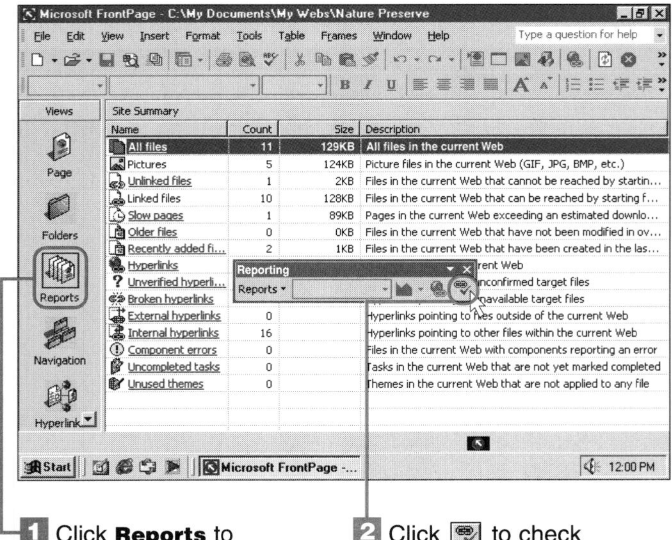

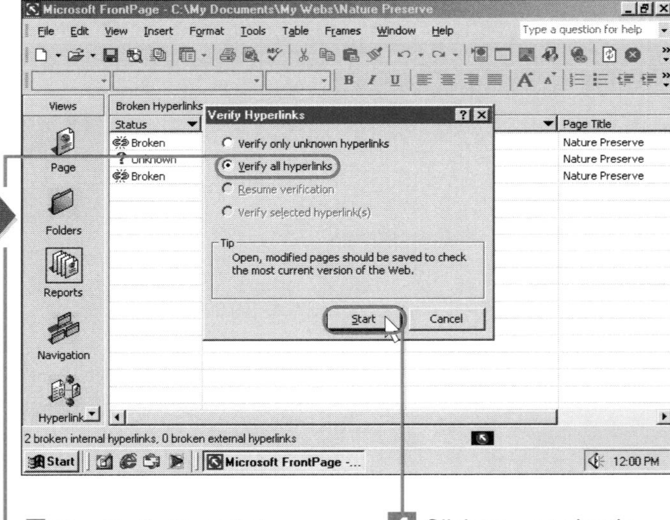

1 Click **Reports** to display your Web site in the Reports view.

2 Click to check all the links in your Web site.

Note: If the Reporting toolbar is not displayed, see page 24 to display the toolbar.

■ The Verify Hyperlinks dialog box appears.

3 Click **Verify all hyperlinks** to check all the links in your Web site (○ changes to ⊙).

4 Click **Start** to begin checking the links.

Note: If you are not connected to the Internet, a dialog box appears that allows you to connect.

Why is a link in my Web site broken?

A link that specifies an incorrect Web page address is called a broken link. When a visitor clicks a broken link, an error message will appear. A link may be broken for the following reasons.

➢ You typed the Web page address incorrectly.

➢ You deleted the Web page in your Web site that the link connects to.

➢ The Web page was moved or deleted on the Web.

Should I manually check the links on my Web pages?

You should manually check the links that connect to Web pages you did not create. Companies and individuals often change the content of their Web pages and the content may no longer relate to your pages.

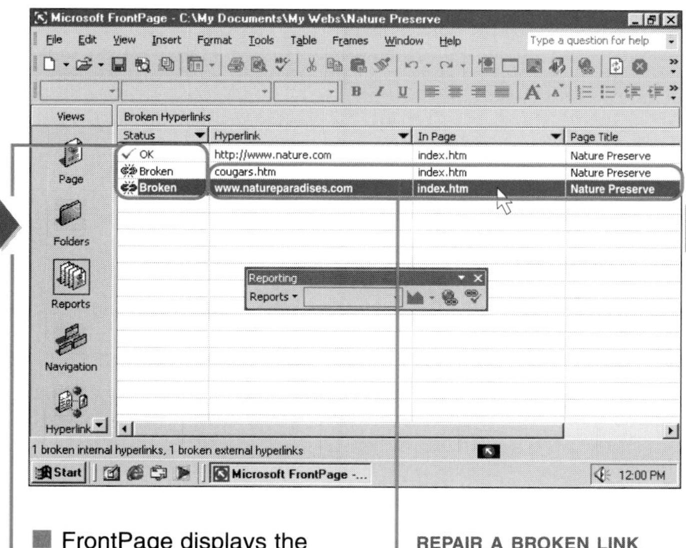

■ FrontPage displays the Broken Hyperlinks report, which displays information about the links in your Web site.

■ As FrontPage checks the links, this column displays the status of the links (✓ OK, Broken).

REPAIR A BROKEN LINK

1 To repair a broken link in your Web site, double-click the broken link.

■ The Edit Hyperlink dialog box appears.

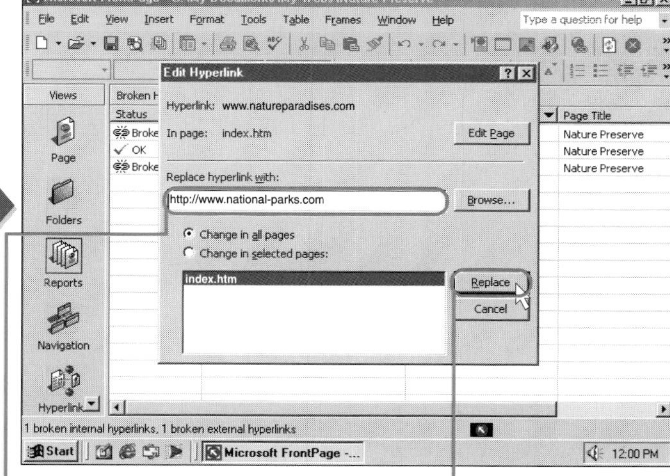

2 If the Web page is on the Web, type the correct Web page address, starting the address with **http://**.

■ If the Web page is on your computer, type the correct location and name of the Web page in your Web site. Make sure you add the **.htm** extension to the end of the Web page name.

3 Click **Replace** to correct the link on all your Web pages.

ADD A LINK BAR

You can add a link bar to a Web page. A link bar displays buttons that visitors can select to display other Web pages.

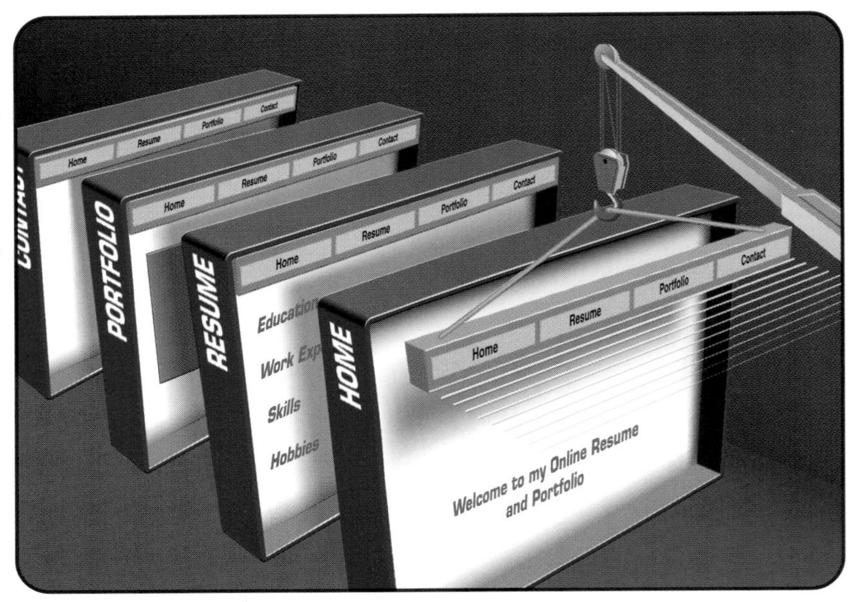

In order for your link bar to work properly when you publish your Web pages, your Web server must have the FrontPage Server Extensions installed. You can determine if your Web server has the FrontPage Server Extensions installed by asking the company that will make your Web pages available on the Web.

ADD A LINK BAR

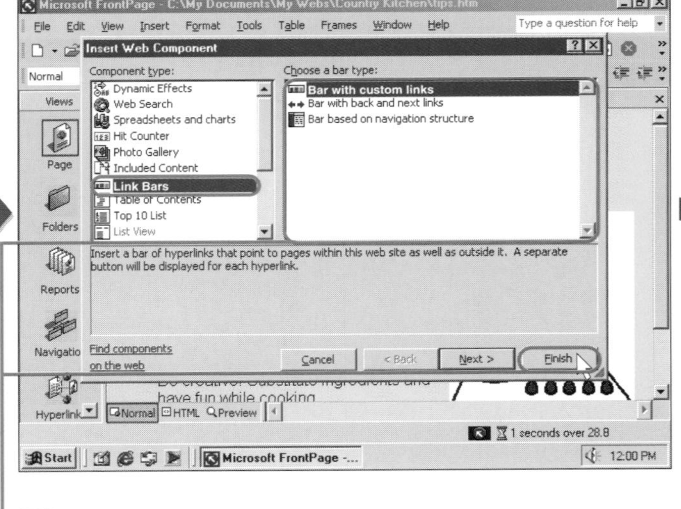

1 Click the location on your Web page where you want to add a link bar.

2 Click [icon] to display a list of components that you can add to your Web page.

■ The Insert Web Component dialog box appears.

3 Click **Link Bars** to add this type of component.

4 Click the type of link bar you want to add to your Web page.

5 Click **Finish**.

*Note: If you selected "Bar based on navigation structure" in step **4**, perform steps **2** to **5** on page 186 to select options in the dialog box that appears. When you finish selecting options in the dialog box, the link bar will appear on your Web page.*

What types of link bars can I add?

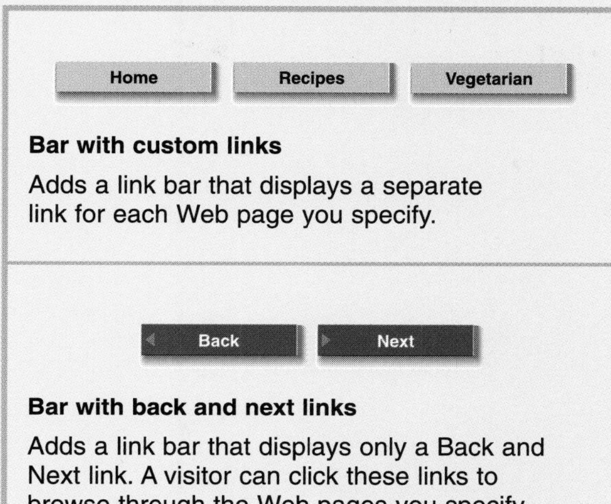

Bar with custom links

Adds a link bar that displays a separate link for each Web page you specify.

Bar with back and next links

Adds a link bar that displays only a Back and Next link. A visitor can click these links to browse through the Web pages you specify.

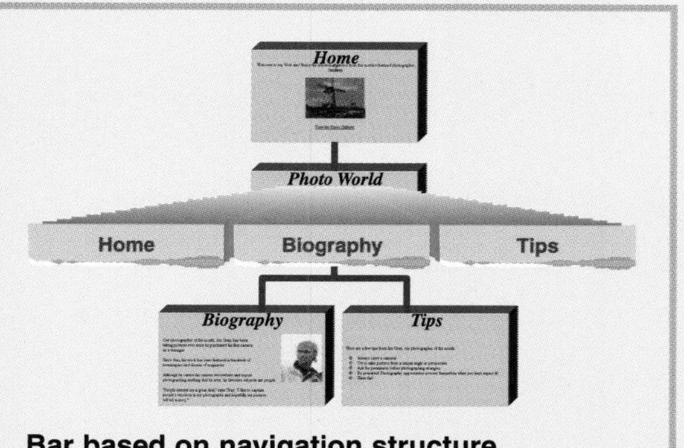

Bar based on navigation structure

Adds a link bar based on the navigational structure of your Web site. For information on working with the navigational structure of your Web site, see pages 178 to 187.

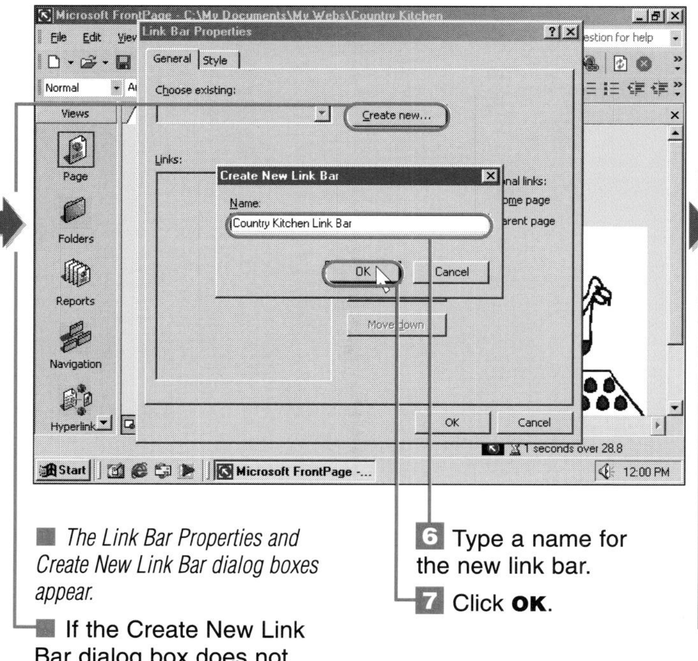

The Link Bar Properties and Create New Link Bar dialog boxes appear.

■ If the Create New Link Bar dialog box does not appear, click **Create new** to display the dialog box.

6 Type a name for the new link bar.

7 Click **OK**.

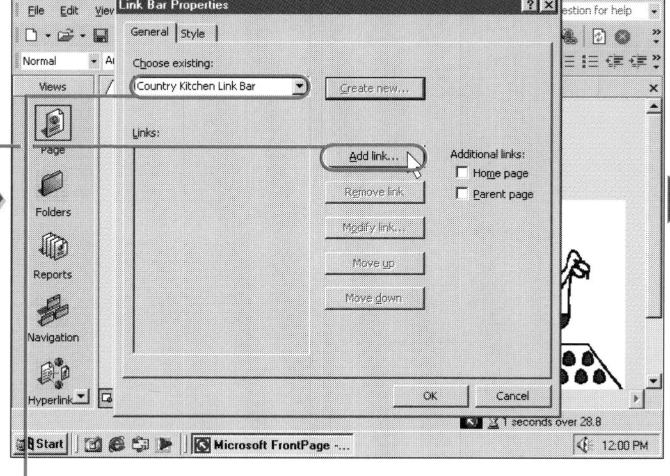

■ This area displays the name of the link bar you created and named.

8 Click **Add link** to add a link to the link bar.

■ The Add to Link Bar dialog box appears.

CONTINUED

You can specify the text you want a link to display on a link bar.

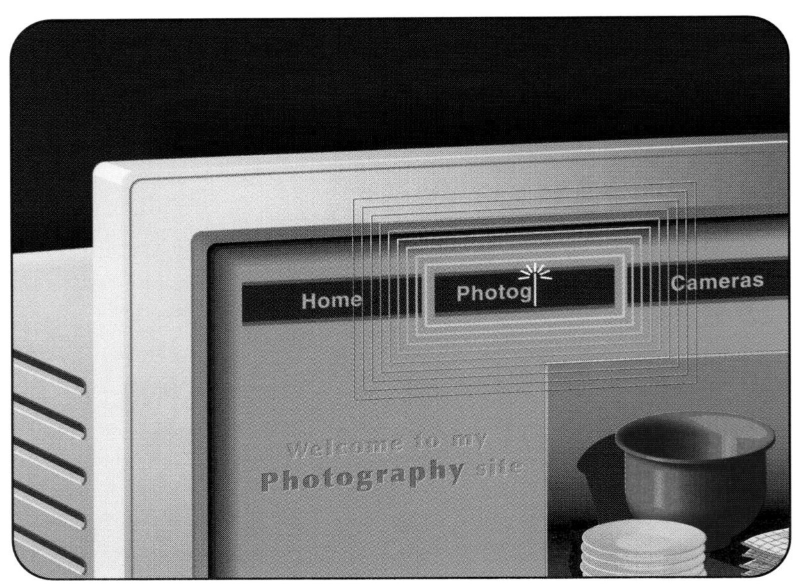

If you do not specify text for a link, FrontPage will use the file name of the linked Web page to label the link.

Make sure you specify text for a link that will clearly indicate where the link will take your visitors.

ADD A LINK BAR (CONTINUED)

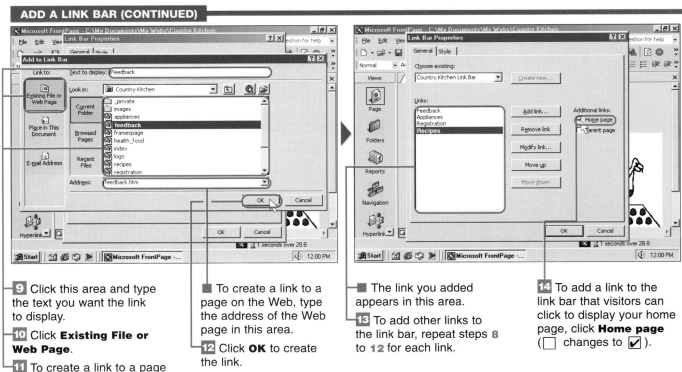

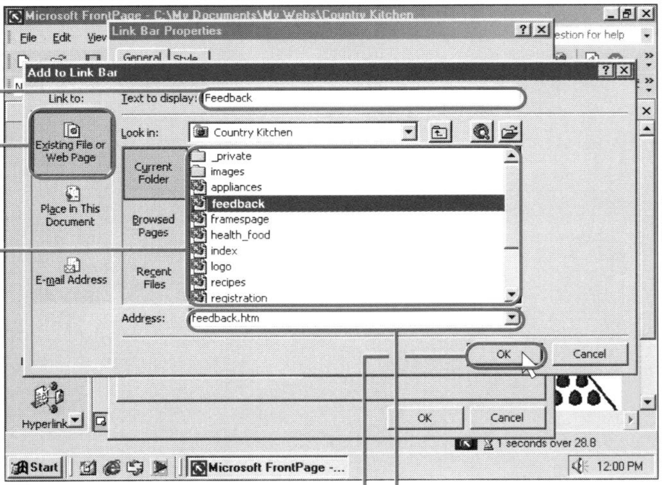

9 Click this area and type the text you want the link to display.

10 Click **Existing File or Web Page**.

11 To create a link to a page in your current Web site, click the Web page ( ) in this area.

■ To create a link to a page on the Web, type the address of the Web page in this area.

12 Click **OK** to create the link.

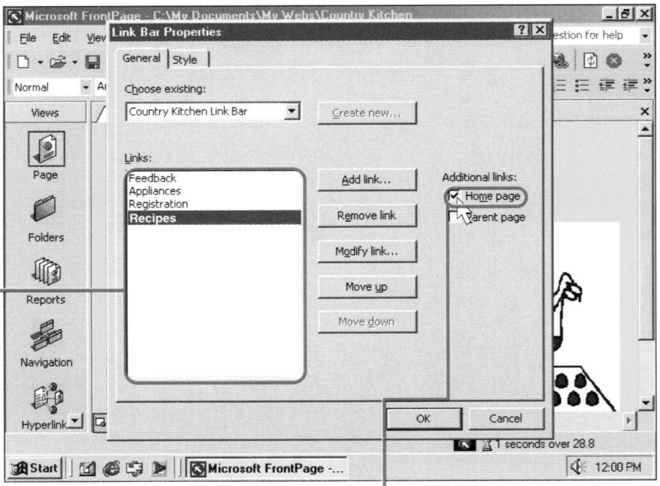

■ The link you added appears in this area.

13 To add other links to the link bar, repeat steps 8 to 12 for each link.

14 To add a link to the link bar that visitors can click to display your home page, click **Home page** (☐ changes to ☑).

Can I add the same link bar to other pages in my Web site?

You can add the same link bar to other pages in your Web site if you selected "Bar with custom links" or "Bar with back and next links" in step 4 on page 150.

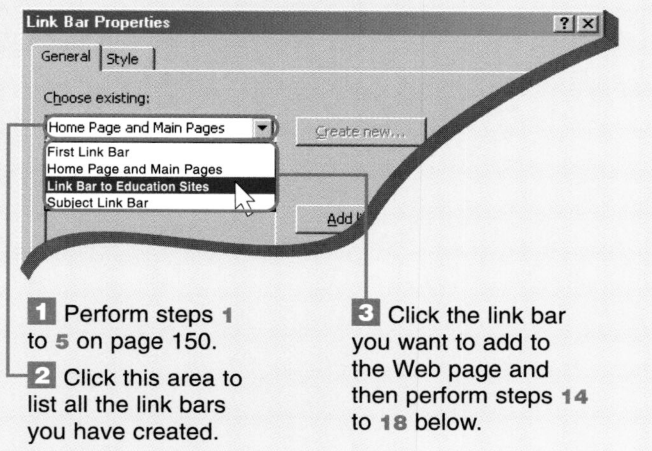

1 Perform steps 1 to 5 on page 150.

2 Click this area to list all the link bars you have created.

3 Click the link bar you want to add to the Web page and then perform steps 14 to 18 below.

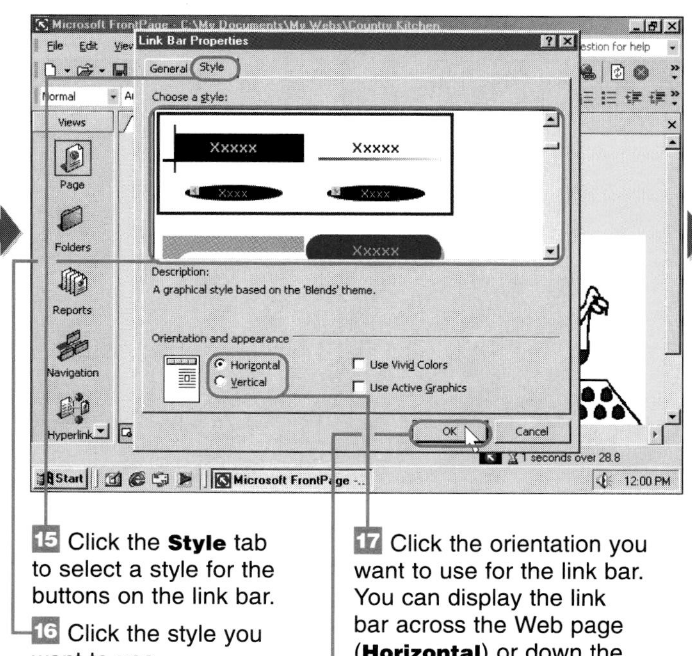

15 Click the **Style** tab to select a style for the buttons on the link bar.

16 Click the style you want to use.

17 Click the orientation you want to use for the link bar. You can display the link bar across the Web page (**Horizontal**) or down the page (**Vertical**).

18 Click **OK** to add the link bar to your Web page.

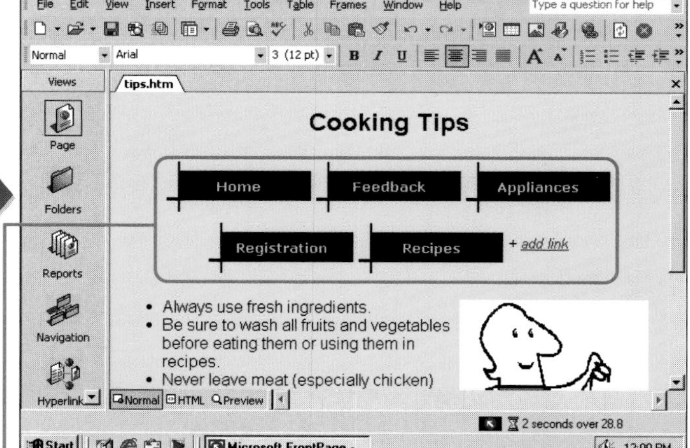

- The link bar appears.
- A visitor can click the links on the link bar to display the Web pages you specified.

Note: To test the link bar, you can use the Preview view. For information on the Preview view, see page 42.

- To make changes to a link bar, double-click the link bar and then perform steps 8 to 18.
- To remove a link bar, click the link bar and then press the Delete key.

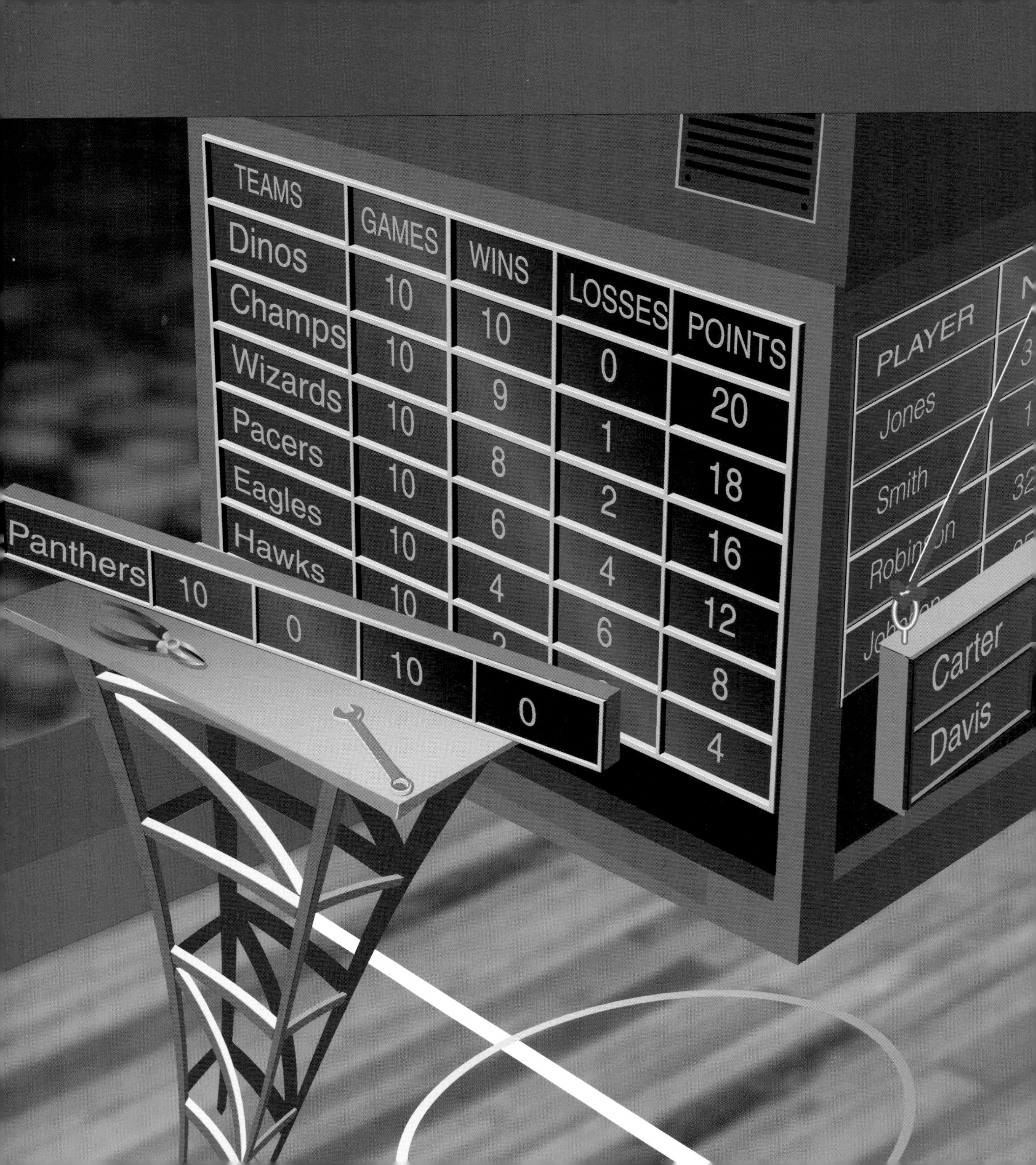

TEAMS
GAMES
WINS
LOSSES
POINTS
Dinos
Champs
Wizards
Pacers
Eagles
Hawks
10
10
10
10
10
10
10
10
9
8
6
4
0
1
2
4
6
20
18
16
12
8
4
Panthers
10
0
10
0
PLAYER
Jones
Smith
Carter
Davis

CHAPTER 9

Create Tables

Do you want to use tables to organize information on your Web pages? Find out how in this chapter.

ADD A TABLE

You can add a table to neatly display information, such as product information or a timetable, on a Web page.

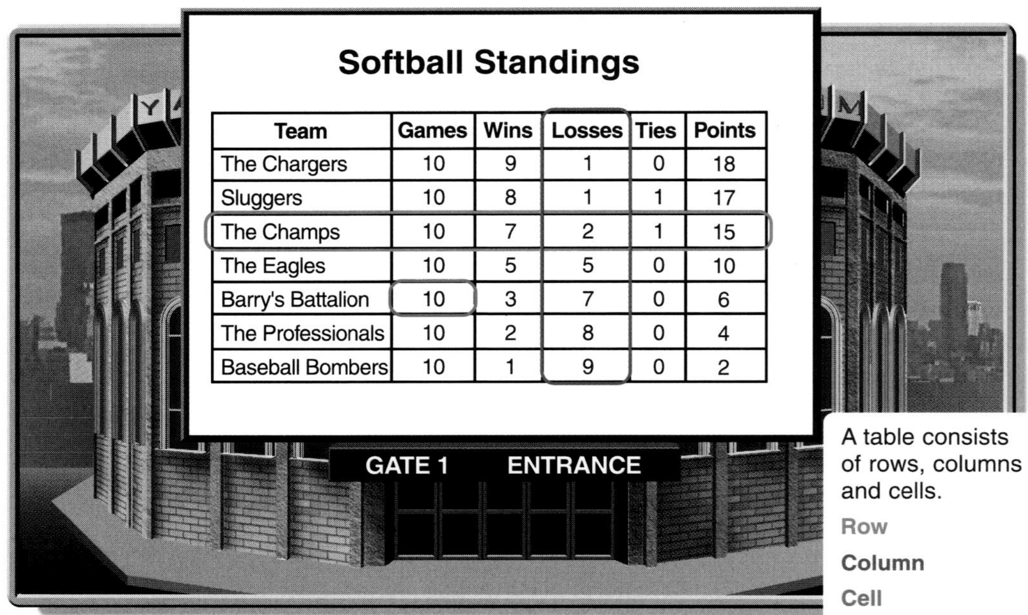

Softball Standings

Team	Games	Wins	Losses	Ties	Points
The Chargers	10	9	1	0	18
Sluggers	10	8	1	1	17
The Champs	10	7	2	1	15
The Eagles	10	5	5	0	10
Barry's Battalion	10	3	7	0	6
The Professionals	10	2	8	0	4
Baseball Bombers	10	1	9	0	2

A table consists of rows, columns and cells.

Row

Column

Cell

ADD A TABLE

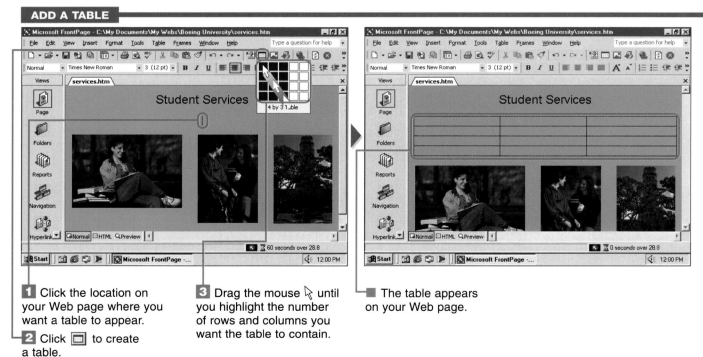

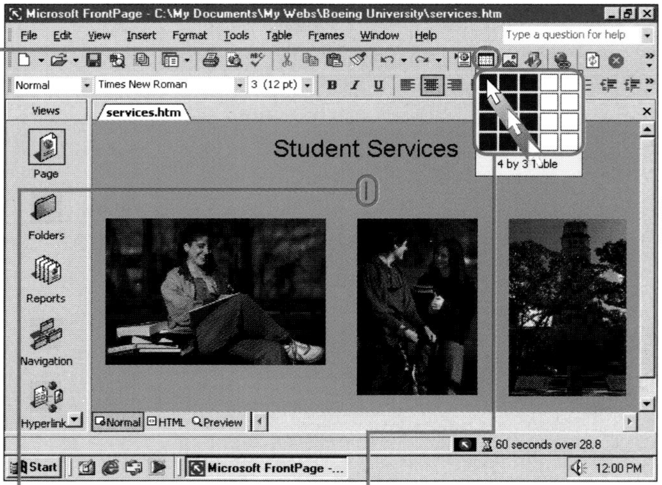

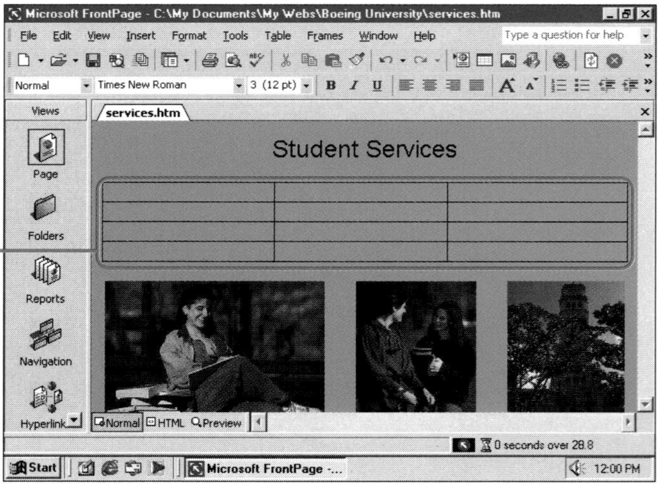

1 Click the location on your Web page where you want a table to appear.

2 Click ▦ to create a table.

3 Drag the mouse ↖ until you highlight the number of rows and columns you want the table to contain.

■ The table appears on your Web page.

What other ways can I use a table on a Web page?

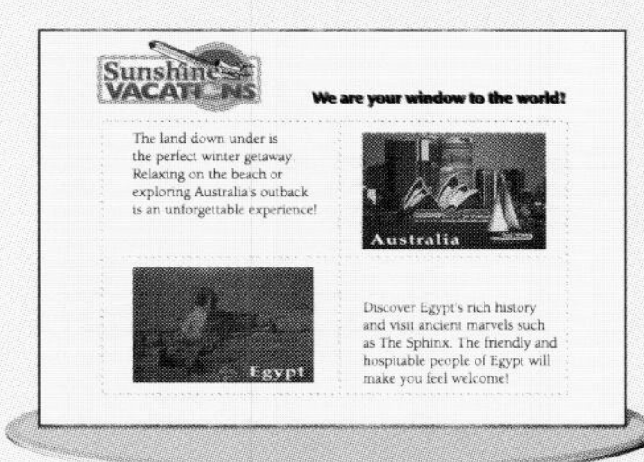

Create Newspaper Columns

You can use tables to present information in columns like those found in a newspaper. For example, to display information in three newspaper columns, you can create a table with one row that contains three cells.

Control Web Page Layout

Tables are useful for controlling the placement of text and images on a Web page. For example, to neatly position two paragraphs and two images, you can create a table with two rows and two columns.

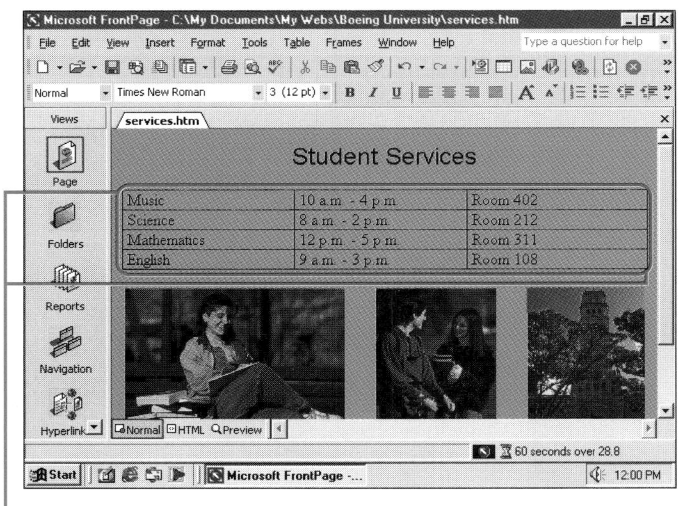

ENTER TEXT IN A TABLE

1 Click the cell where you want to enter text. Then type the text.

2 Repeat step 1 until you finish entering all the text for the table.

Note: You can format text in a table as you would format any text on a Web page. For example, you can change the alignment, font, size and color of text in a table. To format text, see pages 68 to 72.

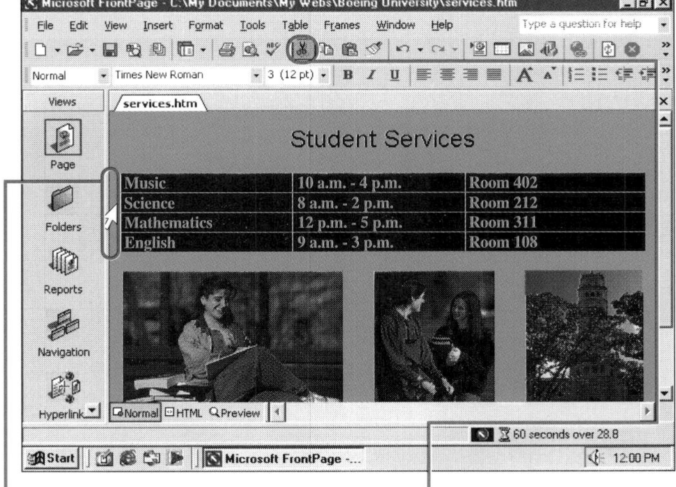

DELETE A TABLE

1 Position the mouse I to the left of the table you want to delete (I changes to ↗). Then double-click to select the table.

2 Click ✂ to delete the table.

■ The table disappears from your Web page.

ADD OR DELETE A ROW OR COLUMN

You can add a row or column to a table to insert additional information. You can also delete a row or column that you no longer want to display in a table.

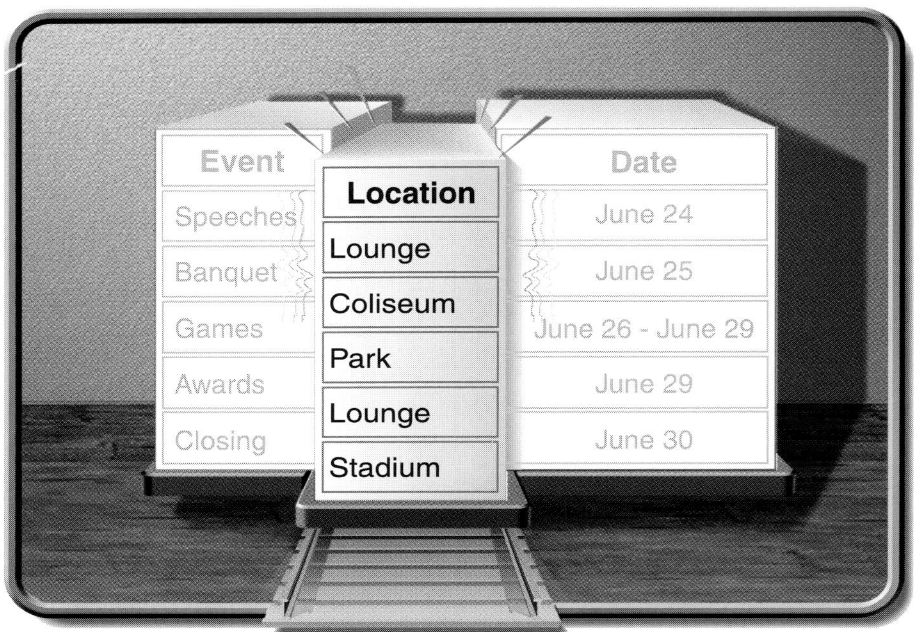

ADD A ROW OR COLUMN

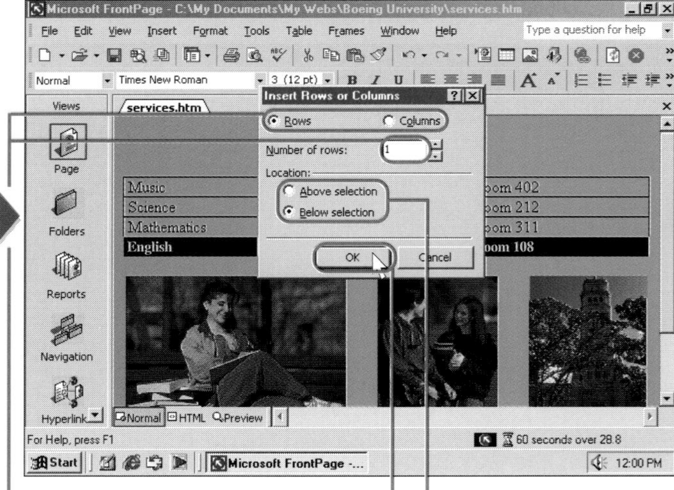

1 Position the mouse I to the left of the row or above the column where you want to add a new row or column (I changes to ➞ or ⬇). Then click to select the row or column.

2 Click **Table**.

3 Click **Insert**.

4 Click **Rows or Columns**.

■ The Insert Rows or Columns dialog box appears.

5 Click an option to add a row or column to the table (○ changes to ⊙).

6 To add more than one row or column, double-click the number in this area and type the number of rows or columns you want to add.

7 Click an option to specify where you want to add the row or column (○ changes to ⊙).

Note: The available options depend on whether you are adding a row or column.

8 Click **OK**.

How can I quickly add a row to the bottom of a table?

To quickly add a row to the bottom of a table, click in the bottom right cell in the table. Then press the Tab key.

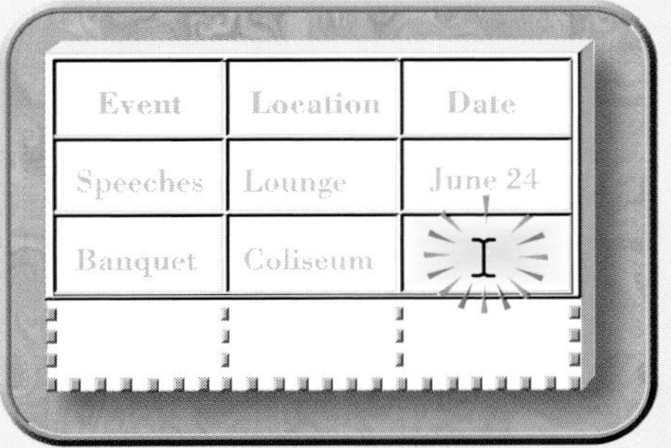

Can I delete the information in a row or column without removing the row or column from a table?

Yes. To select the cells in a table that contain the information you want to delete, drag the mouse I over the cells until the cells are highlighted. Press the Delete key to remove the information.

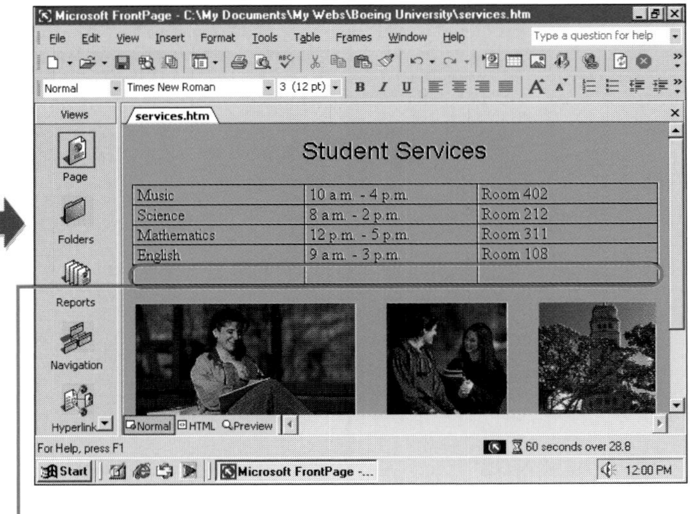

■ The new row or column appears in your table.

■ To deselect a row or column, click outside the table.

DELETE A ROW OR COLUMN

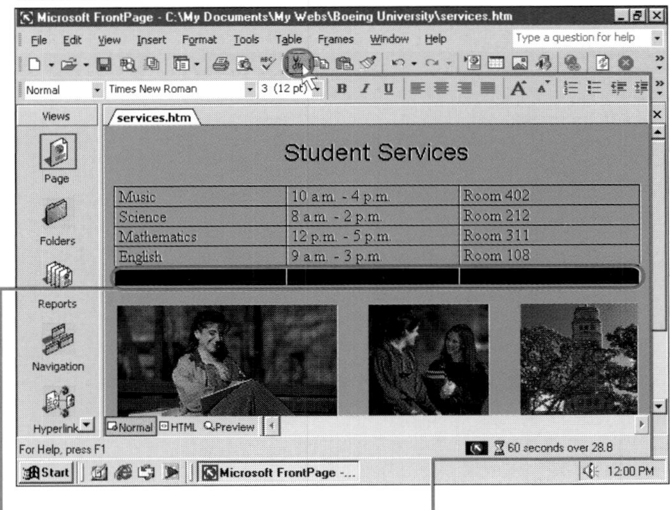

1 Position the mouse I to the left of the row or above the column you want to delete (I changes to ➡ or ⬇). Then click to select the row or column.

2 Click ✂ to delete the row or column you selected.

■ The row or column disappears from your table.

CHANGE ROW HEIGHT OR COLUMN WIDTH

You can change the height of rows and the width of columns to improve the layout of a table.

CHANGE ROW HEIGHT

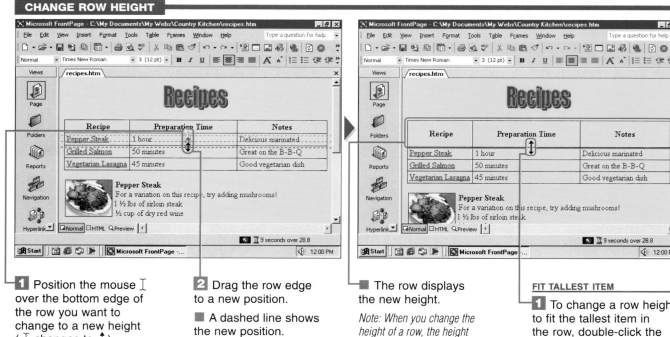

1 Position the mouse I over the bottom edge of the row you want to change to a new height (I changes to ↕).

2 Drag the row edge to a new position.

■ A dashed line shows the new position.

■ The row displays the new height.

Note: When you change the height of a row, the height of the entire table changes.

FIT TALLEST ITEM

1 To change a row height to fit the tallest item in the row, double-click the bottom edge of the row.

Can FrontPage automatically adjust the row height and column width?

When you enter text in a table, FrontPage automatically increases the row height or column width to accommodate the text you type.

Can I make the row height or column width any size?

You can make the row height or column width any size you want. However, FrontPage will not allow you to make a row or column too small to display the text or image in a cell.

CHANGE COLUMN WIDTH

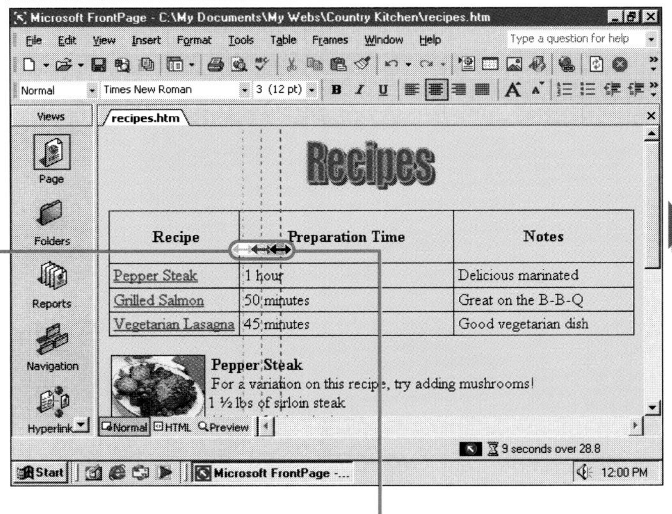

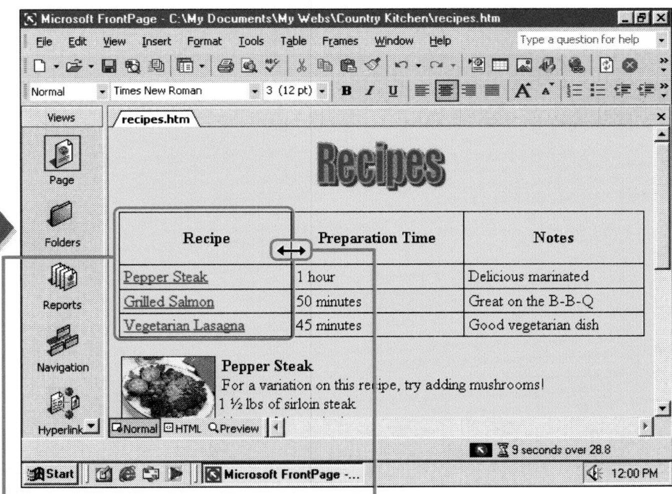

1 Position the mouse I over the right edge of the column you want to change to a new width (I changes to ↔).

2 Drag the column edge to a new position.

- A dashed line shows the new position.

- The column displays the new width.

Note: When you change the width of a column, the width of a neighboring column also changes. When you change the width of the last column, the width of the entire table changes.

FIT LONGEST ITEM

1 To change a column width to fit the longest item in the column, double-click the right edge of the column.

ADD A CAPTION TO A TABLE

You can add a caption to a table to provide a title or a description for the table.

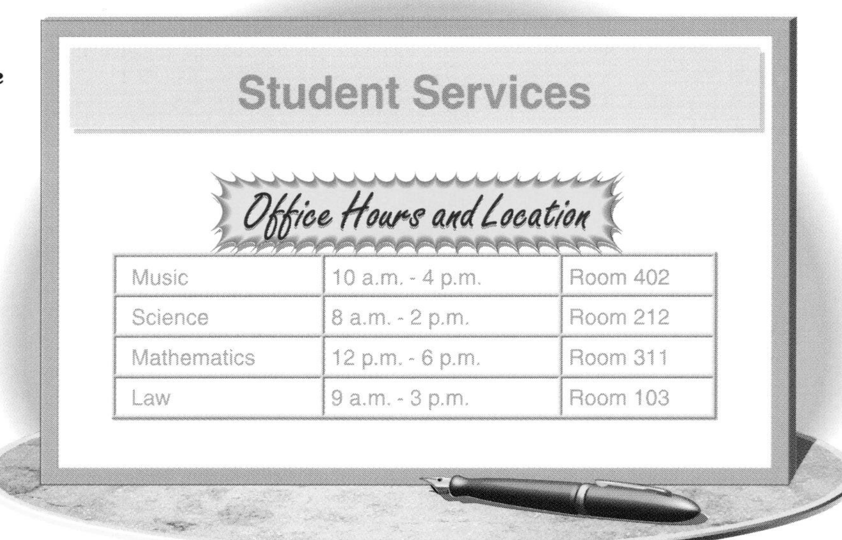

Captions automatically appear centered at the top of a table.

ADD A CAPTION TO A TABLE

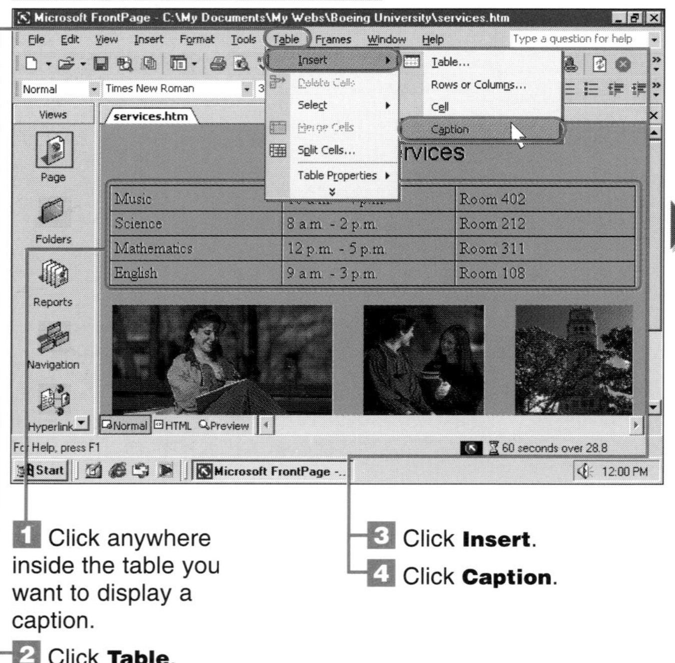

1 Click anywhere inside the table you want to display a caption.

2 Click **Table**.

3 Click **Insert**.

4 Click **Caption**.

■ A flashing insertion point appears above the table.

5 Type the caption you want the table to display.

Note: You can format the caption as you would format any text on a Web page. To format text, see pages 68 to 75.

■ To delete a caption, drag the mouse I over the caption until you highlight the caption. Then press the Delete key twice.

COMBINE CELLS

You can combine two or more cells in a table to make one large cell. This is useful if you want to display a title across the top or down the side of a table.

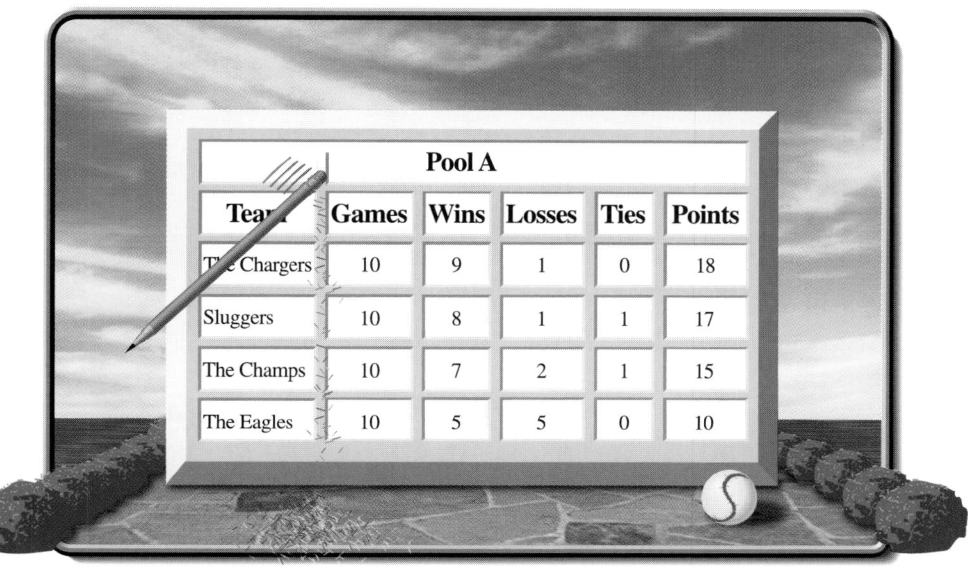

Pool A
Team
Games
Wins
Losses
Ties
Points
The Chargers
10
9
1
0
18
Sluggers
10
8
1
1
17
The Champs
10
7
2
1
15
The Eagles
10
5
5
0
10

COMBINE CELLS

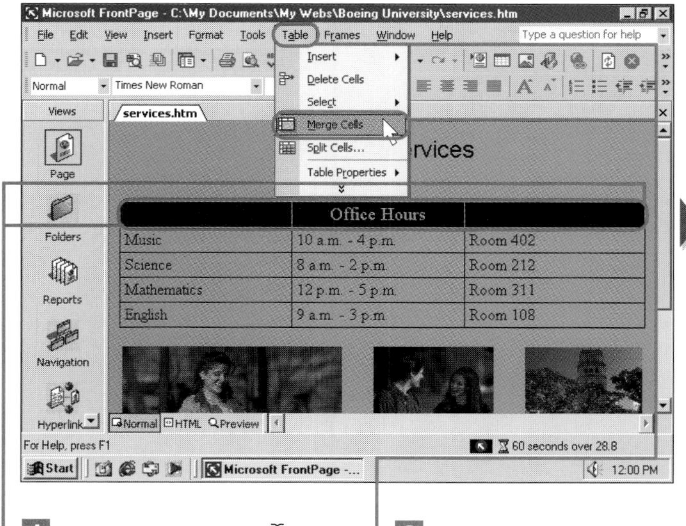

1 Position the mouse I over the first cell you want to merge with other cells.

2 Drag the mouse I until you highlight all the cells you want to merge.

3 Click **Table**.

4 Click **Merge Cells**.

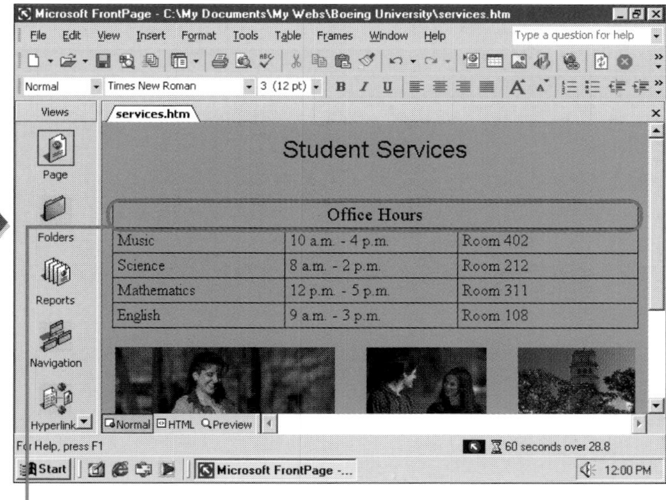

■ The cells combine to create one large cell.

■ To deselect cells in a table, click outside the table.

SPLIT CELLS

You can split one cell in a table into two or more cells.

Splitting cells is useful if you accidentally combined two or more cells or if you are using a table to control the placement of text and images on a Web page. For information on combining cells in a table, see page 163.

SPLIT CELLS

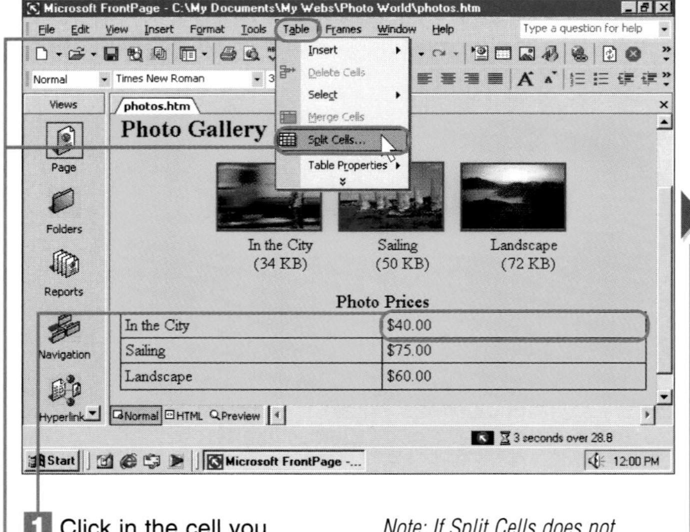

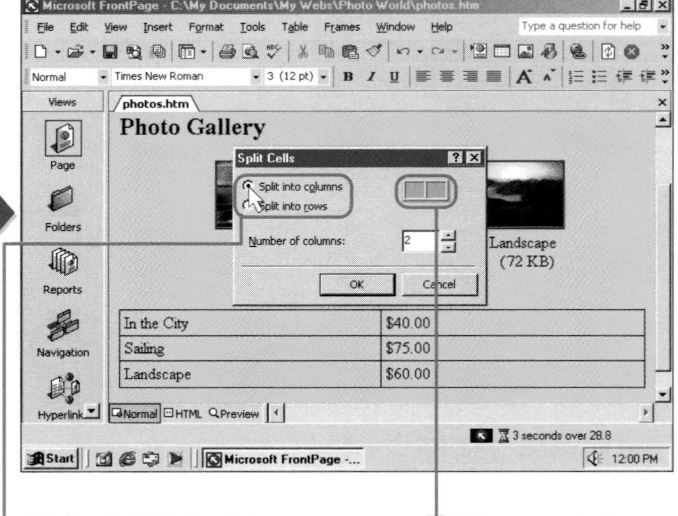

1 Click in the cell you want to split into two or more cells.

2 Click **Table**.

3 Click **Split Cells**.

Note: If Split Cells does not appear on the menu, position the mouse over the bottom of the menu to display all the menu options.

■ The Split Cells dialog box appears.

4 Click an option to split the cell into columns or rows (○ changes to ⊙).

■ This area displays a preview of how the cell will appear.

How can I split cells in a table?

You can split cells into columns or rows.

Columns

Splitting a cell into columns does not change the height of other cells in the same row.

Rows

Splitting a cell into rows increases the height of other cells in the same row.

Can I split more than one cell at a time?

Yes. To split more than one cell at a time, drag the mouse over the cells until you highlight all the cells you want to split. Then perform steps 2 to 6 below.

First Name	Position
John	President
Linda	Vice President
Ken	Director
Deborah	Customer Service

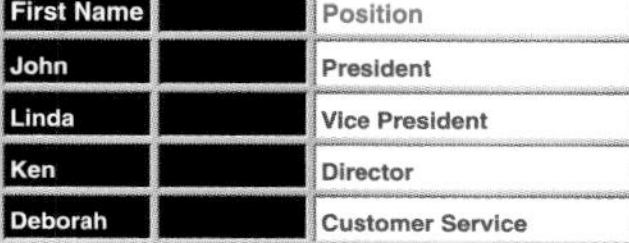

First Name		Position
John		President
Linda		Vice President
Ken		Director
Deborah		Customer Service

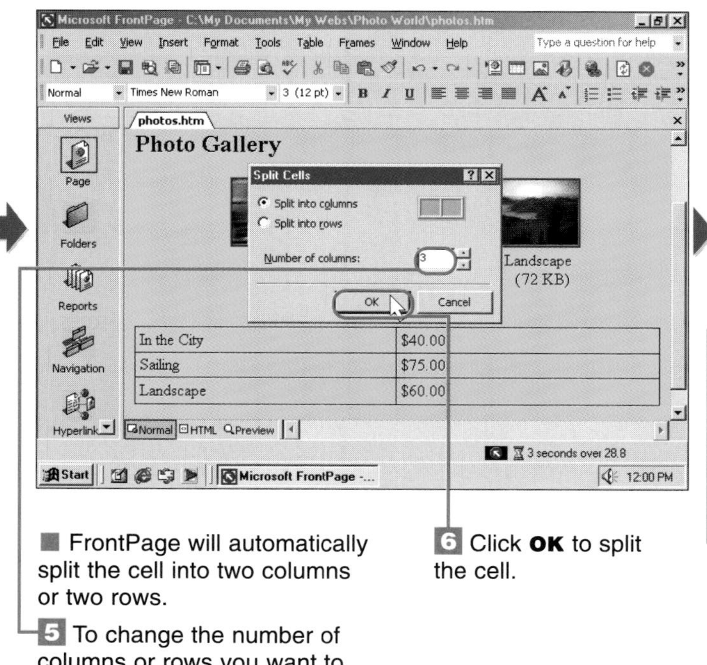

■ FrontPage will automatically split the cell into two columns or two rows.

5 To change the number of columns or rows you want to split the cell into, double-click the number in this area and then type a new number.

6 Click **OK** to split the cell.

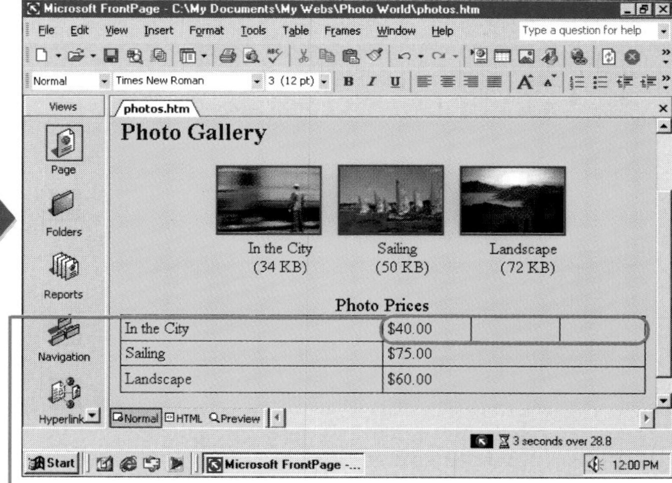

■ The cell splits into the number of columns or rows you specified.

COPY CELL CONTENTS

You can save time by copying information from one cell in a table to other cells in the same row or column.

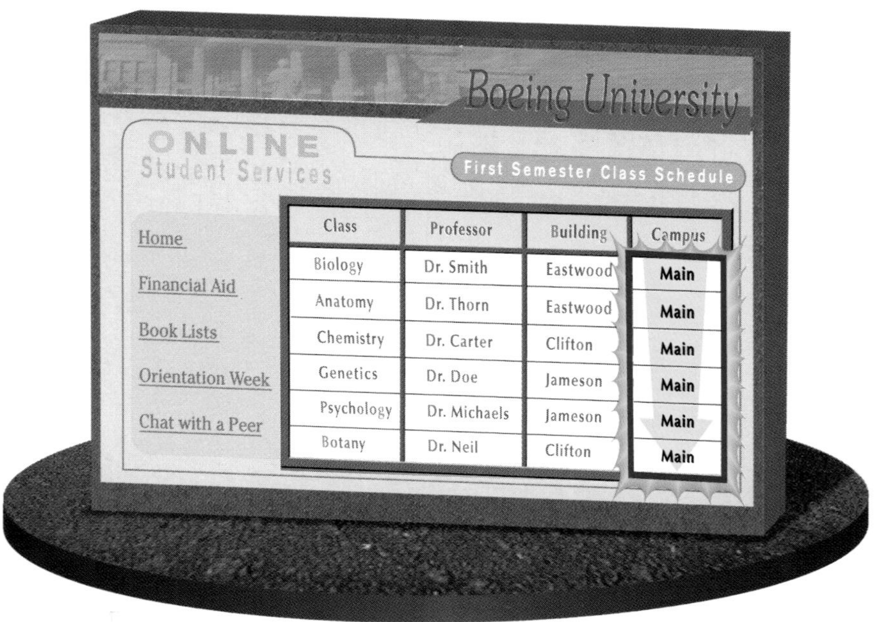

COPY CELL CONTENTS

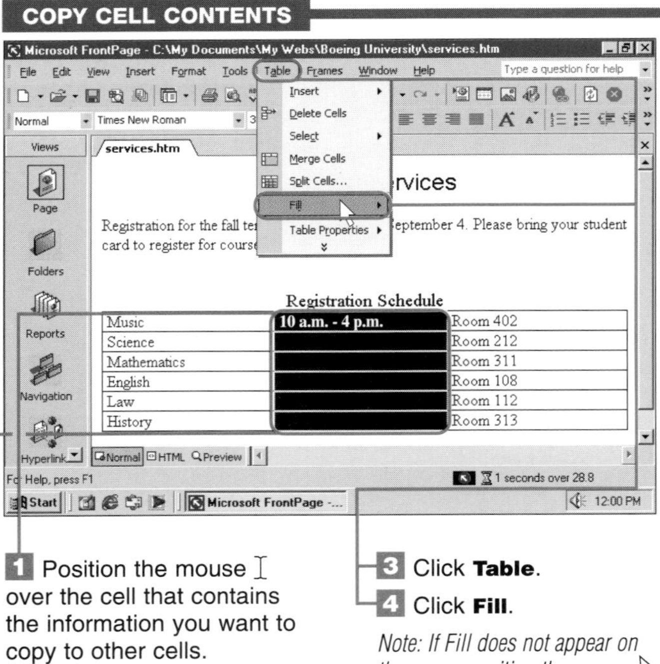

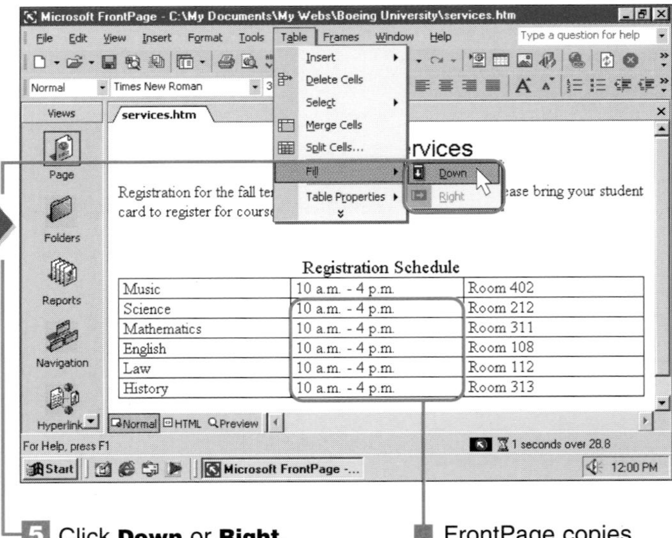

1 Position the mouse I over the cell that contains the information you want to copy to other cells.

2 Drag the mouse I until you highlight all the cells in the row or column you want to copy the information to.

3 Click **Table**.

4 Click **Fill**.

Note: If Fill does not appear on the menu, position the mouse over the bottom of the menu to display all the menu options.

5 Click **Down** or **Right**.

Note: The available option depends on whether you selected cells in a row or column.

- FrontPage copies the information to the cells you selected.

- To deselect cells in a table, click outside the table.

ADD COLOR TO CELLS

You can add color to cells in a table to enhance the appearance of the table.

After you add color to cells, you may want to change the color of the text in the table. To do so, see page 72.

ADD COLOR TO CELLS

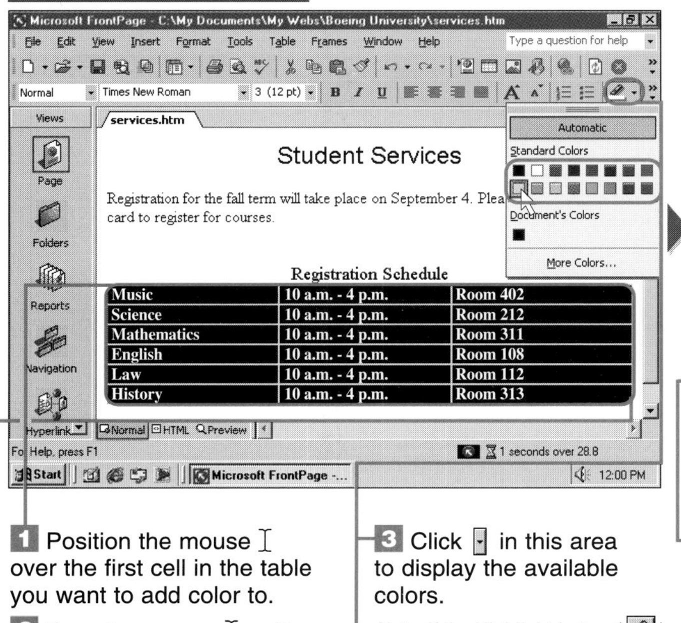

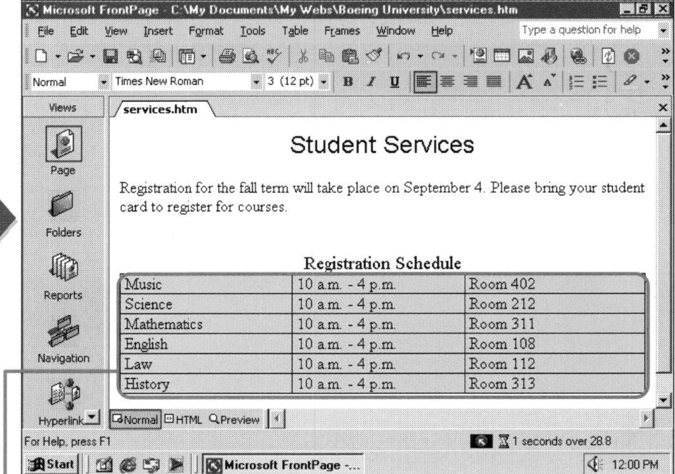

1 Position the mouse I over the first cell in the table you want to add color to.

2 Drag the mouse I until you highlight all the cells you want to add color to.

3 Click ▾ in this area to display the available colors.

Note: If the Highlight button ( ) is not displayed, click » on the Formatting toolbar to display all the buttons.

4 Click the color you want to use.

■ The cells in the table display the color you selected.

■ To deselect cells in a table, click outside the table.

■ To remove color from cells in a table, repeat steps 1 to 4, selecting **Automatic** in step 4.

CHANGE TABLE BORDER

You can change the size of the border that surrounds a table. You can also change the color of the border.

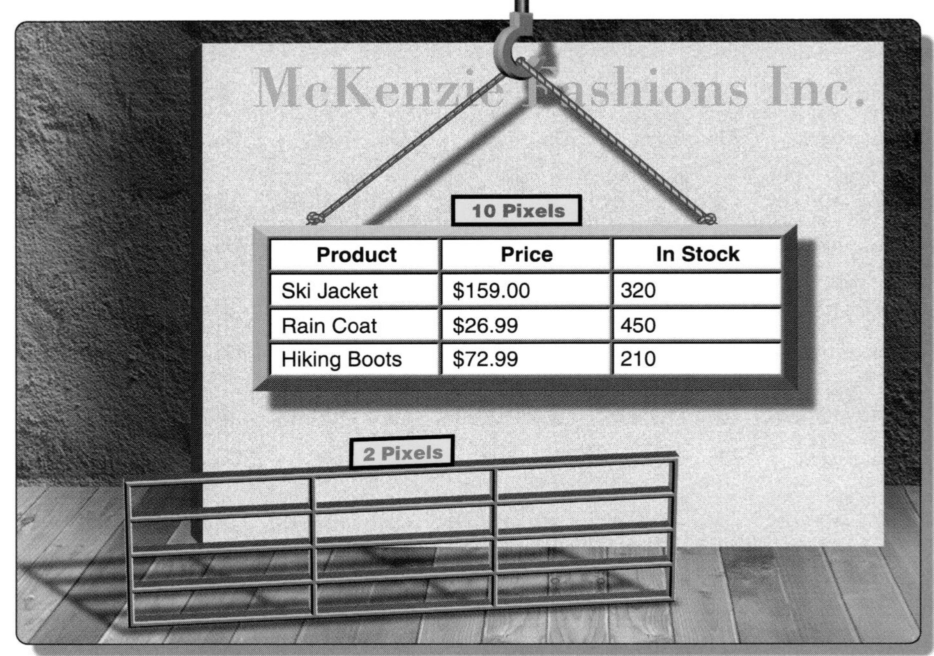

Product	Price	In Stock
Ski Jacket	$159.00	320
Rain Coat	$26.99	450
Hiking Boots	$72.99	210

CHANGE TABLE BORDER

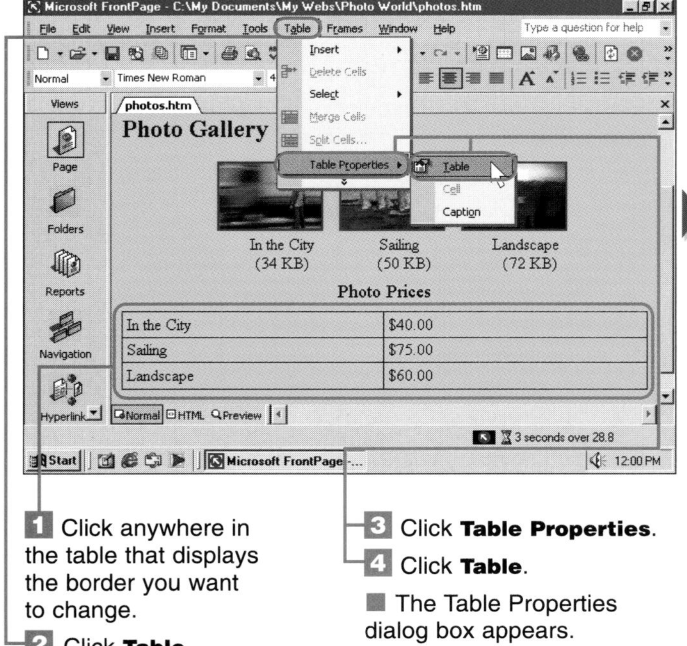

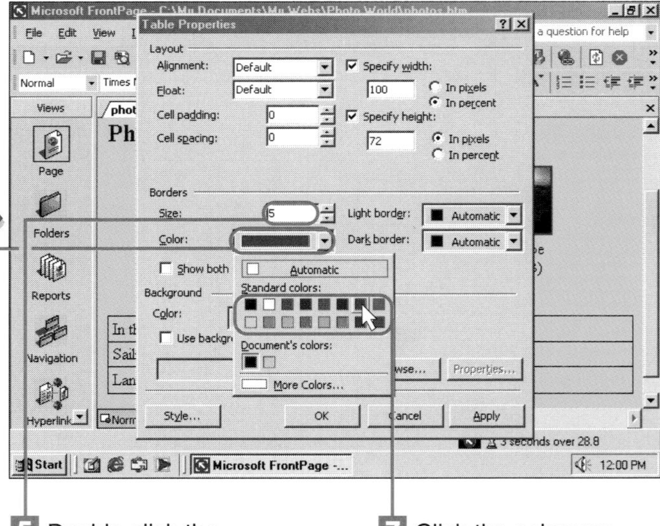

1 Click anywhere in the table that displays the border you want to change.

2 Click **Table**.

3 Click **Table Properties**.

4 Click **Table**.

■ The Table Properties dialog box appears.

5 Double-click the number in this area and then type the size you want to use for the border.

6 To select a color for the border, click this area to display the available colors.

7 Click the color you want to use.

Note: If you added a theme to your Web pages, you will not be able to change the color of the border. For information on themes, see page 88.

How do I specify the size of a border around a table?

You can specify the size of a border around a table in pixels. A pixel is a dot on a computer screen. The word "pixel" comes from **pic**ture **el**ement.

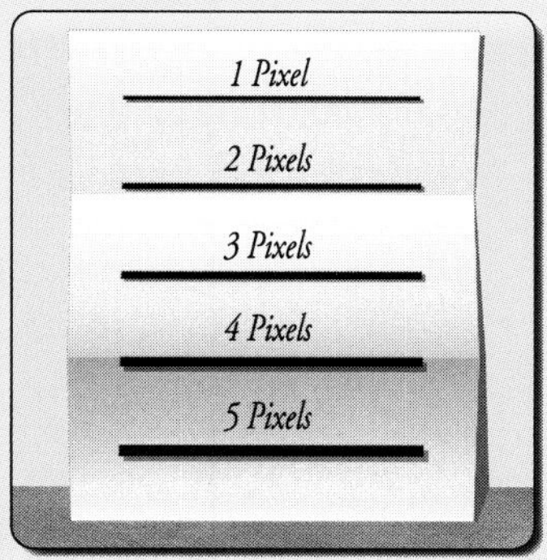

Can I remove a border from a table?

Yes. When you are using a table to organize information on a Web page, you can remove the border to make the table invisible. To remove the border from a table, use a border size of **0** in step **5** below. The border will appear as a dotted line while you are editing the Web page but will not appear when you publish your Web pages.

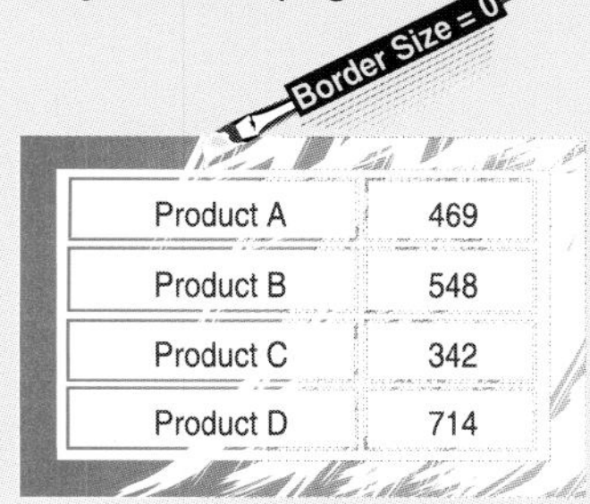

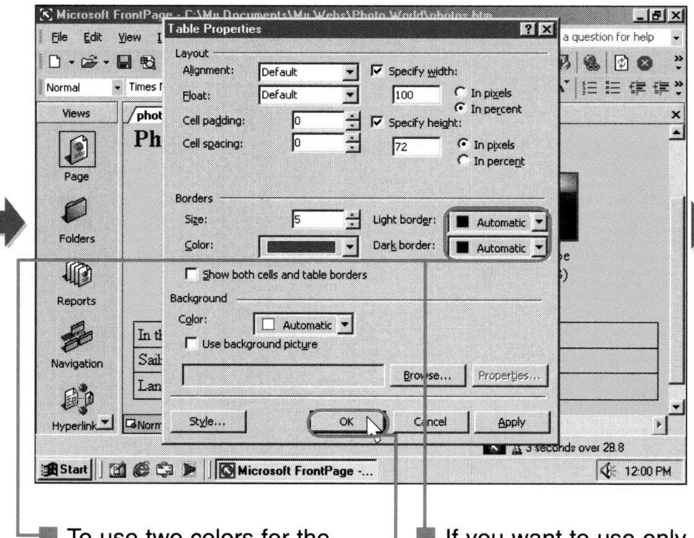

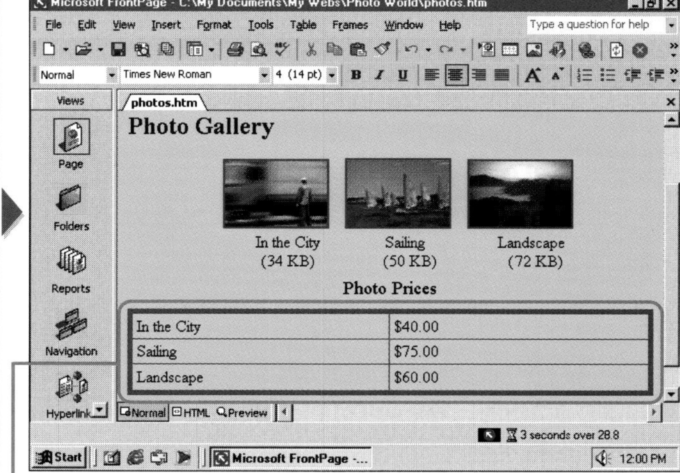

■ To use two colors for the border to give the table a three-dimensional appearance, you can click these areas to select a light and dark border color.

Note: Some Web browsers cannot display a table border with two colors.

■ If you want to use only one color for the border, make sure these options are set to **Automatic**.

8 Click **OK** to confirm your changes.

■ The table displays the border size and color you selected.

■ To return to the original border size, repeat steps **1** to **5**, typing **1** in step **5**. Then perform step **8**.

ADD AN IMAGE TO A TABLE

You can add an image to a cell in a table. For example, you can add photographs of products or pictures of your favorite celebrities.

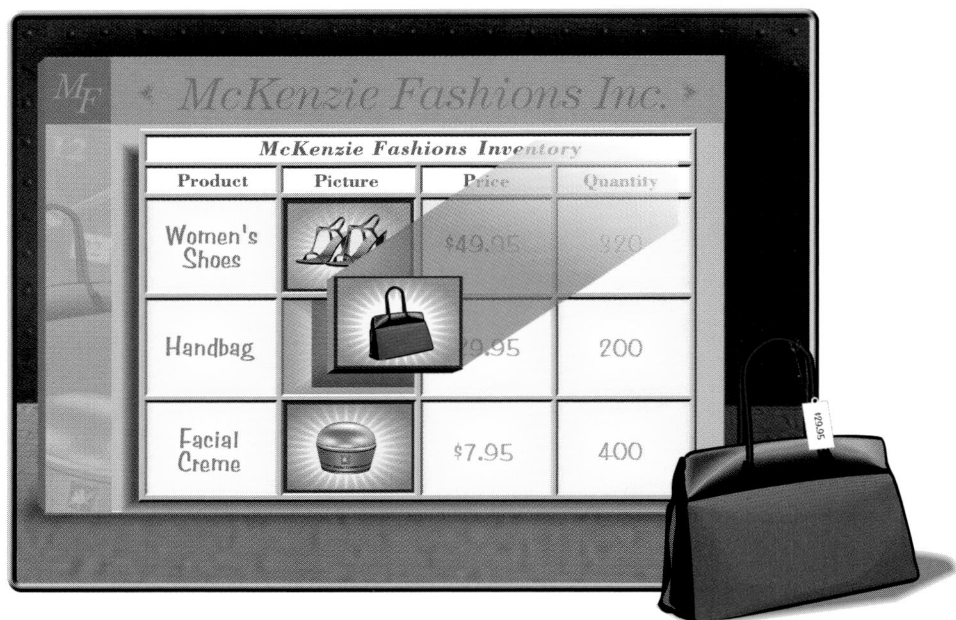

ADD AN IMAGE TO A TABLE

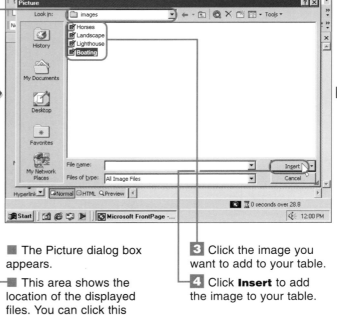

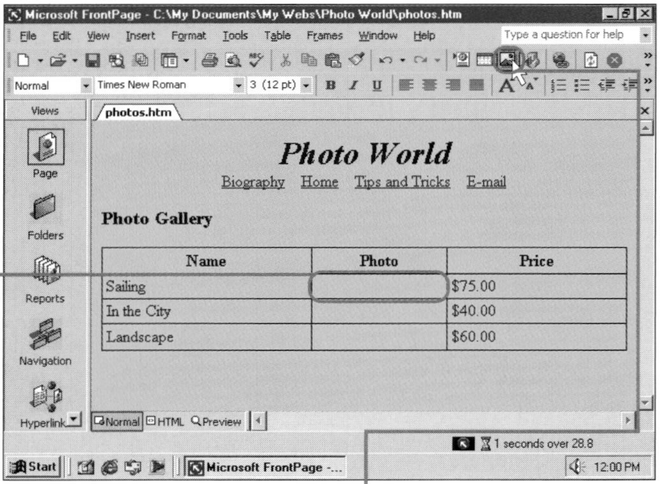

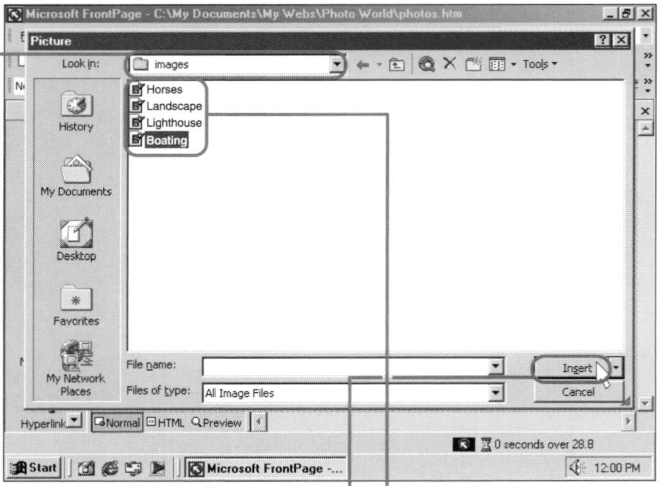

1 Click the cell in the table where you want to add an image.

2 Click the Insert Picture button to add an image.

■ The Picture dialog box appears.

■ This area shows the location of the displayed files. You can click this area to change the location.

3 Click the image you want to add to your table.

4 Click **Insert** to add the image to your table.

When would I add an image to a table?

Tables allow you to control the placement of images and text on a Web page. For example, to neatly position two images and two paragraphs, you can add the images and text to a table with two rows and two columns. When you use a table to organize information on a Web page, you may want to remove the border of the table to make the table invisible. To remove the border from a table, see the top of page 169.

What should I consider when adding images to a table?

Adding large images to a table increases the time a Web page takes to transfer to a visitor's computer. To reduce the time a Web page takes to transfer, you may want to display the images as thumbnail images. For information on thumbnail images, see page 128.

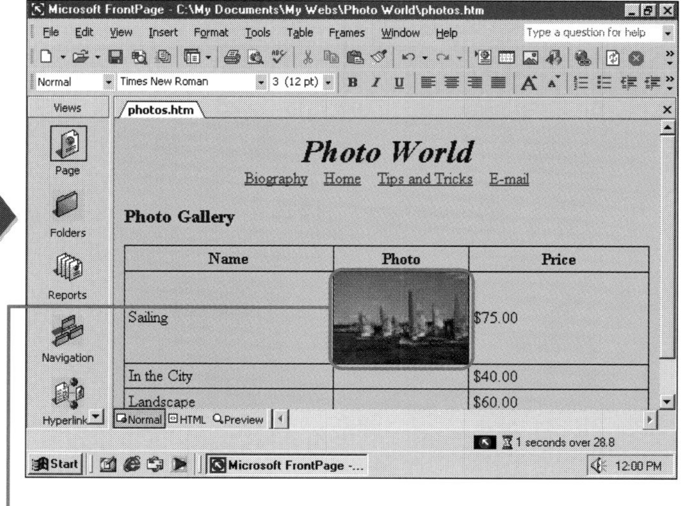

■ The image appears in your table.

■ FrontPage changes the size of the cell to accommodate the image. To resize an image, see page 105.

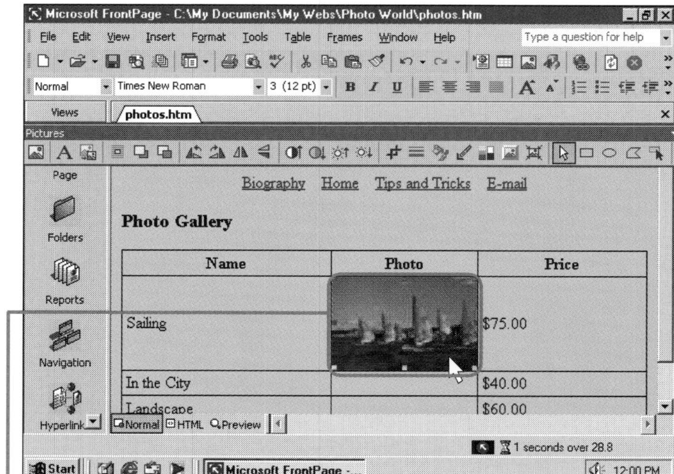

DELETE AN IMAGE FROM A TABLE

1 Click the image you want to delete. Handles (■) appear around the image.

2 Press the Delete key to delete the image.

CHANGE CELL PADDING AND SPACING

You can change the amount of space around the contents of cells and between cells in a table.

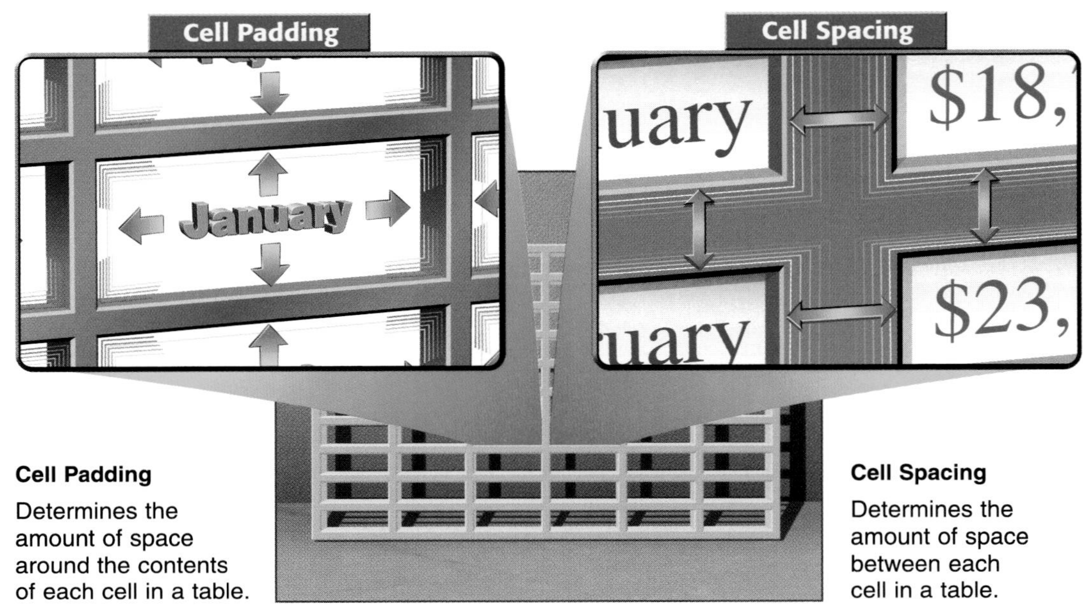

Cell Padding

Determines the amount of space around the contents of each cell in a table.

Cell Spacing

Determines the amount of space between each cell in a table.

CHANGE CELL PADDING AND SPACING

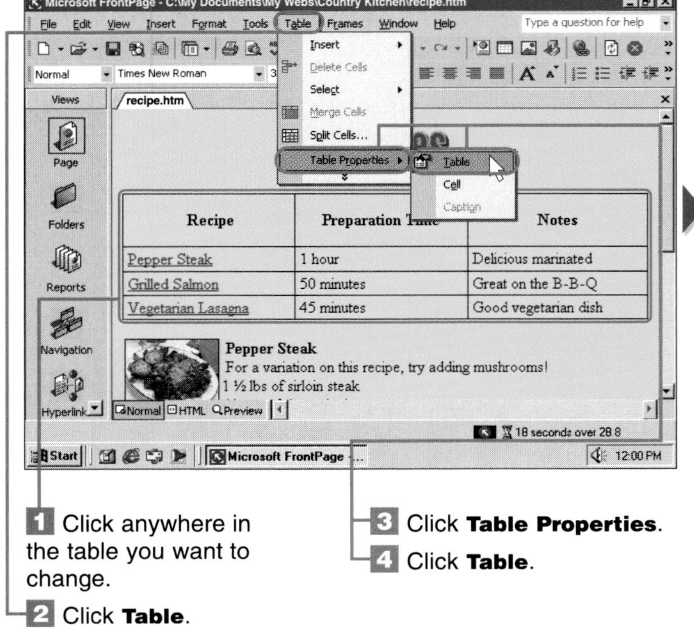

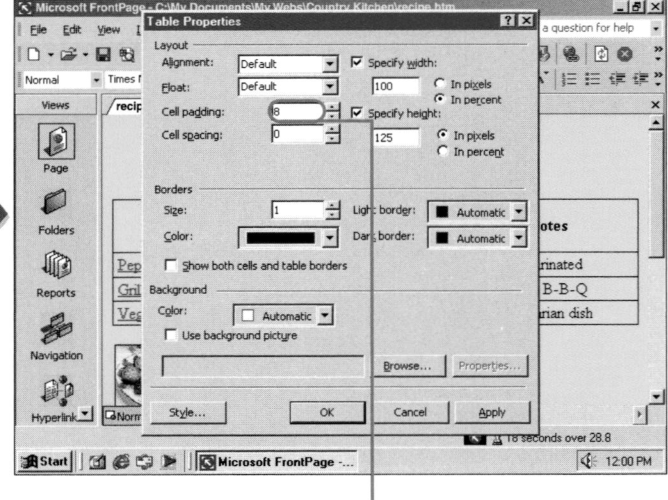

1 Click anywhere in the table you want to change.

2 Click **Table**.

3 Click **Table Properties**.

4 Click **Table**.

■ The Table Properties dialog box appears.

5 To change the amount of space around the contents of each cell, double-click the number in this area and then type a number for the amount of space in pixels.

When would I change the cell padding or spacing in a table?

You may want to change the cell padding or spacing in a table to improve the layout and readability of text in the table. If you are using a table to control the placement of text and images on a Web page, you may want to change the cell padding or spacing to adjust the amount of space that appears between the text and images.

Can I change the cell padding or spacing for one cell in a table?

No. When you change the cell padding or spacing in a table, FrontPage changes every cell in the table. You cannot change the cell padding or spacing for just one cell.

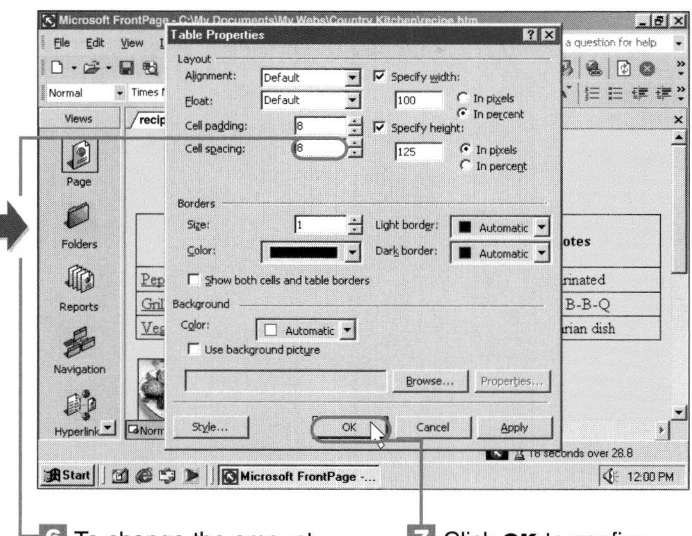

6 To change the amount of space between each cell, double-click the number in this area and then type a number for the amount of space in pixels.

7 Click **OK** to confirm your changes.

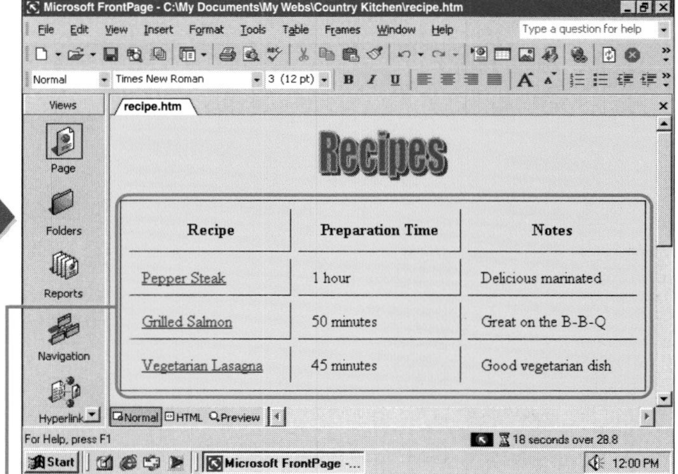

■ The table displays the cell padding and spacing you specified.

■ To return the cell padding and spacing in a table to the original settings, repeat steps 1 to 7, typing **0** in steps 5 and 6.

FORMAT A TABLE

FrontPage offers many ready-to-use designs that you can choose from to give a table a new appearance.

FORMAT A TABLE

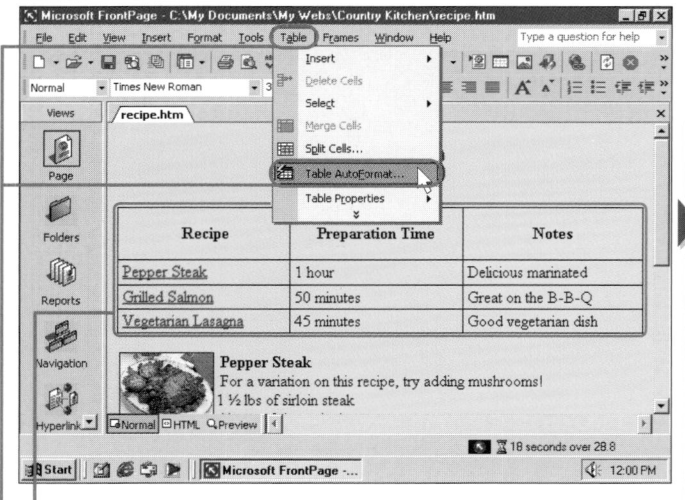

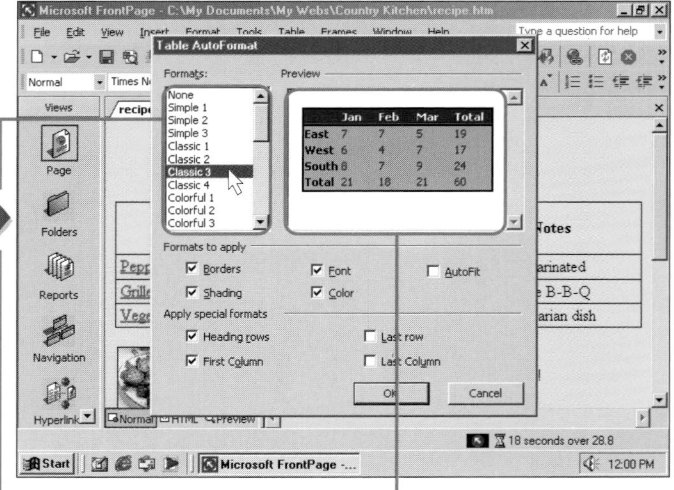

1 Click anywhere in the table you want to format.

2 Click **Table**.

3 Click **Table AutoFormat**.

Note: If Table AutoFormat does not appear on the menu, position the mouse over the bottom of the menu to display all the menu options.

■ The Table AutoFormat dialog box appears.

■ This area displays a list of the available table designs.

4 Click the table design you want to use.

■ This area displays a sample of the table design you selected.

Note: You can repeat step 4 to view a sample of a different table design.

What formatting options can I apply to a table?

The Table AutoFormat dialog box offers many options you can select to customize a table design. Some options will not change the appearance of some table designs.

Salesperson	January	February	March	Total
Joe	25	12	44	81
Dana	36	22	32	90
John	24	54	36	114
Marie	29	21	42	97
Total	114	109	154	1039

Heading Row · First Column · Last Column · Last Row

Formats

You can apply borders, shading, fonts and colors to a table. The AutoFit option changes the size of a table based on the amount of information in the table.

Special Formats

You can apply special formats to the heading row, the first column, the last row and the last column in a table.

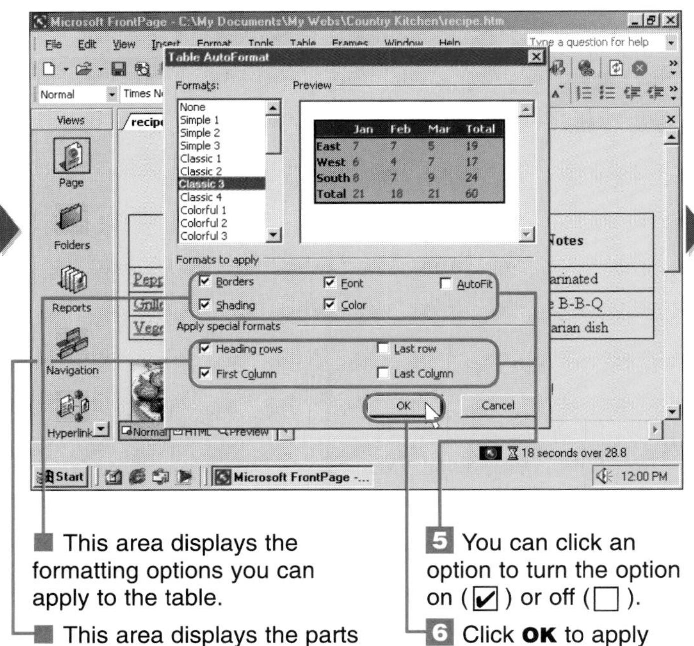

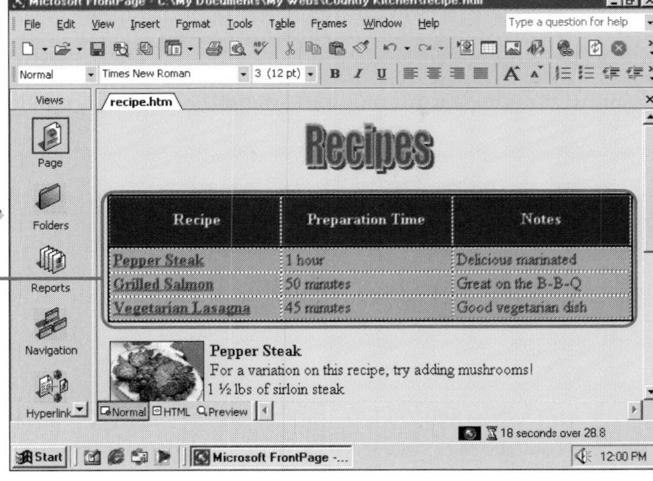

■ This area displays the formatting options you can apply to the table.

■ This area displays the parts of the table you can format.

■ A check mark (☑) beside an option indicates that FrontPage will apply the option to the table.

5 You can click an option to turn the option on (☑) or off (☐).

6 Click **OK** to apply the design to your table.

■ The table displays the design you selected.

■ To remove a table design, repeat steps 1 to 4, selecting **None** in step 4. Then perform step 6.

NAVIGATION VIEW

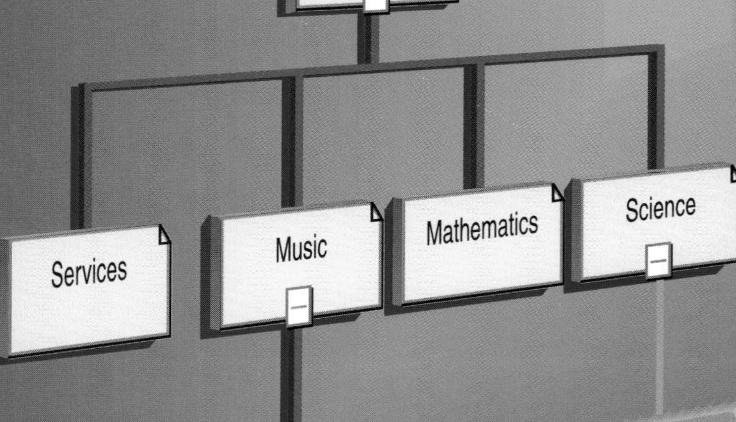
Home Page
Services
Music
Mathematics
Science
School Band
Science Fair
Navigation Buttons
to Appear on Web Pages

CHAPTER 10

Work With Navigational Structure

Are you wondering how to arrange the Web pages in your Web site? This chapter shows you how to build the structure of your Web site.

USING THE NAVIGATION VIEW

You can use the Navigation view to work with the navigational structure of your Web site.

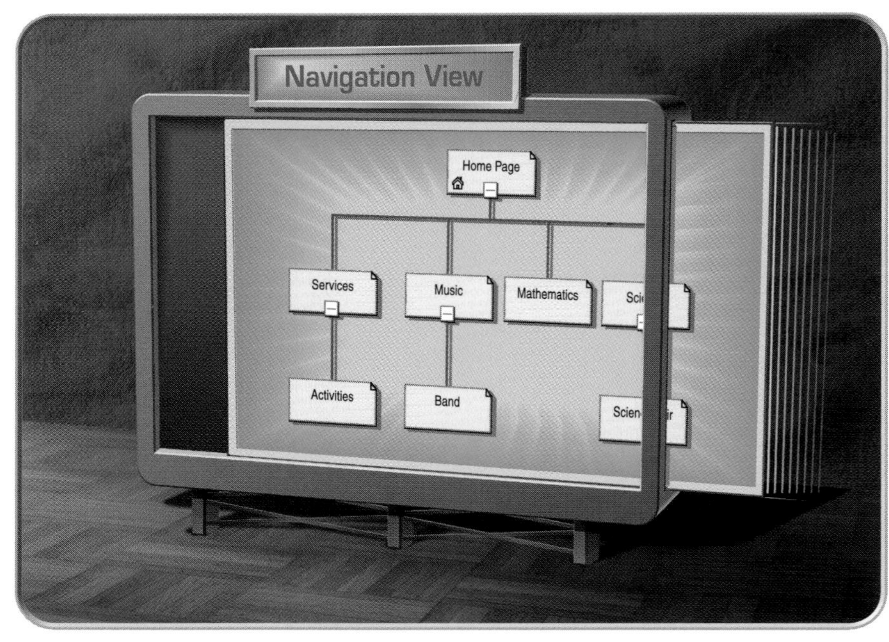

The Navigation view shows how the Web pages in your Web site are related.

USING THE NAVIGATION VIEW

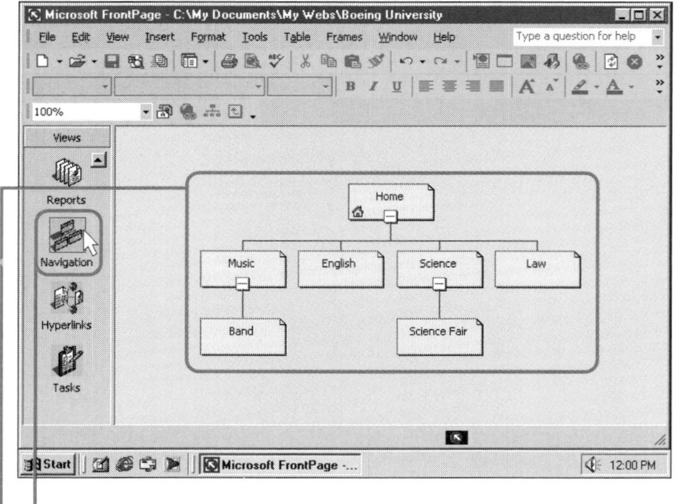

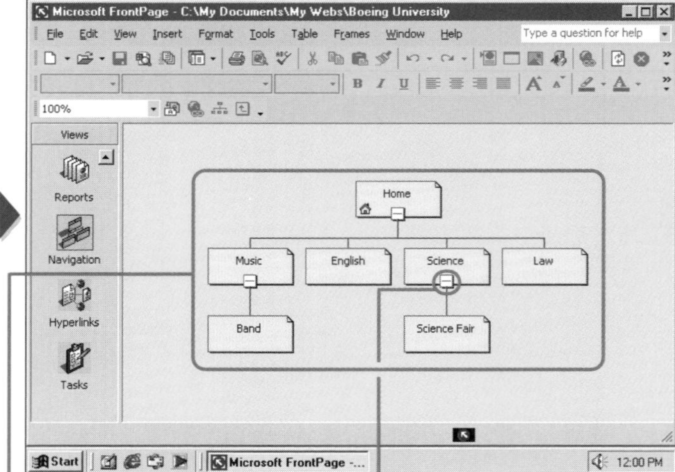

1 Click **Navigation** to display your Web site in the Navigation view.

■ This area displays the navigational structure of your Web site.

Note: When you create a Web site, FrontPage may automatically set up the navigational structure of the Web site for you. If the area appears blank or displays only one Web page, you need to add Web pages to the navigational structure. To add Web pages, see page 180.

■ Each yellow box represents a Web page and displays the title of the page.

■ Lines between the boxes indicate how the Web pages are related.

■ A Web page that displays a minus sign (⊟) has Web pages that appear below the page.

Why should I work with the navigational structure of my Web site?

The navigational structure of your Web site is important if you plan to add navigation buttons to your Web pages. Navigation buttons are links visitors can select to move through the pages in your Web site. FrontPage uses the navigational structure of your Web site to determine which navigation buttons should appear on each Web page. To change the navigational structure of your Web site, see pages 180 to 183. To add navigation buttons to your Web pages, see page 184.

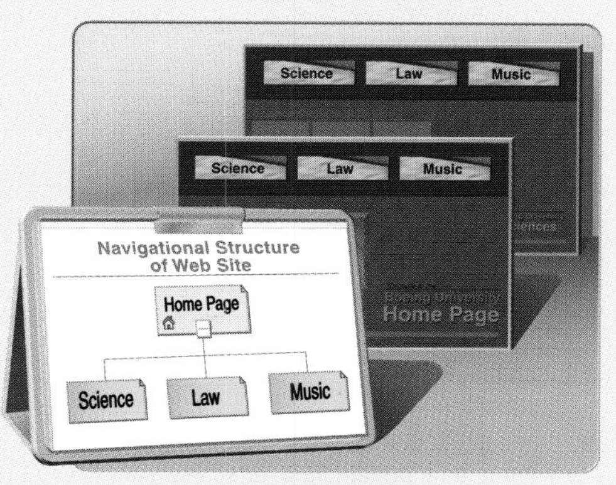

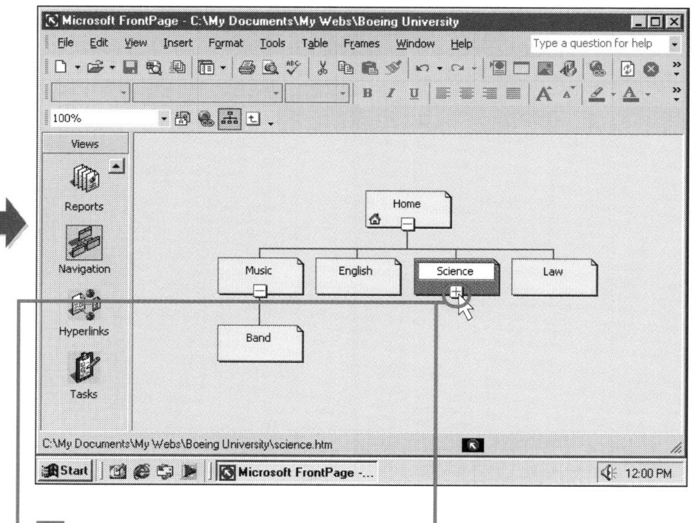

2 To hide the Web pages that appear below a page, click a minus sign (⊟) on a Web page (⊟ changes to ⊞).

Note: Hiding Web pages allows you to temporarily remove pages that are currently not of interest so you can focus on the structure of other pages.

■ To redisplay hidden Web pages, click a plus sign (⊞) on a Web page.

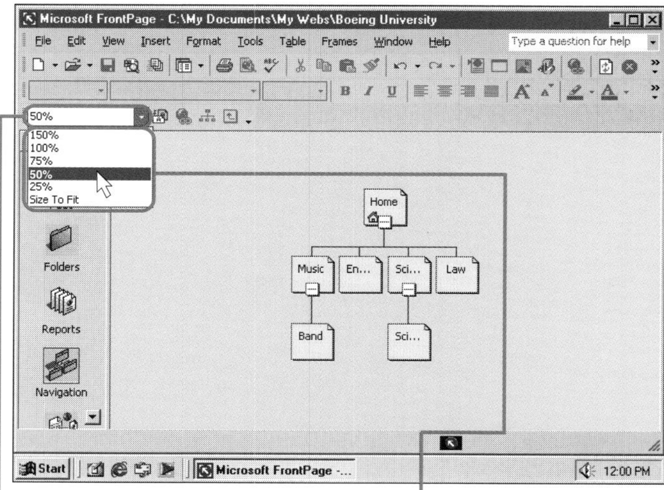

ZOOM IN OR OUT

You can display more or less of the navigational structure of your Web site.

1 Click this area to display a list of zoom settings.

2 Click the zoom setting you want to use.

*Note: To return to the normal zoom setting, repeat steps **1** and **2**, selecting 100% in step **2**.*

ADD A WEB PAGE TO THE NAVIGATIONAL STRUCTURE

You can add Web pages to the navigational structure of your Web site.

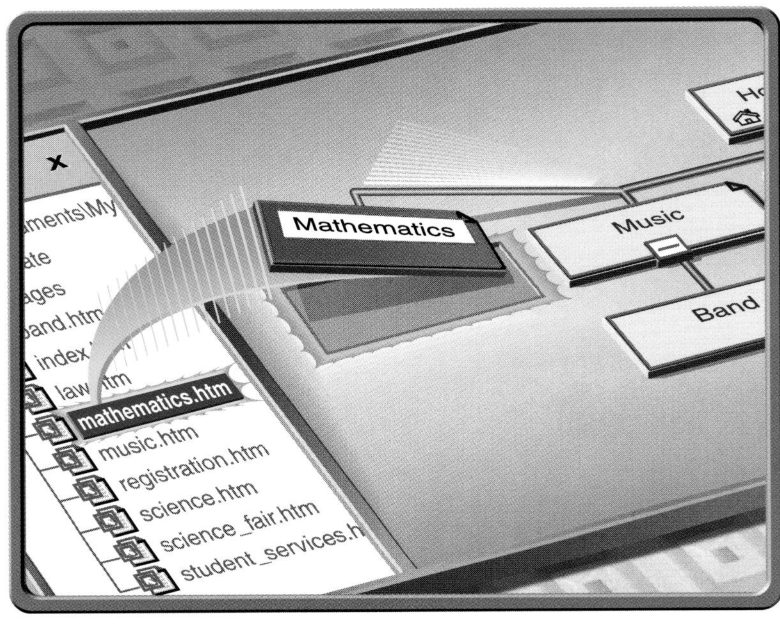

The navigational structure of your Web site determines which navigation buttons appear on your Web pages. Web pages you add to the navigational structure will appear as navigation buttons on your Web pages. To add navigation buttons to your Web pages, see page 184.

ADD A WEB PAGE TO THE NAVIGATIONAL STRUCTURE

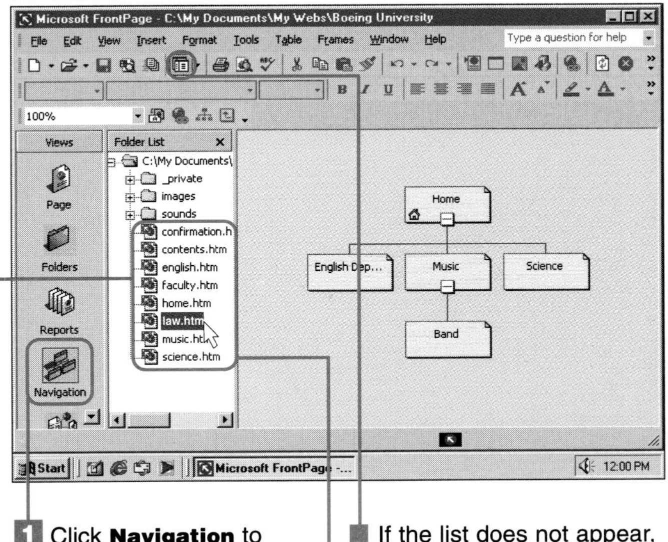

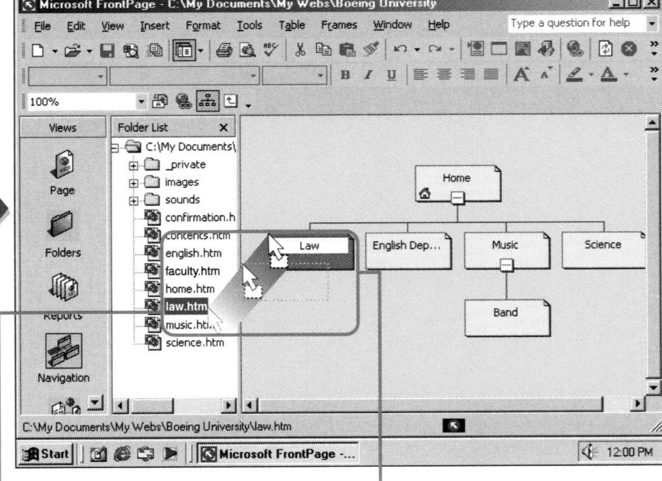

1 Click **Navigation** to display your Web site in the Navigation view.

■ This area lists all the Web pages (📄), folders (📁) and other items in your Web site.

■ If the list does not appear, click ▤ to display the list.

2 Position the mouse ↖ over the Web page you want to add to the navigational structure of your Web site.

3 Drag the mouse to where you want to add the Web page.

Note: A gray outline shows where the Web page will appear.

■ The Web page appears in the navigational structure of your Web site.

■ You can repeat steps **2** and **3** for each Web page you want to add.

REMOVE A WEB PAGE FROM THE NAVIGATIONAL STRUCTURE

You can remove a Web page from the navigational structure of your Web site.

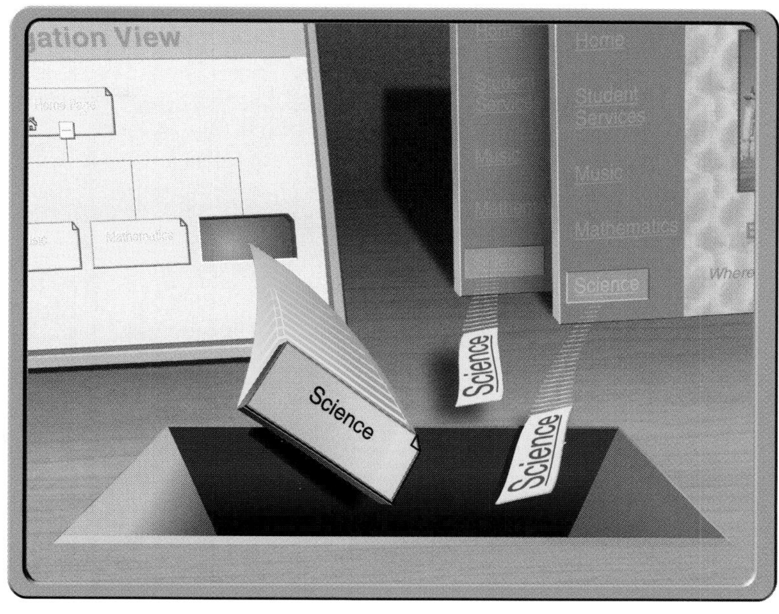

The navigational structure of your Web site determines which navigation buttons appear on your Web pages. Web pages you remove from the navigational structure will no longer appear as navigation buttons on your Web pages. For information on navigation buttons, see page 184.

REMOVE A WEB PAGE FROM THE NAVIGATIONAL STRUCTURE

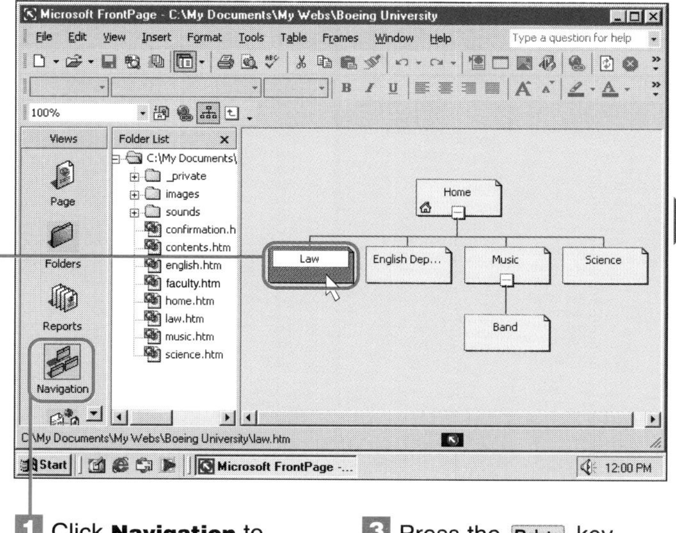

1 Click **Navigation** to display your Web site in the Navigation view.

2 Click the Web page you want to remove from the navigational structure of your Web site.

3 Press the Delete key to remove the Web page.

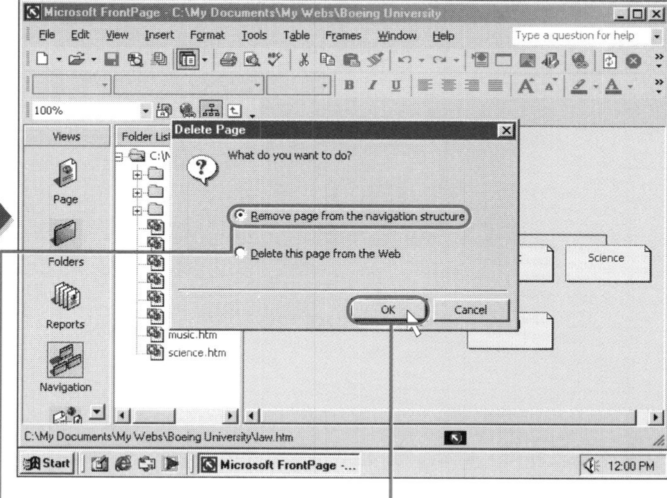

■ The Delete Page dialog box appears.

4 Click this option to delete the Web page from the navigational structure of your Web site (○ changes to ⊙).

5 Click **OK**.

Note: Deleting a Web page from the navigational structure of your Web site will not delete the page from your Web site.

MOVE A WEB PAGE IN THE NAVIGATIONAL STRUCTURE

You can rearrange Web pages to reorganize the navigational structure of your Web site.

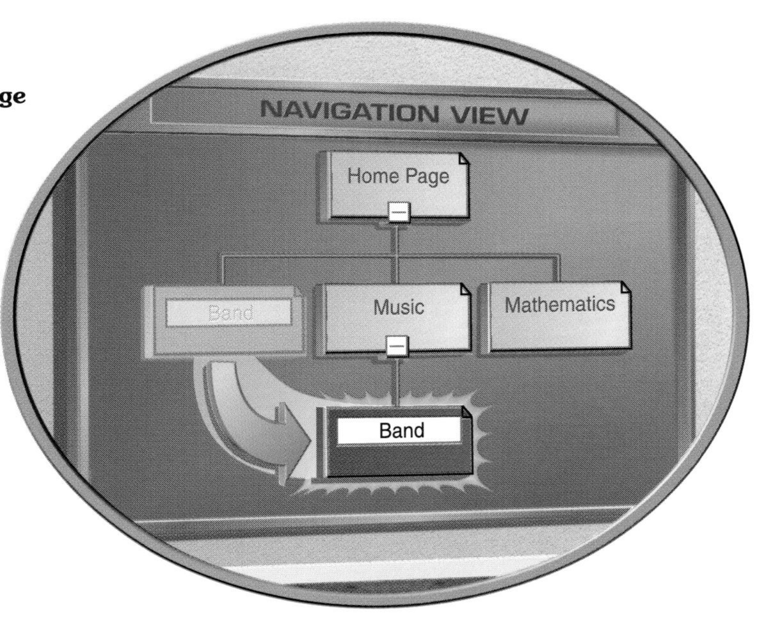

The navigational structure of your Web site determines which navigation buttons appear on your Web pages. Rearranging Web pages in the navigational structure will change which navigation buttons appear on each Web page and the order of the navigation buttons. To add navigation buttons to your Web pages, see page 184.

MOVE A WEB PAGE IN THE NAVIGATIONAL STRUCTURE

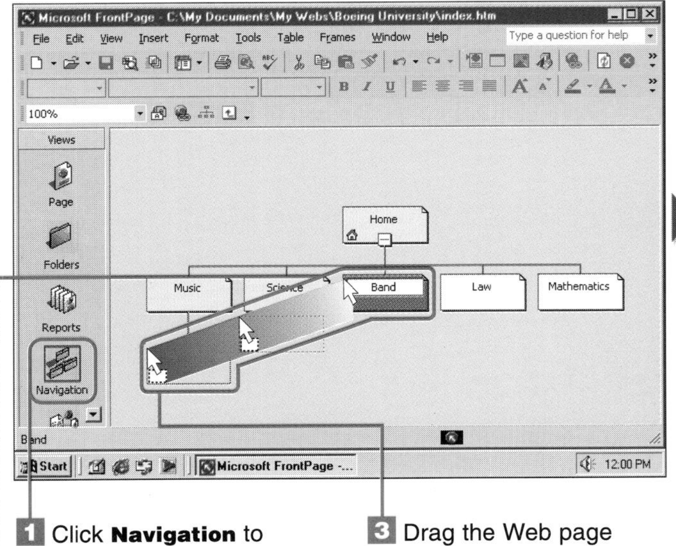

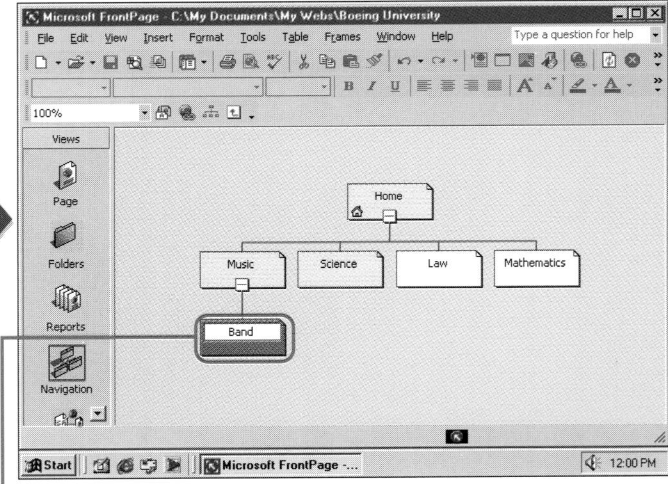

1 Click **Navigation** to display your Web site in the Navigation view.

2 Position the mouse over the Web page you want to move.

3 Drag the Web page to where you want the page to appear in the navigational structure.

Note: A gray outline shows where the Web page will appear.

■ The Web page appears in the new location.

■ You can repeat steps 2 and 3 for each Web page you want to move.

CHANGE A WEB PAGE TITLE IN THE NAVIGATIONAL STRUCTURE

You can change the title of a Web page in the Navigation view to better describe the contents of the page.

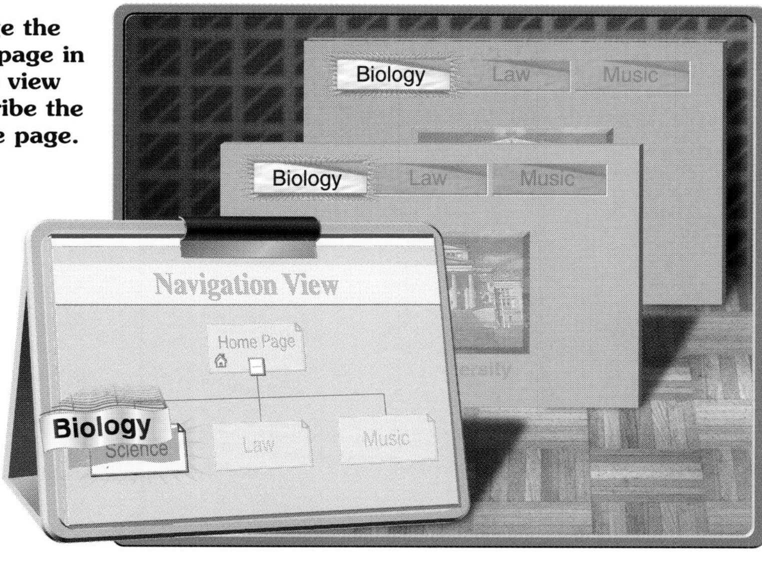

FrontPage will use the Web page titles you specify as the labels for the navigation buttons on your Web pages. To add navigation buttons to your Web pages, see page 184.

Changing the title of a Web page in the Navigation view will change the title that appears at the top of a Web browser window when the page appears on the Web.

CHANGE A WEB PAGE TITLE IN THE NAVIGATIONAL STRUCTURE

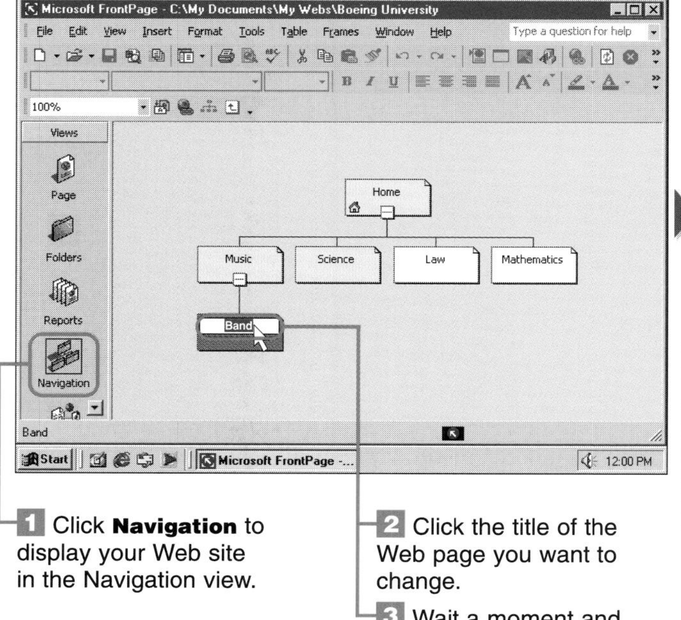

1 Click **Navigation** to display your Web site in the Navigation view.

2 Click the title of the Web page you want to change.

3 Wait a moment and then click the title of the Web page again.

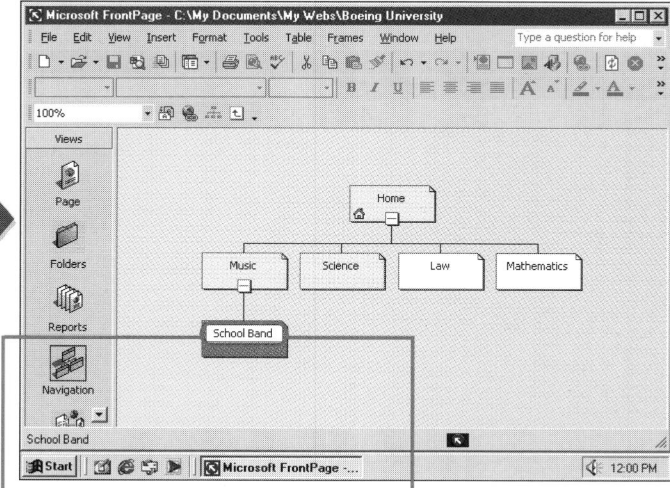

■ The Web page title appears in a box.

4 Type a new title for the Web page and then press the Enter key.

ADD SHARED BORDERS

You can add shared borders to every page in your Web site. Shared borders allow you to display the same information on every Web page.

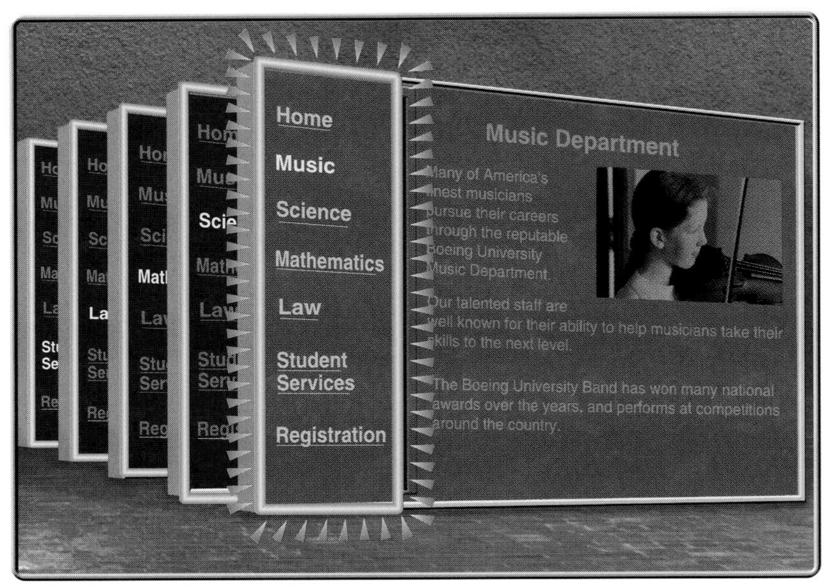

When you add shared borders, you can choose to display navigation buttons in the shared borders. Navigation buttons are links visitors can select to move through the pages in your Web site. You can also add information to shared borders that you want to appear on every Web page, such as a company logo.

ADD SHARED BORDERS

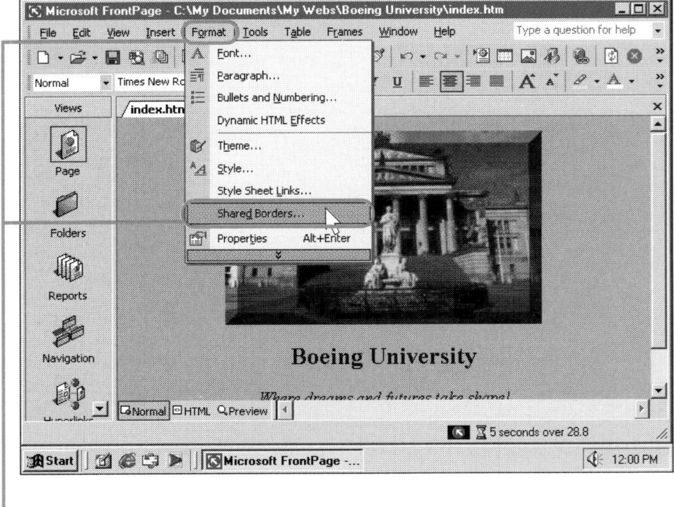

1 Click **Format**.

2 Click **Shared Borders**.

Note: If Shared Borders does not appear on the menu, position the mouse over the bottom of the menu to display all the menu options.

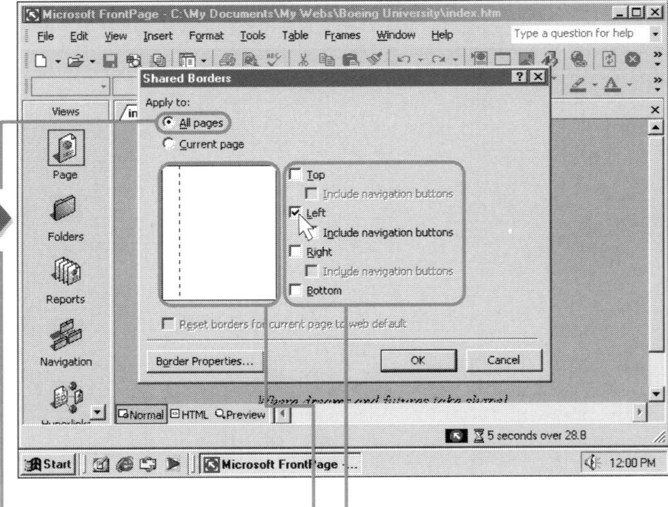

■ The Shared Borders dialog box appears.

3 Click **All pages** to add shared borders to every page in your Web site (○ changes to ⊙).

4 Click an option to specify where you want the shared borders to appear on every Web page (☐ changes to ☑).

■ A dashed line in this area indicates where the shared borders will appear on your Web pages.

How does FrontPage determine which navigation buttons to add to my Web pages?

FrontPage adds navigation buttons to your Web pages based on the navigational structure of your Web site. To work with the navigational structure of your Web site, see pages 178 to 183.

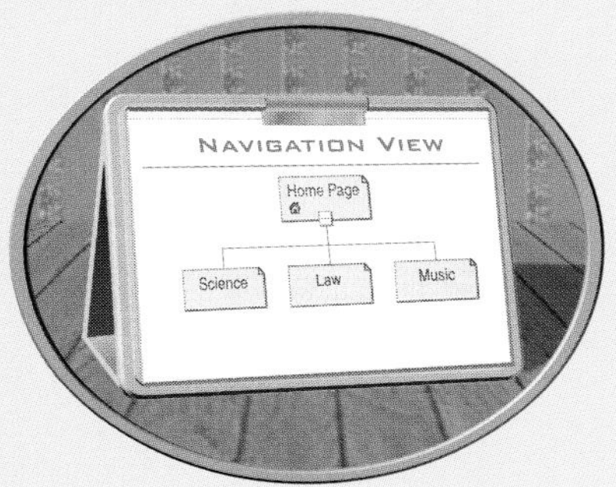

What labels will FrontPage use for the navigation buttons?

The titles of your Web pages in the Navigation view determine the labels that FrontPage will use for the navigation buttons. To change the title of a Web page in the Navigation view, see page 183.

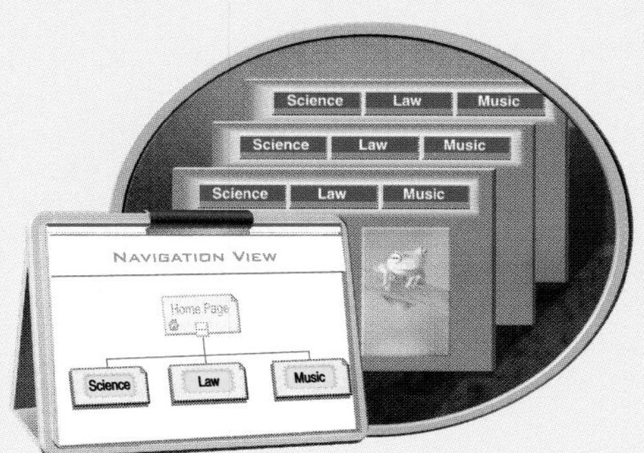

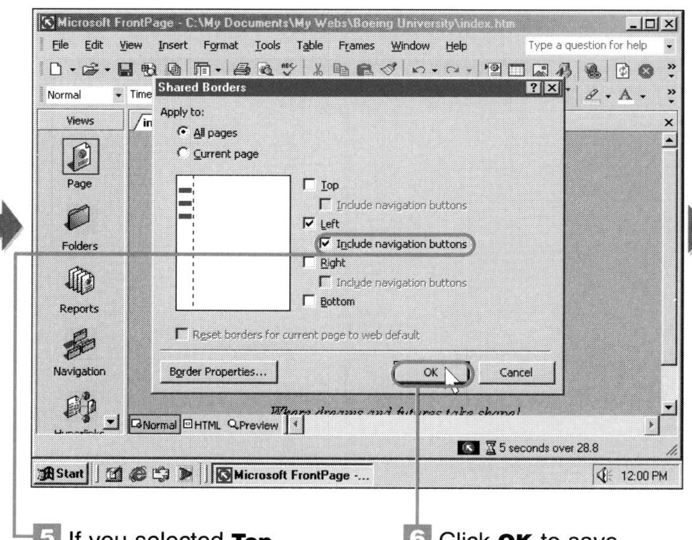

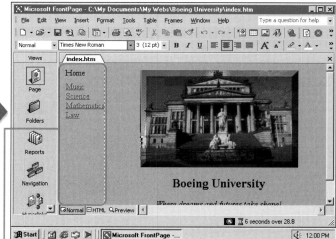

5 If you selected **Top**, **Left** or **Right** in step 4, you can click **Include navigation buttons** to display navigation buttons in the shared borders (☐ changes to ☑).

6 Click **OK** to save your changes.

■ All the Web pages in your Web site display the shared borders.

■ If you chose to include navigation buttons in step 5, the appropriate buttons will appear in the shared borders.

■ Information and images you add to shared borders will appear on every Web page.

■ To remove shared borders from all the pages in your Web site, repeat steps 1 to 4 (☑ changes to ☐ in step 4). Then perform step 6.

CHANGE NAVIGATION BUTTONS IN SHARED BORDERS

After you add navigation buttons to your Web pages, you can specify which navigation buttons you want to appear on the pages. You can also change the appearance of the navigation buttons.

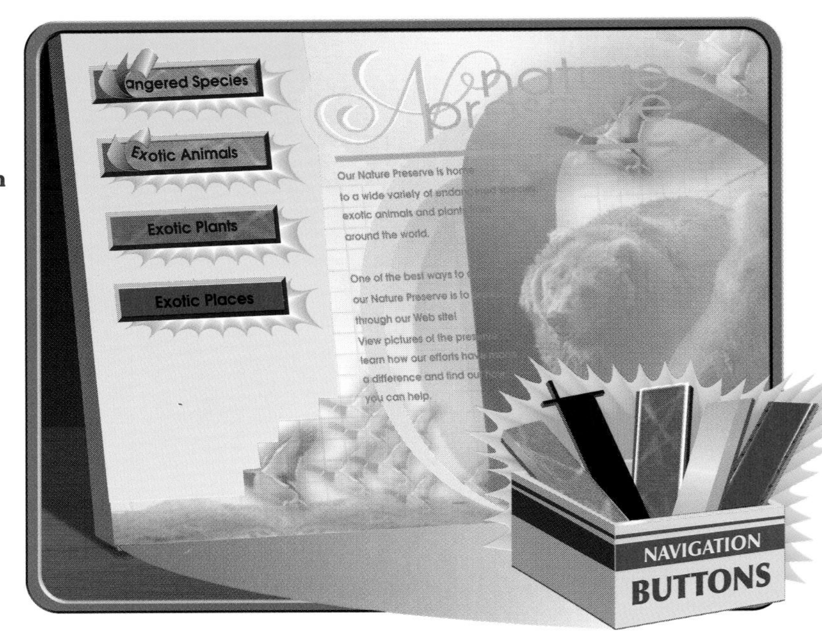

Navigation buttons are links visitors can select to move through the pages in your Web site. To add navigation buttons to your Web pages, see page 184.

CHANGE NAVIGATION BUTTONS IN SHARED BORDERS

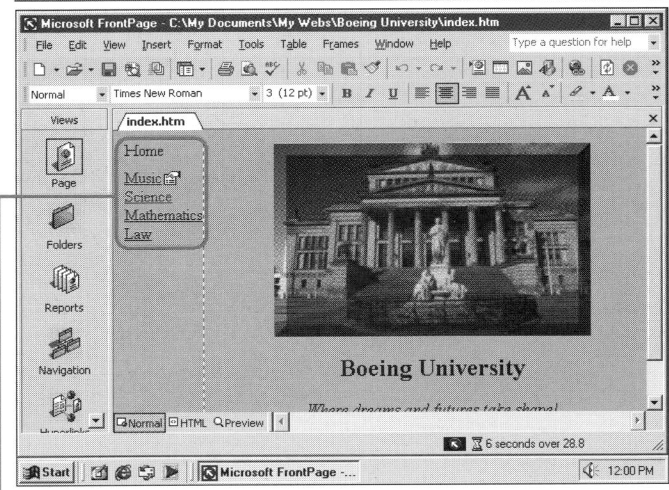

1 Double-click a navigation button on a Web page.

Note: If the displayed Web page does not display navigation buttons, double-click the text that appears in the navigation button area.

■ The Link Bar Properties dialog box appears.

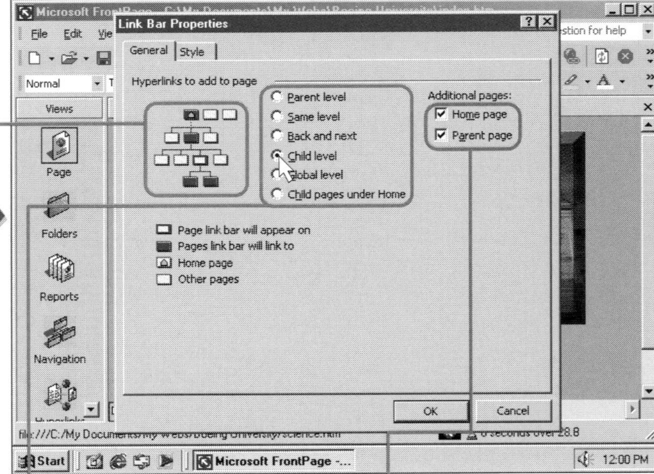

2 Click an option to specify which links you want to appear on your Web pages (○ changes to ⊙).

■ This area shows which links will appear on your Web pages.

■ These options add links to the home page and the page above the current Web page. If you do not want to display these links on your Web pages, click an option to turn the option off (☑ changes to ☐).

What navigation buttons can I add to my Web pages?

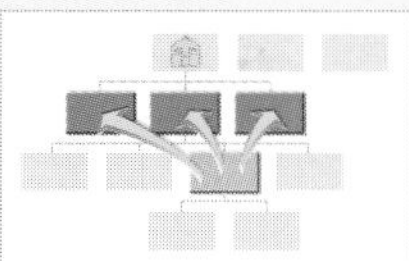

Parent level

Includes links to pages directly above the current page.

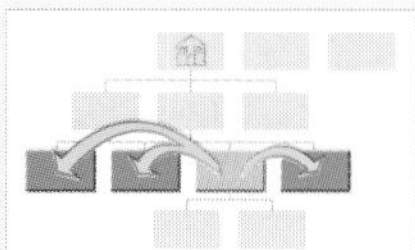

Same level

Includes links to pages on the same level as the current page.

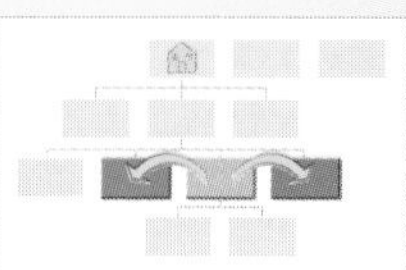

Back and next

Includes links to pages beside the current page.

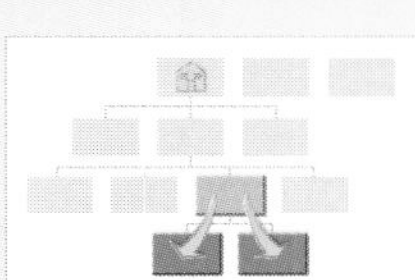

Child level

Includes links to pages directly below the current page.

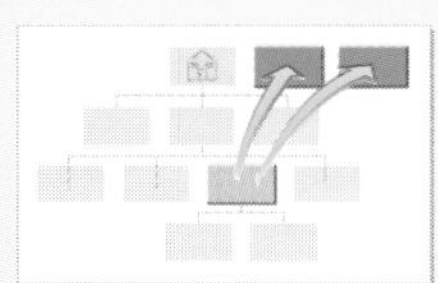

Global level

Includes links to pages on the same level as the home page.

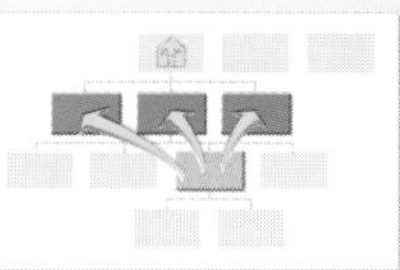

Child pages under Home

Includes links to pages directly below the home page.

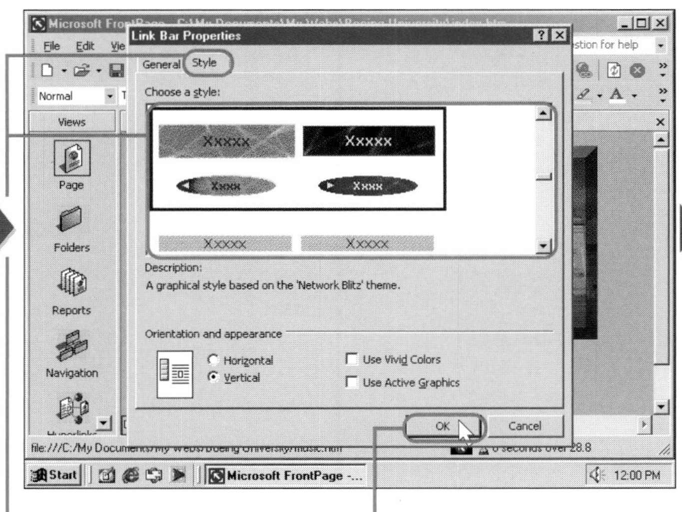

3 Click the **Style** tab to change the appearance of the navigation buttons.

■ This area lists the available styles for the navigation buttons.

4 Click the style you want to use.

*Note: If you applied a theme to your Web pages, you can select the **Use Page's Theme** option to use the navigation button style of the theme. For information on themes, see page 88.*

5 Click **OK** to confirm your changes.

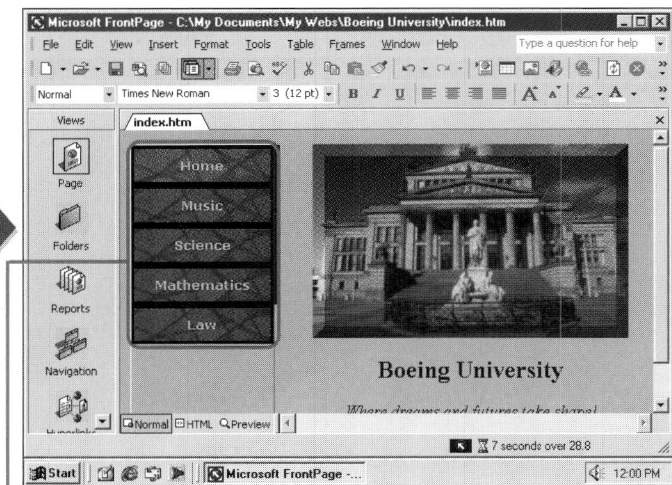

■ The navigation buttons display the changes you specified.

Sunshine VACATIONS
Reservations
Schedules
Travel Tips
Arrivals
Departures
Plan Your Vacation With Us
At Sunshine Vacations, we make all your vacations memorable ones. Call us today to plan your next trip!
Chicago & SouthWestern

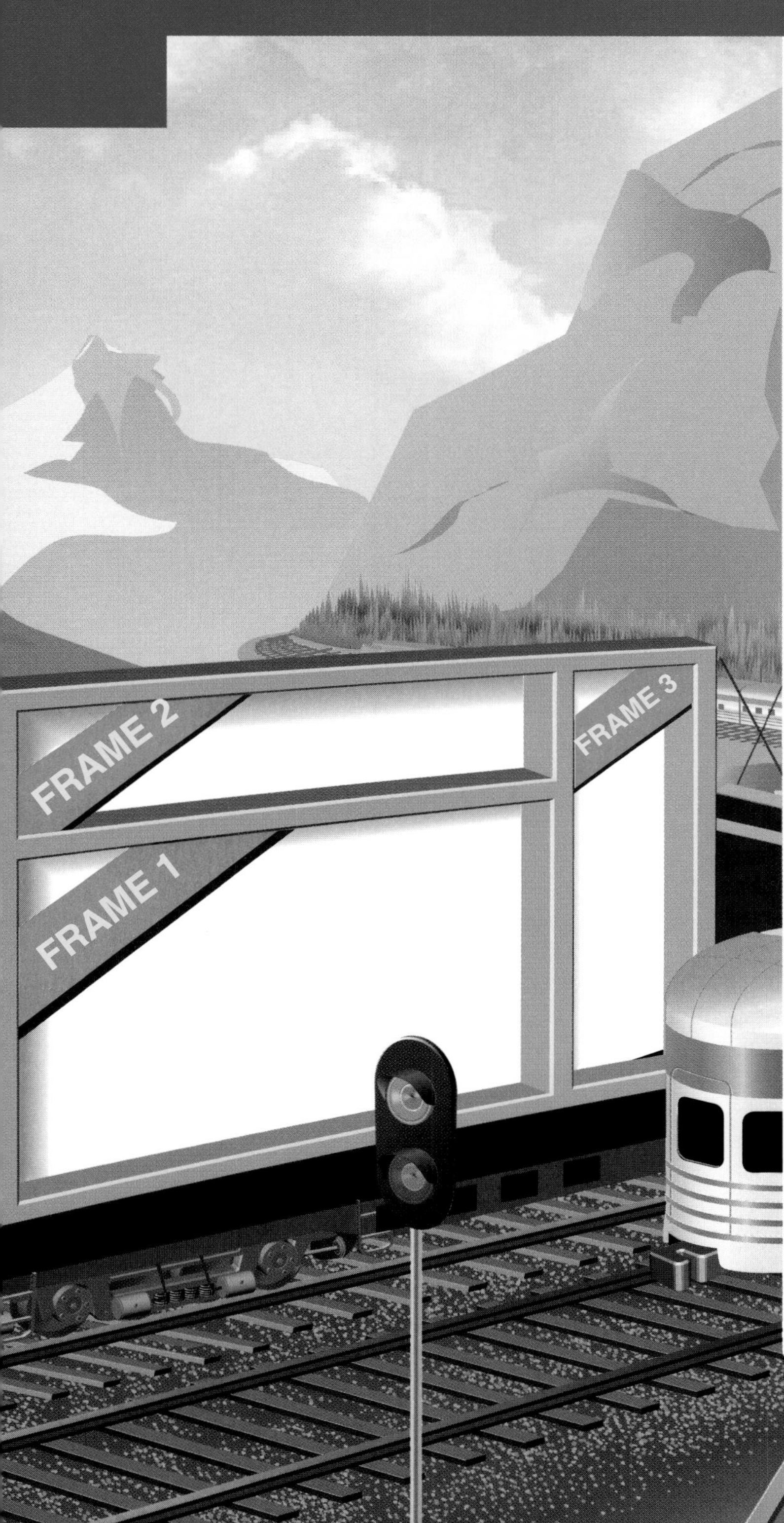

CHAPTER 11

Create Frames

Would you like to display your Web pages in frames? This chapter teaches you how to create and work with frames.

You can create frames to divide a Web browser window into sections. Each section will display a different Web page.

FrontPage offers several ready-to-use templates that you can choose from to quickly create frames.

To create frames, you must create a frames page. A frames page provides the structure for displaying several Web pages at the same time.

CREATE FRAMES

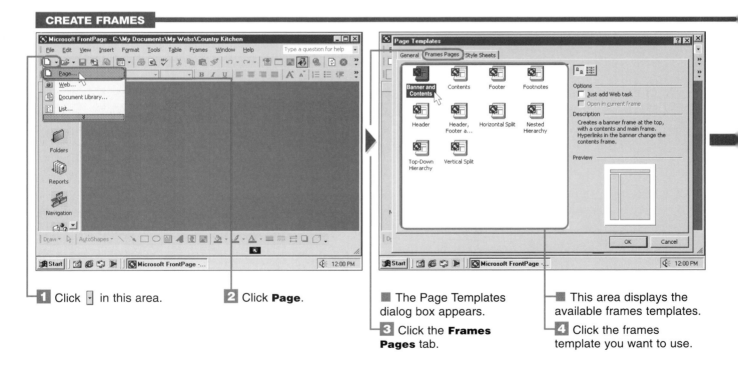

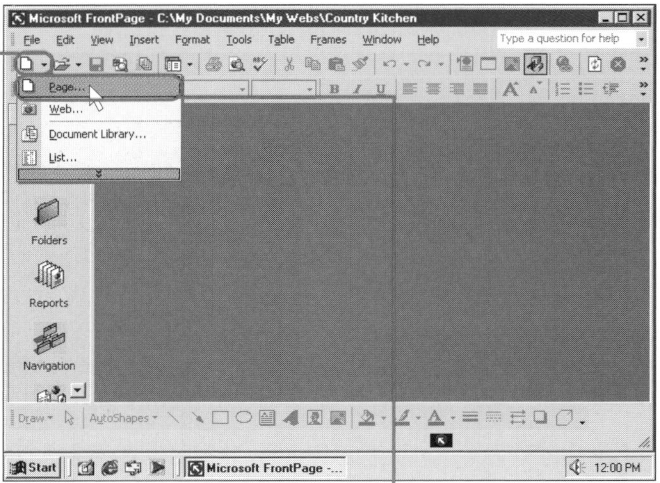

1 Click ▾ in this area.

2 Click **Page**.

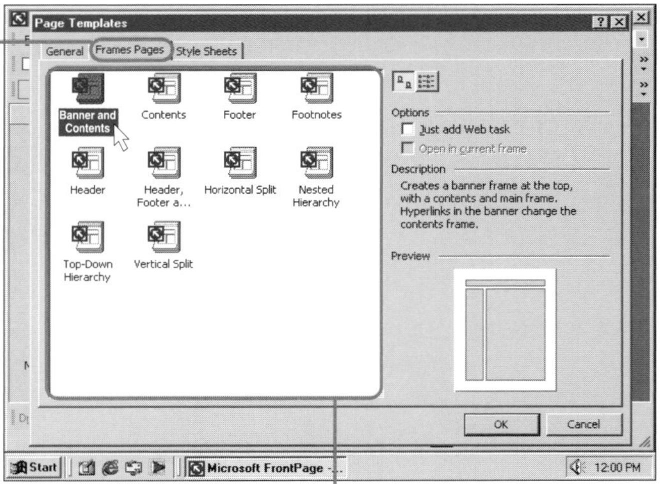

■ The Page Templates dialog box appears.

3 Click the **Frames Pages** tab.

■ This area displays the available frames templates.

4 Click the frames template you want to use.

Why would I use frames?

Frames allow you to display information that will remain on the screen while visitors browse through your Web pages.

Banners

Frames can display information such as an advertisement, a warning message or a company logo.

Navigation

Frames can display a table of contents or navigational tools to help visitors move through your Web pages and find information of interest.

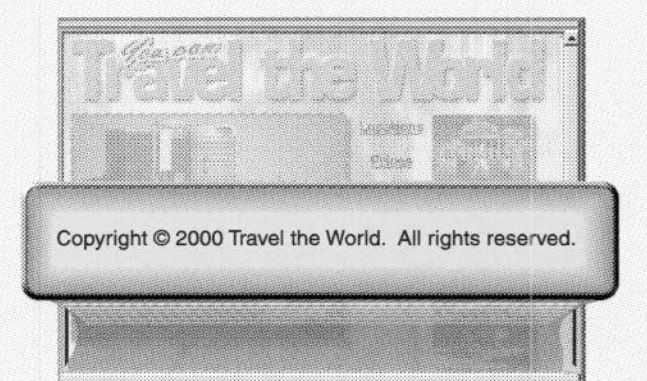

Supporting Information

Frames can display supporting information such as copyright notices or footnotes.

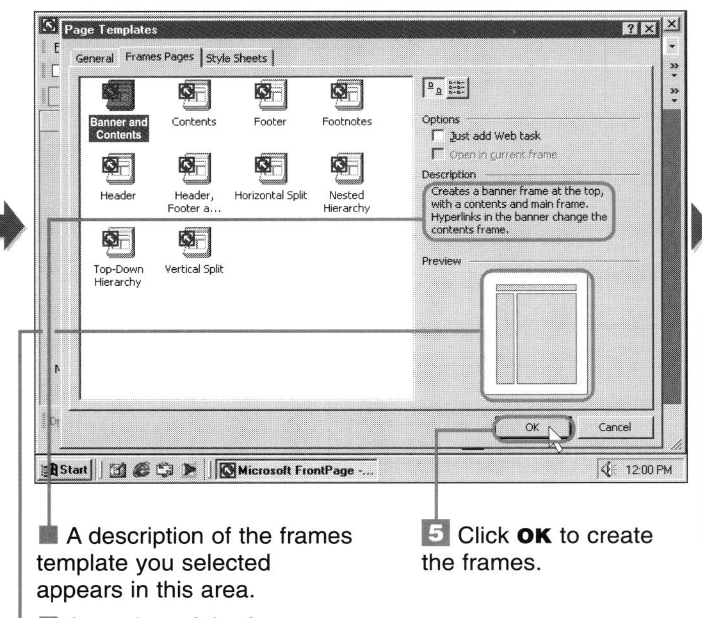

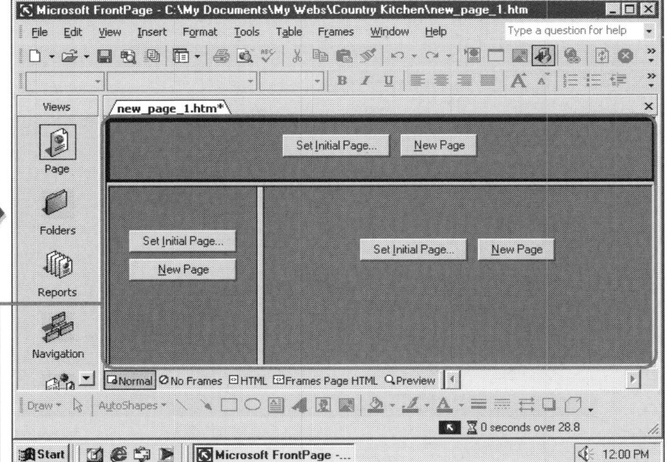

■ A description of the frames template you selected appears in this area.

■ A preview of the frames template appears in this area.

5 Click **OK** to create the frames.

■ FrontPage creates the frames based on the template you selected.

■ To specify which Web page you want to appear in each frame, see pages 192 to 194.

ADD AN EXISTING WEB PAGE TO A FRAME

You can add a Web page you previously created to a frame.

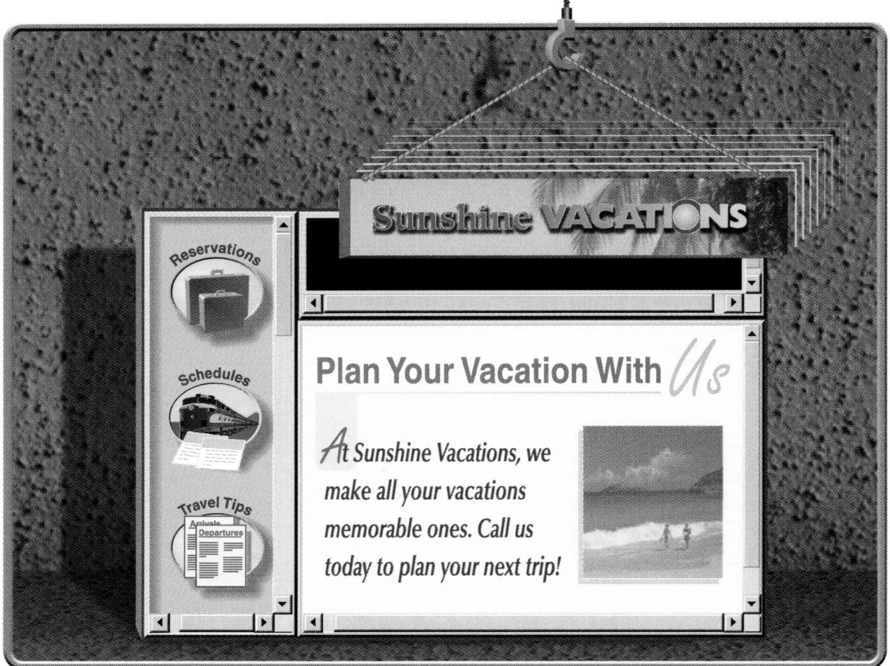

ADD AN EXISTING WEB PAGE TO A FRAME

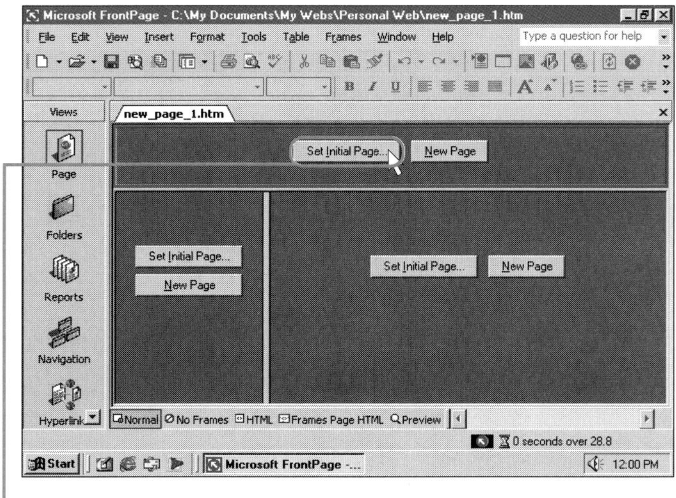

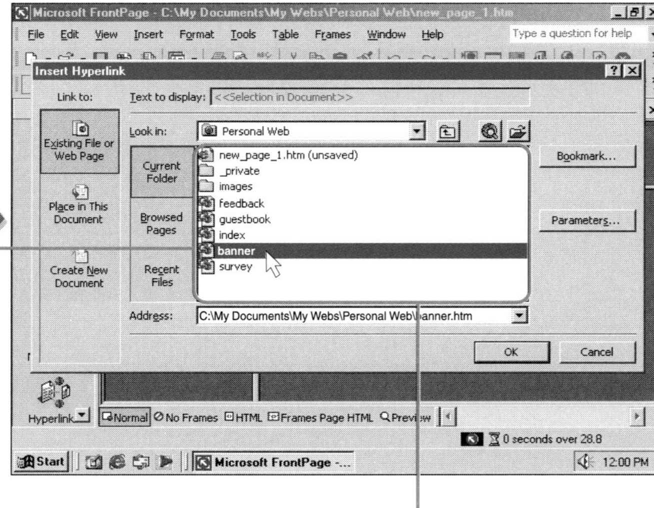

1 Click **Set Initial Page** in the frame you want to display an existing Web page.

Note: If the Set Initial Page button is not displayed, see page 190 to create frames.

■ The Insert Hyperlink dialog box appears.

■ This area lists all the Web pages (), folders () and other items in your Web site.

2 Click the Web page you want to display in the frame.

What should I consider when adding Web pages to frames?

You should check how the Web pages displayed in your frames appear on computer screens using different resolutions. The screen resolution determines the amount of information that will appear in each frame. Computers using lower screen resolutions will show less information in each frame. For example, a heading or image in a frame may not fully appear on a computer screen using a lower resolution.

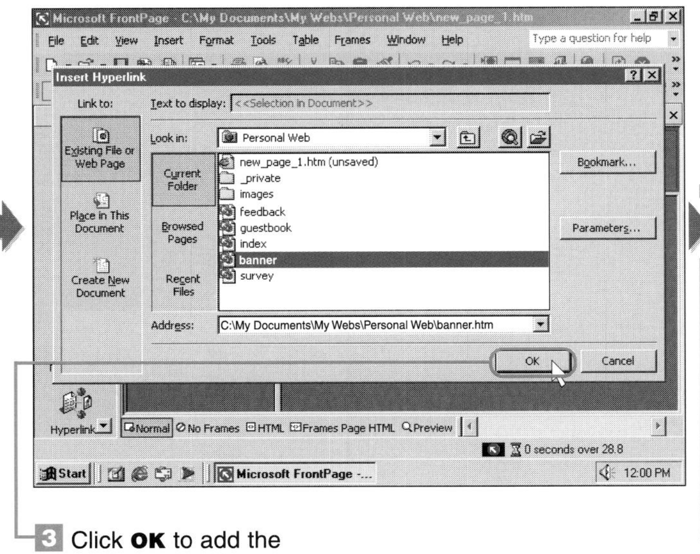

3 Click **OK** to add the Web page to the frame.

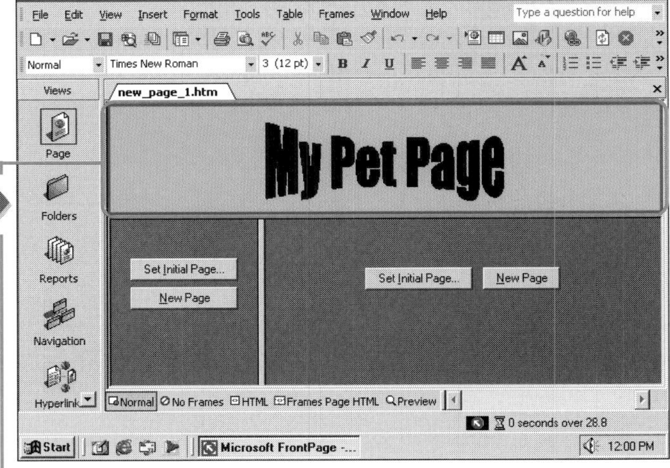

■ The Web page appears in the frame.

■ You can repeat steps 1 to 3 for each frame you want to display an existing Web page.

ADD A NEW WEB PAGE TO A FRAME

After you create frames, you can add a new Web page to a frame.

ADD A NEW WEB PAGE TO A FRAME

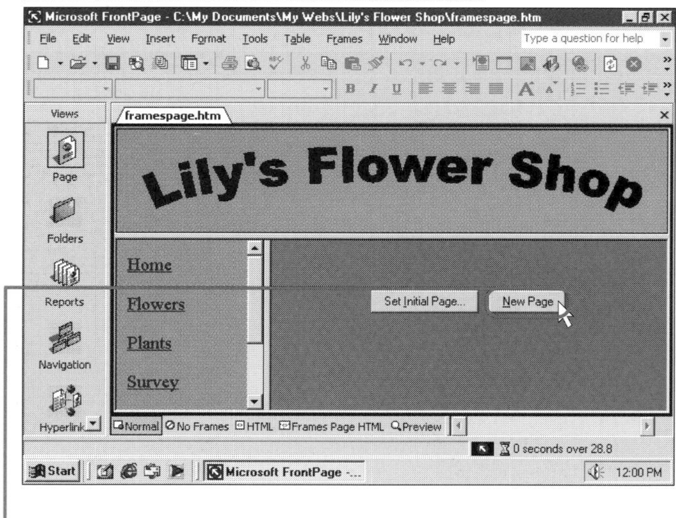

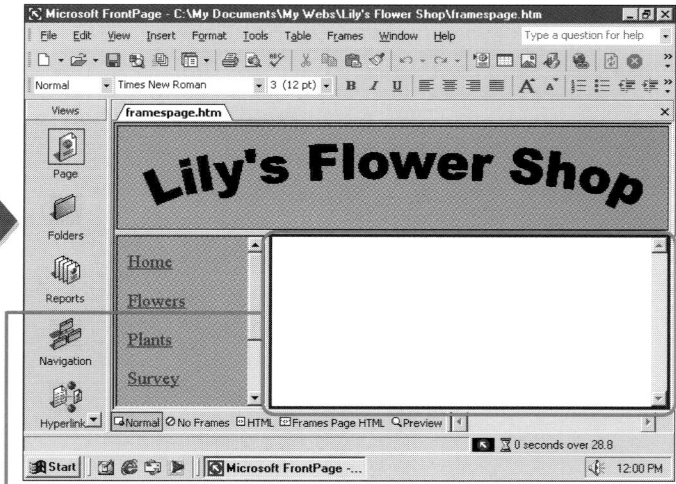

1 Click **New Page** in the frame you want to display a new Web page.

Note: If the New Page button is not displayed, see page 190 to create frames.

■ A new Web page appears in the frame.

■ You can immediately add information to the Web page.

■ You can repeat step 1 for each frame you want to display a new Web page.

You can change the size of a frame to show more or less information in the frame.

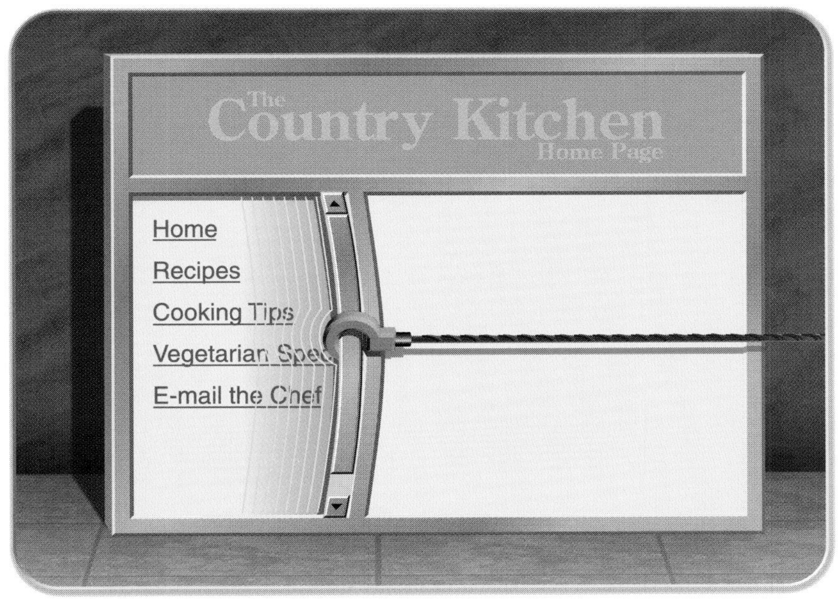

Resizing a frame will not change the information displayed in the frame. Resizing a frame only changes the amount of information the frame displays.

RESIZE A FRAME

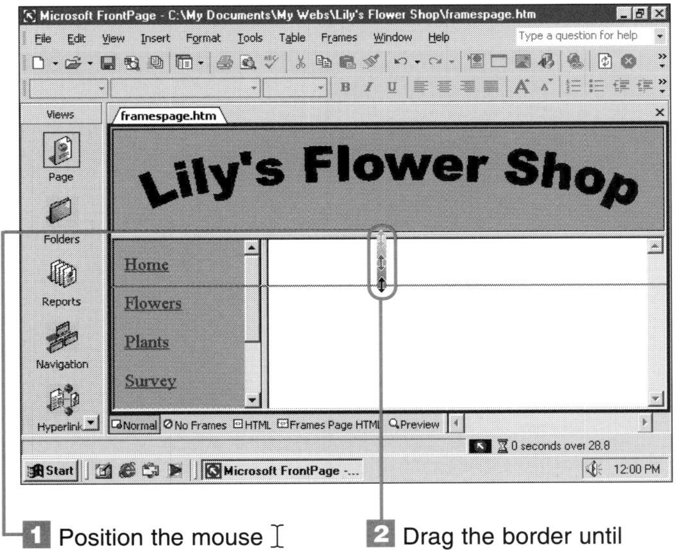

1 Position the mouse I over the border of the frame you want to resize (I changes to ↕ or ↔).

2 Drag the border until the frame is the size you want.

■ A gray line shows the new size of the frame.

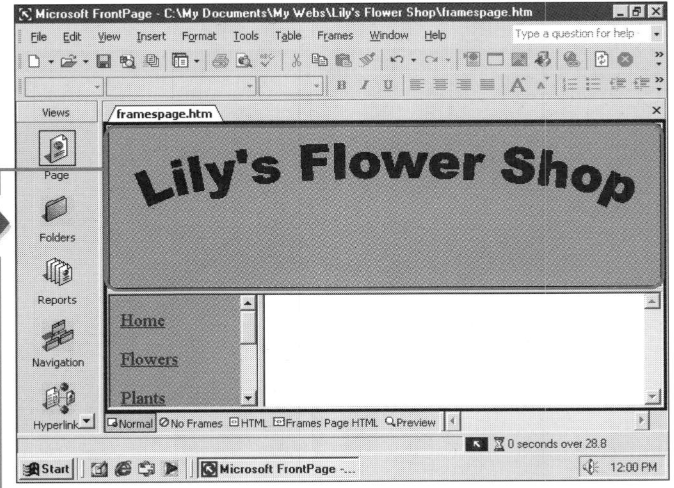

■ The frame displays the new size.

■ When you resize a frame, the size of adjacent frames will also change.

SAVE FRAMES

You should save your frames to store the frames for future use. This allows you to later review and edit the Web pages displayed in the frames.

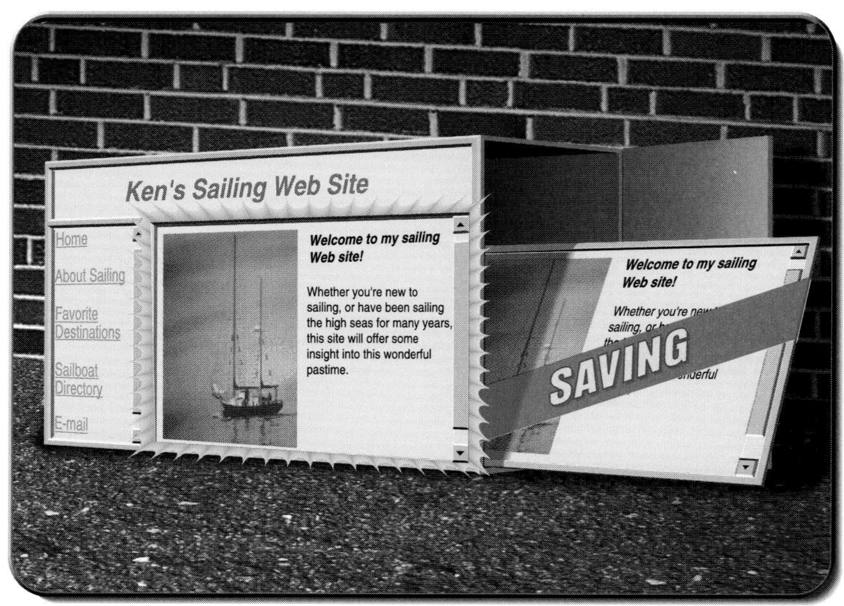

When you save frames, FrontPage will ask you to save each new Web page you added to the frames and the frames page. The frames page provides the structure for displaying several Web pages at the same time.

SAVE FRAMES

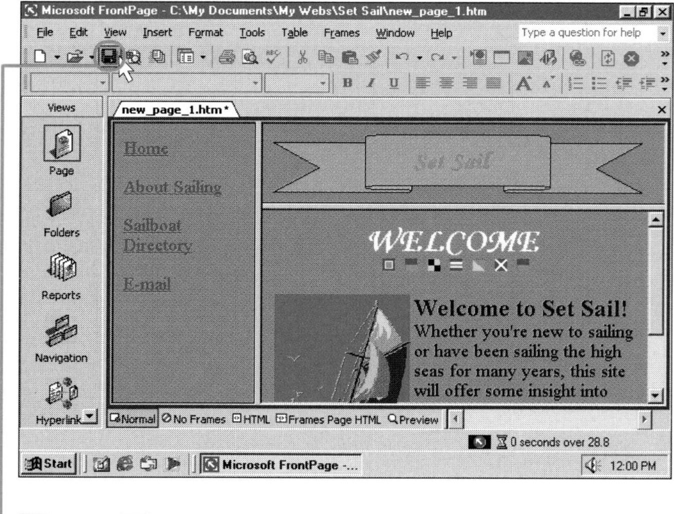

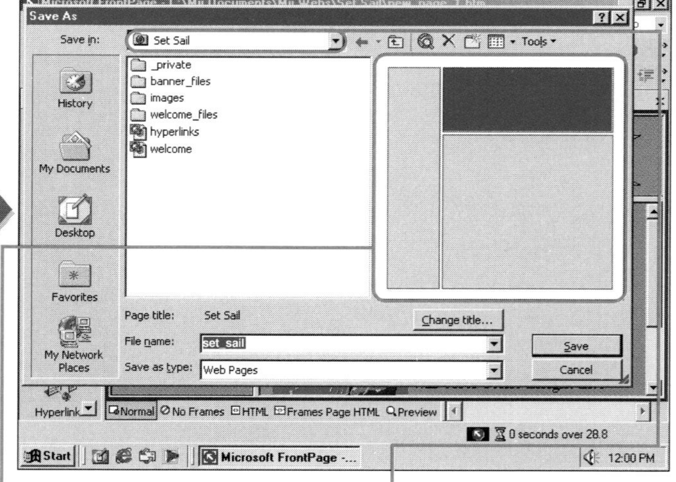

1 Click 💾 to save your frames.

■ The Save As dialog box appears.

■ This area displays the layout of the frames. If you added a new Web page to one of the frames, the frame appears highlighted.

*Note: If you did not add any new Web pages to the frames, skip to step **5**.*

■ This area shows the location where FrontPage will store the new Web page.

Note: FrontPage will automatically store the new Web page in the folder for the current Web site.

Why does the Save Embedded Files dialog box appear when I save my frames?

If you added an image to a Web page displayed in a frame, you must save the image as part of your Web site. FrontPage will place a copy of the image in the same folder that stores all the Web pages for your Web site. This ensures the image will transfer with your Web site when you publish your Web pages.

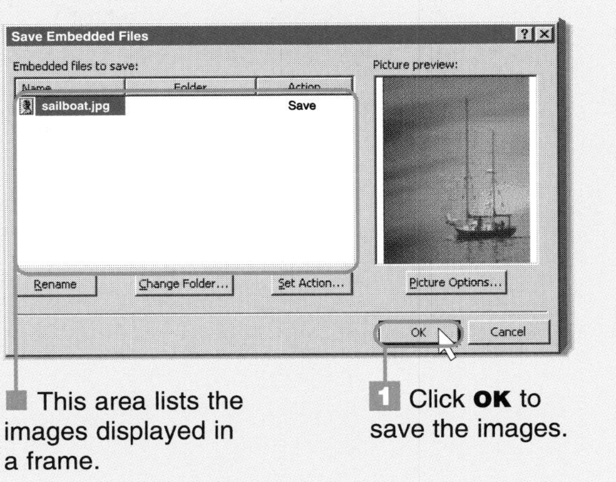

■ This area lists the images displayed in a frame.

1 Click **OK** to save the images.

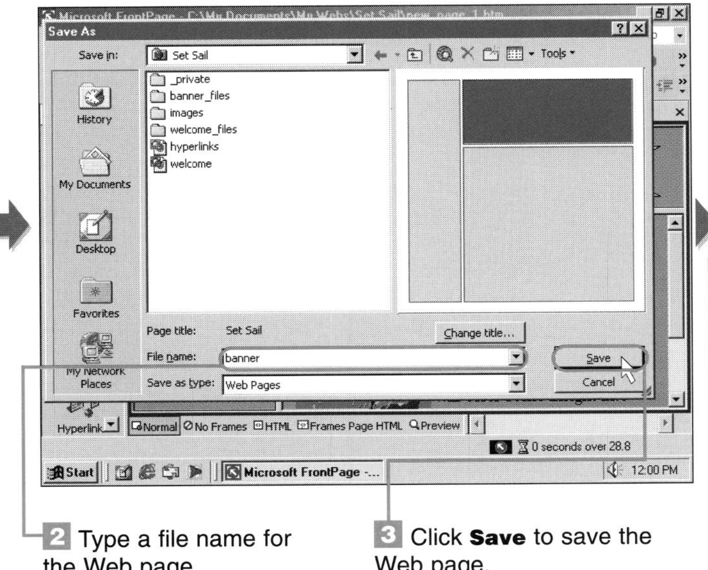

2 Type a file name for the Web page.

*Note: A Web page file name should not include spaces or the characters * : ? # > < | or ".*

3 Click **Save** to save the Web page.

4 Repeat steps 2 and 3 for each new Web page you added to your frames.

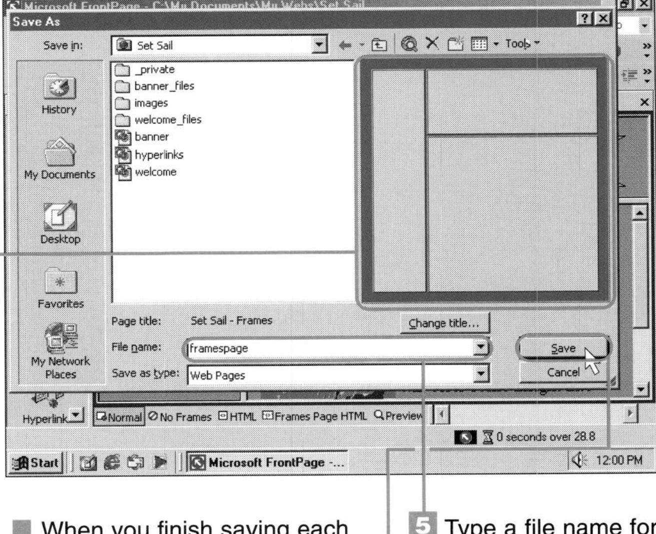

■ When you finish saving each new Web page you added to the frames, FrontPage allows you to save the frames page, which provides the structure for displaying the frames.

■ When saving the frames page, a thick border appears around the frames in this area.

5 Type a file name for the frames page.

6 Click **Save** to save the frames page.

SPLIT A FRAME

You can add another frame by splitting an existing frame into two frames.

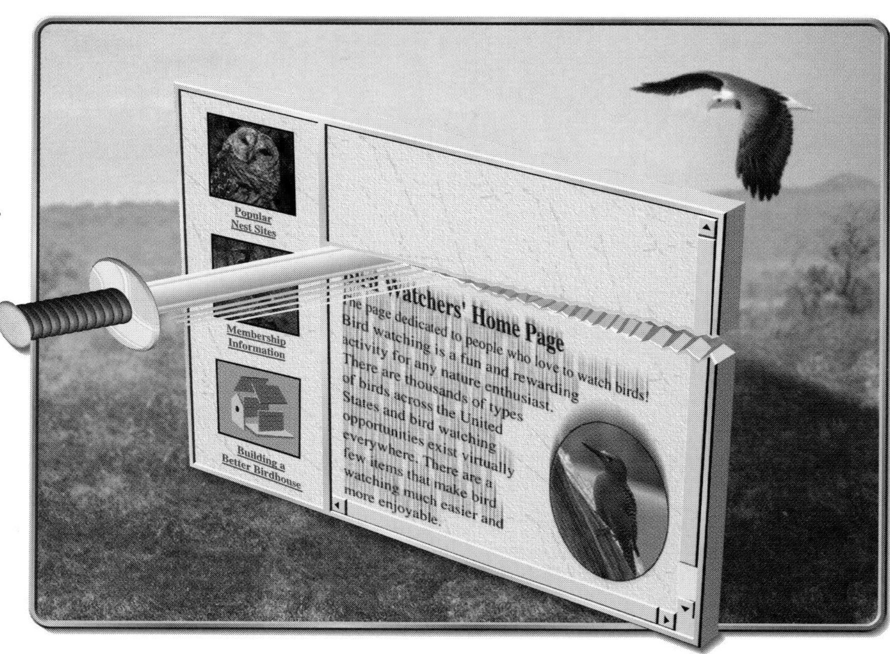

When you split a frame, the content of the original frame is not affected.

SPLIT A FRAME

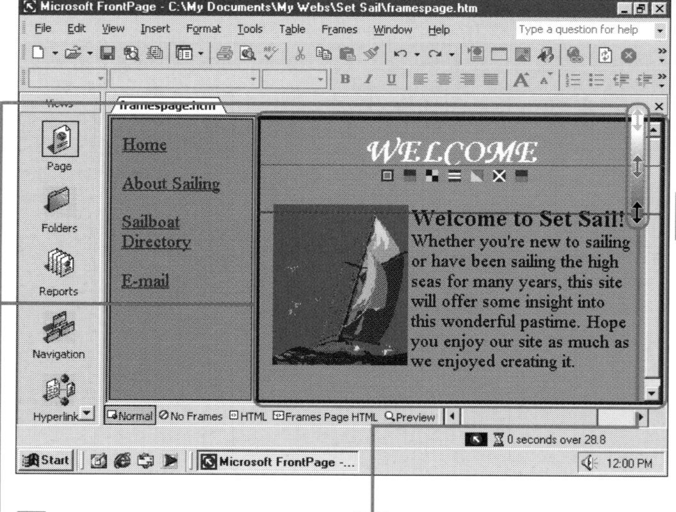

1 Click inside the frame you want to split into two frames.

2 Position the mouse I over the border of the frame you want to use to split the frame.

3 Press and hold down the Ctrl key (I changes to ↕ or ↔) and then drag the frame border to a new location.

Note: A gray line shows where the frame will split into two frames.

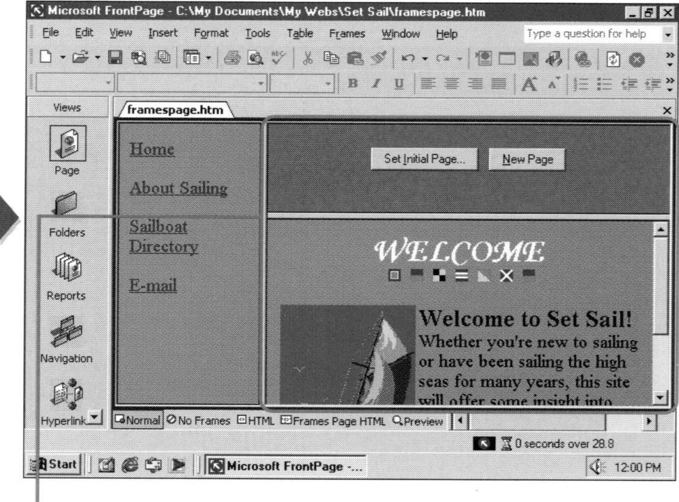

■ The frame splits into two frames.

■ To add an existing Web page to the new frame, see page 192. To add a new Web page to the frame, see page 194.

DELETE A FRAME

You can delete a frame when you no longer want your frames page to display the frame.

DELETE A FRAME

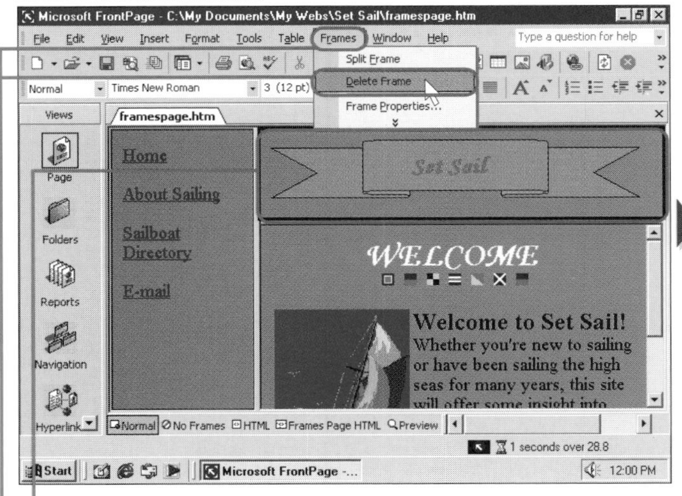

1 Click inside the frame you want to delete.

2 Click **Frames**.

3 Click **Delete Frame**.

*Note: A dialog box may appear, asking you to save changes you made to the Web page displayed in the frame. Click **Yes** to save your changes. For information on saving a Web page, see page 28.*

■ The frame disappears.

Note: Deleting a frame will not delete the Web page displayed in the frame from your Web site.

CREATE A LINK TO A FRAME

You can create a link that visitors can select to display a Web page in another frame.

Creating a link to a frame is useful when you place a table of contents, navigational tools or search tools in one frame and you want the linked Web pages to appear in another frame.

CREATE A LINK TO A FRAME

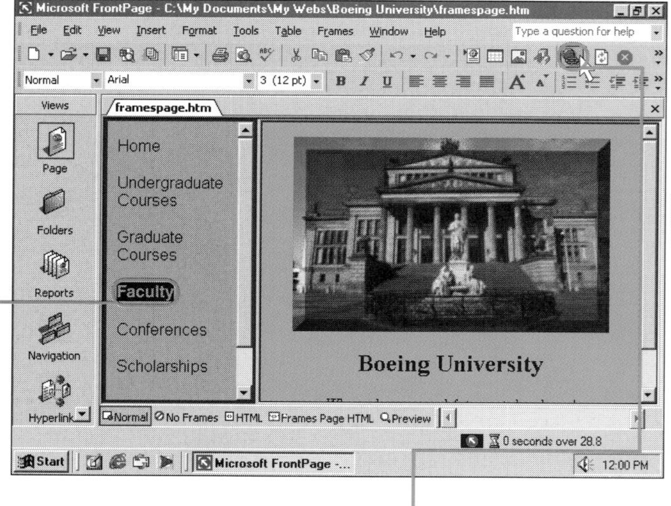

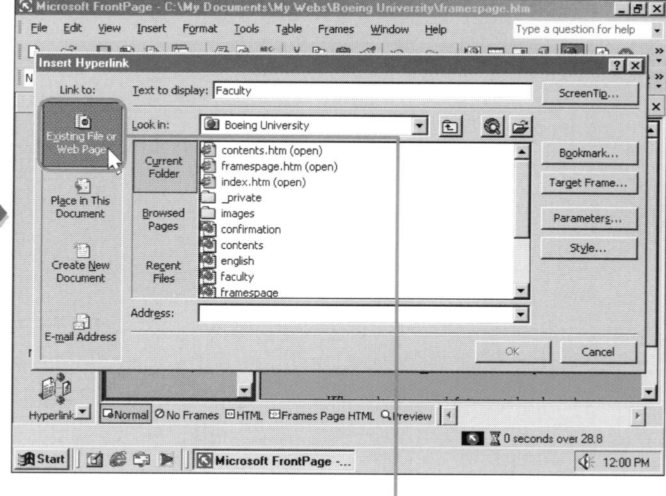

1 Select the text or click the image you want visitors to select to display a Web page in another frame. To select text, see page 54.

2 Click [icon] to create a link.

■ The Insert Hyperlink dialog box appears.

3 Click **Existing File or Web Page** to create a link to another Web page.

What should I consider when creating a link to another frame?

Make sure the text or image you use for a link clearly indicates what information the link will display. Do not use the phrase "Click Here" for a link, since this phrase is not very informative.

When a visitor selects a link, which frame will display the linked Web page?

When you create frames, FrontPage usually sets up one frame to display links and another frame to display the linked Web pages. For example, if you used the Contents template to create frames, FrontPage sets up the left frame to display links and the right frame to display the linked Web pages. To change which frame will display a Web page when visitors select a link, see page 202.

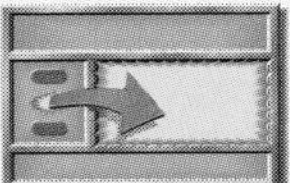

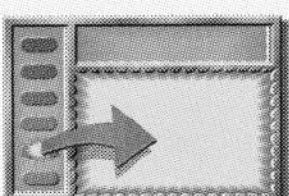

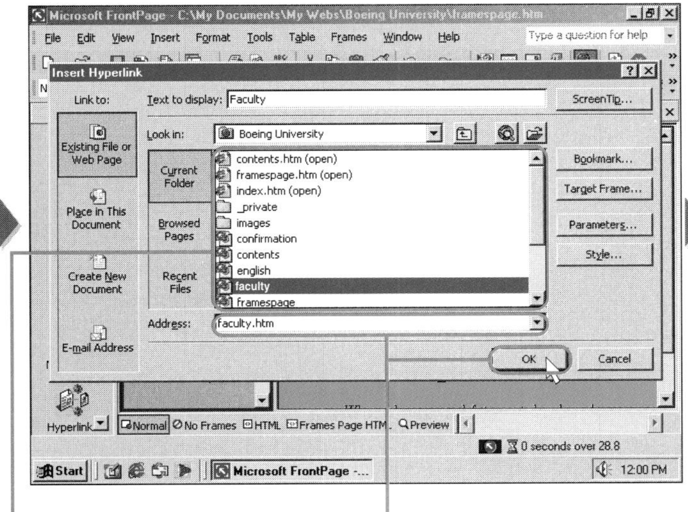

4 To link the text or image to a page in your current Web site, click the Web page ( ) in this area. The area lists all the Web pages in the current Web site.

■ To link the text or image to a page on the Web, type the address of the Web page in this area.

5 Click **OK** to create the link.

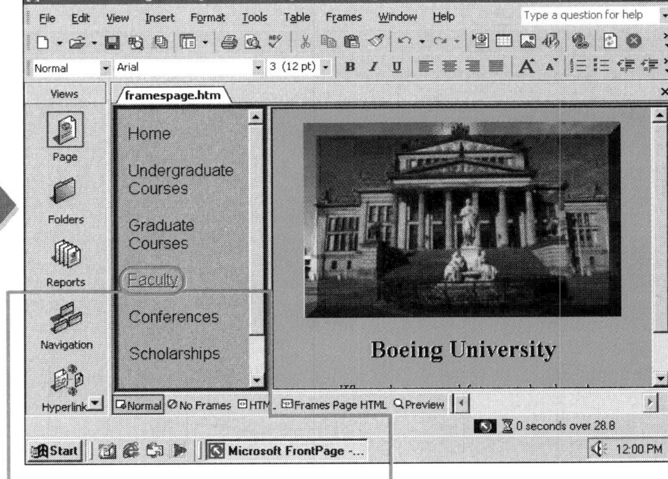

■ FrontPage creates the link. Text links appear underlined and in color.

■ To deselect the link, click outside the link.

■ A visitor can click the link to display the Web page you specified in another frame.

Note: To test the link, you can use the Preview view. For information on the Preview view, see page 42.

CHANGE THE TARGET FRAME

You can change the frame that will display a Web page when visitors select a link. The frame you select is called the target frame.

When you create frames, FrontPage usually sets up one frame to display links and another frame to display the linked Web pages.

CHANGE THE TARGET FRAME

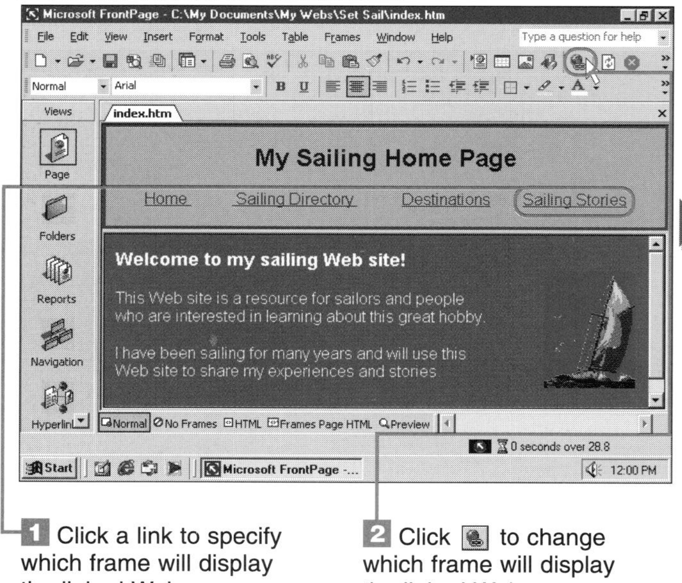

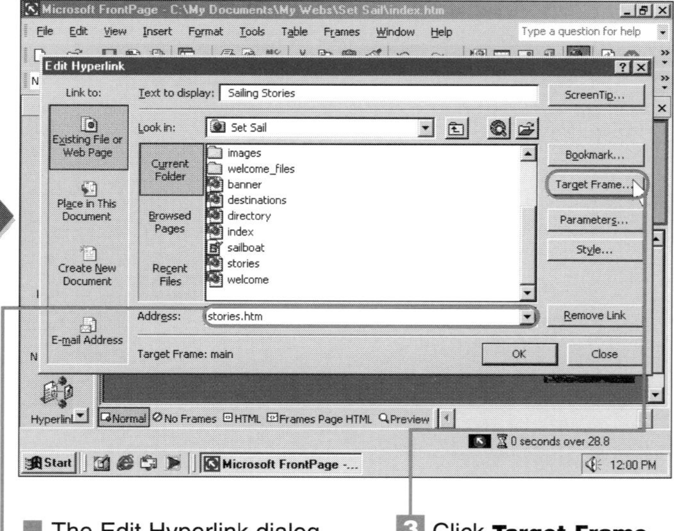

1 Click a link to specify which frame will display the linked Web page.

Note: To create a link, see page 200.

2 Click the hyperlink button to change which frame will display the linked Web page.

■ The Edit Hyperlink dialog box appears.

■ This area indicates the Web page that will appear when visitors select the link.

3 Click **Target Frame** to specify which frame you want to display the linked Web page.

What are some targets that I can use to display a linked Web page?

Page Default

The linked Web page will appear in the frame that FrontPage automatically set up to display linked Web pages.

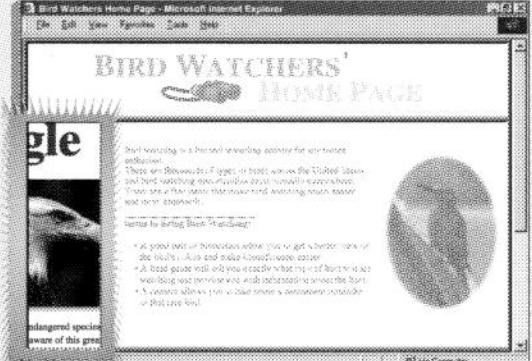

Same Frame

The linked Web page will appear in the same frame that contains the link.

Whole Page

The linked Web page will replace all the frames.

New Window

The linked Web page will appear in its own Web browser window.

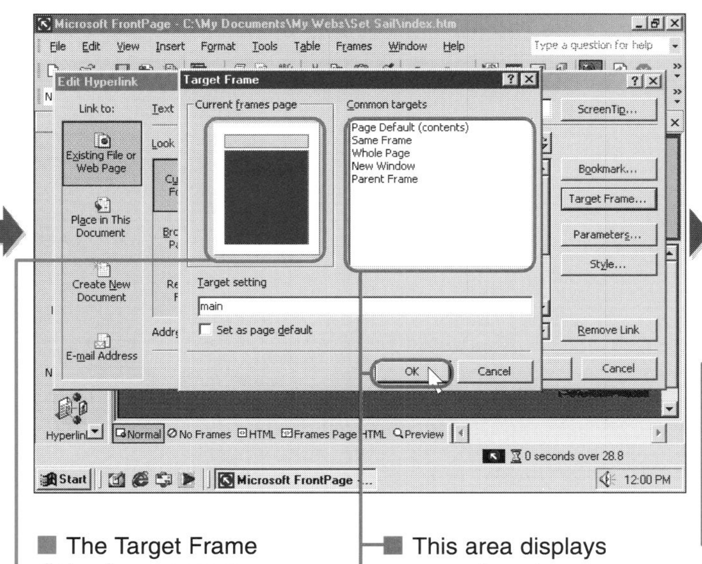

■ The Target Frame dialog box appears.

■ This area displays the layout of the frames.

4 Click the frame you want to display the linked Web page. The frame appears highlighted.

■ This area displays common targets you can use to display the linked Web page. Instead of performing step 4, you can click the target you want to use.

5 Click **OK** to confirm your change.

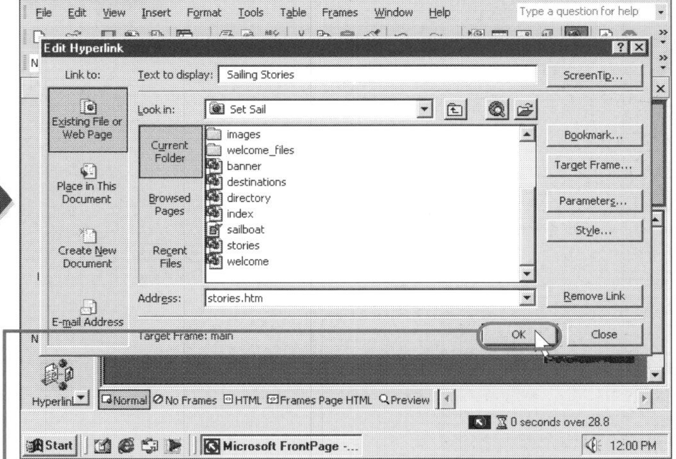

6 Click **OK** to close the Edit Hyperlink dialog box.

■ When a visitor clicks the link, the linked Web page will appear in the frame you specified.

Note: To test the link, you can use the Preview view. For information on the Preview view, see page 42.

HIDE FRAME BORDERS

You can hide the borders between your frames to make the frames invisible. When you hide the frame borders, the contents of the frames will appear as one Web page.

Hiding the frame borders allows information in one frame, such as an advertisement, company logo or table of contents, to appear as part of another frame.

HIDE FRAME BORDERS

1 Click inside one of the frames you no longer want to display borders.

2 Click **Frames**.

3 Click **Frame Properties**.

■ The Frame Properties dialog box appears.

4 Click **Frames Page** to change the properties of all the frames.

When I hide the frame borders, why does FrontPage change the amount of space between the frames to zero (0)?

When you hide the frame borders, FrontPage automatically changes the amount of space between the frames from 2 pixels to 0 pixels. If the frames display a background color or image and the amount of space between the frames is not set to 0 pixels, a white border may appear between the frames.

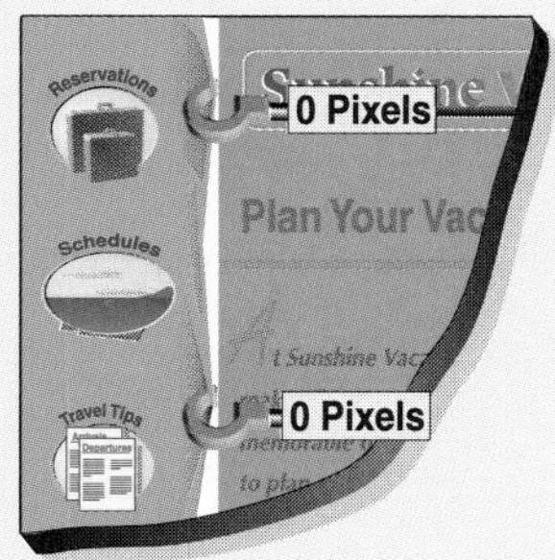

After hiding the frame borders, why do scroll bars still appear?

When visitors view your frames in a Web browser, a scroll bar will appear in a frame that contains more information than can fit in the frame. If you do not want scroll bars to appear in any of your frames, make sure your information will fit in the frames.

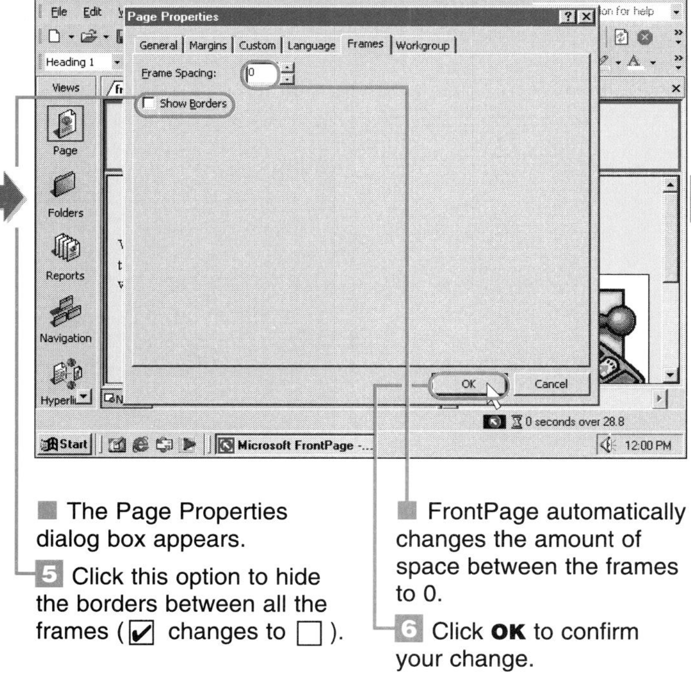

■ The Page Properties dialog box appears.

5 Click this option to hide the borders between all the frames (☑ changes to ☐).

■ FrontPage automatically changes the amount of space between the frames to 0.

6 Click **OK** to confirm your change.

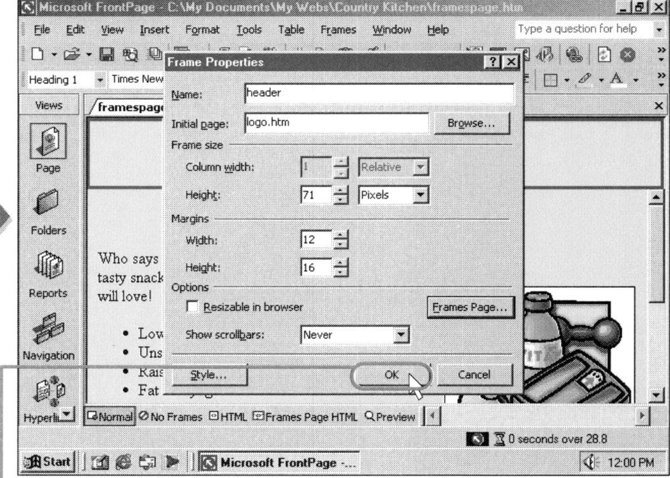

7 Click **OK** to close the Frame Properties dialog box.

■ FrontPage hides the borders between all the frames.

Note: To see how the frames will appear in a Web browser, you can use the Preview view. For information on the Preview view, see page 42.

PROVIDE ALTERNATIVE TEXT FOR FRAMES

You can provide text that you want to appear if a visitor's Web browser cannot display frames. This will give visitors information about the missing frames.

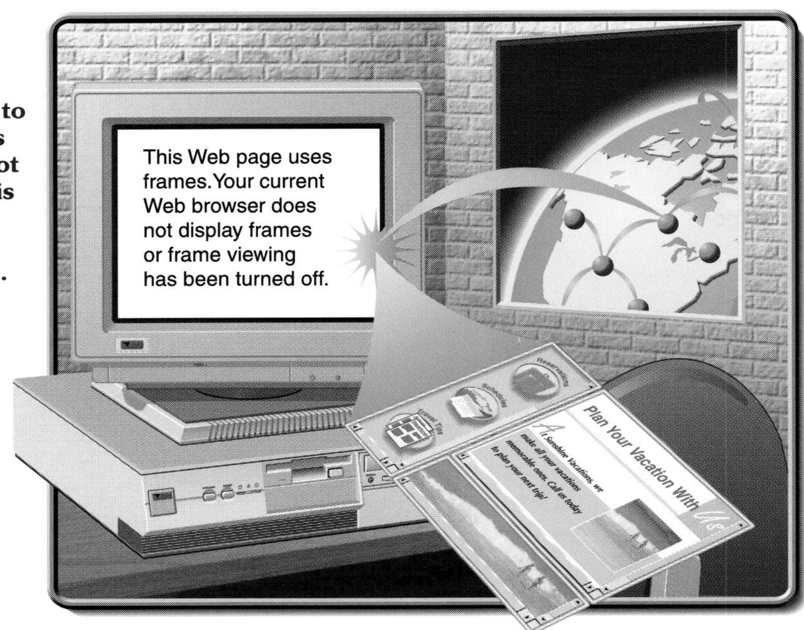

FrontPage automatically provides text that will appear on a Web page if a visitor's Web browser cannot display your frames. You can change the text that FrontPage provides.

PROVIDE ALTERNATIVE TEXT FOR FRAMES

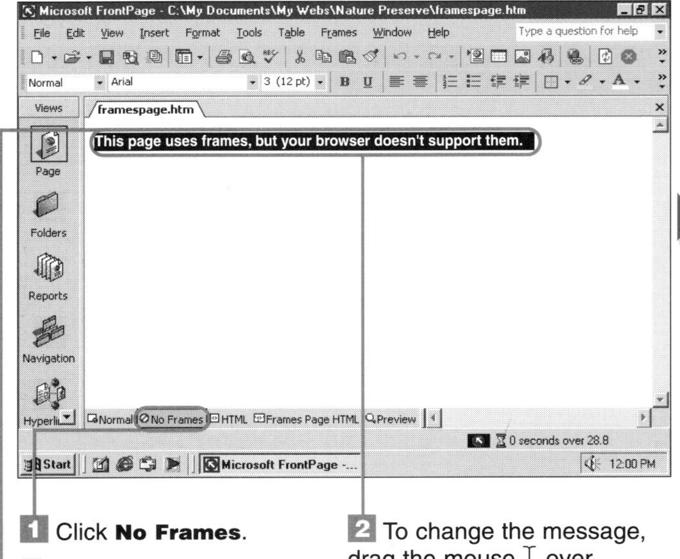

1 Click **No Frames**.

■ This area displays the message that visitors will see if their Web browser cannot display frames.

2 To change the message, drag the mouse I over the existing text until you highlight all the text. Then press the Delete key.

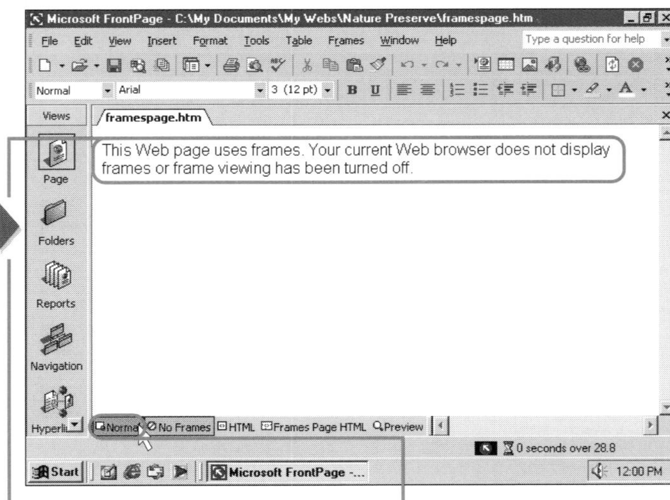

3 Type the text you want to appear if a visitor's Web browser cannot display frames.

Note: You can format the text as you would format text on any Web page. To format text, see pages 68 to 72.

4 To return to the normal view of your Web page, click **Normal**.

PREVENT VISITORS FROM RESIZING A FRAME

You can prevent visitors from resizing a frame. This is useful when you do not want the layout of your frames to change.

Visitors may want to change the size of a frame to display more information in the frame.

FrontPage automatically prevents visitors from resizing some frames, such as a frame displaying a banner.

PREVENT VISITORS FROM RESIZING A FRAME

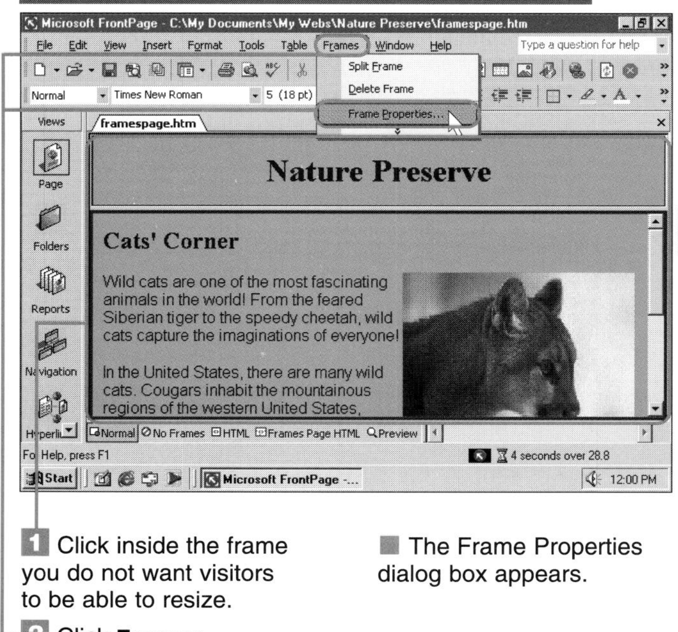

1 Click inside the frame you do not want visitors to be able to resize.

2 Click **Frames**.

3 Click **Frame Properties**.

■ The Frame Properties dialog box appears.

4 Click this option if you do not want visitors to be able to resize the frame (☑ changes to ☐).

5 Click **OK**.

Note: When you prevent visitors from resizing a frame, they will not be able to use the borders of the frame to resize neighboring frames.

■ To once again allow visitors to resize a frame, repeat steps 1 to 5 (☐ changes to ☑ in step 4).

SET A FRAMES PAGE AS YOUR HOME PAGE

If you want your frames page to appear when people first visit your Web site, you need to set the frames page as your home page.

The home page is usually the first page people will see when they visit a Web site. When you create a Web site, FrontPage automatically names your home page index.htm.

SET A FRAMES PAGE AS YOUR HOME PAGE

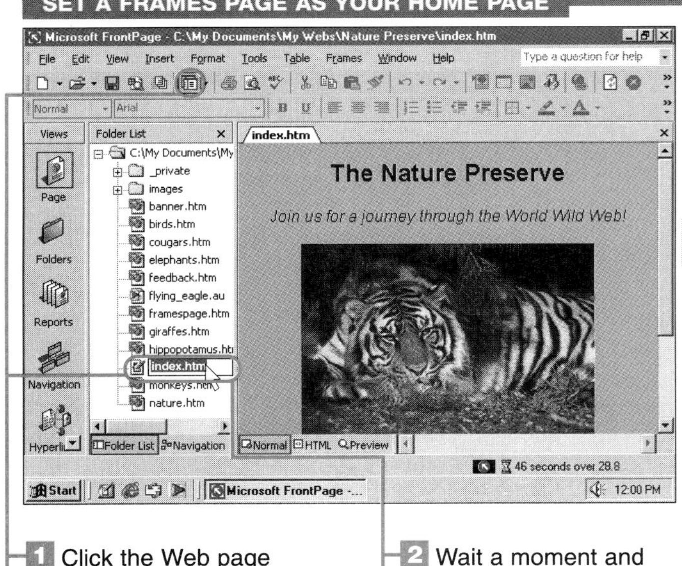

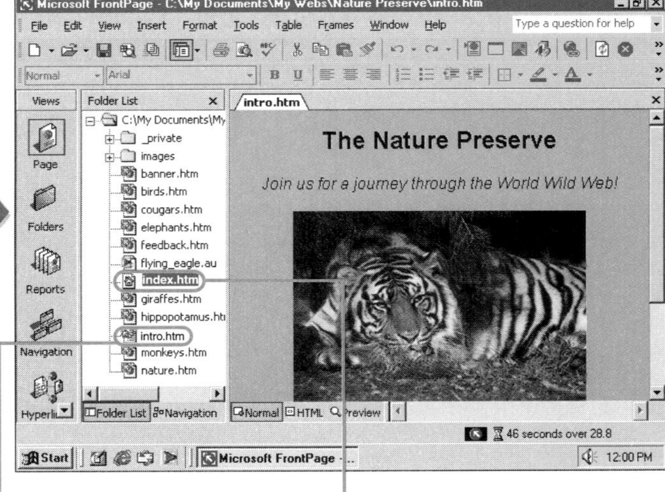

1 Click the Web page named **index.htm**. This page is currently your home page.

■ If the list of Web pages does not appear, click ▤ to display the list.

2 Wait a moment and click the Web page name again.

■ The name of the Web page appears in a box.

3 Type a new name for the Web page. Make sure you add the **.htm** extension to the end of the name. Then press the Enter key.

*Note: A confirmation dialog box appears. Click **Yes** to rename the Web page.*

4 Click the name of your frames page.

5 Wait a moment and click the frames page name again.

6 Type **index.htm** to set the frames page as your home page and then press the Enter key.

CREATE AN INLINE FRAME

You can create an inline frame on a Web page. An inline frame allows you to display a Web page within another Web page.

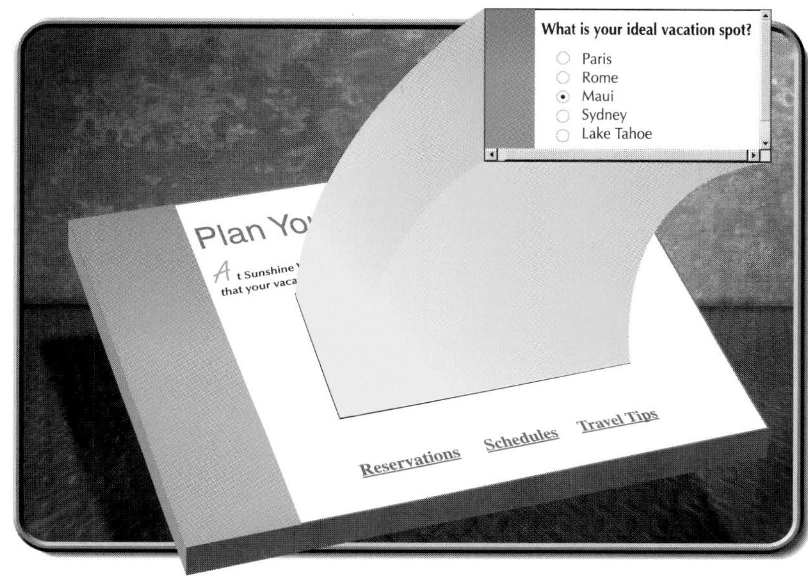

You may want to create an inline frame to display information such as a questionnaire or product descriptions.

CREATE AN INLINE FRAME

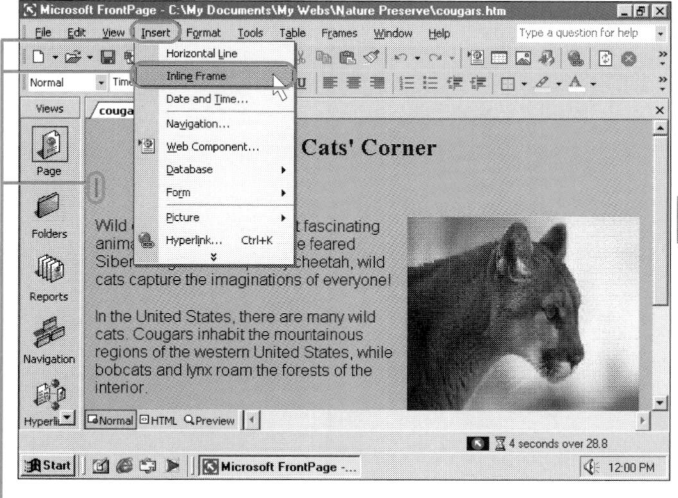

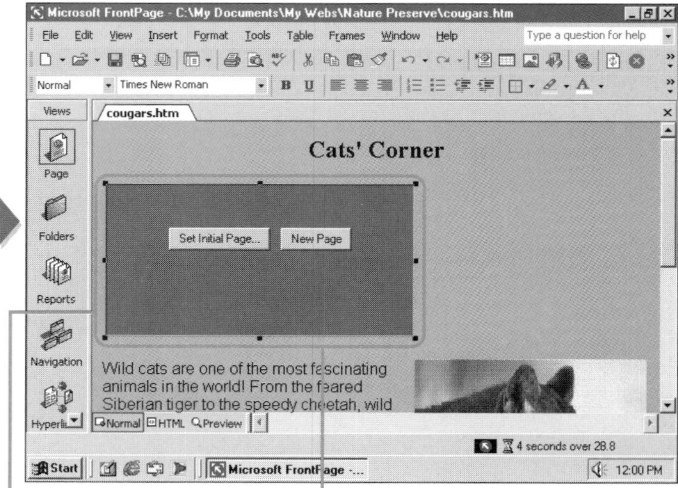

1 Click the location on your Web page where you want to add an inline frame.

2 Click **Insert**.

3 Click **Inline Frame**.

Note: If Inline Frame is not displayed on the menu, position the mouse over the bottom of the menu to display all the menu options.

■ The inline frame appears.

Note: To resize an inline frame, click an edge of the frame and then perform steps 2 and 3 on page 105.

■ To add an existing Web page to the frame, see page 192. To add a new Web page to the frame, see page 194.

■ To delete an inline frame, click an edge of the frame and then press the Delete key.

Form
The Fishing C
CUSTOMER INFORMATION

CHAPTER 12

Create Forms

Would you like to create forms that visitors can use to send you information? Find out how in this chapter.

SET UP A FORM

Forms allow you to gather information from visitors who view your Web pages. Setting up a form allows you to create the basic structure of a form.

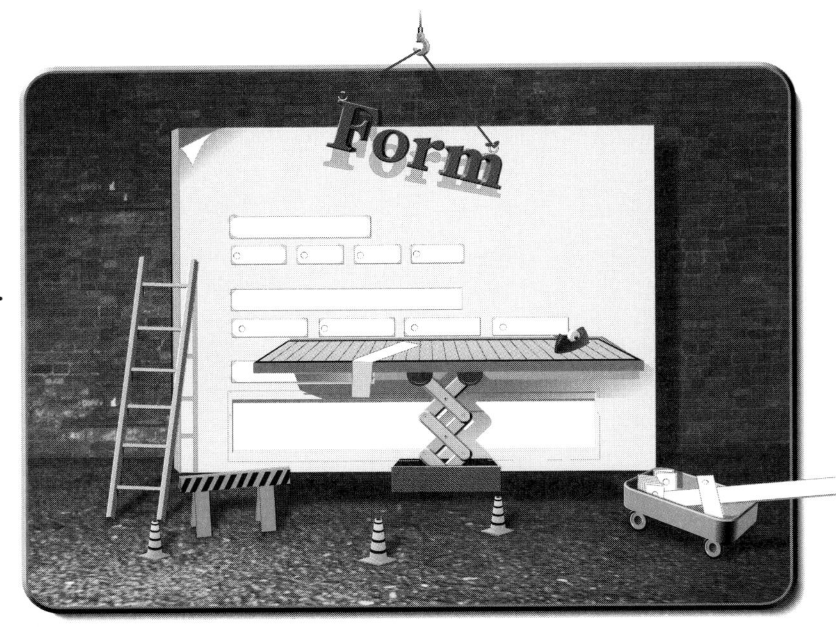

Forms have many uses. For example, you can create a form that allows visitors to send you questions or comments about your Web pages. You can also create a form that allows visitors to purchase your products and services on the Web.

SET UP A FORM

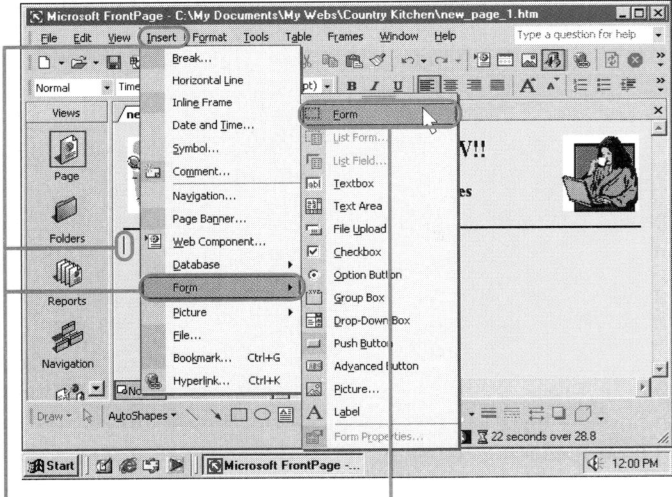

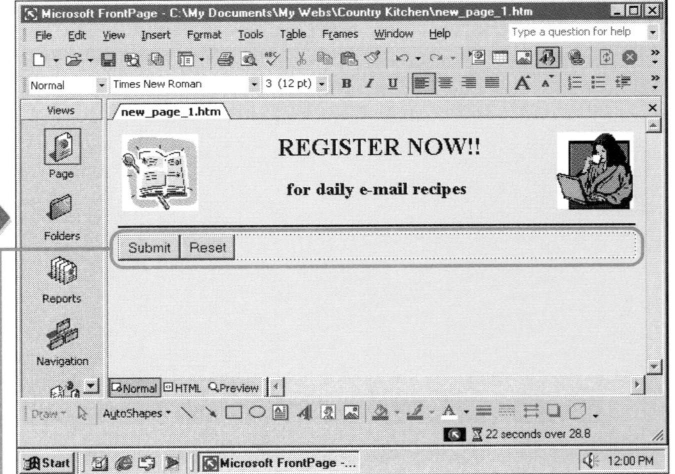

1 Click the location on your Web page where you want the form to appear.

2 Click **Insert**.

3 Click **Form**.

4 Click **Form**.

Note: If all the options are not displayed on a menu, position the mouse over the bottom of the menu to display all the menu options.

■ The form appears on your Web page, displaying the Submit and Reset buttons. A dotted line shows the boundaries of the form.

5 To increase the size of the form so you can easily add information to the form, press the **Enter** key several times.

Note: To add information to the form, see pages 214 to 225.

What should I consider before I set up a form?

For a form to work properly when you publish your Web pages, your Web server must have the FrontPage Server Extensions installed. You can determine if your Web server has the FrontPage Server Extensions installed by asking the company that will make your Web pages available on the Web.

How do forms work?

A visitor can enter information and select options on a form. When a visitor clicks the Submit button, the information entered in the form transfers to your Web server.

When your Web server receives information from a form, the server processes the information. The results of a form are automatically stored in a file on your Web server. To change how you access the results of a form, see page 228.

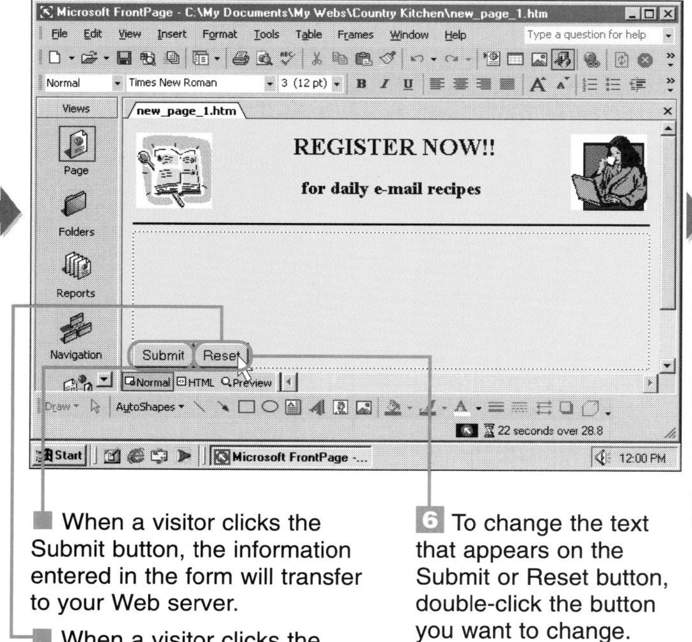

■ When a visitor clicks the Submit button, the information entered in the form will transfer to your Web server.

■ When a visitor clicks the Reset button, the information entered in the form will disappear and the form will display its original settings.

6 To change the text that appears on the Submit or Reset button, double-click the button you want to change.

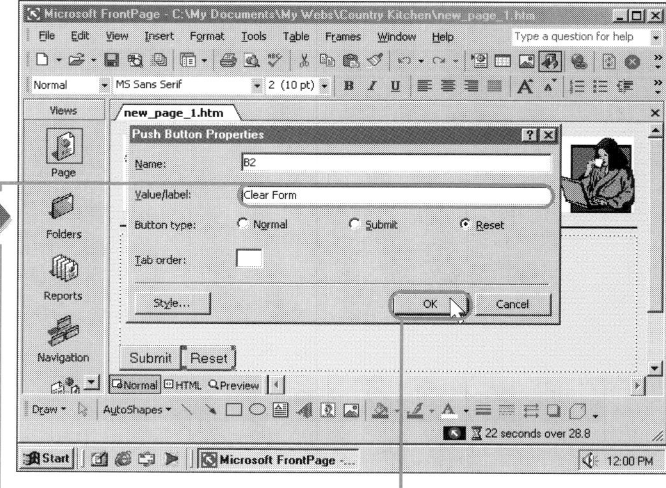

■ The Push Button Properties dialog box appears.

7 Double-click the text in this area and then type the text you want to appear on the button.

8 Click **OK** to confirm your change.

ADD A TEXT BOX

You can add a text box to a form that allows visitors to enter a small amount of text. A text box is commonly used for entering a name, mailing address or e-mail address.

ADD A TEXT BOX

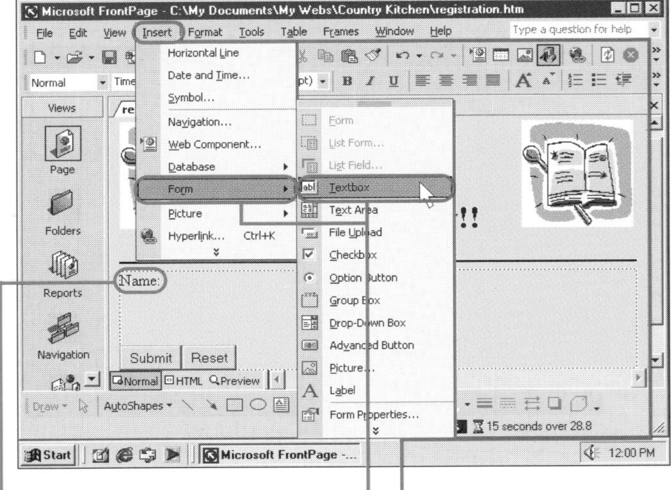

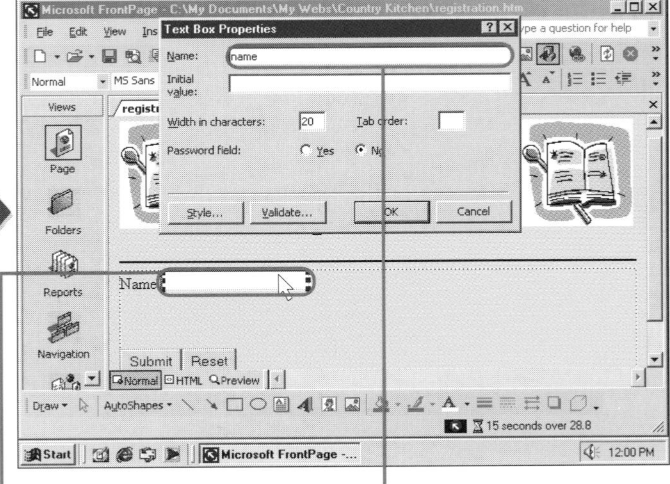

1 Click the area in your form where you want to add a text box.

2 Type the text you want to appear beside the text box.

3 Click **Insert**.

4 Click **Form**.

5 Click **Textbox**.

Note: If all the options are not displayed on a menu, position the mouse over the bottom of the menu to display all the menu options.

■ The text box appears on your Web page.

6 Double-click the text box to change the properties of the text box.

■ The Text Box Properties dialog box appears.

7 Type a name to identify the text box. A name should not contain blank spaces.

Note: The name you enter will not appear on your Web page. The name identifies the information visitors enter in the text box when you view the form results.

Can I create a text box that hides the information visitors enter?

You can create a text box that displays an asterisk (*) for each character visitors type. This is known as a password box. A password box allows visitors to enter confidential information, such as a password or credit card number, without other people viewing the information.

To create a password box, click **Yes** beside Password field in the Text Box Properties dialog box (○ changes to ⊙).

Will the width of a text box affect the number of characters visitors can enter in the text box?

No. The width of a text box only determines the size of the text box on your Web page. If visitors enter more characters than the text box can display, the existing text moves to the left to make room for the new text.

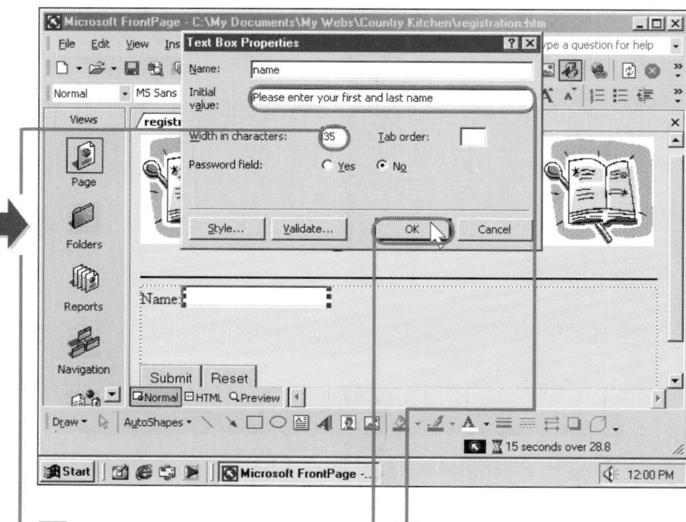

8 To change the width of the text box, double-click the number in this area and type a width for the text box in characters.

9 If you want sample text or instructions to appear in the text box when visitors display the Web page, click this area and type the text.

10 Click **OK** to confirm your changes.

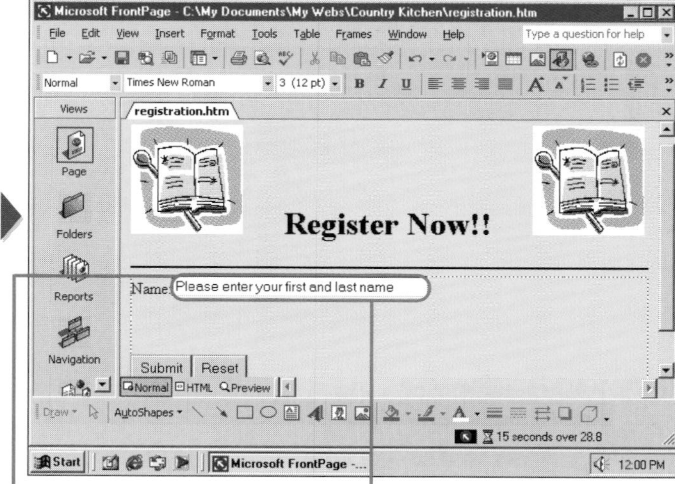

■ A visitor can click in the text box and type the requested information. If you entered sample text or instructions in step 9, the information appears in the text box.

Note: To try entering information into the text box, you can use the Preview view. For information on the Preview view, see page 42.

■ To delete a text box, click the text box and then press the Delete key.

ADD A TEXT AREA

You can add a text area to a form that allows visitors to enter several lines or paragraphs of text.

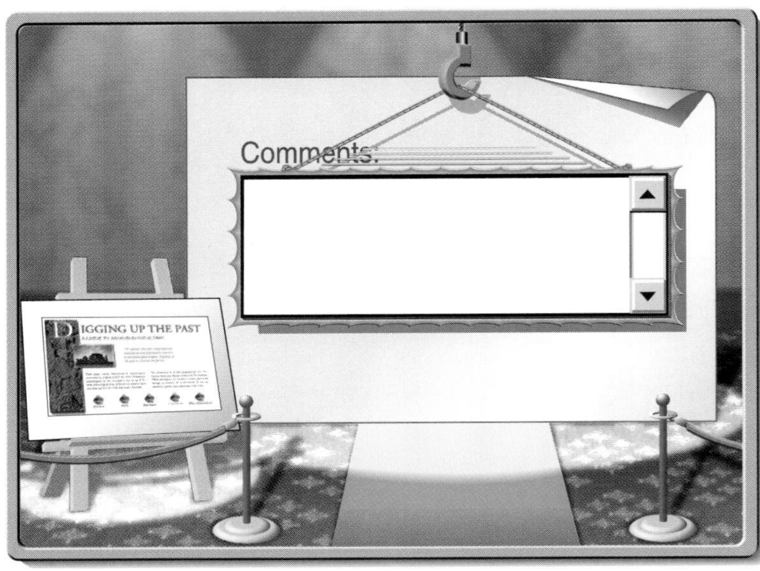

A text area is ideal for gathering comments or questions from your visitors.

ADD A TEXT AREA

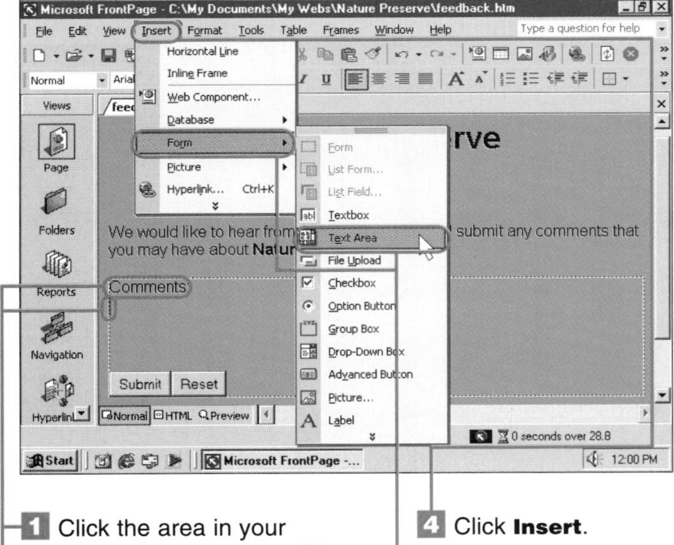

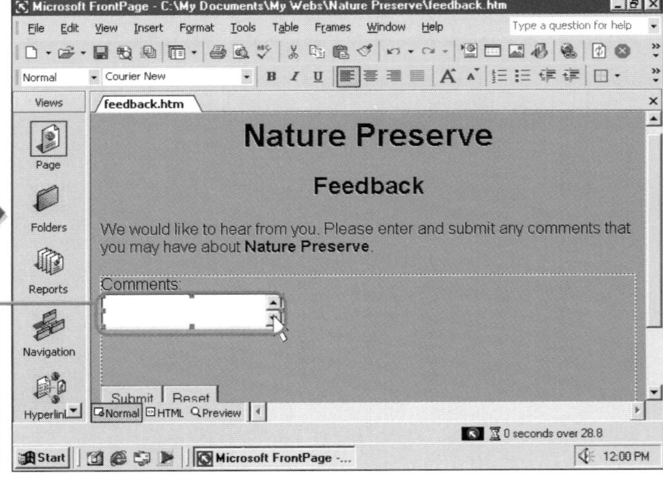

1 Click the area in your form where you want to add a text area.

2 Type the text you want to appear above the text area.

3 To place the text area on a new line, press and hold down the **Shift** key as you press the **Enter** key.

4 Click **Insert**.

5 Click **Form**.

6 Click **Text Area**.

Note: If all the options are not displayed on a menu, position the mouse over the bottom of the menu to display all the menu options.

■ The text area appears on your Web page.

7 Double-click the text area to change the properties of the text area.

■ The TextArea Box Properties dialog box appears.

Can I change the size of a text area?

You can change the size of a text area to change the amount of text that visitors will be able to see in the text area when entering information. If the text visitors type does not fit in the text area, visitors can use the scroll bar to scroll through the text. To change the size of a text area:

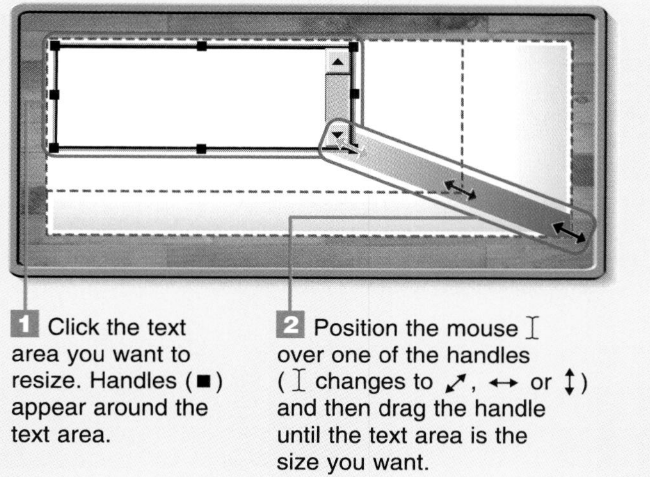

1 Click the text area you want to resize. Handles (■) appear around the text area.

2 Position the mouse I over one of the handles (I changes to ⤢, ↔ or ↕) and then drag the handle until the text area is the size you want.

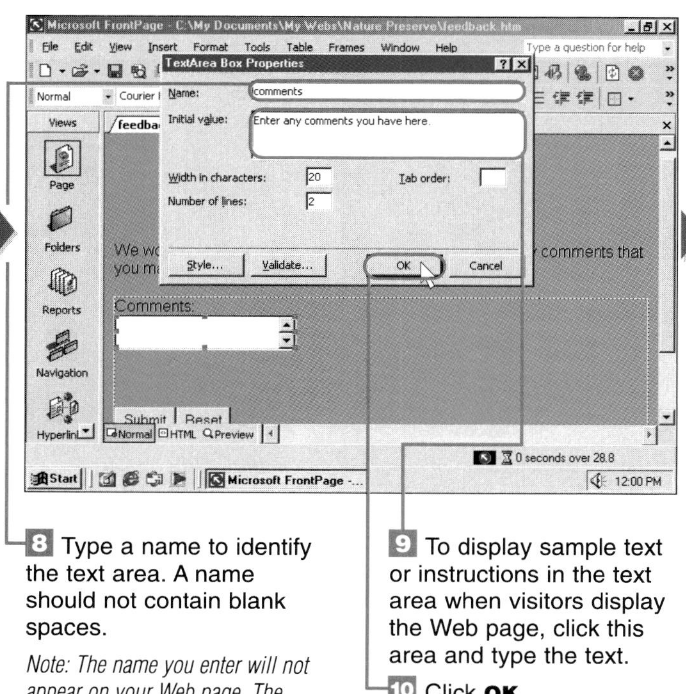

8 Type a name to identify the text area. A name should not contain blank spaces.

Note: The name you enter will not appear on your Web page. The name identifies the information visitors enter in the text area when you view the form results.

9 To display sample text or instructions in the text area when visitors display the Web page, click this area and type the text.

10 Click **OK**.

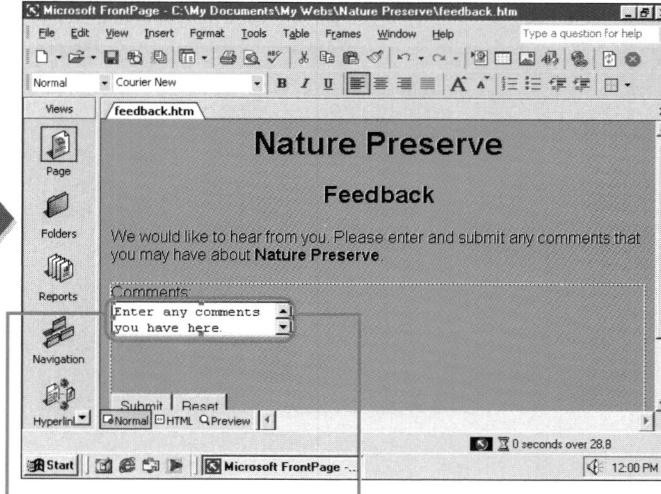

■ A visitor can click in the text area and type the requested information. If you entered sample text or instructions in step 9, the information appears in the text area.

Note: To try entering text into the text area, you can use the Preview view. For information on the Preview view, see page 42.

■ To delete a text area, click the text area and then press the Delete key.

ADD CHECK BOXES

You can include check boxes on a form if you want visitors to be able to select one or more options.

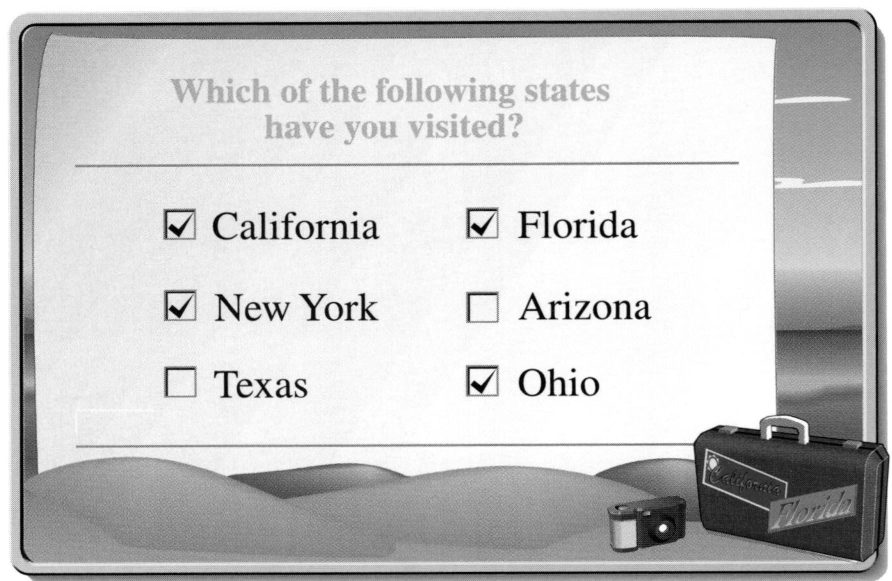

Which of the following states have you visited?
California
Florida
New York
Arizona
Texas
Ohio
California
Florida

ADD CHECK BOXES

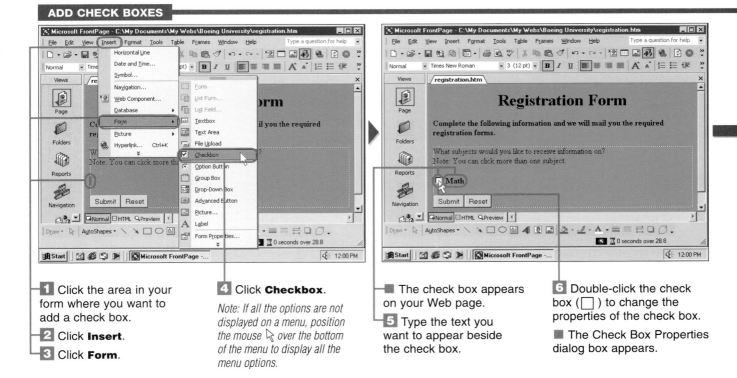

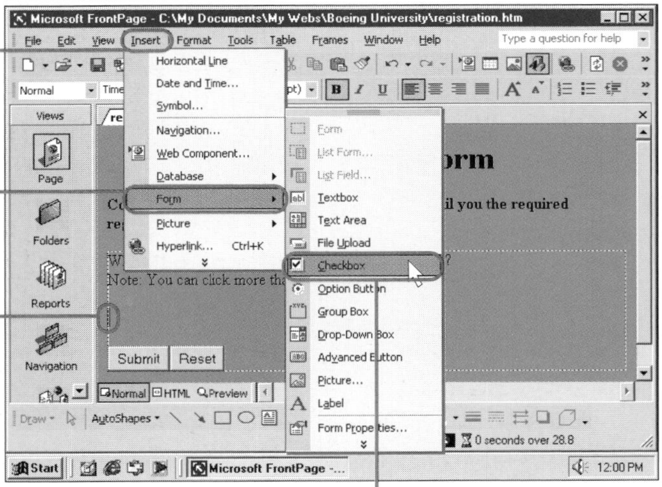

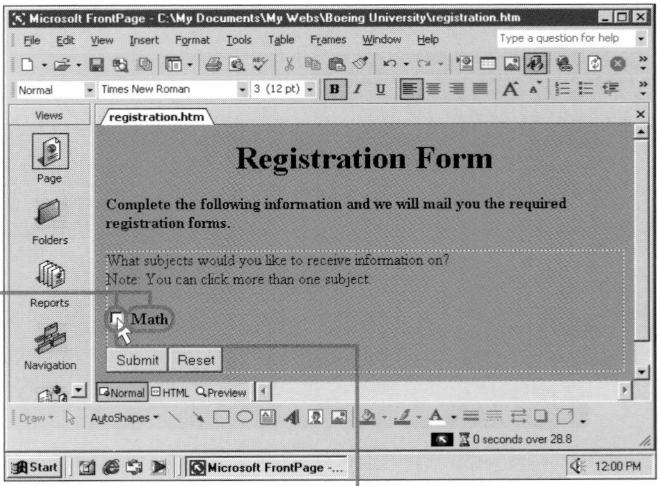

1 Click the area in your form where you want to add a check box.

2 Click **Insert**.

3 Click **Form**.

4 Click **Checkbox**.

Note: If all the options are not displayed on a menu, position the mouse over the bottom of the menu to display all the menu options.

■ The check box appears on your Web page.

5 Type the text you want to appear beside the check box.

6 Double-click the check box (☐) to change the properties of the check box.

■ The Check Box Properties dialog box appears.

What information do I need to specify when creating check boxes?

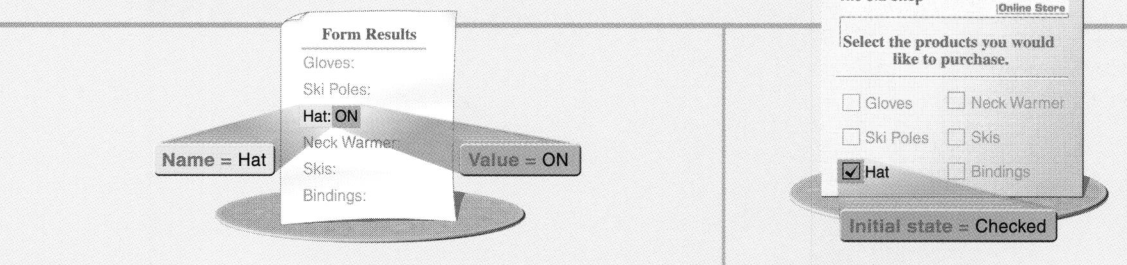

Name
You need to specify a name that describes a check box. The name identifies the check box when you view the results of the form.

Value
You need to specify a value for a check box. When you view the results of the form, the value appears with the name of the check box to indicate the check box was selected.

Initial state
You need to specify if you want a check box to initially appear checked or not checked on the form. If most people will select the option, choose the Checked option.

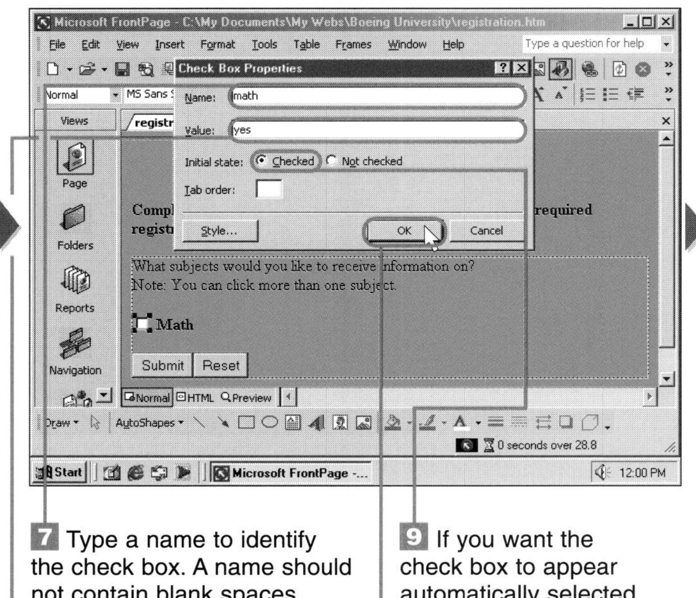

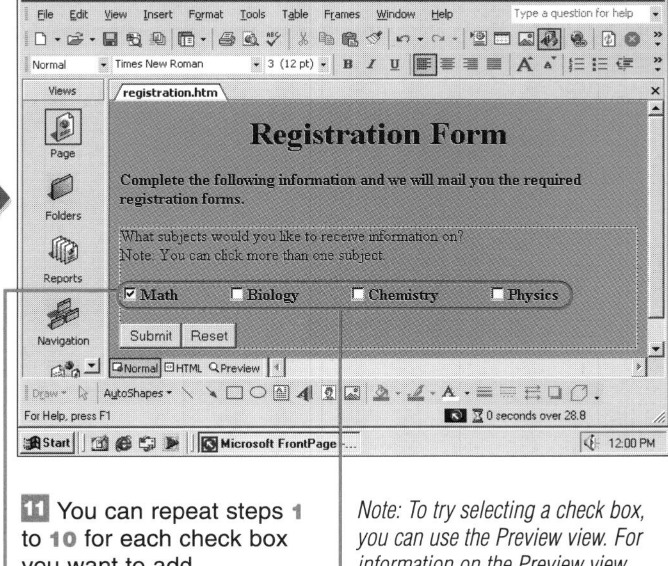

7 Type a name to identify the check box. A name should not contain blank spaces.

8 Double-click this area and type a value for the check box.

Note: The name and value you enter will not appear on your Web page.

9 If you want the check box to appear automatically selected when a visitor displays the Web page, click **Checked** (○ changes to ⊙).

10 Click **OK**.

11 You can repeat steps 1 to 10 for each check box you want to add.

■ A visitor can click the check box for each option they want to select (☐ changes to ☑).

Note: To try selecting a check box, you can use the Preview view. For information on the Preview view, see page 42.

■ To delete a check box, click the check box (☐) and then press the Delete key.

ADD OPTION BUTTONS

You can include option buttons on a form to allow visitors to select only one of several options.

Option buttons are also called radio buttons.

ADD OPTION BUTTONS

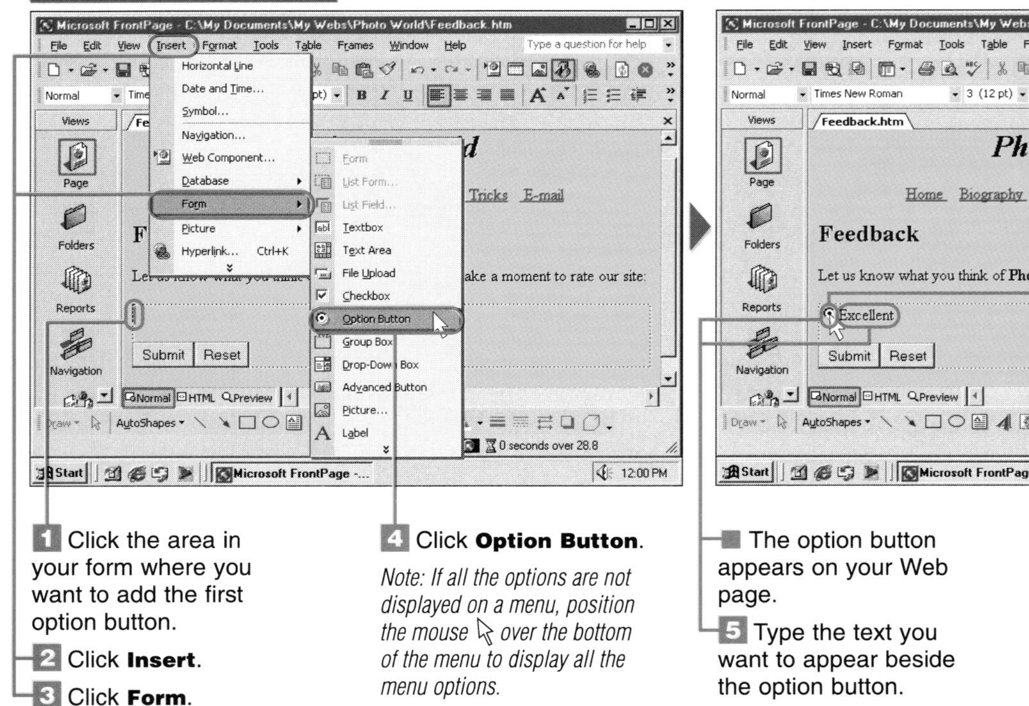

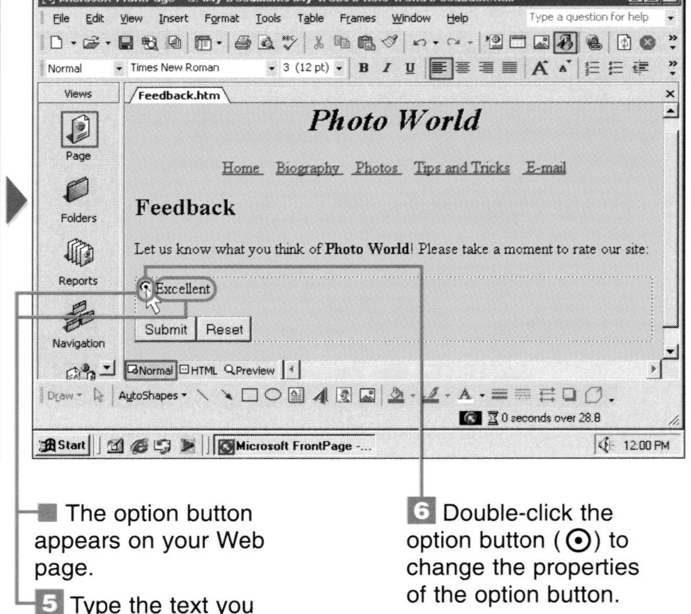

1 Click the area in your form where you want to add the first option button.

2 Click **Insert**.

3 Click **Form**.

4 Click **Option Button**.

Note: If all the options are not displayed on a menu, position the mouse over the bottom of the menu to display all the menu options.

■ The option button appears on your Web page.

5 Type the text you want to appear beside the option button.

6 Double-click the option button (⊙) to change the properties of the option button.

■ The Option Button Properties dialog box appears.

What information do I need to specify when creating option buttons?

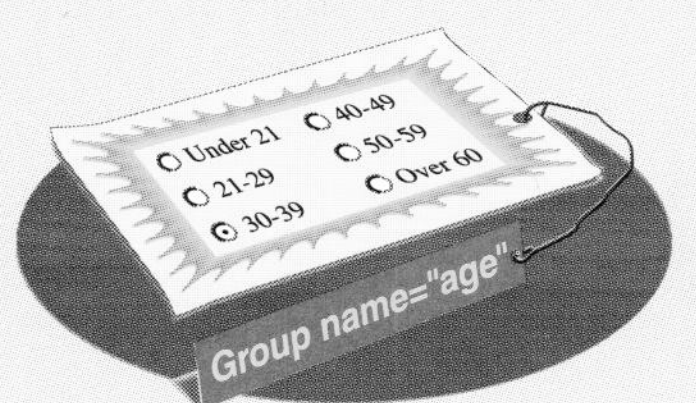

Group name
You need to specify a name that describes the group of option buttons. The name identifies the group of option buttons when you view the results of the form.

Value
You need to specify a value that describes each option button. When you view the results of the form, the value appears with the group name to indicate which option button was selected.

Initial state
You need to specify if you want an option button to initially appear selected or not selected in the form. Only one option button in a group can appear selected.

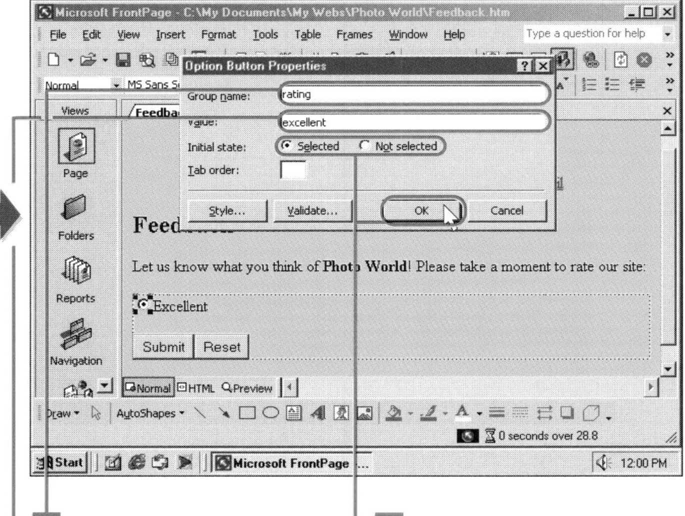

7 Type a name to identify the group of option buttons. A name should not contain blank spaces.

8 Double-click the text in this area and type a value for the option button.

Note: The name and value you enter will not appear on your Web page.

9 Click an option to specify if you want the option button to appear automatically selected when a visitor displays the Web page (○ changes to ⊙).

10 Click **OK**.

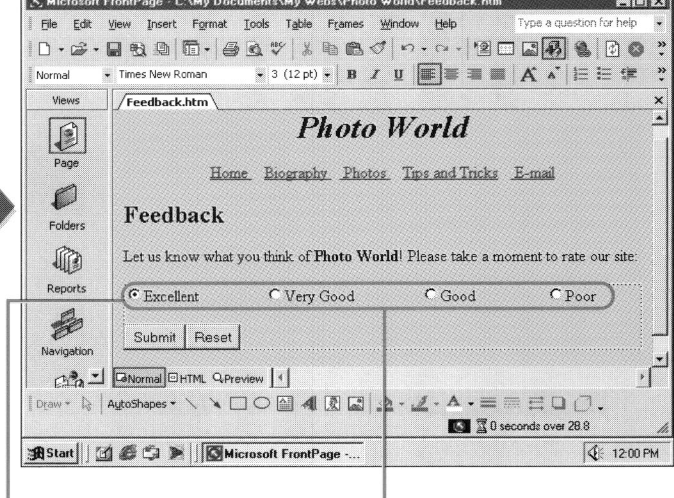

11 You can repeat steps 1 to 10 for each option button you want to add.

■ A visitor can click an option button to select one of several options (○ changes to ⊙).

Note: To try selecting an option button, you can use the Preview view. For information on the Preview view, see page 42.

■ To delete an option button, click the option button (○) and then press the Delete key.

ADD A DROP-DOWN BOX

You can add a drop-down box to a form to provide a list of items that visitors can choose from.

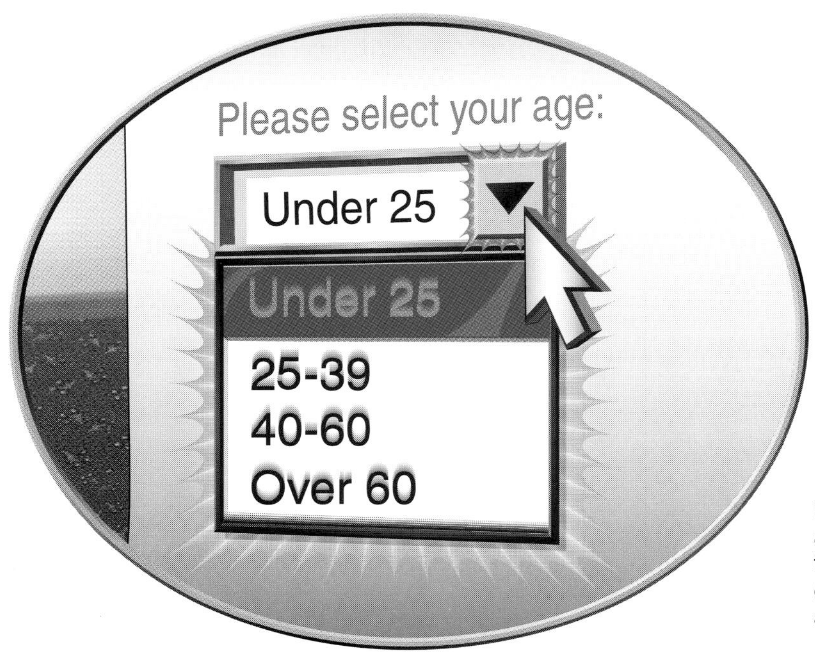

Drop-down boxes are commonly used for displaying lists of states, products and age groups.

ADD A DROP-DOWN BOX

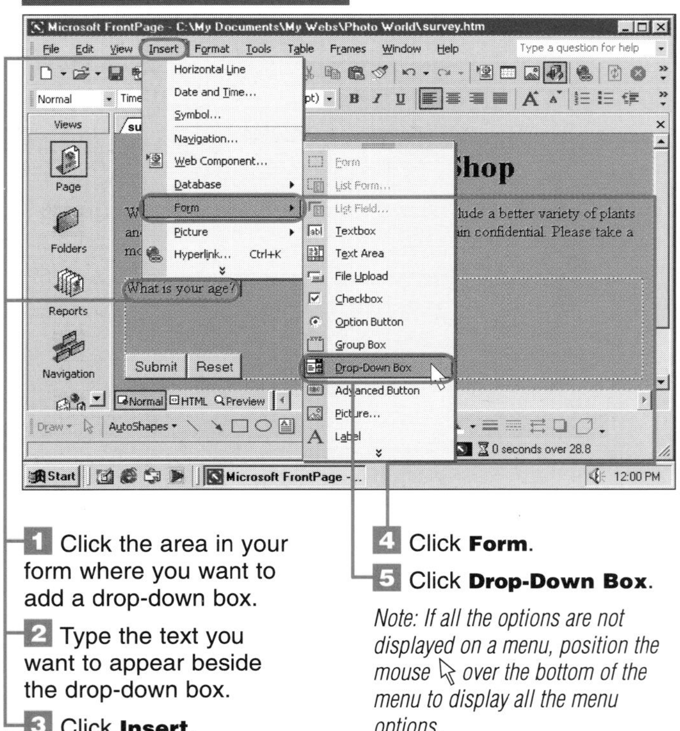

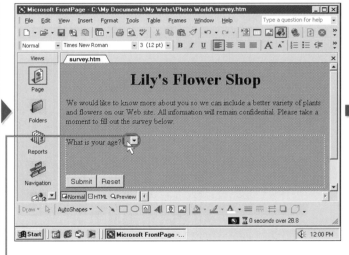

1 Click the area in your form where you want to add a drop-down box.

2 Type the text you want to appear beside the drop-down box.

3 Click **Insert**.

4 Click **Form**.

5 Click **Drop-Down Box**.

Note: If all the options are not displayed on a menu, position the mouse over the bottom of the menu to display all the menu options.

■ The drop-down box appears on your Web page.

6 Double-click the drop-down box to add items to the box.

■ The Drop-Down Box Properties dialog box appears.

What information do I need to specify when creating a drop-down box?

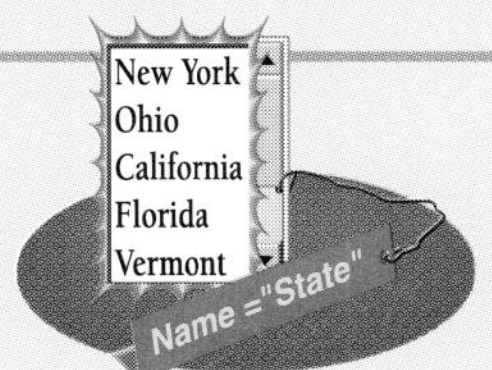

Name

You need to specify a name that describes the drop-down box. The name identifies the drop-down box when you view the results of the form.

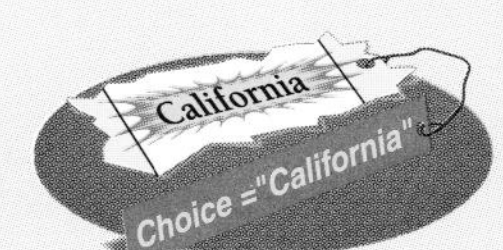

Choice

You need to specify the text you want to appear for each item in the drop-down box.

Value

You can specify a value for each item in the drop-down box. When you view the results of the form, the value identifies the item a visitor selected. The value can be the same as the text displayed in the drop-down box or you can use different text. For example, you can use a more specific or shorter name, such as CA for California.

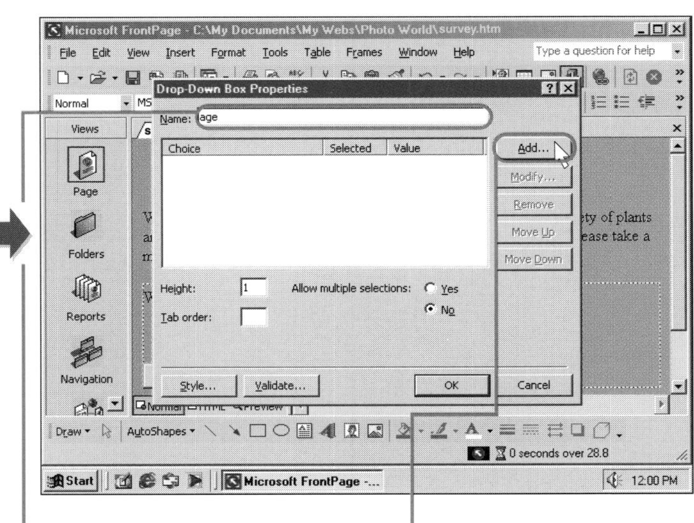

7 Double-click the text in this area and type a name to identify the drop-down box. A name should not contain blank spaces.

Note: The name you enter will not appear on your Web page.

8 Click **Add** to add an item to the drop-down box.

■ The Add Choice dialog box appears.

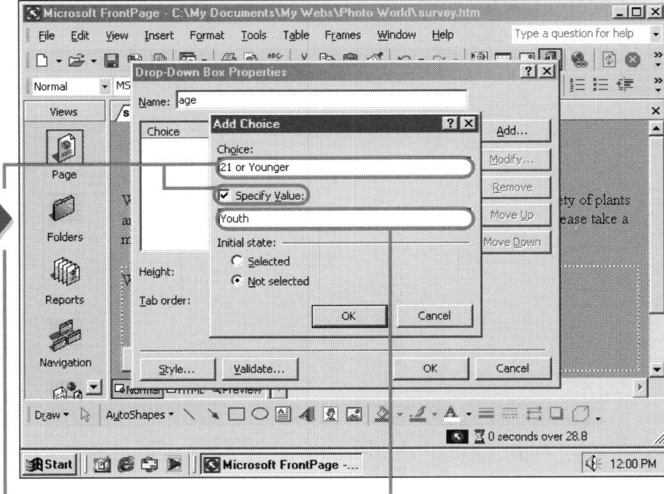

9 Type the first item you want to appear in the drop-down box.

■ The text you typed in step 9 will automatically be the value for the item.

10 To use a different value for the item, click **Specify Value** (☐ changes to ☑).

11 To specify a value for the item, drag the mouse I over the text in this area and then type the value.

CONTINUED

ADD A DROP-DOWN BOX

You can have an item in a drop-down box appear automatically selected on your form. This option is useful if most people will select the item.

ADD A DROP-DOWN BOX (CONTINUED)

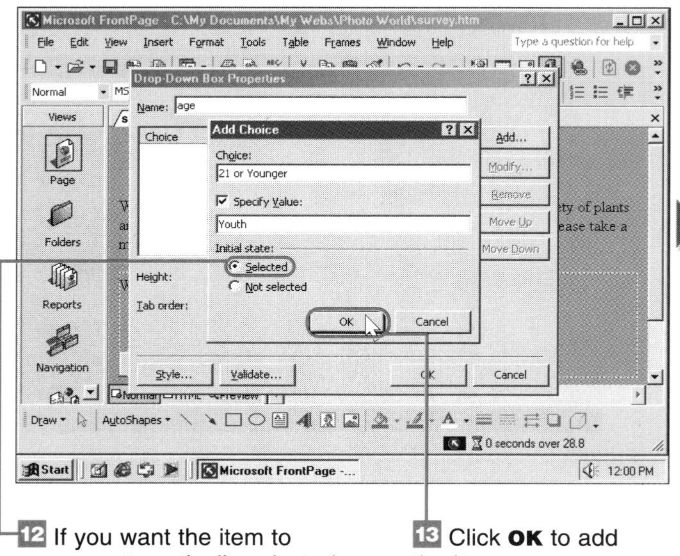

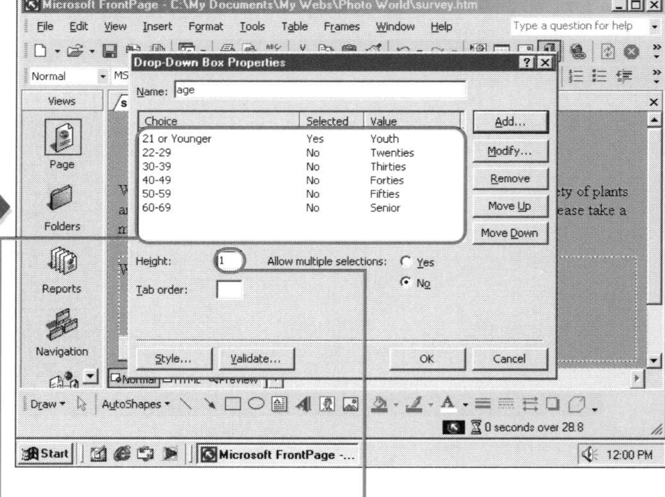

12 If you want the item to appear automatically selected when a visitor displays the Web page, click **Selected** (○ changes to ⊙).

13 Click **OK** to add the item.

■ This area displays the item you added.

14 Repeat steps **8** to **13** for each item you want to add to the drop-down box.

■ This area displays the number of items that visitors will initially see in the drop-down box.

15 To change the number of items that visitors will initially see, double-click the number in this area and type a new number.

Why would I change the number of items visitors initially see in a drop-down box?

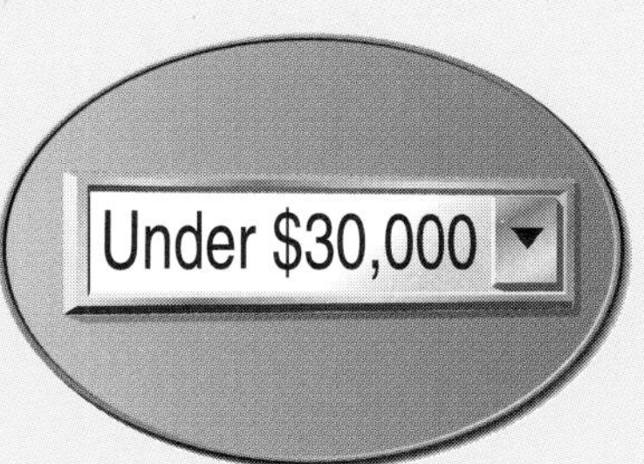

To save space on your form, FrontPage initially sets up a drop-down box to show only the first item. Visitors can click the arrow (▾) to display all the items.

Please select your income:
Under $30,000
$30,000 to $50,000
Over $50,000

If you have a short list of items, you may want a drop-down box to display all the items at once. For example, if your drop-down box contains three items, you can type **3** in step **15** below to display all three items on your form.

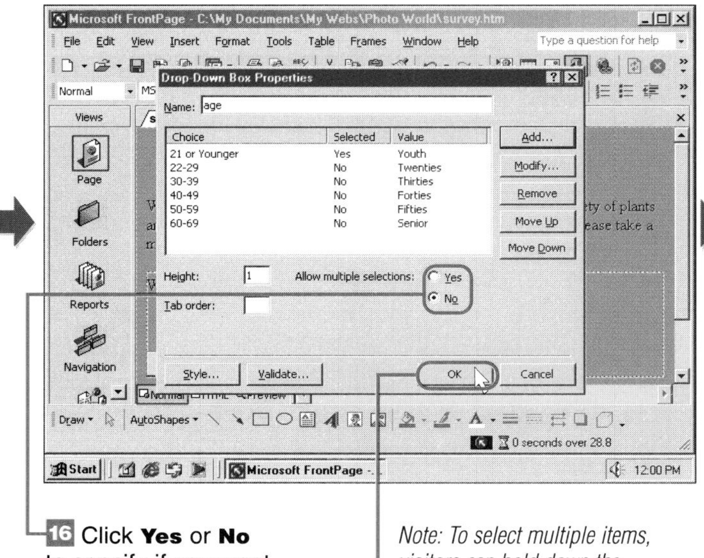

16 Click **Yes** or **No** to specify if you want visitors to be able to select more than one item from the drop-down box (○ changes to ⊙).

Note: To select multiple items, visitors can hold down the Ctrl *key as they click each item.*

17 Click **OK** to confirm all of your changes.

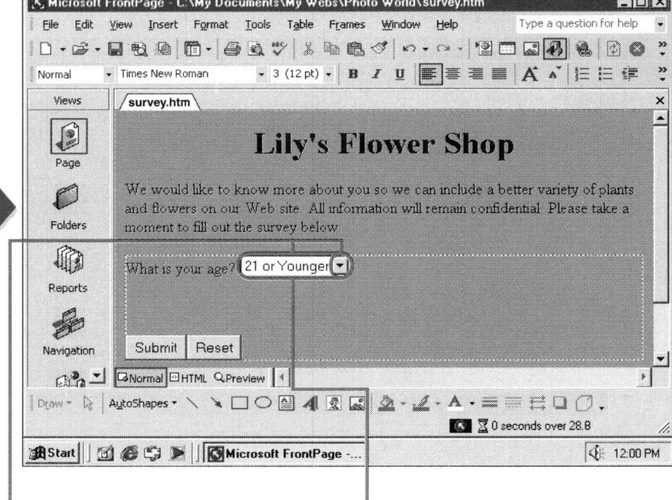

■ The drop-down box displays your changes.

■ In this example, a visitor can click the arrow (▾) to display the items in the drop-down box.

Note: To try selecting an item from a drop-down box, you can use the Preview view. For information on the Preview view, see page 42.

■ To delete a drop-down box, click the drop-down box and then press the Delete key.

CREATE A FEEDBACK FORM

You can quickly create a feedback form that visitors can use to send you questions and comments about your Web pages, products or company.

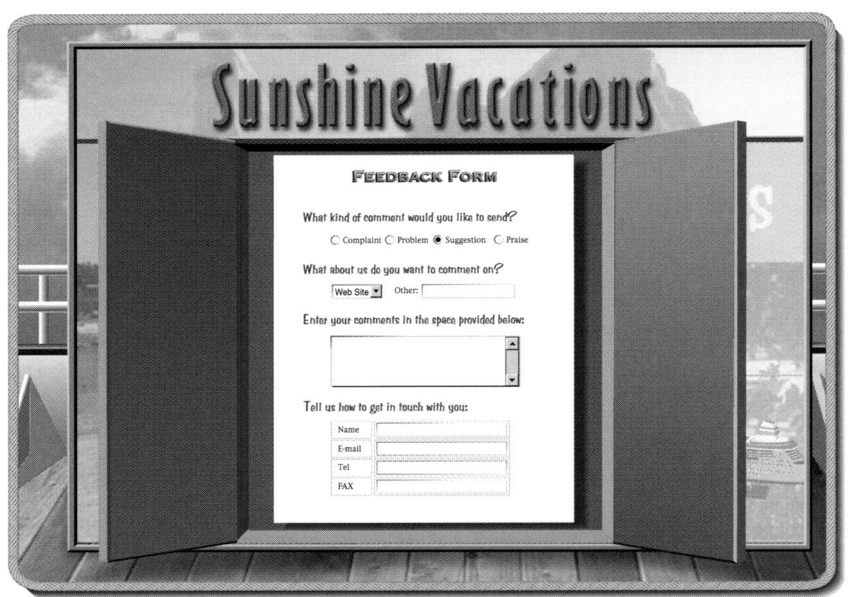

The Feedback Form template included with FrontPage provides the layout, design and text for a feedback form.

CREATE A FEEDBACK FORM

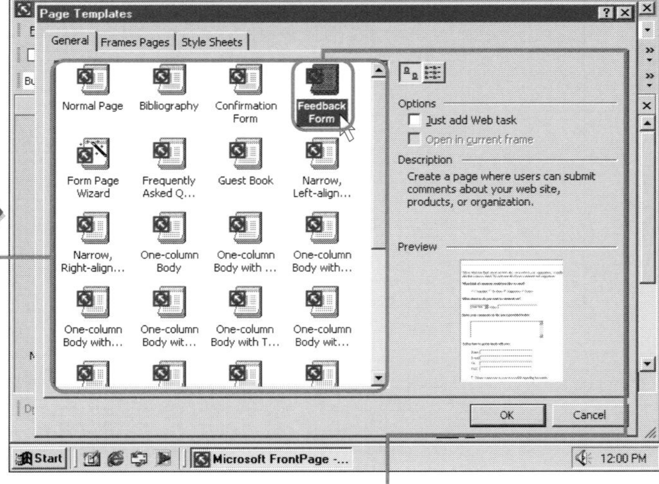

1 Click ▾ in this area.

2 Click **Page**.

■ The Page Templates dialog box appears.

■ This area displays the templates you can use to create a Web page.

3 Click **Feedback Form** to create a Web page that allows visitors to send you questions or comments about your Web pages, products or company.

Can I add additional information to a feedback form?

After you create a feedback form, you can add as many form elements to the form as you wish. For example, you may want to add text boxes that allow visitors to enter their mailing address or a group of option buttons that allows visitors to rate your Web site. To add form elements to a form, see pages 214 to 225.

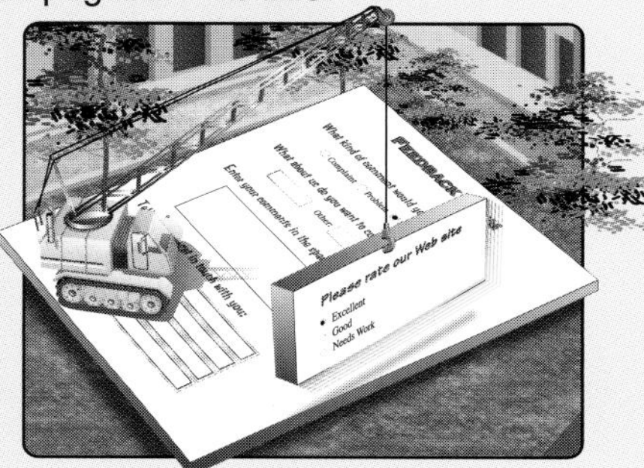

Is there another way that FrontPage can help me create a form?

Yes. FrontPage provides a wizard that will ask you a series of questions about the form you want to create and then use your answers to create a customized form. To create a form using the wizard, perform steps 1 to 4 below, selecting **Form Page Wizard** in step 3.

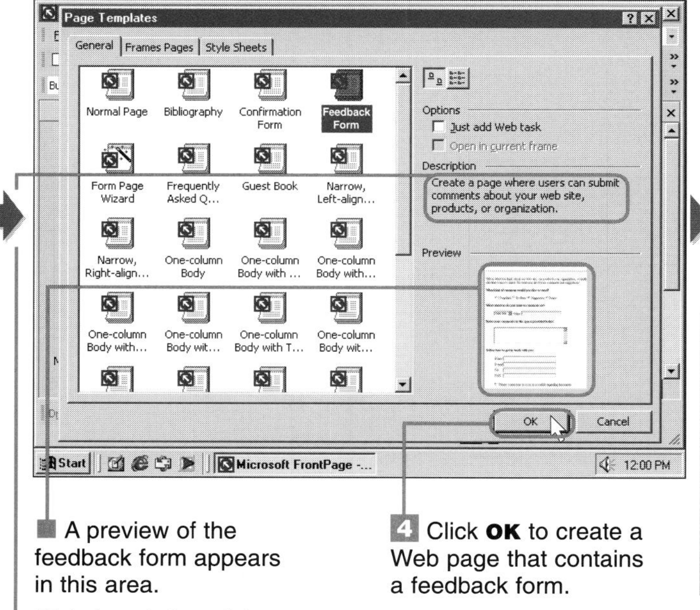

■ A preview of the feedback form appears in this area.

■ A description of the feedback form appears in this area.

4 Click **OK** to create a Web page that contains a feedback form.

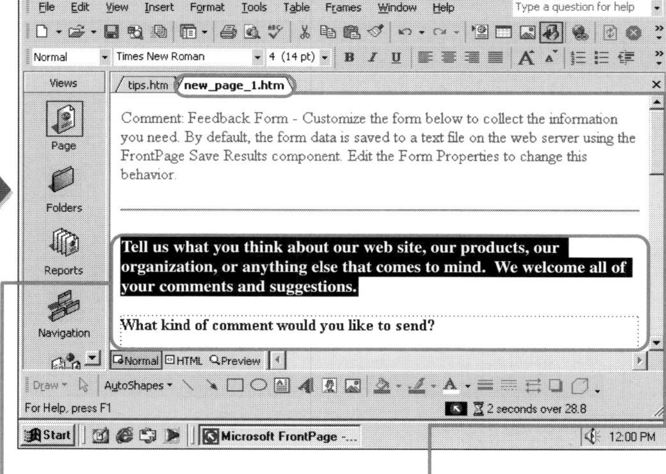

■ A new Web page appears, displaying a feedback form.

5 To replace the sample text on the feedback form with your own information, drag the mouse I over an area of text until you highlight the text and then type your own information.

■ A tab displays a temporary file name for the Web page. To save and name the Web page, see page 28.

ACCESS FORM RESULTS

After you create a form, you need to specify how you want to access the results of the form.

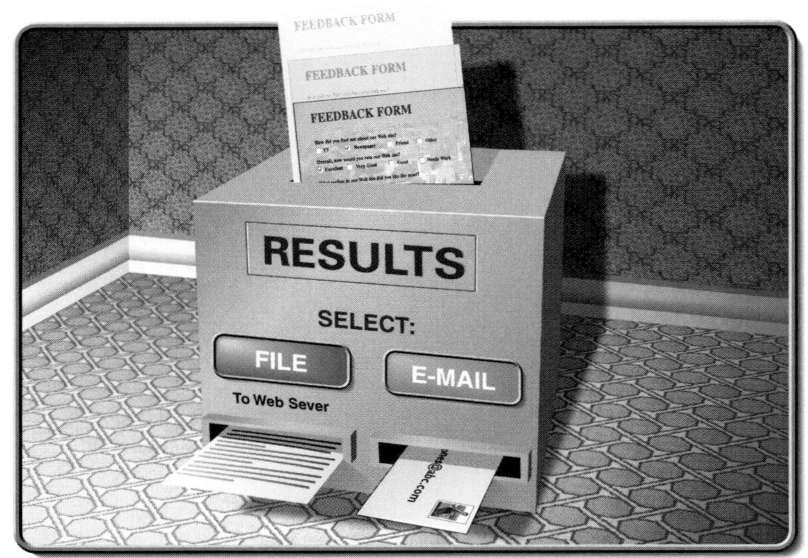

File

You can store the form results in a file on your Web server. When visitors enter information into the form, the information will be added to the file.

E-mail

You can send the form results in e-mail messages. When visitors enter information into the form, the information will be sent to the e-mail address you specify. To use this feature, your Web server must be set up to send the results of forms in e-mail messages.

ACCESS FORM RESULTS

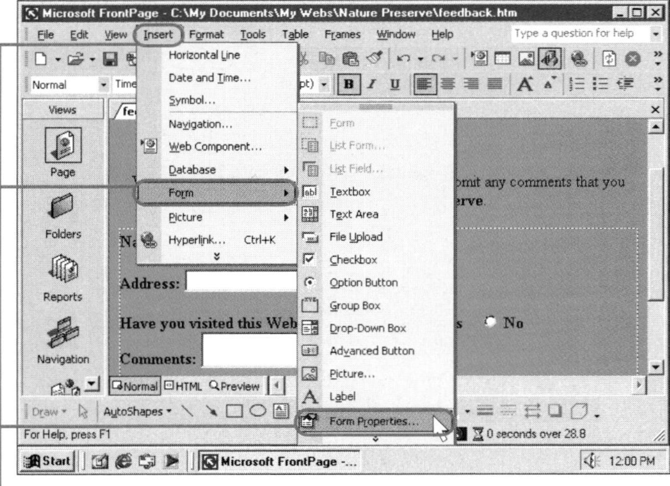

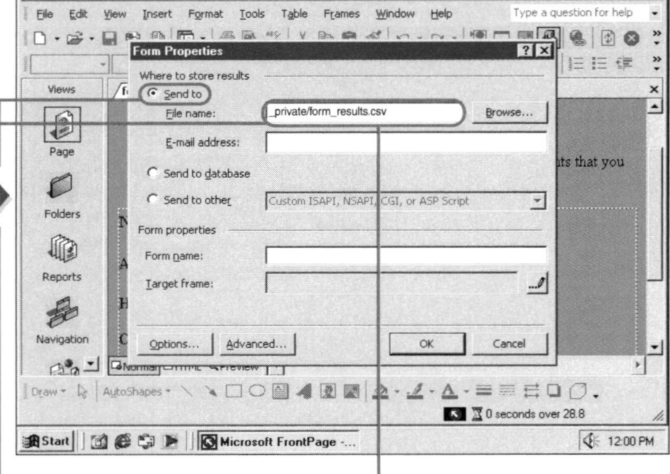

1 To specify how you want to access the results of a form, click anywhere in the form.

2 Click **Insert**.

3 Click **Form**.

4 Click **Form Properties**.

Note: If all the options are not displayed on a menu, position the mouse over the bottom of the menu to display all the menu options.

■ The Form Properties dialog box appears.

5 Click **Send to** (○ changes to ⦿).

■ This area displays the location and name of the file that will store the results of the form.

6 If you do not want to store the form results in a file on your Web server, drag the mouse over the text in this area and then press the Delete key to remove the information.

Can visitors view the file that stores the form results on the Web server?

By default, FrontPage stores the file in the _private folder, which is a hidden folder in your Web site. Visitors browsing through your Web pages cannot view the contents of this folder.

What file format should I use for the file that will store the form results?

You should choose a file format based on the way you plan to use the form results. HTML file formats are useful if you want to view the form results in a Web browser. The other formats are useful if you plan to use the form results in a spreadsheet or database program.

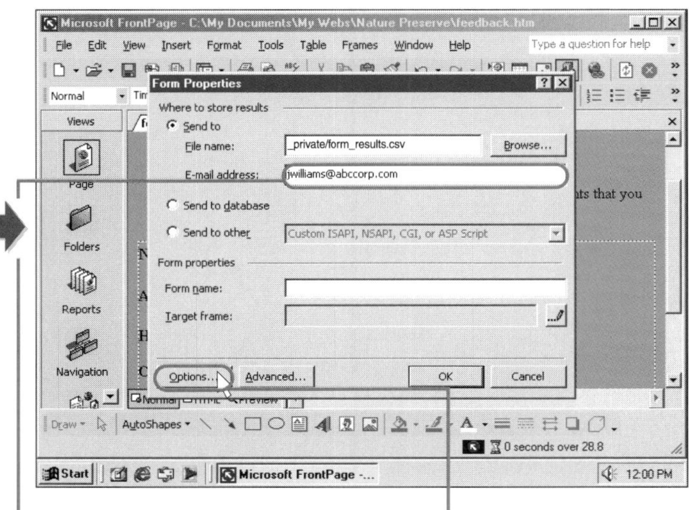

7 To send the results of the form in e-mail messages, click this area and then type the e-mail address you want to send the form results to.

Note: You can store the form results in a file on your Web server as well as send the form results in e-mail messages.

8 Click **Options** to change the settings for the file or e-mail messages that will give you access to the form results.

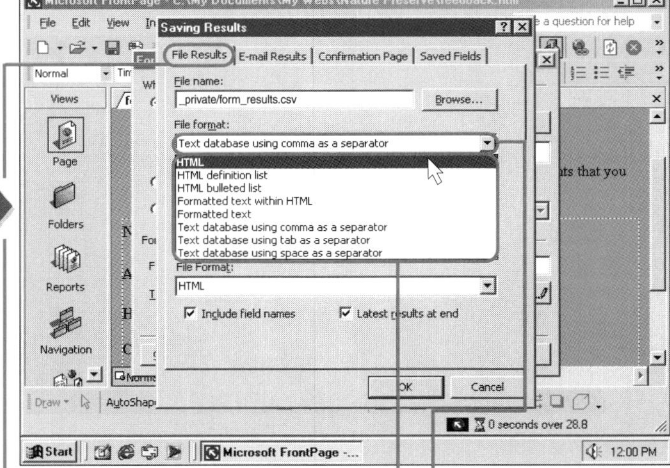

■ The Saving Results dialog box appears.

9 Click the **File Results** tab to change the options for the file stored on your Web server.

Note: If you chose not to store the form results in a file on your Web server in step 6, skip to step 12.

10 Click this area to display a list of the available formats for the file.

11 Click the file format you want to use.

CONTINUED

ACCESS FORM RESULTS

If you are sending the form results in e-mail messages, you can choose the subject you want each e-mail message to display.

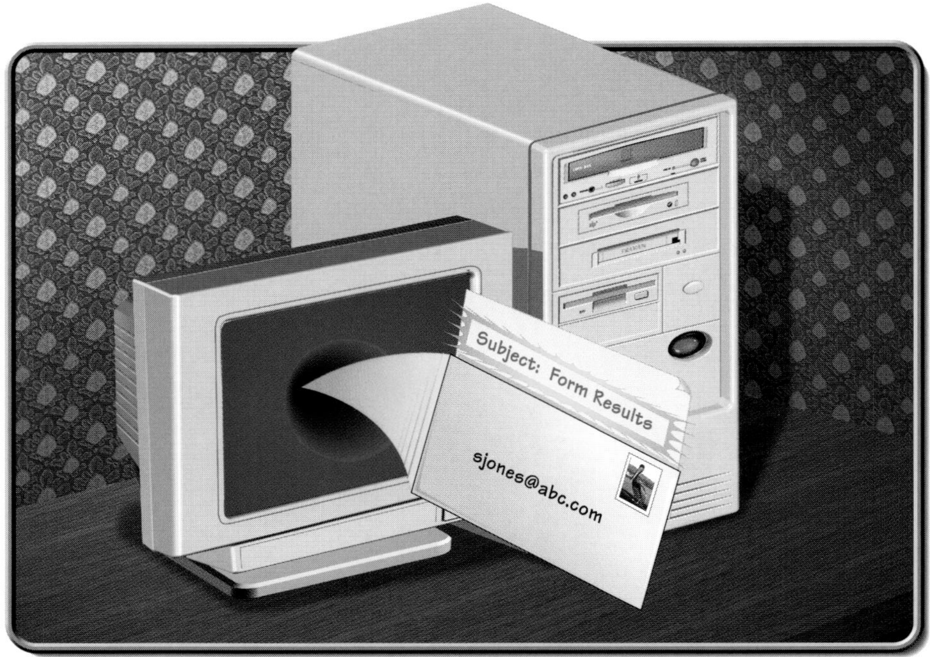

ACCESS FORM RESULTS (CONTINUED)

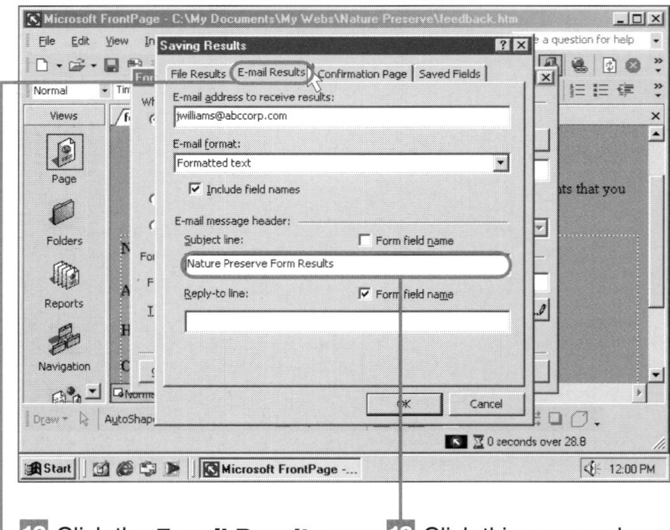

12 Click the **E-mail Results** tab to change the options for sending the form results in e-mail messages.

*Note: If you chose not to send the form results in e-mail messages in step **7**, skip to step **16**.*

13 Click this area and type the subject you want each e-mail message to display.

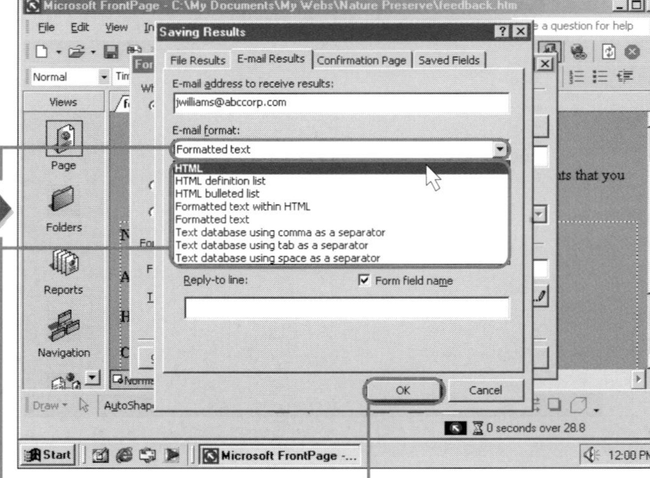

14 Click this area to display a list of the available e-mail formats.

15 Click the e-mail format you want to use.

Note: The e-mail format you should choose depends on the way you plan to use the form results.

16 Click **OK**.

How do I access the file that stores the form results on my Web server?

View File in Web Browser

If you selected an HTML file format for the file in step 11 on page 229, you can view the file in your Web browser.

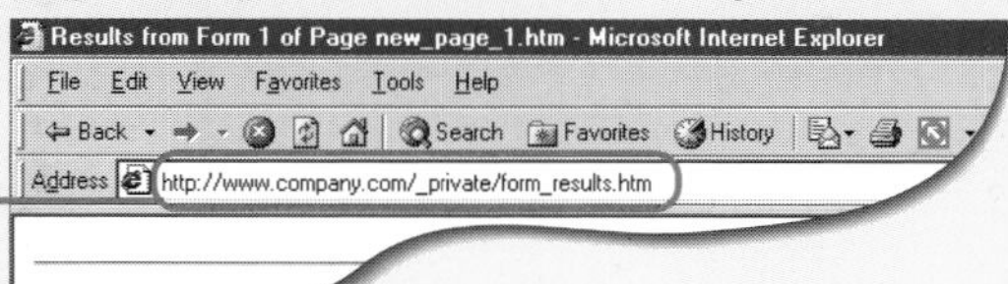

1 Open your Web browser, such as Internet Explorer.

2 Click this area and type the address of the Web server where you published your Web pages followed by **/_private/form_results.htm**.

■ To view the file, you will need to enter the user name and password supplied by the company that publishes your Web pages.

Transfer File to Your Computer

You can use a File Transfer Protocol (FTP) program to transfer the file to your computer. After you transfer the file, you can open and work with the file on your computer. You can obtain a popular FTP program named WS_FTP Pro at the www.ipswitch.com Web site.

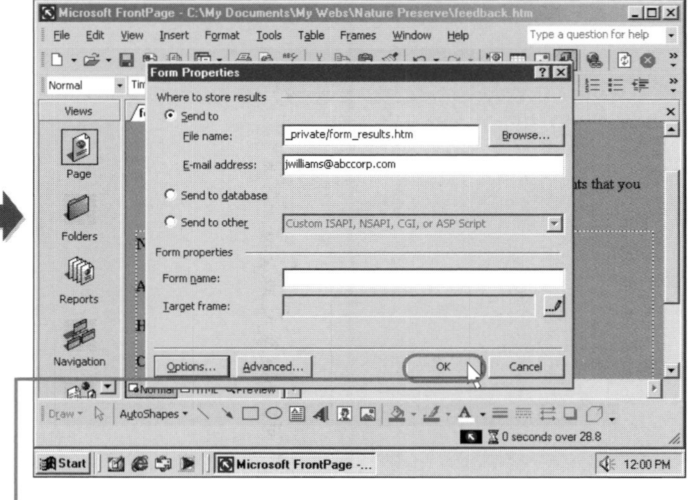

17 Click **OK** to confirm all of your changes.

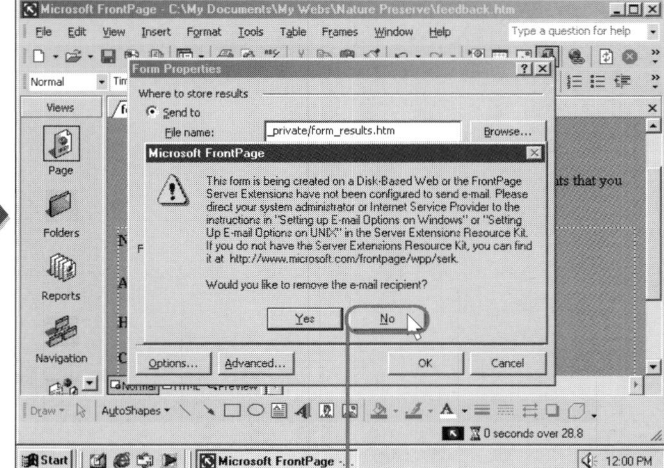

■ If you entered an e-mail address in step 7, a dialog box appears, stating that your computer is not set up to send the results of your form in e-mail messages.

Note: This dialog box only applies to people who will use their own computer to publish their Web pages. If you are using a company to publish your Web pages, you can ignore this message.

18 Click **No** to keep the e-mail address you specified.

CREATE A CONFIRMATION PAGE

You can create a confirmation page that will appear after visitors submit a form. A confirmation page allows visitors to review the information they entered in a form.

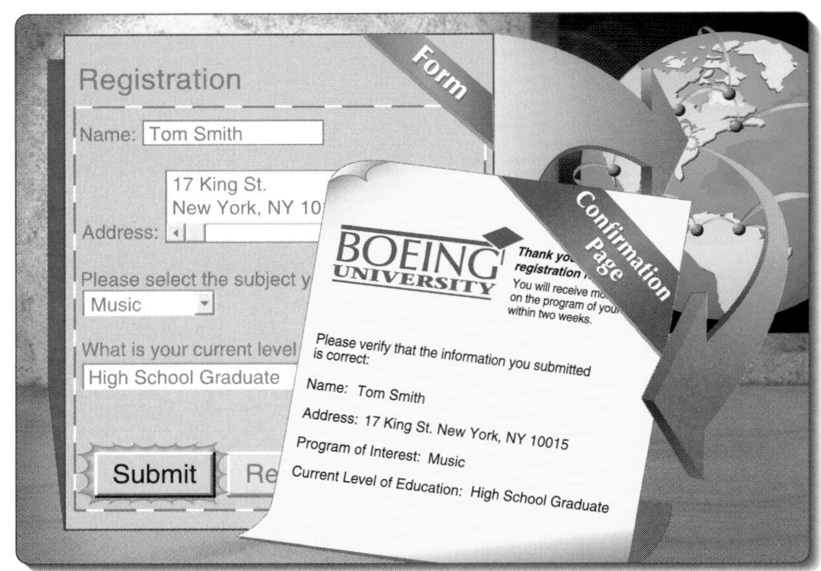

If you do not create a confirmation page, FrontPage will automatically display a basic confirmation page that lists all the information visitors entered in a form.

CREATE A CONFIRMATION PAGE

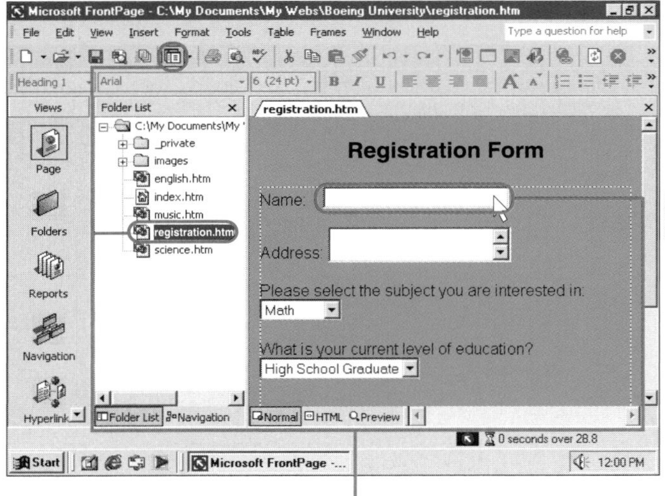

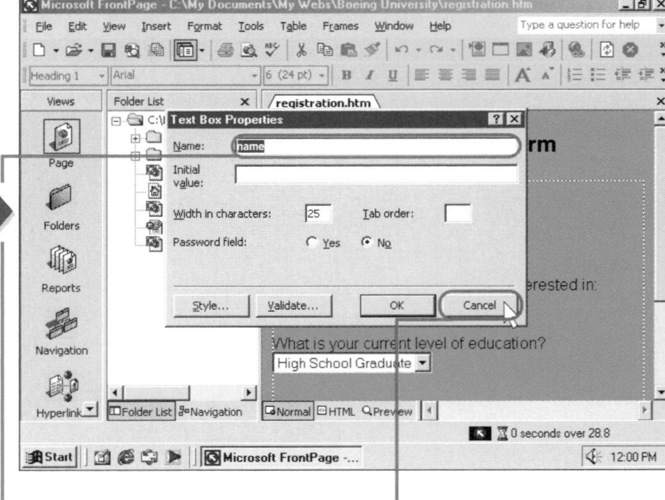

DETERMINE NAMES OF ITEMS ON A FORM

■ Before you can create a confirmation page for a form, you need to write down the name you assigned to each item on the form.

1 Double-click the Web page that contains the form you want to use a personalized confirmation page.

■ If the list of Web pages does not appear, click ▤ to display the list.

2 Double-click an item on the form.

■ A dialog box appears.

■ This area displays the name you assigned to the item.

3 Write down the name of the item on a piece of paper.

4 Click **Cancel** to close the dialog box.

5 Repeat steps 2 to 4 for each item on the form.

What should I consider when creating a confirmation page?

Make sure your confirmation page uses a layout that clearly displays the information that visitors entered in a form. You should place each item that visitors entered on a different line. You may also want to add a background color or image to the confirmation page to differentiate the page from the Web page that contains the form.

You can also add links to a confirmation page that allows visitors to quickly return to specific pages in your Web site. For example, the confirmation page can include a link that allows visitors to return to your home page after submitting a form.

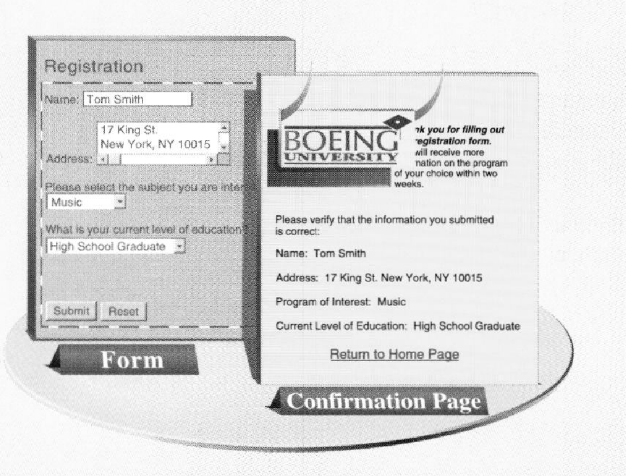

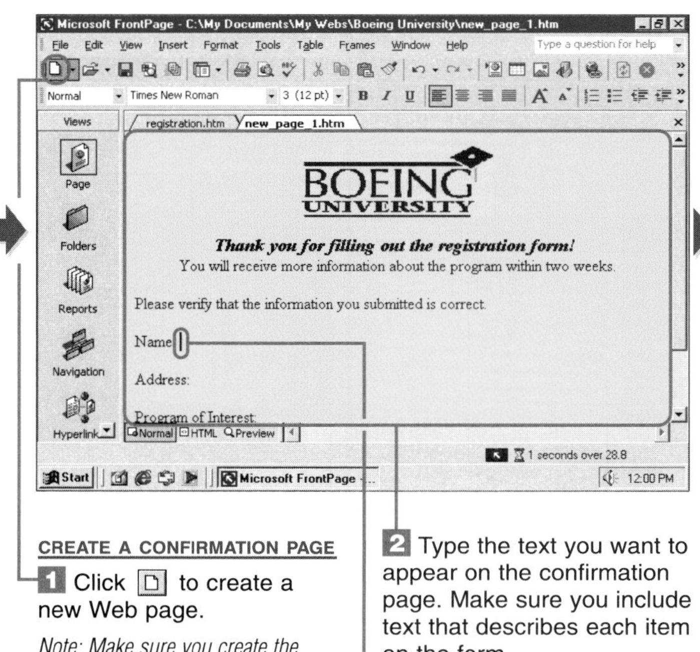

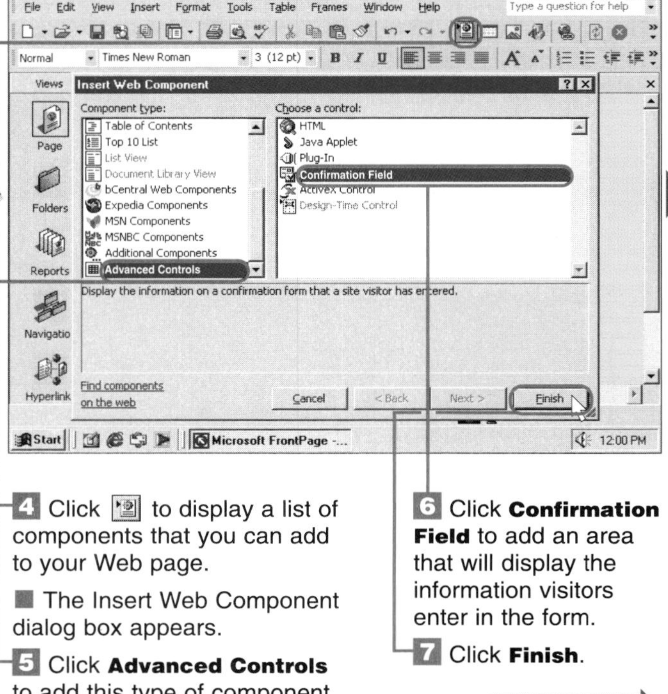

CREATE A CONFIRMATION PAGE

1 Click ▢ to create a new Web page.

Note: Make sure you create the new Web page in the same Web site that contains the form.

2 Type the text you want to appear on the confirmation page. Make sure you include text that describes each item on the form.

3 Click beside an area of text that describes an item on the form.

4 Click ▢ to display a list of components that you can add to your Web page.

■ The Insert Web Component dialog box appears.

5 Click **Advanced Controls** to add this type of component.

6 Click **Confirmation Field** to add an area that will display the information visitors enter in the form.

7 Click **Finish**.

CONTINUED

CREATE A CONFIRMATION PAGE

When creating a confirmation page, you need to enter the name you assigned to each item on the form. When visitors view the confirmation page, each name will be replaced with the information they entered in the form.

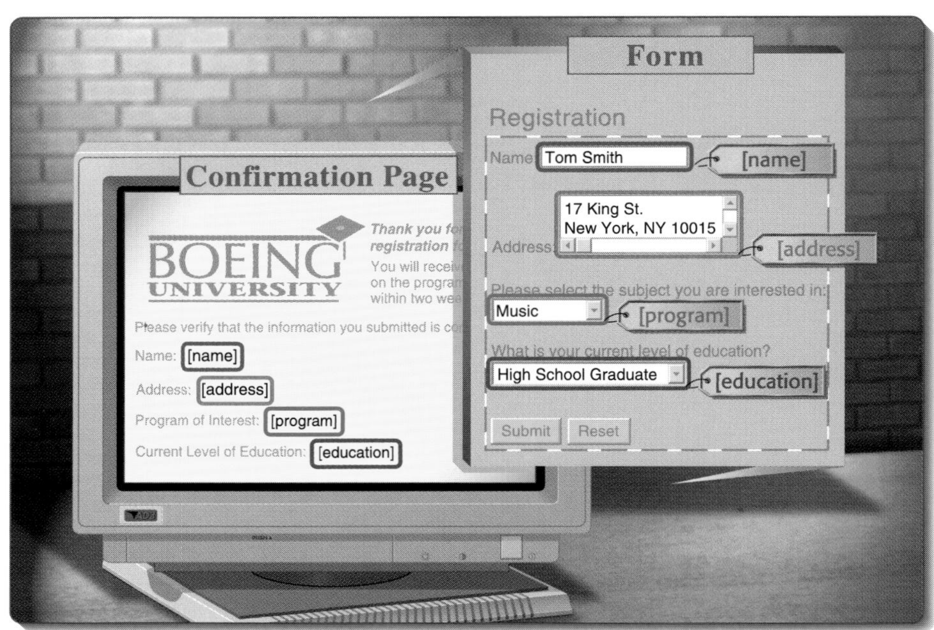

CREATE A CONFIRMATION PAGE (CONTINUED)

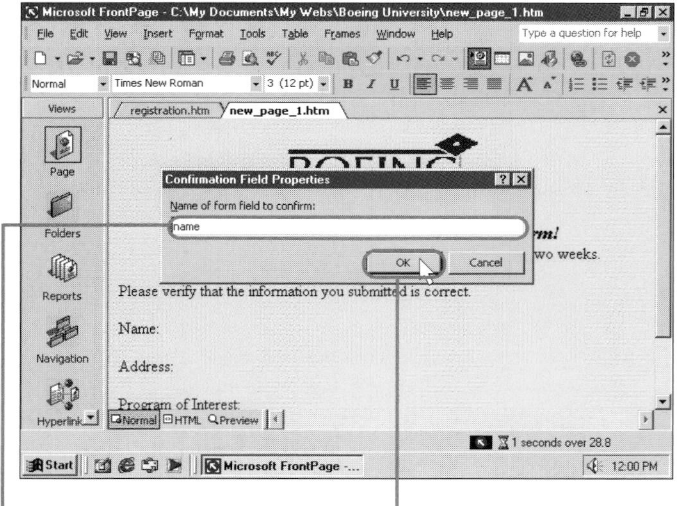

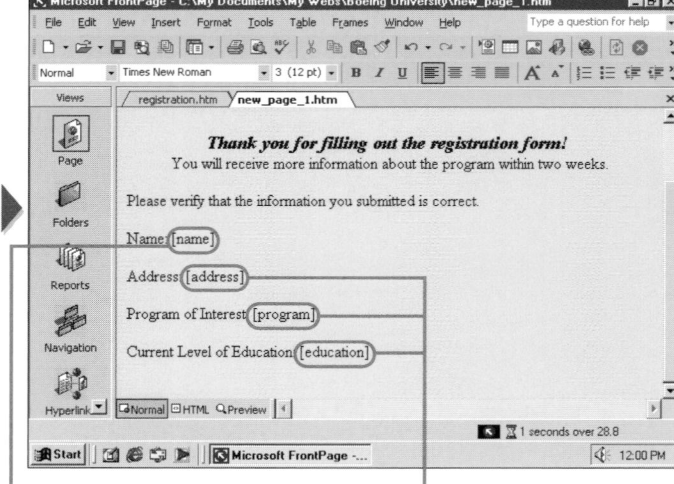

■ The Confirmation Field Properties dialog box appears.

8 Type the name you assigned to the item on the form. Make sure you enter the name exactly.

9 Click **OK** to confirm the information you entered.

■ The name of the item appears in brackets on your Web page.

■ When visitors view the confirmation page, the name of the item will be replaced with the information they entered in the form.

10 Repeat steps **3** to **9** for each area of text that describes an item on the form.

11 Save the Web page. To save a Web page, see page 28.

How can I quickly create a confirmation page?

FrontPage includes the Confirmation Form template that allows you to quickly create a confirmation page. This template provides the layout, design and sample text for a confirmation page. You can add your own information to the appropriate areas of the template. To use the Confirmation Form template to create a confirmation page, see page 26.

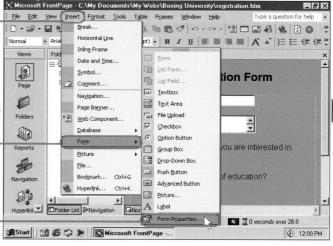

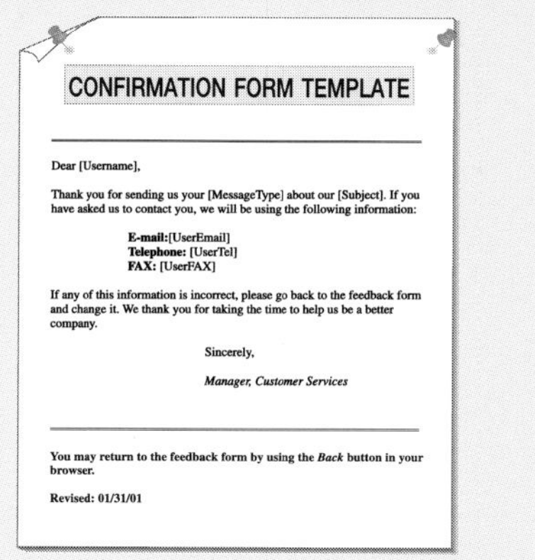

CONFIRMATION FORM TEMPLATE

Dear [Username],

Thank you for sending us your [MessageType] about our [Subject]. If you have asked us to contact you, we will be using the following information:

E-mail:[UserEmail]
Telephone: [UserTel]
FAX: [UserFAX]

If any of this information is incorrect, please go back to the feedback form and change it. We thank you for taking the time to help us be a better company.

Sincerely,

Manager, Customer Services

You may return to the feedback form by using the *Back* button in your browser.

Revised: 01/31/01

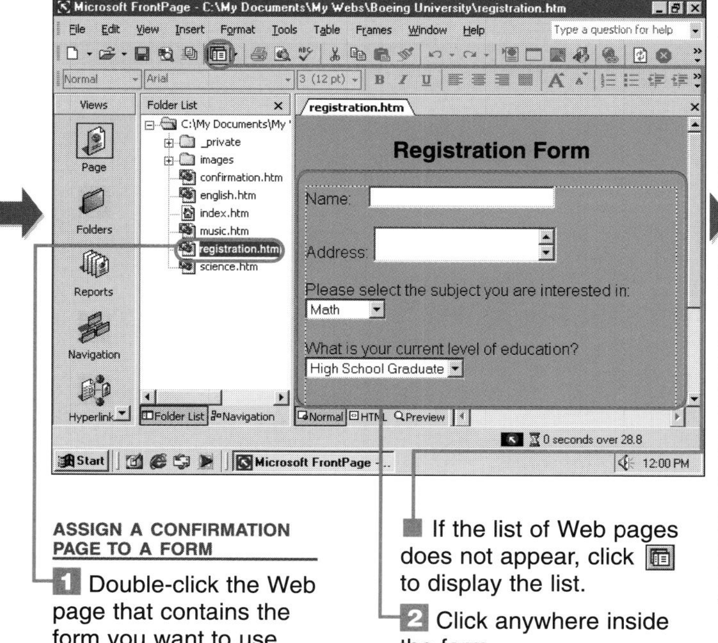

ASSIGN A CONFIRMATION PAGE TO A FORM

1. Double-click the Web page that contains the form you want to use the confirmation page.

■ If the list of Web pages does not appear, click [icon] to display the list.

2. Click anywhere inside the form.

3. Click **Insert**.

4. Click **Form**.

5. Click **Form Properties**.

Note: If all the options are not displayed on a menu, position the mouse [pointer] over the bottom of the menu to display all the menu options.

CONTINUED

CREATE A CONFIRMATION PAGE

After you assign a confirmation page to a form, the page will appear when visitors submit the form.

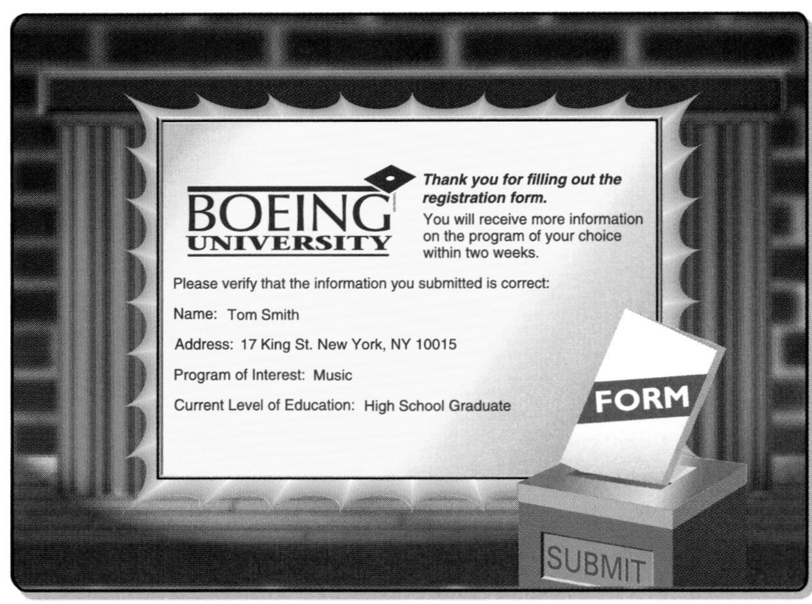

BOEING UNIVERSITY
Thank you for filling out the registration form.
You will receive more information on the program of your choice within two weeks.
Please verify that the information you submitted is correct:
Name: Tom Smith
Address: 17 King St. New York, NY 10015
Program of Interest: Music
Current Level of Education: High School Graduate
FORM
SUBMIT

Visitors cannot edit the information displayed on a confirmation page.

CREATE A CONFIRMATION PAGE (CONTINUED)

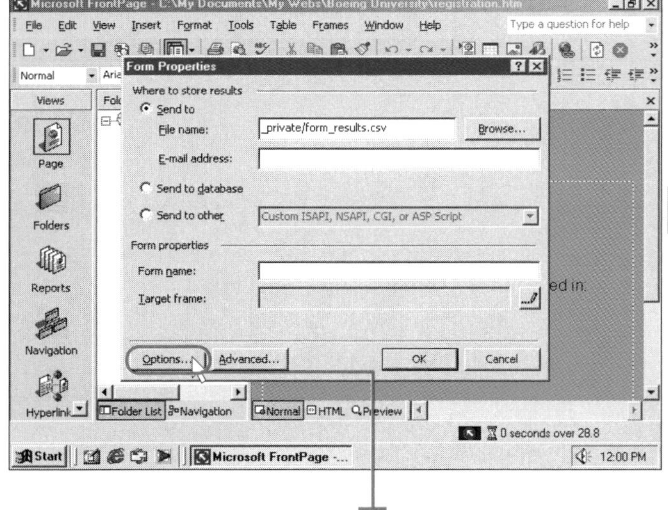

■ The Form Properties dialog box appears.

6 Click **Options** to select the confirmation page you want to assign to the form.

■ The Saving Results dialog box appears.

7 Click the **Confirmation Page** tab.

8 Click **Browse** to locate the confirmation page that you created.

How can I stop a form from using the confirmation page I created?

If you no longer want a form to use the confirmation page you created, you need to delete the connection between the form and the confirmation page. The form will once again use the basic confirmation page that FrontPage provides.

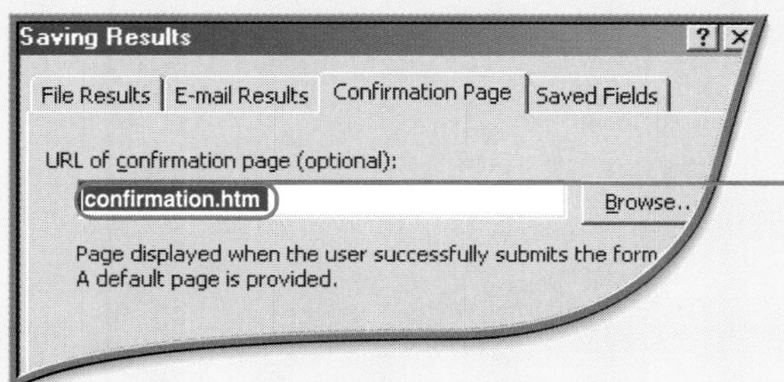

1 Perform steps 1 to 7 starting on page 235 to display the Saving Results dialog box.

2 Press the Delete key to remove the name of the confirmation page displayed in this area. This will delete the connection between the form and the confirmation page.

3 Perform steps 11 and 12 below to confirm your change.

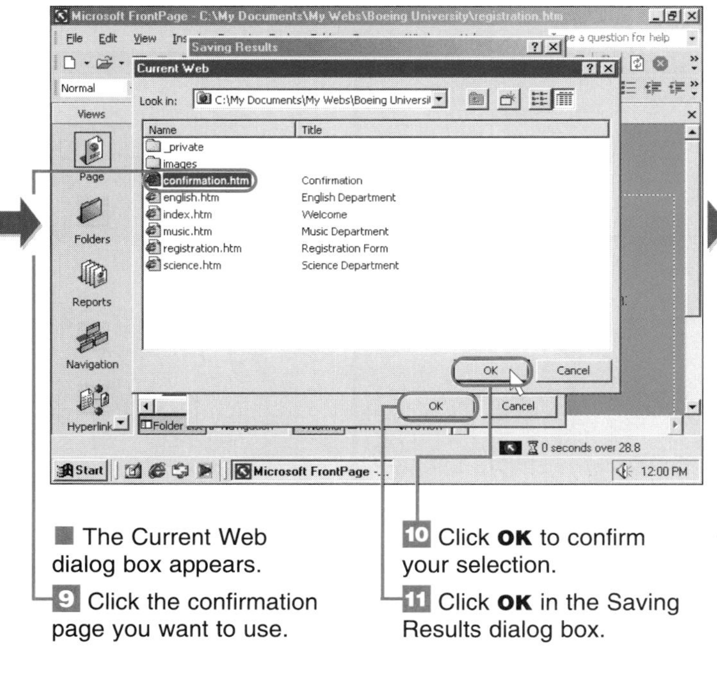

■ The Current Web dialog box appears.

9 Click the confirmation page you want to use.

10 Click **OK** to confirm your selection.

11 Click **OK** in the Saving Results dialog box.

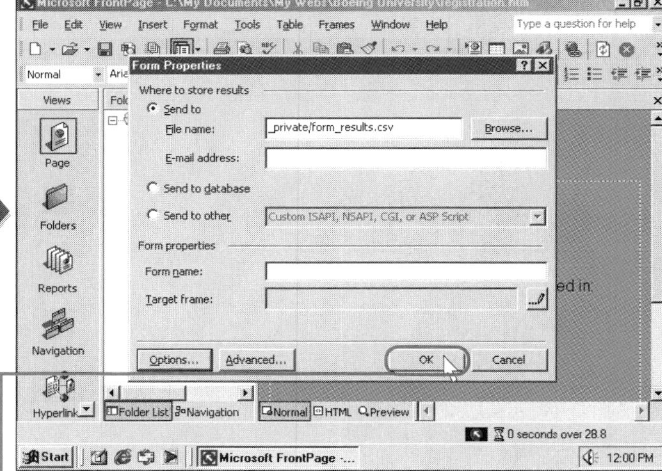

12 Click **OK** in the Form Properties dialog box.

■ When visitors submit the form, the confirmation page you specified will appear.

Note: To test the confirmation page, you must publish your Web pages. To publish your Web pages, see page 292.

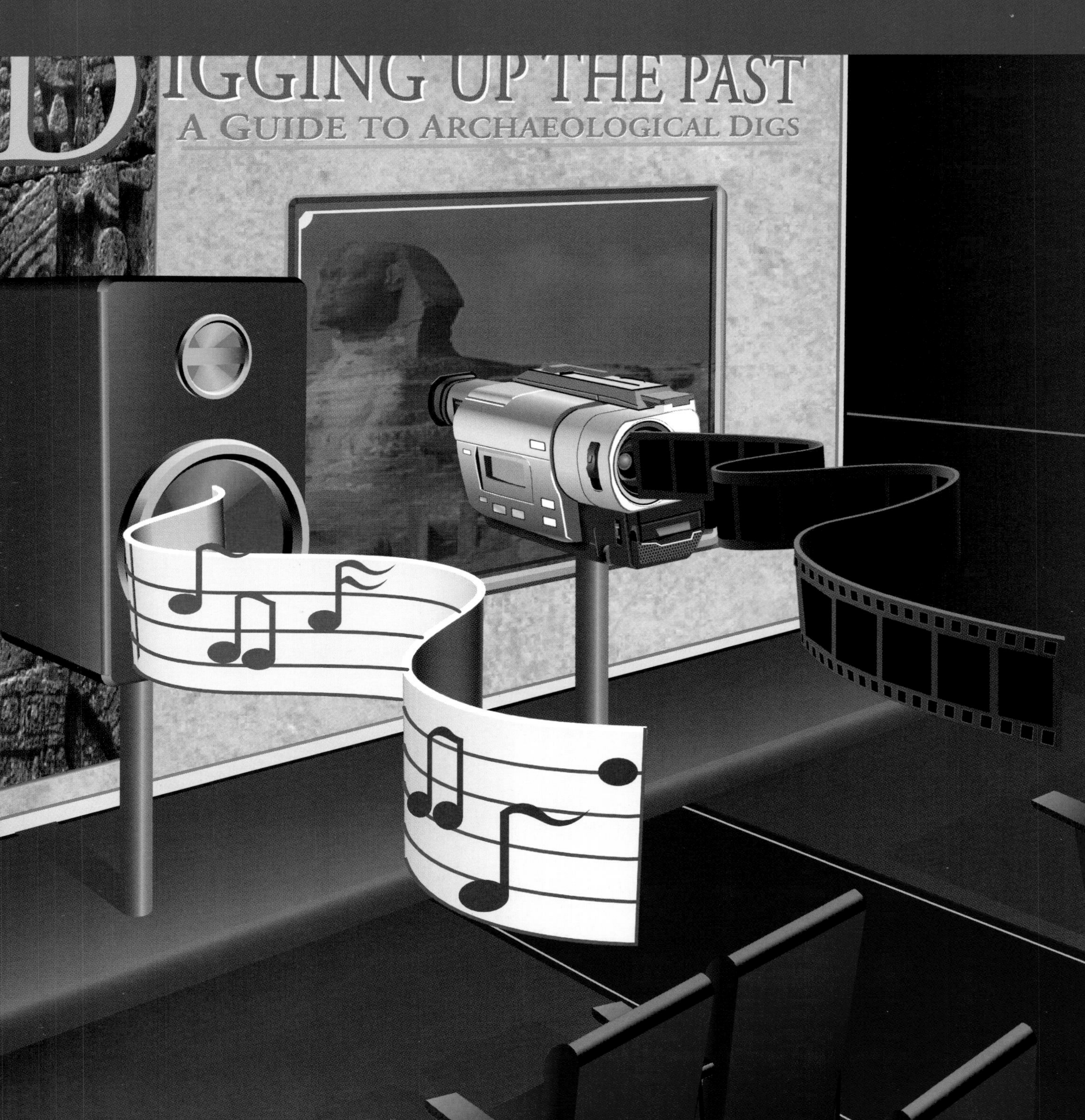
DIGGING UP THE PAST
A GUIDE TO ARCHAEOLOGICAL DIGS

CHAPTER 13

Add Web Page Effects

Are you wondering how to make your Web pages more dynamic and animated? This chapter teaches you how to add sounds, videos and other special effects to your Web pages.

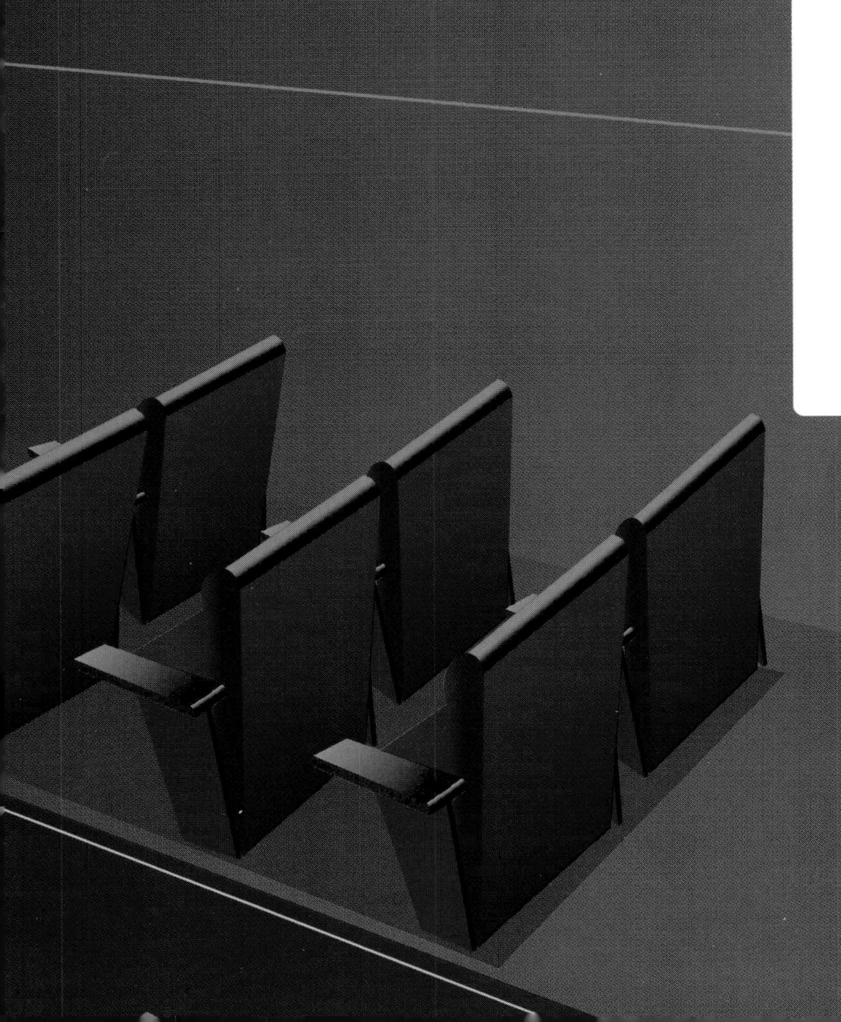

CREATE A LINK TO A SOUND OR VIDEO

You can create a link on a Web page that visitors can select to play a sound or video.

You can provide sound clips from television shows, movies, famous speeches or your own music.

You can provide videos to display visual effects, movie clips, animations, company videos or home movies.

CREATE A LINK TO A SOUND OR VIDEO

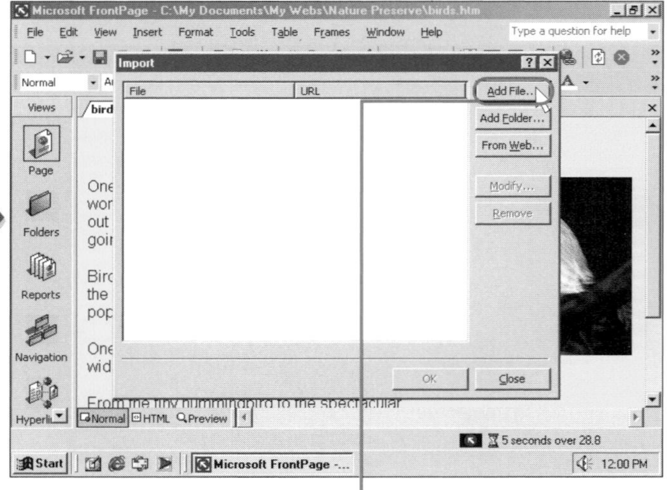

ADD A SOUND OR VIDEO TO A WEB SITE

■ Before you can create a link on a Web page to a sound or video, you must add a copy of the sound or video to your Web site.

1 Click **File**.

2 Click **Import**.

Note: If Import does not appear on the menu, position the mouse over the bottom of the menu to display all the menu options.

■ The Import dialog box appears.

3 Click **Add File** to locate the sound or video on your computer.

Why do I need to add a sound or video to my Web site before I can create a link to the sound or video?

You need to add a copy of a sound or video to your Web site to include the sound or video file in your Web site. This ensures the sound or video will transfer with your Web site when you publish your Web pages. If you do not add the sound or video to your Web site, visitors will not be able to play the sound or video.

What type of sound or video can I create a link to?

You should create a link to a common type of sound or video to ensure that most visitors will be able to play the sound or video. The following chart lists the most common types of sounds and videos on the Web.

SOUNDS	VIDEOS
MIDI	AVI
MP3	MPEG
RealAudio	QuickTime
Wave	RealVideo

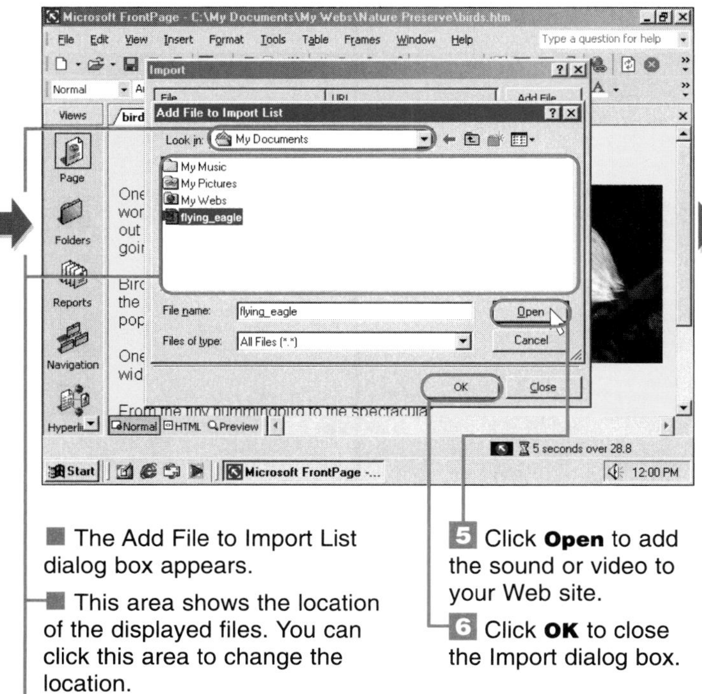

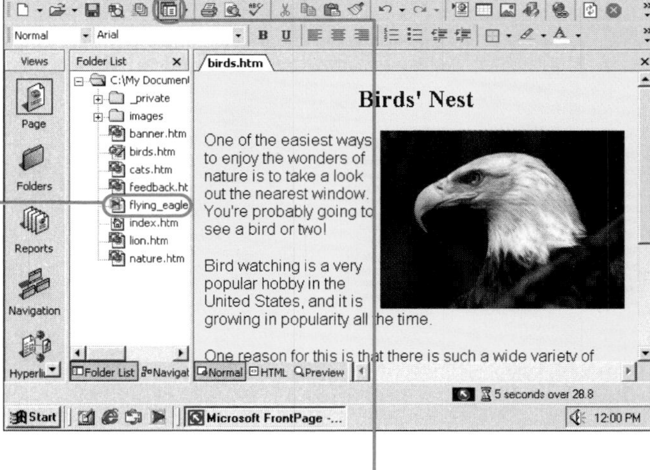

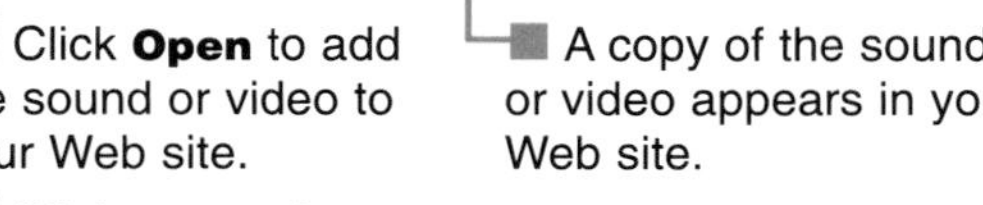

■ The Add File to Import List dialog box appears.

■ This area shows the location of the displayed files. You can click this area to change the location.

4 Click the sound or video you want to add to your Web site.

5 Click **Open** to add the sound or video to your Web site.

6 Click **OK** to close the Import dialog box.

■ A copy of the sound or video appears in your Web site.

■ If the list of Web pages, folders and other items does not appear, click (icon) to display the list.

CONTINUED

CREATE A LINK TO A SOUND OR VIDEO

Whenever possible, you should create a link to a sound or video with a small file size. A sound or video with a large file size can take a long time to transfer and play on a visitor's computer.

You should provide a short description of a sound or video link on a Web page. For example, you should include the file type, size and length of time a sound or video will play. Visitors can use this information to decide if they want to play a sound or video.

CREATE A LINK TO A SOUND OR VIDEO (CONTINUED)

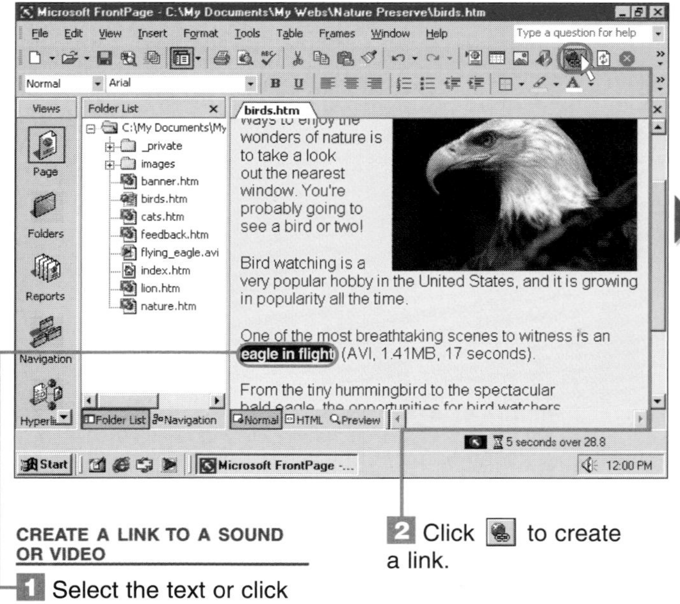

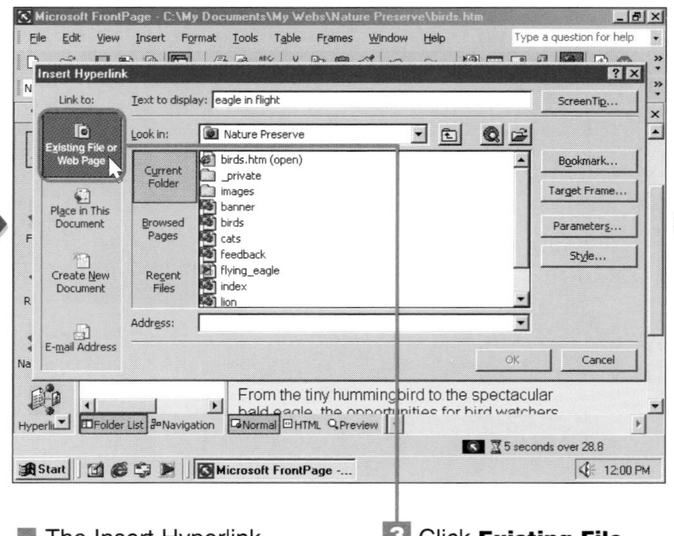

CREATE A LINK TO A SOUND OR VIDEO

1 Select the text or click the image you want visitors to select to play a sound or video. To select text, see page 54.

2 Click [icon] to create a link.

■ The Insert Hyperlink dialog box appears.

3 Click **Existing File or Web Page**.

Where can I obtain sounds and videos?

Sound and Video Collections

You can purchase collections of sounds and videos at computer stores and also obtain sounds and videos on the Web. Make sure you have permission to use any sounds and videos you did not create yourself. You can find sounds and videos at the following Web sites.

www.ultimatemovieclips.com

earthstation1.com

wavcentral.com

www.jurassicpunk.com

Record Your Own Sounds and Videos

You can record your own sounds and videos. With a sound recording program, you can connect a microphone to your computer to record your own voice or connect a CD or cassette player to record music or other sounds. If your computer has a video capture card and video recording software, you can connect a VCR or video camera to your computer to record your own videos.

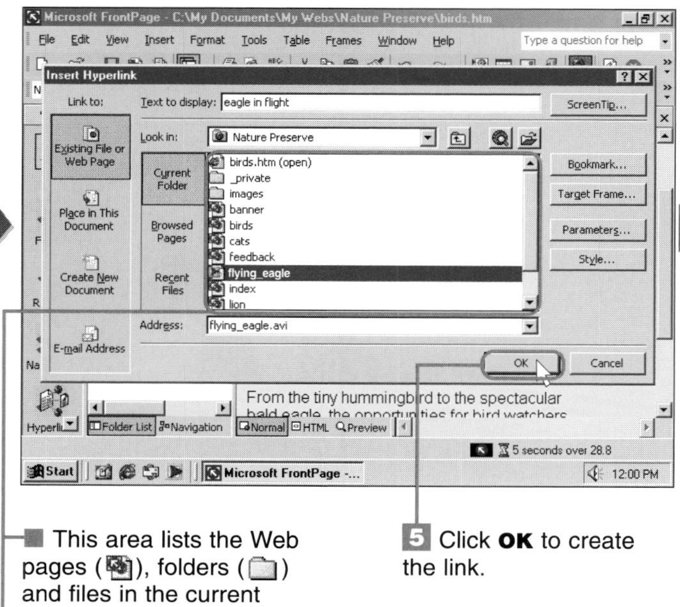

■ This area lists the Web pages (), folders () and files in the current Web site.

4 Click the sound or video you want to link to the text or image.

5 Click **OK** to create the link.

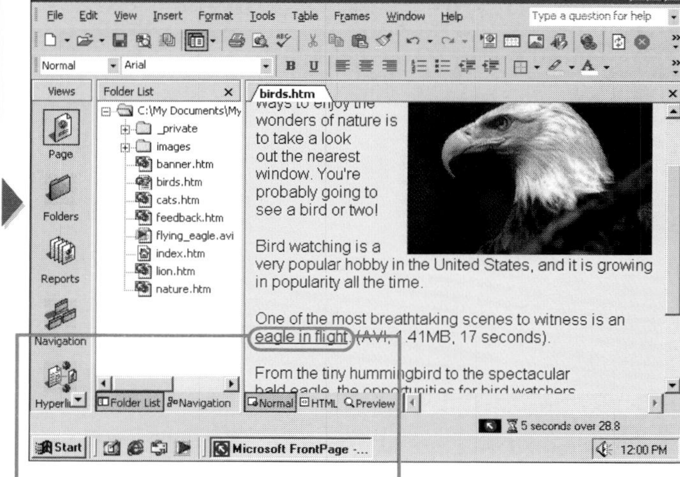

■ FrontPage creates the link. Text links appear underlined and in color.

■ To deselect the link, click outside the selected area.

■ When a visitor selects the link, the sound or video will transfer to their computer and play.

Note: To test the link, you can use the Preview view. For information on the Preview view, see page 42.

ADD A BACKGROUND SOUND

You can add a background sound to a Web page. When visitors display the Web page, the sound will automatically play.

By default, the Netscape Navigator Web browser will not play a background sound that you add to a Web page.

ADD A BACKGROUND SOUND

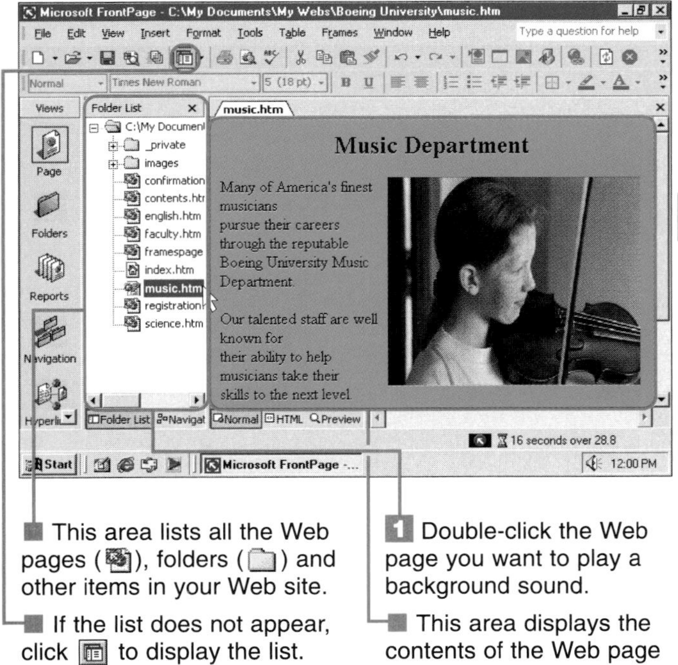

■ This area lists all the Web pages (), folders () and other items in your Web site.

■ If the list does not appear, click to display the list.

1 Double-click the Web page you want to play a background sound.

■ This area displays the contents of the Web page you selected.

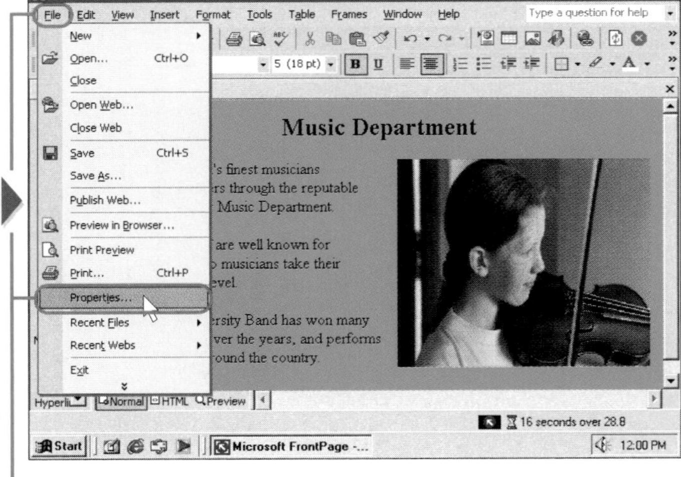

2 Click **File**.

3 Click **Properties**.

■ The Page Properties dialog box appears.

Where can I obtain background sounds?

You can purchase collections of sounds at computer stores and also obtain sounds on the Web. You can find sounds at the following Web sites.

earthstation1.com

wavcentral.com

What types of background sounds can I add to a Web page?

You can add several types of background sounds to a Web page. The most widely accepted types of background sounds are MIDI and Wave. You can determine the type of a sound by the characters that appear after the period in the file name of a sound, such as trumpet.mid (MIDI) and birdchirp.wav (Wave).

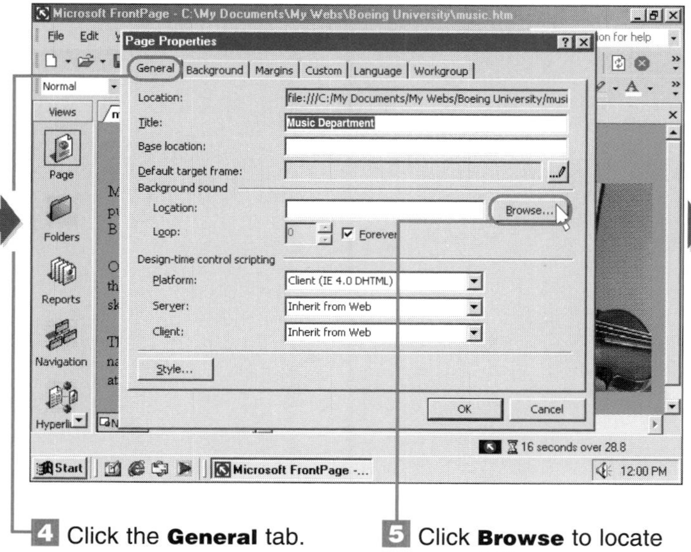

4 Click the **General** tab.

5 Click **Browse** to locate the sound file on your computer that you want to use as the background sound.

■ The Background Sound dialog box appears.

■ This area shows the location of the displayed files. You can click this area to change the location.

6 Click the sound file you want to use as the background sound.

7 Click **Open** to confirm your selection.

CONTINUED

ADD A BACKGROUND SOUND

You can choose to play a background sound continuously or only a specific number of times when a visitor displays your Web page.

Playing a background sound continuously may annoy visitors who display your Web page. Visitors may turn off their speakers or leave your Web page.

ADD A BACKGROUND SOUND (CONTINUED)

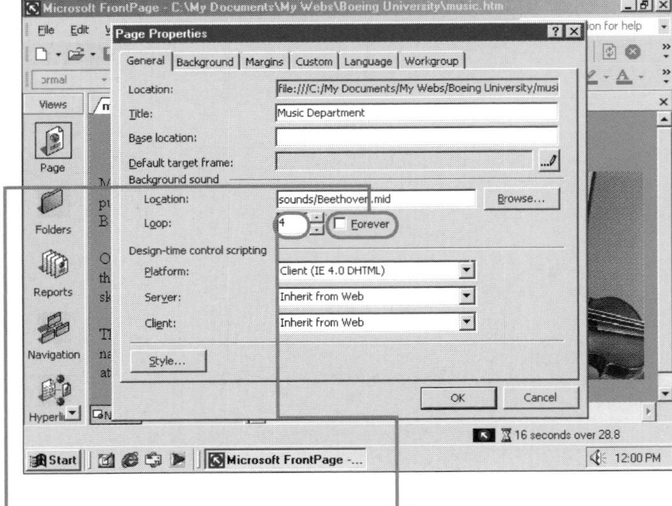

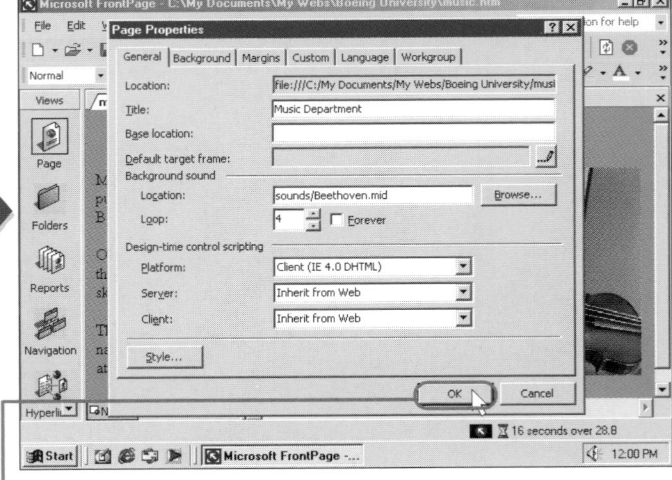

■ This option plays the sound continuously while the Web page is displayed.

8 To play the sound only a specific number of times, click **Forever** to turn off the option (☑ changes to ☐).

9 If you turned off the Forever option in step **8**, double-click the number in this area and type the number of times you want the sound to play.

10 Click **OK** to add the background sound to your Web page.

Note: To test the background sound, you can use the Preview view. For information on the Preview view, see page 42.

■ When you save the Web page, FrontPage will ask you to save the sound file as part of your Web site. To save a Web page, see page 28.

Can I record my own background sounds?

Yes. With a sound recording program, you can connect a microphone to your computer to record your own voice or connect a CD or cassette player to record music or other sounds. Make sure you have permission to use any sounds you did not create yourself.

What should I consider when adding a background sound to a Web page?

Sounds increase the time a Web page takes to appear on a visitor's computer screen. If a Web page takes too long to appear, visitors may lose interest and move to another page. Whenever possible, you should use sounds with small file sizes. Sounds with larger file sizes can take a long time to transfer to a visitor's computer.

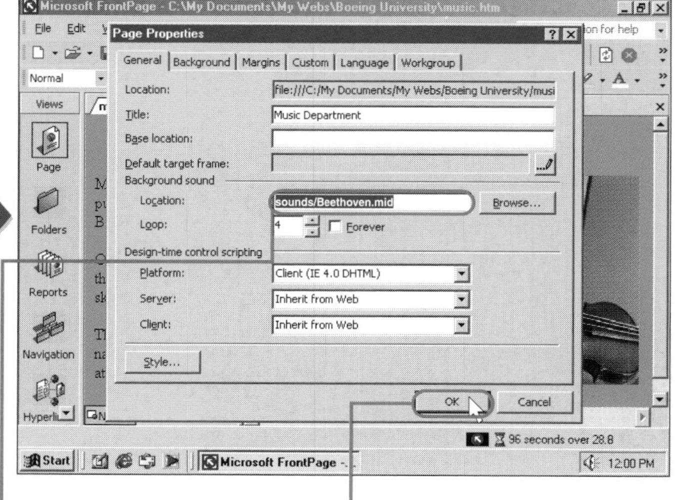

REMOVE A BACKGROUND SOUND

1 Double-click the Web page you no longer want to play a background sound.

2 Click **File**.

3 Click **Properties**.

■ The Page Properties dialog box appears.

4 Drag the mouse over this area until you select all the information.

5 Press the Delete key to remove the background sound from your Web page.

6 Click **OK** to confirm your change.

ADD A VIDEO TO A WEB PAGE

You can add a video to a Web page that will play automatically when a visitor displays the page. A video can liven up a Web page.

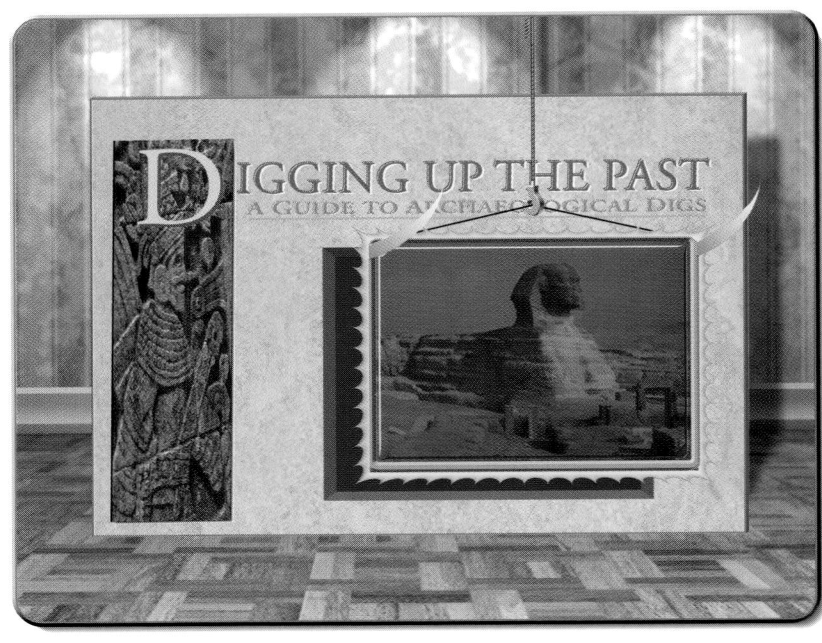

When adding a video to a Web page, you should use AVI videos since most Web browsers can play this type of video.

By default, the Netscape Navigator Web browser will not display or play a video on a Web page.

ADD A VIDEO TO A WEB PAGE

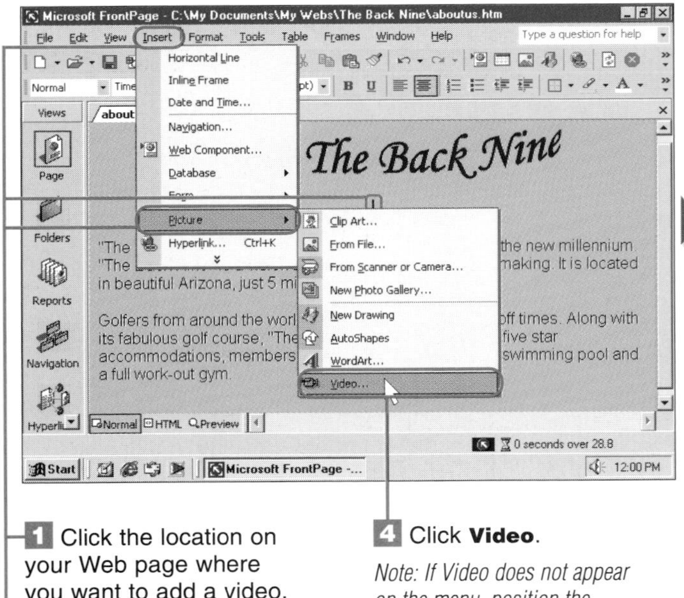

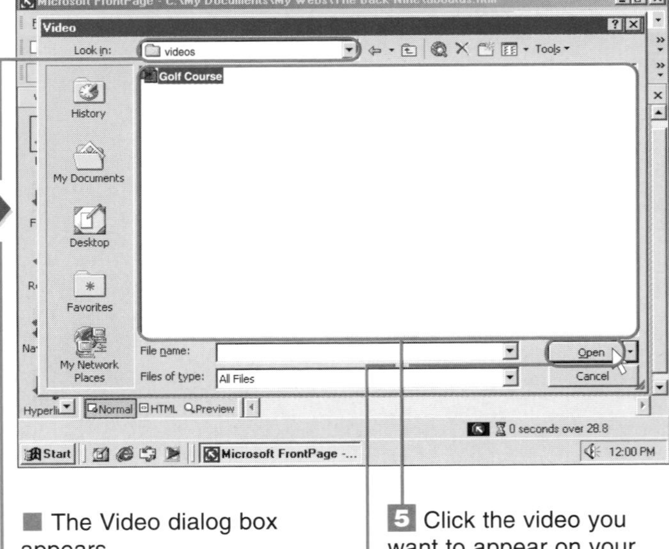

1 Click the location on your Web page where you want to add a video.

2 Click **Insert**.

3 Click **Picture**.

4 Click **Video**.

Note: If Video does not appear on the menu, position the mouse over the bottom of the menu to display all the menu options.

■ The Video dialog box appears.

■ This area shows the location of the displayed files. You can click this area to change the location.

5 Click the video you want to appear on your Web page.

6 Click **Open** to add the video to your Web page.

What should I consider when adding a video to a Web page?

Whenever possible, you should add videos with small file sizes to your Web pages. Videos with large file sizes can take a long time to transfer and play on a visitor's computer.

How can I resize a video on a Web page?

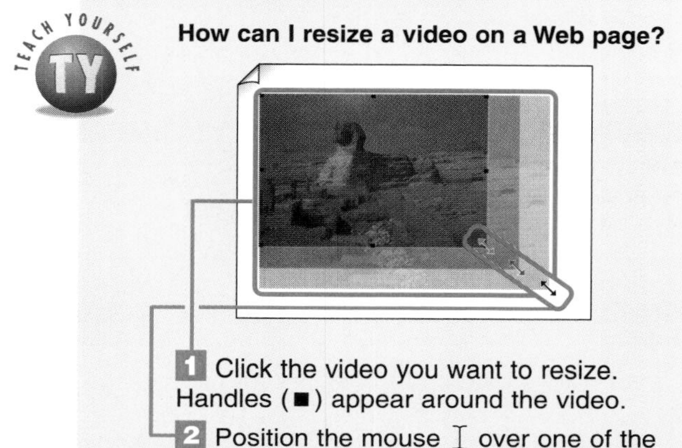

1 Click the video you want to resize. Handles (■) appear around the video.

2 Position the mouse I over one of the handles (I changes to ↘, ↕ or ↔) and then drag the handle until the video is the size you want.

Note: To keep the video in proportion, drag a corner handle.

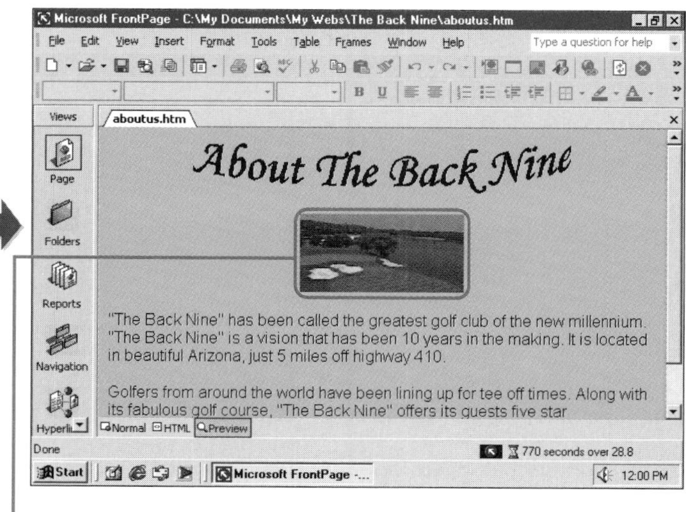

■ The video appears on your Web page.

Note: To test the video, you can use the Preview view. For information on the Preview view, see page 42.

■ When you save the Web page, FrontPage will ask you to save the video as part of your Web site. To save a Web page, see page 28.

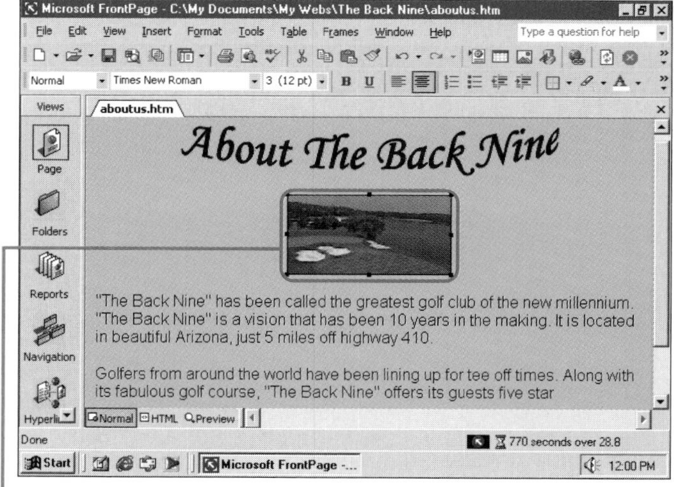

DELETE A VIDEO

1 Click the video you want to delete. Handles (■) appear around the video.

2 Press the Delete key to delete the video.

■ The video disappears from your Web page.

CHANGE VIDEO PROPERTIES

You can change the properties of a video displayed on a Web page. For example, you can change the number of times a video will play and when a video will begin to play.

CHANGE VIDEO PROPERTIES

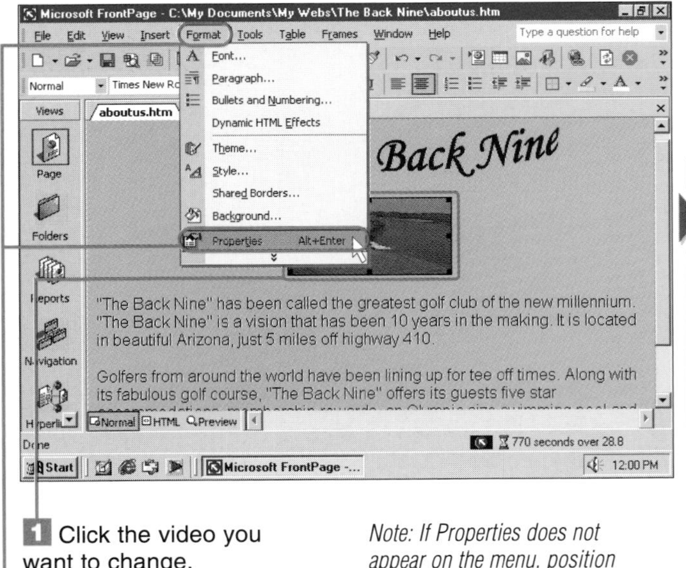

1 Click the video you want to change.

2 Click **Format**.

3 Click **Properties**.

Note: If Properties does not appear on the menu, position the mouse over the bottom of the menu to display all the menu options.

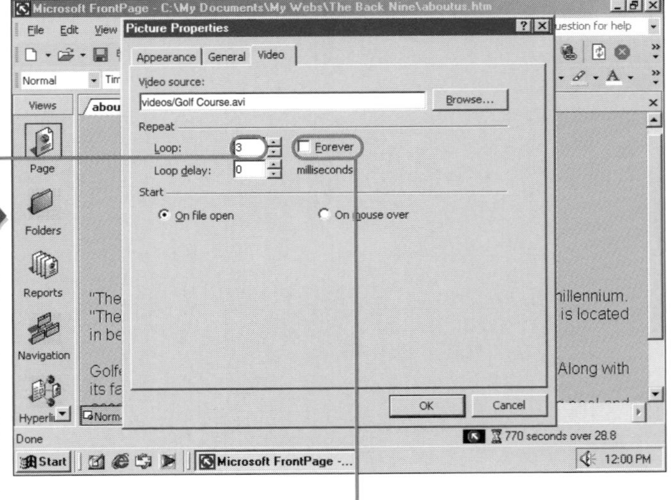

■ The Picture Properties dialog box appears.

4 Double-click this area and type the number of times you want the video to play.

■ If you want the video to play continuously while the Web page is displayed, click **Forever** (☐ changes to ☑).

Note: Playing a video continuously may annoy your visitors. Visitors may turn off their speakers or leave your Web page.

What happens if a visitor's Web browser cannot play a video on a Web page?

If a Web browser cannot play a video, a box will appear where the video should appear on the Web page. If you provide text for the video in step 7 below, the text will appear in the box. This text will provide information about the missing video for visitors who do not see the video.

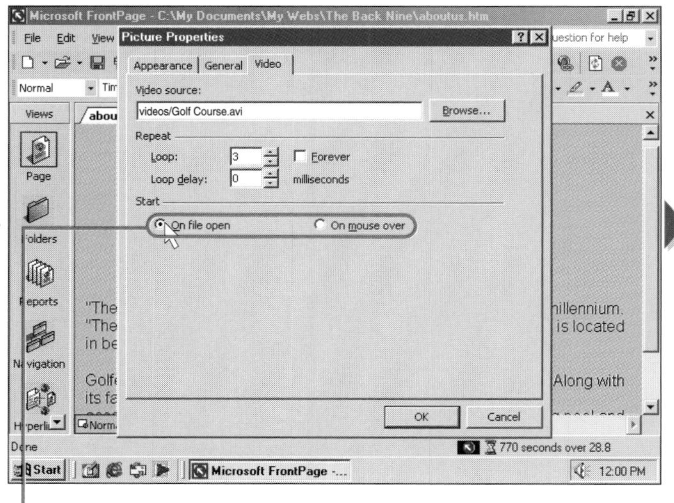

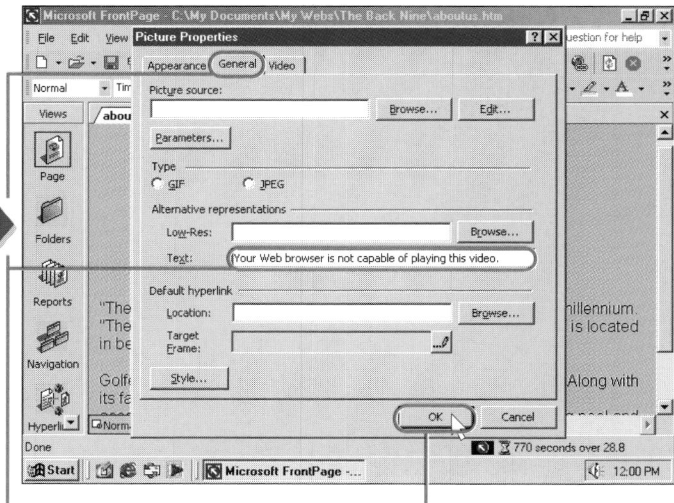

5 Click an option to specify when you want the video to play (○ changes to ⊙).

On file open
The video plays when a visitor first displays the Web page.

On mouse over
The video plays when a visitor moves the mouse over the video.

6 Click the **General** tab.

7 Click this area and type the text you want to appear on the Web page if a visitor's Web browser cannot play the video.

8 Click **OK** to confirm your changes.

ADD A HIT COUNTER

You can add a hit counter to a Web page to keep track of the number of people who visit the page.

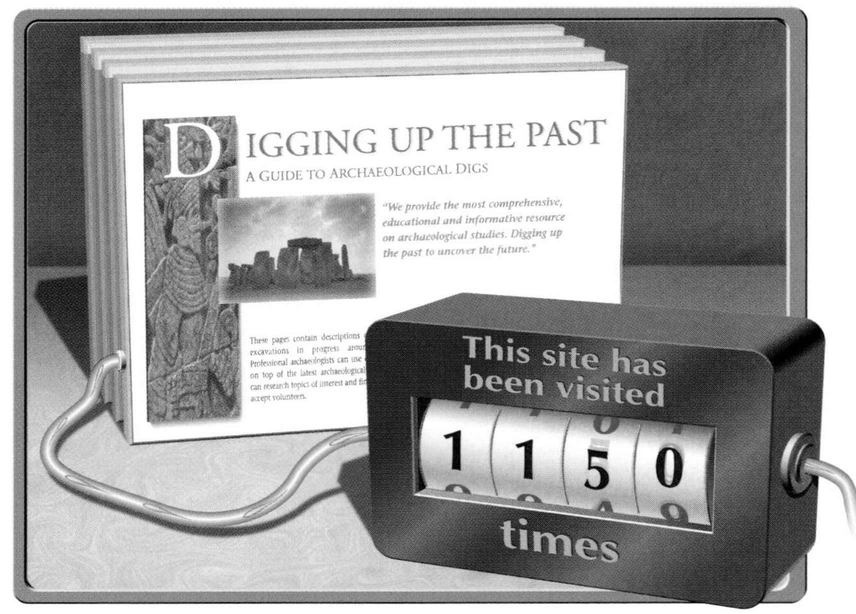

A hit counter displays the number of times a Web page has been visited. For example, a hit counter will display "50" if one person visits the Web page 50 times or if 50 people visit the Web page once.

ADD A HIT COUNTER

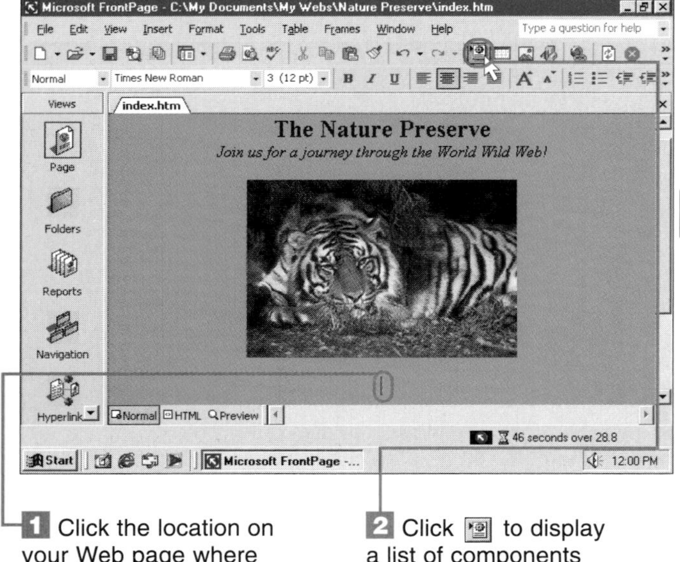

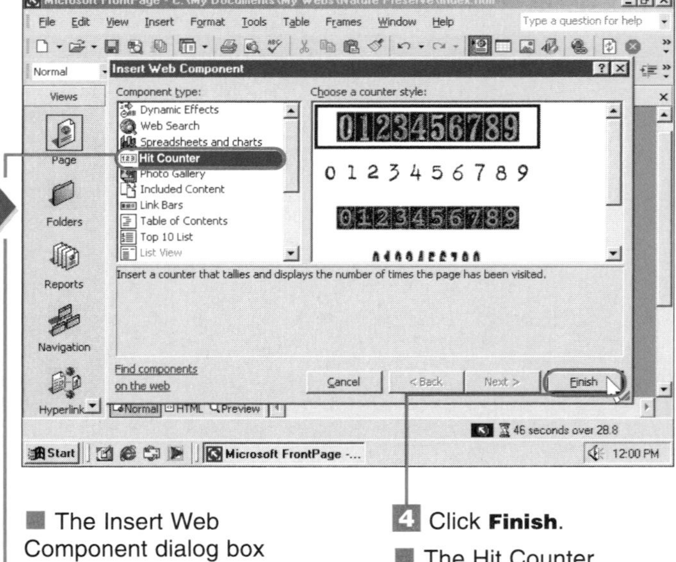

1 Click the location on your Web page where you want to add a hit counter.

2 Click [icon] to display a list of components that you can add to your Web page.

■ The Insert Web Component dialog box appears.

3 Click **Hit Counter** to add a hit counter.

4 Click **Finish**.

■ The Hit Counter Properties dialog box appears.

What should I consider before adding a hit counter to a Web page?

In order for your hit counter to work properly, your Web server must have the FrontPage Server Extensions installed. You can determine if your Web server has the FrontPage Server Extensions installed by asking the company that will make your Web pages available on the Web.

Which Web page should I add a hit counter to?

Most people add a hit counter to their home page since this is the first page visitors usually see when they visit a Web site. The home page is usually named index.htm. You can also add hit counters to other Web pages to determine which pages are the most popular.

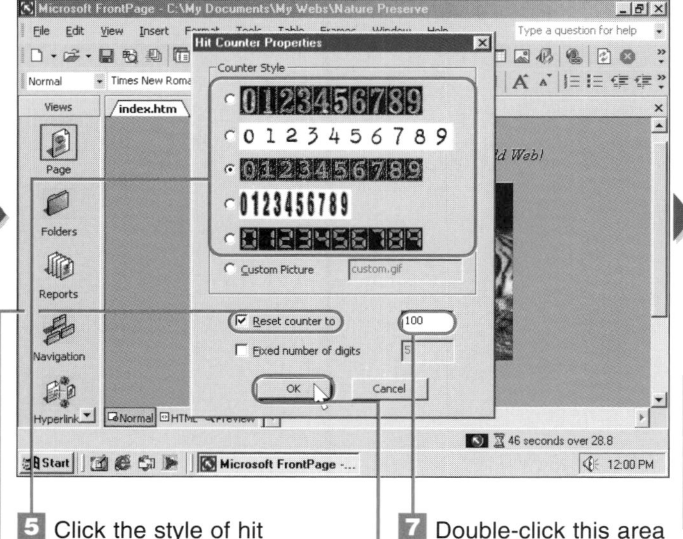

5 Click the style of hit counter you want to use (○ changes to ⊙).

6 To start the hit counter at a specific number, click this option (☐ changes to ☑).

7 Double-click this area and type the starting number you want to use.

Note: FrontPage automatically starts the hit counter at 0.

8 Click **OK** to create the hit counter.

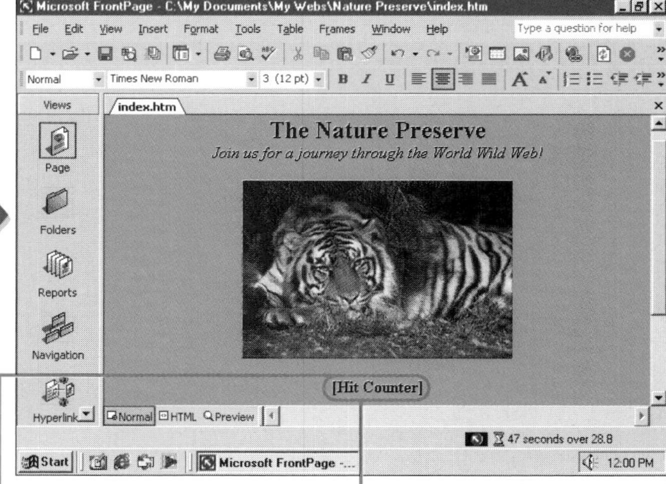

■ The text **[Hit Counter]** appears on your Web page.

■ The hit counter will replace the text when you publish your Web pages.

Note: You must publish your Web pages before you can properly view the hit counter.

■ To remove a hit counter, click **[Hit Counter]** and then press the Delete key.

ADD A MARQUEE

You can add a marquee that displays text that moves across a Web page.

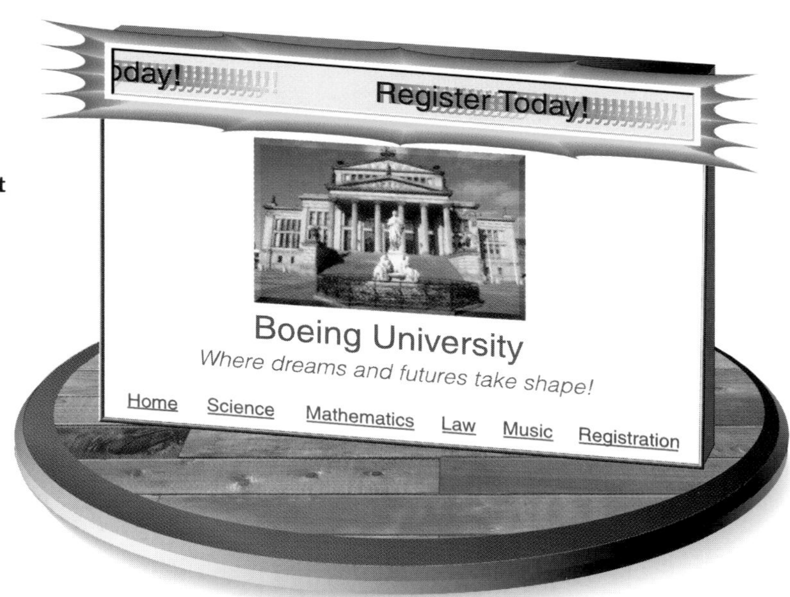

The Netscape Navigator Web browser will not display a marquee properly. The Web browser will display the marquee text, but the text will not move across the Web page.

ADD A MARQUEE

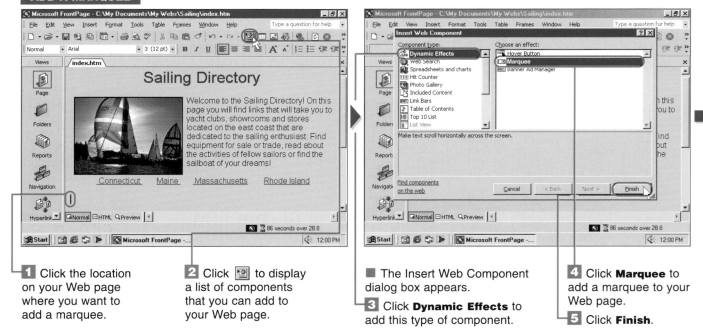

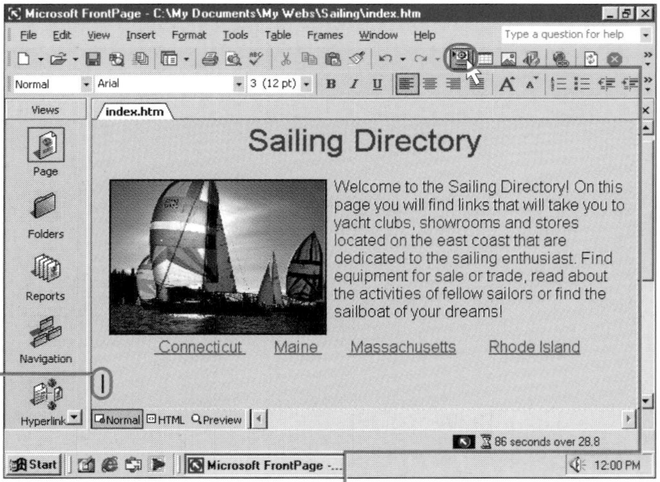

1 Click the location on your Web page where you want to add a marquee.

2 Click [icon] to display a list of components that you can add to your Web page.

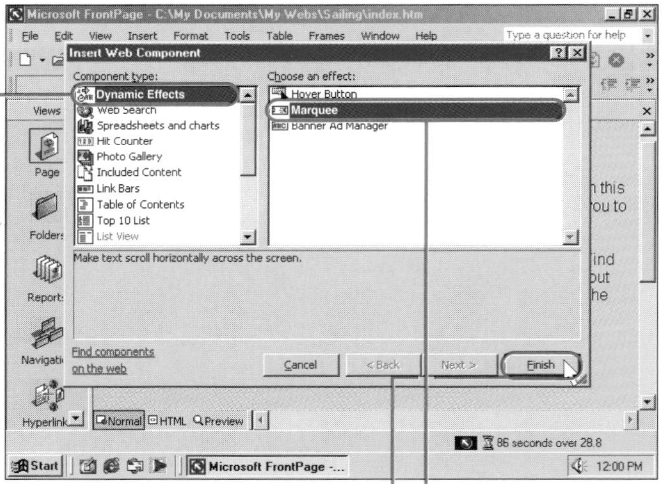

■ The Insert Web Component dialog box appears.

3 Click **Dynamic Effects** to add this type of component.

4 Click **Marquee** to add a marquee to your Web page.

5 Click **Finish**.

How can I move the marquee text across a Web page?

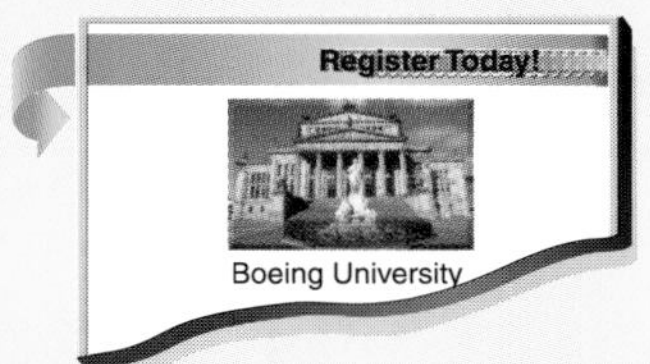

Scroll

The text appears from one side of the Web page, moves across the screen and then disappears on the other side of the page.

Slide

The text appears from one side of the Web page, moves across the screen and then stops at the other side of the page.

Alternate

The text bounces back and forth between the left and right sides of the Web page.

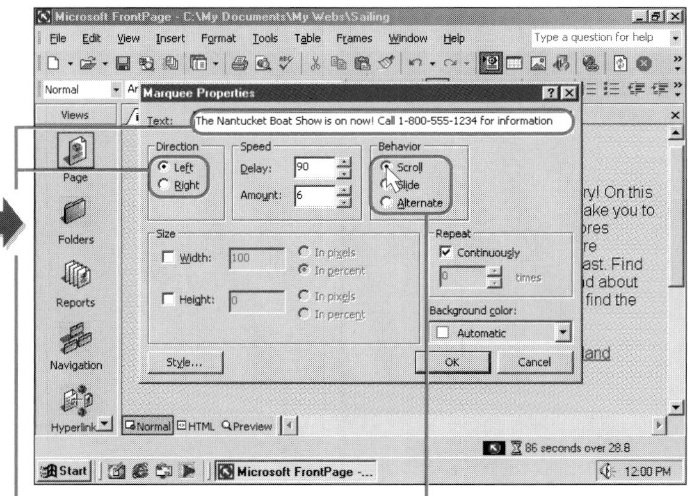

■ The Marquee Properties dialog box appears.

6 Type the text you want the marquee to display.

7 Click **Left** or **Right** to move the text towards the left or right side of the Web page (○ changes to ⊙).

8 Click the way you want to move the text across the Web page (○ changes to ⊙).

Note: For information on the ways you can move the text, see the top of this page.

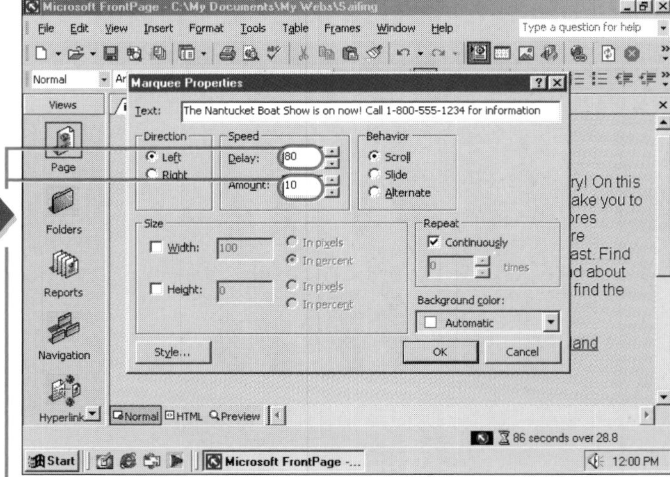

9 Double-click this area and type the number of milliseconds you want to pass between each movement of the text across the Web page.

10 Double-click this area and type the distance in pixels you want the text to move each time the text moves across the Web page.

Note: To move the text more quickly, use a smaller number in the Delay area and a larger number in the Amount area.

CONTINUED

ADD A MARQUEE

You can select the background color you want a marquee to display.

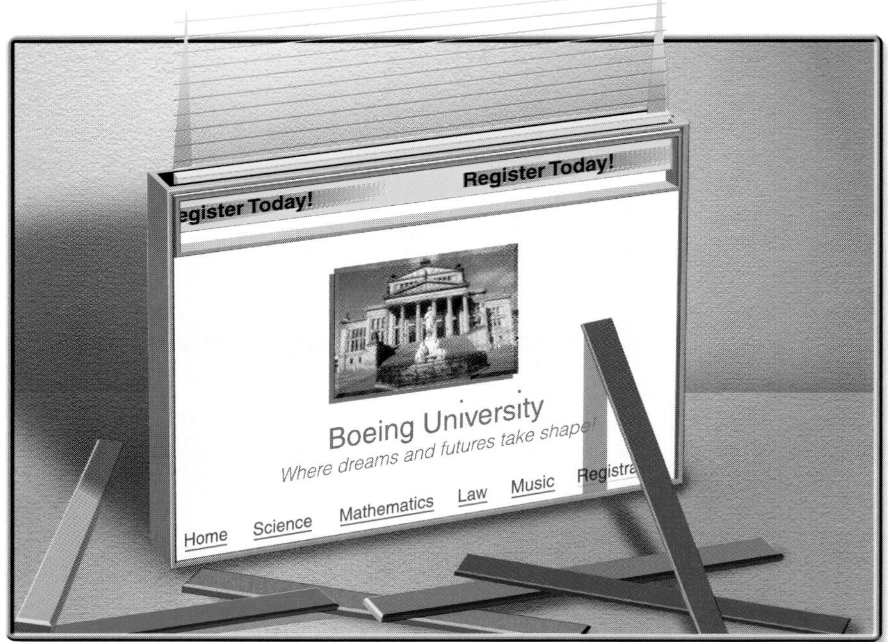

ADD A MARQUEE (CONTINUED)

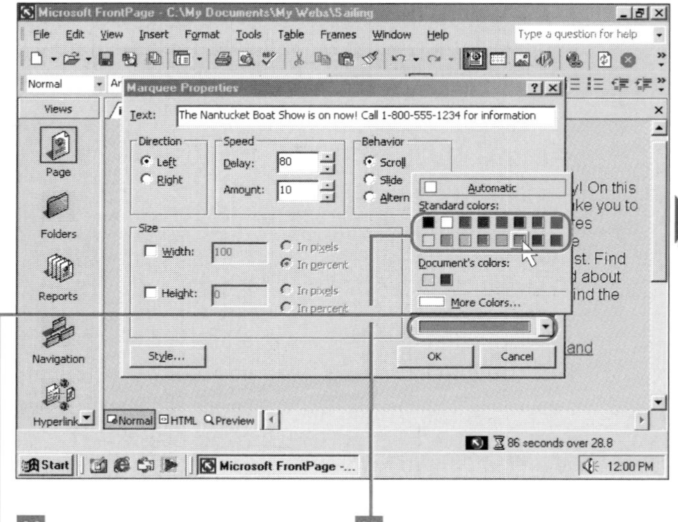

11 Click this area to select the background color you want the marquee to display.

12 Click the background color you want to use.

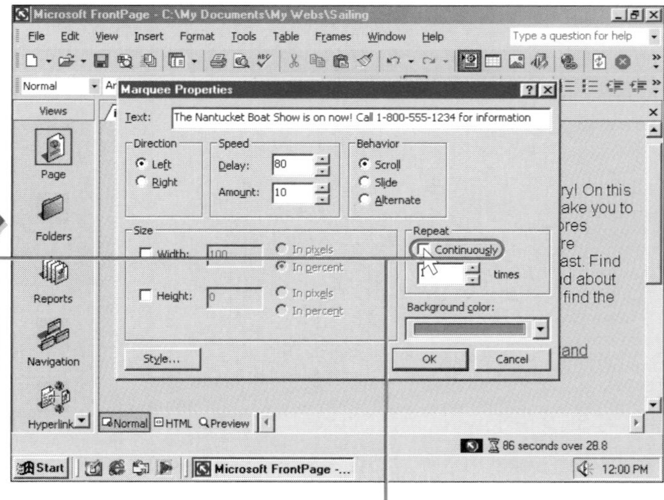

■ This option moves the marquee text continuously across your Web page.

*Note: If you selected Slide in step **8**, the marquee text will not move continuously across your Web page.*

13 If you want the text to move across the Web page only a specific number of times, click **Continuously** to turn off the option (☑ changes to ☐).

How can I change a marquee?

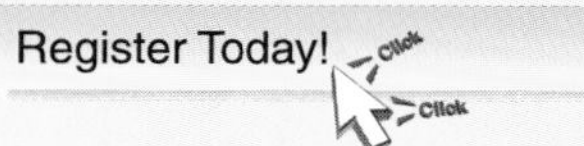

To make changes to a marquee, double-click the marquee to redisplay the Marquee Properties dialog box. Then perform steps **6** to **15** starting on page 255 to change the marquee.

How can I resize a marquee?

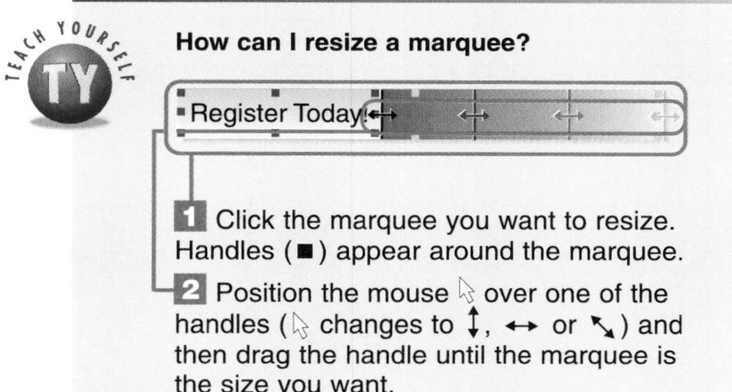

1 Click the marquee you want to resize. Handles (■) appear around the marquee.

2 Position the mouse over one of the handles (changes to ↕, ↔ or ↘) and then drag the handle until the marquee is the size you want.

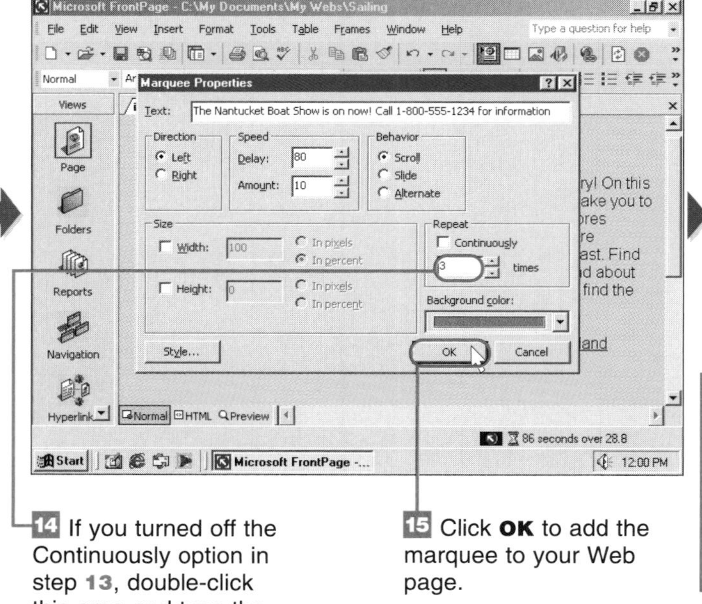

14 If you turned off the Continuously option in step **13**, double-click this area and type the number of times you want the text to move across your Web page.

15 Click **OK** to add the marquee to your Web page.

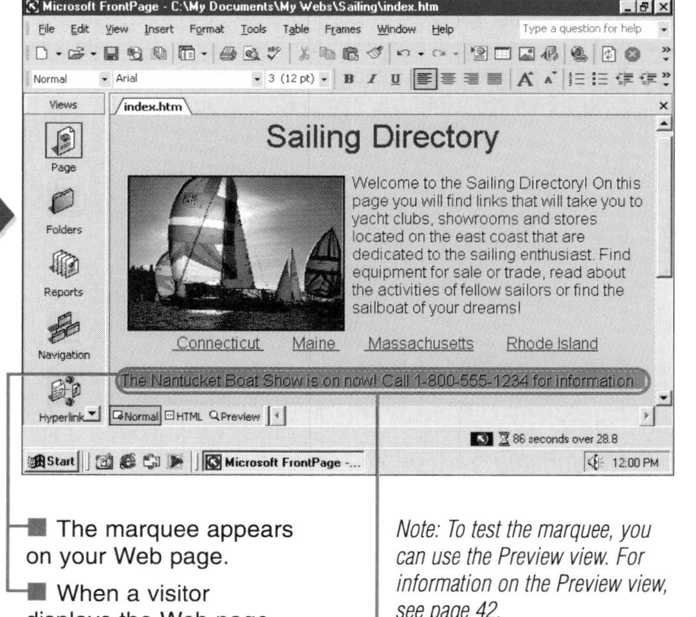

■ The marquee appears on your Web page.

■ When a visitor displays the Web page, the marquee text will move across the page.

Note: To test the marquee, you can use the Preview view. For information on the Preview view, see page 42.

■ To delete a marquee, click the marquee and then press the Delete key.

ADD A HOVER BUTTON

You can create a button that will change appearance when a visitor moves the mouse over the button. This is called a hover button.

A hover button is a link that visitors can select to display another Web page.

ADD A HOVER BUTTON

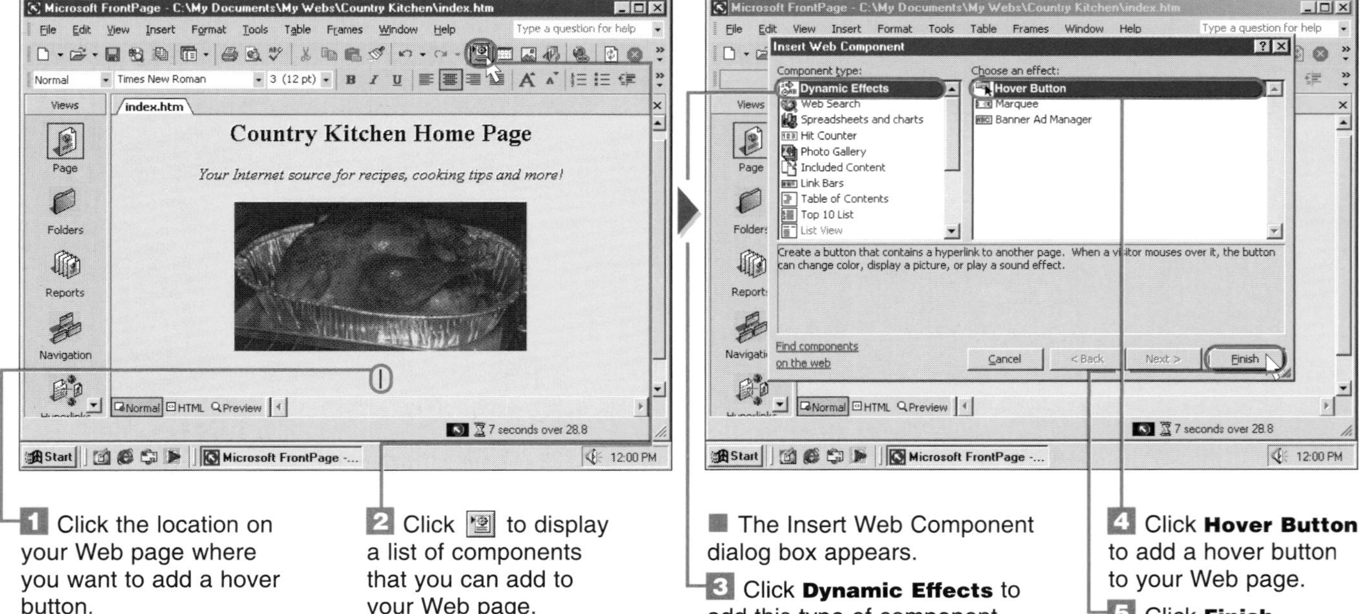

1 Click the location on your Web page where you want to add a hover button.

2 Click [icon] to display a list of components that you can add to your Web page.

■ The Insert Web Component dialog box appears.

3 Click **Dynamic Effects** to add this type of component.

4 Click **Hover Button** to add a hover button to your Web page.

5 Click **Finish**.

When would I use a hover button?

Hover buttons are useful when you want to make your Web pages more interactive. For example, you can create a hover button for each item in a menu. When a visitor moves the mouse pointer over a menu item, the appearance of the item will change. This can help visitors determine which menu item they are selecting.

What should I consider when creating a hover button?

Make sure the text you use for a hover button clearly indicates where the hover button will take your visitors. Do not use the phrase "Click Here" for a hover button, since this phrase is not very informative.

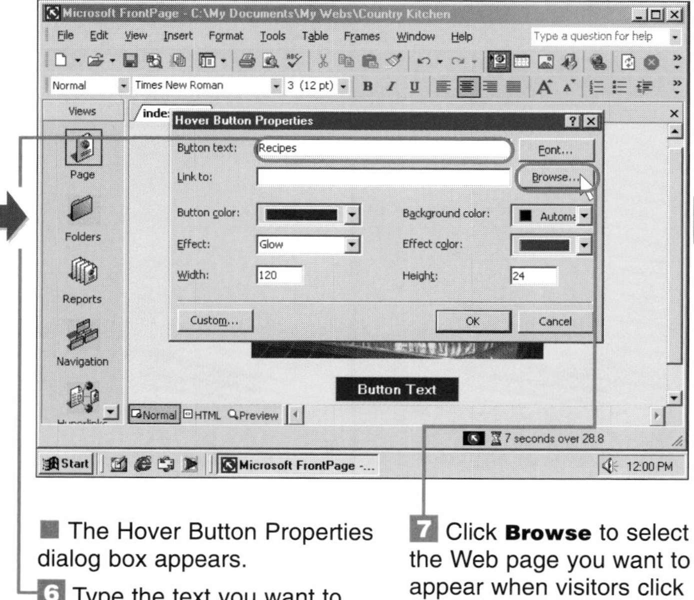

■ The Hover Button Properties dialog box appears.

6 Type the text you want to appear on the hover button.

7 Click **Browse** to select the Web page you want to appear when visitors click the hover button.

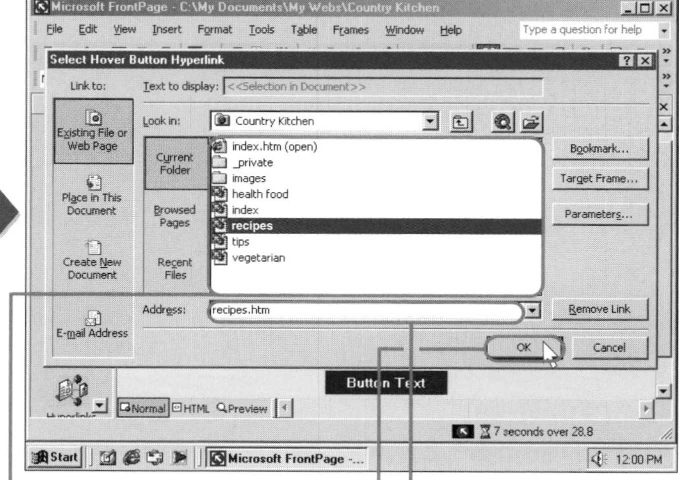

■ The Select Hover Button Hyperlink dialog box appears.

8 To link the hover button to a page in the current Web site, click the Web page (📄) in this area. This area lists all the Web pages in the current Web site.

■ To link the hover button to a page on the Web, type the address of the Web page in this area.

9 Click **OK**.

CONTINUED

ADD A HOVER BUTTON

When adding a hover button, you can choose from several effects that can occur when a visitor moves the mouse over the button.

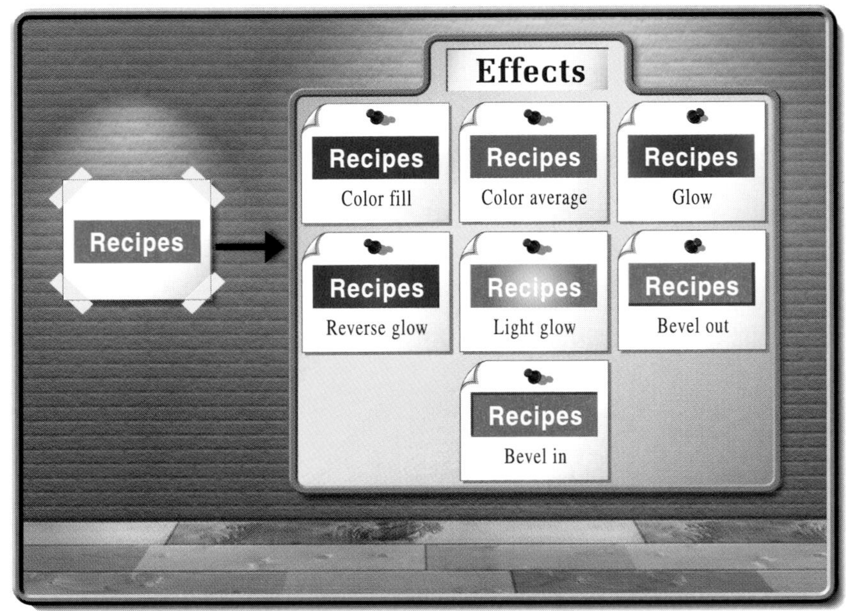

ADD A HOVER BUTTON (CONTINUED)

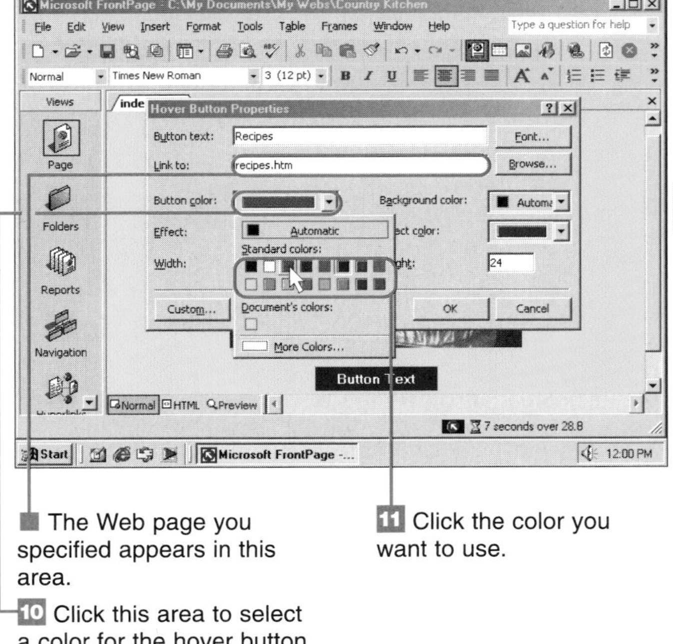

■ The Web page you specified appears in this area.

10 Click this area to select a color for the hover button when the button initially appears on the Web page.

11 Click the color you want to use.

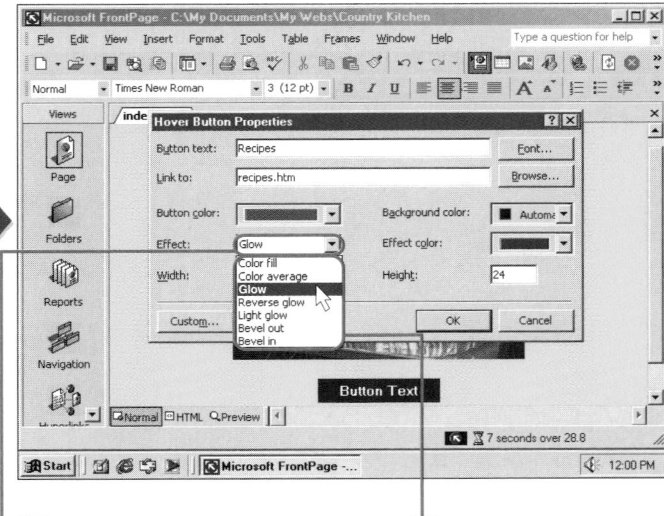

12 Click this area to select the effect you want to occur when a visitor moves the mouse over the hover button.

13 Click the effect you want to use.

How do I change, resize or delete a hover button?

Change a Hover Button

To make changes to a hover button, double-click the button to redisplay the Hover Button Properties dialog box. Then perform steps 6 to 16 starting on page 259 to change the hover button.

Resize a Hover Button

You may need to resize a hover button if the button is not large enough to display the text for the button. You can resize a hover button as you would resize any image on a Web page. To resize an image, see page 105.

Delete a Hover Button

To delete a hover button, click the hover button and then press the Delete key.

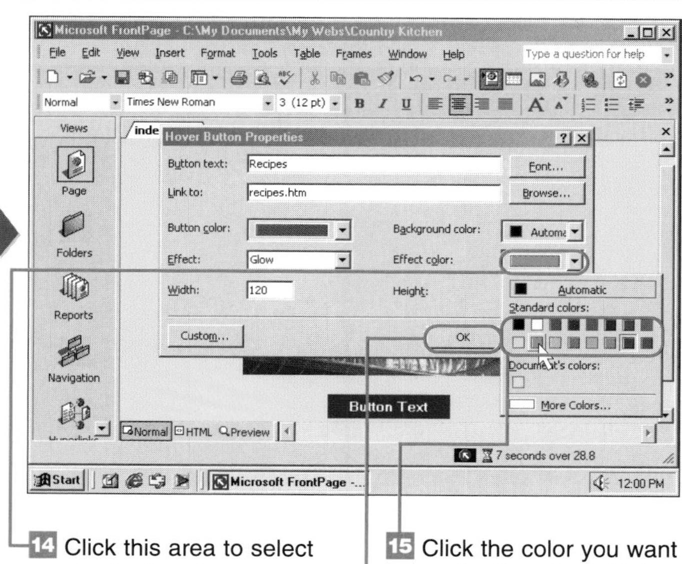

14 Click this area to select a color for the effect.

Note: You do not need to select a color for the effect if you selected Light glow, Bevel in or Bevel out in step 13.

15 Click the color you want to use for the effect. Make sure you choose a different color than the color you selected in step 11.

16 Click **OK** to confirm your selections.

■ When a visitor moves the mouse over the hover button, the appearance of the button will change.

■ A visitor can click the hover button to display the Web page you specified.

Note: To test the hover button, save your Web page and then use the Preview view to test the button. For information on the Preview view, see page 42.

ADD A BANNER AD

You can add a banner ad that continuously rotates a series of images on a Web page.

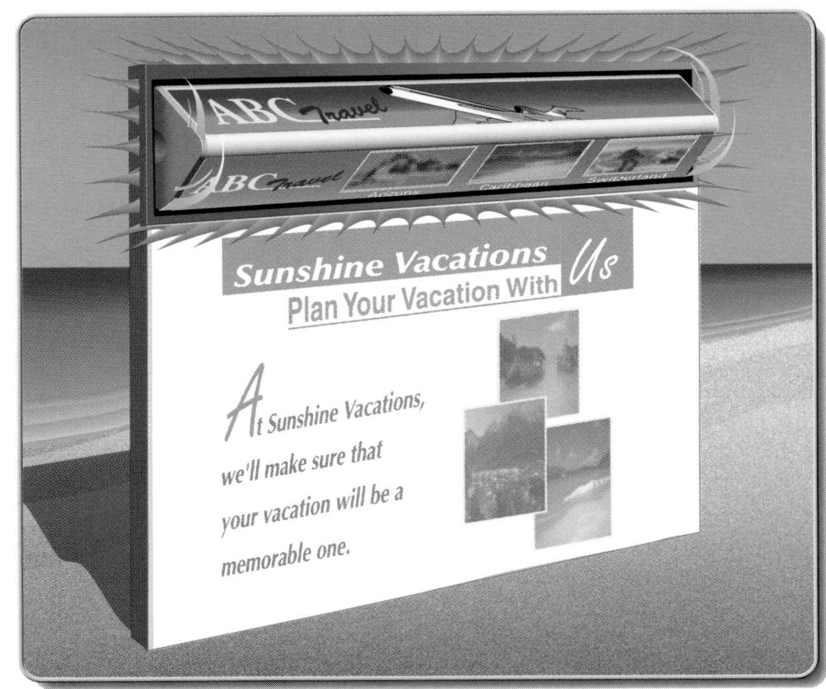

When adding a banner ad, you should use images that are approximately the same size.

ADD A BANNER AD

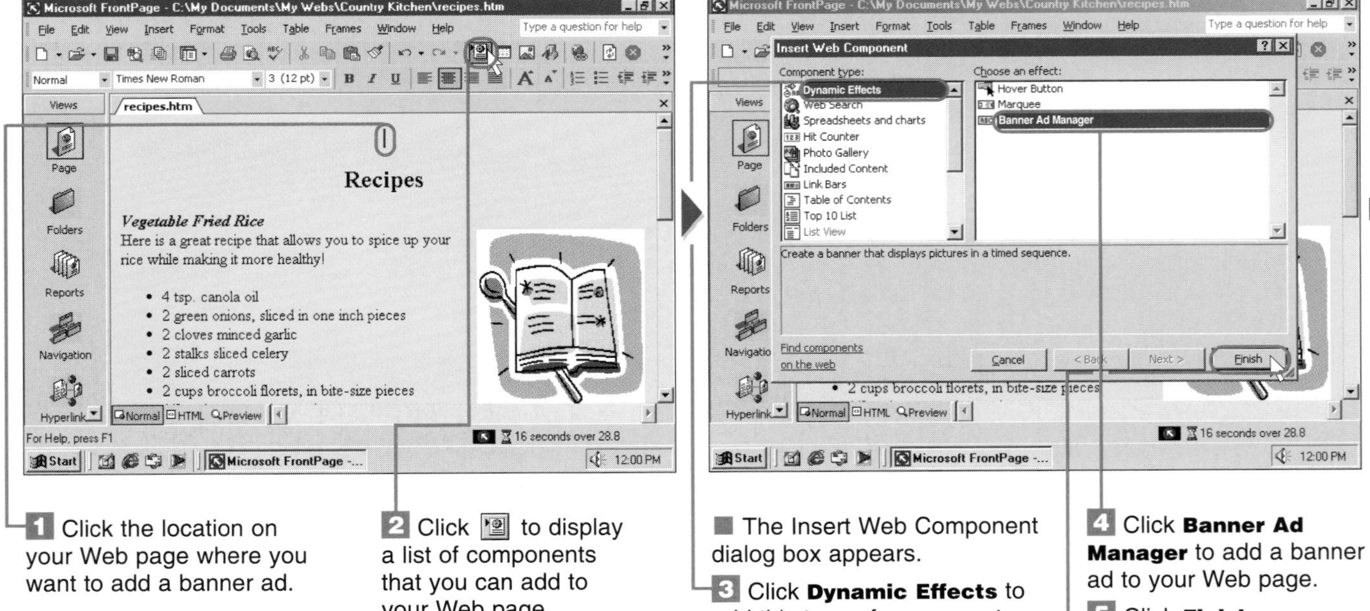

1 Click the location on your Web page where you want to add a banner ad.

2 Click the Web Component button to display a list of components that you can add to your Web page.

■ The Insert Web Component dialog box appears.

3 Click **Dynamic Effects** to add this type of component.

4 Click **Banner Ad Manager** to add a banner ad to your Web page.

5 Click **Finish**.

How can I use a banner ad?

Banner ads are most often used to display advertisements on Web pages. Many companies offer advertising space on their Web pages to earn money. If another Web site offers information, products or services related to your Web site, you can ask the individual or company to include an advertisement for your Web pages if you will do the same. For example, if you are an artist, you can contact the Web sites of local galleries.

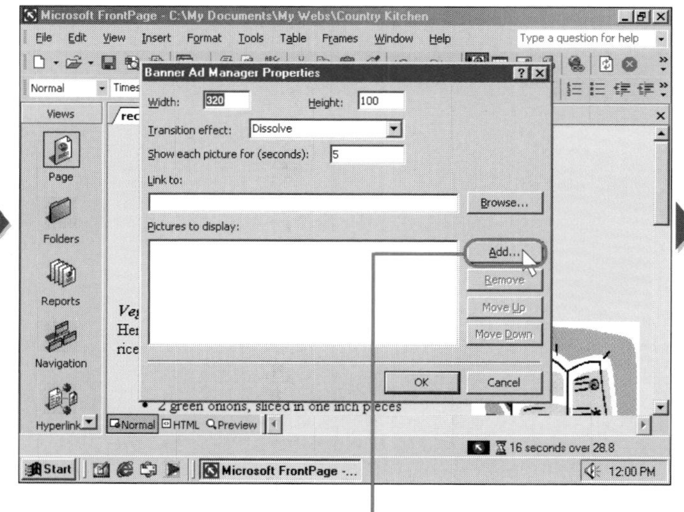

■ The Banner Ad Manager Properties dialog box appears.

6 Click **Add** to select an image that you want to appear on the banner ad.

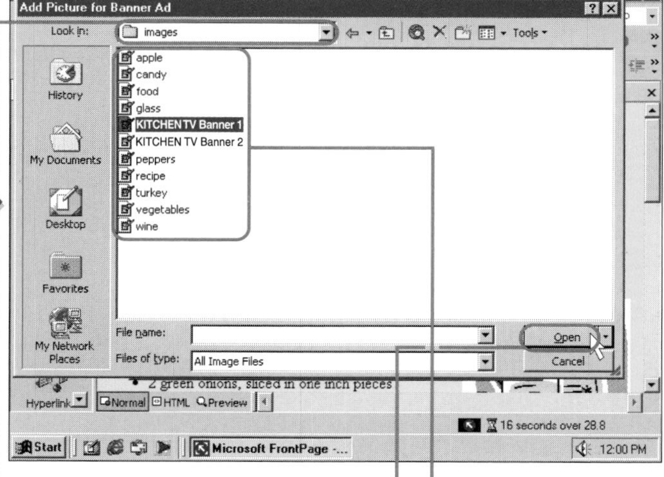

■ The Add Picture for Banner Ad dialog box appears.

■ This area shows the location of the displayed files. You can click this area to change the location.

7 Click the image you want to appear on the banner ad.

8 Click **Open** to confirm your selection.

CONTINUED

You can link a banner ad to a Web page. When visitors click the banner ad, the Web page you specify will appear.

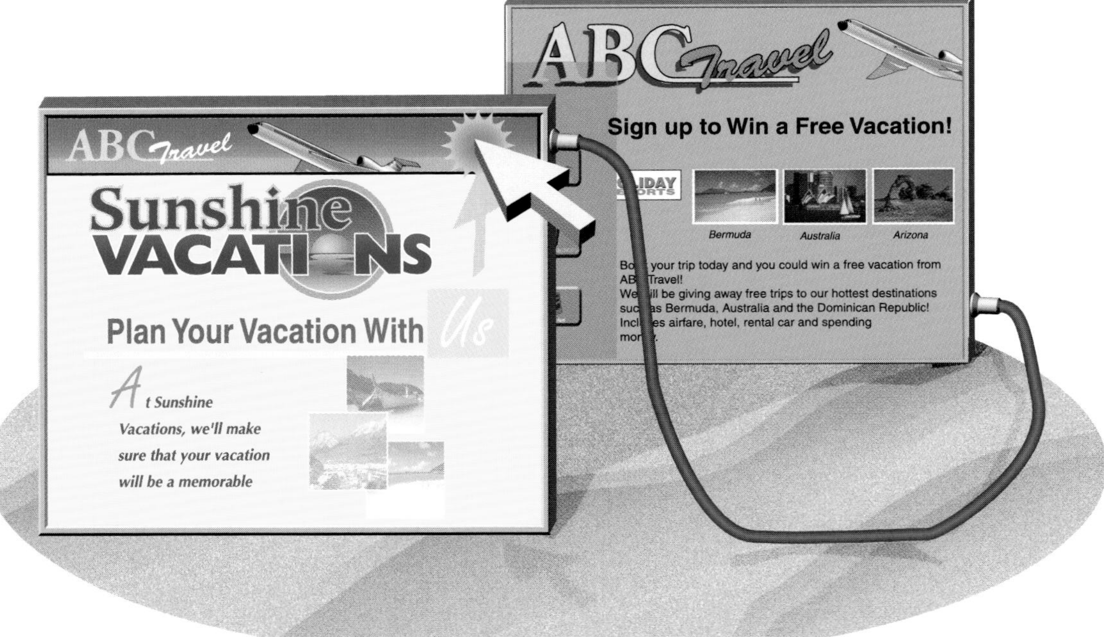

You cannot link the images displayed on a banner ad to different Web pages. Each image can only link to the same Web page.

ADD A BANNER AD (CONTINUED)

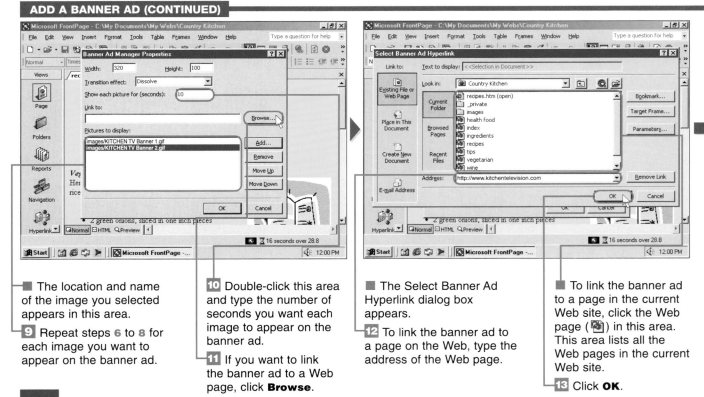

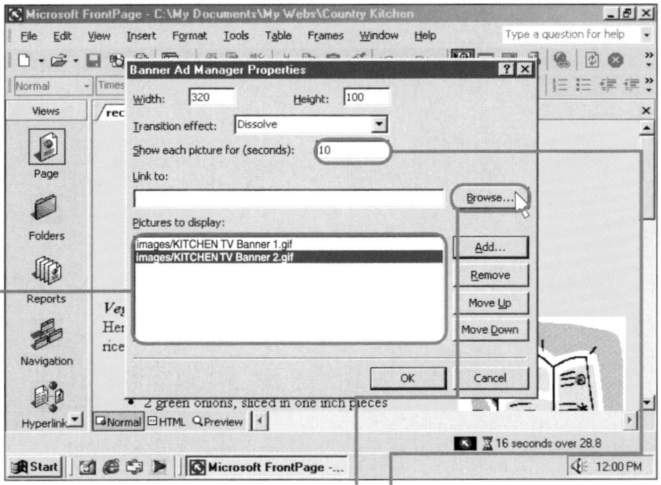

- The location and name of the image you selected appears in this area.

9 Repeat steps 6 to 8 for each image you want to appear on the banner ad.

10 Double-click this area and type the number of seconds you want each image to appear on the banner ad.

11 If you want to link the banner ad to a Web page, click **Browse**.

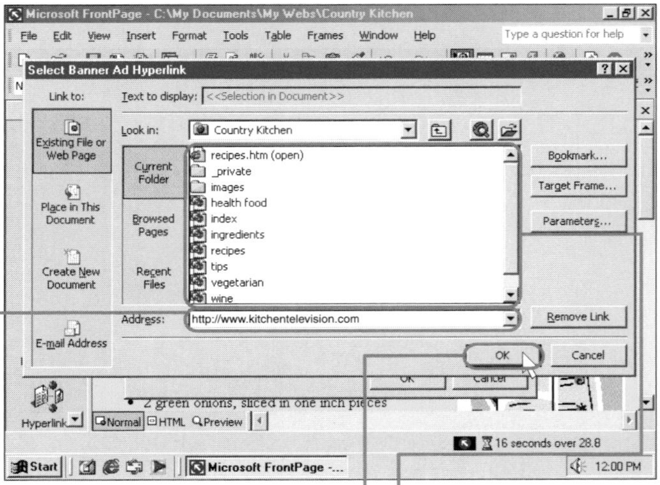

- The Select Banner Ad Hyperlink dialog box appears.

12 To link the banner ad to a page on the Web, type the address of the Web page.

- To link the banner ad to a page in the current Web site, click the Web page in this area. This area lists all the Web pages in the current Web site.

13 Click **OK**.

What is a transition effect?

A transition effect determines how one image moves to the next image on a banner ad. FrontPage offers the Blinds Horizontal, Blinds Vertical, Dissolve, Box In and Box Out transition effects.

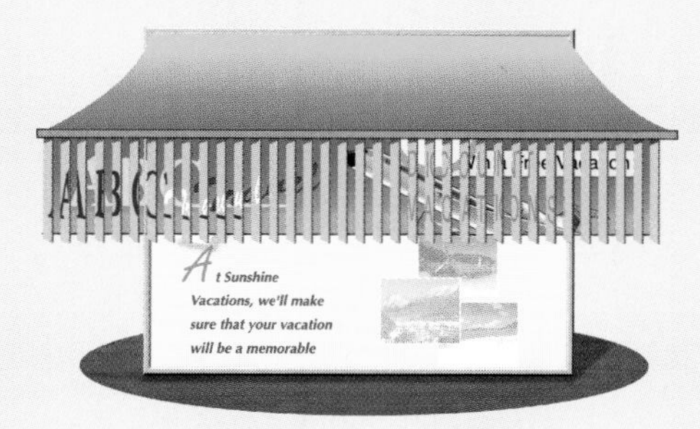

How do I resize a banner ad?

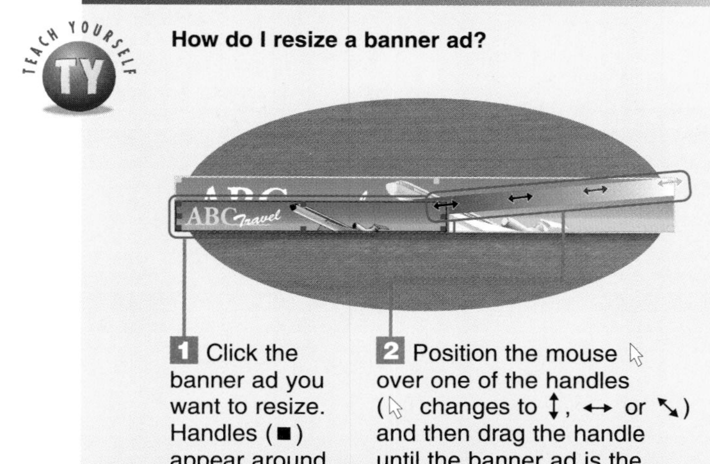

1 Click the banner ad you want to resize. Handles (■) appear around the banner ad.

2 Position the mouse over one of the handles (changes to ↕, ↔ or ↘) and then drag the handle until the banner ad is the size you want.

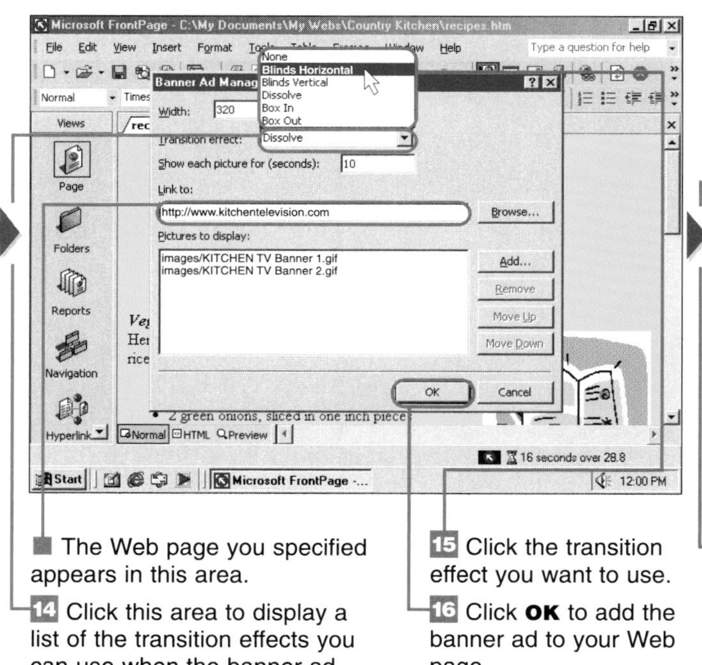

■ The Web page you specified appears in this area.

14 Click this area to display a list of the transition effects you can use when the banner ad moves from one image to another.

15 Click the transition effect you want to use.

16 Click **OK** to add the banner ad to your Web page.

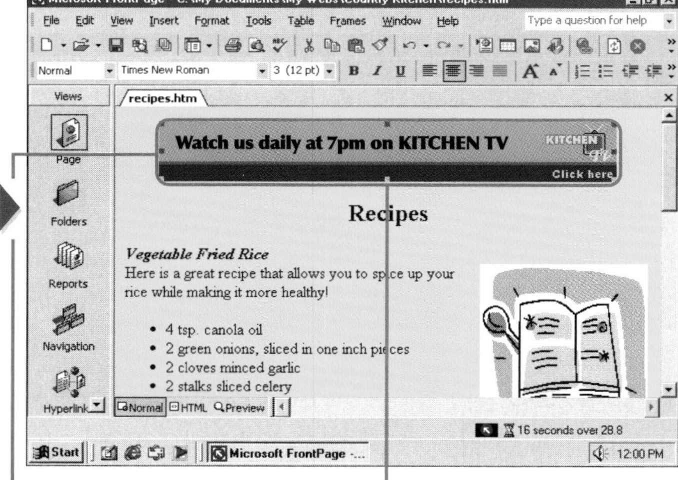

■ The banner ad appears on your Web page.

Note: To test the banner ad, you must display the Web page in a Web browser. To display a Web page in a Web browser, see page 44.

■ To make changes to a banner ad, double-click the banner ad and then perform steps 10 to 16.

■ To delete a banner ad, click the banner ad and then press the Delete key.

ADD A WEB PAGE TRANSITION

You can add a visual effect to a Web page that will appear when visitors display or leave your Web page or Web site. This type of effect is called a transition.

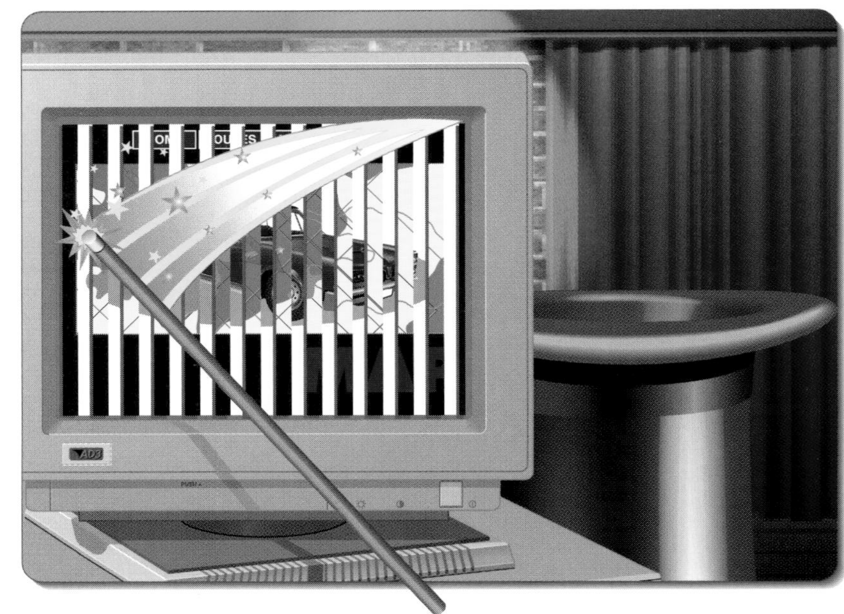

Some Web browsers, such as Netscape Navigator, will not display a transition you add to a Web page.

ADD A WEB PAGE TRANSITION

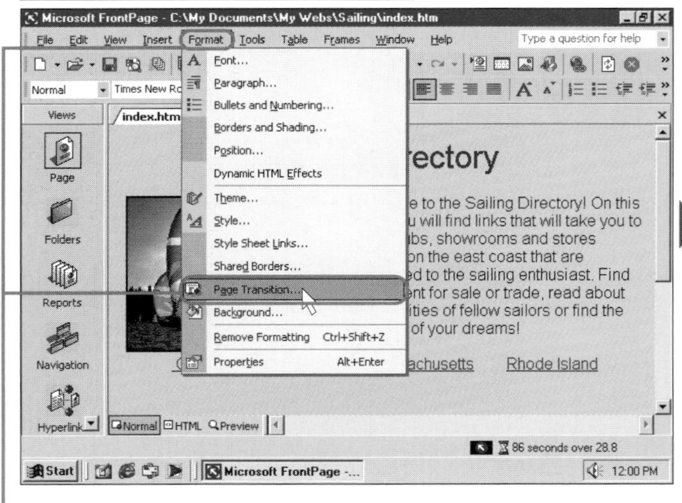

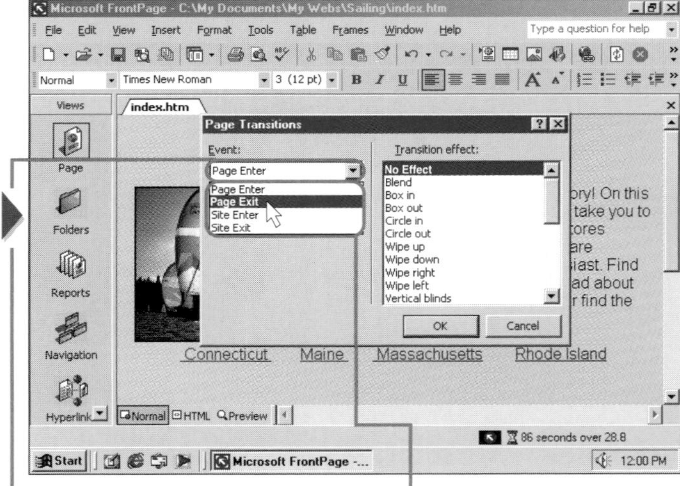

1 Click anywhere on the Web page you want to add a transition to.

2 Click **Format**.

3 Click **Page Transition**.

Note: If Page Transition does not appear on the menu, position the mouse over the bottom of the menu to display all the menu options.

■ The Page Transitions dialog box appears.

4 Click this area to specify when you want the transition to occur.

5 Click the event that describes when you want the transition to occur.

What should I consider when adding a transition to a Web page?

You should set a Web page transition to occur for only a few seconds. Some visitors may leave your Web site if a Web page transition takes a long time to complete. You should also avoid overusing transitions on your Web pages. Visitors may become annoyed with a Web site that displays transitions for every Web page.

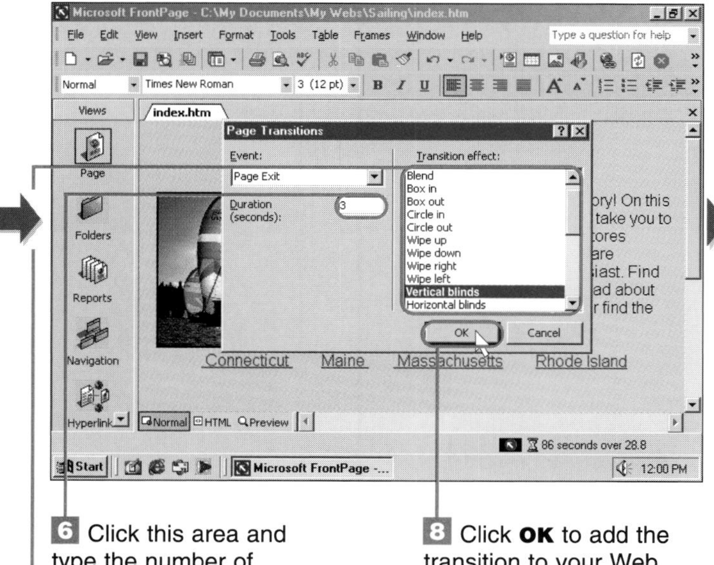

6 Click this area and type the number of seconds you want the transition to occur.

7 Click the transition effect you want to use.

8 Click **OK** to add the transition to your Web page.

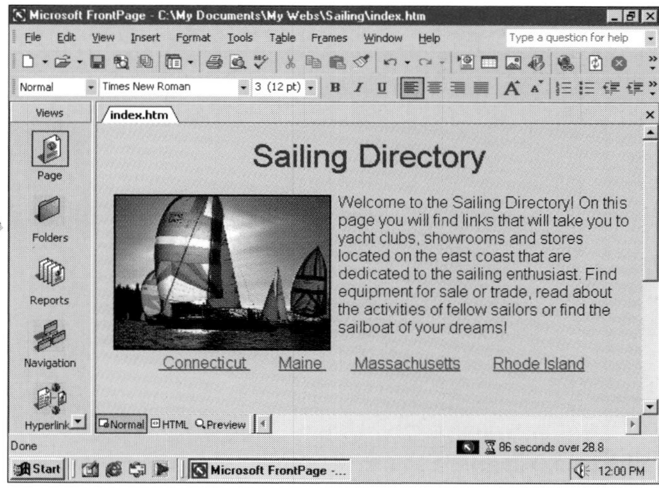

■ When a visitor performs the event you specified in step 5, the transition will occur.

■ To remove a transition from a Web page, repeat steps 1 to 8, selecting **No Effect** in step 7.

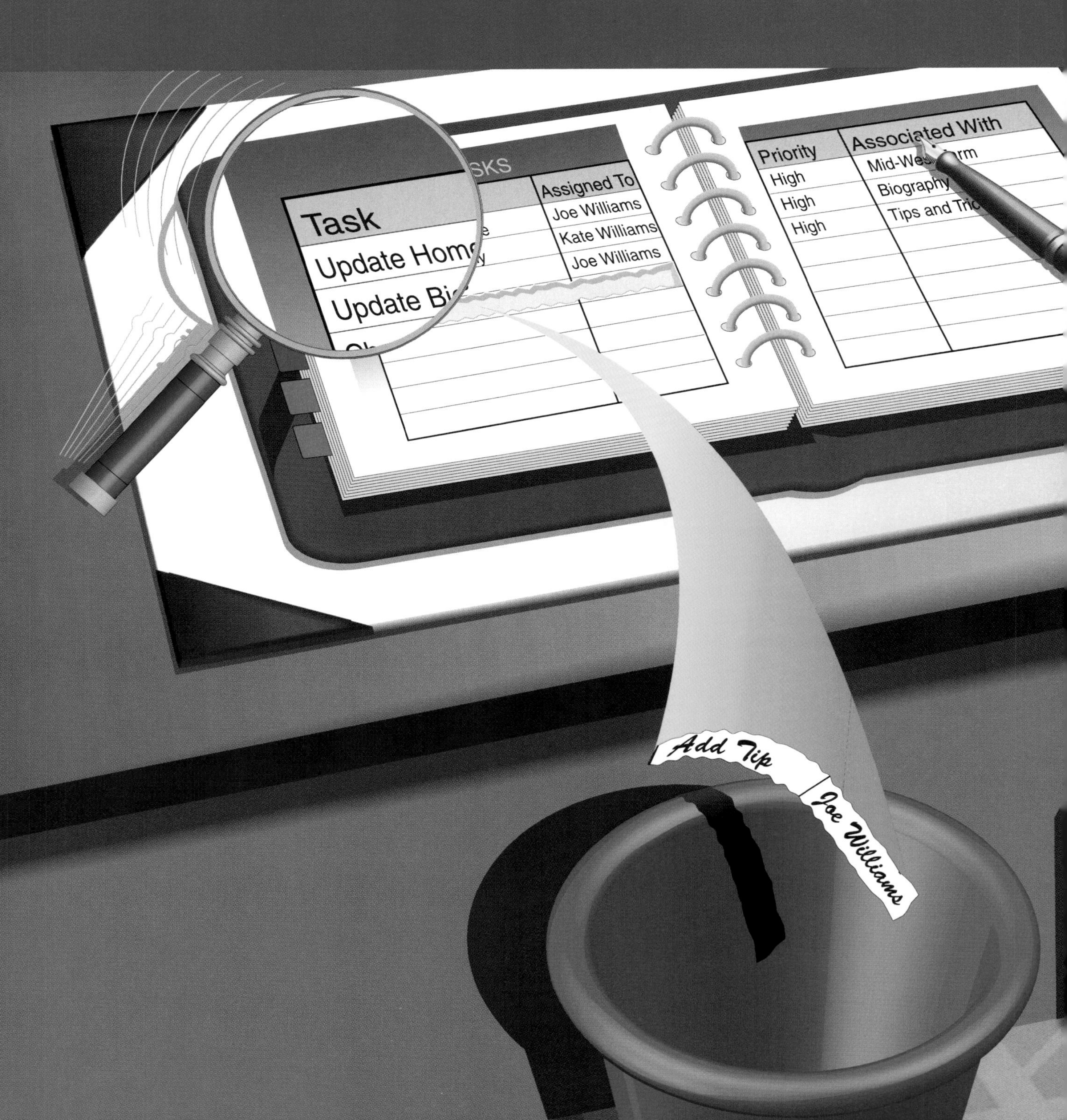
Task
Assigned To
Joe Williams
Kate Williams
Joe Williams
Priority
Associated With
High
High
High
Biography
Add Tip
Joe Williams

CHAPTER 14

Manage Web Pages

Do you want to keep track of your Web site's progress? This chapter shows you how to create and work with tasks, view reports and more.

CREATE A NEW FOLDER

You can create a new folder to help you organize the files in your Web site. For example, you can create a folder named multimedia to store all your sounds and videos.

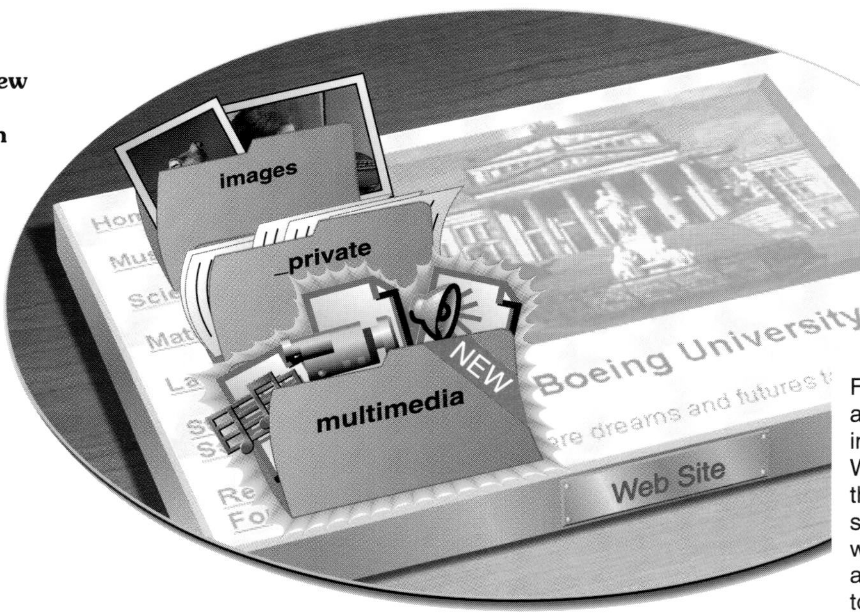

FrontPage automatically adds the _private and images folders to your Web site. You can use the _private folder to store files you do not want visitors to access and the images folder to store images.

CREATE A NEW FOLDER

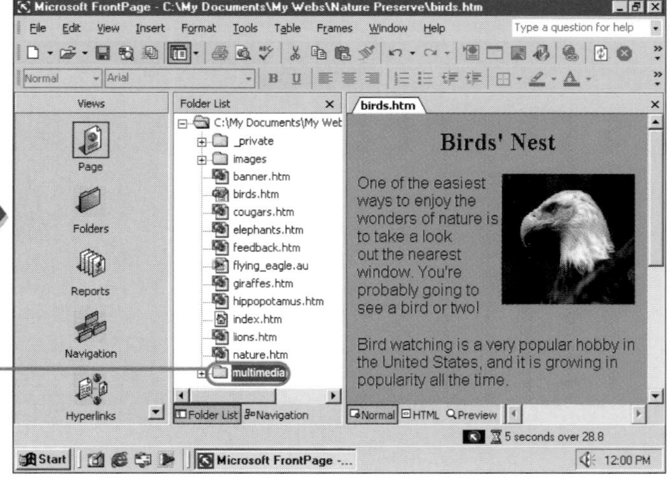

1 Click the folder (📁) you want to contain the new folder.

■ If the list of folders (📁), Web pages and other items does not appear, click ▦ to display the list.

2 Click ▾ in this area.

3 Click **Folder** to create a new folder.

Note: If Folder does not appear on the menu, position the mouse over the bottom of the menu to display all the menu options.

■ The new folder appears.

4 Type a name for the new folder and then press the **Enter** key.

*Note: To delete a folder you created, click the folder and then press the **Delete** key. A dialog box will appear to confirm the deletion. Click Yes to delete the folder.*

MOVE A FILE TO A FOLDER

You can move a file to a folder in your Web site. This allows you to place related files in the same location.

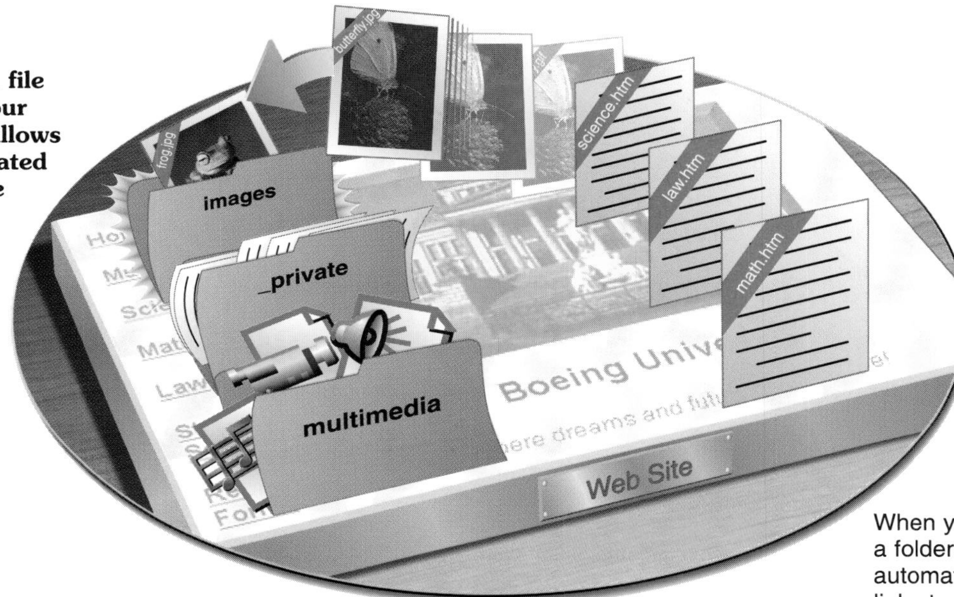

When you move a file to a folder, FrontPage will automatically update all links to the file.

MOVE A FILE TO A FOLDER

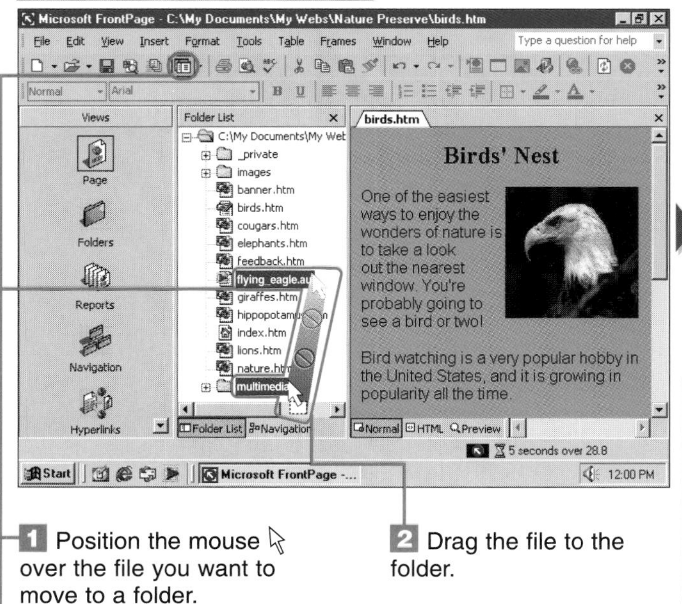

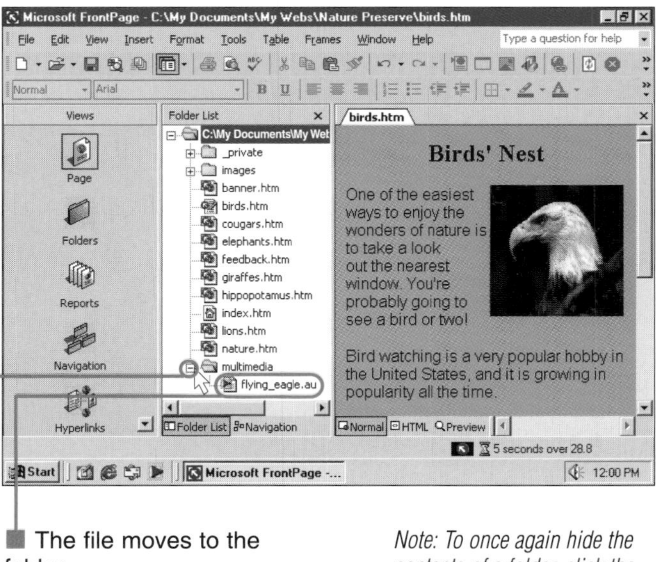

1 Position the mouse over the file you want to move to a folder.

■ If the list of folders (📁), Web pages and other items does not appear, click ▦ to display the list.

2 Drag the file to the folder.

■ The file moves to the folder.

3 To display the contents of a folder, click the plus sign (⊞) beside the folder (⊞ changes to ⊟).

Note: To once again hide the contents of a folder, click the minus sign (⊟) beside the folder.

VIEW REPORTS

You can use the Reports view to display various reports that analyze and summarize information about your Web site.

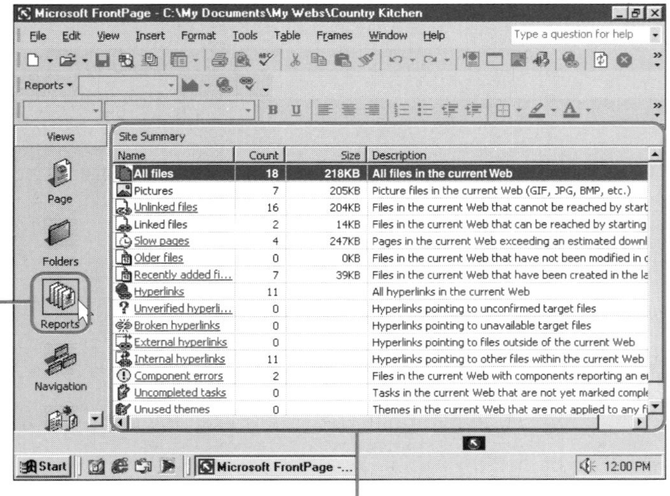

1 Click **Reports** to display your Web site in the Reports view.

■ The Site Summary report appears in this area. This report provides an overview of the information in your Web site, such as the total size of all the files in your Web site.

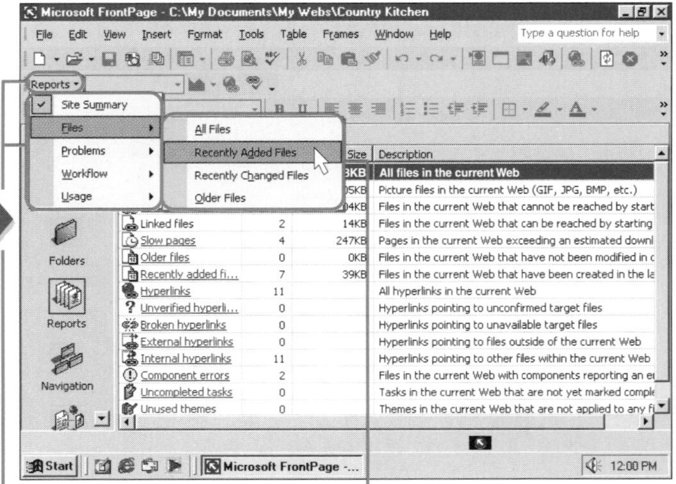

2 To display a different report, click **Reports**.

Note: If the Reporting toolbar is not displayed, see page 24 to display the toolbar.

3 Click the type of report you want to display.

Note: The Usage reports are only useful if you have published your Web pages to a Web server that can provide statistics about your published pages.

4 Click the report you want to display.

What reports does FrontPage offer?

Here are some reports that FrontPage offers to help you review and analyze the information in your Web site.

Report	Description
Site Summary	Provides an overview of the information in your Web site.
All Files	Displays information about each file in your Web site.
Recently Added Files	Displays files added in the last 30 days.
Recently Changed Files	Displays files changed in the last 30 days.
Older Files	Displays files you have not changed in the last 72 days.
Unlinked Files	Displays files you cannot access from your home page.
Slow Pages	Displays Web pages that take at least 30 seconds to download when using a 28.8 Kbps modem.
Broken Hyperlinks	Displays the status of the links in your Web site.

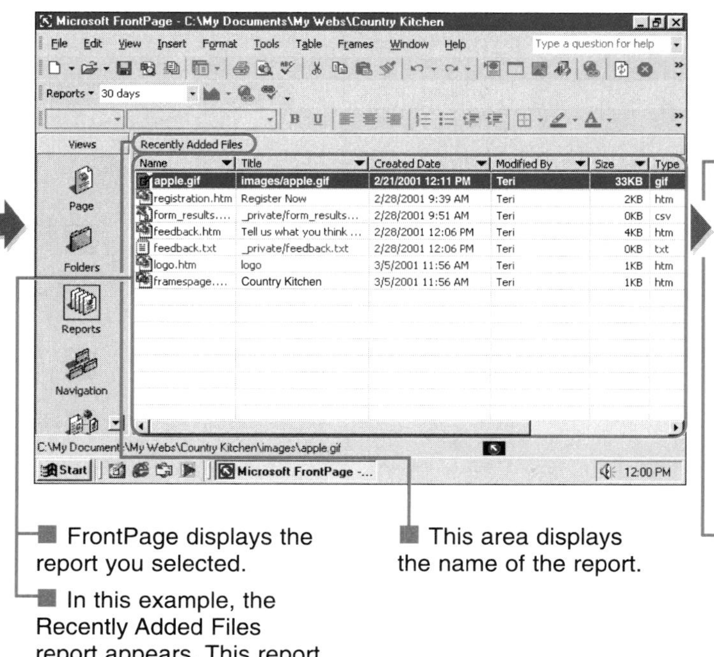

■ FrontPage displays the report you selected.

■ In this example, the Recently Added Files report appears. This report shows information about the files you have added in the last 30 days.

■ This area displays the name of the report.

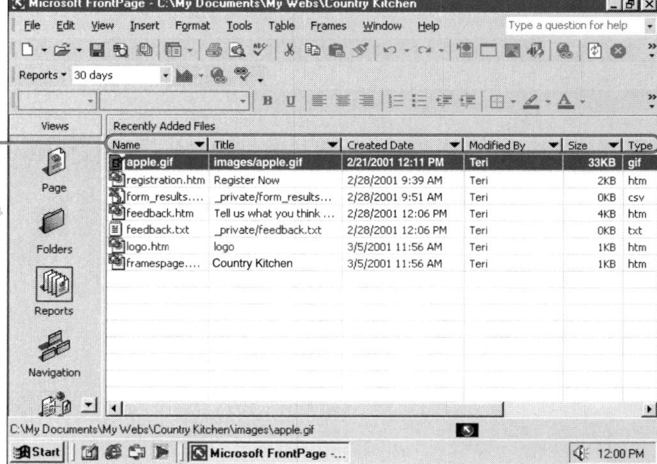

■ To view the files in a different order, click the heading of the column you want to use to sort the files.

Note: To sort the files in the opposite order, click the heading of the column again.

ADD A TASK

You can add tasks to create a to-do list to keep track of Web pages you need to complete.

You can add a task to remind you to add, update, review or confirm information on a Web page at a later time.

You can associate each task you add with a specific Web page in your Web site.

ADD A TASK

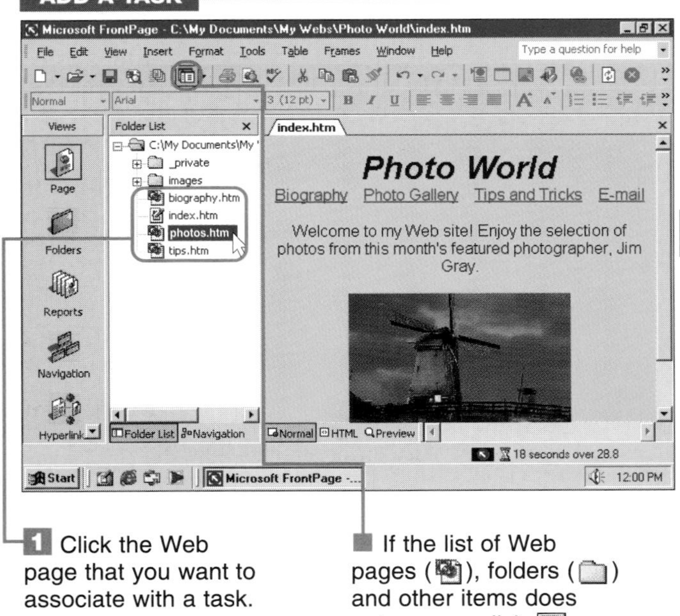

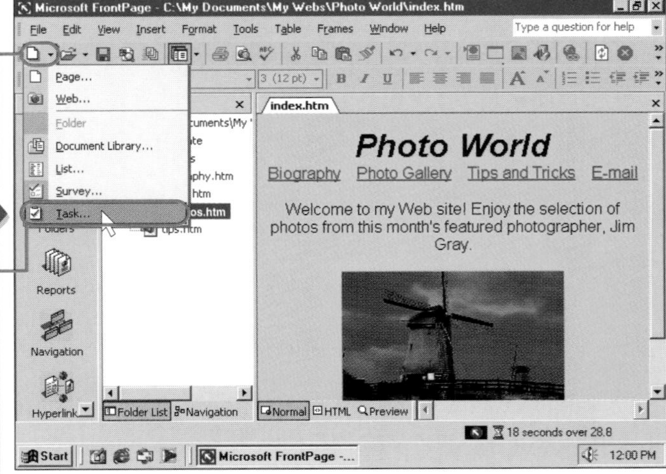

1 Click the Web page that you want to associate with a task.

■ If the list of Web pages (📄), folders (📁) and other items does not appear, click ▤ to display the list.

2 To add a task, click ▾ in this area.

3 Click **Task**.

Note: If Task does not appear on the menu, position the mouse ↖ over the bottom of the menu to display all the menu options.

Can I add a task that is not associated with a specific Web page?

Yes. You may want to add a task that is not associated with a specific Web page if the task relates to more than one page, such as a task for verifying the phone numbers on every page. To add a task that is not associated with a specific Web page, click the Tasks icon and then perform steps 2 to 7 below.

Can I associate a task with any type of file?

You can associate a task with any type of file in your Web site, such as a Web page, image, sound, video or document. This allows you to keep track of specific files you need to complete in your Web site.

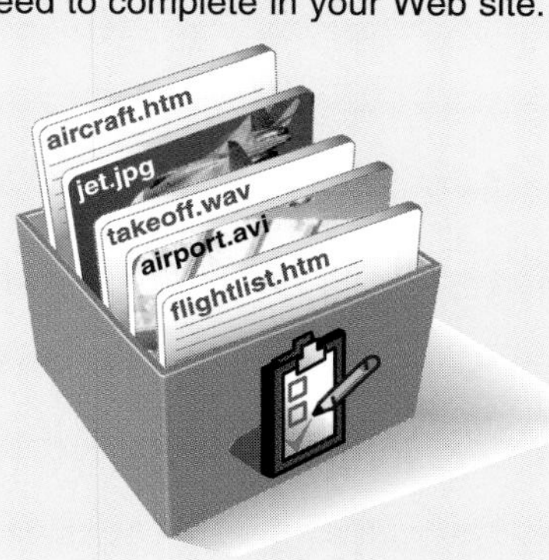

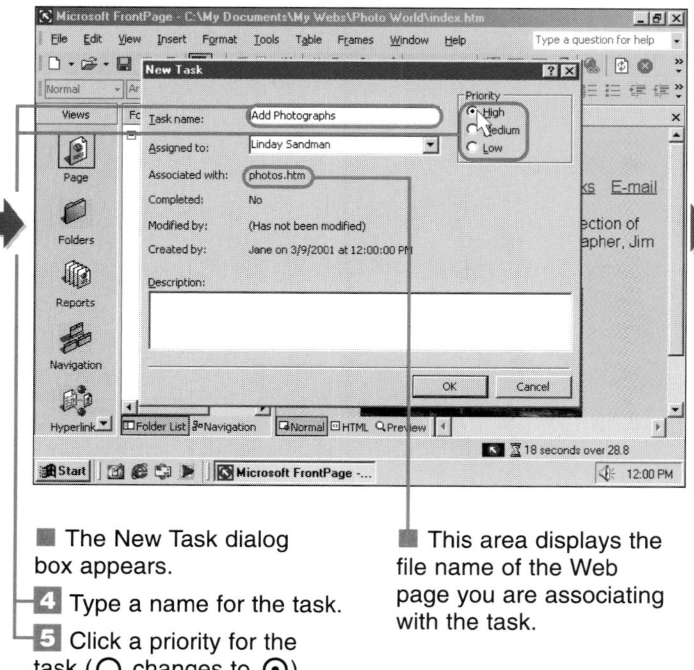

■ The New Task dialog box appears.

4 Type a name for the task.

5 Click a priority for the task (○ changes to ⊙).

■ This area displays the file name of the Web page you are associating with the task.

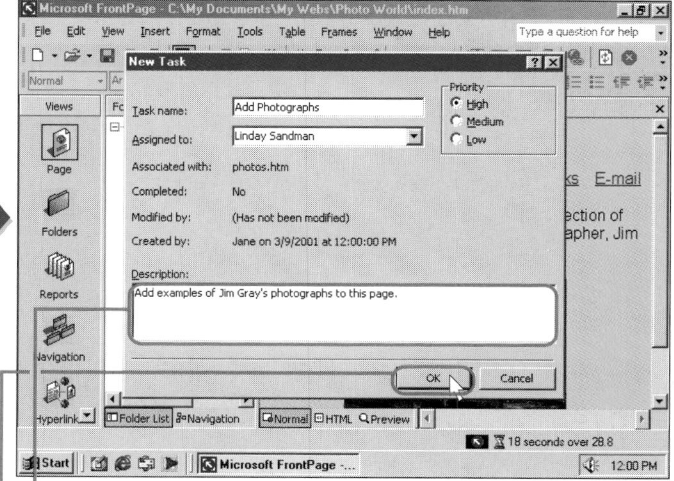

6 Click this area and type a description for the task. The description should include the work you need to perform to complete the task.

7 Click **OK** to add the task.

■ You can repeat steps 1 to 7 for each task you want to add.

Note: To view your tasks, see page 276.

VIEW TASKS

You can view a list of all the tasks you have added to your Web site. Tasks help you keep track of the Web pages you need to complete.

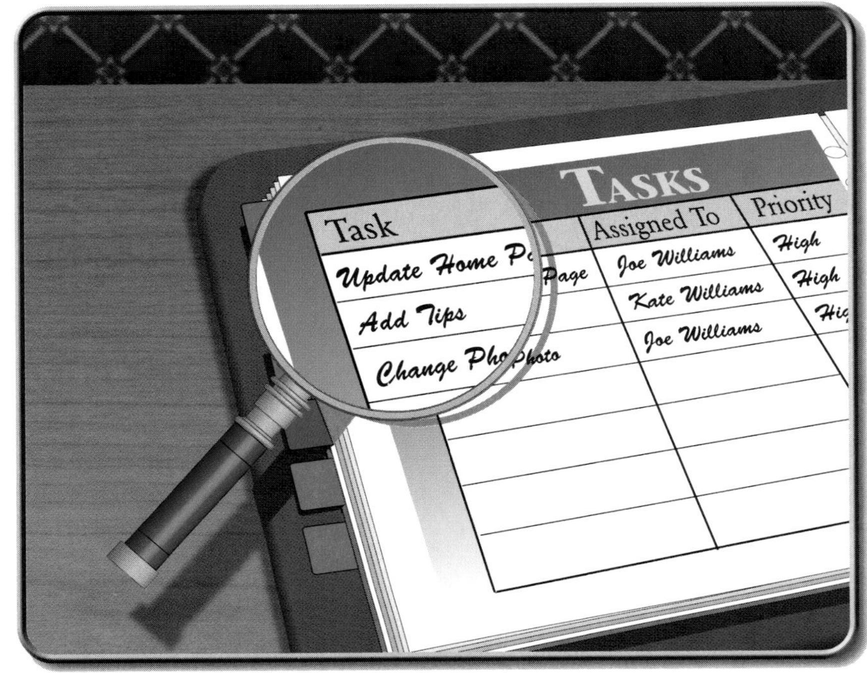

VIEW TASKS

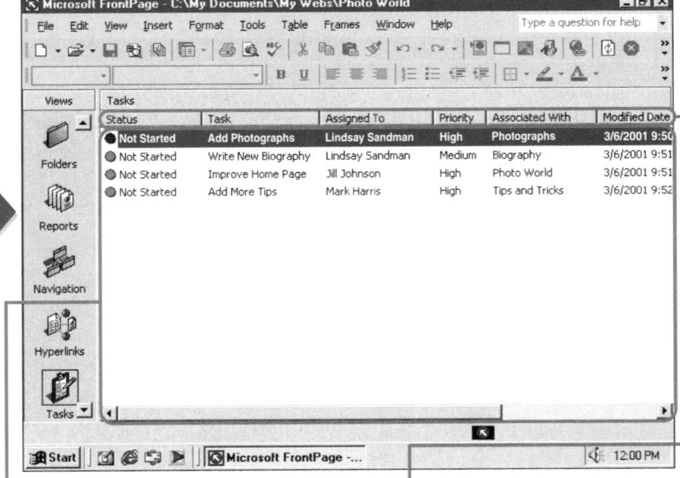

1 Click **Tasks** to view the tasks that you have added to your Web site.

■ If the Tasks icon is not displayed, click ▾ to display the icon.

■ This area displays information about each task you have added, such as the status, name and priority of the tasks as well as the Web pages associated with the tasks.

■ To view the tasks in a different order, click the heading of the column you want to use to sort the tasks.

Note: You can click the heading of the column again to sort the tasks in the opposite order.

EDIT A TASK

You can change the information you specified for a task, such as providing a more accurate name or a more detailed description for a task.

EDIT A TASK

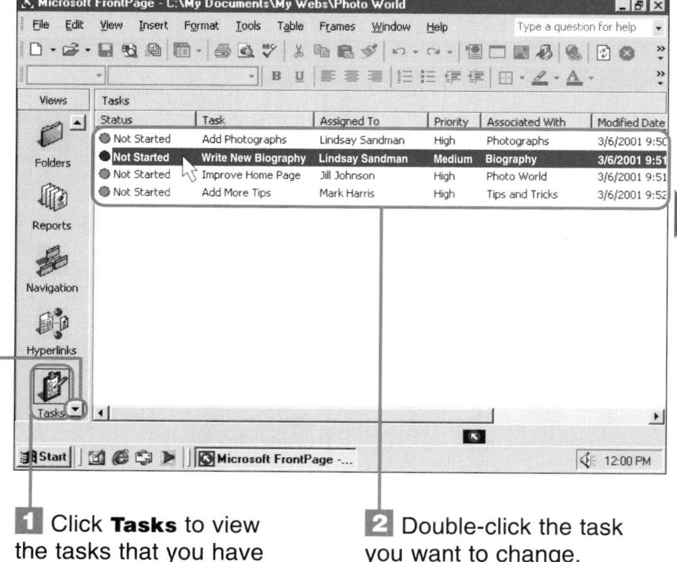

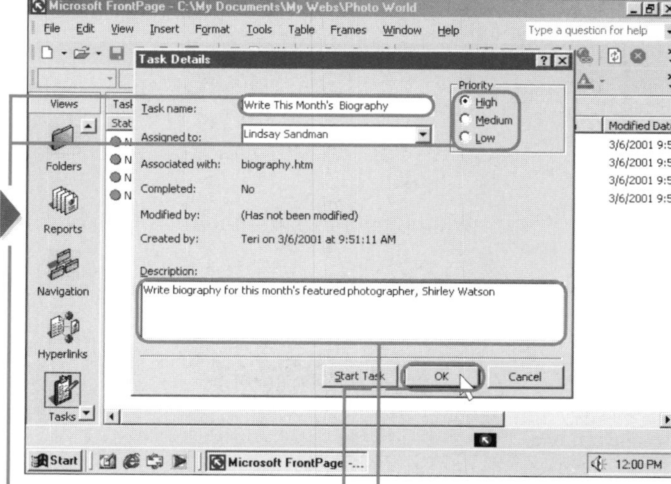

1 Click **Tasks** to view the tasks that you have added to your Web site.

■ If the Tasks icon is not displayed, click ▾ to display the icon.

2 Double-click the task you want to change.

■ The Task Details dialog box appears.

3 To change the name of the task, type a new name.

4 To change the priority of the task, click a different priority (○ changes to ⊙).

5 To change the description of the task, drag the mouse I over the existing description until you highlight the text. Then type a new description.

6 Click **OK** to save your changes.

START A TASK

You can start a task that you associated with a specific Web page. FrontPage will open the Web page so you can complete the task.

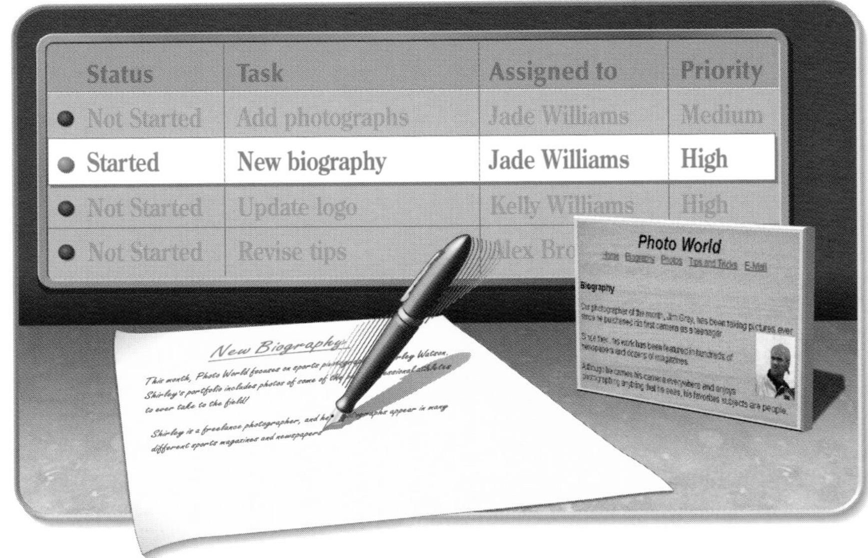

You cannot start a task that you did not associate with a specific Web page.

START A TASK

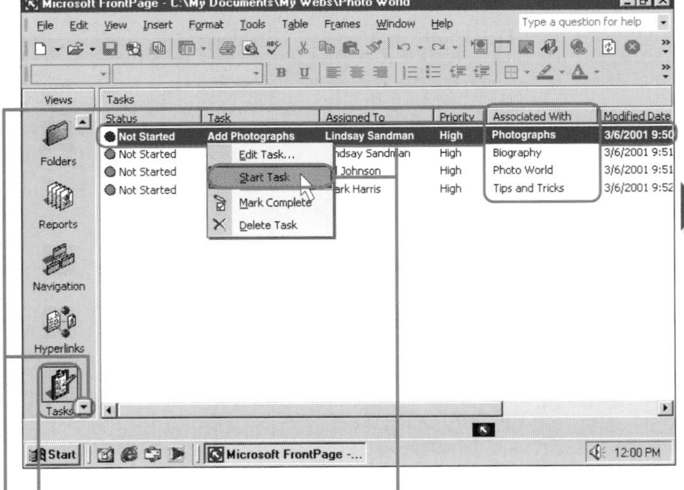

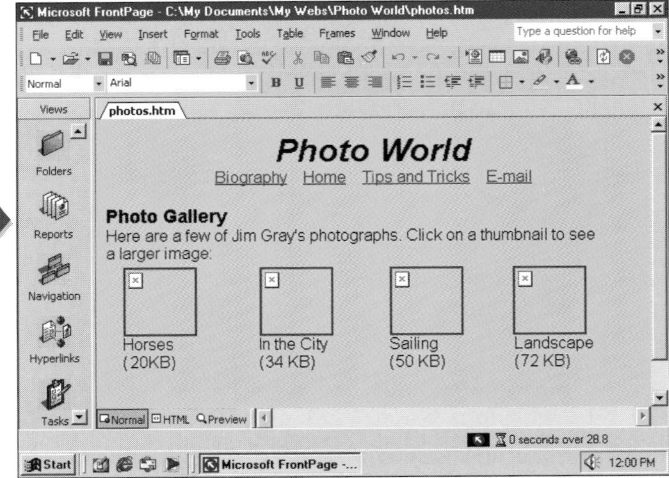

1 Click **Tasks** to view the tasks that you have added to your Web site.

- If the Tasks icon is not displayed, click ▼ to display the icon.

- This column displays the Web page you associated with each task.

Note: If you did not associate a Web page with a task, the area is blank.

2 Right-click the task you want to start. A menu appears.

3 Click **Start Task**.

- The Web page associated with the task appears in the Page view. You can now complete the task.

Note: If you associated the task with another type of file, such as an image, the file will open in a program you can use to view and work with the file.

DELETE A TASK

You can delete a task you have completed to keep your list of tasks up to date.

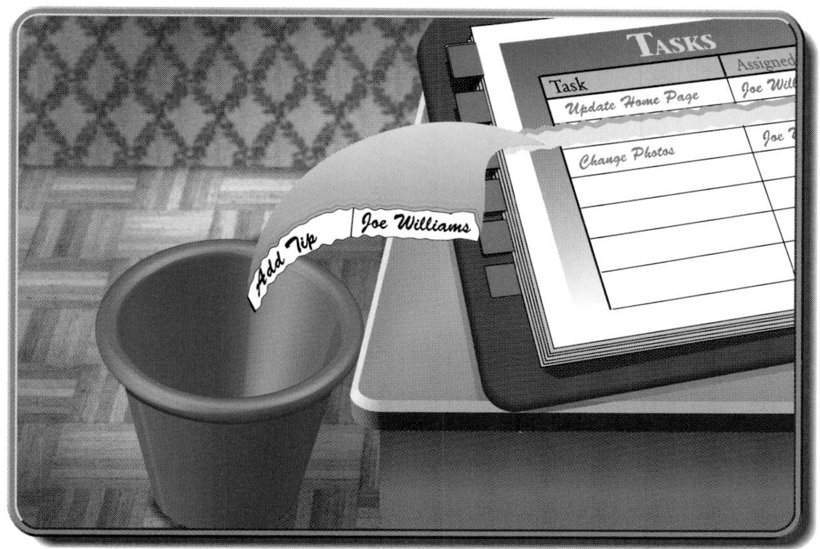

DELETE A TASK

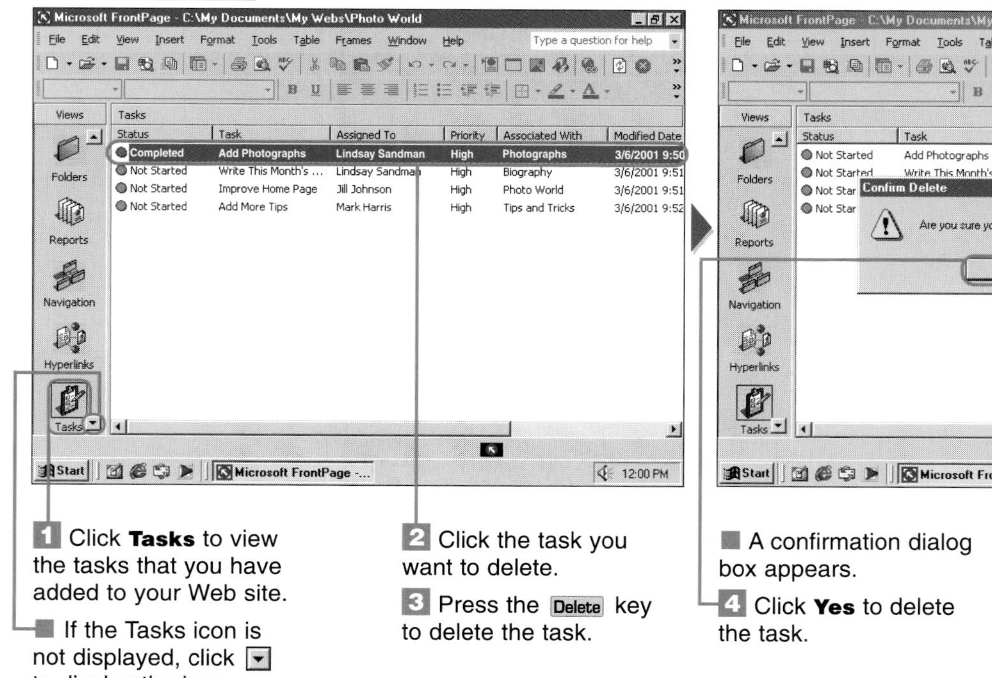

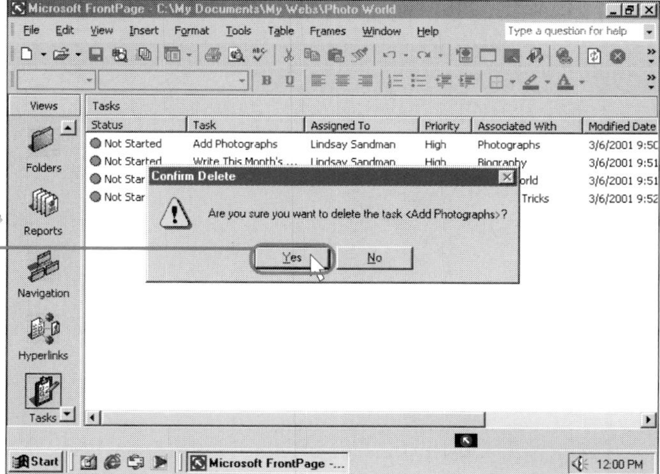

1 Click **Tasks** to view the tasks that you have added to your Web site.

■ If the Tasks icon is not displayed, click ▾ to display the icon.

2 Click the task you want to delete.

3 Press the Delete key to delete the task.

■ A confirmation dialog box appears.

4 Click **Yes** to delete the task.

■ The task disappears from the list of tasks.

Welcome To The
SMITH FAMILY
Web Page
Our Latest Addition
We are pleased to announce there's a new addition to our family. His name is Jack and he was born nine months ago! He is our first child and has brought us nothing but happiness since he arrived.
About Us
We are Jason & Brenda Smith, owners of a 50 acre horse farm. We breed thoroughbred horses and enjoy showing them at national horse shows.

ISP INTERNET SERVICE PROVIDER
Internet Service Provider ISP

CHAPTER 15

Publish Web Pages

Are you ready to publish your Web pages? This chapter will show you how.

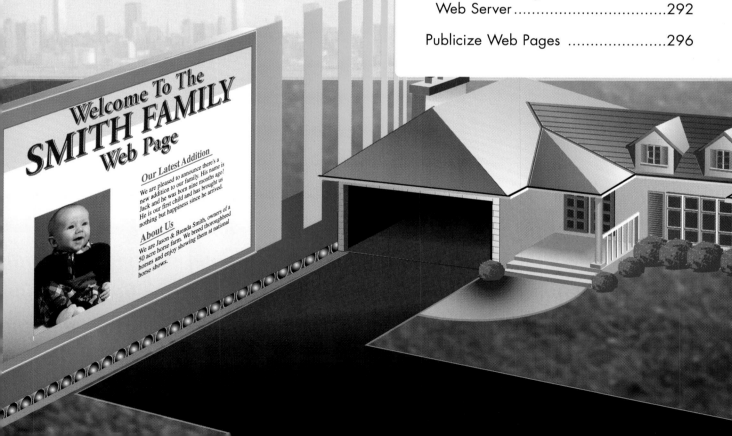

Web hosting services are companies that store Web pages and make them available on the Web for people to view.

Web hosting services store Web pages on computers called Web servers. Web servers monitor and control access to Web pages.

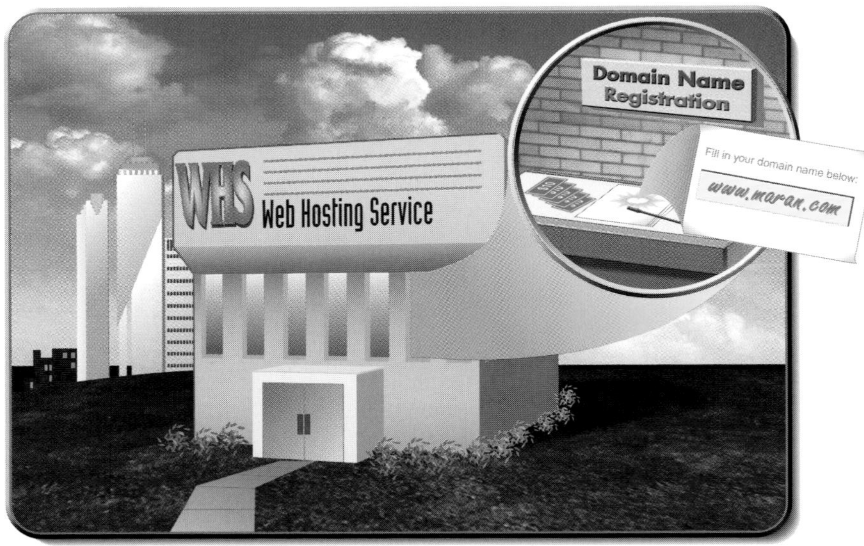

Domain Name Registration

A domain name is the address that people type to access your Web pages, such as www.maran.com. If you want your own personalized domain name, most Web hosting services can register a domain name for you. A personalized domain name is easy for people to remember and will not change if you switch to another Web hosting service. For information on registering your own domain name, visit the internic.net Web site.

INTERNET SERVICE PROVIDERS

Internet service providers are companies that offer people access to the Internet. Most Internet service providers offer space on their Web servers where customers can publish their Web pages. Although an Internet service provider offers the easiest way to publish Web pages, they may not provide all the features or technical support that you require.

FREE WEB HOSTING SERVICES

Some companies on the Web will publish your Web pages for free. These companies offer a limited amount of storage space and usually place advertisements on your Web pages. They also may not offer all the features you need. You can find companies that will publish your Web pages for free at the following Web sites.

geocities.yahoo.com

www.tripod.lycos.com

DEDICATED WEB HOSTING SERVICES

Dedicated Web hosting services are companies that specialize in publishing Web pages. Dedicated Web hosting services are flexible and offer features that other Web hosting services do not offer. You can find dedicated Web hosting services at the following Web sites.

www.hostess.com

www.pair.com

You can search for a Web hosting service in your area at the www.microsoftwpp.com/wppsearch Web site.

YOUR OWN WEB SERVER

Purchasing your own Web server is the most expensive way to publish Web pages and requires a full-time connection to the Internet. Setting up and maintaining your own Web server is difficult but will give you the greatest amount of control over your Web pages.

CHOOSE A WEB HOSTING SERVICE

You should consider several factors when choosing a Web hosting service to publish your Web pages.

TECHNICAL SUPPORT

A Web hosting service should have a technical support department to answer your questions. You should be able to contact a Web hosting service by telephone or e-mail and get a response to your questions within a day.

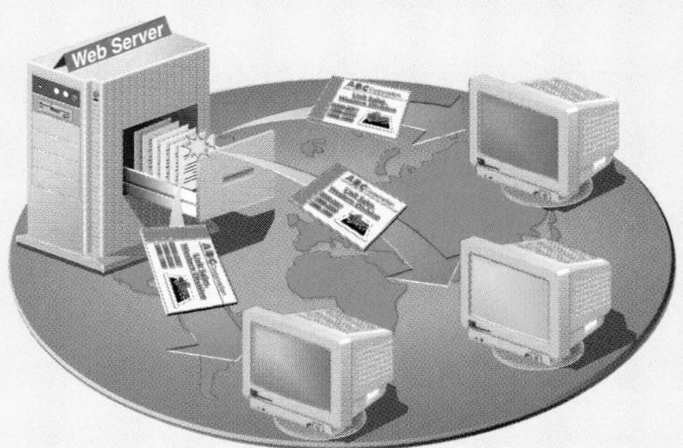

TRAFFIC LIMIT

When visitors view your Web pages, information transfers from the Web server to their computers. The amount of information that transfers from the Web server depends on the number of people that view your Web pages and the file size of your pages.

Most Web hosting services limit the amount of information that can transfer in one month. If more information transfers, you usually have to pay extra. Make sure you choose a Web hosting service that has a traffic limit that meets the needs of your Web site.

RELIABILITY

Make sure the Web hosting service you choose is reliable. A Web hosting service should be able to tell you how often their Web servers shut down. You may want to ask a Web hosting service for customer references. You should take into consideration that Web hosting services occasionally shut down their Web servers for maintenance and upgrades.

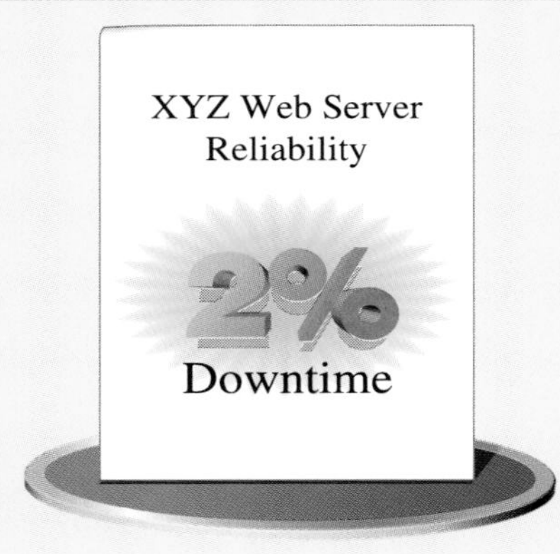

STORAGE SPACE

Most Web hosting services limit the amount of space you can use to store your Web site. If your Web site is larger than the space provided, you will have to pay extra. Choose a Web hosting service that provides enough space to store all the information for your Web site.

ACCESS LOGS

A good Web hosting service will supply you with statistics about your Web pages, such as which Web pages are the most popular and where your visitors are from. You should also be able to view any error messages visitors may see when viewing your Web pages, such as "Page Not Found." Access logs can help you determine if you need to make changes to your Web pages.

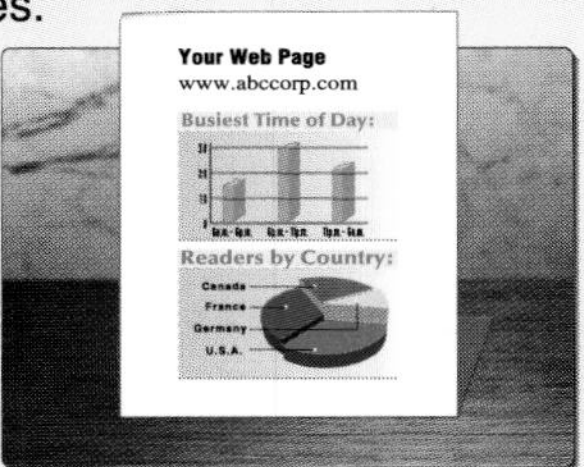

FRONTPAGE SERVER EXTENSIONS

Your Web hosting service must have the FrontPage Server Extensions installed on their Web server for some Web page features to work. For example, your Web server will need the FrontPage Server Extensions installed if you want to use forms and hit counters on your Web pages.

SECURE WEB SERVER

If you require visitors at your Web site to enter confidential information, such as credit card numbers, you will need a Web hosting service with a secure Web server. Secure Web servers encode the information that transfers over the Internet so that only the sending and receiving computers can read the information.

SPECIFY KEYWORDS FOR A WEB PAGE

You can specify keywords to help search tools index your Web pages.

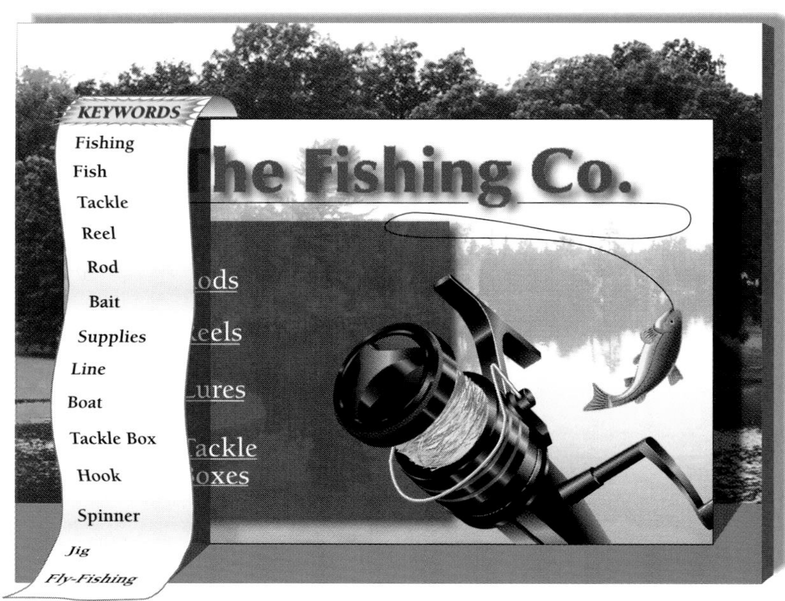

Search tools help people find information on the Web. Popular search tools include AltaVista (www.altavista.com), Lycos (www.lycos.com) and Yahoo! (www.yahoo.com).

When visitors enter words in a search tool that match your keywords, your Web page will more likely appear in the search results.

SPECIFY KEYWORDS FOR A WEB PAGE

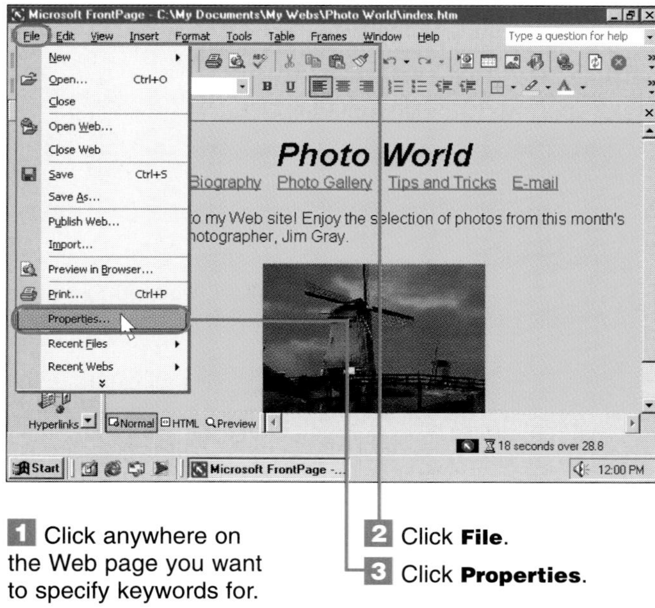

1 Click anywhere on the Web page you want to specify keywords for.

2 Click **File**.

3 Click **Properties**.

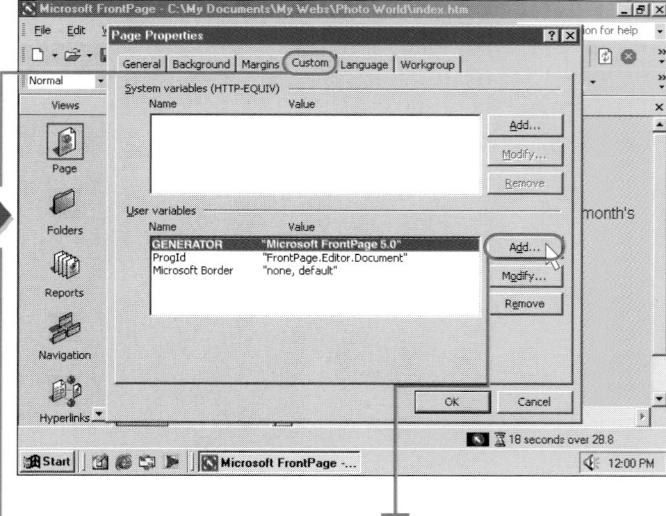

■ The Page Properties dialog box appears.

4 Click the **Custom** tab.

5 Click **Add** to specify keywords for the Web page.

How do search tools find Web pages?

Most search tools use software, called robots, that travel around the Web looking for new Web pages. When search tools find your Web pages, they will use the keywords you specified to help index your pages. You can also submit information about your Web pages to individual search tools or to many search tools at once at the www.submit-it.com Web site.

What words should I specify as keywords?

You should use both general and specific words to describe your Web pages. For example, if a Web page contains information about corvettes, use the keywords "car" and "corvette." You may also want to include misspelled words that people may type, such as "corvete."

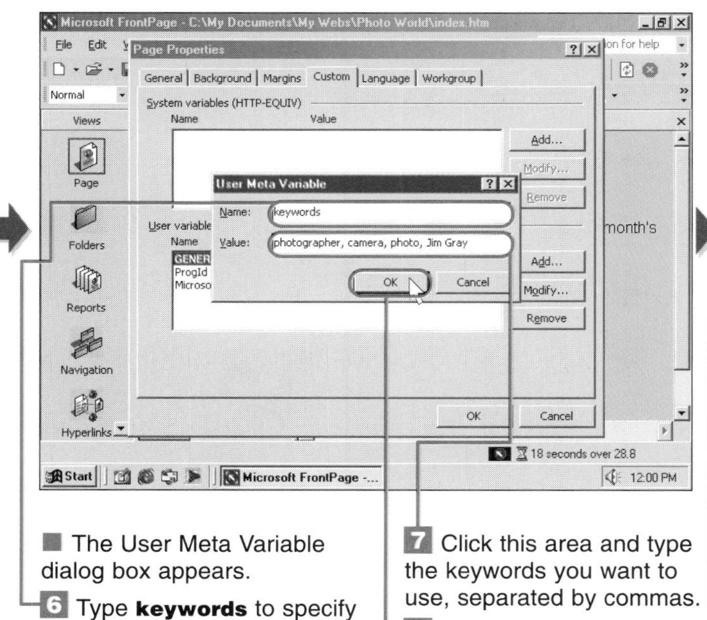

■ The User Meta Variable dialog box appears.

6 Type **keywords** to specify that you want to define keywords for the Web page.

7 Click this area and type the keywords you want to use, separated by commas.

8 Click **OK** to confirm the keywords you entered.

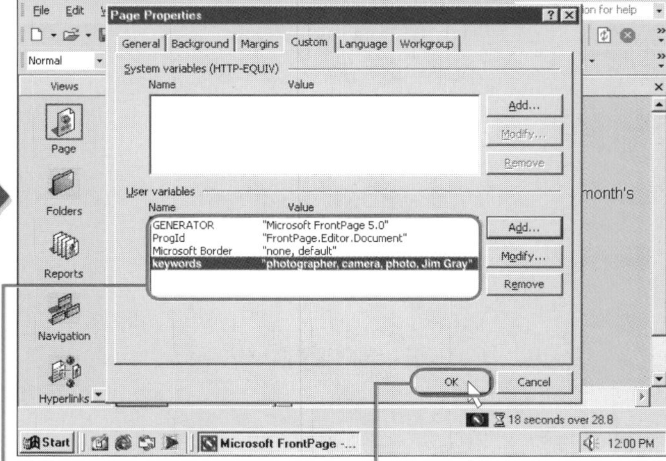

■ The keywords you entered appear in this area.

■ To change the keywords, double-click the keywords and then repeat steps 7 and 8.

9 Click **OK** to close the Page Properties dialog box.

Note: When viewing your Web page, visitors will not see the keywords you entered. Keywords appear in the HTML code for the Web page. To view the HTML code for a Web page, see page 42.

SPECIFY A SUMMARY FOR A WEB PAGE

You can specify a summary that search tools will use to describe a Web page in your Web site.

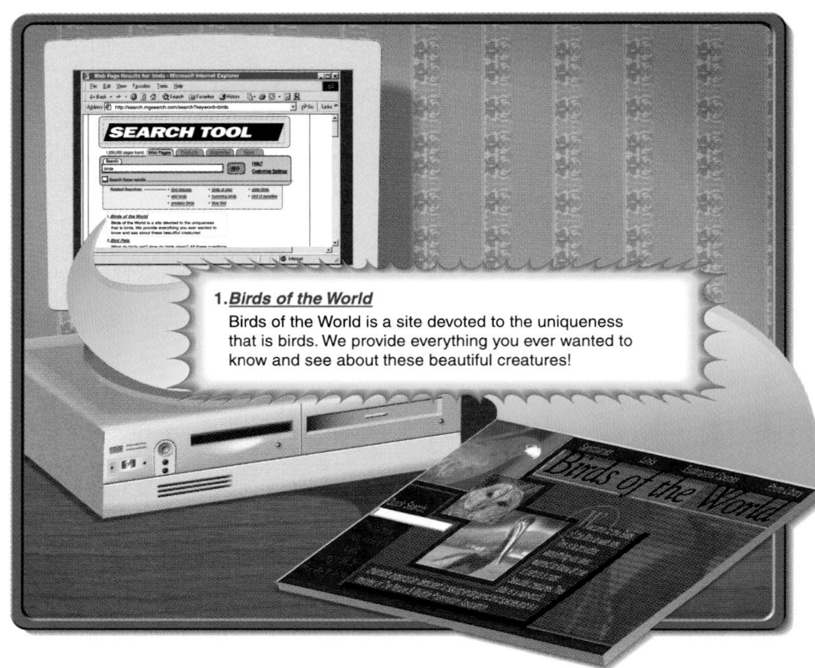

When a visitor uses a search tool to find information on the Web, each Web page that appears in the search results will display a summary. Popular search tools include AltaVista, Lycos and Yahoo!.

SPECIFY A SUMMARY FOR A WEB PAGE

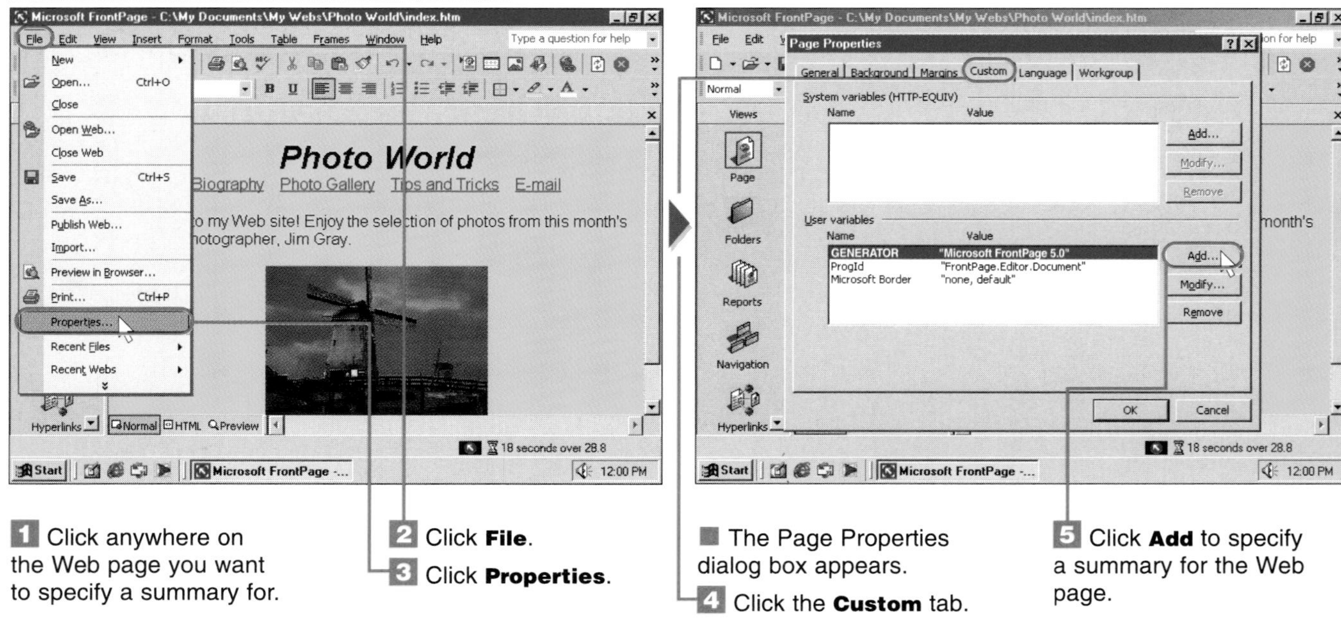

1 Click anywhere on the Web page you want to specify a summary for.

2 Click **File**.

3 Click **Properties**.

■ The Page Properties dialog box appears.

4 Click the **Custom** tab.

5 Click **Add** to specify a summary for the Web page.

What happens if I do not specify a summary for a Web page?

If you do not specify a summary for a Web page, search tools will use text from the top of your Web page for the summary. This may confuse your visitors, particularly if the top of your Web page contains a list of links or a copyright notice rather than a summary.

What should I consider when specifying a Web page summary?

You should try to limit a Web page summary to one or two sentences. Most search tools will not display more than three lines of text for a Web page summary. A brief, descriptive summary can help convince visitors to view your Web page.

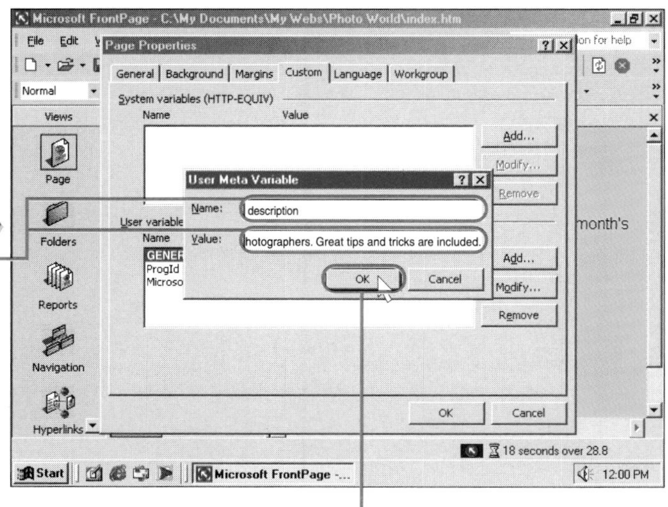

■ The User Meta Variable dialog box appears.

6 Type **description** to specify a summary for the Web page.

7 Click this area and type a summary for your Web page.

Note: If you enter more text than the area can display, the existing text moves to the left to make room for the new text.

8 Click **OK** to confirm the information you entered.

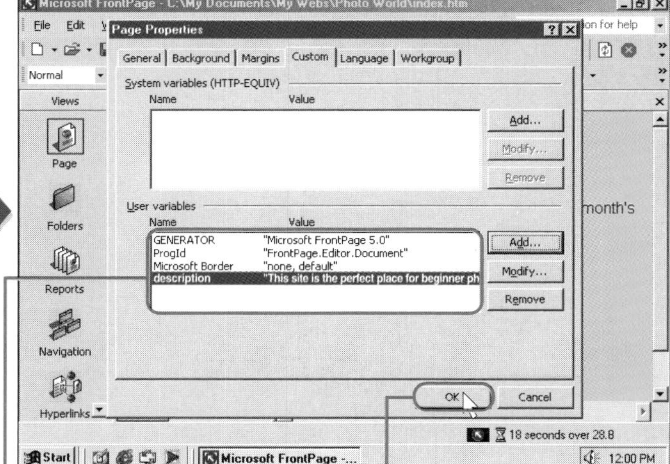

■ The summary you entered appears in this area.

■ To make changes to the summary, double-click the summary and then repeat steps 7 and 8.

9 Click **OK** to close the Page Properties dialog box.

Note: When viewing your Web page, visitors will not see the summary you entered. The summary appears in the HTML code for the Web page. To view the HTML code for a Web page, see page 42.

PREVENT ROBOTS FROM INDEXING A WEB PAGE

Most search tools use programs called robots to find and index new pages on the Web. You can prevent most robots from indexing a Web page, such as a page you created just for your family, friends or company.

Search tools help people find information on the Web. Popular search tools include AltaVista, Lycos and Yahoo!.

PREVENT ROBOTS FROM INDEXING A WEB PAGE

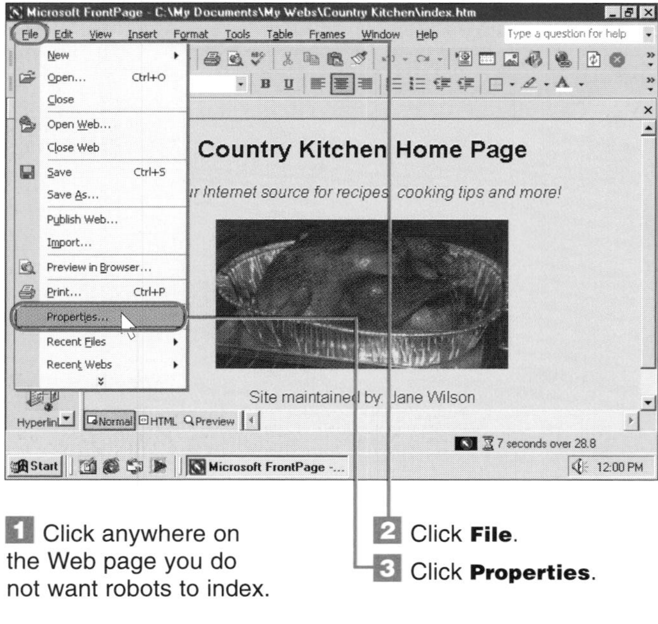

1 Click anywhere on the Web page you do not want robots to index.

2 Click **File**.

3 Click **Properties**.

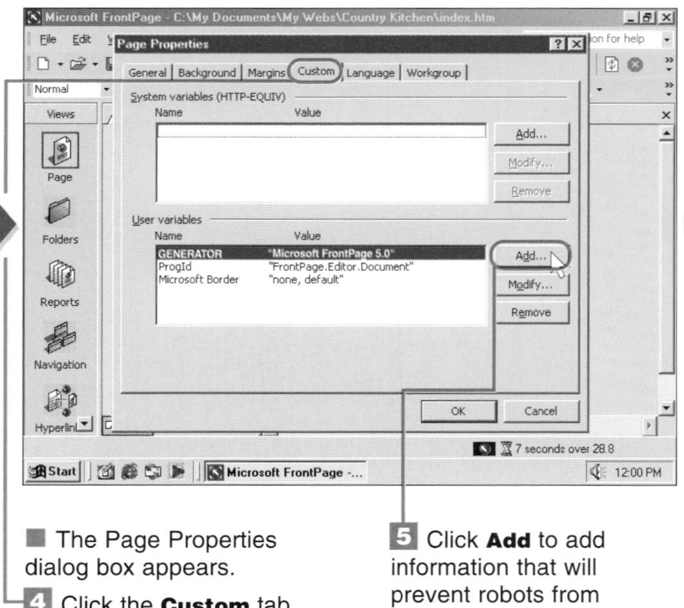

■ The Page Properties dialog box appears.

4 Click the **Custom** tab.

5 Click **Add** to add information that will prevent robots from indexing the Web page.

How do I once again allow robots to index a Web page?

To once again allow robots to index a Web page, perform the following steps.

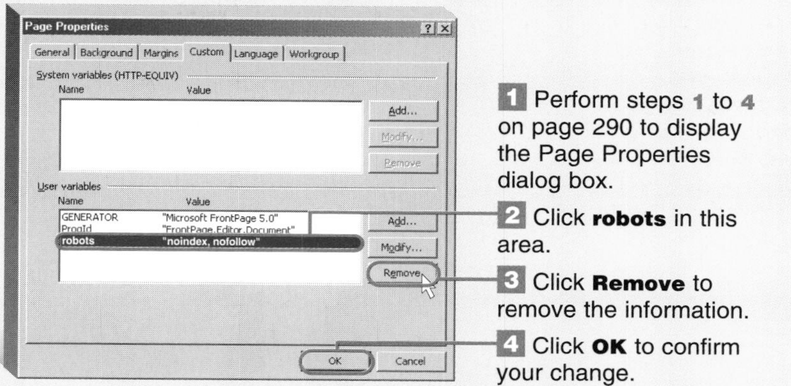

1 Perform steps 1 to 4 on page 290 to display the Page Properties dialog box.

2 Click **robots** in this area.

3 Click **Remove** to remove the information.

4 Click **OK** to confirm your change.

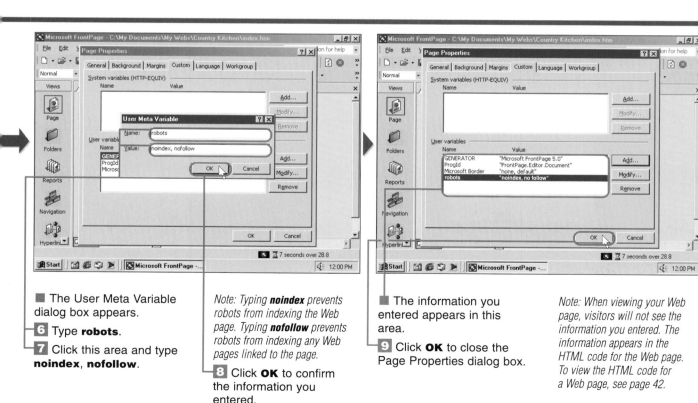

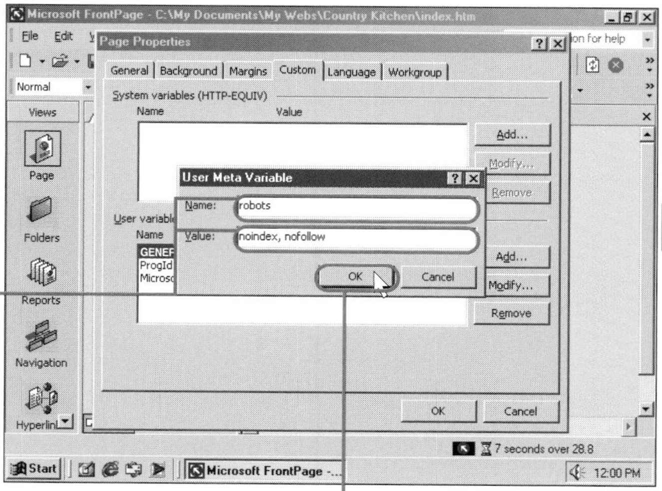

■ The User Meta Variable dialog box appears.

6 Type **robots**.

7 Click this area and type **noindex**, **nofollow**.

*Note: Typing **noindex** prevents robots from indexing the Web page. Typing **nofollow** prevents robots from indexing any Web pages linked to the page.*

8 Click **OK** to confirm the information you entered.

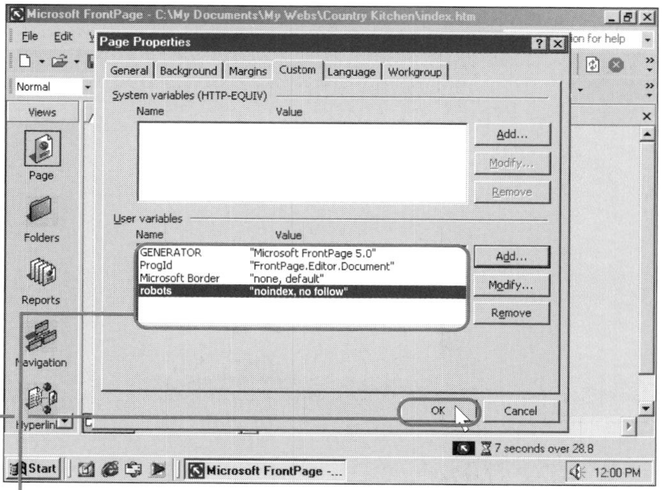

■ The information you entered appears in this area.

9 Click **OK** to close the Page Properties dialog box.

Note: When viewing your Web page, visitors will not see the information you entered. The information appears in the HTML code for the Web page. To view the HTML code for a Web page, see page 42.

TRANSFER WEB PAGES TO A WEB SERVER

When you finish creating your Web pages, you can transfer the pages to a Web server to make the pages available on the Web.

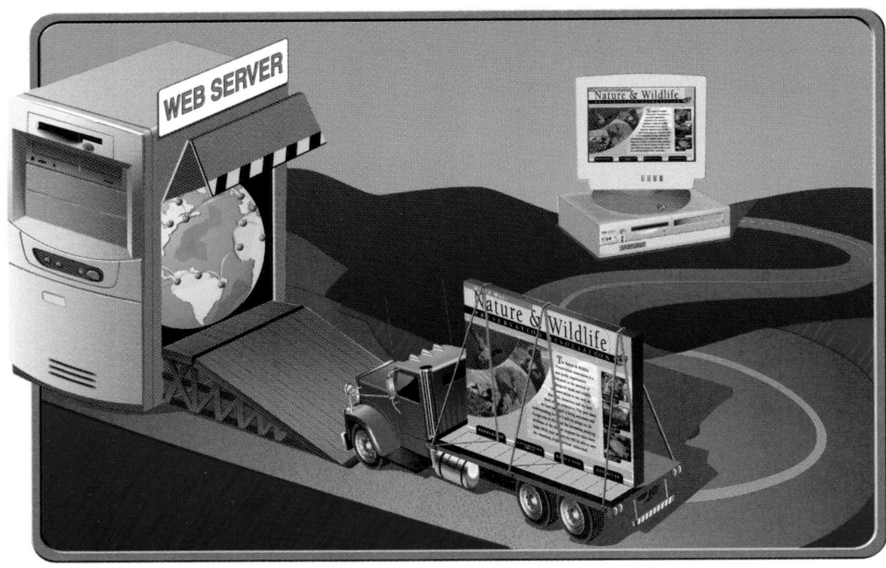

Before you can transfer your Web pages to a Web server, you must choose a Web hosting service to publish your Web pages. For information on Web hosting services, see pages 282 to 285.

TRANSFER WEB PAGES TO A WEB SERVER

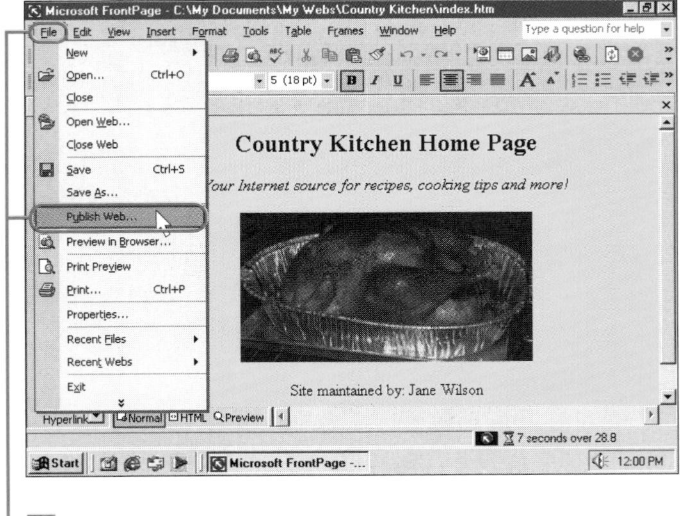

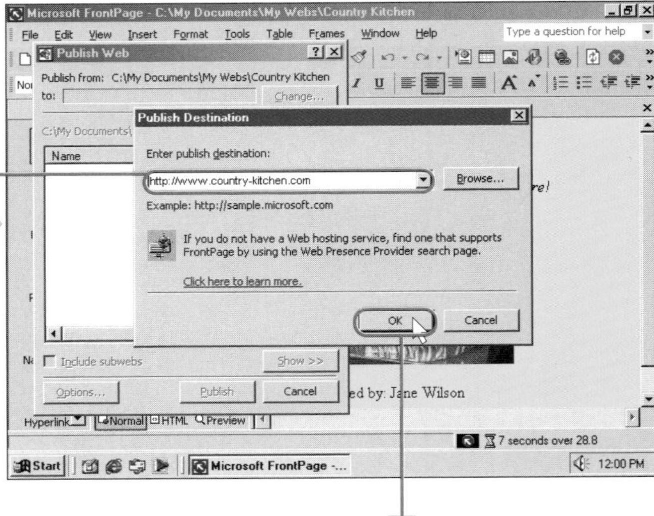

1 Click **File**.

2 Click **Publish Web** to transfer your Web pages to your Web server.

Note: Instead of performing steps 1 and 2, you can click the Publish Web button ( ).

■ The Publish Destination and Publish Web dialog boxes appear.

3 Type the address of the Web server where you want to publish your Web pages.

4 Click **OK** to continue.

Note: If you are not connected to the Internet, a dialog box appears that allows you to connect.

What information do I need to know to transfer my Web pages to a Web server?

You will need to know the address of your Web server and the user name and password required to access your Web server. If you do not know this information, ask your Web hosting service.

What should I do before transferring my Web pages to a Web server?

Before transferring your Web pages to a Web server, make sure you carefully review, test and save all of your Web pages. Saving your Web pages ensures that FrontPage will publish the most recent versions of your pages. Once you publish your Web pages, everyone on the Web will be able to view your pages.

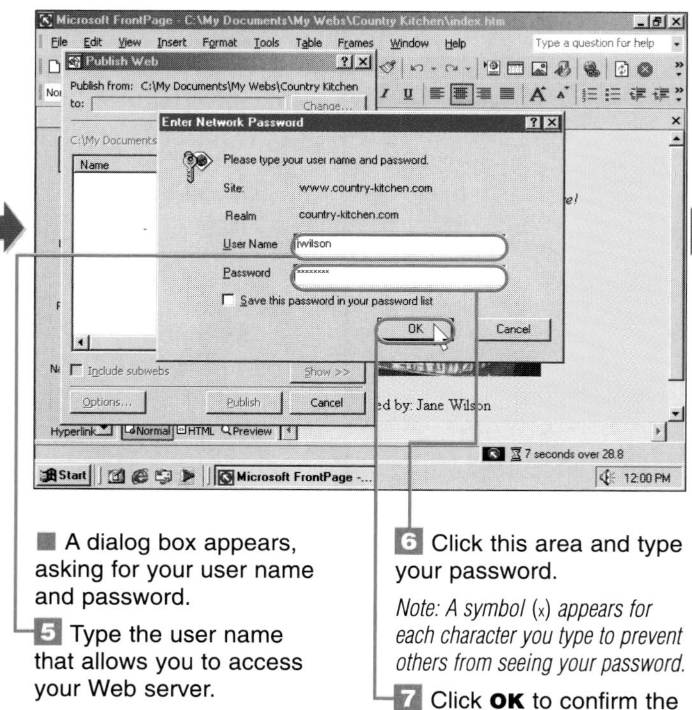

■ A dialog box appears, asking for your user name and password.

5 Type the user name that allows you to access your Web server.

6 Click this area and type your password.

Note: A symbol (x) appears for each character you type to prevent others from seeing your password.

7 Click **OK** to confirm the information you entered.

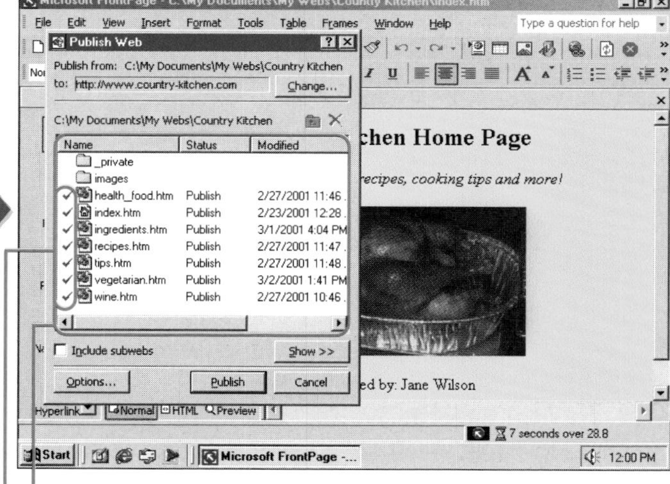

■ This area lists all the folders (📁), Web pages (📄) and other files in your Web site.

■ FrontPage will publish each file that displays a check mark (✓).

Note: The first time you publish your Web pages, FrontPage displays a check mark beside each file.

CONTINUED

TRANSFER WEB PAGES TO A WEB SERVER

You can choose not to publish a specific Web page in your Web site. This is useful if you have not yet completed a Web page, but you want to publish the rest of your pages.

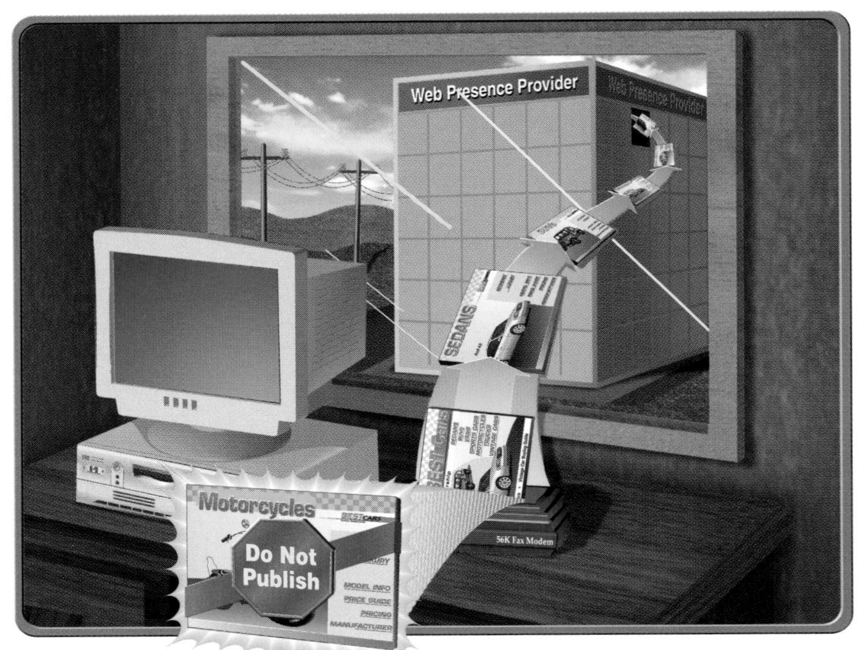

TRANSFER WEB PAGES TO A WEB SERVER (CONTINUED)

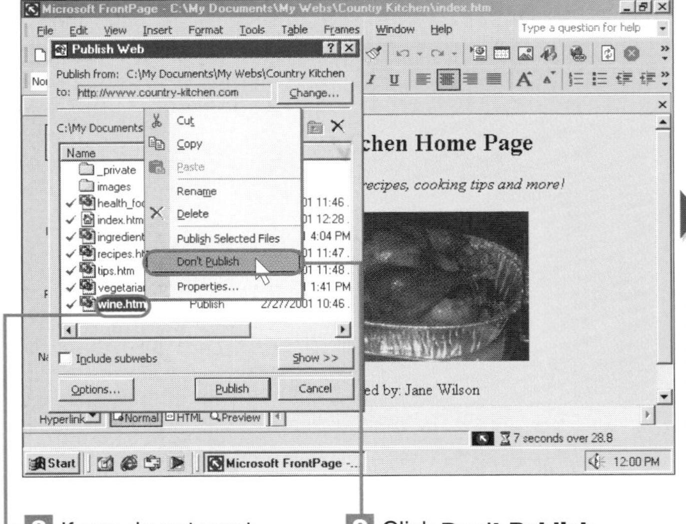

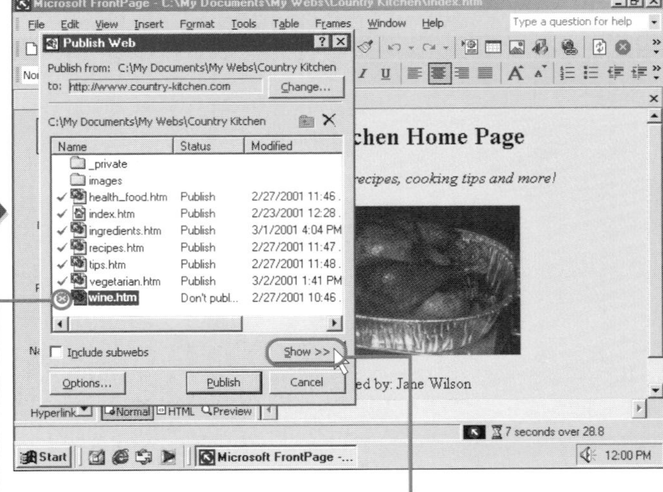

8 If you do not want to publish a specific Web page, right-click the Web page. A menu appears.

9 Click **Don't Publish** to specify that you do not want to publish the Web page.

■ The check mark (✓) beside the Web page changes to an X (⊗).

*Note: If you change your mind, you can repeat steps **8** and **9** to specify that you want to publish the Web page (⊗ changes to ✓ beside the page).*

10 If you want to display the files that are stored on your Web server, click **Show**.

How do I update my Web pages on the Web server?

If you make changes to the Web pages on your computer, you need to transfer the updated pages to your Web server. The updated Web pages will replace the old Web pages on the Web server. If you deleted a Web page on your computer, FrontPage will ask if you want to delete the Web page on the Web server. To transfer the updated Web pages to the Web server, repeat the steps starting on page 292.

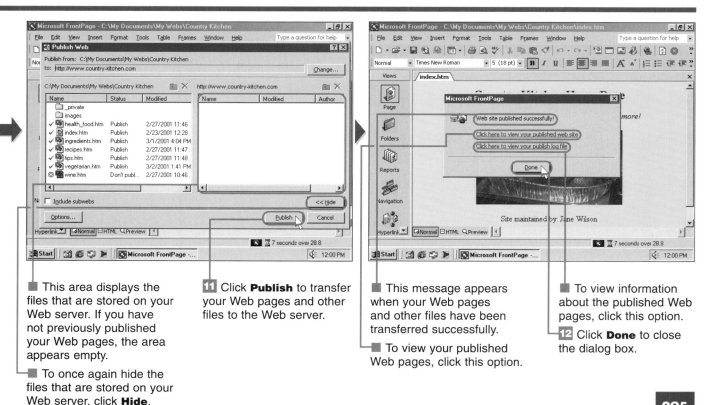

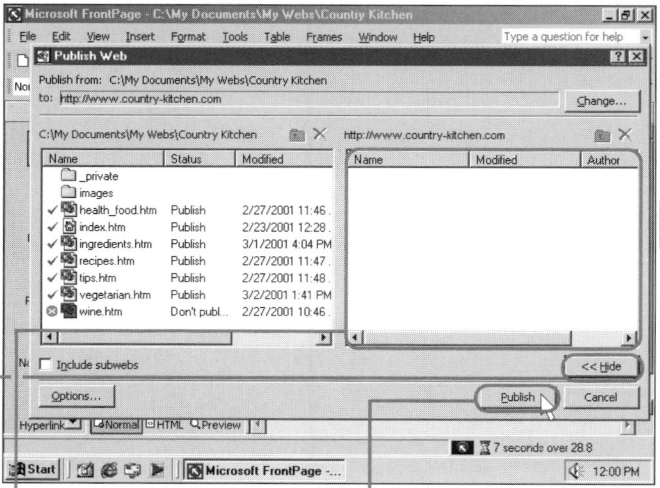

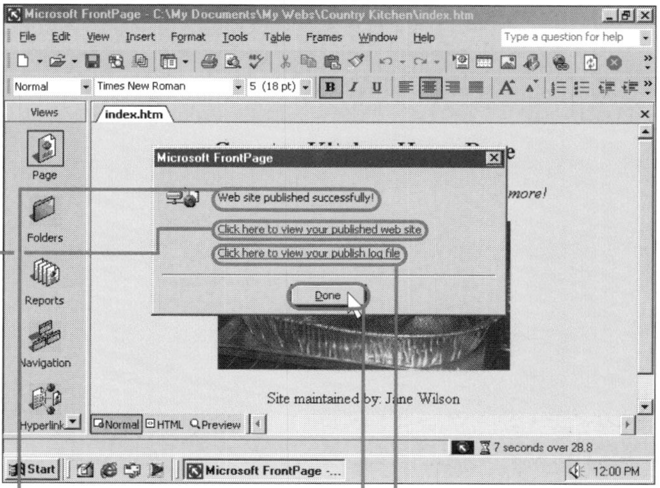

■ This area displays the files that are stored on your Web server. If you have not previously published your Web pages, the area appears empty.

■ To once again hide the files that are stored on your Web server, click **Hide**.

11 Click **Publish** to transfer your Web pages and other files to the Web server.

■ This message appears when your Web pages and other files have been transferred successfully.

■ To view your published Web pages, click this option.

■ To view information about the published Web pages, click this option.

12 Click **Done** to close the dialog box.

PUBLICIZE WEB PAGES

After you publish your Web pages, there are several ways you can let people know about the pages.

TRADITIONAL METHODS

You can mail an announcement about your Web pages to family, friends, colleagues and customers. You can also mail information about your Web pages to local newspapers and magazines that may be interested in your Web pages. If you created Web pages for a company, make sure you include your Web page address on business cards, letterhead and any print advertisements you produce.

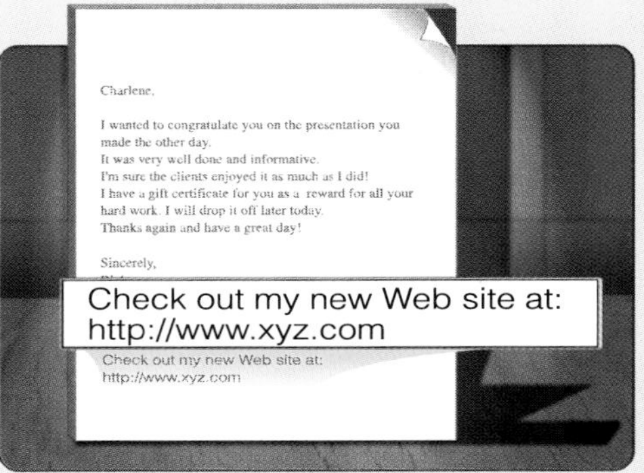

E-MAIL MESSAGES

Most e-mail programs include a feature, called a signature, that allows you to add the same information to the end of every e-mail message you send. You can use a signature to include information about your Web pages in all your e-mail messages.

EXCHANGE LINKS

If another Web site offers information, products or services related to your Web site, you can ask the individual or company to include a link to your Web pages if you will do the same. This allows people reading the other Web pages to easily visit your Web site.

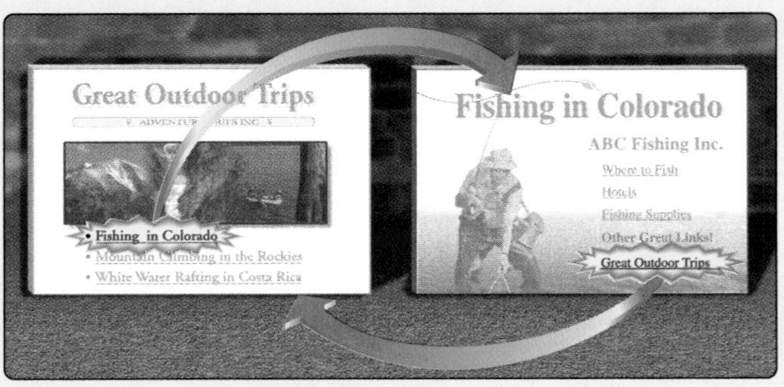

WEB PAGE ADVERTISEMENTS

Many companies set aside areas on their Web pages where you can advertise your Web site for a fee. You can also use the LinkExchange Banner Network, which is a free service that brings organizations together to exchange Web page advertisements. The LinkExchange Banner Network is located at the adnetwork.bcentral.com Web site.

NEWSGROUPS

You can send an announcement about your Web pages to discussion groups on the Internet called newsgroups. Make sure you choose newsgroups that discuss topics related to your Web pages. You can also announce new or updated Web pages by using the comp.infosystems.www.announce newsgroup.

MAILING LISTS

You can send an announcement about your Web pages to carefully selected mailing lists on the Internet. A mailing list is a discussion group that communicates through e-mail. You should read the messages in a mailing list for a week before sending an announcement to make sure the mailing list members would be interested in your Web pages. A directory of mailing lists is available at the www.liszt.com Web site.

SEARCH TOOLS

Search tools help people quickly find information on the Web. Adding your Web pages to various search tools can help people easily find your Web pages. Some popular search tools include:

AltaVista	www.altavista.com
Lycos	www.lycos.com
Yahoo!	www.yahoo.com

The www.submit-it.com Web site allows you to add your Web pages to many search tools at once.

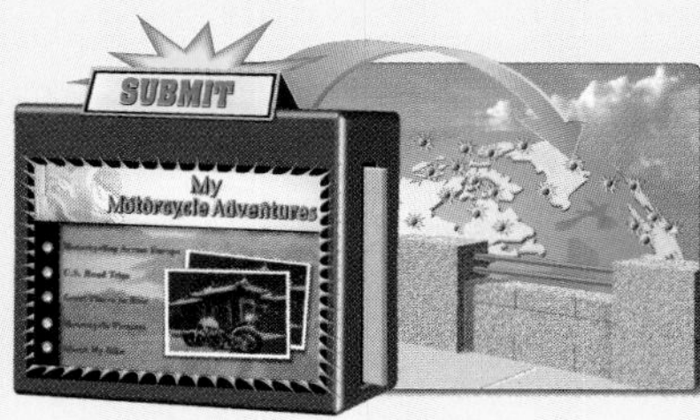

INDEX

A

B

C

D

N

O

P

Q

R

S

T

INDEX

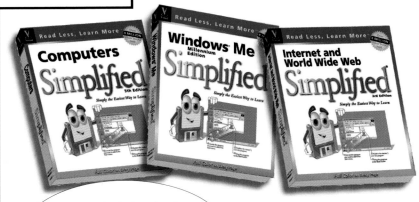

with these full-color Visual™ guides

The Fast and Easy Way to Learn

Discover how to use what you learn with "Teach Yourself" tips

Title	ISBN	Price
Teach Yourself Access 97 VISUALLY™	0-7645-6026-3	$29.99
Teach Yourself FrontPage® 2000 VISUALLY™	0-7645-3451-3	$29.99
Teach Yourself HTML VISUALLY™	0-7645-3423-8	$29.99
Teach Yourself the Internet and World Wide Web VISUALLY™, 2nd Ed.	0-7645-3410-6	$29.99
Teach Yourself Microsoft® Access 2000 VISUALLY™	0-7645-6059-X	$29.99
Teach Yourself Microsoft® Excel 97 VISUALLY™	0-7645-6063-8	$29.99
Teach Yourself Microsoft® Excel 2000 VISUALLY™	0-7645-6056-5	$29.99
Teach Yourself Microsoft® Office 2000 VISUALLY™	0-7645-6051-4	$29.99
Teach Yourself Microsoft® PowerPoint® 97 VISUALLY™	0-7645-6062-X	$29.99
Teach Yourself Microsoft® PowerPoint® 2000 VISUALLY™	0-7645-6060-3	$29.99
Teach Yourself More Windows® 98 VISUALLY™	0-7645-6044-1	$29.99
Teach Yourself Netscape Navigator® 4 VISUALLY™	0-7645-6028-X	$29.99
Teach Yourself Office 97 VISUALLY™	0-7645-6018-2	$29.99
Teach Yourself Red Hat® Linux® VISUALLY™	0-7645-3430-0	$29.99
Teach Yourself VISUALLY™ Computers, 3rd Ed.	0-7645-3525-0	$29.99
Teach Yourself VISUALLY™ Dreamweaver® 3	0-7645-3470-X	$29.99
Teach Yourself VISUALLY™ Fireworks® 4	0-7645-3566-8	$29.99
Teach Yourself VISUALLY™ Flash™ 5	0-7645-3540-4	$29.99
Teach Yourself VISUALLY™ iMac™	0-7645-3453-X	$29.99
Teach Yourself VISUALLY™ Investing Online	0-7645-3459-9	$29.99
Teach Yourself VISUALLY™ Networking, 2nd Ed.	0-7645-3534-X	$29.99
Teach Yourself VISUALLY™ Photoshop® 6	0-7645-3513-7	$29.99
Teach Yourself VISUALLY™ Quicken® 2001	0-7645-3526-9	$29.99
Teach Yourself VISUALLY™ Windows® 2000 Server	0-7645-3428-9	$29.99
Teach Yourself VISUALLY™ Windows® Me Millennium Edition	0-7645-3495-5	$29.99
Teach Yourself Windows® 95 VISUALLY™	0-7645-6001-8	$29.99
Teach Yourself Windows® 98 VISUALLY™	0-7645-6025-5	$29.99
Teach Yourself Windows® 2000 Professional VISUALLY™	0-7645-6040-9	$29.99
Teach Yourself Windows NT® 4 VISUALLY™	0-7645-6061-1	$29.99
Teach Yourself Word 97 VISUALLY™	0-7645-6032-8	$29.99

For visual learners who want to guide themselves through the basics of any technology topic. *Teach Yourself VISUALLY* offers more expanded coverage than our bestselling *Simplified* series.

The Visual™ series is available wherever books are sold, or call

1-800-762-2974.

Outside the US, call

317-572-3993

TRADE & INDIVIDUAL ORDERS

Phone: **(800) 762-2974**
or **(317) 572-3993**
(8 a.m. – 6 p.m., CST, weekdays)
FAX : **(800) 550-2747**
or **(317) 572-4002**

EDUCATIONAL ORDERS & DISCOUNTS

Phone: **(800) 434-2086**
(8:30 a.m.–5:00 p.m., CST, weekdays)
FAX : **(317) 572-4005**

CORPORATE ORDERS FOR VISUAL™ SERIES

Phone: **(800) 469-6616**
(8 a.m.–5 p.m., EST, weekdays)
FAX : **(905) 890-9434**

Qty	ISBN	Title	Price	Total

Shipping & Handling Charges

	Description	First book	Each add'l. book	Total
Domestic	Normal	$4.50	$1.50	$
	Two Day Air	$8.50	$2.50	$
	Overnight	$18.00	$3.00	$
International	Surface	$8.00	$8.00	$
	Airmail	$16.00	$16.00	$
	DHL Air	$17.00	$17.00	$

Subtotal ____________

CA residents add applicable sales tax ____________

IN, MA and MD residents add 5% sales tax ____________

IL residents add 6.25% sales tax ____________

RI residents add 7% sales tax ____________

TX residents add 8.25% sales tax ____________

Shipping ____________

Total ____________

Ship to:

Name ____________

Address ____________

Company ____________

City/State/Zip ____________

Daytime Phone ____________

Payment: □ Check to Hungry Minds (US Funds Only)
□ Visa □ Mastercard □ American Express

Card # ____________ Exp. ____________ Signature ____________